SELECTIONS AND DOCUMENTS
IN ECONOMICS

EDITED BY

WILLIAM Z. RIPLEY, Ph.D.
PROFESSOR OF ECONOMICS, HARVARD UNIVERSITY

SELECTIONS AND DOCUMENTS IN ECONOMICS

TRUSTS, POOLS AND CORPORATIONS
(*Revised Edition*)
By William Z. Ripley, Ph.D., Professor of Political Economy, Harvard University

TRADE UNIONISM AND LABOR PROBLEMS (*Second Series*)
By John R. Commons, Professor of Political Economy, University of Wisconsin

SOCIOLOGY AND SOCIAL PROGRESS
By Thomas N. Carver, Ph.D., Professor of Political Economy, Harvard University

SELECTED READINGS IN PUBLIC FINANCE (*Second Edition*)
By Charles J. Bullock, Ph.D., Professor of Economics, Harvard University

RAILWAY PROBLEMS (*Revised Edition*)
By William Z. Ripley, Ph.D., Professor of Political Economy, Harvard University

SELECTED READINGS IN ECONOMICS
By Charles J. Bullock, Ph.D., Professor of Economics, Harvard University

ECONOMIC HISTORY OF THE UNITED STATES. 1765-1860
By Guy Stevens Callender, late Professor of Political Economy, Yale University

SELECTED READINGS IN RURAL ECONOMICS
By Thomas N. Carver, Ph.D., Professor of Political Economy, Harvard University

READINGS IN SOCIAL PROBLEMS
By Albert Benedict Wolfe, Professor of Economics, University of Texas

SELECTED READINGS IN INTERNATIONAL TRADE AND TARIFF PROBLEMS
By Frank W. Taussig, Henry Lee Professor of Economics, Harvard University

RAILWAY PROBLEMS

EDITED, WITH AN INTRODUCTION

BY

WILLIAM Z. RIPLEY, Ph.D.

ROPES PROFESSOR OF ECONOMICS, HARVARD UNIVERSITY

REVISED EDITION

GINN AND COMPANY
BOSTON · NEW YORK · CHICAGO · LONDON
ATLANTA · DALLAS · COLUMBUS · SAN FRANCISCO

The Athenæum Press
GINN AND COMPANY · PRO-
PRIETORS · BOSTON · U.S.A.

PREFACE TO THE SECOND EDITION

There are two substantial reasons for recasting this collection of reprints originally made up in 1907. The first is that the rapid course of events, legislative and economic, in the United States, especially in the field of transportation, has rendered the old collection obsolete — the later developments having since been described either officially in documents or else in the files of the economic journals. The second, and by no means less important reason to me, as an instructor in the subject forced constantly to face the problem of providing solid reading matter for large classes, is the completion of a systematic treatise upon the subject with which these selections may be closely correlated. Certain chapters of my own in the first edition, having been revised and brought up to date, are now transferred to my Railroads: Rates and Regulation or will appear in the second volume, Railroads: Finance and Organization. Others, like Taussig's classic on the theory of rates, have been so completely incorporated in the text of the former of these volumes, with such amendment as the progress of economic science permits, as to render their separate appearance unnecessary. And certain other chapters on legislation then incomplete, are now, in my judgment, preferably described in a more extended account of such matters in the above-named systematic treatises.

In place of these omissions, a number of substantial additions have been made. The admirable account of early conditions in Pearson's American Railroad Builder is too good to be lost on the shelves of general biography; yet it is impracticable on grounds both of time and expense to place the entire volume in the hands of each student. A number of significant recent opinions of the Interstate Commerce Commission have been added, because of the light they throw upon the radically changed economic and legal conditions since 1905. The admirable description by Theodore Brent of the complexities of railroad rate making and regulation, prepared for the late Robert Mather, president of the Rock Island system, affords an illustration of the manner

v

in which competition generalizes almost at once any set of local conditions. In connection with the proper adjustment of relations between the states and the Federal government, now in process of settlement by the Supreme Court, this chapter is particularly illuminating.

Recent legal developments are also strikingly described in several new chapters added to this edition. The status of the carriers under the Sherman Anti-Trust Act would seem to have been pretty well defined in the course of the extended proceedings dissolving the Union-Southern Pacific merger. A fit sequel to the Northern Securities decision, already described in the first edition, is thus had. A second subject, yet in flux in the courts, is the determination of reasonable rates. The excellent review of judicial findings by Mr. Justice Swayze of the court of last resort in New Jersey covers this topic. And, finally, the most perplexing and interrelated subjects of physical valuation, reasonable rates and conflict of state and Federal authority are authoritatively treated in the recent Supreme Court Minnesota rate decision.

An effort has been made to tie in the illustrative material in this volume with my systematic treatise on the subject above mentioned. For it is believed that an exhaustive examination of a well-chosen set of typical examples — following, in short, the case system of the law schools — affords excellent mental training to the student. For this purpose, the cases may preferably be read before studying the treatise. Then the latter will assist in elucidating the difficult points and providing the proper historical setting. For the mature student of the subject, this order of reading may well be reversed. The bird's-eye view and general discussion may profitably be followed by a careful and minute analysis of particular incidents. Only thus may the great intricacy and the extremely delicate adjustment of commercial affairs in practice be duly appreciated. The detailed account of typical cases is one of the most certain correctives for the *a priori* philosopher and the zealous innovator. These several services to students and men of affairs, it is hoped, will be rendered by an extended set of cross references in all of the volumes above mentioned.

WILLIAM Z. RIPLEY

PREFACE TO THE FIRST EDITION

This collection of reprints, like its predecessor, Trusts, Pools, and Corporations, is directed to the accomplishment of two purposes: not alone to render more easily accessible to the interested public, valuable technical material upon a question of paramount interest and importance at the present time, but also to facilitate the work of the college instructor in the economics of transportation. The worst evil of modern academic life, particularly under the elective system, is that the student may so seldom be called upon to think for himself;—not merely to "cram" and memorize, to absorb information predigested by an instructor, but rather to actively use his reasoning powers in effecting recombinations of ideas. Mere passive contact for a brief period of life with cultivating influences and high ideals, as exemplified in books, general environment, and, it is to be hoped, instructors of the right sort, tends to produce the dilettante, unless at the same time the mind is constantly invigorated by action. This is especially true of the economic and social sciences. To provide material, preferably of a debatable sort, which may be worked over under discussion in the class room, instead of being merely committed to memory, constitutes the pedagogical aim of this book. Some of the extracts, especially the historical ones, are of course not susceptible of such treatment. They are merely reference readings for convenient use. But the others, notably the decisions of the Interstate Commerce Commission, usually provide debatable matter of an admirable sort. This is peculiarly true of cases or decisions with a dissenting minority opinion. Another advantage which many of these economic cases possess, over propositions in mathematics, logic, or even law, as material for training the intelligence, is that they are always charged with human, and often with great public, interest; and that they incidentally involve an acquaintance with the underlying business conditions and trade relations of the country at large.

One point in connection with the reprints from decisions of the Interstate Commerce Commission is peculiarly deserving of note. This volume is a collection of cases in economics and not in law. While legal propositions are sometimes necessarily involved, they are subordinate for our purposes to questions of economic fact. Our interest, for example, in the Import Rate decisions of the Supreme Court arises primarily from the fact that in the settlement of a difficult point at law economic relationships and conditions are revealed. A certain practice may be illegal, and yet sound economically, or the reverse. This explains why many of these reprints have been entirely stripped of legal material in the process of editorial condensation. The case is thereby not only much abridged but at the same time simplified for the use of economic students.

The book is not intended to be used alone in the conduct of courses, but in connection with some standard treatise upon the economics of transportation, such as Hadley's, Johnson's, or the editor's discussion in the Final Report of the United States Industrial Commission of 1900 (pp. 259–485).

For permission to reprint the selections from books and technical journals, acknowledgment is due to the editors of the *Quarterly Journal of Economics*, the *Political Science Quarterly*, and the *Journal of Political Economy*; and to Messrs. McClure, Phillips & Co. and the University of Chicago Press. Honorable Martin A. Knapp, the distinguished chairman of the Interstate Commerce Commission, has in this, as in all other enterprises tending to a further elucidation of the difficult problems of railway economics, rendered most valuable aid. The various authors whose contributions are herein reprinted have given, in all instances, the most cordial permission. I wish, however, to acknowledge my peculiar indebtedness to the Honorable Charles Francis Adams, not alone for his willingness to permit an abbreviated reprint of his Chapters of Erie, now out of print, to be made, but for his friendly aid in the direct accomplishment of that purpose. May the volume, headed by his early contribution to the subject, help to further the public-spirited purpose which inspired his work a generation ago!

WILLIAM Z. RIPLEY

CONTENTS

INTRODUCTION

The first impression conveyed by our historical selections is that they unduly emphasize certain infamous events in the development of the American transportation system. There is surely nothing more discreditable in the economic history of the United States than the defrauding of the government and of innocent investors by the use of development and construction companies, of which the Credit Mobilier was a leading example, by such men as Stanford, Durant, and Crocker; the wrecking of the Erie Railroad by Jay Gould and Jim Fisk; and the utterly unscrupulous manipulation of railroad rates by the Rockefellers and their associates, in order to destroy competition with the Standard Oil Company. Happily such occurrences are exceptional in the economic life of a nation. Nevertheless their description is essential to an understanding of the whole, just as pathological research is needed for a true comprehension of the normal and healthy physiological processes. It would have been far pleasanter to record in detail the course of events by which the wonderful achievement of opening up a great continent to settlement was accomplished. Practically this is impossible within reasonable limits of space. Not the prosaic and normal, but the spectacular, phases of our economic life have been as yet adequately described. The most that can be claimed for the selection of certain of these events is that, while perhaps extreme examples, they are significant as indicating possibilities under the then prevailing state of public opinion and law.

Another less practical, and in fact more important, reason for throwing these infamous events into high light, lies in their instructive character as illustrating the evils generally attendant upon a pioneer stage of development, together with the abuses which naturally arise under conditions of absolutely free competition. The great advance in public morality which to-day refuses to tolerate such abuses becomes at once apparent. In the case of the chapters from the history of the Erie Railroad and its evil spirit, Jay Gould, the corruption of the state judiciary was perhaps the most deplorable feature of the affair. But the necessity of strict financial accountability of the directors of great public-service corporations, both to the government and to the stockholders, is made evident with equal clearness. Public sentiment — more sensitive to financial delinquencies to-day than it was a generation ago — has compelled the creation of governmental agencies for securing publicity. By such means scandalous abuses of trust are more easily detected and punished. Too often in the past, well-merited punishment has not taken place through the agency of the duly constituted legal authorities. The evil doers have received their just deserts only through condemnation by contemporary public opinion, perpetuated afterward by historical record. To keep alive some of these old scandals cannot fail to impress the fact that the evil which men do lives after them. It is not to be condoned, either by purely private morality, or by material success achieved during life, followed by large benefactions after death.

The chapter upon "Standard Oil Rebates" has had a more direct bearing upon contemporary affairs. The undoubtedly typical events therein described were a powerful factor in rousing public sentiment in favor of the original Act to Regulate Commerce of 1887. Their fearless republication, fully authenticated by documentary evidence, in the admirable History of the Standard Oil Company by Miss Tarbell, — confirmed as it was in its main conclusions by the masterly "Report upon the Transportation of Petroleum," by the United States Commissioner of Corporations,[1] — was an equally powerful influence in crystallizing public sentiment in favor of the recently enacted Hepburn Bill of 1906.[2] Public opinion to-day is unanimous in the

[1] Ripley's Railroads: Rates and Regulation, chap. vi, on "Personal Discrimination," gives the necessary historical setting.

[2] *Idem*, chaps xiv–xvii, describes and analyzes this legislation.

demand that railways as common carriers, enjoying inestimably valuable privileges by authority of the government, shall accord substantially equal treatment to all shippers alike, be they great or small.

Rebates and discriminations are not, however, matters of historical but of very present importance. As late as 1900, according to the opinion of experts, personal favoritism had become a thing of the past. This was in large measure probably true so far as the ordinary private businesses of the country were concerned. But a new and highly disturbing factor was the sudden rise of great industrial combinations, incident upon the phenomenal prosperity since 1897. Many of these trusts were floated upon glowing prophecies of economies in production. Prominent among these was to be a saving in freights through division of the market into districts, each supplied by the most conveniently located plant. The results have shown in too many cases that the real saving was not effected in this legitimate way at all. But their size and power were used as a club to force the carriers to grant secret favors in rates which were denied to the independent producers. The exposures of personal discrimination on a large scale started in Wisconsin in 1903, as a corollary to the investigation concerning railroad taxation under Governor La Follette. The so-called Elkins Bill, amending the Interstate Commerce Act in the interest of railroad revenues by greatly increasing the penalties for rebating, was enacted in the same year. Various investigations by the Interstate Commerce Commission since 1904 have uncovered intricate methods for evading even this more drastic prohibition. Prominent among these is the use of terminal railways owned by the shipper, which receive back an undue proportion of the through rate for a merely nominal service. The International Salt Company, the United States Steel Corporation, and the International Harvester Company, for example, have been detected in the utilization of this device. Another method, quite common, especially in securing rebates on grain and flour for the great Minneapolis millers, is the "midnight tariff,"—a low tariff publicly filed but made effective only for one day, for the use of shippers warned and prepared in advance. Discrimination in the use of coal cars, always operating of course in favor of the large shipper, was discovered on the Pennsylvania system even more recently. For years the use of private-car lines by the Chicago packers, known as the Beef Trust, to stifle all effective competition from independents, has been well known; but it was not fully disclosed until the general agitation for railroad reform was taken up by President Roosevelt. And all the time, as it now appears, the plain old-fashioned mode of direct repayment of a part of the published tariff rate has continued in secret. The American Sugar Refining Company (in 1906) and the Colorado Fuel & Iron Company (in 1905) have already been convicted of this offense in the Federal Courts. The climax is now capped by the masterly revelations of the United States Commissioner of Corporations, in his Report upon the Transportation of Petroleum of 1906. That hoary old offender, the Standard Oil Company, is now on trial in the Federal Courts, having been shown by an investigation of the books of the railways by expert accountants, to have been regularly in the enjoyment of preferential rates over competitors in all parts of the country. The evidence upon this point, taken in connection with the public professions of those charged with its management, is one of the most extraordinary exposures of loose business morality which this present generation is likely to witness. This revelation, together with that of the Armstrong Insurance Committee in New York, is unfortunately bound to furnish powerful ammunition for the use of political demagogues, in the furtherance of their selfish ends. For the dispassionate student of public affairs the argument is greatly strengthened in favor of an extension of public regulation both of railroads and trusts. The advantages of an enforced and ample publicity have been most effectively demonstrated by this rather remarkable series of events.

Pooling, or agreements between carriers for obviating competition, was commonly practiced prior to the Interstate Commerce Act of 1887. That law expressly prohibited it; and the courts have also interpreted the Anti-Trust Act of 1890 as applicable to railway contracts of the same kind. Moreover the progress of railway consolidation since 1898 has been such, especially in the southern states, that the necessity for pooling agreements is far less obvious than it was twenty years ago. The enactment of Federal legislation for the prevention of rate cutting and secret discrimination insures a greater measure of stability. Cut-throat competition like that of earlier days has become almost impossible. Competition to-day is rather of service and facilities at established rates, than as between actual rates themselves. Consequently our chapter upon the Southern Railway & Steamship Association,[1] at once the most effective and enduring organization of its kind, is now seemingly of historic interest alone. Yet a cogent reason for describing such a railway pool in detail nevertheless exists, and derives great force from the nature of impending problems in railway operation. Many competent students, other than railroad men, are convinced that the present prohibition of pooling ought to be repealed now that the great principle of public supervision and control of rates has been reaffirmed and securely established by the Hepburn Act of 1906.

The United States Industrial Commission of 1900 in its final report included an elaborate discussion of this topic, leading to the conclusion that agreements between carriers, subject of course to approval by the Interstate Commerce Commission, would not only greatly facilitate railway operation but also contribute powerfully to stability of rates. Since drafting this report, I have been able to investigate the subject further, with particular reference to the economic wastes incident to even normal and healthy railway competition.[2] The conviction that the most certain remedy for many of these economic wastes in transportation will be found in a rehabilitation of pooling under governmental supervision, has been greatly strengthened also by a somewhat extended personal investigation of railway practice in Europe. In the British Isles, the broad principle that railways are essentially natural monopolies, and should both legally and administratively be treated as such, has always

---

[1] *Vide*, p. 128, *infra*.   [2] Ripley's Railroads: Rates and Regulation, chap. viii.

obtained. Pooling agreements are actually enforcible by legal process. This contrasts strongly with our American practice, where we have indiscriminately sought to perpetuate competition by law, both for railways and trusts, regardless of their economic differences. We have, for instance, failed to recognize that in the case of common carriers, as distinguished from industrial combinations, a remedy against unreasonable rates far more secure than competition, namely governmental control, may be exercised. Moreover this method is advantageous because it conduces to stability of rates, never possible under free competition, while at the same time it still permits of competition for business, not by cutting of rates, but under established rates through extension of better service and facilities. The necessity for prohibition of pooling in the United States has largely disappeared, now that the great principle of public regulation by the Federal government is definitely reënacted into law.

Observation in continental Europe, where government ownership of railways prevails, strongly impresses one with the economic advantages of entirely unified systems of operation. No devious routing of traffic is allowed. Certain lines, best situated and equipped for the business, are designated for each kind of traffic, and concentration on them follows to the exclusion of the weak lines, — that is to say, of the lines which are weak for that particular business. No roundabout circuits occur because of the complete absorption of all lines in the government system. No independent roads have to be placated. The sole problem is to cause the tonnage to be most directly and economically transported. The advantage of monopolistic operation is amply demonstrated. But added evidence of the desirability of eliminating competition, except in the matter of service and facilities, is found in the fact that wherever these unified government systems come in contact they immediately resort to pooling agreements with one another. Thus the Prussian system is party to a number of pools with the railways of Austria, Bavaria, and Baden. The emphasis is laid upon securing the most direct and efficient service as well as the maintenance of stable rates.

For all these reasons above stated, it has seemed desirable to reproduce a picture of one of our best old-fashioned pools at work. Had such an organization not been prohibited, so far as rate making is concerned, by the Act of 1887, one may reasonably doubt whether the gigantic consolidations now dominating the southern states would have arisen. This particular chapter is reprinted, therefore, not only because of its historical importance but also in the hope that some day the railway pool under strict governmental supervision and control may be legally restored to favor as an agency for more effective service and greater stability of rates.

Traffic problems may be roughly classified in four groups : those appertaining to the reasonableness of rates in and of themselves without reference to any other tariff ; those which spring from an imputedly unreasonable relativity between rates for different and competing places or markets ; those which concern the relation between rates upon different commodities ; and finally those which deal with differences in rates for the same service between competing shippers. Of these four groups the last one concerning personal discrimination has already been discussed. The third group is mainly concerned with the intricate and technical problems of freight classification, commodity rates, and car-load tariffs. Such matters, decided for example by the Interstate Commerce Commission in a number of important cases,[1] are usually too elaborate for reproduction here, and moreover could subserve no useful purpose, as their decision depends rather upon mere questions of fact than of public policy. One simple concrete case alone, concerning the classification of fur hats,[2] will serve to indicate the principles involved, and their importance in any general scheme of rate making. The problem of relative rates upon grain and grain products, discussed in the Export Rate case,[3] incidentally involves issues of the same sort upon a large scale, as well

[1] Notably, the New York Board of Trade and Transportation Case, Interstate Commerce Commission Reports, Vol. III, pp. 473–511.

[2] P. 522, *infra.*   [3] *Vide*, p. 487, *infra.*

as the St. Louis–Pacific Coast jobbers' controversy.[1] Eliminating personal discrimination and classification, our remaining selections in this field of inquiry are thus narrowed down to two, — namely, absolutely reasonable rates and relative rates for competing markets.

The *inherent reasonableness of railroad rates* is a question less apt to arise with reference to a single commodity than to an entire schedule or tariff. It is a matter of far less concern to an individual merchant or group of traders that the absolute freight rate is high than that it (be it in general high or low) is higher than the rate enjoyed by a competitor. For even if it be unreasonably high, so long as it applies to all traders in the same market, the surcharge can immediately be levied upon the consumer by all dealers alike through an enhancement of prices. In the noted Cincinnati Freight Bureau case,[2] the Middle West was not solicitous for the welfare of the consuming public in the southeastern states when it complained that freight rates from western centers into the South were unduly high. The western merchants were interested in a reduction because their rates were in fact higher than those enjoyed by the Atlantic seaboard cities to the same points. Their complaint concerned itself essentially with the relativity of charges from different competing centers to a common market. The complainant as to the *absolute* reasonableness of southern freight rates should properly be the general consuming public in the region in question. In a similar fashion in another of our cases,[3] Danville complains, not primarily that her freight rates are high, but rather that they are higher than those granted to Richmond, Norfolk, and Lynchburg. The burden of complaint as to the absolute unreasonableness of the rates in question should properly proceed, not from the organized merchants of Danville but from her general consuming population. Nevertheless such questions as concern the absolute level of freight rates do sometimes arise, as in the notable case of the Chicago Stock Yards. In this instance an arbitrary switching charge of two dollars per car was imposed by the railroads in 1894, applicable to all

---

[1] *Vide*, p. 429, *infra.*   [2] *Vide*, p. 153, *infra.*   [3] *Vide*, p. 402, *infra.*

shippers alike. Issue was raised as to whether such an extra charge was justified by the circumstances and conditions under which this particular rate was imposed.[1]

Far more often, however, than in the case of individual or particular charges, for the reasons above outlined, issues of fact concerning the absolute reasonableness of rates in and of them-selves are apt to be raised with reference to entire schedules and tariffs. The Interstate Commerce Commission, as in the case of the freight-rate increases subsequent to 1900, was called upon to act in the general interests of the consuming public. Were these general increases justified by the widespread rise of prices and were they commensurate with the enhancement of costs of operation? The problem in such cases is mainly one of fact, to be discussed and decided by experts. These facts vary in their significance from year to year. Reproduction of such investigations in a volume of this sort would be of little value. Of course the future development of the Interstate Commerce Commission is bound to bring it face to face with just such broad issues. Matters of paramount importance will be involved. But, like matters of classification, they are too technical for our immediate purpose.

While cases suitable for reproduction in this volume rarely turn entirely upon the absolute reasonableness of rates, such an issue is often incidentally involved, as for instance in the Cin-cinnati and St. Louis cases above mentioned and in those of Chattanooga[2] and Savannah.[3] Given the fact that the relativity of two rates is unreasonable, is the one too high or the other too low? Either contingency might give rise to the inequality called in question. A just decision as to relative reasonableness must therefore reckon with the problem of inherent reasonable-ness. But the main interest of such issues for the mere student of railway economics lies less in the bald facts as stated, which may vary from time to time, than in the opposing arguments and principles invoked, which are in their essence permanent.

---

[1] This long-standing controversy, with others concerning the general rates on cattle, seems likely to be made the occasion for a first test of the new Hepburn Act.   [2] P. 266, *infra*.   [3] Pp. 252 and 314, *infra*.

Alleged *relatively unreasonable rates for competing markets* constitute the basis for complaints before the Interstate Commerce Commission far more frequently than do those concerning the absolute amount of the rate charged. The reasons for this have been set forth in the preceding paragraphs. And, common as such complaints have been in the past, it is certain that in future, with the ever-increasing commercial interrelation between different parts of the United States, such alleged grievances will claim a preponderating share of the attention of any administrative commission. Veritable puzzles in rate adjustment constantly arise, which bring out in high relief the economic peculiarities of railway, as distinct from ordinary industrial, competition. For this reason a large number of the cases herein reprinted deal with this phase of the subject.

By and large, these cases may be roughly set apart into two classes corresponding respectively to two distinct aspects of the problem of relative adjustment of rates for competing localities. Of these the first and simplest arises as between two competing markets lying upon and served by the *same* line of railroad. The problem is to adjust with relative fairness the rates to near and distant points on the same line, one often a local or way station, while the other enjoys the benefit of low competitive rates. This is a problem as old as railroading, commonly designated as the long-and-short-haul question. The second class of problems is at once more recent and comprehensive in its scope. It concerns the relativity of rates to or from a common market from various points, not on the same but on *different* lines. A decision in this latter case amounts practically to a delimitation of the entire area of the market. The long-and-short-haul question raises issue as to the extent of a market by one dimension alone, while this second phase of the matter touches the circumscription of the market both in length and breadth, — and one might almost add, in thickness as well. Such is the daily problem of the professional traffic manager. It has not frequently been presented for settlement to the Interstate Commerce Commission, but is certain to do so increasingly often with every increment of regulative power conferred by Congress or sanctioned by the courts. All these classes of problems alike fundamentally involve the principles concerning the element of distance as a factor in the carriage of goods. Transportation is in essence the elimination of the element of distance from markets. The most important and puzzling cases, therefore, naturally turn upon the definition of the due importance of distance as affecting cost of service, in comparison with competition which determines the value of service, and in which mere distance plays no part.[1]

Our cases illustrative of the *long-and-short-haul question* spring mainly from Section 4 of the Act to Regulate Commerce of 1887. That clause of the Federal statute, modeled upon the long-standing legislation of a number of states, prohibited the charging of a greater rate to any intermediate point than was charged to a more distant point on the same line; provided, however, that traffic moved from each under "substantially similar circumstances and conditions."[2] In the celebrated Louisville & Nashville case in 1889, the Interstate Commerce Commission promptly interpreted this latter clause as permitting carriers to charge less to the more distant point in three contingencies: viz., first, when there was water competition; secondly, when there was foreign railway competition at the more distant point; and thirdly, in certain "rare and peculiar cases" not conclusively defined. Under this interpretation of the law, both the railways and the Commission proceeded, until the final decision of the Supreme Court in 1897 in the Alabama Midland case, with which our reprints under this heading begin.[3] In substance this decision held: first, that the existence of railway competition at the more distant point justified the railway in charging what it pleased relatively at intermediate points; and secondly, it seemed to imply that the carrier was a competent

---

[1] This theoretical proposition is discussed in Ripley's Railroads: Rates and Regulation, chaps. iii and x.

[2] For a more elaborate discussion of this topic, *vide*, Final Report United States Industrial Commission, 1900, p. 433.

[3] The original decision of the Interstate Commerce Commission, p. 359; and the opinion of the Supreme Court, p. 378.

judge as to the controlling force of this competition, without reference to the opinion of the Interstate Commerce Commission. How fully this opinion emasculated the original statute is vividly described by Justice Harlan in his dissenting opinion.[1]

The Alabama Midland decision was rendered in 1897. Three cases, — the Savannah Freight Bureau ; [2] Dallas, Texas; and St. Cloud, Minnesota,[3] — decided during the next three years, illustrate the scope of authority exercised by the Commission under the long-and-short-haul clause as thus legally interpreted. In the first two exemption from its provisions was granted; that is to say, the railways were permitted to charge less to the more distant than to the intermediate points; while in the St. Cloud case the Commission held that this ought not to be allowed. For in this last case it appeared that the practice was actually prejudicial to St. Cloud, while in the other two the intermediate points suffered no peculiar damage. Many other interesting comparisons between these cases may be brought out in detailed analysis and discussion. Especial interest is lent to the St. Cloud case, however, because, although granting exemption to the carriers, the Commission was evidently struggling to regain some of the authority and prestige lost by the Alabama Midland decision. The arrogance of the railroads, especially in the southern states, seemed to render necessary either new legislation or a rehabilitation of the old. In the Danville, Virginia, case[4] in 1900 the Commission sought to shift its ground, mainly on the basis of another decision of the Supreme Court, as a reading of the case will show. It thus embarked upon a line of interpretation, not yet at this writing definitely settled by the court of last resort.[5] Appeal to the Supreme Court is still pending. Meantime, however, the entire inadequacy of the law, unless the new powers granted by the Hepburn Bill of 1906 are construed to supplement the old long-and-short-haul clause (which appears doubtful), is amply shown by the Chattanooga case. This, as well as the Danville case, presents a picture of intolerable

---

[1] *Vide*, p. 385.   Compare also p. 288, *infra*, in the Chattanooga case.

[2] P. 314, *infra*.   [3] P. 279, *infra*.   [4] P. 402, *infra*.

[5] Ripley's Railroads: Rates and Regulation, chaps. xiv and xix, brings this to 1912.

monopolistic abuse of power by the railways of the southern states, which would not be permitted in communities where public sentiment is more alert and better organized.[1] Unless some remedy can be found for the injustice indicated by these southern cases, either under a more liberal interpretation of the long-and-short-haul clause or by means of the newly enacted Hepburn Bill of 1906, a constant incentive to popular agitation will exist.

Two cases reprinted herein illustrate the complicated phase of *the distance problem*, wherein several shipping points at various degrees of remoteness from a common market are located, not on the same but on entirely different lines of railway. At Eau Claire, Wis.,[2] for example, it was a question of adjusting rates from a number of lumber-producing centers over a series of different railways converging on a market at the Missouri river. The convergence of these lines upon a common market renders this case somewhat analogous to that of the trunk line rate system, based upon distance percentages.[3] Both are entirely different from the Hutchinson salt case,[4] in which rates to a common market, St. Louis or New Orleans, not on converging lines, but on railways from entirely opposite directions, were called in question. A controversy was here involved as to whether St. Louis and the South should be supplied with salt from the Kansas or the Michigan fields; exactly the same contest involved of late in the struggle of the lumbermen of the far Northwest, of Louisiana, of the far Southeast, and of the northern central states, to gain entry on even terms to the great markets of Chicago and its tributary treeless territory.[5] In such cases as these we attain the climax of complexity in the problems of rate adjustment. Vast areas, a multitude of inter-related rates, and the welfare of large populations depend upon their just settlement. Fortunately in future a divided responsibility between the traffic managers and governmental experts

---

[1] Cf. especially the Savannah Naval Stores case, p. 252. The Troy case (p. 359) and that of Dawson, Ga. (p. 387), are typical of the flagrant discrimination which existed.

[2] P. 231, *infra*.   [3] Ripley's Railroads, chap. x.   [4] P. 216, *infra*.

[5] This is ably discussed with a fine map in the Senate Committee on Interstate Commerce Hearings, 1905, Vol. II.

seems likely to obtain in this work since the enactment of the Hepburn Bill of 1906. The decision no longer rests solely with the traffic manager, representing only one of the many parties in interest.

Certain of our cases are intended to contrast the *general systems of railway rates* prevalent in different sections of the United States. Three main divisions are distinguishable; viz., those of trunk line territory, of the southern states, and of the transcontinental carriers, including the Pacific coast. The trunk line scheme,[1] as might be expected, is the most highly developed system, not only from the point of view of simplicity but of justice as well. It illustrates the dominating importance of distance as a factor in sound rate adjustment. The southern or "basing-point" system, exemplified in the Troy,[2] Dawson,[3] Chattanooga,[4] and Danville [5] cases, lies at the opposite extreme. It shows what evils may result from the exercise of absolutely arbitrary powers by railway managers, acting solely with a view to their own interests and regardless of the general public welfare. To be sure, certain geographical difficulties, no greater than those of trunk line territory, but peculiar to the South, have to be considered. But even making all due allowances, both for the sparseness of its population and the frequency of water competition, the defiance of the fundamental principles of justice in rate making are a constant incentive to governmental interference.

The transcontinental and Pacific coast rate systems are interesting and peculiar, involving as they do constant consideration of the relative merits of transportation by sea and railroad. The San Bernardino case [6] is indicative of this phase of the matter with reference to a particular class of goods; while the important case of the St. Louis jobbers [7] raises the same issue with reference to a long list of commodities. But the latter case is of even wider scope. It discusses an issue which

---

[1] Transferred in this edition to our Railroads: Rates and Regulation, chap. x.

[2] P. 359, *infra*. [5] P. 402, *infra*.

[3] P. 387, *infra*. [6] Interstate Commerce Reports, Vol. IX, pp. 42–60.

[4] P. 266, *infra*. [7] P. 429, *infra*.

constantly arises all over the country with reference to distributive business. Shall California be supplied with hardware, for
example, by means of wholesale shipments to San Francisco,
followed by redistribution from that center; or shall the primary
distribution take place from Chicago and St. Louis direct? The
very existence of San Francisco as a commercial center is involved. It is the everlasting contest for supremacy between the
great cities and those of medium size, as well as the struggle
of each locality for economic independence. All through this
volume issues of this sort are manifest to the observant eye,
underlying what may appear to be relatively trivial complaints
from a financial standpoint. There will be no end to it all until
the firm foundations of a system based upon some scientific principle, as in the trunk line scheme, shall have been devised and
adopted here as well as in the southern states.

The Export Rate case[1] is important as bearing upon a most
difficult problem of commercial adjustment, which is continually cropping up for settlement, not only in the United States
but all over Europe.[2] It might have been better, perhaps, to
have reproduced the noted Import Rate case,[3] in which the Interstate Commerce Commission was finally overruled by a bare
majority opinion in the Supreme Court of the United States,
after having been upheld in the two lower Federal Courts; but
unfortunately both the length of that opinion and its unsatisfactory literary form rendered it impossible for republication.
The issue raised concerned the legality of lower through rates
on imports from Liverpool to San Francisco *via* New Orleans
than were granted on domestic shipments from New Orleans
to the same destination. Thus the rate on books, buttons, and
hosiery, from Liverpool to San Francisco through New Orleans,
was $1.07 per hundred pounds. At the same time the domestic
shipper was compelled to pay $2.88, or two and one-half times
as much, for a haul from New Orleans to San Francisco alone.
In another important ca[ ] tin plate was carried from Liverpool by steamer and rail [ ]rough Philadelphia to Chicago for

[1] P. 487, *infra*.   [2] P. 761, *infra*.
[3] Interstate Commerce Co[ ]mission Reports, Vol. IV, pp. 450–533.

twenty-four cents per hundred pounds. For the American merchant in Philadelphia the rate to the same market was twenty-six cents. For the inland haul alone the Pennsylvania Railroad was receiving sixteen cents on the foreign goods, while coincidently charging American merchants ten cents more for the same service. Discrimination against the American merchant in favor of foreign competition, not infrequently more than sufficient to overbalance any supposed protection afforded by the tariff, has been repeatedly proved in such cases as this. The duty on imported cement is eight cents per hundredweight. In one instance this duty with the total freight rate added amounted to only eighteen cents, as against a rate of twenty cents for the domestic producer from New York to the same point. There are reasons for this grievous discrimination against the domestic shipper, mainly concerned with the vagaries of ocean freight rates. Steamers must have ballast for the return trip to equalize outgoing shipments of grain and other exports, and they will carry heavy commodities, such as salt, cement, crockery, and glass, at extremely low rates. Nevertheless such imported commodities can be sold to advantage in competition with domestic goods only when the railways will contribute equally low rates to complete the shipment.

The Interstate Commerce Commission in this Import Rate case originally held that such discriminations were unlawful. Finally, however, the Supreme Court decided, with three members, including the Chief Justice, dissenting, that the Act to Regulate Commerce as phrased did not expressly prohibit the practice. Everything turned upon the interpretation of certain clauses in the law. No question was ever raised as to the economic issues involved, nor was it competent to these tribunals to pass upon such issues. The question was simply and solely this : When the Act to Regulate Commerce forbade inequality or discrimination between shippers, did it contemplate competition between one shipment originating within the country and others from foreign ports? Was the Interstate Commerce Commission, in other words, empowered, in interpreting this act, to consider circumstances and conditions *without* as well as *within* the boundaries of the United States? If it was entitled to consider solely domestic conditions, it was certainly right and economically sound in forbidding such practices; if, on the other hand, it was required to take account of commercial conditions the world over, irrespective of the effect upon the domestic producer and internal trade, its decision should have been favorable to the railroads. To appreciate fully the extreme nicety of the legal points involved and the delicacy of the economic interests at issue, one must needs read the extended opinions both of the majority of the Supreme Court and of the three dissenting justices, including Chief Justice Fuller. But to interpret the reversal of the original decision of the Interstate Commerce Commission by this tribunal as in the slightest degree involving incompetence or judicial unfairness is a misrepresentation of all the facts involved. As in the preceding cases touching the interpretation of the long-and-short-haul clause, it may fairly be said that the consensus of opinion among business men, and certainly among the professional economists of the country, is on the side of the Commission in condemning such practices. As to the law, that has been decided otherwise by a narrow majority. An important question before the country is as to whether a law thus construed should not be amended so as to permit a reasonable limitation of such abnormal traffic in future.

Governmental regulation, constituting the third division of this volume, is in fact a subject much wider in scope than the mere control of common carriers. It touches and includes the broad field of governmental supervision or control, not of railroads alone but of all public-service corporations. Many of the considerations, for example, in the chapters on "Reasonable Rates"[1] and "The Doctrine of Judicial Review,"[2] as applied to Federal control of railroads, are equally applicable to the problems of state regulation of street railways or of municipal control of gas and electric lighting or any other public service. Great underlying principles of constitutional law, as defined by the Federal Courts, are shown in the making.

[1] P. 597, *infra.*   [2] P. 619, *infra.*

As an episode in the history of governmental regulation of public-service companies the enactment of the Hepburn Bill of 1906 cannot fail to be of note.[1] Not only on account of the scope and magnitude of the interests involved — covering, as the railway net does, the entire country, and representing an investment of $12,000,000,000 — but also because of the powerful and well-organized opposition presented along the entire front, this piece of legislation is unique. It was a convincing demonstration of the power of public opinion when once thoroughly roused and ably led. The problem was vastly more difficult owing to the phenomenal growth of the business. The first law regulating railways was passed in 1887, after an agitation extending over nearly twenty years. Our domestic population from 1889 to 1903 increased slightly less than one third. The railroad mileage grew in about the same proportion. Yet the freight service of American railroads surpassed this rate of growth almost five times over. While population and mileage increased one third, the railroads in 1903 hauled the equivalent of two and one-half times the total volume of freight traffic handled in 1889. In other words, the ton mileage — representing the number of tons of freight hauled one mile — increased from 68,700,000,000 to 173,200,000,000.

Throughout the decade to 1900 the trend of affairs was all in favor of railway interests as against the government. The Alabama Midland decision of 1897 [2] thoroughly emasculated the long-and-short-haul clause of the original act; and the Maximum Rate decision in the Cincinnati Freight Bureau cases [3] deprived the Commission of any effective power to remedy unreasonable rates. During the same period the Anti-Trust Act of 1890 was greatly limited in its scope by a number of legal decisions. The inevitable reaction ensued. Under the leadership of President Roosevelt, public opinion was thoroughly aroused. It became evident to all unprejudiced persons that radical

---

[1] Federal legislation since 1905 is set forth in detail in Ripley's Railroads: Rates and Regulation, pp. 487–627.

[2] P. 378, *infra*.   [3] P. 187, *infra*.

amendment of the law relating to railroad regulation was necessary, not only to protect the shippers and the public but to head off the possibility of government ownership of railways becoming a great political issue in 1908. And yet so powerfully organized was corporate influence that, in spite of aroused public opinion, dilatory and obstructive tactics seemed likely to prevent any effective legislation. Fortunately, however, at this critical juncture came the astounding revelations of fraud and corruption in the great New York life-insurance companies, and of filth and adulteration in the Chicago canning and packing houses. The Senate yielded to the pressure from the President and the House of Representatives, and even outdid the House in zeal for the public welfare by adding amendments of far-reaching importance. The Hepburn Bill of 1906 definitively extending the principle of detailed governmental supervision, previously exercised only in the case of national banks, over the common carriers of the country, is thus worthy of the closest study, not alone in its history and details but in respect of its influence upon the future welfare of the transportation system of the United States.

The chapter upon judicial determination of reasonable rates[1] is of peculiar interest as describing the slow process by which an entire reversal of opinion by the Supreme Court of the United States upon a fundamentally important question may be effected. The right-about-face by this tribunal, respecting the relative power of legislatures and courts in regulating the charges of public-service companies, carries the mind back to the reversal of judgment of that august body a generation ago in the matter of the issue of legal-tender paper. It affords a striking illustration of what, to coin a phrase, one may call the "elastic stability" of our fundamental law. By the enunciation of the " Doctrine of Judicial Review," [2] the power of the legislative branch of our governments, Federal, state, or municipal, is definitely subordinated to that of the judiciary in all questions concerning the rates chargeable for public service. To the courts, therefore, must be submitted for final arbitrament, all controversies touching the reasonableness of railway rates. How

[1] P. 597, *infra*.   [2] Chapter XXIV, p. 619, *infra*.

profoundly this condition affected the form of the Hepburn Bill of 1906 may be seen from the debates in Congress, and particularly in the Senate.

Whether the Doctrine of Judicial Review, subordinating the primary law-making to the law-interpreting branch of the government, will permit of a satisfactory solution of the ever-pressing problem of public regulation of railway rates, is called in question in the chapter upon that subject.[1] The great issue of the opening of the twentieth century, both here and in Europe, concerns individual rights in the narrower sense and private property, on the one hand, as opposed to public welfare, on the other. Always conceding that the success of Anglo-Saxon institutions is attributable in large measure to insistence upon the rights of the individual, it is nevertheless incontrovertible that the swing of the pendulum, for good or ill, is at this time in the direction of the public welfare, more or less regardless of personal or property rights. One sees it in the domain of factory legislation, of taxation, of regulation of trusts and common carriers, of insurance, — a long series of statutes prescribing the conditions under which women and children and even adult men may labor; the quality and even the kind of food and drink which they may consume; the forms in which business enterprises may be organized and the subsequent manner in which they may be conducted; nay, even the precise form in which their accounts shall be kept. Thus the problem of determining which branch of the government shall be supreme in matters of this sort is one which is vital to the stability of our institutions, but also, be it observed, to their capacity for progress. That, within the narrow domain of regulation of railway rates, some modification of present judicial opinion is necessary if such progress — defining progress in the narrow sense of change conformable to the popular will — is to ensue, cannot reasonably be doubted. In any event, the matter is one open to discussion, and of such paramount importance that it cannot long be overlooked or postponed. Of course for the moment the courts stand as the natural champions of individual and

[1] P. 619, *infra.*

property rights, but it should never be forgotten that in truly democratic countries the judges are chosen by the people directly or through the medium of a selected executive, so that this condition is not necessarily an enduring one. The popular will when persistently bent upon a definite goal is bound to prevail in the end. In the best interests of conservatism, therefore, the safest course for the judiciary will be not flatly to dam the course of public opinion when once clearly defined, lest a flood sweeping all before it result. That happened in the case of our Civil War. The true function of the courts should be to hold back the impending waters until the issue is clear, and thenceforth to so shape or divert the current of affairs that both the individual and the public welfare may interact upon one another to the good of both. Reverting to the specific matter of regulation of railway rates, one cannot doubt that some such compromise will be the final outcome.

European conditions and experience in railroad matters, described in the final division of these reprints, have until recently received little attention in the United States. Our problems were unique in themselves; and in so vast an area rail transportation was from the outset so vital to extended existence that the United States has been rather a pioneer than an imitator of Europe in all matters pertaining to construction and operation. But now that affairs are entering upon another stage of development, what with governmental regulation and the increasing density of population, it appears that much valuable information may be gleaned from European experience. At the present time this is peculiarly true of the British Isles, where the economic condition of private ownership and operation prevails as in the United States. On the other hand, owing to its minute area, with omnipresent water carriage by sea, the problems imposed by British geographical conditions are less instructive perhaps than those upon the Continent, especially in Germany and France.

With private ownership and operation of railways, the British government has had an extended experience in regulation by governmental authority. The last fruits of this are set forth in detail, in our chapter upon " The English Railway and Canal Commission." [1] The problem, however, is simpler than ours, by reason of the fact that all control flows from one source, not being divided as in the United States between a Federal Congress and administrative Commission and a host of entirely independent state legislatures and commissions. Moreover, in the British Isles, it should be noted, the difficult questions of authority raised by the presence of a Constitution do not come into play. Parliament is supreme in legislative matters; its word is law. The will of the people may be expressed statutorily, at any time, regardless alike of legislative and judicial precedent. Protection for vested interests lies in a restricted suffrage together with the innate conservatism and sense of fair play of the British people. Thus freed from judicial trammels, it is of interest to observe what has been accomplished in the line of regulation. Among the peculiarities of the situation one notes the entire absence of our great evil of personal discrimination and rebating; [2] and especially that much of the activity of the Railway and Canal Commission is analogous rather to the work of some of the best of our state commissions, Massachusetts and Wisconsin for example, than of the Federal Interstate Commerce Commission. Pooling, likewise, and contracts providing for division of the field, permitting of an avoidance of the evils of excessive competition are allowed, not forbidden as in the United States. The business consists to a far greater degree of small or retail shipments. The problems of classification arising from widely different climatic, industrial, and social conditions do not complicate matters. But, on the other hand, the radical step has been taken of detailed prescription by law both of freight rates and classification. The Dominion of Canada in 1903 has proceeded even farther in this direction, its law upon the subject being based upon the Report upon Railway Rate Grievances of 1902, drawn up by Professor S. J. McLean, author of our chapter upon the English Commission. The

[1] Chapter XXVII, p. 745, *infra.*
[2] Cf. p. 760, *infra.*

Canadian Board of Railway Commissioners combines all the powers of the English Commission with those vested in the British Board of Trade. There is conferred a concentration of power over rates, both in England and Canada, beside which even our amended law of 1906 appears pale and colorless. Altogether the British experience is highly suggestive in all that concerns government regulation.

Government ownership of railroads is so obviously a remote possibility in the United States, so long as administrative regulation is effectively applied, that the experience of Germany in this field would seem to be unimportant. And yet, having due regard to her superb administrative system, and to her peculiar industrial problems, the service is so admirably adapted to her needs that it amply repays close investigation. From the point of view of public finance alone, the Prussian achievement of government ownership is extraordinary. In 1882, with a gross income of about $109,000,000, a clear surplus above expenses and interest on debt of slightly more than $10,000,000 resulted. This net profit has steadily risen. Ten years later it was about $25,000,000; and in 1900 it had increased to $99,000,000. In 1905, with a gross income of approximately $405,000,000 (1,621,000,000 marks) expenses absorbed about $250,000,000, and interest charges about $28,000,000, leaving a net profit on the investment of more than $125,000,000 (503,000,000 marks). A return of something like five and one-half per cent on the capital investment is indeed a notable result in government finance. This has been made possible because of two unique conditions; the wonderful industrial growth of Germany in the last two decades, and the high standard both of technical education and of the personnel of the government service. The railway net comprises only about one seventh of the mileage of our American roads, all operated in a densely populated country with high-grade traffic. No reasonable conclusion can be drawn from these results as to the advantages of government ownership in a vast, sparsely settled region like the United States. But we can learn much from certain features of the management of these German railroads, as set forth in our chapter on the subject.[1] One of the most admirable features is the system of advisory councils, composed jointly of traffic officials and of prominent representatives of shippers. Extended deliberation upon every adjustment of rates ensues; all possible complications are considered, with reference to export trade, fiscal receipts, economy in operation, territorial competition, and the like. Observation in the field strengthens the conclusion that a degree of peace and coöperation between the railroads and the shipping public, far better than that which prevails to-day in the United States, has followed as a result. The avoidance of economic wastes, such as are described in our chapter on the subject, are also strongly in contrast with our American practices. It is my conviction, all things considered, that our American transportation system is the best in the world. All the more reason why we should open our eyes to the excellences of the railroad systems of foreign countries.

WILLIAM Z. RIPLEY

HARVARD UNIVERSITY

---

[1] P. 803, *infra*.

RAILWAY PROBLEMS

I

A CHAPTER OF ERIE [1]

THE history of the Erie Railway has been a checkered one. Chartered in 1832, and organized in 1833, the cost of its construction was then estimated at three millions of dollars, of which but one million was subscribed. By the time the first report was made the estimated cost had increased to six millions, and the work of construction was actually begun on the strength of stock subscriptions of a million and a half, and a loan of three millions from the State. In 1842 the estimated cost had increased to twelve millions and a half, and both means in hand and credit were wholly exhausted. Subscription books were opened, but no names were entered in them; the city of New York was applied to, and refused a loan of its credit; again the legislature was besieged, but the aid from this quarter was now hampered with inadmissible conditions; accordingly work was suspended, and the property of the insolvent corpora tion passed into the hands of assignees. In 1845 the State came again to the rescue; it surrendered all claim to the three millions it had already lent to the company; and one half of their old subscriptions having been given up by the stockholders, and a new subscription of three millions raised, the whole property of the road was mortgaged for three millions more. At last, in 1851, eighteen years after its commencement, the road was opened from Lake Erie to tide water. Its financial troubles had, however, as yet only begun, for in 1859 it could not meet the interest on its mortgages, and passed into the hands of a

[1] From Chapters of Erie and Other Essays, by (Hons.) Charles Francis Adams and Henry Adams, New York, 1886. By permission. The historical setting of these events is given in Ripley's Railroads, both in the volume on Rates (p. 16) and that on Finance (Stock-watering, etc.).

receiver. In 1861 an arrangement of interests was effected, and a new company was organized. The next year the old New York & Erie Railroad Company disappeared under a foreclosure of the fifth mortgage, and the present Erie Railway Company rose from its ashes. Meanwhile the original estimate of three millions had developed into an actual outlay of fifty millions; the 470 miles of track opened in 1842 had expanded into 773 miles in 1868; and the revenue, which the projectors had "confidently" estimated at something less than two millions in 1833, amounted to over five millions when the road passed into the hands of a receiver in 1859, and in 1865 reached the enormous sum of sixteen millions and a half.

*   *   *   *   *   *   *   *

The series of events in the Erie history which culminated in the struggle about to be narrated may be said to have had its origin some seventeen or eighteen years before, when Mr. Daniel Drew first made his appearance in the Board of Directors, where he remained down to the year 1868, generally holding also the office of treasurer of the corporation. Mr. Drew is what is known as a self-made man. Born in the year 1797, as a boy he drove cattle down from his native town of Carmel, in Putnam County, to the market of New York City, and, subsequently, was for years proprietor of the Bull's Head Tavern. Like his contemporary, and ally or opponent, — as the case might be, Cornelius Vanderbilt, he built up his fortunes in the steamboat interest, and subsequently extended his operations over the rapidly developing railroad system. Shrewd, unscrupulous, and very illiterate, — a strange combination of superstition and faithlessness, of daring and timidity, — often good-natured and sometimes generous, — he ever regarded his fiduciary position of director in a railroad as a means of manipulating its stock for his own advantage. For years he had been the leading bear of Wall Street, and his favorite haunts were the secret recesses of Erie. As treasurer of that corporation, he had, in its frequently recurring hours of need, advanced it sums which it could not have obtained elsewhere, and the obtaining of which was a necessity. He had been at once a good friend of the road and the worst enemy it had as yet known. His management of his favorite stock had been cunning and recondite, and his ways inscrutable. Those who sought to follow him and those who sought to oppose him, alike found food for sad reflection; until at last he won for himself the expressive *sobriquet* of the Speculative Director. Sometimes, though rarely, he suffered greatly in the complications of Wall Street; more frequently he inflicted severe damage upon others. On the whole, however, his fortunes had greatly prospered, and the outbreak of the Erie war found him the actual possessor of some millions, and the reputed possessor of many more.

In the spring of 1866 Mr. Drew's manipulations of Erie culminated in an operation which was at the time regarded as a masterpiece; subsequent experience has, however, so improved upon it that it is now looked upon as an ordinary and inartistic piece of what is called " railroad financiering," a class of operations formerly known by a more opprobrious name. The stock of the road was then selling at about 95, and the corporation was, as usual, in debt, and in pressing need of money. As usual, also, it resorted to its treasurer. Mr. Drew stood ready to make the desired advances — upon security. Some twenty-eight thousand shares of its own authorized stock, which had never been issued, were at the time in the hands of the company, which also claimed, under the statutes of New York, the right of raising money by the issue of bonds, convertible, at the option of the holder, into stock. The twenty-eight thousand unissued shares, and bonds for three millions of dollars, convertible into stock, were placed by the company in the hands of its treasurer, as security for a cash loan of $3,500,000. The negotiation had been quietly effected, and Mr. Drew's campaign now opened. Once more he was short of Erie. While Erie was buoyant, — while it steadily approximated to par, — while speculation was rampant, and that outside public, the delight and the prey of Wall Street, was gradually drawn in by the fascination of amassing wealth without labor, — quietly and stealthily, through his agents and brokers, the grave, desponding operator was daily concluding his contracts for the future delivery of stock at current prices. At last the hour had come. Erie was rising, Erie was scarce, the great bear had many contracts to fulfill, and where was he to find the stock? His victims were not kept long in suspense. Mr. Treasurer Drew laid his hands upon his collateral. In an instant the bonds for three millions were converted into an equivalent amount of capital stock, and fifty-eight thousand shares, dumped, as it were, by the cartload in Broad Street, made Erie as plenty as even Drew could desire. Before the astonished bulls could rally their faculties, the quotations had fallen from 95 to 50, and they realized that they were hopelessly entrapped.

The whole transaction, of course, was in no respect more creditable than any result, supposed to be one of chance or skill, which, in fact, is made to depend upon the sorting of a pack of cards, the dosing of a race horse, or the selling out of his powers by a " walkist." But the gambler, the patron of the turf, or the pedestrian represents, as a rule, himself alone, and his character is generally so well understood as to be a warning to all the world. The case of the treasurer of a great corporation is different. He occupies a fiduciary position. He is a trustee, — a guardian. Vast interests are confided to his care; every shareholder of the corporation is his ward; if it is a railroad, the community itself is his *cestui que trust.* But passing events, accumulating more thickly with every year, have thoroughly corrupted the public morals on this subject. A directorship in certain great corporations has come to be regarded as a situation in which to make a fortune, the possession of which is no longer dishonorable. The method of accumulation is both simple and safe. It consists in giving contracts as a trustee to one's self as an individual, or in speculating in the property of one's *cestui que trust,* or in using the funds confided to one's charge, as treasurer or otherwise, to gamble with the real owners of those funds for their own property, and that with cards packed in advance. The wards themselves expect their guardians to throw the dice against them for their own property, and are surprised, as well as gratified, if the dice are not loaded. These proceedings, too, are looked upon as hardly reprehensible, yet they strike at the very foundation of existing society. The theory of representation, whether in politics or in business, is of the essence of modern development. Our whole system rests upon the sanctity of the fiduciary relations. Whoever betrays them, a director of a railroad no less than a member of Congress or the trustee of an orphans' asylum, is the common enemy of every man, woman and child who lives under representative government. The unscrupulous director is far less entitled to mercy than the ordinary gambler, combining as he does the character of the traitor with the acts of the thief.

No acute moral sensibility on this point, however, has for some years troubled Wall Street, nor, indeed, the country at large. As a result of the transaction of 1866, Mr. Drew was looked upon as having effected a surprisingly clever operation, and he retired from the field hated, feared, wealthy, and admired. This episode of Wall Street history took its place as a brilliant success beside the famous Prairie du Chien and Harlem "corners," and, but for subsequent events, would soon have been forgotten. Its close connection, however, with more important though later incidents of Erie history seems likely to preserve its memory fresh. Great events were impending; a new man was looming up in the railroad world, introducing novel ideas and principles, and it could hardly be that the new and old would not come in conflict. Cornelius Vanderbilt, commonly known as Commodore Vanderbilt, was now developing his theory of the management of railroads.

Born in the year 1794, Vanderbilt was a somewhat older man than Drew. There are several points of resemblance in the early lives of the two men, and many points of curious contrast in their characters. Vanderbilt, like Drew, was born in very humble circumstances in the State of New York, and like him also received little education. He began life by ferrying passengers and produce from Staten Island to New York City. Subsequently, he too laid the foundation of his great fortune in the growing steamboat navigation, and likewise, in due course of time, transferred himself to the railroad interest. When at last, in 1868, the two came into collision as representatives of the old system of railroad management and of the new, they were each threescore and ten years of age, and had both been successful in the accumulation of millions, — Vanderbilt even more so than Drew. They were probably equally unscrupulous and equally selfish; but, while the cast of Drew's mind was somber and bearish, Vanderbilt was gay and buoyant of temperament, little given to thoughts other than of this world, a lover of horses and of the good things of life. The first affects prayer meetings, and the last is a devotee of whist. Drew, in Wall Street, is by temperament a bear, while Vanderbilt could hardly be other than a bull. Vanderbilt must be allowed to be by far the superior man of the two. Drew is astute and full of resources, and at all times a dangerous opponent; but Vanderbilt takes larger, more comprehensive views, and his mind has a vigorous grasp which that of Drew seems to want.

* * * * * * * *

Two great lines of railway traverse the State of New York and connect it with the West, — the Erie and the New York Central. The latter communicates with the city by a great river and by two railroads. To get these two roads — the Harlem and the Hudson River — under his own absolute control, and then, so far as the connection with the Central was concerned, to abolish the river, was Vanderbilt's immediate object. First making himself master of the Harlem road, he there learned his early lessons in railroad management, and picked up a fortune by the way. A few years ago Harlem had no value. As late as 1860 it sold for eight or nine dollars per share; and in January, 1863, when Vanderbilt had got the control, it had risen only to 30. By July of that year it stood at 92, and in August was suddenly raised by a "corner" to 179. The next year witnessed a similar operation. The stock which sold in January at less than 90 was settled for in June in the neighborhood of 285. On one of these occasions Mr. Drew is reported to have contributed a sum approaching

half a million to his rival's wealth. More recently the stock
had been floated at about 130. It was in the successful conduct of this first experiment that Vanderbilt showed his very
manifest superiority over previous railroad managers. The
Harlem was, after all, only a competing line, and competition
was proverbially the rock ahead in all railroad enterprise. The
success of Vanderbilt with the Harlem depended upon his getting rid of the competition of the Hudson River Railroad. An
ordinary manager would have resorted to contracts, which are
never carried out, or to opposition, which is apt to be ruinous.
Vanderbilt, on the contrary, put an end to competition by buying up the competing line. This he did at about par, and, in
due course of time, the stock was sent up to 180. Thus his
plans had developed by another step, while through a judicious
course of financiering and watering and dividing, a new fortune
had been secured by him. By this time Vanderbilt's reputation
as a railroad manager — as one who earned dividends, created
stock, and invented wealth — had become very great, and the
managers of the Central brought that road to him, and asked him
to do with it as he had done with the Harlem and Hudson River.
He accepted the proffered charge, and now, probably, the possibilities of his position and the magnitude of the prize within his
grasp at last dawned on his mind. Unconsciously to himself,
working more wisely than he knew, he had developed to its
logical conclusion one potent element of modern civilization.

 *   *   *   *   *   *   *   *

The New York Central passed into Vanderbilt's hands in
the winter of 1866–67, and he marked the Erie for his own in
the succeeding autumn. As the annual meeting of the corporation approached, three parties were found in the field contending for control of the road. One party was represented by Drew,
and might be called the party in possession, that which had
long ruled the Erie, and made it what it was, — the Scarlet
Woman of Wall Street. Next came Vanderbilt, flushed with
success, and bent upon fully gratifying his great instinct for
developing imperialism in corporate life. Lastly, a faction made
its appearance composed of some shrewd and ambitious Wall

Street operators and of certain persons from Boston, who sustained for the occasion the novel character of railroad reformers. This party, it is needless to say, was as unscrupulous, and, as the result proved, as able as either of the others; it represented nothing but a raid made upon the Erie treasury in the interest of a thoroughly bankrupt New England corporation, of which its members had the control. The history of this corporation, known as the Boston, Hartford & Erie Railroad, — a projected feeder and connection of the Erie, — would be one curious to read, though very difficult to write. Its name was synonymous with bankruptcy, litigation, fraud, and failure. If the Erie was of doubtful repute in Wall Street, the Boston, Hartford & Erie had long been of worse than doubtful repute in State Street. Of late years, under able and persevering, if not scrupulous management, the bankrupt, moribund company had been slowly struggling into new life, and in the spring of 1867 it had obtained, under certain conditions, from the Commonwealth of Massachusetts, a subsidy in aid of the construction of its road. One of the conditions imposed obliged the corporation to raise a sum from other sources still larger than that granted by the State. Accordingly, those having the line in charge looked abroad for a victim, and fixed their eyes upon the Erie.

As the election day drew near, Erie was of course for sale. A controlling interest of stockholders stood ready to sell their proxies, with entire impartiality, to any of the three contending parties, or to any man who would pay the market price for them. Nay, more, the attorney of one of the contending parties, as it afterwards appeared, after an ineffectual effort to extort blackmail, actually sold the proxies of his principal to another of the contestants, and his doing so seemed to excite mirth rather than surprise. Meanwhile the representatives of the Eastern interest played their part to admiration. Taking advantage of some Wall Street complications just then existing between Vanderbilt and Drew, they induced the former to ally himself with them, and the latter saw that his defeat was inevitable. Even at this time the Vanderbilt party contemplated having recourse, if necessary, to the courts, and a petition for an injunction had been prepared, setting forth the details of the "corner" of 1866. On the Sunday preceding the election Drew, in view of his impending defeat, called upon Vanderbilt. That gentleman, thereupon, very amicably read to him the legal documents prepared for his benefit; whereupon the ready treasurer at once turned about, and, having hitherto been hampering the Commodore by his bear operations, he now agreed to join hands with him in giving to the market a strong upward tendency. Meanwhile the other parties to the contest were not idle. At the same house, at a later hour in the day, Vanderbilt explained to the Eastern adventurers his new plan of operations, which included the continuance of Drew in his directorship. These gentlemen were puzzled, not to say confounded, by this sudden change of front. An explanation was demanded, some plain language followed, and the parties separated, leaving everything unsettled; but only to meet again at a later hour at the house of Drew. There Vanderbilt brought the new men to terms by proposing to Drew a bold *coup de main*, calculated to throw them entirely out of the direction. Before the parties separated that night a written agreement had been entered into, providing that, to save appearances, the new board should be elected without Drew, but that immediately thereafter a vacancy should be created, and Drew chosen to fill it. He was therefore to go in as one of two directors in the Vanderbilt interest, that gentleman's nephew, Mr. Work, being the other.

This programme was faithfully carried out, and on the 2d of October Wall Street was at once astonished, by the news of the defeat of the notorious leader of the bears, and bewildered by the immediate resignation of a member of the new board and the election of Drew in his place. Apparently he had given in his submission, the one obstacle to success was removed, and the ever-victorious Commodore had now but to close his fingers on his new prize. Virtual consolidation on the Vanderbilt interest seemed a foregone conclusion.

    *   *   *   *   *   *   *   *

The real conflict was now impending. Commodore Vanderbilt stretched out his hand to grasp Erie. Erie was to be isolated and shut up within the limits of New York; it was to be given over, bound hand and foot, to the lord of the Central. To perfect this programme, the representatives of all the competing lines met, and a proposition was submitted to the Erie party looking to a practical consolidation on certain terms of the Pennsylvania Central, the Erie, and the New York Central, and a division among the contracting parties of all the earnings from the New York City travel. A new illustration was thus to be afforded, at the expense of the trade and travel to and from the heart of a continent, of George Stephenson's famous aphorism, that where combination is possible competition is impossible. The Erie party, however, represented that their road earned more than half of the fund of which they were to receive only one third. They remonstrated and proposed modifications, but their opponents were inexorable. The terms were too hard; the conference led to no result; a ruinous competition seemed impending as the alternative to a fierce war of doubtful issue. Both parties now retired to their camps, and mustered their forces in preparation for the first overt act of hostility. They had not long to wait.

  * * * * * * * *

The first open hostilities took place on the 17th of February. For some time Wall Street had been agitated with forebodings of the coming hostilities, but not until that day was recourse had to the courts. Vanderbilt had two ends in view when he sought to avail himself of the processes of law. In the first place, Drew's long connection with Erie, and especially the unsettled transactions arising out of the famous corner of 1866, afforded admirable ground for annoying offensive operations; and, in the second place, these very proceedings, by throwing his opponent on the defensive, afforded an excellent cover for Vanderbilt's own transactions in Wall Street. It was essential to his success to corner Drew, but to corner Drew at all was not easy, and to corner him in Erie was difficult indeed. Very recent experiences, of which Vanderbilt was fully informed, no less than the memories of 1866, had fully warned the public how manifold and ingenious were the expedients through which the coming treasurer furnished himself with Erie, when the exigencies of his position demanded fresh supplies. It was, therefore, very necessary for Vanderbilt that he should, while buying Erie with one hand in Wall Street, with the other close, so far as he could, that apparently inexhaustible spring from which such generous supplies of new stock were wont to flow. Accordingly, on the 17th of February, Mr. Frank Work, the only remaining representative of the Vanderbilt faction in the Erie direction, accompanied by Mr. Vanderbilt's attorneys, Messrs. Rapallo and Spenser, made his appearance before Judge Barnard, of the Supreme Court of New York, then sitting in chambers, and applied for an injunction against Treasurer Drew and his brother directors of the Erie Railway, restraining them from the payment of interest or principal of the three and a half millions borrowed of the treasurer in 1866, as well as from releasing Drew from any liability or cause of action the company might have against him, pending an investigation of his accounts as treasurer ; on the other hand, Drew was to be enjoined from taking any legal steps towards compelling a settlement. A temporary injunction was granted in accordance with the petition, and a further hearing was assigned for the 21st. Two days later, however,— on the 19th of the month, — without waiting for the result of the first attack, the same attorneys appeared again before Judge Barnard, and now in the name of the people, acting through the Attorney-General, petitioned for the removal from office of Treasurer Drew. The papers in the case set forth some of the difficulties which beset the Commodore, and exposed the existence of a new fountain of Erie stock. It appeared that there was a recently enacted statute of New York which authorized any railroad company to create and issue its own stock in exchange for the stock of any other road under lease to it. The petition then alleged that Mr. Drew and certain of his brother directors, had quietly possessed themselves of a worthless road connecting with the Erie, and called the Buffalo, Bradford & Pittsburg Railroad, and had then, as occasion and their own exigencies required, proceeded to supply themselves with whatever Erie stock they wanted, by leasing their own road to the road of which they were directors, and then creating stock and issuing it to themselves, in exchange, under the authority vested in them by law. The uncontradicted history of this transaction, as subsequently set forth on the very doubtful authority of a leading Erie director, affords, indeed, a most happy illustration of brilliant railroad financiering, whether true in this case or not. The road, it was stated, cost the purchasers, as financiers, some $250,000 ; as proprietors, they then issued in its name bonds for two million dollars, payable to one of themselves, who now figured as trustee. This person, then, shifting his character, drew up, as counsel for both parties, a contract leasing this road to the Erie Railway for four hundred and ninety-nine years, the Erie agreeing to assume the bonds ; reappearing in their original character of Erie directors, these gentlemen then ratified the lease, and thereafter it only remained for them to relapse into the rôle of financiers, and to divide the proceeds. All this was happily accomplished, and the Erie Railway lost and some one gained $140,000 a year by the bargain. The skillful actors in this much shifting drama probably proceeded on the familiar theory that exchange is no robbery ; and the expedient was certainly ingenious.

* * * * * * * *

It was not until the 3d of March, however, that any decisive action was taken by Judge Barnard on either of the petitions before him. Even then, that in the name of the Attorney-General was postponed for final hearing until the 10th of the month ; but, on the application of Work, an injunction was issued restraining the Erie board from any new issue of capital stock, by conversion of bonds or otherwise, in addition to the 251,058 shares appearing in the previous reports of the road, and forbidding the guaranty by the Erie of the bonds of any connecting line of road. While this last provision of the order was calculated to furnish food for thought to the Boston party, matter for meditation was supplied to Mr. Drew by other clauses, which specially forbade him, his agents, attorneys, or brokers, to have any transactions in Erie, or fulfill any of his contracts already entered into, until he had returned to the company sixty-eight thousand shares of capital stock, alleged to be the number involved in the unsettled transaction of 1866, and the more recent Buffalo, Bradford & Pittsburg exchange. A final hearing was fixed for the 10th of March on both injunctions.

Things certainly did not now promise well for Treasurer Drew and the bear party. Vanderbilt and the bulls seemed to arrange everything to meet their own views ; apparently they had but to ask and it was granted. If any virtue existed in the processes of law, if any authority was wielded by a New York court, it now seemed as if the very head of the bear faction must needs be converted into a bull in his own despite, and to his manifest ruin. He, in this hour of his trial, was to be forced by his triumphant opponent to make Erie scarce by returning into its treasury sixty-eight thousand shares, — one fourth of its whole capital stock of every description. So far from manufacturing fresh Erie and pouring it into the street, he was to be cornered by a writ, and forced to work his own ruin in obedience to an injunction. Appearances are, however, proverbially deceptive, and all depended on the assumption that some virtue did exist in the processes of law, and that some authority was wielded by a New York court. In spite of the threatening aspect of his affairs, it was very evident that the nerves of Mr. Drew and his associates were not seriously affected. Wall Street watched him with curiosity not unmingled with alarm ; for this was a conflict of Titans. Hedged all around with orders of the court, suspended, enjoined, and threatened with all manner of unheard-of processes, with Vanderbilt's wealth standing like a lion in his path, and all Wall Street ready to turn upon him and rend him, — in presence of all these accumulated terrors of the court room and of the exchange, the Speculative Director was not less speculative than was his wont. He seemed rushing on destruction. Day after day he pursued the same "short"[1] tactics ; contract after contract was put out for the future delivery of stock at current prices, and this, too, in the face of a continually rising market. Evidently he did not yet consider himself at the end of his resources.

[1] An operator is said to be "short" when he has agreed to deliver that which he has not got. He wagers, in fact, on a fall.

It was equally evident, however, that he had not much time to lose. It was now the 3d of March, and the anticipated " corner " might be looked for about the 10th. As usual, some light skirmishing took place as a prelude to the heavy shock of decisive battle. The Erie party very freely and openly expressed a decided lack of respect, and something approaching contempt, for the purity of that particular fragment of the judicial ermine which was supposed to adorn the person of Mr. Justice Barnard. They did not pretend to conceal their conviction that this magistrate was a piece of the Vanderbilt property, and they very plainly announced their intention of seeking for justice elsewhere. With this end in view they betook themselves to their own town of Binghamton, in the county of Broome, where they duly presented themselves before Mr. Justice Balcom, of the Supreme Court. The existing judicial system of New York divides the State into eight distinct districts, each of which has an independent Supreme Court of four judges, elected by the citizens of that district. The first district alone enjoys five judges, the fifth being the Judge Barnard already referred to. These local judges, however, are clothed with certain equity powers in actions commenced before them, which run throughout the State. As one subject of litigation, therefore, might affect many individuals, each of whom might initiate legal proceedings before any of the thirty-three judges ; which judge again might forbid proceedings before any or all of the other judges, or issue a stay of proceedings in suits already commenced, and then proceed to make orders, to consolidate actions, and to issue process for contempt, — it was not improbable that, sooner or later, strange and disgraceful conflicts of authority would arise, and that the law would fall into contempt. Such a system can, in fact, be sustained only so long as coördinate judges use the delicate powers of equity with a careful regard to private rights and the dignity of the law, and therefore, more than any which has ever been devised, it calls for a high average of learning, dignity, and personal character in the occupants of the bench. When, therefore, the ermine of the judge is flung into the kennel of party politics and becomes a part of the spoils of political victory ; when by any chance partisanship, brutality, and corruption become the qualities which especially recommend the successful aspirant to judicial honors, then the system described will be found to furnish peculiar facilities for the display of these characteristics.

*　　*　　*　　*　　*　　*　　*　　*

All this, however, was mere skirmishing, and now the decisive engagement was near at hand. The plans of the Erie ring were matured, and, if Commodore Vanderbilt wanted the stock of their road, they were prepared to let him have all he desired. As usual the Erie treasury was at this time deficient in funds. As usual, also, Daniel Drew stood ready to advance all the funds required, — on proper security. One kind of security, and only one, the company was disposed at this time to offer, — its convertible bonds under a pledge of conversion. The company could not issue stock outright, in any case, at less than par; its bonds bore interest and were useless on the street; an issue of convertible bonds was another name for an issue of stock to be sold at market rates. The treasurer readily agreed to find a purchaser, and, in fact, he himself stood just then in pressing need of some scores of thousands of shares. Already at the meeting of the Board of Directors, on the 19th of February, a very deceptive account of the condition of the road, jockeyed out of the general superintendent, had been read and made public; the increased depot facilities, the projected double track, and the everlasting steel rails, had been made to do vigorous duty; and the board had, in the vaguest and most general language conceivable, clothed the Executive Committee with full power in the premises. . . . Immediately after the Board of Directors adjourned a meeting of the Executive Committee was held, and a vote to issue at once convertible bonds for ten millions gave a meaning to the very ambiguous language of the directors' resolve; and thus, when apparently on the very threshold of his final triumph, this mighty mass of one hundred thousand shares of new stock was hanging like an avalanche over the head of Vanderbilt.

The Executive Committee had voted to sell the entire amount of these bonds at not less than 72½. Five millions were placed upon the market at once, and Mr. Drew's broker became the purchaser, Mr. Drew giving him a written guaranty against loss, and being entitled to any profit. It was all done in ten minutes after the committee adjourned, — the bonds issued, their conversion into stock demanded and complied with, and certificates for fifty thousand shares deposited in the broker's safe, subject to the orders of Daniel Drew. There they remained until the 29th, when they were issued, on his requisition, to certain others of that gentleman's army of brokers, much as ammunition might be issued before a general engagement. Three days later came the Barnard injunction, and Erie suddenly rose in the market. Then it was determined to bring up the reserves and let the eager bulls have the other five millions. The history of this second issue was, in all respects, an episode worthy of Erie, and deserves minute relation. It was decided upon on the 3d, but before the bonds were converted Barnard's injunction had been served on every one connected with the Erie Road or with Daniel Drew. The 10th was the return day of the writ, but the Erie operators needed even less time for their deliberations. Monday, the 9th, was settled upon as the day upon which to defeat the impending "corner." The night of Saturday, the 7th, was a busy one in the Erie camp. While one set of counsel and clerks were preparing affidavits and prayers for strange writs and injunctions, the enjoined vice president of the road was busy at home signing certificates of stock, to be ready for instant use in case a modification of the injunction could be obtained, and another set of counsel was in immediate attendance on the leaders themselves. Mr. Groesbeck, the chief of the Drew brokers, being himself enjoined, secured elsewhere, after one or two failures, a purchaser of the bonds, and took him to the house of the Erie counsel, where Drew and other directors and brokers then were. There the terms of the nominal sale were agreed upon, and a contract was drawn up transferring the bonds to this man of straw, who in return gave Mr. Drew a full power of attorney to convert or otherwise dispose of the bonds, in the form of a promissory note for their purchase money. Mr. Groesbeck, meanwhile, with the fear of injunctions before his eyes, prudently withdrew into the next room, and amused himself by looking at the curiosities and conversing with the lawyers' young gentlemen. After the contract was closed, the purchaser was asked to sign an affidavit setting forth his ownership of the bonds and the refusal of the corporation to convert them into stock in compliance with their contract, upon which affidavit it was in contemplation to seek from some justice a writ of *mandamus* to compel the Erie Railway to convert them, the necessary papers for such a proceeding being then in course of preparation elsewhere. This the purchaser declined to do. One of the lawyers present then said, " Well, you can make the demand now; here is Mr. Drew, the treasurer of the company, and Mr. Gould, one of the Executive Committee." In accordance with this suggestion a demand for the stock was then made, and, of course, at once refused; thereupon the scruples of the man of straw being all removed, the desired affidavit was signed. All business now being finished, the parties separated; the legal papers were ready, the convertible bonds had been disposed of, and the certificates of stock, for which they were to be exchanged, were signed in blank and ready for delivery.

Early Monday morning the Erie people were at work. Mr. Drew, the director and treasurer, had agreed to sell on that day fifty thousand shares of the stock, at 80, to the firms of which Mr. Fisk and Mr. Gould were members, these gentlemen also being Erie directors and members of the Executive Committee. The new certificates, made out in the names of these firms on Saturday night, were in the hands of the secretary of the company, who was strictly enjoined from allowing their issue. On Monday morning this official directed an employee of the road to carry these books of certificates from the West Street office of the company to the transfer clerk in Pine Street, and there to deliver them carefully. The messenger left the room, but immediately returned empty-handed, and informed the astonished secretary that Mr. Fisk had met him outside the door, taken from him the books of unissued certificates, and "run away with them." It was true; — one essential step towards conversion had been taken; the certificates of stock were beyond the control of an injunction. During the afternoon of the same day the convertible bonds were found upon the secretary's desk, where they had been placed by Mr. Belden, the partner in business of Director James Fisk, Jr.; the certificates were next seen in Broad Street.

Before launching the bolt thus provided, the conspirators had considered it not unadvisable to cover their proceedings, if they could, with some form of law. This probably was looked upon as an idle ceremony, but it could do no harm; and perhaps their next step was dictated by what has been called "a decent respect for the opinions of mankind," combined with a profound contempt for judges and courts of law.

Early on the morning of the 9th Judge Gilbert, a highly respected magistrate of the Second Judicial District, residing in Brooklyn, was waited upon by one of the Erie counsel, who desired to initiate before him a new suit in the Erie litigation, — this time, in the name of the Saturday evening purchaser of bonds and maker of affidavits. A writ of *mandamus* was asked for. This writ clearly did not lie in such a case; the magistrate very properly declined to grant it, and the only wonder is that counsel should have applied for it. New counsel were then hurriedly summoned, and a new petition, in a fresh name, was presented. This petition was for an injunction, in the name of Belden, the partner of Mr. Fisk, and the documents then and there presented were probably as eloquent an exposure as could possibly have been penned of the lamentable condition into which the once honored judiciary of New York had fallen. The petition alleged that some time in February certain persons, among whom was especially named George G. Barnard, — the justice of the Supreme Court of the First District, — had entered into a combination to speculate in the stock of the Erie Railway, and to use the process of the courts for the purpose of aiding their speculation; "and that, in furtherance of the plans of this combination," the actions in Work's name had been commenced before Barnard, who, the counsel asserted, was then issuing injunctions at the rate of half a dozen a day.

It is impossible by any criticism to do justice to such audacity as this: the dumb silence of amazement is the only fitting commentary. Apparently, however, nothing that could be stated of his colleague across the river exceeded the belief of Judge Gilbert, for, after some trifling delays and a few objections on the part of the judge to the form of the desired order, the Erie counsel hurried away, and returned to New York with a new injunction, restraining all the parties to all the other suits from further proceedings, and from doing any acts in "furtherance of said conspiracy"; — in one paragraph ordering the Erie directors, except Work, to continue in the discharge of their duties, in direct defiance of the injunction of one judge, and in the next, with an equal disregard of another judge, forbidding the directors to desist from converting bonds into stock. Judge Gilbert having, a few hours before signing this wonderful order, refused to issue a writ of *mandamus*, it may be proper to add that the process of equity here resorted to, compelling the performance of various acts, is of recent invention, and is known as a "mandatory injunction."

All was now ready. The Drew party were enjoined in every direction. One magistrate had forbidden them to move, and another magistrate had ordered them not to stand still. If the Erie board held meetings and transacted business, it violated one injunction; if it abstained from doing so, it violated another. By the further conversion of bonds into stock pains and penalties would be incurred at the hands of Judge Barnard; the refusal to convert would be an act of disobedience to Judge Gilbert. Strategically considered, the position could not be improved, and Mr. Drew and his friends were not the men to let the golden moment escape them. At once, before a new injunction could be obtained, even in New York, fifty thousand shares of new Erie stock were flung upon the market. That day Erie was buoyant, — Vanderbilt was purchasing. His agents caught at the new stock as eagerly as at the old, and the whole of it was absorbed before its origin was suspected, and almost without a falter in the price. Then the fresh certificates appeared, and the truth became known. Erie had that day opened at 80 and risen rapidly to 83, while its rise even to par was predicted; suddenly it faltered, fell off, and then dropped suddenly to 71. Wall Street had never been subjected to a greater shock, and the market reeled to and fro like a drunken man between these giants, as they hurled about shares by the tens of thousands, and money by the million. When night put an end to the conflict, Erie stood at 78, the shock of battle was over, and the astonished brokers drew breath as they waited for the events of the morrow. The attempted " corner " was a failure, and Drew was victorious, — no doubt existed on that point. The question now was, could Vanderbilt sustain himself? In spite of all his wealth, must he not go down before his cunning opponent?

The morning of the 11th found the Erie leaders still transacting business at the office of the corporation in West Street. It would seem that these gentlemen, in spite of the glaring contempt for the process of the courts of which they had been guilty, had made no arrangements for an orderly retreat beyond the jurisdiction of the tribunals they had set at defiance. They were speedily roused from their real or affected tranquillity by trustworthy intelligence that processes for contempt were already issued against them, and that their only chance of escape from incarceration lay in precipitate flight. At ten o'clock the astonished police saw a throng of panic-stricken railway directors, — looking more like a frightened gang of thieves, disturbed in the division of their plunder, than like the wealthy representatives of a great corporation, — rush headlong from the doors of the Erie office, and dash off in the direction of the Jersey ferry. In their hands were packages and files of papers, and their pockets were crammed with assets and securities. One individual bore away with him in a hackney coach bales containing six millions of dollars in greenbacks. Other members of the board followed under cover of the night; some of them, not daring to expose themselves to the publicity of a ferry, attempted to cross in open boats concealed by the darkness and a March fog. Two directors, who lingered, were arrested; but a majority of the Executive Committee collected at the Erie Station in Jersey

City, and there, free from any apprehension of Judge Barnard's pursuing wrath, proceeded to the transaction of business.

Meanwhile, on the other side of the river, Vanderbilt was struggling in the toils. As usual in these Wall Street operations, there was a grim humor in the situation. Had Vanderbilt failed to sustain the market, a financial collapse and panic must have ensued which would have sent him to the wall. He had sustained it, and had absorbed a hundred thousand shares of Erie. Thus when Drew retired to Jersey City he carried with him seven millions of his opponent's money, and the Commodore had freely supplied the enemy with the sinews of war. He had grasped at Erie for his own sake, and now his opponents derisively promised to rehabilitate and vivify the old road with the money he had furnished them, so as more effectually to compete with the lines which he already possessed. Nor was this all. Had they done as they loudly claimed they meant to do, Vanderbilt might have hugged himself in the faith that, after all, it was but a question of time, and the prize would come to him in the end. He, however, knew well enough that the most pressing need of the Erie people was money with which to fight him. With this he had now furnished them abundantly, and he must have felt that no scruples would prevent their use of it.

Vanderbilt had, however, little leisure to devote to the enjoyment of the humorous side of his position. The situation was alarming. His opponents had carried with them in their flight seven millions in currency, which were withdrawn from circulation. An artificial stringency was thus created in Wall Street, and, while money rose, stocks fell, and unusual margins were called in. Vanderbilt was carrying a fearful load, and the least want of confidence, the faintest sign of faltering, might well bring on a crash. He already had a hundred thousand shares of Erie, not one of which he could sell. He was liable at any time to be called upon to carry as much more as his opponents, skilled by long practice in the manufacture of the article, might see fit to produce. Opposed to him were men who scrupled at nothing, and who knew every in and out of the money market. With every look and every gesture anxiously scrutinized, a position more trying than his can hardly be conceived. It is not known from what source he drew the vast sums which enabled him to surmount his difficulties with such apparent ease. His nerve, however, stood him in at least as good stead as his financial resources. Like a great general, in the hour of trial he inspired confidence. While fighting for life he could "talk horse" and play whist. The manner in which he then emerged from his troubles, serene and confident, was as extraordinary as the financial resources he commanded.

Meanwhile, before turning to the tide of battle, which now swept away from the courts of law into the halls of legislation, there are two matters to be disposed of; the division of the spoils is to be recounted, and the old and useless lumber of conflict must be cleared away. The division of profits accruing to Mr. Treasurer Drew and his associate directors, acting as individuals, was a fit conclusion to the stock issue just described. The bonds for five millions, after their conversion, realized nearly four millions of dollars, of which $3,625,000 passed into the treasury of the company. The trustees of the stockholders had therefore in this case secured a profit for some one of $375,000. Confidence in the good faith of one's kind is very commendable, but possession is nine points of the law. Mr. James Fisk, Jr., through whom the sales were mainly effected, declined to make any payments in excess of the $3,625,000, until a division of profits was agreed upon. It seems that, by virtue of a paper signed by Mr. Drew as early as the 19th of February, Gould, Fisk, and others were entitled to one half the profits he should make "in certain transactions." What these transactions were, or whether the official action of Directors Gould and Fisk was in any way influenced by the signing of this document, does not appear. Mr. Fisk now gave Mr. Drew, in lieu of cash, his uncertified check for the surplus $375,000 remaining from this transaction, with stock as collateral amounting to about the half of that sum. With this settlement, and the redemption of the collateral, Mr. Drew was fain to be content. Seven months afterwards he still retained possession of the uncertified check, in the payment of which, if presented, he seemed to entertain no great confidence. Everything, however, showed conclusively the advantage of operating from interior lines. While the Erie treasury was once more replete, three of the persons who had been mainly instrumental in filling it had not suffered in the transaction. The treasurer was richer by $180,000 directly, and he himself only knew by how much more incidentally. In like manner his faithful adjutants had profited to an amount as much exceeding $60,000 each as their sagacity had led them to provide for.

* * * * * * * *

When the Vanderbilt counsel moved to fix a day on which their opponents should show cause why a receiver of the proceeds of the last overissue of stock should not be appointed, the judge astonished the petitioners by outstripping their eagerness, and appointing Vanderbilt's own son-in-law receiver on the spot. Then followed a fierce altercation in court, in which bench and bar took equal part, and which closed with the not unusual threat of impeaching the presiding judge. . . . When Mr. John B. Haskin was placed upon the stand, there ensued a scene which Barnard himself not inaptly characterized the next day as " outrageous and scandalous, and insulting to the court." Upon this occasion the late Mr. James T. Brady seemed to be on the verge of a personal collision with the witness in open court ; the purity of the presiding magistrate was impugned, his venality openly implied through a long cross-examination, and the witness acknowledged that he had himself in the course of his career undertaken for money to influence the mind of the judge privately " on the side of right." All the scandals of the practice of the law, and the private immoralities of lawyers, were dragged into the broad light of day ; the whole system of favored counsel, of private argument, of referees, and of unblushing extortion, was freely discussed. . . . On a subsequent day the judge himself made inquiries as to a visit of two of the directors to one gentleman supposed to have peculiar influence over the judicial mind, and evinced great familiarity with the negotiations then carried on, and even showed some disposition to extend the inquiry indefinitely into periodical literature. . . .

Nor were the lawyers in any way behind the judge. At one moment they would indulge in personal wrangling, and accuse each other of the grossest malpractice, and the next, favor each other with remarks upon manners, more pointed than delicate. All this time injunctions were flying about like hailstones; but the crowning injunction of all was issued, in reference to the appointment of a receiver, by Judge Clerke, a colleague of Judge Barnard, at the time sitting as a member of the Court of Appeals at Albany. The Gilbert injunction had gone, it might have seemed, sufficiently far, in enjoining Barnard the individual, while distinctly disavowing all reference to him in his judicial functions. Judge Clerke made no such exception. He enjoined the individual and he enjoined the judge ; he forbade his making any order appointing a receiver, and he forbade the clerks of his court from entering it if it were made, and the receiver from accepting it if it were entered. The signing of this extraordinary order by any judge in his senses admits of no explanation. The Erie counsel served it upon Judge Barnard as he sat upon the bench, and, having done so, withdrew from the court room ; whereupon the judge immediately proceeded to vacate the order, and to appoint a receiver. This appointment was then entered by a clerk, who had also been enjoined, and the receiver was himself enjoined as soon as he could be caught. Finally the maze had become so intricate, and the whole litigation so evidently endless and aimless, that by a sort of agreement of parties, Judge Ingraham, another colleague of Judge Barnard, issued a final injunction of universal application, as it were, and to be held inviolable by common consent, under which proceedings were stayed, pending an appeal. It was high time. Judges were becoming very shy of anything connected with the name of Erie, and Judge McCunn had, in a lofty tone, informed counsel that he preferred to subject himself to the liability of a fine of a thousand dollars rather than, by issuing a writ of *habeas corpus*, allow his court "to have anything to do with the scandal."

The result of this extraordinary litigation may be summed up in a few words. It had two branches; one, the appointment

of a receiver of the proceeds of the hundred thousand shares
of stock issued in violation of an injunction; the other, the
processes against the persons of the directors for a contempt
of court. As for the receiver, every dollar of the money this
officer was intended to receive was well known to be in New
Jersey, beyond his reach. Why one party cared to insist on
the appointment, or why the other party objected to it, is not
very apparent. Mr. Osgood, the son-in-law of Vanderbilt, was
appointed, and immediately enjoined from acting; subsequently
he resigned, when Mr. Peter B. Sweeney, the head of the Tammany ring, was appointed in his place, without notice to the
other side. Of course he had nothing to do, as there was
nothing to be done, and so he was subsequently allowed by
Judge Barnard $150,000 for his services. The contempt cases
had even less result than that of the receivership. The settlement subsequently effected between the litigants seemed also
to include the courts. The outraged majesty of the law, as represented in the person of Mr. Justice Barnard, was pacified,
and everything was explained as having been said and done in a
" Pickwickian sense"; so that, when the terms of peace had been
arranged between the high contending parties, Barnard's roaring
by degrees subsided, until he roared as gently as any sucking
dove, and finally he ceased to roar at all. The penalty for violating an injunction in the manner described was fixed at the not
unreasonable sum of ten dollars, except in the cases of Mr.
Drew and certain of his more prominent associates; their con-
tumacy His Honor held too gross to be estimated in money,
and so they escaped without any punishment at all. Probably
being as well read a lawyer as he was a dignified magistrate,
Judge Barnard bore in mind, in imposing these penalties, that
clause of the fundamental law which provides that " no excessive fines shall be imposed, or cruel or unusual punishments
inflicted." The legal profession alone had cause to regret the
cessation of this litigation ; and, as the Erie counsel had
$150,000 divided among them in fees, it may be presumed that
even they were finally comforted. And all this took place in
the court of that State over which the immortal Chancellor

Kent had once presided. His great authority was still cited
there, the halo which surrounds his name still shed a glory
over the bench on which he had sat, and yet these, his immediate successors, could

> On that high mountain cease to feed,
> And batten on this moor.

II

It is now necessary to return to the real field of operations,
which had ceased on the morning of the 11th of March to be
in the courts of law. As the arena widened the proceedings
became more complicated and more difficult to trace, embracing
as they did the legislatures of two States, neither of them famed
for purity. In the first shock of the catastrophe it was actually
believed that Commodore Vanderbilt contemplated a resort to
open violence and acts of private war. There were intimations
that a scheme had been matured for kidnapping certain of the
Erie directors, including Mr. Drew, and bringing them by force
within reach of Judge Barnard's process. It appeared that on
the 16th of March some fifty individuals, subsequently described,
in an affidavit filed for the special benefit of Mr. Justice Barnard,
as "disorderly characters, commonly known as roughs," crossed
by the Pavonia Ferry and took possession of the Erie depot.
From their conversation and inquiries it was divined that they
came intending to "copp" Mr. Drew, or, in plainer phraseology,
to take him by force to New York; and that they expected to
receive the sum of $50,000 as a reward for so doing. The exiles
at once loudly charged Vanderbilt himself with originating this
blundering scheme. They simulated intense alarm. From day
to day new panics were started, until, on the 19th, Drew was
secreted, a standing army was organized from the employees of
the road, and a small navy equipped. The alarm spread through
Jersey City ; the militia was held in readiness ; in the evening
the stores were closed and the citizens began to arm ; while a
garrison of about one hundred and twenty-five men intrenched
themselves around the directors, in their hotel. On the 21st

there was another alarm, and the fears of an attack continued, with lengthening intervals of quiet, until the 31st, when the guard was at last withdrawn. It is impossible to suppose that Vanderbilt ever had any knowledge of this ridiculous episode or of its cause, except through the press. A band of ruffians may have crossed the ferry, intending to kidnap Drew on speculation; but to suppose that the shrewd and energetic Commodore ever sent them to go gaping about a station, ignorant both of the person and the whereabouts of him they sought would be to impute to Vanderbilt at once a crime and a blunder. Such botching bears no trace of his clean handiwork.

The first serious effort of the Erie party was to intrench itself in New Jersey; and here it met with no opposition. A bill making the Erie Railway Company a corporation of New Jersey, with the same powers they enjoyed in New York, was hurried through the legislature in the space of two hours, and, after a little delay, signed by the Governor. The astonished citizens of the latter State saw their famous broad-gauge road thus metamorphosed before their eyes into a denizen of the kingdom of Camden and Amboy. Here was another dreadful hint to Wall Street. What further issues of stock might become legal under this charter, how the tenure of the present Board of Directors might be altered, what curious legal complications might arise, were questions more easily put than satisfactorily answered. The region of possibilities was considerably extended. The new act of incorporation, however, was but a precaution to secure for the directors of the Erie a retreat in case of need; the real field of conflict lay in the legislature of New York, and here Vanderbilt was first on the ground.

* * * * * * * *

One favorite method of procedure at Albany is through the appointment of committees to investigate the affairs of wealthy corporations. The stock of some great company is manipulated till it fluctuates violently, as was the case with Pacific Mail in 1867. Forthwith some member of the Assembly rises and calls for a committee of investigation. The instant the game is afoot, a rush is made for positions on the committee. The proposer, of course, is a member, probably chairman. The advantages of the position are obvious. The committee constitutes a little temporary outside ring. If a member is corrupt, he has substantial advantages offered him to influence his action in regard to the report. If he is not open to bribery, he is nevertheless in possession of very valuable information, and an innocent little remark, casually let fall, may lead a son, a brother, or a loving cousin to make very judicious purchases of stock. Altogether, the position is one not to be avoided.

The investigation phase was the first which the Erie struggle assumed at Albany. During the early stages of the conflict the legislature had scented the carnage from afar. There was "money in it," and the struggle was watched with breathless interest. As early as the 5th of March the subject had been introduced into the State Senate, and an investigation into the circumstances of the company was called for. A committee of three was ordered, but the next day a senator, by name Mattoon, moved to increase the number to five, which was done, he himself being naturally one of the additional members. This committee had its first sitting on the 10th, at the very crisis of the great explosion. But before the investigation was entered upon, Mr. Mattoon thought it expedient to convince the contending parties of his own perfect impartiality and firm determination to hold in check the corrupt impulses of his associates. With this end in view, upon the 9th or the 10th he hurried down to New York, and visited West Street, where he had an interview with the leading Erie directors. He explained to them the corrupt motives which had led to the appointment of the committee, and how his sole object in obtaining an increase of the number had been to put himself in a position in which he might be able to prevent these evil practices and see fair play. Curiously enough, at the same interview he mentioned that his son was to be appointed an assistant sergeant-at-arms to aid in the investigation, and proved his disinterestedness by mentioning the fact that this son was to serve without pay. The labors of the committee continued until the 31st of March, and during that time Mr. Mattoon, and at least one other senator, pursued a course of private inquiry which involved further visits to Jersey City. Naturally enough, Mr. Drew and his associates took it into their heads that the man wanted to be bought, and even affirmed subsequently that, at one interview, he had in pretty broad terms offered himself for sale. It has not been distinctly stated in evidence by any one that an attempt was made on his purity or on that of his public-spirited son; and it is difficult to believe that one who came to New York so full of high purpose could have been sufficiently corrupted by metropolitan influences to receive bribes from both sides. Whether he did so or not his proceedings were terribly suggestive as regards legislative morality at Albany. Here was a senator, a member of a committee of investigation, rousing gamblers from their beds at early hours of the morning to hold interviews in the faro-bank parlor of the establishment, and to give "points" on which to operate upon the joint account. Even then the wretched creature could not even keep faith with his very "pals"; he wrote to them to "go it heavy" for Drew, and then himself went over to Vanderbilt, — he made agreements to share profits and then submitted to exposure sooner than meet his part of the loss. A man more thoroughly, shamefacedly contemptible and corrupt, — a more perfect specimen of a legislator on sale haggling for his own price, could not well exist. In this case he cheated every one, including himself. Accident threw great opportunities in his way. On the 31st the draft of a proposed report, exonerating in great measure the Drew faction, was read to him by an associate, to which he not only made no objection, but was even understood to assent. On the same day another report was read in his presence, strongly denouncing the Drew faction, sustaining to the fullest extent the charges made against it, and characterizing its conduct as corrupt and disgraceful. Each report was signed by two of his associates, and Mr. Mattoon found himself in the position of holding the balance of power; whichever report he signed would be the report of the committee. He expressed a desire to think the matter over. It is natural to suppose that, in his eagerness to gain information privately, Mr. Mattoon had not confined his unofficial visits to the Drew camp.

In any case his mind was in a state of painful suspense. Finally, after arranging in consultation on Tuesday for a report favoring the Drew party, on Wednesday he signed a report strongly denouncing it, and by doing so settled the action of the committee. Mr. Jay Gould must have been acquainted with the circumstances of the case, and evidently supposed that Mr. Mattoon was " fixed," since he subsequently declared he was " astounded " when he heard that Mr. Mattoon had signed this report. The committee, however, with their patriotic sergeant-at-arms, whose services, by the way, cost the State but a hundred dollars, desisted at length from their labors, the result of which was one more point gained by Commodore Vanderbilt.

Indeed, Vanderbilt had thus far as much outgeneraled Drew in the manufacture of public opinion as Drew had outgeneraled Vanderbilt in the manufacture of Erie stock. His whole scheme was one of monopoly, which was opposed to every interest of the city and State of New York ; yet into the support of this scheme he had brought all the leading papers of New York City, with a single exception. Now again he seemed to have it all his own way in the legislature, and the tide ran strongly against the exiles of Erie. The report of the investigation committee was signed on April 1st, and may be considered as marking the high-water point of Vanderbilt's success. Hitherto the Albany interests of the exiles had been confided to mere agents, and had not prospered ; but, when fairly roused by a sense of danger, the Drew party showed at least as close a familiarity with the tactics of Albany as with those of Wall Street. The moment they felt themselves settled at Jersey City they had gone to work to excite a popular sympathy in their own behalf. The cry of monopoly was a sure card in their hands. They cared no more for the actual welfare of commerce, involved in railroad competition, than they did for the real interests of the Erie Railway ; but they judged truly that there was no limit to the extent to which the public might be imposed upon. An active competition with the Vanderbilt roads, by land and water, was inaugurated ; fares and freight on the Erie were reduced on an average by one third; sounding proclamations were issued; " interviewers " from the press returned rejoicing from Taylor's Hotel to New York City, and the Jersey shore quaked under the clatter of this Chinese battle. The influence of these tactics made itself felt at once. By the middle of March memorials against monopoly began to flow in at Albany.

While popular sympathy was thus roused by the bribe of active competition, a bill was introduced into the Assembly, in the Erie interest, legalizing the recent issue of new stock, declaring and regulating the power of issuing convertible bonds, providing for a broad-gauge connection with Chicago and the guaranty of the bonds of the Boston, Hartford & Erie, and finally forbidding, in so far as any legislation could forbid, the consolidation of the Central and the Erie in the hands of Vanderbilt. This bill was referred to the Committee on Railroads on the 13th of March. On the 20th a public hearing was begun, and the committee proceeded to take evidence, aided by a long array of opposing counsel, most of whom had figured in the proceedings in the courts of law. In a few days the bill was adversely reported upon, and the report adopted in the Assembly by the decisive vote of eighty-three to thirty-two. This was upon the 27th of March. The hint was a broad one ; the exiles must give closer attention to their interests. So soon as the news of this adverse action reached Jersey City, it was decided that Mr. Jay Gould should brave the terrors of the law, and personally superintend matters at Albany. Neither Mr. Drew nor his associates desired to become permanent residents of Jersey City; nor did they wish to return to New York as criminals on their way to jail. Mr. Gould was to pave the way to a different return by causing the recent issue of convertible bonds to be legalized. That once done, Commodore Vanderbilt was not the man to wage an unavailing war, and a compromise, in which Barnard and his processes of contempt would be thrown in as a makeweight, could easily be effected. A rumor was therefore started that Mr. Gould was to leave for Ohio, supplied with the necessary authority and funds to press vigorously to completion the eighty miles of broad-gauge track between Akron and Toledo, which would open to the Erie the much-coveted connection with Chicago. Having hung out this false light, Mr. Jay Gould went on his mission, the president of the company having some time previously drawn half a million of dollars out of the overflowing Erie treasury.

This mission was by no means unattended by difficulties. In the first place, Judge Barnard's processes for contempt seemed to threaten the liberty of Mr. Gould's person. He left Jersey City and arrived at Albany on the 30th day of March, three days after the defeat of the Erie bill, and two days before Mr. Mattoon had made up his mind as to which report he would sign. Naturally his opponents were well satisfied with the present aspect of affairs, and saw no benefit likely to arise from Mr. Gould's presence in Albany. The day after his arrival, therefore, he was arrested, on the writ issued against him for contempt of court, and held to bail in half a million of dollars for his appearance in New York on the following Saturday. He was immediately bailed of course, and for the next few days devoted himself assiduously to the business he had in hand. On Saturday he appeared before Judge Barnard, and was duly put in charge of the sheriff to answer certain interrogatories. It would seem to have been perfectly easy for him to give the necessary bail, and to return from Barnard's presence at once to Albany; but the simple method seems never to have been resorted to throughout these complications: nothing was ever done without the interposition of a writ and the assistance of a crowd of counsel. In this case Judge Barrett of the Common Pleas was appealed to, who issued a writ of *habeas corpus*, by virtue of which Mr. Gould was taken out of the hands of the sheriff and again brought into court. Of course the hearing of the case was deferred, and it was equally a matter of course that Mr. Gould was bent on returning at once to his field of labor. The officer to whose care Mr. Gould was intrusted was especially warned by the court, in Mr. Gould's presence, that he was not to allow his charge to go out of his sight. This difficulty was easily surmounted. Mr. Gould went by an early train to Albany, taking the officer with him in the capacity of a traveling companion. Once in Albany he was naturally taken ill, —

not too ill to go to the Capitol in the midst of a snowstorm, but much too ill to think of returning to New York. On the 10th the trusty official and traveling companion signified to Mr. Gould that his presence was much desired before Judge Barrett, and intimated an intention of carrying him back to New York. Mr. Gould then pleaded the delicate condition of his health, and wholly declined to undergo the hardships of the proposed journey. Whereupon the officer, stimulated, as was alleged, by Gould's opponents, returned alone to New York, and reported his charge to the court as a runaway. A new spectacle of judicial indignation ensued, and a new process for contempt seemed imminent. Of course nothing came of it. A few affidavits from Albany pacified the indignant Barrett. The application for a *habeas corpus* was discharged, and Mr. Gould was theoretically returned into the custody of the sheriff. Thereupon the required security for his appearance when needed was given; and meanwhile, pending the recovery of his health, he assiduously devoted the tedious hours of convalescence to the task of cultivating a thorough understanding between himself and the members of the legislature.

     *   *   *   *   *   *   *   *

The full and true history of this legislative campaign will never be known. If the official reports of investigating committees are to be believed, Mr. Gould at about this time underwent a curious psychological metamorphosis, and suddenly became the veriest simpleton in money matters that ever fell into the hands of happy sharpers. Cunning lobby members had but to pretend to an influence over legislative minds, which every one knew they did not possess, to draw unlimited amounts from this verdant *habitué* of Wall Street. It seemed strange that he could have lived so long and learned so little. He dealt in large sums. He gave to one man, in whom he said " he did not take much stock," the sum of $5000, " just to smooth him over." This man had just before received $5000 of Erie money from another agent of the company. It would, therefore, be interesting to know what sums Mr. Gould paid to those individuals in whom he did " take much stock." Another individual is reported to have received $100,000 from one side "to influence legislation," and to have subsequently received $70,000 from the other side to disappear with the money; which he accordingly did, and thereafter became a gentleman of elegant leisure. One senator was openly charged in the columns of the press with receiving a bribe of $20,000 from one side, and a second bribe of $15,000 from the other; but Mr. Gould's foggy mental condition only enabled him to be "perfectly astounded" at the action of this senator, though he knew nothing of any such transactions. Other senators were blessed with a sudden accession of wealth, but in no case was there any jot or tittle of proof of bribery. Mr. Gould's rooms at the Develin House overflowed with a joyous company, and his checks were numerous and heavy; but why he signed them, or what became of them, he seemed to know less than any man in Albany. This strange and expensive hallucination lasted until about the middle of April, when Mr. Gould was happily restored to his normal condition of a shrewd, acute, energetic man of business; nor is it known that he has since experienced any relapse into financial idiocy.

About the period of Mr. Gould's arrival in Albany the tide turned, and soon began to flow strongly in favor of Erie and against Vanderbilt. How much of this was due to the skillful manipulations of Gould, and how much to the rising popular feeling against the practical consolidation of competing lines, cannot be decided. The popular protests did indeed pour in by scores, but then again the Erie secret-service money poured out like water. Yet Mr. Gould's task was sufficiently difficult. After the adverse report of the Senate Committee, and the decisive defeat of the bill introduced into the Assembly, any favorable legislation seemed almost hopeless. Both Houses were committed. Vanderbilt had but to prevent action, — to keep things where they were, and the return of his opponents to New York was impracticable, unless with his consent; he appeared, in fact, to be absolute master of the situation. It seemed almost impossible to introduce a bill in the face of his great influence, and to navigate it through the many stages

of legislative action and executive approval, without somewhere giving him an opportunity to defeat it. This was the task
Gould had before him, and he accomplished it. On the 13th
of April a bill, which met the approval of the Erie party, and
which Judge Barnard subsequently compared not inaptly to a
bill legalizing counterfeit money, was taken up in the Senate ;
for some days it was warmly debated, and on the 18th was passed
by the decisive vote of seventeen to twelve. Senator Mattoon
had not listened to the debate in vain. Perhaps his reason was
convinced, or perhaps he had sold out new " points " and was
again cheating himself or somebody else ; at any rate, that
thrifty senator was found voting with the majority. The bill
practically legalized the recent issues of bonds, but made it
a felony to use the proceeds of the sale of these bonds except for
completing, furthering, and operating the road. The guaranty
of the bonds of connecting roads was authorized, all contracts
for consolidation or division of receipts between the Erie and
the Vanderbilt roads were forbidden, and a clumsy provision
was enacted that no stockholder, director, or officer in one of the
Vanderbilt roads should be an officer or director in the Erie,
and *vice versa*. The bill was, in fact, an amended copy of the
one voted down so decisively in the Assembly a few days before,
and it was in this body that the tug of war was expected
to come.

The lobby was now full of animation ; fabulous stories were
told of the amounts which the contending parties were willing
to expend ; never before had the market quotations of votes
and influence stood so high. The wealth of Vanderbilt seemed
pitted against the Erie treasury, and the vultures flocked to
Albany from every part of the State. Suddenly, at the very
last moment, and even while special trains were bringing up
fresh contestants to take part in the fray, a rumor ran through
Albany as of some great public disaster, spreading panic and
terror through hotel and corridor. The observer was reminded
of the dark days of the war, when tidings came of some great
defeat, as that on the Chickahominy or at Fredericksburg. In
a moment the lobby was smitten with despair, and the cheeks

of the legislators were blanched, for it was reported that Vanderbilt had withdrawn his opposition to the bill. The report was true. Either the Commodore had counted the cost and judged it excessive, or he despaired of the result. At any rate, he had yielded in advance. In a few moments the long struggle was over, and that bill which, in an unamended form, had but a few days before been thrown out of the Assembly by a vote of eighty-three to thirty-two, now passed it by a vote of one hundred and one to six, and was sent to the Governor for his signature. Then the wrath of the disappointed members turned on Vanderbilt. Decency was forgotten in a frenzied sense of disappointed avarice. That same night the *pro rata* freight bill, and a bill compelling the sale of through tickets by competing lines, were hurriedly passed, simply because they were thought hurtful to Vanderbilt; and the docket was ransacked in search of other measures, calculated to injure or annoy him. An adjournment, however, brought reflection, and subsequently, on this subject, the legislature stultified itself no more.

The bill had passed the legislature; would it receive the executive signature? Here was the last stage of danger. For some time doubts were entertained on this point, and the last real conflict between the opposing interests took place in the Executive Chamber at Albany. There, on the afternoon of the 21st of April, Commodore Vanderbilt's counsel appeared before Governor Fenton, and urged upon him their reasons why the bill should be returned by him to the Senate without his signature. The arguments were patiently listened to, but, when they had closed, the executive signature placed the seal of success upon Mr. Gould's labors at Albany. Even here the voice of calumny was not silent. As if this remarkable controversy was destined to leave a dark blot of suspicion upon every department of the civil service of New York, there were not wanting those who charged the Executive itself with the crowning act in this history of corruption. The very sum pretended to have been paid was named; the broker of executive action was pointed out, and the number of minutes was specified which should intervene between the payment of the bribe and the signing of the law.[1]

Practically, the conflict was now over, and the period of negotiation had already begun. The combat in the courts was indeed kept up until far into May, for the angry passions of the lawyers and of the judges required time in which to wear themselves out. Day after day the columns of the press revealed fresh scandals to the astonished public, which at last grew indifferent to such revelations. Beneath all the wrangling of the courts, however, while the popular attention was distracted by the clatter of lawyers' tongues, the leaders in the controversy were quietly approaching a settlement.

*　　*　　*　　*　　*　　*　　*　　*

At last, upon the 2d of July, Mr. Eldridge formally announced to the Board of Directors that the terms of peace had been agreed upon. Commodore Vanderbilt was, in the first place, provided for. He was to be relieved of fifty thousand shares of Erie stock at 70, receiving therefor $2,500,000 in cash, and $1,250,000 in bonds of the Boston, Hartford & Erie at 80. He was also to receive a further sum of $1,000,000 outright, as a consideration for the privilege the Erie road thus purchased of calling upon him for his remaining fifty thousand shares at 70 at any time within four months. He was also to have two seats in the Board of Directors, and all suits were to be dismissed and offenses condoned. The sum of $429,250 was fixed upon as a proper amount to assuage the sense of wrong from which his two friends Work and Schell had suffered, and to efface from their memories all recollection of the unfortunate "pool" of the previous December. Why the owners of the Erie Railway should have paid this indemnity of $4,000,000 is not very clear. The operations were apparently outside of the business of a railway company, and no more connected with

[1] It is but justice to Governor Fenton to say, that, though this charge was boldly advanced by respectable journals of his own party, it cannot be considered as sustained by the evidence. The testimony on the point will be found in the report of Senator Hale's investigating committee. Documents (Senate), 1869, No. 52, pp. 146–148, 151–155.

the stockholders of the Erie than were the butchers' bills of the individual directors.

While Vanderbilt and his friends were thus provided for, Mr. Drew was to be left in undisturbed enjoyment of the fruits of his recent operations, but was to pay into the treasury $540,000 and interest, in full discharge of all claims and causes of action which the Erie company might have against him. The Boston party, as represented by Mr. Eldridge, was to be relieved of $5,000,000 of their Boston, Hartford & Erie bonds, for which they were to receive $4,000,000 of Erie acceptances. None of these parties, therefore, had anything to complain of, whatever might be the sensations of the real owners of the railway. A total amount of some $9,000,000 in cash was drawn from the treasury in fulfillment of this *settlement*, as the persons concerned were pleased to term this remarkable disposition of property intrusted to their care.

Messrs. Gould and Fisk still remained to be taken care of, and to them their associates left — the Erie Railway. These gentlemen subsequently maintained that they had vehemently opposed this settlement, and had denounced it in the secret councils as a fraud and a robbery. Mr. Fisk was peculiarly outspoken in relation to it, and declared himself "thunder-struck and dumfounded" that his brother directors whom he had supposed respectable men should have had anything to do with any such proceeding. A small portion of this statement is not wholly improbable. The astonishment at the turpitude of his fellow-officials was a little unnecessary in one who had already seen "more robbery" during the year of his connection with the Erie Railway than he had "ever seen before in the same space of time," — so much of it indeed that he dated his "gray hairs" from that 7th of October which saw his election to the board. That Mr. Fisk and Mr. Gould were extremely indignant at a partition of plunder from which they were excluded is, however, very certain. The rind of the orange is not generally considered the richest part of the fruit; a corporation on the verge of bankruptcy is less coveted, even by operators in Wall Street, than one rich in valuable assets.

Probably at this time these gentlemen seriously debated the expediency of resorting again to a war of injunctions, and carefully kept open a way for doing so; however this may have been, they seem finally to have concluded that there was yet plunder left in the poor old hulk, and so, after four stormy interviews, all opposition was at last withdrawn and the definitive treaty was finally signed. . . . Mr. Eldridge thereupon counted out his bonds and received his acceptances, which latter were cashed at once to close up the transaction, and at once he resigned his positions as director and president. The Boston raiders then retired, heavy with spoil, into their own North country, and there proceeded to build up an Erie influence for New England, in which task they labored with assiduity and success. Gradually they here introduced the more highly developed civilization of the land of their temporary adoption and boldly attempted to make good their private losses from the public treasury. A more barefaced scheme of plunder never was devised, and yet the executive veto alone stood between it and success. These, however, were the events of another year and unconnected with this narrative, from which these characters in the Erie management henceforth disappear. For the rest it is only necessary to say that Mr. Vanderbilt, relieved of his heavy load of its stock, apparently ceased to concern himself with Erie; while Daniel Drew, released from the anxieties of office, assumed for a space the novel character of a looker-on in Wall Street.

III

*   *   *   *   *   *   *   *

The appearance of calm lasted but about thirty days. Early in August it was evident that something was going on. Erie suddenly fell ten per cent; in a few days more it experienced a further fall of seven per cent, touching 44 by the 19th of the month, upon which day, to the astonishment of Wall Street, the transfer books of the company were closed preparatory to the annual election. As this election was not to take place until the 13th of October, and as the books had thus been

closed thirty days in advance of the usual time, it looked very
much as though the managers were satisfied with the present
disposition of the stock, and meant, by keeping it where it was,
to preclude any such unpleasantness as an opposition ticket.
The courts and a renewed war of injunctions were of course
open to any contestants, including Commodore Vanderbilt, who
might desire to avail themselves of them; probably, however,
the memory of recent struggles was too fresh to permit any one
to embark on those treacherous waters. At any rate, nothing
of the sort was attempted. The election took place at the usual
time, and the ring in control voted itself, without opposition, into
a new lease of power. Two new names had meanwhile appeared
in the list of Erie directors, — those of Peter B. Sweeney and
William M. Tweed, the two most prominent leaders of that
notorious ring which controls the proletariat of New York City
and governs the politics of the State. The alliance was an
ominous one, for the construction of the new board can be
stated in few words, and calls for no comment. It consisted
of the Erie ring and the Tammany ring, brought together in
close political and financial union; and, for the rest, a working
majority of supple tools and a hopeless minority of respectable
figureheads. This formidable combination shot out its feelers
far and wide: it wielded the influence of a great corporation
with a capital of a hundred millions; it controlled the politics
of the first city of the New World; it sent its representatives
to the Senate of the State, and numbered among its agents,
the judges of the courts. Compact, disciplined, and reckless, it
knew its own power and would not scruple to use it.

It was now the month of October, and the harvest had been
gathered. The ring and its allies determined to reap their harvest
also, and that harvest was to be nothing less than a contribution
levied, not only upon Wall Street and New York, but upon all
the immense interests, commercial and financial, which radiate
from New York all over the country. Like the Cæsar of old,
they issued their edict that all the world should be taxed. The
process was not novel, but it was effective. A monetary stringency may be looked for in New York at certain seasons of every

year. It is generally most severe in the autumn months, when the crops have to be moved, and the currency is drained steadily away from the financial center towards the extremities of the system. The method by which an artificial stringency is produced is thus explained in a recent report of the Comptroller of the Currency:

It is scarcely possible to avoid the inference that nearly one half of the available resources of the national banks in the city of New York are used in the operations of the stock and gold exchange; that they are loaned upon the security of stocks which are bought and sold largely on speculation, and which are manipulated by cliques and combinations, according as the bulls or bears are for the moment in the ascendency. . . . Taking advantage of an active demand for money to move the crops West and South, shrewd operators form their combination to depress the market by "locking up" money, — withdrawing all they can control or borrow from the common fund; money becomes scarce, the rate of interest advances, and stocks decline. The legitimate demand for money continues ; and, fearful of trenching on their reserve, the banks are strained for means. They dare not call in their demand loans, for that would compel their customers to sell securities on a falling market, which would make matters worse. Habitually lending their means to the utmost limit of prudence, and their credit much beyond that limit, to brokers and speculators, they are powerless to afford relief ; — their customers by the force of circumstances become their masters. The banks cannot hold back or withdraw from the dilemma in which their mode of doing business has placed them. They must carry the load to save their margins. A panic which should greatly reduce the price of securities would occasion serious, if not fatal, results to the banks most extensively engaged in such operations, and would produce a feeling of insecurity which would be very dangerous to the entire banking interest of the country.[1]

All this machinery was now put in motion ; the banks and their customers were forced into the false position described, and towards the end of October it had become perfectly notorious in Wall Street that large new issues of Erie had been made, and that these new issues were intimately connected with the sharp stringency then existing in the money market. It was at last determined to investigate the matter, and upon the 27th of the month a committee of three was appointed by the Stock Exchange to wait upon the officers of the corporation with the

[1] Finance Report, 1868, pp. 20, 21.

view of procuring such information as they might be willing to impart. The committee called on Mr. Gould and stated the object of their visit. In reply to their inquiries Mr. Gould informed them that Erie convertible bonds for ten millions of dollars had been issued, half of which had already been, and the rest of which would be, converted into stock; that the money had been devoted to the purchase of Boston, Hartford & Erie bonds for five millions, and also — of course — to payments for steel rails. The committee desired to know if any further issue of stock was in contemplation, but were obliged to rest satisfied with a calm assurance that no new issue was just then contemplated except "in certain contingencies;" from which enigmatical utterances Wall Street was left to infer that the exigencies of Messrs. Gould and Fisk were elements not to be omitted from any calculations as to the future of Erie and the money market. The amount of these issues of new stock was, of course, soon whispered in a general way; but it was not till months afterwards that a sworn statement of the secretary of the Erie Railway revealed the fact that the stock of the corporation had been increased from $34,265,300 on the 1st of July, 1868, the date when Drew and his associates had left it, to $57,766,300 on the 24th of October of the same year, or by two hundred and thirty-five thousand shares in four months.[1] This, too, had been done without consultation with the board of directors, and with no other authority than that conferred by the ambiguous resolution of February 19th. Under that resolution the stock of the company had now been increased one hundred and thirty-eight per cent in eight months. Such a process of inflation may, perhaps, be justly considered the most extraordinary feat of financial legerdemain which history has yet recorded.

[1] In April, 1871, although the stock was then nominally registered, a further secret issue was made by which some $600,000 in cash was realized on $3,000,000 of stock. Periodical issues had then carried the gross amount up to the neighborhood of $86,500,000; or from a total of 250,000 shares, when the management changed at the election of October 17, 1867, to 865,000 shares within four years. Apparently Mr. Fisk was more correct than usual in his statement, when he remarked, that, having once joined the robbers, "he had been with them ever since."

Now, however, when the committee of the Stock Exchange had returned to those who sent them, the mask was thrown off, and operations were conducted with vigor and determination. New issues of Erie were continually forced upon the market until the stock fell to 35 ; greenbacks were locked up in the vaults of the banks, until the unexampled sum of twelve millions was withdrawn from circulation ; the prices of securities and merchandise declined ; trade and the autumnal movement of the crops were brought almost to a standstill ; and loans became more and more difficult to negotiate, until at length even one and a half per cent a day was paid for carrying stocks. Behind all this it was notorious that some one was pulling the wires, the slightest touch upon which sent a quiver through every nerve of the great financial organism, and wrung private gain from public agony. . . . The very revenues of the government were affected by the operations of gamblers. They were therefore informed that, if necessary, fifty millions of additional currency would be forthcoming to the relief of the community, and then, and not till then, the screws were loosened.

The harvest of the speculators, however, was still but half gathered. Hitherto the combination had operated for a fall. Now was the moment to change the tactics and take advantage of the rise. The time was calculated to a nicety. The London infatuation had wonderfully continued, and as fast as certificates of stock were issued they seemed to take wings across the Atlantic. Yet there was a limit even to English credulity, and in November it became evident that the agents of foreign houses were selling their stock to arrive. The price was about 40 ; the certificates might be expected by the steamer of the 23d. Instantly the combination changed front. As before they had depressed the market, they now ran it up, and, almost as if by magic, the stock, which had been heavy at 40, astonished every one by shooting up to 50. New developments were evidently at hand.

At this point Mr. Daniel Drew once more made his appearance on the stage. As was very natural, he had soon wearied of the sameness of his part as a mere looker-on in Wall Street, and had relapsed into his old habits. He was no longer treasurer of the Erie, and could not therefore invite the public to the game, while he himself with somber piety shook the loaded dice. But it had become with him a second nature to operate in Erie, and once more he was deep in its movements. At first he had combined with his old friends, the present directors, in their "locking-up" conspiracy. He had agreed to assist them to the extent of four millions. The vacillating, timid nature of the man, however, could not keep pace with his more daring and determined associates, and, after embarking a million, becoming alarmed at the success of the joint operations and the remonstrances of those who were threatened with ruin, he withdrew his funds from the operators' control and himself from their councils. But though he did not care to run the risk or to incur the odium, he had no sort of objection to sharing the spoils. Knowing, therefore, or supposing that he knew, the plan of campaign, and that plan jumping with his own bearish inclinations, he continued, on his own account, operations looking to a fall. One may easily conceive the wrath of the Erie operators at such a treacherous policy; and it is not difficult to imagine their vows of vengeance. Meanwhile all went well with Daniel Drew. Erie looked worse and worse, and the golden harvest seemed drawing near. By the middle of November he had contracted for the delivery of some seventy thousand shares at current prices, averaging, perhaps, 38, and probably was counting his gains. He did not appreciate the full power and resources of his old associates. On the 14th of November their tactics changed, and he found himself involved in terrible entanglements, — hopelessly cornered. His position disclosed itself on Saturday. Naturally the first impulse was to have recourse to the courts. An injunction — a dozen injunctions — could be had for the asking, but, unfortunately, could be had by both parties. Drew's own recent experience, and his intimate acquaintance with the characters of Fisk and Gould, were not calculated to inspire him with much confidence in the efficacy of the law. But nothing else remained, and, after hurried consultations among the victims, the lawyers were applied to, the affidavits

were prepared, and it was decided to repair on the following
Monday to the so-called courts of justice.

Nature, however, had not bestowed on Daniel Drew the steady
nerve and sturdy gambler's pride of either Vanderbilt or of his
old companions at Jersey City. His mind wavered and hesitated
between different courses of action. His only care was for himself, his only thought was of his own position. He was willing
to betray one party or the other, as the case might be. He had
given his affidavit to those who were to bring the suit on the
Monday, but he stood perfectly ready to employ Sunday in
betraying their counsels to the defendants in the suit. A position more contemptible, a state of mind more pitiable, can hardly
be conceived. After passing the night in this abject condition,
on the morning of Sunday he sought out Mr. Fisk for purposes
of self-humiliation and treachery.[1] He then partially revealed the
difficulties of his situation, only to have his confidant prove to
him how entirely he was caught, by completing to him the revelation. He betrayed the secrets of his new allies, and bemoaned
his own hard fate; he was thereupon comforted by Mr. Fisk
with the cheery remark that " he (Drew) was the last man who
ought to whine over any position in which he placed himself in
regard to Erie." The poor man begged to see Mr. Gould, and
would take no denial. Finally Mr. Gould was brought in, and
the scene was repeated for his edification. The two must have
been satiated with revenge. At last they sent him away, promising to see him again that evening. At the hour named he again
appeared, and, after waiting their convenience, — for they spared
him no humiliation, — he again appealed to them, offering them
great sums if they would issue new stock or lend him of their
stock. He implored, he argued, he threatened. At the end of
two hours of humiliation, persuaded that it was all in vain, that
he was wholly in the power of antagonists without mercy, he
took his hat, said, " I will bid you good night," and went his way.

*   *   *   *   *   *   *   *

[1] It ought perhaps to be stated that this portion of the narrative has no stronger
foundation than an affidavit of Mr. Fisk, which has not, however, been publicly
contradicted.

But to return to the course of events. With the lords of Erie forewarned was forearmed. They knew something of the method of procedure in New York courts of law. At this particular juncture Mr. Justice Sutherland, a magistrate of such pure character and unsullied reputation that it is inexplicable how he ever came to be elevated to the bench on which he sits, was holding chambers, according to assignment, for the four weeks between the first Monday in November and the first Monday in December. By a rule of the court, all applications for orders during that time were to be made before him, and he only, according to the courtesy of the Bench, took cognizance of such proceedings. Some general arrangement of this nature is manifestly necessary to avoid continual conflicts of jurisdiction. The details of the assault on the Erie directors having been settled, counsel appeared before Judge Sutherland on Monday morning and petitioned for an injunction restraining the Erie directors from any new issue of stock or the removal of the funds of the company beyond the jurisdiction of the court, and also asking that the road be placed in the hands of a receiver. The suit was brought in the name of Mr. August Belmont, who was supposed to represent large foreign holders. The petition set forth at length the alleged facts in the case, and was supported by the affidavits of Mr. Drew and others. Mr. Drew apparently did not inform the counsel of the manner in which he had passed his leisure hours on the previous day; had he done so, Mr. Belmont's counsel probably would have expedited their movements. The injunction was, however, duly signed, and, doubtless, immediately served.

Meanwhile Messrs. Gould and Fisk had not been idle. Applications for injunctions and receiverships were a game which two could play at, and long experience had taught these close observers the very great value of the initiative in law. Accordingly, some two hours before the Belmont application was made, they had sought no less a person than Mr. Justice Barnard, caught him, as it were, either in his bed or at his breakfast, whereupon he had held a *lit de justice*, and made divers astonishing orders. A petition was presented in the name of one

McIntosh, a salaried officer of the Erie Road, who claimed also to be a shareholder. It set forth the danger of injunctions and of the appointment of a receiver, the great injury likely to result therefrom, etc. After due consideration on the part of Judge Barnard, an injunction was issued, staying and restraining all suits, and actually appointing Jay Gould receiver, to hold and disburse the funds of the company in accordance with the resolutions of the Board of Directors and the Executive Committee. This certainly was a very brilliant flank movement, and testified not less emphatically to Gould's genius than to Barnard's law; but most of all did it testify to the efficacy of the new combination between Tammany Hall and the Erie Railway. Since the passage of the bill "to legalize counterfeit money," in April, and the present November, new light had burst upon the judicial mind, and as the news of one injunction and a vague rumor of the other crept through Wall Street that day, it was no wonder that operators stood aghast and that Erie fluctuated wildly from 50 to 61 and back to 48.

The Erie directors, however, did not rest satisfied with the position which they had won through Judge Barnard's order. That simply placed them, as it were, in a strong defensive attitude. They were not the men to stop there: they aspired to nothing less than a vigorous offensive. With a superb audacity, which excites admiration, the new trustee immediately filed a supplementary petition. Therein it was duly set forth that doubts had been raised as to the legality of the recent issue of some two hundred thousand shares of stock, and that only about this amount was to be had in America; the trustee therefore petitioned for authority to use the funds of the corporation to purchase and cancel the whole of this amount at any price less than the par value, without regard to the rate at which it had been issued. The desired authority was conferred by Mr. Justice Barnard as soon as asked. Human assurance could go no further. The petitioners had issued these shares in the bear interest at 40, and had run down the value of Erie to 35; they had then turned round, and were now empowered to buy back that very stock in the bull interest, and in the name and with the funds of the corporation, at par. A law of the State distinctly forbade corporations from operating in their own stock; but this law was disregarded as if it had been only an injunction. An injunction forbade the treasurer from making any disposition of the funds of the company, and this injunction was respected no more than the law. These trustees had sold the property of their wards at 40; they were now prepared to use the money of their wards to buy the same property back at 80, and a judge had been found ready to confer on them the power to do so. Drew could not withstand such tactics, and indeed the annals of Wall Street furnished no precedent or parallel.

*   *   *   *   *   *   *   *

When this last, undreamed-of act was made public on Wednesday at noon, it was apparent that the crisis was not far off. Daniel Drew was cornered. Erie was scarce and selling at 47, and would not become plenty until the arrival of the English steamer on Monday; and so, at 47, Mr. Drew flung himself into the breach to save his endangered credit, and, under his purchases, the stock rapidly rose, until at five o'clock Wednesday afternoon it reached 57. Contrary to expectation, the "corner" had not yet culminated. It became evident the next morning that before two o'clock that day the issue would be decided. Drew fought desperately. The Brokers' Board was wild with excitement. High words passed; collisions took place; the bears were savage, and the bulls pitiless. Erie touched 62, and there was a difference of sixteen per cent between cash stock and stock sold to be delivered in three days, — when the steamer would be in, — and a difference of ten per cent between stock to be delivered on the spot and that to be delivered at the usual time, which was a quarter after two o'clock. Millions were handled like thousands; fabulous rates of interest were paid; rumors of legal proceedings were flying about, and forays of the Erie chiefs on the Vanderbilt roads were confidently predicted. New York Central suddenly shot up seven per cent under these influences, and Vanderbilt seemed about to enter the field. The interest of the stock market centered in the combatants and on these two great corporations. All other stocks were quiet and neglected while the giants were fighting it out. The battle was too fierce to last long. At a quarter before three o'clock the struggle would be over. Yet now, at the very last moment, the prize which trembled before them eluded the grasp of the Erie ring. Their opponent was not saved, but they shared his disaster. Their combination had turned on the fact, disclosed to them by the Erie books, that some three hundred thousand shares of its stock had been issued in the ten-share certificates which alone are transmitted to London. This amount they supposed to be out of the country ; the balance they could account for as beyond the reach of Drew. Suddenly, as two o'clock approached, and Erie was trembling in the sixties, all Broadway — every tailor and bootmaker and cigar vender of New York — seemed pouring into Broad Street, and each new-comer held eagerly before him one or more of those ten-share certificates which should have been in London. Not only this, but the pockets of the agents of foreign bankers seemed bursting with them. Bedlam had suddenly broken loose in Wall Street. It was absolutely necessary for the conspirators to absorb this stock, to keep it from the hands of Drew. This they attempted to do, and manfully stood their ground, fighting against time. Suddenly, when the hour had almost come, — when five minutes more would have landed them in safety, — through one of those strange incidents which occur in Wall Street and which cannot be explained, they seemed smitten with panic. It is said their bank refused to certify their checks for the suddenly increased amount; the sellers insisted on having certified checks, and, in the delay caused by this unforeseen difficulty, the precious five minutes elapsed, and the crisis had passed. The fruits of their plot had escaped them. Drew made good his contracts at 57, the stock at once fell heavily to 42, and a dull quiet succeeded to the excitement of the morning. The hand of the government had made itself felt in Wall Street.

The Broad Street conflict was over, and some one had reaped a harvest. Who was it? It was not Drew, for his losses, apart from a ruined prestige, were estimated at nearly a million and a half of dollars. The Erie directors were not the fortunate men, for their only trophies were great piles of certificates of Erie stock, which had cost them " corner " prices, and for which no demand existed. If Drew's loss was a million and a half, their loss was likely to be nearer three millions. Who, then, were the recipients of these missing millions? There is an ancient saying, which seems to have been tolerably verified in this case, that when certain persons fall out certain other persons come by their dues. The " corner " was very beautiful in all its details, and most admirably planned; but, unfortunately, those who engineered it had just previously made the volume of stock too large for accurate calculation. For once the outside public had been at hand and Wall Street had been found wanting. A large portion of the vast sum taken from the combatants found its way into the pockets of the agents of English bankers, and a part of it was accounted for by them to their principals; another portion went to relieve anxious holders among the American outside public; the remainder fell to professional operators, probably far more lucky than sagacious. Still, there had been a fall before there was a rise. The subsequent disaster, perhaps, no more than counterbalanced the earlier victory; at any rate, Messrs. Gould and Fisk did not succumb, but preserved a steady front, and Erie was more upon the street than ever. In fact, it was wholly there now. The recent operations had proved too outrageous even for the Brokers' Board. A new rule was passed, that no stock should be called, the issues of which were not registered at some respectable banking-house. The Erie directors declined to conform to this rule, and their road was stricken from the list of calls. Nothing daunted at this, these Protean creatures at once organized a new board of their own, and so far succeeded in their efforts as to have Erie quoted and bought and sold as regularly as ever.

Though the catastrophe had taken place on the 19th, the struggle was not yet over. The interests involved were so enormous, the developments so astounding, such passions had been aroused, that some safety valve through which suppressed wrath could work itself off was absolutely necessary, and this the courts of law afforded. The attack was stimulated by various motives. The *bona fide* holders of the stock, especially the foreign holders, were alarmed for the existence of their property. The Erie ring had now boldly taken the position that their duty was, not to manage the road in the interests of its owners, not to make it a dividend-paying corporation, but to preserve it from consolidation with the Vanderbilt monopoly. This policy was openly proclaimed by Mr. Gould, at a later day, before an investigating committee at Albany. With unspeakable effrontery, — an effrontery so great as actually to impose on his audience and a portion of the press, and make them believe that the public ought to wish him success, — he described how stock issues at the proper time, to any required amount, could alone keep him in control of the road, and keep Mr. Vanderbilt out of it; it would be his duty, therefore, he argued, to issue as much new stock, at about the time of the annual election, as would suffice to keep a majority of all the stock in existence under his control; and he declared that he meant to do this. . . . The strangest thing of all was, that it never seemed to occur to his audience that the propounder of this comical sophistry was a trustee and guardian for the stockholders, and not a public benefactor; and that the owners of the Erie Road might possibly prefer not to be deprived of their property, in order to secure the blessing of competition. So unique a method of securing a reëlection was probably never before suggested with a grave face, and yet, if we may believe the reporters, Mr. Gould, in developing it, produced a very favorable impression on the committee. It was hardly to be expected that such advanced views as to the duties and powers of railway directors would favorably impress commonplace individuals who might not care to have their property scaled down to meet Mr. Gould's views of public welfare. These persons accordingly, popularly supposed to be represented by Mr. Belmont, wished to get their property out of the hands of such fanatics in the cause of cheap transportation and plentiful stock, with the least possible delay. Combined with these were the operators who had suffered in the late "corner," and who desired to fight for better terms and a more equal division of plunder. Behind them all, Vanderbilt was supposed to be keeping an eager eye on the long-coveted Erie. Thus the materials for litigation existed in abundance.

On Monday, the 23d, Judge Sutherland vacated Judge Barnard's order appointing Jay Gould receiver, and, after seven hours' argument and some exhibitions of vulgarity and indecency on the part of counsel, which vied with those of the previous April, he appointed Mr. Davies, an ex-chief-justice of the Court of Appeals, receiver of the road and its franchise, leaving the special terms of the order to be settled at a future day. The seven hours' struggle has not been without an object; that day Judge Barnard had been peculiarly active. The morning hours he had beguiled by the delivery to the grand jury of one of the most astounding charges ever recorded; and now, as the shades of evening were falling, he closed the labors of the day by issuing a stay of the proceedings then pending before his associate. . . . Tuesday had been named by Judge Sutherland, at the time he appointed his receiver, as the day upon which he would settle the details of the order. His first proceeding upon that day, on finding his action stayed by Judge Barnard, was to grant a motion to show cause, on the next day, why Barnard's order should not be vacated. This style of warfare, however, savored altogether too much of the tame defensive to meet successfully the bold strategy of Messrs. Gould and Fisk. They carried the war into Africa. In the twenty-four hours during which Judge Sutherland's order to show cause was pending three new actions were commenced by them. In the first place, they sued the suers. Alleging the immense injury likely to result to the Erie Road from actions commenced, as they alleged, solely with a view of extorting money in settlement, Mr. Belmont was sued for a million of dollars in damages. Their second suit was against Messrs. Work, Schell, and others, concerned in the litigations of the previous spring, to recover the $429,250 then paid them, as was alleged, in a fraudulent settlement. These actions were, however, commonplace, and might have been brought by ordinary men. Messrs. Gould and Fisk were always displaying the invention of genius. The same day they carried their quarrels into the United States courts. The whole press, both of New York and of the country, disgusted with the parody of justice enacted in the State courts, had cried aloud to have the whole matter transferred to the United States tribunals, the decisions of which might have some weight, and where, at least, no partisans upon the bench would shower each other with stays, injunctions, vacatings of orders, and other such pellets of the law. The Erie ring, as usual, took time by the forelock. While their slower antagonists were deliberating, they acted. On this Monday, the 23d, one Henry B. Whelpley, who had been a clerk of Gould's, and who claimed to be a stockholder in the Erie and a citizen of New Jersey, instituted a suit against the Erie Railway before Judge Blatchford, of the United States District Court. Alleging the doubts which hung over the validity of the recently issued stock, he petitioned that a receiver might be appointed, and the company directed to transfer into his hands enough property to secure from loss the plaintiff as well as all other holders of the new issues. The Erie counsel were on the ground, and, as soon as the petition was read, waived all further notice as to the matters contained in it; whereupon the court at once appointed Jay Gould receiver, and directed the Erie Company to place eight millions of dollars in his hands to protect the rights represented by the plaintiff. Of course the receiver was required to give bonds with sufficient sureties. Among the sureties was James Fisk, Jr. The brilliancy of this move was only surpassed by its success. It fell like a bombshell in the enemy's camp, and scattered dismay among those who still preserved a lingering faith in the virtue of law as administered by any known courts. The interference of the court was in this case asked for on the ground of fraud. If any fraud had been committed, the officers of the company alone could be the delinquents. To guard against the consequences of that fraud, a receivership was prayed for, and the court appointed as receiver the very officer in whom the alleged frauds, on which its action was based, must have originated. It is true, as was afterwards observed by Judge Nelson in setting

it aside, that a *prima facie* case, for the appointment of a receiver
" was supposed to have been made out," that no objection to the
person suggested was made, and that the right was expressly
reserved to other parties to come into court, with any allegations
they saw fit against Receiver Gould. The collusion in the case
was, nevertheless, so evident, the facts were so notorious and so
apparent from the very papers before the court, and the character of Judge Blatchford is so far above suspicion, that it is hard
to believe that this order was not procured from him by surprise, or through the agency of some counsel in whom he reposed
a misplaced confidence. The Erie ring, at least, had no occasion to be dissatisfied with this day's proceedings.

The next day Judge Sutherland made short work of his
brother Barnard's stay of proceedings in regard to the Davies
receivership. He vacated it at once, and incontinently proceeded, wholly ignoring the action of Judge Blatchford on the
day before, to settle the terms of the order, which, covering as it
did the whole of the Erie property and franchise, excepting only
the operating of the road, bade fair to lead to a conflict of jurisdiction between the State and Federal courts.

And now a new judicial combatant appears in the arena. It
is difficult to say why Judge Barnard, at this time, disappears
from the narrative. Perhaps the notorious judicial violence of
the man, which must have made his eagerness as dangerous to
the cause he espoused as the eagerness of a too swift witness,
had alarmed the Erie counsel. Perhaps the fact that Judge
Sutherland's term in chambers would expire in a few days had
made them wish to intrust their cause to the magistrate who
was to succeed him. At any rate, the new order staying proceedings under Judge Sutherland's order was obtained from
Judge Cardozo, — it is said, somewhat before the terms of the
receivership had been finally settled. The change spoke well
for the discrimination of those who made it, for Judge Cardozo is
a very different man from Judge Barnard. Courteous but inflexible, subtle, clear-headed, and unscrupulous, this magistrate
conceals the iron hand beneath the silken glove. Equally
versed in the laws of New York and in the mysteries of

Tammany, he had earned his place by a partisan decision on the excise law, and was nominated for the bench by Mr. Fernando Wood, in a few remarks concluding as follows : " Judges were often called on to decide on political questions, and he was sorry to say the majority of them decided according to their political bias. It was therefore absolutely necessary to look to their candidate's political principles. He would nominate, as a fit man for the office of Judge of the Supreme Court, Albert Cardozo." Nominated as a partisan, a partisan Cardozo has always been, when the occasion demanded. Such was the new and far more formidable champion who now confronted Sutherland, in place of the vulgar Barnard. His first order in the matter — to show cause why the order of his brother judge should not be set aside — was not returnable until the 30th, and in the intervening five days many events were to happen.

Immediately after the settlement by Judge Sutherland of the order appointing Judge Davies receiver, that gentleman had proceeded to take possession of his trust. Upon arriving at the Erie building, he found it converted into a fortress, with a sentry patrolling behind the bolts and bars, to whom was confided the duty of scrutinizing all comers, and of admitting none but the faithful allies of the garrison. It so happened that Mr. Davies, himself unknown to the custodian, was accompanied by Mr. Eaton, the former attorney of the Erie corporation. This gentleman was recognized by the sentry, and forthwith the gates flew open for himself and his companion. In a few moments more the new receiver astonished Messrs. Gould and Fisk, and certain legal gentlemen with whom they happened to be in conference, by suddenly appearing in the midst of them. The apparition was not agreeable. Mr. Fisk, however, with a fair appearance of cordiality, welcomed the strangers, and shortly after left the room. Speedily returning, his manner underwent a change, and he requested the newcomers to go the way they came. As they did not comply at once, he opened the door, and directed their attention to some dozen men of forbidding aspect who stood outside, and who, he intimated, were prepared to eject them forcibly if they sought to prolong their unwelcome

stay. As an indication of the lengths to which Mr. Fisk was
prepared to go, this was sufficiently significant. The movement, however, was a little too rapid for his companions; the
lawyers protested, Mr. Gould apologized, Mr. Fisk cooled down,
and his familiars retired. The receiver then proceeded to give
written notice of his appointment, and the fact that he had
taken possession ; disregarding, in so doing, an order of Judge
Cardozo, staying proceedings under Judge Sutherland's order,
which one of the opposing counsel drew from his pocket, but
which Mr. Davies not inaptly characterized as a " very singular
order," seeing that it was signed before the terms of the order
it sought to affect were finally settled. At length, however, at
the earnest request of some of the subordinate officials, and
satisfied with the formal possession he had taken, the new
receiver delayed further action until Friday. He little knew
the resources of his opponents, if he vainly supposed that a
formal possession signified anything. The succeeding Friday
found the directors again fortified within, and himself a much
enjoined wanderer without. The vigilant guards were now no
longer to be beguiled. Within the building, constant discussions and consultations were taking place ; without, relays of
detectives incessantly watched the premises. No rumor was too
wild for public credence. It was confidently stated that the
directors were about to fly the State and the county, — that the
treasury had already been conveyed to Canada. At last, late
on Sunday night, Mr. Fisk with certain of his associates left
the building, and made for the Jersey Ferry; but on the way
he was stopped by a vigilant lawyer, and many papers were
served upon him. His plans were then changed. He returned
to the office of the company, and presently the detectives saw
a carriage leave the Erie portals, and heard a loud voice order
it to be driven to the Fifth Avenue Hotel. Instead of going
there, however, it drove to the ferry, and presently an engine,
with an empty directors' car attached, dashed out of the Erie
station in Jersey City, and disappeared in the darkness. The
detectives met and consulted; the carriage and the empty
car were put together, and the inference, announced in every

New York paper the succeeding day, was that Messrs. Fisk and Gould had absconded with millions of money to Canada.

That such a ridiculous story should have been published, much less believed, simply shows how utterly demoralized the public mind had become, and how prepared for any act of high-handed fraud or outrage. The libel did not long remain uncontradicted. The next day a card from Mr. Fisk was telegraphed to the newspapers, denying the calumny in indignant terms. The eternal steel rails were again made to do duty, and the midnight flitting became a harmless visit to Binghamton on business connected with a rolling mill. Judge Balcom, however, of injunction memory in the earlier records of the Erie suits, resides at Binghamton, and a leading New York paper not inaptly made the timid inquiry of Mr. Fisk, "If he really thought that Judge Balcom was running a rolling mill of the Erie Company, what did he think of Judge Barnard?" Mr. Fisk, however, as became him in his character of the Mæcenas of the bar, instituted suits claiming damages in fabulous sums, for defamation of character, against some half dozen of the leading papers, and nothing further was heard of the matter, nor, indeed, of the suits either. Not so of the trip to Binghamton. On Tuesday, the 1st of December, while one set of lawyers were arguing an appeal in the Whelpley case before Judge Nelson in the Federal courts, and another set were procuring orders from Judge Cardozo staying proceedings authorized by Judge Sutherland, a third set were aiding Judge Balcom in certain new proceedings instituted in the name of the Attorney-General against the Erie Road. The result arrived at was, of course, that Judge Balcom declared his to be the only shop where a regular, reliable article in the way of law was retailed, and then proceeded forthwith to restrain and shut up the opposition establishments. The action was brought to terminate the existence of the defendant as a corporation, and, by way of preliminary, application was made for an injunction and the appointment of a receiver. His Honor held that, as only three receivers had as yet been appointed, he was certainly entitled to appoint another. It was perfectly clear to him that it was his duty to enjoin the defendant corporation from delivering the possession of its road, or of any of its assets, to either of the receivers already appointed; it was equally clear that the corporation would be obliged to deliver them to any receiver he might appoint. He was not prepared to name a receiver just then, however, though he intimated that he should not hesitate to do so if necessary. So he contented himself with the appointment of a referee to look into matters, and, generally, enjoined the directors from omitting to operate the road themselves, or from delivering the possession of it to "any person claiming to be a receiver."

This raiding upon the agricultural judges was not peculiar to the Erie party. On the contrary, in this proceeding it rather followed than set an example; for a day or two previous to Mr. Fisk's hurried journey, Judge Peckham of Albany had, upon papers identical with those in the Belmont suit, issued divers orders, similar to those of Judge Balcom, but on the other side, tying up the Erie directors in a most astonishing manner, and clearly hinting at the expediency of an additional receiver to be appointed at Albany. The amazing part of these Peckham and Balcom proceedings is, that they seem to have been initiated with perfect gravity, and neither to have been looked upon as jests, nor intended by their originators to bring the courts and the laws of New York into ridicule and contempt. Of course the several orders in these cases were of no more importance than so much waste paper, unless, indeed, some very cautious counsel may have considered an extra injunction or two very convenient things to have in his house; and yet, curiously enough, from a legal point of view, those in Judge Balcom's court seem to have been almost the only properly and regularly initiated proceedings in the whole case.

These little rural episodes in no way interfered with a renewal of vigorous hostilities in New York. While Judge Balcom was appointing his referee, Judge Cardozo granted an order for a reargument in the Belmont suit, — which brought up again the appointment of Judge Davies as receiver, — and assigned the hearing for the 6th of December. This step on his part bore a curious resemblance to certain of his performances in the notorious case of the Wood leases, and made the plan of operations perfectly clear. The period during which Judge Sutherland was to sit in chambers was to expire on the 4th of December, and Cardozo himself was to succeed him; he now, therefore, proposed to signalize his associate's departure from chambers by reviewing his orders. No sooner had he granted the motion, than the opposing counsel applied to Judge Sutherland, who forthwith issued an order to show cause why the reargument ordered by Judge Cardozo should not take place at once. Upon which the counsel of the Erie Road instantly ran over to Judge Cardozo, who vacated Judge Sutherland's order out of hand. The lawyers then left him and ran back to Judge Sutherland with a motion to vacate this last order. The contest was now becoming altogether too ludicrous. Somebody must yield, and when it was reduced to that, the honest Sutherland was pretty sure to give way to the subtle Cardozo. Accordingly the hearing on this last motion was postponed until the next morning, when Judge Sutherland made a not undignified statement as to his position, and closed by remitting the whole subject to the succeeding Monday, at which time Judge Cardozo was to succeed him in chambers. Cardozo, therefore, was now in undisputed possession of the field.

*   *   *   *   *   *   *   *

It was now very clear that Receiver Davies might abandon all hope of operating the Erie Railway, and that Messrs. Gould and Fisk were borne upon the swelling tide of victory. The prosperous aspect of their affairs encouraged these last-named gentlemen to yet more vigorous offensive operations. The next attack was upon Vanderbilt in person. On Saturday, the 5th of December, only two days after Judge Sutherland and Receiver Davies were disposed of, the indefatigable Fisk waited on Commodore Vanderbilt, and, in the name of the Erie Company, tendered him fifty thousand shares of Erie common stock at 70. . . . As the stock was then selling in Wall Street at 40, the Commodore naturally declined to avail himself of this liberal offer. He even went further, and, disregarding his usual wise policy of silence, wrote to the New York Times a short communication, in which he referred to the alleged terms of settlement of the previous July, so far as they concerned himself, and denied them in the following explicit language : " I have had no dealings with the Erie Railway Company, nor have I ever sold that company any stock or received from them any *bonus*. As to the suits instituted by Mr. Schell and others, I had nothing to do with them, nor was I in any way concerned in their settlement." This was certainly an announcement calculated to confuse the public ; but the confusion became confounded, when, upon the 10th, Mr. Fisk followed him in a card in which he reiterated the alleged terms of settlement, and reproduced two checks of the Erie Company, of July 11, 1868, made payable to the treasurer and by him indorsed to C. Vanderbilt, upon whose order they had been paid. These two checks were for the sum of a million of dollars. He further said that the company had a paper in Mr. Vanderbilt's own handwriting, stating that he had placed fifty thousand shares of Erie stock in the hands of certain persons, to be delivered on payment of $3,500,000, which sum he declared had been paid. Undoubtedly these apparent discrepancies of statement admitted of an explanation ; and some thin veil of equivocation, such as the transaction of the business through third parties, justified Vanderbilt's statements to his own conscience. Comment, however, is wholly superfluous, except to call attention to the amount of weight which is to be given to the statements and denials, apparently the most general and explicit, which from time to time were made by the parties to these proceedings. This short controversy merely added a little more discredit to what was already not deficient in that respect. On the 10th of December the Erie Company sued Commodore Vanderbilt for $3,500,000, specially alleging in their complaint the particulars of that settlement, all knowledge of or connection with which the defendant had so emphatically denied.

None of the multifarious suits which had been brought as yet were aimed at Mr. Drew. The quondam treasurer had apparently wholly disappeared from the scene on the 19th of November. Mr. Fisk took advantage, however, of a leisure day, to remedy this oversight, and a suit was commenced against Drew, on the ground of certain transactions between him, as treasurer, and the railway company, in relation to some steamboats concerned in the trade of Lake Erie. The usual allegations of fraud, breach of trust, and other trifling and, technically, not State prison offences, were made, and damages were set at a million of dollars.

*   *   *   *   *   *   *   *

It was not until the 10th of February that Judge Cardozo published his decision setting aside the Sutherland receivership, and establishing on a basis of authority the right to overissue stock at pleasure. The subject was then as obsolete and forgotten as though it had never absorbed the public attention. And another "settlement" had already been effected. The details of this arrangement have not been dragged to light through the exposures of subsequent litigation. But it is not difficult to see where and how a combination of overpowering influence may have been effected, and a guess might even be hazarded as to its objects and its victims. The fact that a settlement had been arrived at was intimated in the papers of the 26th of December. On the 19th of the same month a stock dividend of eighty per cent in the New York Central had been suddenly declared by Vanderbilt. Presently the legislature met. While the Erie ring seemed to have good reasons for apprehending hostile legislation, Vanderbilt, on his part, might have feared for the success of a bill which was to legalize his new stock. But hardly a voice was raised against the Erie men, and the bill of the Central was safely carried through. This curious absence of opposition did not stop here, and soon the two parties were seen united in an active alliance. Vanderbilt wanted to consolidate his roads; the Erie directors wanted to avoid the formality of annual elections. Thereupon two other bills went hastily through this honest and patriotic legislature, the one authorizing the Erie board, which had been elected for one year, to classify itself so that one fifth only of its members should vacate office during each succeeding year, the other consolidating the Vanderbilt roads into one colossal monopoly. Public interests and private rights seem equally to have been the victims.

II

EARLY AMERICAN CONDITIONS[1]

WHAT happened in Michigan was typical of the whole western situation. In the early days of its statehood it had planned and partly built two lines of railroad across its lower peninsula, from east to west. So severely, however, was the state shaken by the panic that in spite of its heroic efforts to meet its obligations the word Michigan became a scarecrow to eastern capital. As the years went on and there proved to be no possibility of completing the roads or even of procuring the money necessary to keep them in repair, it grew plain that the state must get rid of them. One, the Michigan Central, one hundred and forty-five miles long, ran from Detroit to Kalamazoo. The other, the Michigan Southern, also ran nowhere, but achieved the same result with less effort, being only seventy-five miles long. The roads together had cost $3,500,000. Accordingly, placing its dilapidated property on the bargain-counter, the state waited for customers.

At last, in 1845, the railroads attracted the attention of two young men, both easterners who had gone West, and both persuaded not only that the day of prosperity for the West was about to dawn, but that, if the right means were taken, eastern capital could be brought to look upon a western road with favor. One of the men was James F. Joy, a graduate of Dartmouth College and the Harvard Law School, who had come to Detroit and was waiting for his practice to grow. The other was John W. Brooks, the superintendent of the Auburn and Rochester Railroad in New York. They believed that if the Michigan Central could be rehabilitated and completed for the remaining third of the distance to Lake Michigan, it would prove a profitable investment. It would open up the rich farming land of

---

[1] From An American Railroad Builder: John Murray Forbes, by Henry G. Pearson, Boston, 1911. By permission.

Michigan; better still, it would constitute a link in the shortest route from the East to Chicago and the Mississippi Valley. At that time the traveller left the cars at Buffalo, where he took a steamer which conveyed him, by the roundabout way of Lake Huron and the Straits of Mackinaw, to the head of Lake Michigan. If he had good luck, his boat reached Chicago in four days and a half; not infrequently six days were needed. With the railroad completed across Michigan, the time from Buffalo could be reduced to thirty-six hours. Of course, Brooks reasoned, it was conceivable that as years went on a railroad might be built along the southern shore of Lake Erie to Toledo, and from there to Chicago; but the cost of such an undertaking would be so stupendous and the returns so uncertain that he dismissed the possibility from his calculations. The Michigan Central was, it is true, a railroad in the wilderness; nevertheless its strategic position was such that it could hold its own against the circuitous water route. With eastern capital and eastern control, it was practically certain to succeed. Filled with this conviction Brooks, then twenty-six years old, set forth in the winter of 1845-46 to make the acquaintance of men of means in Boston and New York in the hope of interesting them in his scheme.

Good luck led Brooks, in the course of his labors, to the counting-room of John M. Forbes. Forbes had already made experiments, most of them financially unsuccessful, in the application of steam to ocean transportation;[1] but he was ready to listen to possibilities more promising in connection with steam transportation on land. In those days, of course, there was nowhere any expert knowledge of railroading; yet, judged even by the standards of that time, his notions of the problems of railroad management were, as he took delight in recalling in later years, naïvely rudimentary. He reasoned, for example,

[1] For the most part the vessels used steam only as auxiliary power, having hinged propeller-shafts, by means of which, in good sailing weather, the propeller could be turned up out of harm's way. The Midas, built and owned by the Forbes brothers, was the first steamer to navigate Chinese waters; the Massachusetts was one of the earliest ocean steamers on the Atlantic. The Iron Witch, an iron paddle-wheel steamer, designed for fast service on the Hudson, was an expensive failure.

that in all probability the presidency of a railroad company was like that of an insurance company, — a dignified office which, at that time, was given to "honest and reliable though unsuccessful merchants," the work being done by a secretary. Such a position he wished to find for his elder brother Bennet, whose daring and brilliant career as a sea captain had not proved the best preparation for success in mercantile affairs.

Drawn on partly by this fraternal motive and partly by the fascination of the enterprise itself, Forbes went so far as to employ Daniel Webster to draft a charter embodying the wisdom that had been gleaned from eastern railroad experience, and to send Brooks back to Michigan to secure the passage of the charter by the legislature.

The discussion of this bill, with its momentous consequences to the exhausted treasury of Michigan, was naturally the chief event of the legislative session of 1846. But so ignorant were both the public at large and the legislators themselves concerning railroad charters that the point on which local interest centred was the danger that the pagan capitalists of the East should attempt to run trains "on the Sabbath"; and every day petitions bearing on this point were presented. When, however, the time came for voting on this section, amendments were offered requiring that the corporation should observe the other nine commandments also, and that the directors should attend church at least twice every Sunday, and the section was laughed to defeat.[1] The true guardian of the state's interests proved to be the governor, Alpheus Felch, an able and honest executive, who more than once during this session had to restrain the legislature from giving away to corporations the property of the people. Thus the charter as passed retained for the state a measure of legislative supervision and control.[2] Yet even so, Brooks and

---

[1] Journal of the Senate of Michigan, 1846, pp. 274, 275.

[2] By the act of incorporation (Laws of Michigan, 1846, pp. 37–64) the Michigan Central Railroad was granted the property of the road forever; but the state might repurchase it after a lapse of twenty years, and after thirty years the legislature might alter, amend, or repeal the charter. For the first four years the road was to pay a tax of one-half of one per cent, after that, of three-fourths of one per cent on the capital stock and loans for construction

Joy knew that, with the price of the road fixed at $2,000,000, they had not the worst of the bargain.

Everything now depended on the skill and force of the man who took hold of the financiering. Boston capital, which had been principally invested in the China trade, was now beginning to be put into mills in Massachusetts and New Hampshire and into short lines of railroad along the Atlantic coast. In New Bedford, owing to the decline in profits from the whaling industry, there was also a considerable amount of capital that might be drawn into new projects. Through family connections in these two cities Forbes could make a good beginning, and in New York he got a large measure of help from his former partner in China, John C. Green. Moreover, he was sure of aid from the forlorn holders of Michigan bonds and internal-improvement warrants, who were only too glad to jump from their present fire into the frying-pan of railroad stocks. As one person after another looked into the facts about this worn-out railroad in the wilderness, it became plain that it was, indeed, a bargain. Brooks's report showed that there had been an increase of one hundred per cent in the receipts within the past year, and there was every prospect of even more satisfactory returns when the road should

purposes. Its annual report to the secretary of the state was to contain tables showing its financial condition, its physical condition, and the amount and character of its business. The amount of the capital stock was set at five million dollars, with permission to increase it to eight million.

The rates existing under state management were to continue in force until July 1, 1848, from which time a reduction of twenty-five per cent was to be made on flour and grain ; the tariff for no article was to be higher than the average of the tariffs charged for that article on the Boston and Lowell, the Boston and Providence, and the Boston and Worcester railroads, during September and October of 1845. An exception might be made if the secretary of state of Michigan, the auditor, and the attorney-general gave their consent. There was provision for a commission to determine what was the average rate on the New England railroads, and in case of disagreement a final decision was to be rendered by the court of chancery. Furthermore, not oftener than once in ten years the legislature might require such a commission to review all the rates of the road. The road was required to " transport merchandise and property . . . without showing partiality or favor, and with all practical despatch." The maximum passenger tariff was fixed at three cents per mile. No publication of rates was required ; nevertheless, for eight years, from 1850 to 1857 inclusive, these schedules were given in the annual report of the railroad.

be built across the state and properly equipped. Finally, there
was the assurance that it was to be controlled by eastern capitalists of proved honesty and ability. Advantages such as these
did not suffer when presented by a man like Forbes, who had
vision, will, and above all the faculty of "pitching in"; and as
the six months allowed for the formation of the company drew
to an end, his tense and tireless efforts brought success. "I shall,
I hope," he wrote when it was all over, "have cause to look
back upon this September as one of the best spent months of
my life." He had, indeed, opened the door upon his true career.

On September 23, 1846, the Michigan Central Railroad took
possession of its property. Forbes was president, having consented to take the office only because he found that otherwise
the necessary capital could not be secured; but he arranged to
put the burden of his work on the treasurer, George B. Upton,
to whom he made over his salary. John W. Brooks, at Detroit,
was to have charge of the running of the road.

Promising as were the prospects of the Michigan Central, the
road itself, as Brooks's report made clear, was a shabby piece of
property. The one hundred and forty-five miles of track from
Detroit to Kalamazoo were in bad condition, and fifty-six miles
more were needed to complete the line to the nearest point on
Lake Michigan. There were only four passenger "depots" along
the line, and at Detroit nothing but a small freight depot and
an engine-house, both inconveniently situated at some distance
from the water front. The value of the rolling stock was $68,000,
the largest single item being $4000 for a locomotive of twelve tons.

The track, like that of all early railroads, consisted of beams
of wood six inches square, to which were fastened strips of iron
half an inch thick by two and a quarter inches wide. The beams
were fastened to cross-ties laid three feet apart, which in turn
were laid upon under-sills, "the whole being supported upon
short blocks of different lengths, varying according to the distance between the bottom of the under-sills and a firm foundation." [1] On the first thirty miles out of Detroit the wooden part

---

[1] Brooks's Report upon the Merits of the Michigan Central Railroad as an
Investment for Eastern Capitalists, p. 4.

of the track, which had been in use for eight years, had never been renewed, and was naturally much decayed. The iron, worn out and broken, curved up at the ends; and when one of these up-springing pieces thrust itself through the floor of the car between the feet of a passenger, it was expressively known as a "snake-head." Such a form of track, best described by the phrase "a barrel-hoop tacked to a lath," was already passing; and the charter of the new company required the road to be laid with a heavy H rail of iron, weighing sixty pounds a yard.[1]

When the directors held their first annual meeting at Detroit in June, 1847, the road had already proved prosperous enough to justify them in beginning at once to build toward Lake Michigan. They accordingly sanctioned expenditures amounting to over two million dollars, which should give them a road fully equipped to handle its rapidly growing business. The actual cost, it may be added, was more than four million dollars.

It was at the time of this meeting that Forbes and some of his associates received their first lesson in practical railroading. They travelled on the road, explored so-called harbors on Lake Michigan in the search for a western terminus, went on to Chicago, and returned by steamer through the Straits of Mackinaw. Forbes, a born traveller, with a keen eye and a zest for every experience, described the trip in a journal letter to his wife, which deserves a place here for the picture it gives of the rawness of the country which the railroad was to do so much to develop.

Steamer Empire, Mackinaw, June 11, 1847

We reached Detroit 1.30 in the night and landed in the mud, slept an hour or two, and had to get up and go to find T. Howe; Brooks, our mainstay, having gone West. We decided to follow, and started at eight or so on our railroad. . . .

For the first few miles the country was dreary; flat, with a great deal of surface water, through forests mostly, but dense and melancholy ones, water under foot and huge decaying trees lying about; the trees generally tall and with no foliage until near the top.

We found the road in a most deplorable condition, the iron broken up often into pieces not a foot long, and sometimes we could not see any

---

[1] The present weight of the heaviest steel rails is more than one hundred pounds a yard.

iron for some feet, only wood; in other places short pieces of iron, almost athwartships, but our protection was in its being so short that no snake-heads could reach the cars. This bad road lasted about eighty miles, the bad country about thirty, when we came to a little drier soil and passed through several flourishing villages.

Here we began to see the famous oak openings, — noble oak trees just far enough apart to let each take its handsome natural shape, just as a park should be; but, sad to tell, we seldom saw the openings in their beauty, for the trees had generally been girdled and stood naked and dead (some of them dying, having been cut this year), and fine fields of wheat growing right up to their trunks, and fields varying in size from twenty to two hundred acres each; but few flowers to be seen, and the houses far from our New England houses in neatness. At night we reached a dirty country tavern at Kalamazoo, where the road terminates. . . .

At K. we found Brooks was gone to Niles; and we resolved to follow him, and arranged to start with a barouche and four horses at 4 A.M. We sat up till half-past eleven talking with our engineers, whom we sent for to get information from them about our routes, and then turned in. In an hour Brooks arrived, and came to my room, and after one hour's talk we decided to take him with us and push for the celebrated city of St. Joseph, fifty-six miles distant, which we accordingly did at 4 A.M. With few exceptions, our ride was like that of the day before, the roads execrable, full of deep holes and gullies, where we had a right to expect a capsize; but the weather was lovely beyond measure, and on the whole we enjoyed our drive, excepting that, not daring to drink the water, our tongues were parched like fever patients.

At four we reached the marsh which surrounds St. Joseph. Figure to yourself a pestilential black mud, quivering and shaking under its own weight, with tufts of grass, rank and uneven, a deep river in the midst, and sand-banks where the mud ceases. . . . Rising up from this was a steep but small bluff, extending into the lake, on which the city stands. Two handsome houses built in 1837, and I believe now empty, two large wooden taverns, one now untenanted, and a few other indifferent looking palaces, with some stray houses along the river, complete the *coup d'œil* of this famous city, which sprung up in a night and withered next day. The only pleasant thing was the fine view of Lake Michigan, blue, like the ocean, and wide.

We started out to make our observations, accompanied by pretty much all the town, some half-dozen people, who took care we should not be alone a moment for fear we should not appreciate fully the beauties of the place. We went over to Uncle Sam Russell's "Eden," which has a fine map of land laid out into cities, and is called North St. Joseph. Drifting sand near the lake and the aforesaid marsh in shore. Nothing would induce me to visit this place again, unless I could carry Mr. Russell with me and witness his first interview with his domain.

June 12

. . . We left [St. Joseph] on Sunday A.M. for Niles, 26 miles, and arrived there to dinner; the country dull for 12 miles, then tolerable. . . . We started at 7 along the lake shore for Michigan City; a beautiful day, the lake just like the ocean, plenty of deer tracks. Got there at 11 and examined the harbor to our satisfaction, and at 2 P.M. embarked in the steamer for Chicago, taking leave of Brooks who was bound back to Detroit. Found Mr. Ogden [William B. Ogden, first Mayor of Chicago] on board, a very agreeable man who came to Chicago 12 years ago, when it was a wilderness, and now there are 15,000 to 20,000 people there. Arrived at Chicago at 5 P.M. — hotter than Tophet. Established ourselves at an immense hotel, and the pangs of thirst being unbearable, we here broke into lake water astonishingly, and happily without bad effect. Mr. Ogden came for us at 6 or 7 in his carryall, and took us to drive about the town. Some of the houses are on a bluff (like that at Brooklyn) looking out on the blue lake, and it was lovely at sunset beyond imagination; few trees, however, and the ground under foot dampish, being called " Wet Prairie." Mr. O. offered to drive us next day to the " Grand Prairie," 20 miles distant, but the roads were bad, the weather hot, and after a week's train we did not think it worth while.

Ogden's attentions, it soon appeared, were by way of inducing the eastern capitalists to buy land for which he was the agent. The " wet prairie," within a mile of the hotel, he offered at $1.25 an acre. "Sheltered by our absurd prejudices against land," wrote Forbes thirty-five years later, " we were proof against Ogden's seductions, and I do not think any of us ever bought a foot of land in Chicago for ourselves while the road was in course of construction. My hotel bill of one hundred and twenty-five dollars would have bought one hundred acres, now worth $8,000,000 to $12,000,000."

This rawness of the land which the Michigan Central was to serve was matched by the inexperience of the settlers in the obligations of a railroad public. Having had things pretty much their own way in the days when the road belonged to the state, they did not take kindly to the regulations that were necessary to put the road on a business basis. The turbulent element which is found in every frontier community, being here well organized and determined to rule or ruin, precipitated a fierce struggle which was the precursor of the granger difficulties of later decades.

In the early days of the road the locomotives had proceeded with such obliging caution that live-stock could browse between the rails in entire safety. Naturally, when under the new management the speed was accelerated, with the consequent destruction of cattle, the outcry was at first great. But the balm of damages easily obtained opened the eyes of the settlers to new tactics, and soon they took their pigs to the railroad track as to a market. As a counter move, when the line of track had been properly fenced in, Brooks issued notice to the effect that hereafter the road would pay only one-half the value of any animal killed. The contest was then joined. Trains found their progress blocked by logs on the track, and on grades the rails were often greased, so that the passengers had to get out and work their passage. In his Reminiscences Forbes tells the story of the struggle.

In the country next west of Detroit the lawbreakers were so strong that it was said no judge or jury dared to convict any of the prominent men among them; and it was soon evident that here was the battle-ground between order and disorder. Mr. Brooks at once took his measures with his characteristic foresight and decision. When almost powerless, he maintained the best truce possible, protecting his property and trade by special police raised from his own men, and usually running a hand car ahead of every train, as I remember was still done the first time my wife and I went over the railroad. But Brooks laid his plans for more thorough work. His shrewd lawyer sent on colonists to settle on the line of road in that county as farmers, and at the same time to get evidence against the conspirators, who had determined either to destroy or control our road. He also quietly took measures to get the legislature to change the general law, so that criminals could, when circumstances justified it, be tried in counties other than those in which their offences were committed. While thus accumulating evidence and getting ready for enforcing his rights, he went on extending and rebuilding the road with vigor. The conspirators were led by a man named Fitch, supposed to be quite rich for the country, who boasted that no court would give a verdict against him or his men. Misled perhaps by Brooks's quiet methods, he extended his operations from putting obstruction on the track and firing upon trains, to burning wood-piles and depots, destroying at one fire $75,000 worth of property. . . .

When in due time Mr. Brooks's plan was ripe, he one night sent out a train-load of special officers, chiefly enlisted among his own men, and captured [thirty-five] of the conspirators without a blow being struck or any resistance attempted. They expected only to be carried to their county town, there to be bailed out; but, when they approached Detroit, they found for the first time that the law had been changed, and that they could be tried in a place where justice was possible. They hired William H. Seward to come from New York and defend them, which he did in a speech worse than any made by himself or any other demagogue in this country. The trial lasted all summer, Fitch and one or two others dying in jail, it was said in consequence of medicine taken to produce illness and prolong the trial in hopes of a disagreement of the jury. Mr. Brooks's measures for getting evidence and working up his case were so good that in spite of Seward's help and of all the disadvantages of a great corporation prosecuting individuals and farmers, all the worst members of the gang were . . . convicted. . . . It was the great railroad trial of this century, and settled many practical questions for all Mr. Brooks's successors in railroad building and management.

In the operation of the road, Brooks, as this episode makes clear, was the guiding spirit. Besides being an experienced engineer, he was an executive full of energy and resource. For very little of what he was called upon to do was there any precedent; conditions were so exceptional that his inventive genius was heavily drawn upon. It was, in fact, a typical instance of the way in which mother wit and Yankee ingenuity can save a situation and establish order out of chaos.

Such success as Brooks achieved in his own department, however, would have been impossible if the financial management of the road also had not been masterly. The older railroads in the East yielded every six months a wreckage of embarrassments and disasters, all due to the mental or moral incompetence of the men who undertook to guide them through the uncharted waters of railroad finance. To find and to keep the channel under such circumstances required a remarkable measure of alertness, faith, and courage. Railroading is preëminently an enterprise in which men must think in decades and scores of years ; yet at this time the oldest road in Massachusetts had been running barely fifteen years. So it was that, in these hobble-de-hoy days of railroads, the Michigan Central owed no little of its brilliant success to the fact that its financial affairs were guided by a man so sound and resolute as John M. Forbes.

In the first three years of Forbes's presidency more than $6,000,000 were required for the purchase, construction, and equipment of the road. It was his business to secure this money, and the limits within which he could work were narrow enough. With Baring Brothers and with bankers in Europe, it is true, he was in close touch through his ventures in the China trade, and to such men he was constantly expressing the hope that the high rates of interest prevailing in the United States might prove more tempting than the three or four per cent they could get at home. " You are probably aware," he wrote in March, 1849, to a merchant in Hamburg, " that for 18 months past the *best* paper, such as that, for instance, of my good uncle, T. H. Perkins, Esq., with other names on the notes, has been selling here at from 10 to 18% per annum." But foreign bankers, making no distinction between enterprises backed by poor and irresponsible western states, and those financed by reliable eastern merchants, were proof against his allurements; and in these first years, except for one small loan obtained at the very beginning, not a cent of foreign capital went into the Michigan Central Railroad. On the other hand, the continuing decline of the China trade and the whaling industry in New England was an opportunity of which Forbes made the most. By his persistent and persuasive application to his friends, and by the action of the directors in applying to construction the eight per cent dividend of $176,000, earned in 1848, and issuing a dividend of stock, the cash needed to complete the road was raised.

Thus, thanks to the faith and works of Brooks and Forbes, when, in the spring of 1849, the line was completed from Detroit to New Buffalo on Lake Michigan, the stockholders had every reason to be satisfied with their investment. Not only was the road well constructed: it was adequate in its provisions for increase of traffic. Moreover, the company had built the Mayflower, one of the largest and fastest steamers in the country, to run between Buffalo and Detroit, and thus it controlled the only quick route to the West. With the assurance of a large amount of through traffic to be added to its already profitable and rapidly growing business, the road promised to become without further delay a highly remunerative investment. Forbes and Brooks, to be sure, perceived that their very success, taken with the quickened development of the West, was bringing the danger of competition nearer and nearer. They could not expect to keep their advantage much longer to themselves. But the conservative majority looked upon any such possibility as chimerical; and the directors, confident that the road would never need to go beyond the western boundary of the state, even rejected a chance to obtain for a song a railroad charter which had been granted by the Indiana legislature. They had made their investment; the railroad was finished; they now wanted the profits to come in.

Within a year, however, these illusions of security were dispelled. A group of New York capitalists bought the Michigan Southern, the straggling zigzag bit of line, once the property of the state, which has already been mentioned, snapped up the Indiana charter which the Michigan Central had rejected, and prepared to build a cheap railroad from Toledo to Chicago. At the same time it became apparent to the most conservative minds that the construction of a railroad along the southern shore of Lake Erie was only a few years distant. If the Michigan Central were not to become an isolated piece of road, picking up what business it could between its two lake terminals, it must extend its influence both east and west. Its owners must, in fact, double their investment if they were to save what they had already put in.

Among the causes that accounted for the extraordinary development of the period upon which the Middle West was just entering were such obvious ones as the steady increase of the population, particularly after 1848, by immigration from Germany, and the general introduction of the McCormick reaper, which made possible the increase of the grain harvest twenty or thirty fold. Furthermore, commerce between this region and the cotton-raising states had outgrown the capacity of the rivers and demanded a railroad from the Lakes to the Gulf. So imperative was this last need, that in 1850 Congress granted aid from the public lands along the line of the proposed route. With this magnificent gift, the roads that were to compose the system — the Illinois Central and the Mobile and Ohio — could make a successful appeal for capital.

But perhaps the chief reason for the rapid development of these years, especially as regards railroads, was the call of the Far West. With the discovery of gold in California in 1849, the nation took a continental view of itself. Its first thought was to abridge the journey, long and wearisome whether by land or by sea, to the Pacific coast, and every railroad in the Mississippi Valley entertained schemes of laying its track westward over the prairies. "The discoveries of gold," wrote Forbes in 1854, "have been the direct cause of the construction of four-fifths of the western railways begun since 1849. The success of a few which had been previously constructed gave confidence, it is true, and the West had been fast developing; but not much faster than it had been in four years previously, when hardly anything was done in railways there. This sudden success of western enterprises was also in the face of the failure or the depreciation of the eastern railways."[1]

By the year 1850 eastern financiers were fully awake to these marvellous opportunities for the investment of capital. Their own resources being still inadequate, they again appealed to Europe. "As money seems to be a drug on your side," wrote Forbes, in May of 1852, to the merchant in Hamburg to whom three years before he had turned in vain, "while we have still use for it here at a fair price, I cannot help repeating the suggestion which I then made for your consideration. When I see quotations on your side and on ours for money, I feel just as you would if old *Java Coffee* were selling here at four cents, and a drug at that, while *fifteen days* distant it was worth eight cents in your market."

And to Russell Sturgis in London he wrote in September, 1851, concerning the prospects of railroad building in Illinois: "Imagine a deep black soil, almost every acre of which can be entered at once with the plough, and an enormous crop secured the first season, but where the very fertility and depth of the soil make transportation on common roads almost impracticable at the season when produce ought to be sent to market, and this region now for the first time opened to a market by railroad.

[1] February 20, 1854.

The farmer himself in the interior of the state will be nearer New York *in time* and even in cheapness of transporting his produce than the fertile Genesee valley was before the Erie Canal was made, and where poorer land is now worth one hundred dollars per acre and upwards — nearer in time than many parts of the interior of New York and Ohio *now are.*"

The result of this constant hammering and of such a fact — patent to all — as the success of the Michigan Central, was that the English threw their hesitation to the winds, and after it their discretion too. The same British lack of discrimination which, after the panic of 1837, had lumped together all investments in the Middle West as bad, now lumped them all together as good.

Whatever the remote danger from this state of things, — and, as will presently appear, it was a danger that Forbes saw clearly, — the immediate advantage to the Michigan Central was the assurance of an adequate supply of money for its westward extension. Its first move was to build some ten miles of track, from New Buffalo, in Michigan, to Michigan City, in Indiana. There remained fifty-five miles to be constructed to Chicago, — work which had to be done under conditions of irritation and excitement, for their rival in the race, the Michigan Southern, proved to be both alert and slippery. To build in Indiana, the Michigan Central put money into the New Albany and Salem road, a local affair which had thirty-five miles of track in the southern part of the state and a charter conveniently vague, and which, in return for the grateful inflow of eastern capital, consented to begin building at once a " branch " around Lake Michigan, in the northwestern corner of the state. The " Southrons " protested, and persistently sought injunctions; the Michigan Central men, to prove their good faith, had to put their hands deeper into their pockets, with the result that the New Albany and Salem achieved the glory of becoming the first line to connect Lake Michigan and the Ohio River.

In building the twenty miles of track in Illinois between the state line and Chicago, even greater difficulties were in the way. Partly from proper reasons of economy, but chiefly because it had no charter and the legislature would not meet for a year and a half, the Michigan Central desired to build and use a track in common with the Illinois Central; and a secret agreement was made between the two companies by which the Illinois road, in building its branch from Chicago, was to deflect its line some half a dozen miles to the east, touching the Indiana boundary at the point where the Michigan Central stopped. In return for this favor, the Illinois Central, as yet barely organized, acquired the universal desideratum, eastern capital, and could begin to build at once.

At the mere suspicion of such plans, Chicago burst into wrath. Hitherto its isolation had greatly retarded its growth. Islanded in "wet prairie" and Illinois mud, it was practically inaccessible by land; by water the route from the East was long and round-about, while from the West the Illinois and Michigan Canal had been open for only a few years. Thus in 1850, though it had increased by 10,000 in the preceding decade, its population was still under 30,000, a pitiable showing when compared with the great river cities of Cincinnati with 115,000, and St. Louis with 78,000. Through railroads it hoped for salvation; and yet even here there was danger. Lying fifteen miles to the north of the southern end of Lake Michigan, it had fears lest the main line of traffic to the west and the southwest might pass it by alto-gether; and it shuddered at the prospect of becoming a mere way-station on a branch. Therefore, when in the spring of 1851 the city discovered that three railroad companies were making plans for entering it, it assumed an attitude of aggressive sensi-tiveness, — perhaps not unknown since, — and sought to dictate terms. Newspapers, city officials, and business men insisted that no through passengers or freight should be transferred at any junction-point outside the city, but that all should be brought within its gates for tribute. Furthermore, the hack-drivers and teamsters, fearing that their prospective trade might be nothing but a Tantalus glimpse, raised a cry that each railroad must enter the city on its own tracks and have its own station.

These matters all came to a head in July, 1851, when two "railroad conventions" were held in Chicago, at which the plans of the roads for reaching the city were made known to the public.

The commotion, it is true, never reached the intensity of the "Erie War," that famous contest for a break in gauge in order that the piemen of Erie, Pennsylvania, might sell their wares to passengers changing cars; but it is amusingly characteristic of this period in railroad-building. Indeed, for a season the lustre of even the great Judge Douglas was dimmed in Chicago by reason of his attitude on the railroad question.

The Michigan Southern smoothed its way diplomatically. Having secured the charter of a plank-road company which was alleged to have railroad privileges, it proposed to come into the city on its own track, thus making sure of a gracious reception by the Chicagoans and of a generous subscription from them to its stock. The Illinois Central and the Michigan Central, for proposing to come in together, were looked upon with disfavor. The directors of the Illinois road accordingly did not dare to carry out their agreement to swing their track eastward to the Indiana line and there connect with the Michigan road. The nearest that they would consent to come left a gap of six and a half miles, over which Brooks and Joy proposed to build without a charter, trusting to the next legislature to legalize their action.

Forbes protested. "Going without a charter a quarter-section is as bad as the Atlantic would be." Unused prairie though the land was, he argued, their enemies would be sure to build a highway across their proposed line to block them. Nevertheless, as the months went on this unsatisfactory scheme proved to be the only basis on which it was possible to go ahead.

Meanwhile in Indiana each company was racing to get its line completed first. The Michigan Southern men had the advantage of a good start, and were not retarded by scruples as to building solidly, but the seasons in their courses fought against them. The rails for the last section of their track reached Dunkirk, on Lake Erie, after the lake was closed to navigation, and, as luck would have it, in the following spring the lake was not clear until a month later than usual. So, although the Chicago end of the line was completed, in Indiana passengers and freight must be transported a distance of thirteen miles over a plank road. The Michigan Central, on the other hand, having ordered its iron in good season from England, built steadily and achieved the triumph of beginning its regular through service on May 21, 1852, a day ahead of the first through train on the Michigan Southern, and a week before that road was in regular running order. A month later, at a special session of the Illinois legislature, the six-mile bit of track in Illinois was legalized.

In the midst of this struggle to extend its road to the west, the Michigan Central was forced to look also to the matter of eastern connections. A line of roads between Buffalo and Toledo connecting with the Michigan Southern was already under construction. Therefore the Michigan Central stockholders were urged, in the most persuasive of circulars, to subscribe to the stock of the Canada Great Western, which was to run from Windsor, opposite Detroit, through Ontario to Niagara Falls, there crossing the river by a suspension-bridge. Although the scheme had many advantages, notably in the shortness of the route, Forbes and his friends were hampered by the necessity of working with a foreign corporation. First, the Canadian road insisted on a different gauge of track from that of the Michigan Central. Then, at the instigation of sharp citizens of Detroit, with an eye for making a penny out of delayed travellers, it attempted to locate its station in Windsor at a point as remote as possible from the station of the Michigan Central.

A later and more serious cause of trouble was the attempt of its Canadian directors to sell the road to the Grand Trunk. Journeys to Canada on the part of Forbes and other American directors were constantly necessary " to kill off some rascals "; but as troubles continued and multiplied, and as it was found inexpedient to make an appeal to the English government, the Michigan Central men, after a few years, withdrew altogether.

In these labors to make the Michigan Central a link in an all-rail route from the East to Chicago, the directors of the road had assumed heavy burdens and run great risks. Besides adding a million and a half to the cost of their own road, they had been obliged to purchase bonds of the Illinois Central and the Indiana roads to the amount of $600,000 and $800,000 respectively, and they had contributed no less heavily to the Canadian line. But they had been face to face with the emergency of competition. Not to have accepted the challenge would have been to throw away all the money and labor that they had put into the road — a mocking of their visions. And from the competition which they had spent so much to enter there lay a further danger, in that their rivals were unscrupulous.

For the next five years operating expenses were heavily increased by the necessity of more frequent and more rapid passenger trains, and of "runners" at various Eastern passenger stations, and earnings were cut into by reduced freight rates. Every truce made in the shape of an agreement as to rates was secretly violated by the Michigan Southern, and then followed open war. This state of things continued until the Michigan Southern was wrecked in the panic of 1857. After that, with a new management in control, an arrangement that proved permanent was made between the two roads by which the steamboat lines of both on Lake Erie were withdrawn, the number and the speed of the through passenger trains were reduced, and the freight earnings pooled on a basis of fifty-eight per cent for the Michigan Central and forty-two per cent for the Michigan Southern. In this fashion these financiers discovered the laws of competition and combination in the field of railroading.

In spite of the weight of the burdens caused by construction and competition, the prosperity of the Michigan Central in the years from 1852 to 1857 was sufficient to carry them easily. In a résumé of the history of the road made by Forbes in December, 1855, after nine years of operating under private ownership, he told the story of its success in striking figures.

The history of railroad enterprise in the West, up to that time [1846], was one of almost universal failure, and we were entering upon ground that was worse than untried; it had been prematurely tried under the auspices of the state governments, and isolated embankments at various points stood as monuments of disaster. . . .

With very good management it [the Michigan Central] was capable of earning as a maximum $400,000 per annum; it has now grown to be 269 miles long, with a power of earning over $2,500,000.

During our first winter, say December, January and February, 1846–1847, our *total* receipts were about $53,000. For the first winter after our completion to Chicago, say December, January and February, 1852–1853, our receipts had grown to be $164,000. While we have earned during the *first two weeks* of this month, December, 1855, $114,000.

The present termini of our road then claimed to have, Detroit and Chicago, each about 14,000 inhabitants, the former now claims 49,600, and the latter 80,000. . . .

The whole number of miles of railroad west of Buffalo and north of the Ohio River was only about 500 miles, and these laid with a flat rail; where there are now over 7300 miles of road finished with heavy rails, besides a large amount of unfinished roads.

Detroit was then three days' journey from the seaboard in the summer, and five or six days in winter. It can now be reached in about twenty-seven hours.

With an addition to construction of thirty-eight per cent, the business of the road had grown one hundred and forty per cent. The increase in gross earnings in 1855 over 1854 was forty per cent, and the limit of its capacity as a single-track road was fast being reached. Moreover, the increase of traffic from the new roads in Illinois which were in alliance with the Michigan Central — the Illinois Central and the Chicago, Burlington, and Quincy — was only just beginning to be felt.

*   *   *   *   *   *   *   *

The result of the rapid railroad expansion after the war was seen as early as 1870 in the existence of three lines — of which the C. B. & Q. and the Burlington and Missouri in Iowa constituted one — connecting Chicago and Omaha, and in the formation of the "Omaha pool" for the purpose of dividing equally the profits of the business done between the two cities. Though the evils of competition were checked here, they cropped out elsewhere in the constant temptations offered to the trunk lines to purchase small branch roads. The usual method was for a group of towns considering themselves worthy of the privileges of a railroad to vote for its construction sums which often ran as high as ten thousand dollars a mile, and then to take their proposed line to market. The trunk line which they first approached rarely refused to pay the sum, however large, which might be needed to attach the new road to its system; little as it might be able to afford the expense, — for these branches usually proved "suckers" instead of "feeders," — it could still less afford to see the branch grafted upon a rival trunk. Eastern directors had as yet hardly heard of pools, such things being minor mysteries, with which western managers alone were concerned; but the proposals for the purchase of branch roads came within their cognizance, and they were inclined to suspect that these schemes were often sheer imposition. Forbes's certainty on this point was pithily put at the time in story fashion, and he was fond of telling the anecdote in later years.

It had become quite common [he writes in his " Reminiscences "] for [the President] to come from the West with a plan for a hundred or two miles of new road, which then meant about $30,000 of seven or eight per cent bonds per mile; and on one occasion, when such a branch was about being authorized, I related a story of my Naushon experience. We had been troubled with cats, which destroyed our birds, and so we put a bounty on killing them of so much for every cat's tail brought in; which amount proving insufficient we raised the price until we found, or thought we found, that they were raising cats to bring in to sell to us. " Now," said I to the directors, "I am convinced that the contractors and speculators are building roads merely to sell to us, and the more we buy of them, the more cats' tails will be brought in to us!" That cat was not bought; the story got around, and in Boston circles the Chicago, Burlington, and Quincy branches were known as the C. B. & Q. cats' tails.[1]

Still another difficulty connected with railroad management in these years was the insistent need of pushing out into new territory at a rate and in a direction that should prove far enough and yet not too far ahead of the oncoming flow of population. Here was a problem containing so many chances for error in its solution that the interests of the company as a whole must be considered from every point of view before it was safe for the road to commit itself. The B. & M. in Nebraska, organized as a separate corporation to build from the Missouri River at Plattsmouth to the recently completed Union Pacific at Kearney, besides having a land grant of 2,365,864 acres, easily justified itself as being certain to obtain a good share of business from and to the Union Pacific. Another plan for building a road up the west bank of the Mississippi River into what was then the far Northwest, that is to say, southern Minnesota, was agreed to

[1] Letters and Recollections, Vol. II, p. 213.

by the C. B. & Q. board, and was put into execution in similar fashion by the organization of two independent companies known as the Dubuque, or River, Roads. The directors of the C. B. & Q. recommended to their stockholders the bonds of these roads to the extent of some four and a half millions of dollars, and took a considerable share for themselves. The bonds bore six per cent interest and were sold at 90. In this case, however, the caution of the eastern directors had given way too easily before the enthusiasm of the western officials: the promise of local aid and a land grant of 40,000 acres could not make up for the fact that the roads were built nearly ten years too soon. Charles E. Perkins, Forbes's cousin, who had been associated with the B. & M. in Iowa since 1859, showed his clearer understanding of the situation at the moment in the ironical remark that the directors of the C. B. & Q. might as well have endorsed the bonds of a railroad to be built in the valley of the Red River of the North.[1] From this error, as will presently appear, came a train of disastrous consequences.

Consolidation naturally went hand in hand with rapid physical development. On January 1, 1873, the C. B. & Q., with its 825 miles of track, and the B. & M. in Iowa, with its 443 miles, were united, the new corporation, which held property worth more than fifty millions of dollars, being one of the largest in the country. But this was only a first step. Though the new C. B. & Q. stood high in the financial world and commanded the services of able men in its several departments, its organization was extremely haphazard. It had no definite method for securing harmonious and united action between the financial management in Boston and the operating management in Chicago, and its system of auditing belonged to *ante-bellum* days. Furthermore, as with the directors in Boston the care of C. B. & Q. interests was only one of several irons in the fire, so the executive officers in Chicago gave to the road only a portion of their time. Nowhere was there a man of experience and force in high position devoting himself exclusively to the service of the road.

[1] MS. Recollections of C. E. Perkins.

The dangers of such a situation came upon Forbes with cumulative effect in June, 1873, after his return from a yachting trip to the Azores and a visit to California which had kept him away from Boston and business for a year and a half. Long trusted as his co-workers and fellow counsellors had been, their acquiescence in the methods and routine of smaller days continued under the new conditions became a trouble that he could not shake off. Reports from his sharp-eyed and critical cousin in the West, who now, as vice-president of the B. & M. in Nebraska, could speak more freely of C. B. & Q. men and measures, helped to make Forbes feel that matters should no longer be allowed to drift. The bonded indebtedness of the combined roads needed badly to be got into satisfactory shape, and there was a floating debt of a million and a half dollars. His uneasiness is expressed in a letter written to a fellow director not long after his return.

I do think we need more control at this end over our 50-million property.

We know next to nothing and we trust the administration of this mammoth enterprise 1000 miles off to a man who has no experience in the details of R. R. business, and who represents at least two other companies, whose interests *may be* conflicting: 1st, the coal co. of whom we buy our fuel; 2d, a R. Road which, with or without his fault, has managed to get largely into a debt to us which it cannot pay.

I don't know how many other things he may be in, which are suckers instead of feeders, but if the stockholders ever look into their affairs and find that in one way and another — with the Board's assent and without it — the present administration have used over a million of *their* money for the protection of other enterprises in which some of the Directors are concerned, and all the stockholders are not, we shall find ourselves in a very awkward position. It was only at the June meeting of the Board that I knew of this accumulation of indebtedness. It was my fault that I did not know and try to prevent it, but I don't feel like going on in the same road much farther.

Anybody may make one such blunder in trusting others' management, but the man that makes it a second time with his eyes thus opened becomes a party to the mismanagement, and I confess I see nothing to prevent the same sort of thing being done right over again — except that our credit is not quite so good.[1]

[1] July 13, 1873.

The disquiet here expressed was not allayed when Forbes learned of the pass to which the two River Roads had been brought. From the outset misfortune had attended them. The Chicago and Northwestern, which owned the railroad bridge over the Mississippi at Clinton, acting with pardonable consideration for its own interests, refused to permit the lower of the two to make connection over it with the C. B. & Q.; and thus a portion of the additional traffic expected went to increase the profits of a rival trunk line. As if this were not bad enough, extravagant construction and careless management had done their worst, and early in 1873 the River Roads were in such condition that they were unable to pay the interest on their bonds. In this emergency, the directors of the C. B. & Q. undertook to save the situation by voting the sum necessary for this payment from the funds of their company. When Forbes discovered where the cash for his coupons came from, his first impulse was to express his disapprobation and disgust by returning the money. To one of the directors who protested against this course he wrote:

Not wishing to do anything in haste which so wise a man as you disapproves of, I withdraw my letter . . . for the moment; but when you get time I wish you would give me in ten lines the grounds upon which you expect to justify the payment of the Dubuque Bonds coupons.

That it will eventually come out and be challenged is just as sure as that we live, and now is the time for any of us who were not responsible for the transaction to take their ground.

I am open to conviction; but while I can guess at many good reasons for paying out such a large sum to outsiders, I am utterly at a loss for reasons justifying our voting it to ourselves.[1]

On this point Forbes yielded for the moment. In the meantime, his passion for having things sound and right, and his sense of responsibility, now thoroughly awakened, drove him to work over plans for getting the indebtedness of the road into shape by a large issue of mortgage bonds which Baring Brothers might be induced to take. This, of course, they would not do " without giving C. B. & Q. a good sifting," and thus the reforms in the

[1] August 7, 1873.

management which Forbes desired could be accomplished. In such manner the summer wore away.

The panic of September, 1873, with its widespread wrecking of railroads, when the River Roads went completely under, and the C. B. & Q. stood firm chiefly through the strength brought to it by the B. & M., was to Forbes a trumpet-call to action. As of old, nothing roused him so completely as the threat of disaster. Within a week he was off for the Mississippi Valley, impatient and relentless, to do a little "sifting" on his own account. With him went John N. A. Griswold, who had lately been added to the board and on whom he relied implicitly. A batch of telegrams scattered notice of their coming. "If we cannot do any good we can say we have *tried!*" he wrote.

The investigation included a trip over the River Roads from Clinton to La Crescent. With the two men from the East were J. K. Graves, the president of the roads, and various high officials of the C. B. & Q. system. In the course of the journey, Graves explained to one member of the party that the work of building the roads, as yet incomplete, had been undertaken by a construction company, of which several of the directors of the C. B. & Q. were stockholders.[1] Other facts given in the same conversation were such as to lead Forbes, when it was repeated to him, to determine on a session of rigid cross-examination. Here follows, in his own vivid and vigorous language, the story of the interview, as he wrote it out in detail within the next forty-eight hours for the benefit of one of the directors in Boston.

Returning Friday night from our survey we passed the evening at the company's offices in an interview (and a course of inquiries) with the president, Mr. Graves, the treasurer, General Booth, and the superintendent, Mr. Hudson, which developed the most remarkable condition of things which I have thus far found upon any living railroad company. The president is a sharp merchant, full of various enterprises, from gas-works up to building railroads, pretty bright, but loose in his notions of administration, loose beyond the imagination of the ordinary mind to conceive of.

General Booth, on the other hand, seems tighter and more technical than any West Point martinet; his accounts beautifully correct in form,

[1] MS. Recollections of C. E. Perkins.

and (as he says) kept distinct in bank from his private or from any outside mixings; but he is and professes to be simply an automaton. . . . To our questions whether he used any discretion in the application of the funds or any supervision of their use, he replied frankly: —

"None whatever. I simply pay the money when called for by the president and the superintendent."

"What has been done with the $140,000, more or less, earned by the roads since December 1, 1872?"

"It has been paid to the superintendent's order for expenses, and the balance has been paid to the president. What the president does with it is no concern of mine."

Question to the president: "What have you been doing with the company's money?"

Answer. "I have been paying the notes which I have given as president."

"What are the notes? Where is the record of them? Is it in the treasurer's account?"

"It is not in the company's books, but can be ascertained."

"What were the notes given for?"

Answer. "Chiefly to meet the obligations of two construction companies, of which I was president also, and which built the roads of each company by contract."

"Then you, as president of the railroad company, are paying yourself as president of the construction company, without the supervision of the treasurer or of any one else, and without any auditing of your accounts?"

"Yes."

"Have the construction company received the full amount of money, of stocks, of lands, for which they agreed to construct and equip the roads?"

"Yes, they have, leaving unfinished about forty miles of Turkey Branch and twelve miles on the lower road."

"Have any of your directors besides yourself been interested in these contracts?"

The answer to this was not definite, but left the impression that some of the directors had been, and he promised to send me a copy of the contracts, and a list of the stockholders in the construction company. He asserts that all the assets of the construction company have been expended, except a part of the land grant, which remains unsold; and to my question whether this remaining land ought not to be returned to the company, he answered that he thought the contractors would do whatever is fair, but that they had been large cash losers by the contract, and have nothing but a little land and a good deal of railroad stock to show for it.

Exactly how much cash from our earnings had been paid over to the contractor president, we had not time to investigate, but of course if the superintendent's figures are right, about $140,000; and the railroad president seems to be expecting to go on paying to the contractor president our earnings as they come in, until he has paid off the debts of the construction company. . . .

What the equities or the elements of expediency are, I know not, but it is perfectly clear to me that the board, which I now understand is transferred to Boston, ought at once to direct the treasurer to apply the earnings, first, to paying off legitimate operating expenses, and next to hold the balance for such uses as the board may direct, — or, better still, remit it to Boston, instead of holding it to the order of Mr. Graves — an active merchant and the representative, first, of contractors, and second, of another railroad, the Iowa Pacific, to whose use he has already applied $170,000 of the funds of our two companies, or of the contractors, which are all mixed up together. Mr. Graves (to his credit be it said) seemed to appreciate the absurdity of his position, and expressed a desire to have his accounts audited and to have a settlement; but, in our judgment (I speak of Griswold and myself), the blame will be transferred to the board, if, after knowing this state of things, they allow the funds of the company to remain a day longer under the control of a man who has so many other uses for them, however honest and however rich he may be on paper.

As an instance of what may happen, the pay-roll was postponed a month in order to pay some of the debts, but whether it was for the debts of the railroad company or for the contractor, or the Iowa Pacific, or Mr. Graves's personal ones, we had not time to investigate, and nobody can tell until an auditor (and a very good and forcible one) settles what Mr. Graves's account stands at, and who ought to pay the notes. He has signed as president, probably without any vote of the board, and certainly without having them recorded in the books of the company.[1]

The director to whom Forbes poured out this story of mismanagement, in the hope of eliciting his sympathetic indignation, was himself, such is the irony of circumstance in the business world, one of the members of the construction company, — a fact which soon came to light. Indeed, it presently transpired that six out of the twelve members of the C. B. & Q. board were in this position, and five of the six were Boston men. Being persons of integrity, who had conceived that, in their two-fold capacity as contractors and directors, they were fully able to deal with themselves justly, they took offence at Forbes's pointed questions concerning their acts, and refused to give information. This secrecy, based on a natural though mistaken wish not to seem to flinch under fire, of course aroused suspicion, and led the way

[1] November 9, 1873.

to a demand for an investigation. Finally, the resentment felt
by the contractor-directors that Forbes should seem to impugn
their honesty as well as their judgment had the effect of uniting
them in defence of the old régime in the C. B. & Q. board and
its methods.

The point of Forbes's criticism of his associates is perhaps
best seen from a letter written during the long course of these
difficulties to his friend S. G. Ward, agent of Baring Brothers.
" Either you or George once made a very pertinent remark about
C. B. & Q., to the effect that we had *honest* enough management, everybody said, but that it took something besides honesty
to run a big railroad, and that the smart rogues around us
would beat us in net profits to their stockholders after having
stolen all they wanted ! I have often thought of it, and recognized the soundness of your view. Skill, talent, courage, honesty
are *all* essential to railroad management, and especially so in distant ones which are apt to be managed after the fashion of the
Roman viceroys." When therefore he found that the contractor-
directors either could not or would not see their fault, there
was nothing for him but deliberately to range himself against
them. His clear sense of the welfare of the great corporation,
the reorganization of which he now deemed more important
than ever, and his feeling of responsibility toward the hundreds of
investors whose money it was using, both drove him on to action.

Though he and his supporters were a minority in the C. B.
& Q. board, they, as bondholders of the River Roads, were able
to stir up their fellow victims. An authorized investigating committee from this group of men made considerable progress in
ascertaining the true condition of things, and at last unearthed
the contract for building the roads, by the terms of which the
construction company was released from any obligation to complete them after it had used up all its money. It then appeared
that the railroad companies had paid at the rate of $25,000 a
mile for fifty-five miles of road which had not been constructed.
From time to time Forbes, to prevent if possible an open breach
in the C. B. & Q. board, had tried to get the directors who were
members of the construction company to agree to some act of

restitution to the bondholders, proposing to join them as a fellow director in bearing his share of the burden and the blame; but now, the bringing to light of this contract, of the vicious clause in which the Boston contractor-directors declared that they had been wholly ignorant, at the same time that it was further proof of the need of a new dispensation, rendered a peaceful adjustment highly improbable. Nevertheless, as the following appeal to one of these men shows, Forbes left nothing undone to prevent the personal estrangements that, to a man of his sense of loyalty, seemed nothing short of a calamity.

The proposition which I made yesterday would, I think, preserve sufficient harmony in our circle to enable us, or most of us, to work together for the common good. If the investigating committee will agree to accept it and recommend it as the best thing practicable, it will relieve them of the necessity of presenting to the bondholders the alternative; what blame their report must involve I shall, under this proposition, take my just share of.

You who went into the construction company then holding a contract for getting possession of all the bonds and assets of the River Roads, with a clause added relieving them from any obligation to *build* the roads, and under which the bonds you recommended have scattered ruin among large numbers of innocent people, have placed yourselves in a most unfortunate position. No matter how thoughtlessly you assumed this position, no matter how innocent of intended harm to others, you have done the harm, and by concealing from me the fact that you had an interest as contractor behind your interest as a bondholder of the River Roads and director of C. B. & Q., you have led me to join in causing the mischief.

I have offered to join you in a very slight measure of reparation for our folly and neglect — I now once more ask you in the name of our long tried friendship to accept my offer.[1]

Feeling as strongly as he did the pain of a personal breach, Forbes held back, till almost too late, from the alternative of war, — that is, a campaign to oust enough of the opposing directors at the coming annual election of the C. B. & Q. board to give his party control. But when fight was at last forced upon him, he flung himself into the struggle with all his wonted zest and relentlessness. His two battlefields were the meeting of the Dubuque bondholders in Boston on February 17, to hear

[1] February 13, 1875.

the report of the investigating committee, and the annual meeting of the C. B. & Q. stockholders in Chicago on February 24. The story of the contests is best given in the animated narrative of the general-in-chief, written to a member of his family while the glow of battle was still on him.

We had on the whole quite a lively time, of which the scraps sent will give you some hints. Perhaps the most dramatic performance was our meeting, a week ago Wednesday, of Dubuque victims (our second Dubuque). At the first one, two weeks earlier, I had given our associates the first of the Sibylline leaves, to accept a very soft path opened to them ; but S—— the magnificent, wrapped in his panoply of law and self-sufficiency, coolly declined, as if he had spoken and the world must bow (and no small dog like me must bow-wow !). Well, when the second day of fate was approaching, I spent Sunday in cooking another dish which I offered them, a good deal harder to digest than the first but still eminently proper and quite within limits. This I begged B—— to accept, adopt and advocate, and thus avoid [a fight]. This was declined as indigestible, but with less confidence, for the skies had begun to lower and my appeal to B—— was solemn. They were blinded and obstinate, so on Wednesday we went to the meeting ignorant whether they would skulk' or fight. In a room full of some one hundred or one hundred and fifty indignant bondholders, we found my old friend —— at the front like a lion at bay, the others deserting him and keeping in the background. Clifford was chairman; and Charles Bowditch, secretary of the investigating committee, read the report, which might well be called the indictment, and which was very considerably made up of my testimony — the C. B. & Q. directors having dodged the most important points. This brought —— to his feet, and you have read his speech, fired directly at me, so that the chair had frequently to call him to address the chair. He is a very powerful speaker, and of course I was like a small mouse under the whiskers of grimalkin, or of a fierce bull-terrier ! You have had the speeches, so I will only give you these outlines of the scene, which lasted from eleven to about three. My best speeches amounted to two or three words, interjected here and there in the chinks of ——'s oratory, but which found the holes in his armor. Getting through this, wearied and full of bad air, Griswold and Will [W. H. Forbes] and I had to take up the question of what next? Should we go on fighting from the outside, or should we, with only three days' time, try to change the Board ? . . .

They had been getting proxies for the annual meeting of 24th February ever since 20th January, while we had Thursday, Friday, and Saturday to work our *coup d'état* in, as Will and Griswold had to leave Saturday afternoon for Chicago, if we were to make the fight! We determined to try it, and at once had to frame advertisements, choose our list of directors and get them all into the New York, Albany, and Boston papers by telegraph, also to get the stenographer to write out the pithy parts of his Dubuque report and send this off to New York by telegraph. We did not know then how much the press were interested in the subject. We found afterwards that they had one or two stenographers, and the *Tribune* reporter sent on 1000 words by wire that afternoon. Then I had to write letters and telegrams, and talk, and do everything but sleep! In brief we had a good old war-time. P. W. Chandler says there had not been so much excitement in Boston any day for thirty-five years (he meant in business circles) as the day our advertisement came out. On Wednesday 24th, Will and Griswold in Chicago had 22,000 majority or say about 90,000 votes out of 155,000 that were thrown, and carried our whole ticket except T. J. Coolidge — that tender-hearted old Green ordering his large batch of votes thrown for D——, and thus electing him. He however is, I guess, docile as a kitten, and I have no doubt we can now have our own way on all reasonable things, and you know I never want any other. Will got back last night, and now, the fight being over, the work begins, for with victory will, I fear, come responsibility and care. It would have been far easier, just to have stepped out and sold my stock, and had an easy life; and I expect to repent not doing so.[1]

The significance of this victory was shown in the immediate appointment of George Tyson as auditor, "a very good and forcible one," and with his arrival in Chicago a new era began in the company's methods of accounting. The River Roads were sold to the Chicago, Milwaukee, and St. Paul, and the claims of the bondholders of these roads upon the C. B. & Q. directors who had recommended the bonds were recognized, though the amount of money restored to the victims was necessarily small. Since those of the contractor-directors who still remained on the board could not fail to see that the success of the men and measures that they had opposed had put their property on a solider basis than ever before, it was worth while for them to swallow their pride for the sake of remaining in the family and sharing in its prosperity.

HENRY G. PEARSON

[1] February 26 and 28, 1875.

III

STANDARD OIL REBATES[1]

THE apathy and inaction which naturally flow from a great defeat lay over the Oil Regions of Northwestern Pennsylvania long after the compromise with John D. Rockefeller in 1880, followed, as it was, by the combination with the Standard of the great independent seaboard pipe line which had grown up under the oil men's encouragement and patronage. Years of war with a humiliating outcome had inspired the producers with the conviction that fighting was useless, that they were dealing with a power verging on the superhuman, — a power carrying concealed weapons, fighting in the dark, and endowed with an altogether diabolic cleverness. Strange as the statement may appear, there is no disputing that by 1884 the Oil Regions as a whole looked on Mr. Rockefeller with superstitious awe.

* * * * * * * *

The effect of this dread was deplorable, for it intensified the feeling, now widespread in the Oil Regions, that it was useless to make further effort at a combined resistance. And yet these men, who were now lying too supine in Mr. Rockefeller's steel glove even to squirm, had laid the foundation of freedom in the oil business. It has taken thirty years to demonstrate the inestimable value of the efforts which in 1884 they regarded as futile — thirty years to build even a small structure on the foundation they had laid, though that much has been done.

The situation was saved at this critical time by individuals scattered through the oil world who were resolved to test the validity of Mr. Rockefeller's claim that the coal-oil business belonged to him. "We have a right to do an independent business," they said, "and we propose to do it." They began

[1] From The History of the Standard Oil Company, by Ida M. Tarbell, published by McClure, Phillips & Co., New York, 1904. By permission. Rebating in general is treated historically and critically in Ripley's Railroads: Rates and Regulation, chap. vi.

this effort by an attack on the weak spot in Mr. Rockefeller's armor. The twelve years just passed had taught them that the realization of Mr. Rockefeller's great purpose had been made possible by his remarkable manipulation of the railroads. It was the rebate which had made the Standard Oil Trust, the rebate, amplified, systematized, glorified into a power never equaled before or since by any business of the country. The rebate had made the trust, and the rebate, in spite of ten years of combination, Petroleum Associations, Producers' Unions, resolutions, suits in equity, suits in quo warranto, appeals to Congress, legislative investigations — the rebate still was Mr. Rockefeller's most effective weapon. If they could wrest it from his hand they could do business. They had learned something else in this period — that the whole force of public opinion and the spirit of the law were against the rebate, and that the railroads, knowing this, feared exposure of discrimination, and could be made to settle rather than have their practices made public. Therefore, said these individuals, we propose to sue for rebates and collect charges until we make it so harassing and dangerous for the railroads that they will shut down on Mr. Rockefeller.

The most interesting and certainly the most influential of these private cases was that of Scofield, Shurmer & Teagle, of Cleveland, one of the firms which, in 1876, entered into a "joint adventure" with Mr. Rockefeller for limiting the output and so holding up prices. The adventure had been most successful. The profits were enormous. Scofield, Shurmer & Teagle had made thirty-four cents a barrel out of their refinery the year before the "adventure." With the same methods of manufacture, and enjoying simply Mr. Rockefeller's control of transportation rates and the enhanced prices caused by limiting output, they made $2.52 a barrel the first year after. This was the year of the Standard's first great coup in refined oil. The dividends on 88,000 barrels this year were $222,047, against $41,000 the year before. In four years Scofield, Shurmer & Teagle paid Mr. Rockefeller $315,345 on his investment of $10,000 — and rebates.

After four years the Standard began to complain that their partners in the adventure were refining too much oil — the first year the books showed they had exceeded their 85,000-barrel limitation by nearly 3000, the second year by 2000, the third by 15,000, the fourth by 5000. Dissatisfied, the Standard demanded that the firm pay them the entire profit upon the excess refined; for, claimed Mr. Rockefeller, our monopoly is so perfect that we would have sold the excess if you had not broken the contract, consequently the profits belong to us. Scofield, Shurmer & Teagle paid half the profit on the excess, but refused more, and they persisted in exceeding their quota; then Mr. Rockefeller, controlling by this time the crude supply in Cleveland through ownership of the pipe lines, shut down on their crude supply. If they would not obey the contract of their own will they could not do business. The firm seems not to have been frightened. " We are sorry that you refuse to furnish us crude oil as agreed," they wrote Mr. Rockefeller; " we do not regard the limitation of 85,000 barrels as binding upon us, and as we have a large number of orders for refined oil we must fill them, and if you refuse to furnish us crude oil on the same favorable terms as yourselves, we shall get it elsewhere as best we can and hold you responsible for its difference in cost."

Mr. Rockefeller's reply was a prayer for an injunction against the members of the firm, restraining them individually and collectively " from distilling at their said works at Cleveland, Ohio, more than 85,000 barrels of crude petroleum of forty-two gallons each in every year, and also from distilling any more than 42,500 barrels of crude petroleum of forty-two gallons each, each and every six months, and also from distilling any more crude petroleum until the expiration of six months from and after July 20, 1880, and also from directly and indirectly engaging in or being concerned in any business connected with petroleum or any of its products except in connection with the plaintiff under their said agreement, and that on the final hearing of this case the said defendants may in like manner be restrained and enjoined from doing any of said acts until the expiration of said agreement, and for such other and further relief in the premises as equity can give." In this petition, really remarkable for its unconsciousness of what seems obvious — that the agreement was preposterous and void because confessedly in restraint of trade — the terms of the joint adventure are renewed in a way to illustrate admirably the sort of tactics with refiners which, at this time, was giving Mr. Rockefeller his extraordinary power over the price of oil.[1]

Scofield, Shurmer & Teagle did not hesitate to take up the gauntlet, and a remarkable defence they made. In their answer they declared the so-called agreement had at all times been "utterly void and of no effect as being by its terms in restraint of trade and against public policy." They declared that the Standard Oil Company had never kept the terms of the agreement, that it had intentionally withheld the benefits of the advantages it enjoyed in freight contracts, and that it now was pumping crude oil from the oil regions to Cleveland at a cost of about twelve cents a barrel and charging them (Scofield, Shurmer & Teagle) twenty cents. They denied that the Standard had sustained any damage through them, but claimed that their business had been carried on at a large profit. "There is such a large margin between the price of crude oil and refined," declared the defendants, "that the manufacture and sale of refined oil is attended with large profit; it is impossible to supply the demand of the public for oil if the business and refineries of both plaintiff and defendant are carried on and run to their full capacities, and if the business of the defendants were stopped, as prayed for by the plaintiff, it would result in a still higher price for refined oil and the establishment of more perfect monopoly in the manufacture and sale of the same by plaintiff." To establish such a monopoly, the defendants went on to declare, had been the sole object of the Standard Oil Company in making this contract with them, and similar ones with other firms, to establish a monopoly and so maintain unnaturally high prices,[2] and

[1] See Appendix, Number 42, Standard Oil Company's Petition for Relief and Injunction.

[2] See Appendix, Number 43, Answer of William C. Scofield et al.

certainly Scofield, Shurmer & Teagle knew whereof they swore, for they had shared in the spoils of the winter of 1876 and 1877, and at this very period, October, 1880, they were witnessing an attempt to repeat the coup.

The charge of monopoly Scofield, Shurmer & Teagle sustained by a remarkable array of affidavits — the most damaging set for the Standard Oil Company which had ever been brought together. It contained the affidavits of various individuals who had been in the refining business in Cleveland at the time of the South Improvement Company and who had sold out in the panic caused by it. It contained a review of the havoc which that scheme and the manipulation of the railroads by the Standard which followed it had caused in the refining trade in Pennsylvania, and it gave the affidavits of Mrs. B—— and of her secretary and others concerning the circumstances of her sale in 1878. The affidavits filed by John D. Rockefeller, Oliver H. Payne, and Henry M. Flagler in reply to the set presented by Scofield, Shurmer & Teagle are curious reading. From the point of view of our present knowledge they deny a number of things now known to be true.[1]

It was not necessary, however, for the defendants to have presented their elaborate array of evidence to support the charge of intended monopoly. The character of the agreement itself was sufficient to prevent any judge from attempting to enforce it. The amazement was that the Standard Oil Company ever had the hardihood to ask for its enforcement. "That it should venture to ask the assistance of a court of equity to enforce a contract to limit the production and raise the price of an article of so universal use as kerosene oil," said the Chicago Tribune, "shows that the Standard Oil Company believed itself to have reached a height of power and wealth that made it safe to defy public opinion." This case is not the only one belonging to the period which goes to support the opinion of the Tribune.

Scofield, Shurmer & Teagle were now obliged to stand on their own feet. They could refine all the oil they wished, but

[1] See Appendix, Number 44, Affidavit of John D. Rockefeller.

they must make their own freight contracts, and they found
rates when you worked with Mr. Rockefeller were vastly different from rates when you competed with him. The agent of
the Lake Shore Railroad, by which most of their shipments
went, told them frankly that they could not have the rates of
the Standard unless they gave the same volume of business.
The discrimination against them was serious. For instance, in
1880, when the Standard paid sixty-five cents a barrel from
Cleveland to Chicago, Scofield, Shurmer & Teagle paid eighty.
From April 1 to July 1, 1881, the Standard paid fifty-five cents
and their rival eighty cents; from July 1 to November 1, 1881,
the rates were thirty-five and seventy cents respectively, and so
it went on for three years, when the firm, despairing of any
change, took the case into court. This case, fought through
all the courts of Ohio, and in 1886 taken to the Supreme Court
of the United States, is one of the clearest and cleanest in
existence for studying all the factors in the rebate problem —
the argument and pressure by which the big shipper secures
and keeps his advantage, the theory and defence of the railroad in granting the discrimination, the theory on which the
suffering small shipper protests, and finally the law's point of
view. The first trial of the case was in the Court of Common
Pleas, and the refiners won. The railroad then appealed to the
District Court (the present Circuit Court), where it was argued.
So "important and difficult" did the judges of the District
Court find the questions involved to be, that on the plea of the
railroad they sent their findings of the facts in the case to the
Supreme Court of the state for decision, — a privilege they had
under the law in force at that time.

* * * * * * * *

Now, as a matter of fact, other propositions in this same set
from which the above are quoted, find that Scofield, Shurmer
& Teagle offered the railroad exactly the same facilities as the
Standard, a switch, loading racks, exemption from loss by fire
or accident.[1] "The manner of making shipments for plaintiffs
and for the Standard Oil Company was precisely the same,

[1] See Appendix, Number 45.

and the only thing to distingnish the business of the one
from the other was the aggregate yearly amounts of freight
shipped," said Judge Atherton, of the Supreme Court, who gave
the decision on the findings of fact, and he held in common
with his predecessors that a rebate on account of volume of
business only was "a discrimination in favor of capital," and
contrary to a sound public policy, violation of that equality of
rights guaranteed to every citizen, and a wrong to the dis-
favored person. "We hold, . . ." he said, "that a discrimination in the rate of freights resting extensively on such a basis
ought not to be sustained. The principle is opposed to sound
public policy. It would build up and foster monopolies, add
largely to the accumulated power of capital and money, and
drive out all enterprise not backed by overshadowing wealth.
With the doctrine, as contended for by the defendants, recognized and enforced by the courts, what will prevent the great
grain interest of the Northwest, or the coal and iron interests
of Pennsylvania, or any of the great commercial interests of
the country bound together by the power and influence of aggregated wealth and in league with the railroads of the land,
driving to the wall all private enterprises struggling for existence, and with an iron hand thrusting back all but themselves?"
Judge Atherton was scathing enough in his opinion of the contract between the Lake Shore and the Standard. Look at it, he
said, and see just what is shown. In consideration of the company giving to the railroad its entire freight business in oil,
they transport this freight about ten cents a barrel cheaper
than for any other customer. "The understanding was to keep
the price *down* for the favored customer, but *up* for all others,
and the inevitable tendency and effect of this contract was to
enable the Standard Oil Company to establish and maintain an
overshadowing monopoly, to ruin all other operators and drive
them out of business in all the region supplied by the defendant's road, its branches, and connecting lines."

Judge Atherton was particularly hard on the portion of the
contract [1] which pledged the Standard to give the Lake Shore

[1] Number 20, Findings of Facts. See Appendix, Number 45.

all its freight in return for the rebates, and for this reason: In 1883 a new road Westward was opened from Cleveland, the New York, Cincinnati & St. Louis. It might become an active competitor in transporting petroleum for customers other than the Standard Oil Company. It might establish such a tariff of rates that other operators in oil might successfully compete with the Standard Oil Company. To prevent this, the Lake Shore road, on the completion of the new road, entered into a tariff arrangement giving to it a portion of the Westward shipments of the Standard Oil Company, on condition of its uniting in carrying out the understanding in regard to rebates to the Standard Oil Company. " How peculiar ! " exclaimed Judge Atherton. " The defendant, by a contract made in 1875, was entitled to all the freights of the Standard Oil Company, and yet, say the District Court, ' for the purpose of securing the *greater part* of said trade,' they entered into a contract to divide with the new railroad, if the latter would only help to keep the rates *down* for the Standard and *up* for everybody else." Such a contract so carried out was, in the opinion of the court, " not only contrary to a sound public policy, but to the lax demands of the commercial honesty and ordinary methods of business."

Another fact found by the District Court incensed Judge Atherton. This was that the contract " was not made or continued with any intention on the part of the defendant to injure the plaintiffs in any manner." It does not " make any difference in the case," he declared. " The plaintiffs were not doing business in 1875, when the contract was entered into, and, of course, it was not made to injure them in particular. If a man rides a dangerous horse into a crowd of people, or discharges loaded firearms among them, he might, with the same propriety, select the man he injures and say he had no intention of wounding him. And yet the law holds him to have intended the probable consequences of his unlawful act as fully as if purposely directed against the innocent victim, and punishes him accordingly. And this contract, made to build up a monopoly for the Standard Oil Company and to drive its competitors from the field, is just as unlawful as if its provisions had been aimed directly against the interests of the plaintiffs." [1]

Having lost their case in the Supreme Court of the state, the Lake Shore now appealed to the Supreme Court of the United States, and the record was filed in November, 1886. It was never heard; the railroad evidently concluded it was useless, and finally withdrew its petition, thereby accepting the decision of the Supreme Court of Ohio restraining it from further discrimination against Scofield, Shurmer & Teagle.

This case, which was before the public constantly during the six or seven years following the breaking up of the Producers' Union, in which the Oil Regions presented no united front to Mr. Rockefeller, served to keep public attention on the ruinous effect of the rebate and to strengthen the feeling that drastic legislation must be taken if Mr. Rockefeller's exploit was to be prevented in other industries.

One other case came out in this war of individuals on the rebate system, which heightened the popular indignation against the Standard. It was a case showing that the Standard Oil Company had not yet abandoned that unique feature of its railroad contracts by which a portion of the money which other people paid for their freight was handed over to them! This peculiar development of the rebate system seems to have belonged exclusively to Mr. Rockefeller. Indeed, a careful search of all the tremendous mass of materials which the various investigations of railroads produced shows no other case — so far as the writer knows — of this practice. It was the clause of the South Improvement contracts which provoked the greatest outcry. It was the feature of Mr. Cassatt's revelations in 1877 which dumfounded the public and which no one would believe until they saw the actual agreements Mr. Cassatt presented. The Oil Regions as a whole did not hesitate to say that they believed this practice was still in operation, but, naturally, proof was most difficult to secure. The demonstration came in 1885, through one of the most aggressive and violent independents which the war in oil has produced, George Rice, of

[1] Ohio State Reports, Vol. 43, pp. 571–623.

Marietta, Ohio. Mr. Rice, an oil producer, had built a refinery at Marietta in 1873. He sold his oil in the state, the West, and South. Six years later his business was practically stopped by a sudden raise in rates on the Ohio roads — an advance of fully 100 per cent being made on freights from Marietta, where there were several independent refineries, although no similar advance was made from Wheeling and Cleveland, where the Standard refineries were located. These discriminations were fully shown in an investigation by the Ohio State Legislature in 1879. From that time on Mr. Rice was in constant difficulty about rates. He seems to have taken rebates when he could get them, but he could never get anything like what his big competitors got.

In 1883 Mr. Rice began to draw the crude supply for his refinery from his own production in the Macksburg field of Southeastern Ohio, not far from Marietta. The Standard had not at that time taken its pipe lines into the Macksburg field; the oil was gathered by a line owned by A. J. Brundred, and carried to the Cincinnati & Marietta Railroad. Now, Mr. Brundred had made a contract with this railroad by which his oil was to be carried for fifteen cents a barrel, and all other shippers were to pay thirty cents. Rice, who conveyed his oil to the railroad by his own pipe line, got a rate of twenty-five cents by using his own tank car. Later he succeeded in getting a rate of $17\frac{1}{2}$ cents a barrel. Thus the rebate system was established on this road from the opening of the Macksburg field. In 1883 the Standard Oil Company took their line into the field, and soon after Brundred retired from the pipe line business there. When he went out he tried to sell the Standard people his contract with the railroad, but they refused it. They describe this contract as the worst they ever saw, but they seem to have gone Mr. Brundred one better, for they immediately contracted with the road for a rate of ten cents on their own oil, instead of the fifteen cents he was getting, and a rate of thirty-five on independent oil. And in addition they asked that the extra twenty-five cents the independents paid *be turned over to them!* If this was not done the

Standard would be under the painful necessity of taking away its shipments and building pipe lines to Marietta. The Cincinnati & Marietta Railroad at that time was in the hands of a receiver, one Phineas Pease, described as a "fussy old gentleman, proud of his position and fond of riding up and down the road in his private car." It is probably a good description. Certainly it is evident from what follows that the receiver was much "fussed up" ethically: Anxious to keep up the income of his road, Mr. Pease finally consented to the arrangement the Standard demanded. But he was worried lest his immoral arrangement be dragged into court, and wrote to his counsel, Edward S. Rapallo, of New York City, asking if there was any way of evading conviction in case of discovery.

Upon my taking possession of this road [the receiver wrote], the question came up as to whether I would agree to carry the Standard Company's oil to Marietta for ten cents a barrel, in lieu of their laying a pipe line and piping their oil. I, of course, assented to this, as the matter had been fully talked over with the Western & Lake Erie Railroad Company before my taking possession of the road, and I wanted all the revenue that could be had in this trade.

Mr. O'Day, manager of the Standard Oil Company, met the general freight agent of the Western & Lake Erie Railroad and our Mr. Terry, at Toledo, about February 12, and made an agreement (verbal) to carry their oil at ten cents per barrel. But Mr. O'Day compelled Mr. Terry to make a thirty-five cent rate on all other oil going to Marietta, and that we should make the rebate of twenty-five cents per barrel on all oil shipped by other parties, and that the rebate should be paid over to them (the Standard Oil Company), thus giving us ten cents per barrel for all oil shipped to Marietta, and the rebate of twenty-five cents per barrel going to the Standard Oil Company, making that company say twenty-five dollars per day clear money on George Rice's oil alone.

In order to save the oil trade along our line, and especially to save the Standard Oil trade, which would amount to seven times as much as Mr. Rice's, Mr. Terry verbally agreed to the arrangement, which, upon his report to me, I reluctantly acquiesced in, feeling that I could not afford to lose the shipment of 700 barrels of oil per day from the Standard Oil Company. But when Mr. Terry issued instructions that on and after February 23 the rate of oil would be thirty-five cents per barrel to Marietta, George Rice, who has a refinery in Marietta, very naturally called on me yesterday and notified me that he would not submit to the advance, because the business would not justify it, and that the move was made by

the Standard Oil Company to crush him out. (Too true.) Mr. Rice said:
" I am willing to continue the 17½ cent rate which I have been paying from
December to this date."

Now, the question naturally presents itself to my mind, if George Rice
should see fit to prosecute the case on the ground of unjust discrimination,
would the receiver be held, as the manager of this property, for violation
of the law? While I am determined to use all honorable means to secure
traffic for the company, I am not willing to do an illegal act (if this can
be called illegal), and lay this company liable for damages. Mr. Terry is
able to explain all minor questions relative to this matter.[1]

Mr. Rapallo, after consulting his partner and "representative bondholders," " fixed it " for the receiver in the following
amazing decision:

You may, with propriety, allow the Standard Oil Company to charge
twenty-five cents per barrel for all oil transported through their pipes to
your road ; and I understand from Mr. Terry that it is practicable to so
arrange the details that the company can, in effect, collect this direct without its passing through your hands. You may agree to carry all such oil
of the Standard Oil Company, or of others, delivered to your road through
their pipes, at ten cents per barrel. You may also charge all other shippers
thirty-five cents per barrel freight, *even though they deliver oil to your road
through their own pipes;* and this, I gather from your letter and from
Mr. Terry, would include Mr. Rice.[2]

Now, how was this to be done " with propriety"? Simply
enough. The Standard Oil Company was to be charged ten
cents per barrel, less an amount equivalent to twenty-five cents
per barrel upon all oil shipped by Rice. " Provided your accounts, bills, vouchers, etc., are consistent with the real arrangement actually made, you will incur no personal responsibility
by carrying out such an arrangement as I suggest." Even in
case the receiver was discovered nothing would happen to *him*,
so decided the counsel. " It is possible that, by a proper application to the court, some person may prevent you, in future,
from permitting any discrimination. Even if Mr. Rice should
compel you, subsequently, to refund to him the excess charge

[1] Proceedings in Relation to Trusts, House of Representatives, 1888, Report
No. 3112, pp. 575–576.

[2] See Appendix, Number 46, Letter of Edward S. Rapallo to General
Phineas Pease, receiver Cleveland & Marietta Railroad Company.

over the Standard Oil Company, the result would not be a loss to your road, taking into consideration the receipts from the Standard Oil Company."

Fortified by his counsel, Receiver Pease put the arrangement into force, and beginning with March 20, 1885, a joint agent of the Standard pipe line and of the Cincinnati & Marietta road collected thirty-five cents per barrel on the oil of all independent shippers from Macksburg to Marietta. Ten cents of this sum he turned over to the receiver and twenty-five cents to the pipe line. When Mr. Rice found that the rate was certainly to be enforced he began to build a pipe of his own to the Muskingum River, whence he was to ship by barge to Marietta. By April 26 he was able to discontinue his shipments over the Cincinnati & Marietta road. This was not done until a rebate of twenty-five cents a barrel had been paid to the Standard Oil Company on 1360 barrels of his oil, — $340 in all.

Mr. Rice, outraged as he was by the discrimination, was looking for evidence to bring suit against the receiver, but it was not until October that he was ready to take the matter into court. On the 13th of that month he applied to Judge Baxter of the United States Circuit Court for an order that Phineas Pease, receiver of the Cleveland & Marietta Railroad, report to the court touching his freight rates and other matters complained of in the application. The order was granted on the same day the application was made. It was specific. Mr. Pease was to report his rates, drawbacks, methods of accounting for discrimination, terms of contracts, and all other details connected with his shipment of oil. No sooner was this order of the court to Receiver Pease known than the general freight agent, Mr. Terry, hurried to Cleveland, Ohio, to meet Mr. O'Day of the Standard Oil Company, with whom he had made the contract. The upshot of that interview was that on October 29, twelve days *after* the judge had ordered the contracts produced, a check for $340, signed by J. R. Campbell, Treasurer (a Standard pipe-line official), was received from Oil City, headquarters of the Standard pipe line, by the agent who had been collecting and dividing the freight money. This

check for $340 was the amount the pipe line had received on
Mr. Rice's shipments between March 20 and April 25. The
agent was instructed to send the money to the receiver, and
later, by order of the court, the money was refunded to Mr.
Rice. But the Standard was not out of the scrape so easily.

Receiver Pease filed his report on November 2, but the judge
found it "evasive and unsatisfactory," and further information
was asked for. Finally the judge succeeded in securing the
correspondence between Mr. Pease and Mr. Rapallo, quoted
above, and enough other facts to show the nature of the discrimination. He lost no time in pronouncing a judgment, and
he did not mince his words in doing it:

But why should Rice be required to pay 250 per cent more for the
carriage of his oil than was exacted from his competitor? The answer is
that thereby the receiver could increase his earnings. This pretense is not
true; but suppose it was, would that fact justify, or even mitigate, the
injustice done to Rice? May a receiver of a court, in the management of
a railroad, thus discriminate between parties having equal claim upon him,
because thereby he can accumulate money for the litigants? It has been
repeatedly adjudged that he cannot legally do so. Railroads are constructed
for the common and equal benefit of all persons wishing to avail themselves of the facilities which they afford. While the legal title thereof is
in the corporation of individuals owning them, and to that extent private
property, they are by the law and consent of the owners dedicated to the
public use. By its charter and the general contemporaneous laws of the
state which constitute the contract between the public and the railroad
company — the state, in consideration of the undertaking of the corporators to build, equip, keep in repair and operate said road for the public
accommodation, authorized it to demand reasonable compensation from
every one availing himself of its facilities, for the service rendered. But
this franchise carried with it other and correlative obligations.

Among these is the obligation to carry for every person offering business
under like circumstances, at the same rate. All unjust discriminations are
in violation of the sound public policy, and are forbidden by law. We have
had frequent occasions to enunciate and enforce this doctrine in the past few
years. If it were not so, the managers of railways in collusion with others in
command of large capital could control the business of the country, at least
to the extent that the business was dependent on railroad transportation
for its success, and make and unmake the fortunes of men at will.

The idea is justly abhorrent to all fair minds. No such dangerous
power can be tolerated. Except in the modes of using them, every citizen

has the same right to demand the service of railroads on equal terms that they have to the use of a public highway or the government mails. And hence when, in the vicissitudes of business, a railroad corporation becomes insolvent and is seized by the court and placed in the hands of a receiver to be by him operated pending the litigation, and until the rights of the litigants can be judicially ascertained and declared, the court is as much bound to protect the public interests therein as it is to protect and enforce the rights of the mortgagers and mortgagees. But after the receiver has performed all obligations due the public and every member of it — that is to say, after carrying passengers and freight offered, for a reasonable compensation not exceeding the maximum authorized by law, if such maximum rates shall have been prescribed, upon equal terms to all, he may make for the litigants as much money as the road thus managed is capable of earning.

But all attempts to accumulate money for the benefit of corporators or their creditors, by making one shipper pay tribute to his rival in business at the rate of twenty-five dollars per day, or any greater or less sum, thereby enriching one and impoverishing another, is a gross, illegal, inexcusable abuse of a public trust that calls for the severest reprehension. The discrimination complained of in this case is so wanton and oppressive it could hardly have been accepted by an honest man having due regard for the rights of others, or conceded by a just and competent receiver who comprehended the nature and responsibility of his office; and a judge who would tolerate such a wrong or retain a receiver capable of perpetrating it ought to be impeached and degraded from his position.

A good deal more might be said in condemnation of the unparalleled wrong complained of, but we forbear. The receiver will be removed. The matter will be referred to a master to ascertain and report the amount that has been as aforesaid unlawfully exacted by the receiver from Rice, which sum, when ascertained, will be repaid to him. The master will also inquire and report whether any part of the money collected by the receiver from Rice has been paid to the Standard Oil Company, and if so, how much, to the end that, if any such payments have been made, suit may be instituted for its recovery.[1]

On December 18 George K. Nash, a former governor of Ohio, was appointed master commissioner to take testimony and clear up the point doubtful in the judge's mind — to whom had the extra money paid by Rice been paid; the receiver declared that he never paid the Standard Oil Company any

[1] Proceedings in Relation to Trusts, House of Representatives, 1880, Report No. 3112, pp. 577–578.

part of Rice's money. Mr. Nash summoned a large number of witnesses and gradually untangled the story told above. Mr. Pease spoke truly, he had never paid the Standard Oil Company any part of Mr. Rice's money. A joint agent of the railroad and the pipe line had been appointed, at a salary of eighty-five dollars a month, sixty dollars paid by Pease and twenty-five dollars by the Standard, who collected the freight on independent shipments and divided the money between the two parties. It was from this agent that it was learned that, twelve days *after* Judge Baxter ordered Receiver Pease to bring his contracts into court, the money paid on Mr. Rice's oil had been returned by the Standard Oil Company.[1] While the investigation in regard to Mr. Rice's oil was going on, complaints came to Commissioner Nash from two other oil works at Marietta that they had been suffering a like discrimination for a much longer time. The commissioner investigated the cases and found the complaints justified. The Standard Oil Company had received $649.15 out of the money paid by one concern to the railroad for carrying its oil, and $639.75 out of the sum paid by another concern! Both of these sums were returned by the Standard.[2]

Of course the case aroused violent comment. In 1888 it came before the Congressional Committee which was investigating trusts, and an effort was made to explain the twenty-five cents extra as a charge of the pipe line for carrying oil to the railway. Now, the practice in vogue in the Oil Regions then and now is that the *purchaser of the oil pays the pipe-line charge.* The railroad has nothing to do with it. Even if the Standard Oil Company puts a tax on railroads for allowing them to take oil carried by its pipe lines — thus collecting double pay — the tax would not apply in Mr. Rice's case, for the oil came to the Cincinnati & Marietta road not through Standard pipes but through Mr. Rice's own pipes.

[1] See Appendix, Number 47, Testimony of F. G. Carrel, freight agent of the Cleveland & Marietta Railroad Company.

[2] See Appendix, Number 48, Report of the Special Master Commissioner George K. Nash to the Circuit Court.

IV

THE BUILDING AND THE COST OF THE UNION PACIFIC [1]

IT was not long after the passage of the Act of 1862 that work under it began. The Central Pacific Railroad Company, to which the building of the western end of the line was assigned, had been organized, in 1861, under California state law. On October 7, 1862, it formally accepted the terms offered by Congress, and the work of construction began January 8, 1863.

The Union Pacific Railroad Company, which was to build the eastern part of the line, effected its temporary organization according to the terms of the act, and books for stock subscriptions were opened in the leading cities of the country. Thirty-one shares [2] of $1000 each were subscribed for, and $17,300 paid in. There the matter stopped. Railway men knew that a mile of road in Illinois cost $33,000; in Iowa, $35,000; in the level parts of California, $34,000. [3] A considerable proportion of the able-bodied men of the country was in the army, and the prices of both labor and materials were abnormally high. Between the eastern system of railways and the initial point of the proposed road was a gap of hundreds of miles, making it necessary to carry materials by way of the Missouri River, a hazardous and costly mode of transportation. Under the circumstances, the capitalists of the country did not consider the Union Pacific a promising investment.

Meanwhile, Thomas C. Durant, of New York, a man of wide experience in railway building and of large resources, became

---

[1] From History of the Union Pacific Railway by Henry Kirke White. The University of Chicago Press, 1895. By permission.

[2] Forty-second Congress, third session; House Report No. 78, February 20, 1873 (Affairs of the Union Pacific Railroad Company — Mr. J. M. Wilson, Chairman), Testimony taken by the Committee, p. 604.

[3] *Congressional Globe*, Fortieth Congress, second session, p. 2427.

interested in the enterprise and took hold of it with characteristic vigor. He not only made a stock subscription of his own, but also secured subscriptions among his friends. To do this he advanced for them the 10 per cent required by law to be paid in before the permanent organization could be effected, and agreed to find persons to take it off their hands in case they wished to withdraw from the venture. On October 29, 1863, 2177 shares of $1000 each had been subscribed for [1] and a board of thirty directors was chosen. In the list we find such names as August Belmont, of New York; C. A. Lambard, of Boston; C. S. Bushnell, of New Haven ; Joseph H. Scranton, of Scranton, Pennsylvania; J. Edgar Thompson, of Philadelphia; S. C. Pomeroy, of Atchison, Kansas, besides those who were next day chosen officers. These were : President, General John A. Dix ; Vice President, Thomas C. Durant; Secretary, H. V. Poor, and Treasurer, J. J. Cisco, all of New York. Immediately after organization was effected men were put to work, ground being broken at Omaha December 2, 1863.[3] The sum of $218,000 which had been paid in on stock subscriptions was used up, and debts contracted for from $200,000 to $300,000 more. The company was so hard pressed on these debts that it finally resorted to the expedient of selling part of the materials and cars to raise funds.[4]

The line as first projected ran west from Omaha, but as heavy grades would thus be encountered, a somewhat circuitous route was finally settled upon, starting south from the city.[5] Still the first thirty or forty miles were expensive.

As this section of the road approached completion it was seen that New York capitalists were not to be induced to put the enterprise through;[6] work must soon cease for lack of funds. On May 12, 1864, therefore, a committee was appointed to let a contract for building one hundred miles of road.[7]

[1] Affairs of the Union Pacific Railroad Company, p. 599.

[3] Report of the Directors of the Union Pacific Railroad Company for 1884.

[4] Affairs of the Union Pacific Railroad Company, p. 63.

[5] *Ibid.*, p. 39.   [6] *Ibid.*, p. 39.

[7] Forty-second Congress, third session ; House Report No. 77, February 18, 1873 (Credit Mobilier Investigation — Mr. Poland, Chairman), Testimony taken by the Committee, p. 365.

The enactment of the Act of 1864 followed soon after this, doubling, as has been said, the funds from which to build the road.

Even then the friends of Durant were so doubtful of the success of the enterprise that they availed themselves of the offer made them when they subscribed, and Durant was made responsible for three fourths of the sum ($2,000,000) required to be subscribed before organization was authorized.[1]

As a result of the labors of the committee appointed in the preceding May, a proposal was received on August 8, 1864, from H. M. Hoxie, to build one hundred miles of road at $50,000 per mile. This matter was arranged at New York between Durant and H. C. Crane, who acted as Hoxie's attorney.[2] Crane was intimately connected with the Union Pacific as stockholder, director and otherwise; Hoxie was an employee of the road. Oliver Ames says distinctly that Hoxie was a man of no means,[3] of no responsibility.[4] Still Durant declares that the Hoxie contract was made in good faith.[5] At any rate it was accepted,[6] and October 4, 1864, Hoxie proposed its extension to cover the line from Omaha to the one hundredth meridian. This proposal was likewise accepted.[7] So H. M. Hoxie, whatever his financial standing may have been, stood bound to construct for the Union Pacific Company $247\frac{45}{100}$ miles of road, for which he was to receive over $12,000,000.

Aside from the relations existing between Durant, Crane and Hoxie, the terms of the contract would lead one to suspect that there was some purpose in mind other than that which appeared on the face of the matter. The contractor was specifically exempted from paying more than $85,000 for any one bridge; the excess in price of iron above $130 per ton at Omaha was to be borne by the Company; if required to Burnetize[8] ties, an

---

[1] Credit Mobilier Investigation, p. 388; Affairs of the Union Pacific Railroad Company, p. 515.

[2] Affairs of the Union Pacific Railroad Company, Part II, p. 2.

[3] *Ibid.*, p. 256.   [5] *Ibid.*, p. 69.

[4] *Ibid.*, p. 285.   [6] *ibid.*, Part II, p. 4.

[7] *Ibid.*, Part II, p. 4.

[8] A process by which cottonwood ties were made more durable.

additional 16 cents per tie was to be paid; and, most important, acceptance of the contract bound the contractor to subscribe, or cause to be subscribed to the capital stock of the
Union Pacific, $500,000.[1]

As early as September 30, 1864, that is, some time before its
extension had been voted, Hoxie had agreed with Durant to
assign his contract to such parties as he (Durant) might designate. October 7, 1864, an agreement was drawn up binding its
signers to take the contract from Hoxie and to subscribe for carrying it out the sum of $1,600,000. This liability was divided
as follows: Thomas C. Durant, $600,000; C. S. Bushnell,
$400,000; Charles A. Lambard, $100,000; H. S. McComb,
$100,000; H. W. Gray, $200,000; etc.[2] According to the terms
of the agreement one fourth of the sums subscribed was paid in,
$400,000 in all, and this amount was used on the road. The
men who had assumed the Hoxie contract now stood in the relation of partners, liable not only for the sums subscribed, but to
the extent of their fortunes. Some of them became fearful and
concluded that it would be better to lose the sums already sunk
in the enterprise than to go on and take greater risks.[3] They
therefore failed to respond to the call for the second installment
of their subscriptions.[4]

About this time, August 1865, an important step was taken
in getting the brothers, Oakes and Oliver Ames, to take hold of
the project.[5] Oakes Ames had become interested in the Pacific
railway while a member of the Committee on Railroads in the
House of Representatives,[6] and his personal influence in Massachusetts, together with his great financial strength, made him a
valuable ally of those who had started the road. Plans for proceeding were again discussed, and it was agreed that the only
feasible way to enlist the necessary capital was to make use of
a construction company. The scheme of building railways by

[1] Affairs of the Union Pacific Railroad Company, Part II, p. 2.
[2] Ibid., Part II, p. 5.
[3] Ibid., p. 64, and Credit Mobilier Investigation, p. 365.
[4] Affairs of the Union Pacific Railroad Company, p. 365.
[5] Ibid., p. 4.
[6] Oakes Ames Memoir, p. 5.

construction companies organized among the stockholders was not new; it had been tried successfully in Iowa.[1] Exhaustive contracts were not a new device.[2] So all the Union Pacific people had to do was to adapt to their own uses methods which others had elaborated.

It having been decided to make use of a construction company, an examination of charters followed. This led to the rejection of one which Bushnell had bought in Connecticut,[3] and to the choice of a Pennsylvania corporation as better meeting their needs. This was the Pennsylvania Fiscal Agency, which had been chartered to build railways in the South and West[4] by an act of the state legislature of Pennsylvania, approved November 1, 1859.[5] On the fifth of the same month books had been opened in Philadelphia and stock subscribed for.[6] Later it became known that the organization then effected was irregular, and it was treated as a nullity.[7] May 29, 1863, books were again opened, stock subscribed, the required per cent paid in, and organization properly effected.[8] March 2, 1864, Durant opened negotiations for the purchase of the charter rights of the Fiscal Agency, and on the following day the bargain was closed, Durant paying to the original subscribers what they had invested, they assigning their stock.[9] Previous to this time there had been no connection whatever between the men of the Union Pacific and of the Fiscal Agency.

On March 26, 1864, an amendatory act changed the name from the Pennsylvania Fiscal Agency to the Credit Mobilier of America,[10] and as such it later became widely known. Thus the Credit Mobilier became an adjunct of the Union Pacific Railroad Company.

The reason for securing such a company as the Credit Mobilier is obvious. No firm could be induced to undertake

---

[1] Affairs of the Union Pacific Railroad Company, p. 164.
[2] *Ibid.*, p. 420.   [3] *Ibid.*, p. 39.
[4] Credit Mobilier Investigation, p. 199.
[5] Affairs of the Union Pacific Railroad Company, p. 7.
[6] *Ibid.*, p. 144.   [8] *Ibid.*, p. 146.
[7] *Ibid.*, p. 146.   [9] *Ibid.*, p. 147.
[10] Affairs of the Union Pacific Railroad Company, p. 9.

the building of the road if each member was liable to the extent of his property.[1] The risk was too great. But it was believed that if a company was secured in which the liability was limited to the amount of the subscription to stock, as in the Credit Mobilier, capital could be enlisted. This proved to be the case, and the necessary funds were quickly subscribed.

As a matter of convenience the offices of the Credit Mobilier were to be in New York, where the headquarters of the railway were located, but under the terms of its charter it could not cease to be a Pennsylvania corporation. To get around this difficulty, the device of a New York branch was resorted to. The corporate existence of the Credit Mobilier was maintained in Pennsylvania, the board of directors, the officers, and the executive committee being elected at meetings held in Philadelphia. This executive committee then chose from among the stockholders of the Credit Mobilier and of the Union Pacific, a number of men to constitute what they called a railway bureau.[2] This body had its office in a room adjoining the offices of the Union Pacific.[3] The executive committee attended to all the larger fiscal transactions, while the railway bureau had charge of the construction of the road, payments for work, and other details.[4] Under this arrangement the work progressed satisfactorily. Part of the necessary capital of the Credit Mobilier was secured by transferring to its books the subscriptions which had been made for carrying out the Hoxie contract by the men who assumed it.[5] They were relieved of their former obligations by the transfer of the Hoxie contract to the corporation of which they had just become stockholders. This change was made March 15, 1865,[6] some six months after they had taken the contract off Hoxie's hands. The transferred subscriptions, $1,600,000, were supplemented by others, securing for the Credit Mobilier a working capital of upwards of $2,000,000,[7]

[1] Affairs of the Union Pacific Railroad Company, pp. 39–40.
[2] *Ibid.*, pp. 131, 148.
[3] *Ibid.*, p. 153. [4] *Ibid.*, p. 148.
[5] Credit Mobilier Investigation, p. 366.
[6] Affairs of the Union Pacific Railroad Company, p. 64.
[7] Credit Mobilier Investigation, p. 366.

and the work, which otherwise must have stopped within sixty days, was pushed vigorously.[1]

But note how incongruous was this arrangement. The Credit Mobilier was nominally a Pennsylvania corporation, while at the Pennsylvania office no business was done. The New York concern was in form only a branch of the Pennsylvania corporation, yet it transacted all the business which the Credit Mobilier ever had. The Union Pacific Railroad was being built, not by the Union Pacific Company, but by the Credit Mobilier, and the Union Pacific officers simply got the resources into available shape and turned them over to the Credit Mobilier. The United States bonds it sold and transferred the cash. Sometimes it turned over the proceeds of the sale of first-mortgage bonds, sometimes the bonds themselves.

This state of affairs was in part due to the unfortunate looseness with which the Pennsylvania legislature had framed the Credit Mobilier charter. The practice of granting charters containing almost no limitations was at that time common. Unfortunately it is not yet unknown.

Under the new impulse which the Credit Mobilier gave to the enterprise, the work of construction was carried forward so rapidly that during the year 1866 the government passed upon and accepted 270 miles of track as meeting the requirements of the law.

About the time when the road had reached the one hundredth meridian, quite a number of the stockholders of the Credit Mobilier had become large stockholders of the Union Pacific, among them Mr. Ames, Mr. Dillon, and Mr. Duff. Naturally they desired to be represented on the Union Pacific board, and Oliver Ames and two or three others, at the election of October 3, 1866, went into the directory of the Union Pacific.[2] From this time on there were two factions among the Union Pacific people, one headed by Durant, the other by Oakes Ames. Durant's claim to leadership lay in the importance of what he had already accomplished. Ames had yet to win his spurs. It

[1] Affairs of the Union Pacific Railroad Company, p. 659.
[2] *Ibid.*, p. 598.

has repeatedly been said that the struggle between Durant and Ames was due to their different views as to the Union Pacific enterprise and their different motives in taking it up. Durant is said to have believed that the road would be a commercial failure, and that the only money to be made out of it was to be made on construction contracts; while Ames believed in the future of the road and looked to the legitimate business of the road after its completion for his profit. The evidence as to contracts made by these men for construction, however, does not exhibit any great rapacity on Durant's part, nor any great tenderness toward the road on Ames's part. It seems that the friction between these men was rather of a personal nature. Durant carried the enterprise as far as his resources would allow, and then had to give way to Ames. Whoever had succeeded him as leader would probably have aroused Durant's jealousy and had his opposition to contend with.

Be that as it may, the decided friction between the two parties manifested itself repeatedly when the letting of contracts was under discussion, and the execution of several engagements which had been formally entered into was prevented. Of this sort were five which deserve attention. Their history shows the internal difficulties of the company, which were at times so serious as to carry the questions into court. It also shows the evolution of the terms of the contract under which the most difficult parts of the road were built, the Ames contract.

The first of these never-executed agreements is known as the Boomer contract.[1] Late in 1866 Durant made a contract with L. B. Boomer, of Chicago, which called for the building of 150 miles of road, beginning at the one hundredth meridian. East of the North Platte River the price stipulated was $19,500 per mile, exclusive of equipment. The bridge over that stream was to be paid for at actual cost. West of the river the price was $20,000 per mile. By paying for work already done and giving ten days' notice, Durant could at any time terminate this

[1] On the books it is called the Gessner contract. Boomer appointed Gessner his agent and later sold the contract to him (Affairs of the Union Pacific Railroad Company, p. 69).

arrangement.[1] President Dix, Treasurer Cisco, and other conservative members of the board sustained Durant in his action
in regard to this contract,[2] but it was never approved by the
board as a whole.[3] Oliver Ames afterward declared that the
Boomer contract was a secret arrangement, a bogus thing of
Dr. Durant's, and that Boomer was a man of no responsibility.[4]
At any rate, the Credit Mobilier, although it had received no new
contract, continued to build the road west of the one hundredth
meridian precisely as it had done east of that point. This was
done in expectation of another contract on the same terms as the
Hoxie contract, and as the stockholders of the Credit Mobilier
and of the Union Pacific were the same persons[5] this expectation was not likely to prove without foundation.

Durant's move in regard to the Boomer contract having been
successfully met, the next one was made by the other side.
There was presented to the board of directors of the Union
Pacific, on the 5th of January 1867, a resolution extending the
Hoxie contract to the point then completed, namely, 305 miles
west of Omaha, and authorizing the officers to settle with the
Credit Mobilier for the added 58 miles at $50,000 per mile.
By a vote of eight to four the resolution was passed.[6] According to the Act of 1864, the President of the United States
appointed five members of the board of directors of the Union
Pacific who should protect the interests of the government.
The four votes against the extension of the Hoxie contract
were cast by government directors, one voting in favor of it.[7]
Durant, who was absent on necessary business of the company
when this resolution was passed, entered a protest against its
being carried out, and also served an injunction on the officers
to prevent their making the proposed payments. His objections
were that, although the Hoxie contract was originally let in
good faith, no one being interested in it, the Credit Mobilier
and the Union Pacific had since become identical in interest,

[1] Affairs of the Union Pacific Railroad Company, Part II, p. 7.
[2] Credit Mobilier Investigation, p. 368.
[3] Affairs of the Union Pacific Railroad Company, p. 67.
[4] *Ibid.*, p. 285.
[5] *Ibid.*, p. 284.   [6] *Ibid.*, p. 67.   [7] *Ibid*, p. 67.

and that this extension was simply letting a contract to themselves; that no new subscriptions to the Union Pacific stock were required because of this extension; that this strip of road, built at much less cost than the proposed price, had been accepted by the government as completed, and so that carrying out this contract would entail heavy loss upon the company, as the actual cost of this part of the road, when fully equipped, was about $27,500 per mile. January 24, nineteen days after its passage, the order to extend the contract was rescinded.[1]

The condition of the finances of the two closely allied corporations made it necessary, early in 1867, earnestly to attempt measures of betterment. One form which this effort took is shown by a letter of February 13. The Credit Mobilier proposed to purchase of the Union Pacific, land-grant bonds to the amount of $3,000,000, at 80; first-mortgage bonds to the amount of $2,060,000, at 85; certificates convertible into first-mortgage bonds to the amount of $750,000, at 80, these certificates to bear 6 per cent interest until exchanged. The Credit Mobilier further proposed to loan or procure to be loaned to the Union Pacific $1,250,000 on four months' time, at 7 per cent annual interest and $2\frac{1}{2}$ per cent commission, with first-mortgage bonds at $66\frac{2}{3}$ per cent as security. On the other hand, the Union Pacific was to pay to the Credit Mobilier the balances due on previous debts at least as soon as the Credit Mobilier had paid for the securities named above. It was also provided that the Hoxie contract should be extended 100 miles west of the one hundredth meridian at $42,000 per mile.[2] This arrangement would have given the Union Pacific $6,001,000 of ready funds. As the contract price was considerably in excess of what this part of the road was actually costing, it would have given the Credit Mobilier a profit in hand on that part of the 100 miles of road which had at that time been completed, and an inconsiderable risk on the remainder of what the contract covered. The executive committee of the Union Pacific accepted this proposition,[3] but it was not carried out.

---

[1] Affairs of the Union Pacific Railroad Company, pp. 68–70.
[2] Credit Mobilier Investigation, p. 171.
[3] Affairs of the Union Pacific Railroad Company, p. 172.

However, an understanding was reached about this time that whenever a contract was entered into, it should be so placed that the benefit would inure to the stockholders of the Credit Mobilier. On the strength of this understanding the capital stock of the Credit Mobilier was increased. This was originally intended to be $2,000,000; September 21, 1865,[1] it was made $2,500,000 nominally, although not all of the new stock was taken up;[2] now, in February 1867, it was increased to $3,750,000. The difficulty in getting the old subscribers to take this new stock was met in this way: for $1000 in cash there was promised $1000 in Credit Mobilier stock and a $1000 first-mortgage bond of the Union Pacific. That this offer would prove attractive will appear when it is considered that the first-mortgage bonds were then worth 85, thus leaving the Credit Mobilier stock to represent 15 per cent of the price paid. On these terms the new stock was all taken and the cash turned over to the Union Pacific in payment for bonds. The $1,250,000 thus put into the Union Pacific treasury was used to cancel a part of the $3,500,000 or $4,000,000 of debt which it then owed.[3]

Having spent this sum, things came to a standstill again almost as bad as before. The Union Pacific then allowed Bushnell to undertake the sale of a large block of first-mortgage bonds which it had on hand and on which it was borrowing money at extravagant rates of interest, up to $14\frac{1}{2}$ per cent.[4] By wide advertising and great diligence Bushnell met with marked success, and in less than six months bonds were sold to the amount of $10,000,000, the price being put up from 90 to 95.[5] Thus the financial difficulties were removed.

To carry out the tacit agreement made in February, that the Credit Mobilier stockholders should have the profits on constructing the road, attempts were made to let contracts direct to that corporation, but Durant objected on account of the identity of the two organizations and twice prevented such action by injunctions.[6]

---

[1] Affairs of the Union Pacific Railroad Company, p. 78.
[2] Ibid., p. 15.   [4] Ibid., p. 41.   [6] Ibid., p. 41.
[3] Ibid., p. 40.   [5] Ibid., p. 42.

One of these attempts gave rise to what is known as the Williams contract. March 1, 1867, John M. S. Williams proposed to the company to take the building of 267.57 miles of road westward from the one hundredth meridian as the initial point, the price for the first 100 miles being $42,000 per mile, for the remainder $45,000 per mile. As another feature of the contract Williams was to bind himself to procure subscriptions for Union Pacific stock to the amount of $1,500,000. The board accepted his offer and gave instructions that a contract be drawn up on this basis. Williams assigned the contract to the Credit Mobilier, and the Credit Mobilier accepted the assignment. Then Durant, on March 27, entered a protest against letting this contract, stating as grounds that part of the road was already built and accepted by the government, that the price was too high, that no time limit for completing the work was specified. His protest was backed up by an injunction, so nothing was done in the matter. This protest shared the same fate as his previous one — both were expunged from the minutes.[1]

June 24, 1867, Williams again made a written proposal to the Union Pacific. It was this: To build the road from the one hundredth meridian to the base of the Rocky Mountains, 267.52 miles, at $50,000 per mile, the work to be completed before January 1, 1868. The provision for a stock subscription was omitted this time. Another proposal accompanying this one was to assign the contract, if received, to the Credit Mobilier.[2] The June proposal, like the one made in March, came to naught. This ends the series of failures at contract making.

It had been anticipated that great difficulty and heavy expense would be met in crossing the Rocky Mountains, but during 1867 it became generally known that there was an easy route by way of the Black Hills, requiring no grade heavier than ninety feet to the mile, and knowledge of this fact greatly strengthened confidence in the completion of the road. This route lay through what had previously been called the Cheyenne Pass, Cheyenne and Sherman being located there. From this time on it was

---

[1] Affairs of the Union Pacific Railroad Company, pp. 70–71.
[2] Ibid., pp. 162–163.

called the Evans Pass, it having been discovered by an engineer named Evans, acting under the guidance of the chief engineer of the road, General Dodge.

Meanwhile construction was being pushed. The Hoxie contract had been completed to the one hundredth meridian October 5, 1866,[1] and beyond that point the Union Pacific made all its bargains for work subject to any future contract which might be let.[2] By August 16, 1867, 188 miles more had been built,[3] and a letter of that date from Oakes Ames proposed the terms on which he would become responsible for building the 667 miles of road beginning at the one hundredth meridian.[4] The board passed a resolution the same day directing the officers to obtain the written consent of the stockholders, a provision upon which Durant insisted,[5] and then to ratify the contract, giving Ames the option of extending it westward to Salt Lake if he chose.[6] The prices specified were: 100 miles at $42,000 per mile, 167 at $45,000, 100 at $96,000, 100 at $80,000, 100 at $90,000, 100 at $96,000.[7] Thus Ames assumed a contract aggregating $47,915,000.

These prices, although high for the eastern sections of the part which they covered, were, on the whole, perhaps not exorbitant. The rates for the western sections would undoubtedly have been made considerably higher if the eastern part with its assured profit had not been included. Moreover, this contract insured the building of the difficult portions by providing that when the proceeds of the bonds were not sufficient to pay the contract prices, the contractor should subscribe for enough stock to furnish the money for paying the balance. In other words, Ames was bound to take in stock, at par, that part of his pay which was not produced by selling the two kinds of bonds. In no other way could security have been obtained for the building of the difficult and risky portions of the road. In fact, it was impossible to let contracts to outsiders for even the

---

[1] Affairs of the Union Pacific Railroad Company, p. 65.   [2] Ibid., p. 115.
[3] Ibid., p. 113.   [4] Credit Mobilier Investigation, p. 365.
[5] Affairs of the Union Pacific Railroad Company, p. 542.
[6] Ibid., Part II, p. 12.   [7] Ibid., p. 10.

easy portions of the road. John Duff, who had done a great deal of work of this sort, made repeated efforts to let contracts among experienced and competent contractors, appealing to his own subcontractors in his attempts to find some one who would do the work, but he was unable to get any one to go out there.[1] Horace Clarke said, in 1873, that he thought the Ames contract the wildest contract he ever knew to be made by a civilized man.[2] Be that as it may, the work was pushed to completion under it.

Although this contract did not intimate in its terms that any one besides Oakes Ames and the Union Pacific Railroad Company was in any way concerned in the matter, there undoubtedly existed a more or less definite understanding that the persons to profit thereby were the stockholders of the Credit Mobilier.[3] The arrangement by which the profits were distributed to them is described in the tripartite agreement, which was signed October 15, 1867.[4] General Benjamin F. Butler suggested this form of contract as obviating the difficulty which would arise if any single stockholders of the Credit Mobilier should object to the transfer of responsibility to that organization.[5] The party of the first part was Oakes Ames, who then held the contract, and who assigned it to the party of the second part. Seven trustees constituted the party of the second part, and they bound themselves to carry out the contract according to its terms, and to distribute the profits thereupon among those stockholders of the Credit Mobilier who should execute to them an irrevocable proxy on at least six tenths of any Union Pacific stock which they then owned, or which they in future might own. This power to vote a majority of the Union Pacific stock insured the trustees against the election of a Union Pacific board hostile to the interests of the Credit Mobilier. The men named as trustees were Oliver Ames, T. C. Durant, J. B. Alley, Sidney Dillon, C. S. Bushnell, H. S. McComb, and Benjamin E. Bates. The party of the third part was the Credit Mobilier, which guaranteed the carrying out of the contract and bound

[1] Affairs of the Union Pacific Railroad Company, p. 493.
[2] *Ibid.*, p. 405. [4] *Ibid.*, Part II, pp. 13–16.
[3] *Ibid.*, p. 5. [5] *Ibid.*, p. 684.

itself to loan the trustees what funds they needed, receiving therefor 7 per cent interest and $2\frac{1}{2}$ per cent commission.

Noteworthy changes in the standing of the Union Pacific enterprise had taken place since 1864. Then the Credit Mobilier had to be secured in order to limit liability and get enough capital to continue construction. In 1868 there was no difficulty in getting capital to take hold of the Ames contract. The proxies which were required, and which were readily given to the trustees, were so worded that they made each stockholder of the Credit Mobilier a partner in the enterprise — just what the Credit Mobilier had been made use of to avoid — and the trustees went to work with $50,000,000 back of them. Until the connection of the Credit Mobilier with the Ames contract was known, the stock of that corporation had never had a market value. Then it immediately went far above par, and what few sales were made were at fancy figures like 260.

As has already been said, the Credit Mobilier continued to build the road beyond the one hundredth meridian, where its contract ceased, knowing that proper credit for its work would be given when the final contract was let. We have seen that when Ames's proposal was made, 188 miles had already been built. By the time he assigned the contract to the trustees, 50 miles more had been finished.[1] This first part of the work embraced under the Ames contract was not expensive, and what was to be paid for it was some $2,500,000 or $3,000,000 in excess of its cost to the builder.[2] So the trustees, with this sum in hand, made haste to carry out their obligations.

As Ames did not wish to extend his contract beyond the 667 miles which it originally covered,[3] Durant, to avoid delay, made a contract in November 1868, with James W. Davis, a subcontractor, to build the remainder of the road. The Davis contract took the Ames contract as its basis, and an accompanying agreement provided for its assignment to the same trustees who executed the Ames contract. A resolution of the board of directors of the Union Pacific approved Durant's action, and a committee

[1] Affairs of the Union Pacific Railroad Company, p. 114.
[2] *Ibid.*   [3] *Ibid.*, p. 4.

was appointed to obtain the necessary consent of the Union Pacific stockholders.[1] Thus without any change of machinery the work went on.

Construction on the western part of the road was pushed with unprecedented vigor, winter not being allowed to stop work. There were several reasons for this haste. Public opinion, which the government directors voiced, urged it.[2] To put capital into the road and postpone its productiveness by not opening it to traffic until 1875, the limit set by the Act of 1864, would have crushed the company under the accumulation of interest. The Salt Lake business and a "governing point" for the traffic of that region was a prize to be gained only by rapid work.[3] Late in the construction period the desire to meet the Central Pacific as far west as possible became a motive. So the work was done with marvelous speed. Four or five miles of track were laid per day, and items of expense which should have been $600 per mile were made $1500 instead.[4] By such methods the Union Pacific and the Central Pacific were joined May 10, 1869.[5]

[1] Affairs of the Union Pacific Railroad Company, p. 17.
[2] Ibid., p. 664.   [3] Ibid., p. 563.   [4] Ibid., p. 510.
[5] The facts of the construction period thus far related may be brought together by the aid of the accompanying diagram :

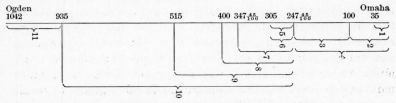

1. Built by Union Pacific Company, largely with Durant's money.
2. Hoxie Contract.
3. Hoxie Contract Extension.
4. Assigned to Credit Mobilier.
5. Built by Credit Mobilier.
6. First proposed extension to Hoxie Contract.
7. Proposed Hoxie Contract extension, coupled with purchase of $6,000,000 of securities.
8. Boomer Contract.
9. I. Williams Contract of March 1, 1867.
   II. Williams Contract of June 24, 1867.
10. Ames Contract.
11. Davis Contract.

This saving of six years of the time allowed by the law for completing the road doubled the cost to the builders. By increasing the working force the chance of accidental delays was increased, and the costliness of such delays likewise increased. Just before the Ames contract was let, the Union Pacific was obliged to borrow money in New York to use on the road, for which it paid 18 or 19 per cent.[1] By pushing the road out beyond the bounds of civilization and not waiting for the slower pace of the settler, it often became necessary for one half the force to stand guard while the other half worked.[2] Hundreds of workmen were killed by the Indians.[3]

Thus far the managers of the enterprise were responsible for the increased cost; they could have avoided it by adopting a different policy. But there were other items of needless cost which they could not avoid. For these the government alone was to blame.

The requirement that only American iron be used on the road increased the cost $10 for every ton of rails laid.[4] An incident, typical rather than intrinsically important, is that of two government directors who insisted that a cut should be made through each rise in the Laramie plains, giving the track a dead level, instead of conforming it to the profile of the ground. As snow blockades made it necessary to refill these cuts later, there was a waste of from $5,000,000 to $10,000,000. At the crossing of the North Platte, machine shops were called for which cost perhaps $300,000. To the company they were not worth three cents.[5] Another of a worse sort concerned a government commissioner, Cornelius Wendell, appointed to examine the road and report whether or not it met the requirements of the law, who flatly demanded $25,000 before he would proceed to perform his duty. As a considerable section of road awaited acceptance, and as acceptance must precede the drawing of subsidies, his demand was paid in the same spirit in which it was made — as just so much blood money.[6] Such results were

---

[1] Affairs of the Union Pacific Railroad Company, p. 252.
[2] Ibid., p. 431.　　　　　　　　[3] Ibid., p. 494.
[4] Credit Mobilier Investigation, p. 255.
[5] Affairs of the Union Pacific Railroad Company, p. 432.　[6] Ibid., p. 471.

bound to follow when the government made its power to appoint commissioners a means of distributing political patronage.[1]

As steps toward answering the question, What did the building of the Union Pacific yield as profit? the capitalization and the cost must be considered.

The property, at the close of the period of construction, stood burdened with four kinds of bonds — United States bonds, its own first-mortgage bonds, land-grant bonds, and income bonds. Of the government bonds there were issued the full quota — $27,266,512 on 1038.68 miles of road.[2] The aggregate of first-mortgage bonds was slightly less than this sum, $27,213,000.[3] Of land-grant bonds there were outstanding $10,400,000, and of income bonds, $9,355,000. Thus the total indebtedness represented by the four kinds of bonds was $74,204,512.

The stock of the road subscribed for when organization was effected was slightly in excess of the $2,000,000 required,[4] and was owned in various quarters. As early as December 1, 1864, the Credit Mobilier began to buy in these shares, and succeeded in acquiring almost all of them.[5] By the time the Ames contract was let, the $2,000,000 had increased to about $5,000,000.[6] Under the Ames and Davis contracts the trustees subscribed, at various times as the work proceeded, according to the terms of those contracts, for $30,096,000 of stock,[7] and when the road was done the stock issued was $36,762,300. Thus the total capitalization of the road was $110,966,812.

But this sum does not represent the cost of the road. From the books of the Union Pacific and the Credit Mobilier, it appears that the expenditures by the Union Pacific directly amounted to $9,746,683.33; and that the actual expenditures under the Hoxie, Ames, and Davis contracts were $50,720,957.94, making the total cost of the road $60,467,641.27.[8]

---

[1] Affairs of the Union Pacific Railroad Company, p. 431.

[2] Ibid., p. 738.   [4] Ibid., p. 599.   [6] Ibid., p. 72.

[3] Ibid., p. 590.   [5] Ibid., p. 20.   [7] Ibid., p. 642.

[8] The figures upon which this estimate is based were compiled by Mr. Benjamin F. Ham, who was assistant secretary and treasurer of the Credit Mobilier during most of the period of its active existence (Affairs of the Union Pacific Railroad Company, p. 371).

This should be compared with the sum received for bonds, which is shown by the following table : [1]

First-mortgage bonds	$27,213,000.00	
Loss on same	3,494,991.23	
		$23,718,008.77
Land-grant bonds	10,400,000.00	
Loss on same	4,336,007.96	
		6,063,992.04
Government bonds	27,236,512.00	
Loss on same	91,348.72	
		27,145,163.28
Income bonds	9,355,000.00	
Loss on same	2,818,400.00	
		6,536,600.00
Total		$63,463,764.09
Cost of road		$60,467,641.27
Excess of receipts from bonds over cost of road		$2,993,122.82

There must be added to this sum, in order to get the cash profit on building the road, the amount which was paid to the Union Pacific by the Central Pacific for the section of road lying between Promontory, which had been settled upon as the meeting place of the two roads, and the point which is now the end of the Union Pacific, some four or five miles west of Ogden.[2] For this transfer of the ownership of some fifty miles of road the Union Pacific received the sum of $2,698,620. This makes the cash profit on the enterprise $5,691,742.82.

Then, in order to ascertain the total profit on construction, there must be added the value of the whole amount of stock issued. But what that value is cannot be said. The leading men of the enterprise seemed unanimous in the opinion that a fair valuation was 30. But Union Pacific stock has certainly

[1] Affairs of the Union Pacific Railroad Company, p. 590.

[2] Those provisions of the chartering acts which were intended to spur the eastern and the western companies to rapid building, in competition for the subsidies offered, worked only too well. Instead of bringing the ends of the road together as soon as possible, the two construction parties passed within sight of each other, and graded two parallel lines. The Central Pacific went almost to Ogden and the Union Pacific to Humboldt — points 170 miles apart — before a compromise was effected. The terms of the compromise are indicated in the text (Affairs of the Union Pacific Railroad Company, p. 11).

been above that point repeatedly, and it was down at one time to 9. It has always been a speculative stock, the sales amounting in a year to several times the total amount outstanding. But, for the sake of getting an estimate of the profits made by the builders of the Union Pacific, even though that estimate be admittedly unreliable, the valuation given above may be taken. At 30, the $36,762,300 of stock would be worth $11,028,690. Adding this to the cash profit as stated above, the total profit appears to be $16,710,432.82, or slightly above $27\frac{1}{2}$ per cent of the cost of the road. Considering the character of the undertaking and the time when it was carried through, this does not seem an immoderate profit.

V

THE SOUTHERN RAILWAY & STEAMSHIP ASSOCIATION [1]

A TYPICAL POOL

ABOUT the year 1860, after the railroads from the East had been pushed through to Chicago, and the short independent roads began to be united in interest and in management, the sharp competition that has become such a marked feature in modern railroad operations first came into prominent notice. Up to that time, each road had used only its own cars, the freight and passengers being transferred at the terminus. As it became necessary for connecting roads to work together, and make through lines requiring no transfers, each road began to work for the whole line of which it formed a part as against other similar lines or combinations.

The development in the South was much slower; and combination and competition, though inevitable, came more tardily. It was not till the Southern country had been laid waste by the contending armies, and its business brought to a standstill, that really sharp competition became the rule. Then the country was found to be supplied with more roads than were needed. According to Mr. Powers, afterwards Commissioner of the Southern Railway & Steamship Association, "there was not as much business as all could do. Indeed, any one of these lines, with a comparatively small output for rolling stock, can do all the business to any, indeed to all, competitive points named in our circulars." [2] With such a condition of affairs, it

---

[1] From the *Quarterly Journal of Economics*, Vol. V, 1891, pp. 70–94. Circular Letters of the Southern Railway Steamship Association are simply referred to hereafter as Circular Letters. The number preceding the title indicates the volume. Pooling and combination in general are discussed in Ripley's Railroads: Finance and Organization. [2] 3 Circular Letters, 991.

was inevitable that each road should try to get all the business possible. This was done by means of rebates or open cutting of rates, which soon brought them to a ruinously low range. At this stage of events, agreements to restore and maintain rates were not infrequently made; but, as Mr. Fink subsequently remarked in one of his reports to the Association, these agreements were generally made by the managers "with the purpose merely of practising deception upon each other. Starting from a higher scale of rates, they secured, for a short period at least, some remuneration for the work performed, until the low rates were reached again."[1] Mr. Fink estimated that by means of these rate wars the gross earnings of the Southern railroads were reduced about forty-two per cent below what regular rates would have yielded.[2] This forty-two per cent was in many cases equal to the whole net earnings which could have been derived from the competitive business at the regular rates, showing that the business was really unprofitable. The roads in the South were, in consequence, practically worthless to their owners. The following language was used in 1876 by a committee of the stockholders of the Central Railroad & Banking Company of Georgia: "It is conceded that the property of your stockholders is on the brink of being sunk forever; and the bankruptcy of a number of your roads is imminent, if not even now a fact."[3] This was the condition of affairs which led to the formation of the Southern Railway & Steamship Association.

Several isolated attempts were made to bring about a division of business before the final comprehensive scheme was adopted. Thus, in 1873, the roads running out of Atlanta, the Central, the Georgia, the Western & Atlantic, and the Atlanta & Charlotte Air Line, agreed upon divisions of the cotton business.[4] The accounts were kept by the superintendent of the Western & Atlantic, and were settled after some delay and dispute. This agreement covered only the cotton season of 1873.

On December 21, 1874, a meeting of the Southern roads was held at Macon, Georgia, to devise some permanent means of

[1] 1 Circular Letters, 277.   [2] 1 Ibid., 278.   [3] 2 Ibid., 338.
[4] 22 Ibid., 1619 (Report of the General Commissioner).

settling the difficulties that were constantly arising between them. Adjourned meetings were held in January, 1875, when an agreement was drawn up and a provisional division of business agreed upon for the principal competitive points. Several meetings for perfecting the agreement were held during 1875; and on October 13 of that year Mr. Albert Fink was elected General Commissioner.[1] This was in itself a favorable omen for the experiment; for Mr. Fink had been General Superintendent of the Louisville & Nashville Road, and was familiar with the railroad business of the South. Furthermore, it was largely on a plan laid down by him in a letter to the president of the convention that the Association was formed. He accepted office only for the purpose of organizing the pool and setting it in motion, and served but six months. Notwithstanding his short term of office, it is to Mr. Fink that the Association owes much of its success. The Southern Association was his first experiment in arranging railroad pools and agreements, and was, in fact, with one exception, the first practical pooling arrangement in this country.[2]

The Association, as its name implies, was intended to include all of the Southern transportation companies. Any road south of the Ohio and Potomac Rivers and east of the Mississippi could become a member. Any steamship company connecting these roads with Boston, Providence, New York, Philadelphia, or Baltimore was eligible. Its main object was to remedy the evil of excessive competition, which was working the destruction of all Southern roads, by maintaining rates and securing a fair distribution of business. To accomplish these ends, an annual convention was held, to which each road sent a representative. This convention elected the President, a permanent General Commissioner, a Secretary and Auditor, a Board of Arbitration, and an Executive Committee. It voted on the admission of new members, and adjusted all matters that could not be determined by the General Commissioner, a two-thirds vote being necessary for any action.

[1] 1 Circular Letters, 18.
[2] The exception was the so-called "Omaha Pool," first formed in 1870 between the Burlington, Rock Island, and North-Western Roads.

The Commissioner had general charge of the business of the Association, but referred to the convention, or to the managers of the roads interested, whatever delicate matters he did not feel able himself to deal with. His decisions, orders, recommendations, statistics, together with the minutes of the conventions and committee meetings, were communicated to the various roads by means of circular letters. These have been collected, and the twenty-four volumes in which they are preserved form the chief source of information regarding the history of the Association.

The practice of referring details to the convention, adopted in the first agreement, proved cumbersome and impracticable. Accordingly, there were occasional informal meetings of the various managers; and in 1883 [1] an Executive Committee was appointed, consisting of the manager or executive officer of each of the principal lines in the Association. This Executive Committee was given jurisdiction over all matters relating to the joint traffic, but could act only by unanimous consent. It could delegate to subcommittees jurisdiction over matters especially committed to their charge. Such a subcommittee was the Rate Committee; though a Rate Committee, with powers derived from a different source (the convention), had existed for several years before this. Having charge, in the first instance at least, of rates and classifications, this subcommittee became one of the most important branches of the organization. It consisted of the general freight agents of each of the lines in the Association. The Rate Committee, like the Executive Committee, could act only by a unanimous vote; and any member could demand that a question be referred to the Executive Committee.[2] This condition of a unanimous vote was probably meant to prevent any combination or clique of lines from bettering themselves at the expense of the others. But the result, as might be expected, was that it was often impossible to reach a decision, even on comparatively unimportant matters. The question would then go to the Executive Committee, where a similar state of affairs was likely to be met, and finally to the Board of Arbitration.

---

[1] 22 Circular Letters, 352.
[2] See the Agreement, Articles 7 and 10.

This involved much time and expense, even in cases where a majority vote in either committee should have been amply sufficient. But it may be said, on the other side, that by this reference of the matter to arbitration the dissenting roads were sure of an entirely impartial decision, and would be much more likely to abide by it than when outvoted in the committees.

By the first agreement (1875),[1] provision was made for reference of any disputes that might arise to the Commissioner as arbitrator. Then, if any member disapproved of his decision, the matter was referred to outsiders selected by the contestants in the case. In one case, Mr. Charles Francis Adams was so chosen as referee.[2] But this scheme of bringing in strangers, busy with affairs of their own, was not always practicable. Accordingly, some years later, an Arbitrator was elected as a permanent officer of the Association. His duty was to receive written arguments, and, in connection with the Commissioner, to decide all cases that might be referred to him. At the ninth annual convention,[3] October 24, 1883, the number of the Arbitrators was increased to three, the present number.

As soon as possible after the completion of the organization and the election of the Commissioner, a permanent division of business was agreed upon for Atlanta, Augusta, and Macon. This was put into effect on November 19, 1875. Each road was expected to carry, as nearly as possible, the appointed amount. In case the exact proportions could not be secured, one half a cent per ton per mile was allowed each road for any excess carried by it, to cover the expense of carriage; and the remainder of the revenue was paid to the Commissioner to be transferred to the credit of those roads carrying less than their proportions.[4] Daily returns of the competitive business were made to the Commissioner, whose duty it was to publish monthly tables of the amount of freight carried by each road.

This would have done very well if all the roads had honestly performed their part. But such was not the case. Down to

---

[1] 1 Circular Letters, 7.   [2] 14 *Ibid.*, 35.   [3] 14 *Ibid.*, 45.
[4] This was changed later. Twenty per cent of the revenue was allowed in the last years of the pooling arrangement.

July 31, 1876, when Mr. Virgil Powers took the place of Mr. Fink, only $62\frac{1}{2}$ per cent of the merchandise balances had been settled.[1] The remaining $37\frac{1}{2}$ per cent, and all the balances on cotton, still remained unpaid. A compromise was arranged for the remainder, and the amount agreed upon was at last nearly all paid. But, as the same trouble was likely to recur, the Commissioner proposed that each road should deposit to his order a certain percentage of the revenue on each waybill of pooled business. In June, 1877, a convention of the roads agreed to a deposit of twenty per cent.[2] In 1887, in his annual report,[3] the Commissioner was able to say that "since 1877 all balances have been paid and rates thoroughly maintained, except for about a month from February 14 to March 15, 1878, during which time there was a war of rates between the roads."

At the outset the pool covered only the business with the Eastern cities. The Western business was not pooled till the year before the Interstate Commerce Act was passed. On this unpooled business, rates were being constantly cut, and there was much complaint both by the roads and by the public. To remedy this evil, another organization of Southern roads was formed in 1886, known as the "Associated Roads of Kentucky, Alabama, and Tennessee,"[4] and the pooling arrangement, which had operated so successfully with the Eastern business, was extended to the business to and from the West. In 1887, the new organization was united with the Southern Railway & Steamship Association; and the Commissioner of the former Association, Mr. J. R. Ogden, was elected Vice-Commissioner of the latter and given charge of the Western business.[5]

One further point in the history of the organization needs to be spoken of before we turn to its practical workings. The agreement contemplated putting both passenger and freight business under the rules of the Association. At first, however, freight traffic alone was regulated. In 1885 the Commissioner

---

[1] 21 Circular Letters, 1679.   [3] 21 *Ibid.*, 1620.
[2] 3 *Ibid.*, 861.   [4] 21 *Ibid.*, 1620.
[5] 22 *Ibid.*, 138, 1621. At the end of the year, however, this office of Vice-Commissioner was abolished.

was asked to submit a plan for bringing the passenger business
under the control of the Association, and in November a plan
was submitted to the Executive Committee.[1] It was never
acted on by the Association as such ; but it was taken in hand
by the roads, and another Association was formed, called the
Southern Passenger Association. It is distinct more in name
than in practice. The two Associations are composed of the
same roads, and the same person is their General Commissioner.
The Southern Passenger Association is now practically a part
of the Southern Railway & Steamship Association.

So much for the history and general organization of the
Association. The Commissioner, the Executive and Rate Committees, and the Arbitrators are the effective parts of the machinery; and to their functions and the modes of exercising them
we will now turn.

The General Commissioner has always been the executive
officer of the Association. His duty was primarily to carry out
all laws passed by the convention or the committees. But
it went beyond this. He had a conditional legislative power.
By written authority he was actually made a special agent
of each of the roads, and was supposed to look after the interests of all alike. One of his most important duties was, in
connection with the Auditor, to collect and publish accounts
of the business transacted, and statistics on any other matters
that would be of assistance to the roads. As an example of
this function, we may mention certain tables in regard to the
capacity of the different Tank Line cars for the transportation
of oils. It had often been impossible to ascertain the exact
weight of shipments of oil; and it was arranged that in future
the capacity of the cars, as given in these tables, should be
taken as the basis in calculating the charges.[2]

The Commissioner and Auditor were to keep accounts of the
business done. To enable them to do this the agents of the
initial roads were ordered to forward daily to the Commissioner
copies of all waybills of through business.[3] At the same time,

---

[1] 17 Circular Letters, 1622 ; 18 *Ibid.*, 193.
[2] 20 *Ibid.*, 107 ; and 22 *Ibid.*, 391.   [3] See the Agreement, Article 18.

they were to deposit in bank to the order of the Commissioner twenty per cent of the revenue from such business. The accounts, which were to be made out and published monthly, were divided into nine tables. Table A showed the movements of merchandise during the month from each Eastern city to all division points; the route, amount performed in pounds and revenue, allowance for carriage and net revenue to be divided, percentages and revenue allotment, excess in the amount carried, and the cash deposited to the order of the Commissioner.[1] Table B gave similar information for the two months previous, enabling a manager to tell whether his road was gaining or falling behind the other lines. Tables C and D gave similar information about the cotton business. E and F showed the gross revenue and balances for the month at each point and at all points combined, for merchandise and cotton respectively.

[1] By way of illustration, I give the Commissioner's Table A for October, 1882, on New York traffic: —

NEW YORK TO ATHENS, GA. Name of Road and Route	Gross Pounds	Gross Revenue	Allowance for Transportation	Net Revenue Divided. Debit	Per cent agreed on for Each Line	Net Revenue Allotted. Credit	Revenue in Excess. Net Debit	Revenue in Deficit. Net Credit	General Com'r's Deposit, 20%
N. E. R.R. via Pied. A. L. . Ga. R.R. via	149,687	$1,045.85	$209.17	$836.68	57.5%	$1,029.69	. . .	$193.01	$201.55
Savannah . Ga. R.R. via	18,800	181.85	36.37	145.48	17.	304.43	. . .	158.95	34.18
Charleston . Ga. R.R. via	149,332	971.94	194.39	777.55	17.	304.43	$473.12	. . .	194.12
A. C. L. . . Ga. R.R. via	2,205	22.11	4.42	17.69	5.1	91.33	. . .	73.64	4.43
Port Royal	2,280	16.70	3.34	13.36	3.4	60.88	. . .	47.52	3.34
Totals . .	322,304	$2,238.45	$447.69	$1,790.76	100%	$1,790.76	$473.12	$473.12	$437.62

To keep these various accounts, of course a larger force of clerks was necessary, entailing a considerable expense. This expense was met, first, by a yearly membership fee of $300 for each road, and, second, by assessments on the various roads in proportion to their revenue from competitive business. For the year ending May 31, 1889, the expenses of the Association were a little more than $51,000.

G gave the gross revenue and balances for merchandise and cotton combined, at all points, and the cash deposited for the month. This is the table upon which the settlements were made. H gave the gross revenue from merchandise and cotton, and the two combined, for the two months previous. I gave the amount of the Commissioner's deposits, where deposited, the character of the business on which deposit was made, and by whom it was made. In 1883 another set of tables was added, showing the movements of cotton factory goods. By means of these various tables, the manager of each road was enabled to see at a glance just what business there was to compete for, and what share his road was getting. They showed him, also, the basis on which the percentages of division were calculated.

Having informed the roads by means of these tables of the amount of their indebtedness, and of the business from which it arose, the Commissioner and Auditor acted as clearing-house agents for the settlement of the accounts. The twenty per cent deposit of the debtor companies was applied as far as possible to paying their balances, and sight drafts were drawn by the Commissioner for any excess. The deposits were relied on, however, to pay the greater part of the indebtedness. In September, 1884, — to take a month at random, — out of the sixty lines (routes) for which accounts were kept, twenty-one had carried more than their share of freight. Out of these twenty-one, ten had deposits large enough to cover all indebtedness. With five more, the excess was less than $100; while only six of the twenty-one owed more than $100 in addition to what their deposits would cover. The deposit practically assured a prompt settlement of all balances. Whatever remained of the twenty per cent after paying the debts was returned monthly to the depositing companies.

The Commissioner's accounts and statements obviously could not be accepted as conclusive unless the right was given him to examine the books of any member of the Association, as a safeguard against fraudulent or irregular reports. This right was given by Article 18 of the Agreement. Some instances of the mode in which it was enforced will serve to illustrate the practical working of the Association. In the fall of 1886, one of the Inspectors, at the order of the Auditor, attempted to examine the books of the Alabama Great Southern Road at Chattanooga, in order to trace some cotton shipped from Atlanta. The officials of the road refused to allow this examination; and the matter was brought up in the Executive Committee. A vote of censure on the road was there passed, and the action of the Alabama Great Southern in this case was treated by the committee simply as a breach of the agreement.[1] In 1883, however, the power was more vigorously exercised. It had been charged that rebates were being paid on compressed cotton via the Atlantic ports; and the Commissioner was instructed by the Executive Committee to examine the books of the railroad companies and the steamship companies carrying to and from these ports, for the purpose of ascertaining whether such rebates had been paid.[2] Another case, even more striking, came up in July, 1885.[3] The matter of rates and rebilling from the West was under discussion. The Rate Committee requested the Commissioner to examine the rebilling records of the Nashville, Chattanooga & St. Louis Railroad, and to report the extent of such business, making a separate statement of each class of freight rebilled, under what divisions and to what points; and also a statement of the quantity of similar business shipped at Nashville rates. The examination was made, and a report of fifteen or more printed pages presented a few weeks later.[4]

---

[1] 20 Circular Letters, 121.

[2] 14 *Ibid.*, 213.

[3] 17 *Ibid.*, 1625.

[4] 18 *Ibid.*, 364. Other statistics were collected by the Commissioner. Among them were some that must have been gathered in any case; but the matter was much simplified when one man gathered the information for all the roads. Such, for example, were the tables of the "arbitraries" charged by the Northern roads. The Southern Association made rates to New York, Providence, Boston, and other cities. To find the rates on cotton (the chief North-bound business) to the interior New England manufacturing town, the arbitraries given in these tables were added to the regular Boston rates, and gave a desirable uniformity in the rates.

We turn now to another important part of the Commissioner's functions. The object of the Association was primarily to maintain rates. Theoretically, this was done; but in practice there were many irregularities. Goods were often classified wrongly or were underweighed. Shippers often misrepresent the goods when the railroad agents are unable to ascertain for themselves their quality and class. Often the agents are willfully negligent; by not being too watchful in classifying and weighing, they cut rates and draw the traffic to their lines. To remedy this evil, in 1886 (July 16) the Commissioner was empowered[1] to appoint two Inspectors of Weights and Classifications. The same experiment had been tried by the South-western Association, and some others, and had proved very successful.[2] The need that had existed for some such check is shown by the following table of the work accomplished by the Inspectors in the first year after they were appointed:[3] —

	NUMBER OF SHIPMENTS CORRECTED	WEIGHT CORRECTED	INCREASE IN REVENUE
Oct. 1, 1886, to June 1, 1887	10,173	11,992,037	$32,057.35
One month, May, 1887 . .	1,829	1,649,348	5,112.21

This of itself shows a substantial increase in revenue. But the effect of the new method was much greater than the figures of corrections would indicate. " The knowledge that checks have been provided makes shippers more careful than they would be otherwise. Hence attempts to evade the classification are not so numerous as they formerly were, or as they would be, did not the shippers know that we were watching to prevent irregularities."[4] Whenever the Commissioner suspected that fraudulent practices were being followed, he would

[1] 19 Circular Letters, 1717. The number of Inspectors has since been increased.   [2] 19 *Ibid.*, 1689.   [3] 21 *Ibid.*, 1627.

[4] Letter from J. W. Midgeley, Commissioner of the South-western Association, to Mr. Powers, in 19 *Ibid.*, 1690.

send an Inspector to examine and, if possible, stop them. The Inspectors were also sent to examine the books of a company, if it was suspected that business was done without being reported. In 1886, the East Tennessee, Virginia & Georgia road was charged with failing to report all the cotton carried to Brunswick. An Inspector examined the books of the company, and watched the shipments for some time, in this case without bringing to light any irregularity.

*   *   *   *   *   *   *   *

The second important part of the machinery of the Association consists of the Executive Committee and the Rate Committee, whose formation and powers have already been described. We may now examine some particular cases illustrative of these powers. It will be most convenient to describe them irrespective of whether they came up in the Rate Committee or Executive Committee. The reader will remember that the Executive Committee is the higher court, as it were, and that any matter can be appealed to it from the Rate Committee.

Of course, the first duty of the Rate Committee is to make rates to and from the competitive points. This statement seems simple, but it involves more than appears at the first glance. It brings up the questions of (1) division of the business on which rates have been made ; (2) differentials between different towns; (3) classification of goods.

A fixed rate having been agreed upon for the competitive business, a division of the business follows almost of necessity. There are always differences in the position or equipment of the competing roads. The best equipped and most convenient road would naturally get most of the business. This would ordinarily lead to a cutting of rates, and that, too, as is usual in such cases, by the road least able to give low rates. The only way to prevent a continual struggle is to assure the weaker road a certain proportion of the business. In the early days of the Association, divisions were agreed upon by the managers of the roads for eight points, — Atlanta, Augusta, Macon, Newnan, West Point, Opelika, Montgomery, and Selma. These divisions were based on the normal carrying capacity of the roads, as shown in the business of the years past. For example, the divisions for Atlanta were : [1] —

	COTTON	MERCHANDISE
Central R.R.	31.7%	$26\frac{2}{3}\%$
Georgia R.R.	31.7	40
Atlantic & Richmond Air Line R.R.	15.8	$16\frac{2}{3}$
Western & Atlantic R.R.	15.8	$16\frac{2}{3}$
Atlanta & West Point R.R.	5.	. . . .

As new roads were built, new allotments of business were demanded or allotments at new places. In 1886, the merchandise business of 15 places was pooled; and at Atlanta the number of pooled routes had grown from 5 to 12.

Again, some of the old lines, by offering greater facilities, might feel able to demand a larger proportion of the business. There was an important case of this sort in 1884, on the Montgomery cotton business. From January, 1881, to August, 1883, the business had been pooled on the following percentages : [2] —

East Tennessee, Virginia & Georgia, via Calera 14%
Louisville & Nashville, via Mobile, and North, via Louisville & Nashville 48
Montgomery & Eufaula and Western of Alabama 38

In 1883, the East Tennessee became dissatisfied with this division, and refused to renew the agreement, asserting that, to avoid paying the heavy penalty of $1.50 per bale for excess carried, they had been compelled to turn over to their competitors several thousand bales of cotton. In 1883–84, the cotton business from the point in question was not pooled, and the East Tennessee Road carried over twenty-seven per cent of the business, even though full Association rates had been charged. The next year, the matter came up in the Executive Committee,

[1] 1 Circular Letters, 1.
[2] Argument before the Board of Arbitration by the East Tennessee, Virginia & Georgia Railroad.

where an attempt was made to settle it. This failing, it went to the Arbitrators for a decision. They gave a division of the business as follows: [1] —

	NEW DIVISION	OLD
East Tennessee	22%	14%
Louisville & Nashville	42	48
Western of Alabama and Montgomery & Eufaula	36	38

A similar dispute arose at about the same time over the Selma cotton business. The Executive Committee agreed to refer the matter to an arbitrator. Immediately thereafter, the initial roads entered into a contract, as provided in Article 20 of the Agreement, dividing the business according to his decision.

In close connection with the making of rates is the matter of classification. In the classification of the Association, as it stood in 1886, there were specified in round numbers 1250 articles. The classification of the Association was adopted in the first instance by the annual convention of 1878, but since then has been in the hands of the Rate Committee. Even the first classification was drawn up and proposed by a committee corresponding to the present Rate Committee.[2] The result has been a single uniform classification for the whole Southern territory, in place of the chaos which had existed before. " In July, 1876, the Eastern lines had two classifications. The Savannah line used 9 classes, and the Charleston and Coast lines worked 5 and 6 classes. The Western lines were using the ' Green Line ' classification, with a number of ' Specials.' " [3] The advantage of having one classification for all the roads in

[1] 16 Circular Letters, 41.

[2] 19 *Ibid.*, 1687.

[3] 19 Circular Letters, 1687. In January, 1888, a committee was appointed by our Association to confer with the Joint Classification Committee of the Trunk Lines Association and others, for the purpose of ascertaining what possibility existed for establishing a uniform classification. But thus far none has been agreed upon ; and it is questionable whether an agreement is reached at an early day, unless the Interstate Commerce Commission succeeds in bringing enough pressure on the roads.

a section of the country, or even for the whole country, if that were possible, is obvious.

The third task involved in the making of rates is the fixing of the differentials between neighboring cities. The general object in fixing the differentials was to make such rates that all cities similarly situated should have the same chance in the competition of trade. Thus a New York merchant would have to pay the same rates, whether he shipped his goods to Chattanooga, Dalton, Rome, Atlanta, Athens, Gainesville, Anniston, or Birmingham. On the other hand, Boston, New York, Philadelphia, were treated alike, the rates to and from any given Southern point being the same. Norfolk, Portsmouth, and Richmond formed another group ; and, again, Charleston, Port Royal, Savannah, and Brunswick. From the West, rates were the same from Chicago to all Eastern ports, such as Jacksonville, Fernandina, Charleston, Port Royal, Savannah, and Brunswick ; and in like manner from either Louisville or Memphis to the Eastern ports. These examples suffice to indicate the principle on which differentials were adjusted. As new roads were built, of course new places had to be considered. Thus, in 1886, the East Tenenssee, Virginia & Georgia moved, in the Rate Committee, that the rates to and from Rockmart, Georgia, be the same as to Cedartown, Georgia. The two towns were between ten and twenty miles apart, and were doing substantially the same business. The motion was lost, and the matter referred to the Executive Committee. There again it was lost, and referred to the Arbitrators, who finally directed that the rates to Rockmart be the same as to Rome and Cedartown.[1] At another time, in August, 1886, a question arose as to differentials on cotton from Atlanta to New Orleans and to Savannah. The old differentials had been 7 cents per 100 pounds in favor of Savannah. The motion now was to reduce this to 3 cents. The Arbitrators finally agreed on a compromise differential of 5 cents, the rate to New Orleans being put at 50 cents per 100 pounds, and that to Savannah at 45 cents.[2]

*   *   *   *   *   *   *   *

[1] 20 Circular Letters, 102, 114, 121, 467.
[2] 19 Ibid., 2041 ; 20 Ibid., 47.

Next, as to the relations of the Association lines with outside lines. In its dealings with these, the Association has not always been lenient, especially when there was competition between its members and the outsiders. In the revised rules adopted in December, 1876, there was the following provision : " If any company owning or operating a line of transportation in connection with the roads or lines of companies, parties hereto, shall refuse to become a member of the Association, . . . such line shall, as far as practicable, be refused recognition as part of a through line." [1] This practically amounted to boycotting such lines. The provision for a boycott does not appear in the later agreement, though there have been recent cases where some such rule would, no doubt, have been very acceptable to the roads of the Association; as when the Chesapeake & Ohio was completed to Newport News, and again when the Kansas City, Memphis & Birmingham was built to Birmingham. These roads, being outside of the Association, often reduced the rates and materially affected the business. Following up the policy here indicated, the Commissioner, in August 6, 1877, issued a circular authorizing greatly reduced rates to Boston and New York and to the South Atlantic ports. The reason was that the steamship lines to and from these points had refused to co-operate with the Association in carrying out its rules. Within three weeks, all the steamship lines had signed the agreement, and rates were restored.[2]

Equally troublesome was the competition of the river steamboat lines. Often the differentials between two cities, such as St. Louis and East Cairo, were sufficient to allow the boats to cut rates, even after paying insurance. To prevent this, in the case referred to, the rates to East Cairo were advanced enough to make them the same as to Cairo, across the river, thereby reducing the differential between East Cairo and St. Louis two cents per hundred pounds on Classes C and D, and four cents per barrel on flour.[3] Rates to Selma and Montgomery from the East were cut in a similar way by the New York & Mobile Steamship Line. The Association changed their rates to stop

[1] 2 Circular Letters, 598.   [2] 3 *Ibid.*, 897, 931.   [3] 22 *Ibid.*, 131.

this : a few months later, the competition being withdrawn, they were restored.[1]

Next, let us turn our attention to the Board of Arbitration. The duties of the Board have already been referred to in a general way, and in treating of other subjects examples have incidentally been given of the exercise of their powers. It will be helpful to give other examples, illustrating the variety of cases which come before them.

Perhaps the matter that they had to consider most often was that of making divisions of the competitive business, of which one instance, the Montgomery and Selma pool settlement, was considered on page 110. We there saw that the business from these points was pooled from 1881 to 1883. Then, the East Tennessee, Virginia & Georgia becoming dissatisfied with its share, a year followed without the pool. But in 1884 a new division of the business was made by the Arbitrators, whereby the East Tennessee got more nearly the share of the business which it demanded. In 1886 this question came before the Arbitrators again, but in a more complicated form.[2] In the first place, the East Tennessee renewed its claim for a larger share of the business from these points. This was refused in the case of Montgomery, but from Selma the East Tennessee got one per cent in addition to its previous proportion. Next, when the annual convention was held, and the agreement presented as usual for signature, the Louisville & Nashville refused to sign, on the ground that balances to the amount of $5500 were still due it on the Montgomery and Selma pool. This amount was said to be due from the East Tennessee Road, which had lately gone out of existence by the foreclosure of a mortgage, becoming the East Tennessee, Virginia & Georgia Railway Company, and from which, in consequence, the money could not be collected. After having been debated in the Executive Committee, the matter was handed over to the Arbitrators to decide what balances, if any, were due, and how they were to

[1] 22 Circular Letters, 21.
[2] 20 *Ibid.*, 53.

be divided among the several roads. They agreed that the condition of the accounts before August 31, 1884, the date on which the second pool went into effect, was too confused to admit of any unraveling. Hence all balances before that date were considered canceled and discharged. On the business after that date, they decided that a balance of $3700 was due the Louisville & Nashville, of which the East Tennessee should pay $976. These had been the precise amounts given in the accounts of the Commissioner.[1]

Another typical case, showing the usefulness of the Arbitrators in allotting business, came up in connection with the traffic of Memphis and Nashville. There had been no previous division of the business to these points, and rates had been irregular for a considerable time. Finally, in the summer of 1885, an agreement was made by the East Tennessee and the Louisville & Nashville Roads, the competitors for the business, to maintain rates, and ask the Arbitrators to allot the business. This allotment was made, and accepted by both roads.[2]

Another case, of a somewhat different sort, was brought up by the Louisville & Nashville[3] at a later period. Under the terms of the agreement, the initial lines from any point " shall determine the subdivisions of its business among its connections." The Louisville & Nashville claimed that it was not receiving from the Atlanta & West Point, with which it connected, its fair share of the Atlanta cotton, and so demanded an apportionment, extending back to 1877, or at least to 1884–85. The two claims differed only in regard to the dates. In regard to the second, it was decided that a fixed share of the Atlanta & West Point business should be given to the Louisville & Nashville, the share to be determined by the Auditors' accounts.[4] In regard to the other, no division was allowed, on the grounds that previous to January 17, 1883, the part of the Louisville & Nashville for which this claim was made had not been a member of the Association; that until 1884 it would not have been obliged to pay over the receipts from any

[1] 19 Circular Letters, 2048; 20 *Ibid.*, 55.
[2] 17 *Ibid.*, 1490.

[3] 20 *Ibid.*, 263.
[4] 20 *Ibid.*, 469.

excess that might have fallen to it, and so should have no claim for a deficit of freight carried.[1]

At another time, cotton was shipped from a local station to Montgomery, a competitive point, on a local bill of lading, and then reshipped. This was held to be subject to the regular pool divisions of Montgomery, according to the agreement, by which " all business from or to a crossing or meeting point of two or more roads is joint traffic." [2]

A peculiar dispute, important as illustrating one of the articles of the agreement, came before the Board in 1887.[3] It is spoken of here because closely connected with the matter of allotting business. Complaint had been made that the East Tennessee Road had carried some cotton from Selma which it had failed to report for division. In answer, it was stated that the cotton in question had been refused by the Western Railroad of Alabama and others. The Board held that, according to Article 19 of the Agreement, this cotton should be eliminated from the pool, and need not be reported. Article 19 reads that " each company shall be required to carry, as nearly as possible, its allotted proportion," but " no penalty shall be imposed upon a company or line which carries an excess for the benefit of any company that refuses or willfully neglects to carry its allotted proportion." The object of the article was, of course, to keep all the roads in the market. Its effect was to maintain competition, notwithstanding the pool.

Next in number, but less varied in character, are the cases relating to rates and differentials. Some of these have already been noted. The dispute on New Orleans and Savannah differentials, and the difficulties that arose in regard to steamship competition on Ohio and Mississippi River points, were in the end settled by the Board. Another, of a typical sort, referred to the rates on iron from Birmingham and Chattanooga to St. Louis.

---

[1] These cases are interesting in another way. The Louisville & Nashville were dissatisfied with the decisions given, and asked for a reopening of the matter. Although such a thing may be allowed, and at times has been allowed, the Arbitrators at this time did not see fit to grant the rehearing. 21 *Ibid.*, 1107.

[2] 18 *Ibid.*, 205.   [3] 22 *Ibid.*, 155.

The Kansas City, Memphis & Birmingham Railroad (not in the Association) had lowered the rate from Birmingham to St. Louis. This was followed by a similar reduction by the Association, but without a corresponding reduction in the Chattanooga rates. On reference to the Arbitrators, it was decided that the old differential of $0.25 between Chattanooga and Birmingham should continue in force, and that any reduction in the rates from Birmingham should carry with it a corresponding reduction from Chattanooga.[1]

The Board of Arbitration have also had to consider various other questions. Points in regard to classification have arisen, as in regard to the classification of cotton goods, the products of Southern mills. These goods, which had been favored from the outset by a low classification, were raised in 1887 from the sixth to the fourth class, thereby removing in part one of the "protective" features of the system. Even after this change the rates were not the same both ways. Cotton factory goods South bound went first class at $1.14 per 100 pounds, New York to Atlanta. Southern factory goods North bound paid now, as fourth class, instead of 49 cents, 73 cents. "But for the fact," the Arbitrators said, in giving their decision, "that finer fabrics shipped South bound, some of them without discovery, are of higher value than those shipped North bound, the still existing inequality would be unjustifiable."[2] Another minor matter which has come before the Board has been the question of insured bills of lading. The agreement provides, in Article 21, that, "in cases of competition between all rail lines and water or combined water and rail lines, the latter may assume the whole burden of insuring against marine risks ; and bills of lading to that effect may be issued." The Arbitrators decided that such insured bills of lading could be issued in competition with all rail lines only, the privilege not applying between two combined rail and water lines.[3] Another decision was as to what were "initial roads" under the agreement. It was held that the phrase "initial roads" is not used in distinction to "terminal roads," but that the responsible road at any given point was

[1] 22 Circular Letters, 363.   [2] 20 *Ibid.*, 261 ; 21 *Ibid.*, 1105.   [3] 16 *Ibid.*, 45.

the initial road.[1] Still another decision was in regard to " milling in transit," which was held to be a form of rebilling, and hence prohibited.[2]

These cases have been cited, not because in themselves of great importance, but because they show the great variety of matters which the Arbitrators had to deal with. They are all types of cases that come up often. They include, either directly or indirectly, nearly all the matters over which the Association had control. The task of the Board has been by no means an easy one. There were many masters to please, but it has performed its functions without even a suspicion of dishonesty or partiality.

We have thus far been considering in detail the organization and workings of the Association as it existed down to 1887. It now remains to note the changes which were brought about by the Interstate Commerce Act passed in that year.[3] The Act, first of all, stopped the pooling feature of the Association. The twenty per cent deposits were no longer called for, and the payment by one road to another of any excess of earnings above allotment was put an end to. The daily reports of business and the monthly tables, however, were still continued. The act also required some readjustment of rates. While each road reported its rates to the Interstate Commerce Commission directly, and aimed to keep them, as nearly as possible, in line with the decisions of that Commission, yet the through rates were, in the main, discussed and arranged as before by the Rate Committee of the Association. At first the committee of the Association had some difficulty in arranging rates so as to compete successfully with the river lines, and therefore asked for and obtained a suspension for ninety days of the long and short haul clause of the act. The delay was asked mainly to give time for rearranging the rates without disturbing more than was necessary the interests of the shippers. In making the rearrangement, a partial reclassification was necessary; and the number of places

---

[1] 18 Circular Letters, 203.   [2] 20 *Ibid.*, 259.

[3] Later details are given in the Cincinnati Freight Bureau Cases, *vide*, p. 154, *infra.* — Ed.

to which through rates were made was somewhat reduced, in order to get more nearly in line with the requirements of the law. The Association was recognized by the Interstate Commerce Commission, and on several cases has been summoned to appear before it for examination.[1] Complaints have also been brought against the Association before the Commission for illegal rates. At times the roads over which the rates in question were given were joined as codefendants, but this has not always been the case.

The prohibition of pooling by the Interstate Commerce Act by no means put an end to the power of the Association. It still continues, having for its object the saving of revenue by the maintenance of rates. Though pool divisions may no longer be made use of, fines may be imposed to accomplish the same end. A recent case will serve to show how this is done.

In the adjustment of rates from Eastern cities to Southeastern points, it happened that a combination of "locals" from Baltimore to some of these cities was less than the through rates. This was not true from any other city. The business, however, from Baltimore to the points in question was so small that the differences amounted to nothing. One road, without consulting the Commissioner, reduced the through rates to this combination of locals, thereby affecting all through rates from New York and Philadelphia to these Southeastern points. The Interstate Act requires that notice of reductions of rates must be filed in the office of the Commission at least three days before they can go into effect ; for the Southern Railway & Steamship Association territory the practice is that all changes are made by the Rate Committee, and notice is given at Washington by the Commissioner. The road in question filed notice of reduction itself with the Interstate Commerce Commission, and then notified the Commissioner of the Southern Association of the intended change. That officer at once notified the other roads interested ; but these protested against the reduction as unnecessary and unwise, and asked that the rates be not put into effect until the matter could be brought before the Rate Committee. Notwithstanding

[1] Interstate Commerce Reports, Vol. III, p. 7.

these remonstrances, the rates were put into force as originally planned. Thereupon one road, connecting with a water line, in retaliation issued insured bills of lading; another refused to authorize the reduced rates except upon order of the Commissioner of the Association. Permission to use them was given by the Commissioner; but, as the rates were not officially announced by him, the road still refused to use the reduction or honor bills of lading given at the reduced rates. The matter was very soon brought before the Executive Committee in the shape of a complaint. It was referred by them to the Arbitrators, who, after a full hearing, ordered the original rates to be restored and the offending road to pay a fine of $5000. The fine was paid, and rates were restored within three weeks after the original reduction.

This brings the Association to date. Let us now glance at its effects on the roads and on the public.

There can be no doubt that it has been of great benefit to the roads. It has secured the maintenance of rates, and an adjusted share of business to each line. The stronger lines would perhaps have survived without this division, but hardly the weaker. As to the public, the regularity of rates has helped the growth of the country, and this has reacted in turn to the benefit of the roads. The traffic has increased enormously. The amount of cotton carried North from all pooled points has more than doubled from 1877–78 to 1885–86. In 1877 it was 297,284 bales; in 1885–86 it was 664,337.[1] The amount of merchandise South bound has increased in the same time from seventy million pounds to nearly one hundred and fifty million. The total of merchandise carried South in this time to all pooled points was 1,285,928,199 pounds, with a revenue of $8,747,564. The total cotton revenue in this time was $10,905,000. During the same period, the General Commissioner's deposits, referred to above, were $1,636,270.

The regularity of rates under the Association is the advantage to the public most distinctly due to its existence. Changes in rates have been comparatively few, and secret rebates rare.

[1] 21 Circular Letters, 1626.

Such changes as took place have been almost uniformly downward; and, as reasonable notice of these has been given, there has been no offset to the public's gain such as sudden and fluctuating reductions bring. The figures in the note show the steady downward trend of rates, and prove at least that the effect of the Association was not to maintain rates at any fixed high figure.[1] Certainly, that part of the public which had to do directly with the roads in the Association was not dissatisfied with the working of the pool. In 1887 the General Commissioner was able to say at the annual convention, "There has been literally no complaint of discrimination between individuals in the same locality, and very little (and that unreasonable) between localities."[2]

In conclusion, a word may be said of the effect of the Association in maintaining rather than suppressing competition among the roads. Pools of which this is a type do indeed limit competition. But it is a great mistake to suppose that they destroy competition. On the contrary, as Professor Seligman puts it,[3] "they maintain the advantages of a healthy competition. Each of the roads will still attempt to procure as much

[1] The rates, in cents per hundred pounds on numbered classes, from Eastern cities to Atlanta on the first of January of each year, have been : —

YEAR	FROM BOSTON, NEW YORK, PHILADELPHIA						FROM BALTIMORE					
	1	2	3	4	5	6	1	2	3	4	5	6
1875 . .	170	140	110	90	80	70	160	130	100	85	75	65
1876 . .	170	140	110	90	80	70	160	130	100	85	75	65
1877 . .	145	125	100	80	60	50	135	115	90	75	55	45
1878 . .	145	125	100	80	60	50	135	115	90	75	55	45
1879 . .	125	110	85	75	60	45	119	104	79	71	56	41
1880 . .	125	110	85	75	60	45	119	104	79	71	56	41
1881 . .	126	110	94	81	65	41	119	104	89	76	61	46
1882 . .	100	90	80	70	58	48	95	85	75	65	55	45
1883 . .	125	108	93	78	63	49	118	102	88	73	59	46
1884 . .	114	98	86	73	60	49	107	92	81	68	56	46
1885 . .	114	98	86	73	60	49	107	92	81	68	56	46
1886 . .	114	98	86	73	60	49	107	92	81	68	56	46
1887 . .	114	98	86	73	60	49	107	92	81	68	56	46

[2] 21 Circular Letters, 1620.

[3] In the *Political Science Quarterly*, Vol. II, p. 389.

business as can possibly be obtained in a fair and open manner." The agreement of the Southern Railway & Steamship Association was renewed yearly, and most of the contracts for division of business were made for a year at a time. Each road tried to carry as much freight as possible, so that, when the next contract came to be made, it might demand with some show of reason a larger share of the business. It is competition of this sort that is advantageous, not competition with little or no regard to the cost of doing the work.

HENRY HUDSON

VI

UNREASONABLE RATES

The Cincinnati Freight Bureau Case[1]

CLEMENTS, *Commissioner :*

The complaints in these cases, which were heard and may be disposed of together, were filed, respectively, by the Freight Bureau of the Cincinnati Chamber of Commerce and the Chicago Freight Bureau. The former will hereinafter be referred to as the Cincinnati case, and the latter as the Chicago case.

In both complaints, Baltimore, Philadelphia, New York, Boston and contiguous territory, are designated "Eastern Seaboard territory;" Knoxville and Chattanooga, Tenn., Rome and Atlanta, Ga., Birmingham, Anniston and Selma, Ala., Meridian, Miss., and contiguous territory, "Southern territory;" and Cincinnati, Ohio, Louisville, Ky., Indianapolis and Evansville, Ind., Chicago and Cairo, Ill., St. Louis, Mo., and contiguous territory, "Central territory." These designations will be so applied in this opinion.

The general ground of complaint in the Cincinnati case is that the rates of freight established by the defendant carriers from the Eastern Seaboard and Central territories, respectively, to Southern territory, "unjustly discriminate in favor of the merchants and manufacturers whose business is located and transacted in Eastern Seaboard territory and against the merchants and manufacturers whose business is located and transacted in Cincinnati and other points in Central territory." It is stated that "the burden of the complaint lies against the *relation* which exists between the current rates of freight on *manufactured*

---

[1] Decided May 29, 1894. Interstate Commerce Reports, Vol. VI, pp. 195–256. Overruled by the Supreme Court, *vide*, p. 187, *infra*. The final disposition of it at p. 198, *infra*. The entire history of this suggestive case may be traced by means of the index in Ripley's Railroads : Rates and Regulation.

articles and merchandise" (numbered classes) "from Eastern
Seaboard territory to Southern territory, and the current rates
of freight exacted upon like commodities when shipped from
Central territory to the South, and against the unfair basis of
general construction of the tariffs under consideration whereby
the rates charged for transportation of commodities classified
under ' numbered classes ' bear a much higher percentage relation
to the rates from New York than do the rates on commodities
enumerated under the lettered classes " (food products and similar heavy traffic) ; and it is alleged, "that this improper relation
between rates has the effect of restraining and impeding the
growth of productive industries in Central territory and encouraging and promoting similar industries in Eastern Seaboard territory, and is the direct result of an agreement established by
convention between the officers of defendants, whereby in order
to secure stability in rates and to prevent competition between
the lines leading respectively from the Eastern Seaboard and
Central territories to the South, it was decided to secure to the
Eastern lines and Eastern territory the traffic in merchandise
and manufactured articles and to the Western territory the
traffic in food products and similar heavy commodities." In
support of these charges as to the alleged "improper relation "
between the rates from Eastern territory and Central territory
to Southern territory, and between those on the numbered and
lettered classes, tabular statements are given of the distances,
and class rates from leading points in the Eastern and Central
territories to the points named above in Southern territory and
of the percentage relation borne by rates and distances from
Cincinnati to those from New York.

The complaint in the Chicago case contains similar tabular
statements and charges, made applicable to Chicago, and in
addition calls in question the *reasonableness in themselves* of the
through rates from Chicago to Southern territory by the aver-
ments "that traffic between Chicago and the Southern territory
is through traffic and it is unjust to Chicago that rates from that
point should be exacted by defendants based upon unreasonably
high rates between Cincinnati and other Ohio river crossings

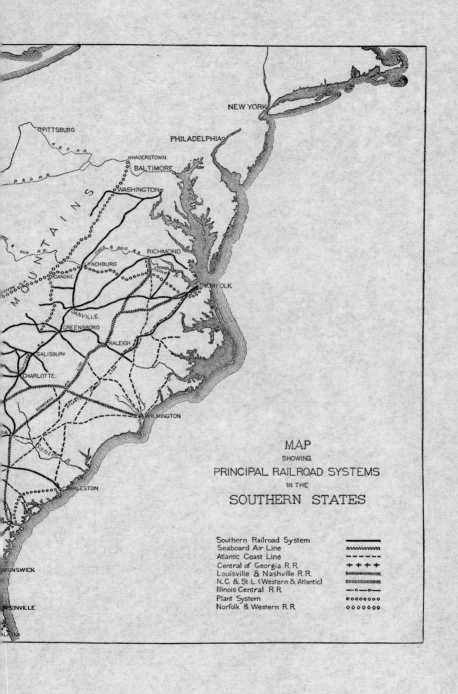

MAP

SHOWING

PRINCIPAL RAILROAD SYSTEMS

IN THE

SOUTHERN STATES

Southern Railroad System	
Seaboard Air Line	
Atlantic Coast Line	
Central of Georgia R. R.	
Louisville & Nashville R.R.	
N. C. & St L. (Western & Atlantic)	
Illinois Central R. R.	
Plant System	
Norfolk & Western R. R.	

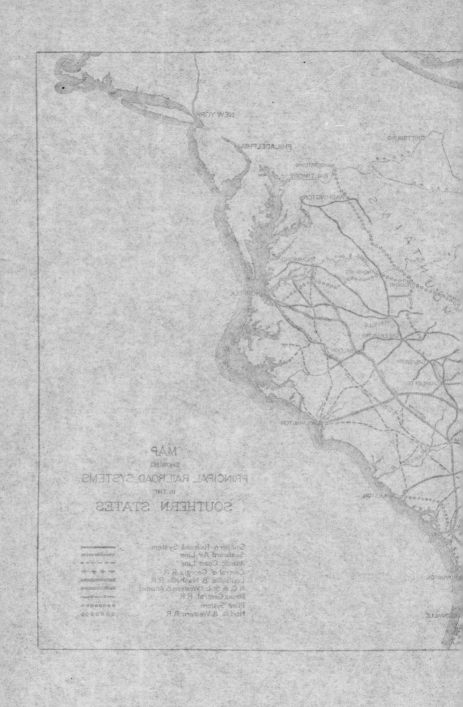

and Southern territory, to which are added substantially the
local rates in effect from Chicago to Cincinnati and said other
Ohio river crossings," and that "if Cincinnati rates are to be
taken as a basis, the rates from Chicago to Southern territory
should be some fair percentage above the rates from Cincinnati,
or some other arbitraries above the Cincinnati rates as the
present New York and Boston rates are above the rates from
Baltimore." It is also alleged that " the same rates are charged
from New York and from Boston to points in Southern territory
whose distances vary more than 500 miles," and it is claimed,
that "if equal rates prevail from points widely separated in
Eastern territory such as New York and Boston to Southern
territory, the same basis should govern in rate making to the
same Southern points from stations in Central territory, such as
Cincinnati and Chicago, which are much nearer together than
New York and Boston." The prayer of the complainants in
both cases is for an order commanding the defendants to desist
from the alleged violations of the Act to Regulate Commerce
and requiring them to so adjust their several freight tariffs as
to afford the merchants and manufacturers of Cincinnati and
Chicago and other points in contiguous territory " a fair and
equal opportunity to deliver their products to consumers in the
South upon such terms of equality compared with their competitors in Eastern Seaboard territory, as their geographical
position, commercial ability and ample transportation facilities
will justify."

In the Cincinnati case answers are filed by the Cincinnati,
New Orleans & Texas Pacific Railway Company *et al.* . . . They
all deny the general charge, that the rates over the respective
lines of transportation from the Central and Eastern Seaboard
territories to Southern territory unjustly discriminate against
Central territory in favor of Eastern Seaboard territory. It is
alleged in substance that the all rail rates from Eastern Seaboard
to Southern territory are determined by the combined rail and
water rates from Boston, New York, Philadelphia and Baltimore
via Steamship lines to Charleston and Savannah and thence by
rail to the interior, and that the rates from Cincinnati and other

points in Central territory are not thus controlled by water competition. The other allegations of the complaint stated above are also denied, and it is claimed by most of the respondents that the transportation in which they, as members of through lines from their respective territories to the South, are engaged, is not *"under a common control, management or arranagement, for a continuous carriage or shipment,"* within the meaning of those words as used in the first section of the Act to Regulate Commerce.

In the Chicago case answers are filed by the following railway companies: the Louisville, New Albany & Chicago, *et al.* . . . These answers present substantially the same issues as are raised in the Cincinnati case. It will be noted, that in addition to the railroad and steamship companies made parties defendants in the Cincinnati case, the complaint in the Chicago case is filed against a number of railroad companies running from Chicago to Cincinnati and other Ohio river points. These roads allege that their " rates are confined to the Ohio river, and that the through rate to any point south of the Ohio river is made by adding their rates to the Ohio (exclusively made by them) to the rates established by the lines south thereof, to the point of destination, over which rates south of the Ohio they neither possess nor exercise any control whatever, either as to the making or enforcement thereof." They also affirm the reasonableness of their rates north of the Ohio.

*   *   *   *   *   *   *   *

Facts

1. The tabular statements mentioned above as being contained in the complaints purporting to show distances and class rates from Cincinnati and Chicago in Central territory and from Boston, New York, Philadelphia and Baltimore, in Eastern Seaboard territory, to the points designated as being in Southern territory, and also giving the percentage relation borne by such distances and rates from Cincinnati and Chicago to those from New York are found to be correct with a few immaterial exceptions. The following are those statements corrected and showing current rates and percentages: [Abridged. — ED.]

TABULAR STATEMENT OF DISTANCES, CURRENT RATES, AND PER-
CENTAGES BETWEEN CINCINNATI AND CHICAGO AND NEW
YORK, PHILADELPHIA, BOSTON AND BALTIMORE AND SOUTH-
ERN POINTS

To KNOXVILLE, TENN.

FROM	DIST.	1	2	3	4	5	6	A	B	C	D	E	F	H
Cincinnati . .	290	76	65	57	47	40	30	20	26	23	19	34	38	33
Chicago . . .	560	116	99	82	64	55	42	32	38	33	29	47	58	48
New York . .	735	100	85	70	55	48	40	36	40	36	36	48	55	72
Philadelphia .	645	108	92	83	71	58	47	34	46	38	37	56	74	66
Boston . . .	948	100	85	70	55	48	40	36	40	36	36	48	72	55
Baltimore . .	549	95	80	65	50	45	37	33	37	33	33	45	66	52
Percentage														
Chic. of N. Y. .	78	116	116	117	116	115	105	89	95	92	81	98	105	67
Cinn. of N. Y. .	39	76	76	81	85	83	75	56	65	64	53	71	69	46

To CHATTANOOGA, TENN.

FROM	DIST.	1	2	3	4	5	6	A	B	C	D	E	F	H
Cincinnati . .	335	76	65	57	47	40	30	20	26	23	19	34	38	33
Chicago . . .	595	116	99	82	64	55	42	32	38	33	29	47	58	48
New York . .	847	114	98	86	73	60	49	36	48	40	39	58	78	68
Philadelphia .	757	108	92	84	71	58	47	34	46	38	37	56	74	66
Boston . . .	1060	114	98	86	73	60	49	36	48	40	39	58	78	68
Baltimore . .	661	106	90	83	70	57	46	33	45	37	36	55	72	65
Percentage														
Chic. of N. Y. .	70	102	101	95	88	92	86	89	79	82	74	81	74	70
Cinn. of N. Y. .	40	67	66	66	64	67	61	56	54	58	49	59	49	49

To ATLANTA, GA.

FROM	DIST.	1	2	3	4	5	6	A	B	C	D	E	F	H
Cincinnati . .	475	107	92	81	68	56	46	28	35	28	24	48	48	53
Chicago . . .	733	147	126	106	85	71	58	40	47	38	34	61	68	68
New York . .	876	114	98	86	73	60	49	36	48	40	39	58	78	68
Philadelphia .	786	114	98	86	73	60	49	36	48	40	39	58	78	68
Boston . . .	1089	114	98	86	73	60	49	36	48	40	39	58	78	68
Baltimore . .	690	107	92	81	68	56	46	34	45	37	36	55	72	65
Percentage														
Chic. of N. Y. .	84	129	128	123	116	118	118	111	98	95	87	105	87	100
Cinn. of N. Y. .	54	94	94	94	93	93	94	78	73	70	62	83	62	78

2. The distances from the Eastern Seaboard cities in the above statements are *all rail*, while the rates are *rail and water*, or based on the rail and water rates ; both the distances and rates from Cincinnati and Chicago are *all rail*. There are a number of steamship lines running from the Eastern Seaboard to Charleston, Savannah and other southern ports, namely, the Ocean Steamship, the Mallory, the Morgan, the Clyde, and the Merchants and Miners ; and the above combined *rail and water* rates appear to be made by adding the rate of the steamer lines to the rate of the rail lines from the ports to interior points. The actual mileage by water from New York to Charleston and Savannah is estimated at about 750 miles, but the rates of the steamer lines are made on the basis of what is termed by the witnesses a "constructive mileage" of 230 miles to Charleston and 250 miles to Savannah, that is, the water rate from New York to Charleston is equal to the rail rate for 230 miles by land, and to Savannah, to the rail rate for 250 miles. The all rail distance from New York to Charleston is 799 miles and to Savannah 914 miles. The following are the distances from Charleston and Savannah by rail to the interior points named :

FROM CHARLESTON TO	MILES	FROM SAVANNAH TO	MILES
Knoxville	533	Knoxville	520
Chattanooga	446	Chattanooga.	433
Atlanta.	308	Atlanta	295
Rome	367	Rome	367
Birmingham	475	Birmingham.	462
Anniston	412	Anniston	399
Selma (*via* E. T. V. & G.) . .	561	Selma (*via* S. F. R. R.) . .	462
Meridian (*via* E. T. V. & G.) .	671	Meridian (*via* E. T. V. & G)	669

The sums of the "constructive" mileages of 230 miles from New York to Charleston and 250 miles to Savannah, plus the actual rail mileages to interior points above given, are shown by the following table :

From N.Y. via Charleston to	Miles	From N.Y. via Savannah to	Miles
Knoxville	763	Knoxville	770
Chattanooga	676	Chattanooga	683
Atlanta	538	Atlanta	545
Rome	597	Rome	617
Birmingham	705	Birmingham	712
Anniston	642	Anniston	649
Selma	791	Selma	712
Meridian	901	Meridian	919

These are what are termed the "rate-making mileages" from New York by water to Charleston and Savannah and thence by rail to the interior points named, upon which the combined *rail and water* rates from New York are based. The rail and water rates from the Eastern Seaboard cities to Southern territory practically control the all rail rates. The all rail rates are the same as the rail and water rates to Knoxville, Chattanooga, Birmingham, Selma and Meridian, but to Rome, Atlanta, Anniston and points east of a line drawn from Chattanooga through Birmingham, Selma and Montgomery to Pensacola, the all rail rates are higher than the rail and water rates by the following differentials.

Classes	1	2	3	4	5	6	A	B	C	D	E	H	F
Differentials in cents	8	6	5	4	3	2	2	2	2	2	3	4	4

3. The lines regularly engaged in the transportation of traffic from Cincinnati, Chicago and contiguous territory, to Southern territory, are *all rail.* There appears to be no through water or rail and water line in regular operation for the transportation of traffic in the numbered classes between those territories. There is a line by lake from Chicago to Buffalo and from that point by rail or canal to New York, which has a *direct* effect on the rail rates between Chicago and the seaboard — particularly the rates on grain and grain products. As to rates on articles of the higher classes, the influence of the water competition does not appear to be so controlling. The rates from Chicago to New

York are the basis of the rates from Central and Trunk Line
territory to the Northeastern seaboard, the latter being percentages of the former, and the water competition by lake and canal
thus *indirectly* exerts an influence upon the rates to the seaboard
from as far south as St. Louis and Cincinnati. Traffic may be
transported by the lake and canal or lake and rail line from
Chicago to New York and thence on the Atlantic to Charleston,
Savannah and other southern ports, and thence by rail to interior
points in Southern territory, and there is evidence tending to
show that in the past, some shipments have been made that way,
but mostly of grain and heavy articles such as are embraced in
Class 6 of the Official Classification and the lettered classes of
the Southern Classification. The traffic shipped from Chicago
by lake to Buffalo and from that point by canal or rail to New
York is principally wheat, corn and other grains, which can be
transferred through an elevator at Buffalo to the canal boat, or
car. If the transportation be continued by ocean to a southern
seaport the same process of transfer is necessary at the seaboard
and these transfers add to the expense. . . .

Merchandise may also be carried from Central territory by
rail to Baltimore and thence by steamer to Charleston, Savannah
and other southern ports for shipment by rail to the interior.
The class rates from Cincinnati to Baltimore are :

Class	1	2	3	4	5	6
Rates in cents per 100 lbs. . . .	62	53½	40½	27½	23	18½

4. The rates on through shipments from Chicago *via* the
Ohio river crossings, Cincinnati, Louisville and Evansville, to
points in Southern territory, are not prorated the entire distance
but are the sum of the regular rate to the Ohio, of the roads
north of that river, plus that of those south. The shipments
are almost invariably, however, under a through bill of lading,
quoting a total through rate (made up as above stated) and
issued at Chicago by the agent of the initial carrier, and the
goods when in car loads are carried through without transfer or

"breaking bulk" at the river. When shipments are in less than car loads, it is stated a transfer is generally made at the river because of the disinclination of the southern roads to pay for the use of cars of other roads. The rates both north and south of the river appear to be influenced to a large extent by competition of the various railway lines, and are not, strictly speaking, local rates. The rates of the roads north of the river are lower per mile than those of the southern roads, this being attributed to the greater volume of tonnage in the territory of the former than in that of the latter. The effect of prorating on a mileage basis the rate from Chicago to points in Southern territory would be to advance the proportion of the lines north of the Ohio and to reduce the proportion of the lines south. The rates for transportation between Chicago and the Ohio are what are known as Trunk Line rates, and are governed by the Official Classification and those for transportation between the Ohio and Southern territory are governed by the Classification of the Southern Railway & Steamship Association. The class rates and distances by the short lines from Chicago to the Ohio river points, Cincinnati, Louisville, and Evansville, and to Cairo, are shown below :

To	Distances	RATES IN CENTS PER 100 POUNDS					
		1	2	3	4	5	6
Cincinnati . . .	298 miles	40	34	25	17	15	12
Louisville . . .	304 "	42	36	27	19	17	14
Evansville . . .	287 "	40	34	25	17	15	12
Cairo	364 "	45	35	25	20	15	12

(The distances and rates from Cincinnati to points in Southern territory, are hereinbefore given in the tables taken from the complaints.)

In the tables of rates which we have given, those containing only the six numbered classes are under the Official Classification, which is applied east of Chicago and the Mississippi and north of the Ohio and Potomac rivers, and those embracing also lettered classes are under the Classification of the Southern Railway & Steamship Association, which applies south of the Ohio and Potomac and east of the Mississippi rivers. As above stated, grain and grain products fall under Class 6 of the Official Classification; in the Southern Classification, grain and its products and heavy freight are in the lettered classes. Manufactures and costly commodities are in the higher classes.

5. It appears from tariffs on file with the Commission that there were in existence when the Interstate Commerce Law was passed and up to April 17, 1893, through rates from New York *via* Cincinnati to Chattanooga, Meridian and Birmingham, less than the sum of the rates to Cincinnati and the rates thence on to those cities, and there are such rates still in effect to Nashville, Memphis, Mobile, and a number of Mississippi river points.

Those through rates to Chattanooga, Meridian, and Birmingham, were as follows :

1	2	3	4	5	6
114	98	86	73	60	49

The following are the rates from New York to Cincinnati :

1	2	3	4	5	6
65	57	44	30	26	22

* * * * * * * *

9. All the defendants (including the steamship lines) in the Cincinnati case are also defendants in the Chicago case and are for the most part members of the Southern Railway & Steamship Association. The latter case, as before stated, embraces as defendants, in addition to those in the former, roads north of the Ohio participating in the transportation of traffic from Central territory to that river. *None of these are members of the Southern Railway & Steamship Association except the Illinois Central Railroad*, which, as we have seen, extends into territory south of the Ohio. This Association is composed of

transportation lines (including the steamship lines from northeastern cities to southern ports) engaged in the traffic of the
territory south of the Potomac and Ohio rivers and east of the
Mississippi, and the rates involved in these cases from both Eastern and Central to Southern territory are established and maintained under its rules and regulations. As to the origin of this
Association,[1] it is set forth in a report of March 4, 1891, by
Commissioner Wilson to the Cincinnati Freight Bureau (which
report was put in evidence), that " subsequent to the close of
the war and closely following the reëstablishment of transportation lines and through rates into the South, there arose lively
competition between what are known as Eastern Coastwise Lines
and the Western lines which reached the South from the West
via Ohio and Mississippi river gateways. Each commenced
operations in the territory of the other, and while corn from
Chicago was carried *via* Boston and Charleston to Atlanta and
Chattanooga, the manufactured products of the East were not
infrequently brought west *via* Cincinnati and Louisville, or Chicago and Cairo, for delivery to southern destinations. Rate
wars were much more fierce and frequent than they are now.
It was to check competition of this character and to protect
the revenues of transportation lines generally that the Southern
Railway & Steamship Association was established."

The records of proceedings of the Association from as far
back as 1878 and up to January 14, 1892, have been introduced in evidence. From these records, it appears that in
1878, the roads leading south from Chicago, St. Louis, Cincinnati, Louisville and other western cities (then combined in
an organization known as the " Green Line ") met in convention with the steamer lines from eastern cities and the roads
south of the Potomac engaged in the transportation of eastern
traffic. At this meeting its object was disclosed to be " to protect to the Green Line Roads *the business which is peculiar to
the Northwest* and to the Eastern lines, the *business peculiar to
their territory*, and to maintain equal rates on business common
to the two sections." The Green Line rates appear to have then

---

[1] *Vide*, Chapter V.

been advanced and the rates of the two systems of carriers adjusted with a view to the transportation by western lines of *western products* (that is, products from territory west of Pittsburg and east of the Mississippi and between the Ohio and the lakes) and the transportation by eastern lines of *eastern manufactures.*

Up to 1885 this adjustment of rates appears to have been the means employed to carry out the above-stated object of the convention of 1878. In 1885 a division of territory was established and a provision was inserted in the agreement for that year requiring the exaction of local rates by the eastern and western lines, with a view to the protection to those lines, respectively (so far as it was possible in that way), of what is termed " the revenue derived by them from transportation."

By a resolution adopted by the Executive Committee of the Association in April, 1885, it was provided in connection with the division of territory above referred to that " in case eastern lines take western business or western lines take eastern business, they are to pay the *pool* the entire revenue accruing thereon from points of junction with Association roads, to be given to the lines composing the eastern or western lines as the case may be." The agreement of that year and those of subsequent years up to at least as late a date as that of the agreement which terminated July 1, 1887, make provision for such pooling or as it is termed " actual apportionment." In those agreements two methods of apportionment are provided for — namely, apportionment of *tonnage* and apportionment of *revenue.* Subsequent agreements do not so distinctly provide for pooling, but in the last agreement introduced in evidence (that of January 14, 1892), it is declared that " the principle of an apportionment of business subject to arbitration shall be recognized in the operation of the Association so far as this can be *lawfully* done." Provision is, also, made in that and the last agreement entered into since the hearing in these cases, for raising a fund for payment of what are termed fines for violations of the agreement, as will hereinafter appear.

The provisions as to division of territory and the exaction of local rates have been carried forward in the various agreements entered into from 1885 to the present time. The last agreement introduced in evidence is that dated, January 14, 1892, and it is substantially the same as those of preceding years as far back as 1885. Its clauses as to the exaction of local rates and division of territory are as follows :

Art. II, sec. 2. For the mutual protection of the various interests, and for the purpose of securing the greatest amount of net revenue to all the companies parties to this agreement, it is agreed that what are termed western lines shall protect the revenue derived from transportation by what are known as eastern lines, *under the rates as fixed by this Association*, so far as can be done by the exaction of local rates, and that eastern lines shall in like manner protect *like* revenue of western lines.

Sec. 3. That a line from Buffalo through Salamanca, Pittsburg, Wheeling and Parkersburg, to Huntington, West Virginia, be made the dividing line between eastern and western lines for the territory hereinafter outlined. That the western lines shall not make joint rates from points east of that line for any points east of a line drawn from Chattanooga through Birmingham, Selma and Montgomery to Pensacola.

Sec. 4. The eastern lines, including the Richmond & Danville railroad *via* Strasburg or points east of Strasburg, and the East Tennessee, Virginia & Georgia Railway *via* Bristol, shall not make joint rates on traffic from points west of that line (Buffalo, etc.) to any points on or west of a line drawn from Chattanooga through Athens, Augusta and Macon, to Live Oak, Florida.

Sec. 5. The traffic from Buffalo through Salamanca, Pittsburg, Wheeling and Parkersburg to Huntington, West Virginia, and points on that line, to and east of Chattanooga, Calera and Selma, shall be carried by either the eastern or western lines only at such rates as may be agreed upon.

Sec. 6. It is understood that the eastern and western lines will coöperate in the enforcement of the 3d and 4th sections of this second article.

The objects of the Association as alleged in the preamble to this agreement, are " the establishment and maintenance of tariffs of uniform rates, to prevent unjust discrimination such as necessarily arises from the irregular and fluctuating rates which inevitably attend the separate and independent action of transportation lines " and the securing as to business in which the carriers have a common interest " a proper co-relation of rates, such as will protect the *interests of competing markets* without unjust discriminations in favor of or against any city or section."

*   *   *   *   *   *   *   *

The agreement provides for an annual convention of the representatives of the several companies, members of the Association, at which each company shall have one vote, two thirds of the whole vote of the members present being required to make the action of the convention binding. At this meeting, among other business to be transacted, there are to be elected a President, a Commissioner, a Secretary and three Arbitrators. The members of the Association are each required to designate a representative, authorized " to represent them in all matters of business with the Association or its members," and the representatives so designated constitute an " Executive Board." The " Executive Board," it is provided, " shall have jurisdiction over all matters relating to traffic covered by the agreement, but shall act only by *unanimous consent* of all its members " and " in the event of failure to agree, the questions at issue shall be settled by the Board of Arbitration." The " Executive Board " are authorized " at their discretion to appoint *Rate Committees* and other subcommittees, either of their own number or from among the officers and agents of the Companies; members of the Association." It is provided that, " with a view to a proper relative adjustment of all rates, and especially a proper relative adjustment of rates on similar articles from the East and West to common territory, the *Rate Committees* shall have *sole authority to make all rates and classifications on all traffic covered by the agreement*, subject to decision of the Commissioner, the Executive Board or Board of Arbitration in case such Rate Committees cannot agree." If the " Rate Committees " fail or omit to make rates, the Commissioner is given authority to make such rates, so that, it is stated, " there shall be properly authenticated tariffs of rates on all traffic covered by the agreement." The subcommittees appointed by the " Executive Board " can " only act by *unanimous consent*, and failing to agree, the questions at issue may, upon demand of any member, be referred to the Executive Board for action at their next meeting, and such questions may be submitted direct to the Board of Arbitration, when so authorized by a majority of the Executive Board. The decisions of the Board of Arbitration are made " final and conclusive on all questions which may be submitted to them under the agreement or by consent of the parties." The Commissioner is Chairman of the Executive Board, and also of the subcommittees and is authorized to represent absent members of subcommittees as well as of the Executive Board, and " during the interim between the reference of any matter of difference from a subcommittee to the Executive Board and the final determination of such matter," he is given authority " if he deem it a matter requiring prompt action, to decide it temporarily " and his decision is made " binding on all parties until reversed by the Executive Board or by arbitration ; " he is declared to be " the chief executive officer of the Association, and as a representative of its members, both *severally and jointly*," is empowered to " act for them in all matters which come within the jurisdiction of the Association, in conformity with the requirements of the agreement and the instructions of the Executive Board and subcommittees, but *exercising his discretion in all cases* which are not provided for either by the agreement or by the Executive Board and committees acting under its authority and sanction ; " and he is also authorized " to reduce the rates when necessary to meet the competition of lines or roads not parties to the agreement and at the same time to make corresponding reductions from other points from which relative rates are made," and is given " such authority over the traffic officers and their subordinates and over the accounting departments of the parties to the agreements as may be necessary to enforce its terms relative to the maintenance of rates." When rates have been fixed under the provisions of the agreement by the Rate Committees, the Commissioner, the Executive Board or by arbitration, there is to be " no reduction from such rates without the consent of the Commissioner " and in all cases changes therein are to be made by the Rate Committees or the Commissioner. The agreement declares " that the maintenance of rates as established under the rules of the Association is of its very essence and that the parties thereto pledge themselves to require all their connections to maintain such rates, and in the event of any company or line, or its connections, not members of the Association, failing to conform to this obligation, the other parties in interest *pledge themselves to increase their proportion of through rates sufficiently to protect the authorized rate whenever required by the Commissioner, to do so ;* " and further, that it is "one of the fundamental principles of the agreement that no party thereto shall take *separate* action in any matter affecting the interests of one or more of the other parties, contrary to the spirit and intent of the agreement," and that "all measures necessary to carry out the purpose of the agreement shall be taken *jointly* by the parties thereto." In cases of violation of the agreement, the Board of Arbitration, after hearing, is required to "impose such penalties therefor as it may deem proper and necessary to secure the maintenance of the rates of the Association." These penalties are to be enforced by the Commissioner, and "in order to provide for the prompt payment of any fines that may be assessed against any member of the Association for violating its rules, each company is required to deposit with the Commissioner an amount equivalent to five dollars ($5.00) for each mile of the road operated by said company under the provisions of the agreement, or in case a company operates a water line, five dollars ($5.00) for each mile allowed as a prorating distance in the division of through rates — provided such amounts shall not exceed the sum of five thousand dollars ($5000.00) for any one company." Of this fund thus raised it is provided, that "any surplus over and above the *amount that may be awarded by the Board of Arbitration to indemnify any members for losses sustained* shall be applied to the payment of the expenses of the Association."

The agreement now in force (made July 14, 1893, since the hearings in these cases) extends the territorial line commencing at Buffalo and terminating at Huntington to "Toronto on the north shore of Lake Ontario, through Lewiston and Niagara Falls," and provides that points on this line (from Toronto to Huntington) "shall be common to lines through the eastern and western gateways, together with such points adjacent thereto from which the rates shall be the same as from the points above named" (points on said line) "through the gateways of Cincinnati and Louisville, the Rate Committees to agree upon the common points adjacent to said line." To the clause requiring members of the Association " to increase their proportions of through rates sufficiently to protect the authorized rates " in the event of any company or line or its connections not members of the Association failing to conform to the rates established by the Association, it adds the further requirement, that they (members of the Association interested) shall " *apply full local rates upon all traffic subject to the Association Agreement coming from or going to such offending lines, when required by the Commissioner to do so.*" The clause requiring the Board of Arbitration in cases of violations of the Agreement by any member, to impose " such penalties therefor as it may deem proper and necessary to secure the *maintenance of the rates of the Association*," is altered so as to read " such penalties therefor as it may deem proper and *commensurate with the injuries inflicted upon the Association and of competing lines parties to this Agreement.*" The other material terms of this agreement are substantially the same as those of the agreement of January 14, 1892, above given.

* * * * * * * *

10. At the convention of the eastern and western lines in 1878, it was announced by Mr. Peck, General Manager of the Southern Railway & Steamship Association, that the western lines " concede that the transportation of manufactured articles into the territory embraced by the Association should be left to the eastern lines and undertake by *prohibitory* rates to prevent such articles from eastern cities reaching Association points over their lines." Accordingly a basis of rates was then adopted, by which rates on the western lines for " articles peculiar to the East" were to be at least 10 cents higher than the rates on the eastern lines and rates on eastern lines for " western products " were to be at least 10 cents higher than the rates on western lines. At the time of this adjustment it appears that the west (or Central territory) contributed " principally food products in the solid and liquid forms of corn, bacon, flour, whiskey, etc.," for southern consumption, while "manufactured articles and notions " came for the most part from the Eastern Seaboard. These conditions have, however, materially changed ; " the cen-

ters of food production have moved westward" and Central territory has engaged much more extensively in manufacturing enterprises. In the Annual Report made to the Southern Railway & Steamship Association by its Commissioner, July 6, 1889, he says: "Formerly, agricultural products constituted a large excess of the western business, but the proportion of miscellaneous commodities—traffic formerly from the East—is steadily growing from the West. Especially is this true in all manufactured articles of wood, such as furniture, wagons, carriages of all kinds, etc., and manufactures from the cheap grades of iron from the South, such as stoves, agricultural implements, etc." Central territory has also entered upon the manufacture on a large scale and shipment South of boots, shoes, clothing, saddlery, harness and other articles of general merchandise. It is estimated that manufactures in Central territory have increased 100 per cent in twenty years.

These manufactured articles are shipped south from Central territory under the rates applied to the numbered classes in the Southern Railway & Steamship Association Classification, and bagging, ties, grain (and its products including liquors) and packing-house products are shipped under the rates applied to the lettered classes. The testimony is to the effect that articles falling within the lettered classes are of more general consumption in the Southern territory than those in the numbered classes. No reliable data is furnished as to the proportion the south-bound tonnage of the former bears to that of the latter, but it appears to be much larger. In their reports on file with the Commission the railways do not give separately the south-bound and north-bound tonnage, but it appears that boots, shoes, clothing, wooden ware, furniture, saddlery, harness, groceries and "everything that goes under the head of general merchandise" constituted in 1891 not quite 25 per cent of the total south-bound tonnage of the Cincinnati, New Orleans & Texas Pacific Road, and that bagging, ties, grain (and its products) and packing-house products, "covered the bulk of the business south-bound."

Articles in the numbered classes manufactured in Wisconsin, Michigan, Illinois, Indiana and Ohio, are sold as far east as

Rochester and Albany, New York, as far west as the Pacific coast, and to a greater or less extent over the South from Texas and Arkansas to the Virginias. The testimony tends to show that in the Southeast, in the territory embracing Alabama, East Tennessee, Florida, Georgia, the Carolinas and Virginias, and particularly at points near the Atlantic coast, the merchants and manufacturers of Central territory meet with strong competition in the sale of these goods from New York and the other Eastern Seaboard cities. They do not appear to be driven out of this territory altogether by this competition, but their business and the profit on it are not so great as a general rule as in other markets reached by them. In some instances they are required by their customers to " equalize the rates," or in other words, to refund the excess of the rates on their goods over those on goods of the same kind and class from Eastern Seaboard territory.

11. L. R. Brockenborough, General Freight Agent of the Chicago & Eastern Illinois Railway Company (whose road runs from Chicago to the Ohio at Evansville) stated that " his impression (is) that the general impression seems to be that the rates from the Central territory into Southern territory are out of line with those from the seaboard," and that his road "would be willing to reduce its rate to bring the through rate in line with the New York rate." John C. Gault, General Manager of the Queen & Crescent System (in which are defendants, the Cincinnati, New Orleans & Texas Pacific and the Alabama Great Southern Companies) stated that he " always thought rates from Chicago to southern points on higher classes ought to be the same as those from Boston and New York ; " and that this " would not harm New York and hardly be enough in favor of the west." He also, under date of August 14, 1888, wrote to the Commissioner of the Chicago Board of Trade, that " the roads interested in Chicago business ought in my (his) judgment to take such action as is necessary to insure a reduction of the rates " from the West. M. C. Markham, Assistant Traffic Manager of the Illinois Central R.R. Co., testified that he had made an effort to have the Southern Railway & Steamship

Association reduce the rates from Central territory, and said, " Looking at the disparity between the rates from Eastern and Central territories, it appears there might be in them an element of unfairness to the latter. If it is true, that rates from Eastern territory into the southeast were made on account of water competition along the Atlantic seaboard, and if all rail lines leading from the East into that territory can afford to carry the goods for those rates made by water lines, then the western through lines *could afford to carry for the same rates a less distance*, provided all conditions governing the matter were equal." S. R. Knott, Traffic Manager of the Louisville & Nashville Road in a letter to G. J. Grammar of April 14, 1890, wrote that " While the adjustment may be *unfair, as we think it is*, yet it can hardly be said to be arbitrary or wholly unreasonable ; " and that his company, "together with other lines interested in western traffic, then members of the Southern Railway & Steamship Association, urged a modification of the difference " (between eastern and western rates) " and succeeded in having the matter brought, under the rules of the Association, before the Board of Arbitration;" and that " the question was fully presented from both sides of the case and the decision of the Board at that time (May, 1888) was that the best protection of *all interests* did not warrant the change in the adjustment of rates which we, with the other western lines, had requested, that is, changing the adjustment from Ohio river points and points north as compared with the rates from eastern cities." B. E. Hand, Assistant General Freight Agent of the Michigan Central Road, stated that he had made " repeated efforts with railroads operating in Southern territory for a reduction of rates on manufactures from the West to the Southeast." G. J. Grammar, Chairman of the Central Traffic Association's Committee on relations with southern roads, in a letter to N. G. Iglehart, of April 2, 1890, says, " All our efforts thus far have been unavailing to get the southern roads to more justly equalize the rates. You doubtless understand southern roads' rates from the Ohio river are arbitrary, their rates on all classes south-bound being from 50 to 100 per cent greater per mile than by lines north of the River on similar traffic." In a letter, dated April 8, 1890, to S. R. Knott, he says, "The injustice of the present basis of rates" (from the Ohio) "must of necessity be apparent."

Conclusions

The principal charge in both cases it is stated is based on the first paragraph of section 3 of the Act to Regulate Commerce, which declares,

"That it shall be unlawful for any common carrier subject to the provisions of this Act to make or give any undue or unreasonable preference or advantage to any particular person, company, firm, corporation, or locality, or any particular description of traffic, in any respect whatsoever, or to subject any person, company, firm, corporation or locality, or any particular description of traffic, to any undue or unreasonable prejudice or disadvantage in any respect whatsoever."

The specific ground of complaint under this charge is in substance that the rates on *manufactured* goods from Eastern Seaboard territory to Southern territory, and those on the same classes of goods from Central territory to Southern territory, are so fixed or adjusted with reference to each other as to give to merchants and manufacturers in Eastern Seaboard territory an "undue or unreasonable preference or advantage" over those in Central territory, and consequently subject the latter to "an undue or unreasonable prejudice or disadvantage" with respect to the former, when they meet in competition in the southern markets.

*   *   *   *   *   *   *   *

The reasonableness in themselves of the rates from Central territory is a matter material to the issue raised by the charge in both cases, that the relation between those rates and the eastern rates is *unjustly* prejudicial to Central territory, and the question is directly presented in the Chicago case by the allegation that the rates from Cincinnati and other Ohio river crossings to Southern territory are "unreasonably high." Where the reasonableness of rates is in question, comparison may be made, not only with rates on another line of the same carrier, but also with those on the lines of other and distinct carriers—

the value of the comparison being dependent in all cases upon the *degree* of similarity of circumstances and conditions attending the transportation for which the rates compared are charged. It appears from the tabular statements in our findings of fact, giving *all rail* distances and class rates from Cincinnati and Chicago in Central territory and from New York and other northeastern cities, to points in Southern territory, that on a *mileage* basis the rates from the former (particularly, those on the higher or numbered classes) are largely in excess of those from the latter. For the purpose of illustration the following table is given, which shows the current rates on goods of Class 1 from Cincinnati and Chicago and from New York to points named in Southern territory, and what the rates from Cincinnati and Chicago would be on the basis of the (all rail) mileage rates from New York:

To	CURRENT CLASS 1 RATES			RATES ON BASIS OF MILEAGE RATES FROM NEW YORK	
	From Cincinnati	From Chicago	From New York	From Cincinnati	From Chicago
Knoxville	76	116	100	39	78
Chattanooga	76	116	114	45	79
Rome	107	147	114	51	83
Atlanta	107	147	114	61	95
Meridian	122	134	124	62	71
Birmingham	89	119	114	54	75
Anniston	107	147	114	57	85
Selma	108	138	114	62	78

The excess of the Class 1 rates in the above table from Cincinnati and Chicago over the New York rates from a mileage standpoint is, as follows:

To	FROM CINCINNATI	FROM CHICAGO	To	FROM CINCINNATI	FROM CHICAGO
Knoxville . .	37	38	Meridian . .	60	63
Chattanooga .	31	37	Birmingham	35	44
Rome . . .	56	64	Anniston .	50	62
Atlanta . .	46	52	Selma . .	46	60

As to the other *numbered* classes and the other northeastern cities, the relation or difference between the two sets of rates is to a large extent substantially the same as shown in the above tables.

Many striking disparities in rates will be observed on an inspection of the tabular statements of rates and distances in our findings of facts, and particularly, in the Class 1 rates from Chicago, on the one hand, and Boston and New York, on the other — the latter two cities being given for the most part the same rates. For example, while the distance from Chicago to Chattanooga is 595 miles, and from Boston and New York, respectively, 1060 and 847 miles, the rate from Chicago is 116 cents and from Boston and New York, 114 cents, and while the distance from Chicago to Meridian, Miss., is 723 miles and from Boston and New York, respectively, 1355 and 1142 miles, the rate from Chicago is 134 cents, and from Boston and New York, 124 cents. Under the rate last named, a shipper of a car load of 25000 pounds, of Class 1 goods from Boston and New York to Meridian would pay $25.00 less than a shipper of a like car load from Chicago, notwithstanding the relative proximity of the latter city to the common point of destination. (Up to March 16, 1894, the rate from New York and Boston to Meridian was 114 cents.) Further examples of similar import might be taken from the tabular statements of rates and distances, but the above are deemed sufficient.

*   *   *   *   *   *   *   *

The plea that the all rail lines from northeastern cities to Southern territory are subjected to water competition *via* the Atlantic and that this competition has naturally a controlling influence on their rates, is sustained by the proof.

*   *   *   *   *   *   *   *

The defendants in their proof have furnished a measure or given *their estimate* of the influence of the water competition from the northeastern cities to the southeastern ports. It is that, while the distance by water from New York to Charleston and Savannah is approximately 750 miles, the rates by the steamer lines are made on the basis of what is termed a " constructive mileage " of 230 miles to Charleston and 250 miles to Savannah, or, in other words, the water rate from New York to Charleston is equal to the rail rate for 230 miles by land, and to Savannah, to the rail rate for 250 miles by land. These " constructive mileages " plus the actual distances by rail from those ports to interior points in Southern territory are called the " rate-making mileages," upon which the combined rail and water rates from New York to the interior points are based. As is claimed by defendants, the proof tends to show that the rail and water rates regulate the all rail rates, and the rail and water and all rail rates are the same to all the points named in Southern territory except *Rome*, *Anniston* and *Atlanta*, to which the all rail rates are higher than the rail and water by certain differentials ranging from 2 to 8 cents per 100 pounds as appears from our findings of facts. A comparison of these " rate-making mileages " (rail and water) with the all rail distances from New York to southern points may be instructive as indicating the *estimate by the roads* of the extent of the influence of water competition on the eastern rates. Those " mileages " (*via* Charleston) and all rail distances are given in the following table :

To	FROM NEW YORK	
	All Rail Distances	" Rate-making Mileages " *via* Charleston — Rail and Water
Knoxville	735 miles	763 miles
Chattanooga	847 "	676 "
Rome	925 "	597 "
Atlanta	876 "	538 "
Meridian	1142 "	901 "
Birmingham	990 "	705 "
Anniston	949 "	642 "
Selma	1080 "	791 "

From the following table a comparison may be made of the " rate-making mileages," rail and water, from New York to southern points, with the actual all rail distances from Cincinnati and Chicago to the same.

To	FROM NEW YORK "Rate-making Mileages" *via* Charleston — Rail and Water	FROM CHICAGO All Rail Distances	FROM CINCINNATI All Rail Distances
Knoxville	763 miles	560 miles	290 miles
Chattanooga . . .	676 "	595 "	335 "
Rome	597 "	673 "	413 "
Atlanta	538 "	733 "	475 "
Meridian	901 "	723 "	630 "
Birmingham . . .	705 "	652 "	478 "
Anniston	642 "	715 "	476 "
Selma	791 "	746 "	598 "

It will be seen from the above table that the "rate-making mileages" from New York, *which are arrived at by an allowance for the estimated effect of water competition — the estimate being that of the defendants,* are greater than the actual all-rail distances from Chicago, as follows: to Knoxville, by 203 miles; to Chattanooga, by 81 miles; to Meridian, by 178 miles; to Birmingham, by 53 miles; and to Selma, by 45 miles. They are less to Rome by 76 miles, to Anniston by 73 miles and to Atlanta by 195 miles. They are in every instance much greater than the distances by rail from Cincinnati. The all rail distances from Cincinnati and Chicago are the following percentages of the "rate-making mileage" from New York:

To	FROM CINCINNATI	FROM CHICAGO
Knoxville	38%	73%
Chattanooga	50	88
Rome	69	112
Atlanta	88	136
Meridian	70	80
Birmingham	68	92
Anniston	74	111
Selma	80	94

On the above basis — that is, making the rates from Cincinnati and Chicago the same percentages of the current New York

rates as the distances by rail from the former cities are of the
" rate-making mileages " from the latter — the rates from Cincinnati will be materially less than they now are on the *numbered* classes in all cases and also from Chicago, *except those to
Atlanta and those on classes 4, 5, and 6 to Birmingham and 4
and 6 to Chattanooga.* They will also be less to a large, but
not so great an extent, on the lettered classes. It thus appears
that, giving full weight to the claim of defendants that water
competition *via* the Atlantic necessitates rates from the East
relatively lower than those from the West and as a consequence
rates from the West relatively higher than those from the East,
it does not with the exceptions above named account for or
justify the existing disparity between them.

The evidence shows that the rates from Eastern Seaboard and
Central territories, respectively, were adjusted with reference to
each other by mutual agreement between the eastern and western carriers through the medium of the Southern Railway &
Steamship Association and that in making this adjustment *other
considerations* than those of water competition, or other dissimilarity of circumstances or condition affecting transportation, had
a controlling influence. It appears that lively competition resulting in rate wars had arisen between the eastern and western lines
in the transportation into the South by each of traffic from territory claimed by the other. This led to the convention in 1878
(referred to in our statement of facts) of the carriers interested,
the object of which was stated to be the establishment of such
a co-relation of rates as would " protect to the eastern lines the
business peculiar to their territory" and to the western lines (then
known as the " Green Line Roads ") the business relating to
" *their peculiar commodities* "— in other words, to secure to the
eastern lines the transportation of " articles manufactured in the
East, and in other countries and imported into eastern cities,
embraced under the general terms of dry goods, groceries, crockery and hardware " and classified for the most part under the
first four of the numbered classes, and to the western lines,
the transportation of " articles of western produce, comprising
the produce of animals and the field " and embraced principally

in the lettered classes. The only way to accomplish this result through the agency of rate adjustment or manipulation was to place relatively high rates on manufactured articles and relatively low rates on food products shipped from or *via* the West, and *vice versa*, as to such shipments from or *via* the East ; and at the opening of the convention, Mr. Peck, the General Manager of the Association, being called on by the chairman to state its object, said among other things, that the western lines conceded that the transportation of manufactured articles "into the territory embraced by the Southern Railway & Steamship Association should be left to the eastern lines, and *undertake by prohibitory rates to prevent such articles from eastern cities reaching the Association points over their lines.*" A basis of rates, at least ten cents higher by the eastern lines than the western on western products and at least ten cents higher by the western lines than the eastern on "articles peculiar to the East," was then adopted, with a view to effecting the announced object of the convention. It is manifest that at that time the influence of water competition on the eastern rates was not regarded as a controlling factor in determining what the excess of the western should be over the eastern rates on manufactured goods and the reasonableness in themselves of those western rates was a matter of secondary, if any, consideration. While there have since been fluctuations and changes in the two sets of rates, the principle regulating their co-relation or adjustment with reference to each other has remained practically the same to the present time. The leading idea of securing to each system of carriers the traffic of what is termed its territory by the adjustment and manipulation of rates and in other ways, is prominent throughout all the Association Agreements. In the last, as in those preceding, it distinctly appears, and the provisions, among others, for a geographical division of territory, for the exaction of local rates to protect Association rates, and for penalties, all look to this end. It is, also, apparent on an inspection of the current rates themselves, which disclose the broad distinction made between the rates on the numbered and lettered classes — the relation between the two sets of rates on the former being advantageous to the East, while that between the rates on the latter are not nearly so favorable to that territory. As a fair illustration, the rates from Chicago to Chattanooga on the lettered classes are from seventy to eighty-nine per cent of the New York rates, while on the numbered classes 1, 2 and 3, — they are respectively, 102, 101 and 95 per cent. It is true, rates upon the heavy and cheap articles in the lettered classes should be less than rates upon the comparatively light weighted and valuable articles in the numbered classes, because, as respects the latter, the value of the service to the shipper and the risk to the carrier are greater. These considerations, however, apply equally to shipments of traffic from both territories, and do not, therefore, justify or account for the distinction to which we have just adverted. The fact, that the tonnage of traffic in the lettered classes from Central territory is larger than of traffic in the numbered classes, and doubtless, also, larger than the tonnage of traffic in the lettered classes from Eastern territory is not in our opinion sufficient to authorize or account for the great difference apparent on the face of the tariffs. This difference finds a natural solution in the avowed purposes of the Southern Railway & Steamship Association to secure, by an adjustment of rates calculated to bring about that result, the transportation by the eastern lines of goods in the numbered classes from the territory set apart as theirs and to the western lines the transportation of traffic in the lettered classes from the territory apportioned to them.

The relation established between the eastern and western rates in 1878 was, doubtless, suggested by, and found a plausible pretext in, the fact that at that time the West contributed principally articles in the lettered classes for southern consumption, while goods in the numbered classes came for the most part from the East. The situation in this respect has, however, as appears from our statement of facts, materially changed, and it is estimated that the manufacture in Central territory of goods in the numbered classes has increased 100 per cent in twenty years. If, therefore, the condition as to manufactures and products in 1878 could have been set up in justification of

the adjustment of rates then made, that justification no longer
exists and the change in those conditions is an argument in favor
of a corresponding change in the rate adjustment. We are of opinion, however, that the situation in 1878 in the respect named constituted no justification. The tendency of such an adjustment
of rates was to encourage and build up manufactures in the
East and discourage and retard them in the West and thus maintain the *status quo.* In this connection may be noticed the claim
of the defendants, that the great growth in Central territory of
the manufacture and sale of articles in the numbered classes
shows that the rates in question to Southern territory have not
been prejudicial to manufacturers and shippers in Central territory. This does not appear to be a legitimate inference in view
of the fact that Central territory is not limited to Southern territory as a market, but also sells its manufactures and products
as far west as the Pacific coast, as far east as Rochester and
Albany, and in the Southwest. The proof is that the shipments
of goods in the numbered classes from Central to Southern territory (the Southeast) are small in comparison with those of goods
in the lettered classes and this may be, in part at least, due to
the rate adjustment complained of. If the fact, that one section
is a large producer and another a small producer of certain
classes of traffic, is a factor to be considered in fixing rates from
them to a common market, which is not conceded, it would seem
that it should operate to give more favorable rates to the latter
with a view of stimulating and increasing its production. Considerations of this character, however, if they are to be allowed
any weight by carriers in fixing rates from rival territories,
should always be held in strict subordination to the invariable
rule, that in all cases rates shall be reasonable in themselves.
No departure from this rule can be justified on the ground, that
it is necessary in order to maintain existing trade relations, or
to "protect the interests of competing markets," or to "equalize
commercial conditions," or to secure to carriers traffic from certain
territory assumed to be exclusively theirs. It is not the duty of
carriers, nor is it proper, that they undertake by adjustment of
rates or otherwise to impair or neutralize the natural commercial

advantages resulting from location or other favorable condition of one territory in order to put another territory on an equal footing with it in a common market. Each locality competing with others in a common market is entitled to reasonable and just rates at the hands of the carriers serving it and to the benefit of all its natural advantages. *James & M. Buggy Co.* v. *Cincinnati N. O. & T. P. R. Co.*, 3 Inters. Com. Rep. 682, 4 I. C. C. Rep. 744; *Raworth* v. *Northern Pac. R. Co.*, 3 Inters. Com. Rep. 857, 5 I. C. C. Rep. 234; *Eau Claire Board of Trade* v. *Chicago, M. & St. P. R. Co.*, 4 Inters. Com. Rep. 65, 5 I. C. C. Rep. 264; *Chamber of Commerce of Minneapolis* v. *Great Northern R. Co.*, 4 Inters. Com. Rep. 230, 5 I. C. C. Rep. 571. If this result in prejudice to one and advantage to another, it is not the *undue* prejudice or advantage forbidden by the statute, but flows naturally from conditions *beyond the legitimate sphere of legal or other regulation.* "Carriers," moreover, "in making rates cannot arrange them from an exclusive regard to their own interests, but must respect the interests of those who may have occasion to employ their services, and *subordinate their own interests to the rules of relative equality and justice which the Act prescribes.*" (Second Annual Report.) The provision in the Association Agreements for the "*exaction* of local rates " to "protect" to each system of carriers the revenue which would come to them, respectively, under a strict enforcement of Association rates and under the division of territory between them, is stated to be for "the purpose," among others, " of securing the *greatest amount of net revenue* to *all* the companies parties to the agreement." This is, doubtless, the *controlling* consideration. The interests of the public, certainly, cannot be subserved in this way. The division of territory is wholly without warrant in law and is practically a denial to shippers in such territory of the right to ship their goods or produce to market by the line or route they may prefer. The exaction of higher rates on certain articles shipped from Central to Southern territory *than would otherwise prevail,* for the purpose of securing to eastern lines the transportation of that traffic from territory apportioned to them, is manifestly unlawful, and results in injury to both Central and Southern territory.

RATES PER TON PER MILE ON THE NUMBERED CLASSES FROM CHICAGO
TO CINCINNATI

1	2	3	4	5	6
2 68 cents	2 28 cents	1 68 cents	1 14 cents	1 00 cents	80 cents

RATES PER TON PER MILE ON THE NUMBERED CLASSES FROM CINCINNATI

To	1	2	3	4	5	6
	Cents	Cents	Cents	Cents	Cents	Cents
Knoxville . .	5 24	4 48	3 93	3 24	2 75	2 06
Chattanooga .	4 53	3 88	3 40	2 80	2 38	1 79
Rome . . .	5 18	4 45	3 92	3 29	2 71	2 22
Atlanta . . .	4 50	3 87	3 41	2 86	2 35	1 93
Meridian . .	3 87	3 23	2 82	2 38	1 96	1 71
Birmingham .	3 72	3 30	2 84	2 30	1 96	1 50
Anniston . .	4 49	3 86	3 40	2 85	2 35	1 93
Selma . . .	3 61	3 41	2 94	2 37	1 97	1 57

The fact, which clearly appears, that rates on the numbered classes from Central territory are made *higher than they otherwise would* be, for the purpose of securing to the eastern lines the transportation of that traffic from the territory set apart to them under the Southern Railway & Steamship Association Agreement, itself raises a *prima facie* presumption of the unreasonableness of those rates. In the Cincinnati case, the complainant does not directly question the reasonableness of the rates from Cincinnati, but in the Chicago case it is charged, that the rates on through traffic from Chicago to Southern territory are made up of " substantially the local rates in effect from Chicago to Cincinnati and other Ohio river crossings " and " *unreasonably high* rates " from the Ohio on to Southern territory. It appears that the Chicago rates are made up of the two rates as charged — the rates from that city to the Ohio being the regular Trunk Line rates and from the Ohio southward, the Southern Railway & Steamship Association rates. The shipments being through shipments, under a through bill of lading quoting a total through rate, and without breakage of bulk at the river, this method of making up the rates is a departure from the general rule under which through rates established by two or more connecting carriers *are less than the sum of their separate rates*. The Trunk Line rates per ton per mile from Chicago to Cincinnati and the Association rates per ton per mile from Cincinnati to Southern territory are given in the tables on page 175.

From these tables it will be seen that the rates per ton per mile from Cincinnati south are in all cases much higher, and in many instances a hundred per cent or more higher, than those from Chicago to Cincinnati.

The averages of the rates per ton per mile on all the classes, lettered as well as numbered, from Cincinnati, are approximately:

FROM CINCINNATI TO	AVERAGE OF RATES PER TON PER MILE ON ALL CLASSES
	Cents
Knoxville	2 70
Chattanooga	2 33
Rome	2 62
Atlanta	2 31
Meridian	2 00
Birmingham	1 96
Anniston	2 27
Selma	1 85

By reference to the tables in our statement of facts giving freight revenue per ton per mile and cost per ton per mile, it will be seen that the above averages are largely in excess of that revenue and cost on the roads taken as a whole in, respectively, Southern territory, Central territory, and the country at large.

*   *   *   *   *   *   *   *

The weight of the testimony of railroad officials connected with the roads and lines leading from Central territory to the South, as appears from our finding of facts, tends to show that the idea is prevalent in western railroad circles, that the adjustment of rates from Central and Eastern territories is unjustly prejudicial to the former, and that those roads and lines, south as well as north of the Ohio, are disposed to favor a readjustment of their rates on a basis more favorable to Central territory, but that they have not done so on account of their alliance with the eastern lines as members of the Southern Railway & Steamship Association, the latter lines not being willing to agree to such readjustment.

Our conclusion upon the whole is, that, as charged in the complaint in the Chicago case, the rates on the numbered classes from Cincinnati and the Ohio river crossings to the south are "unreasonably high," and as they enter into the through rates from Chicago, that those through rates, as well as the rates from Cincinnati, are excessive. There is no complaint that the rates from Chicago to Cincinnati and the other crossings are unreasonable in themselves and no evidence authorizing us to so find. They are the regular Trunk Line rates and are *not* subject to the objection, as in the case of the Association rates south of the river, that they are made higher than they otherwise would be for the purpose of securing to the Eastern Seaboard lines traffic from territory set apart to them. The cost on freight in general per ton per mile on the roads south of the river appears to have been for the years named in the tables heretofore given about 25 per cent on an average greater than the cost per ton per mile on the roads from Chicago to the river. The tonnage of the latter roads is also greater than that of the former as shown in the tables. Rates from Cincinnati to Southern territory from 35 to 50 per cent higher per ton per mile than those from Chicago to Cincinnati and other Ohio river crossings will, in our opinion, make full allowance for these differences in cost and tonnage, and be at least not unreasonably low as maximum rates. The rates in cents per 100 pounds given below are approximately upon this basis.

FROM CINCINNATI TO	1	2	3	4	5	6
Knoxville	53	45	37	27	22	20
Chattanooga . . .	60	54	40	30	24	22
Rome	75	64	54	44	34	24
Atlanta	86	73	60	45	35	27
Meridian	114	98	80	62	49	38
Birmingham . . .	87	74	60	46	36	28
Anniston	86	73	60	45	35	27
Selma	108	92	78	60	48	36

* * * * * * * *

An order will be issued directing the defendants engaged in transporting traffic from Chicago and Cincinnati to Southern territory to desist from charging higher rates on the traffic embraced in the numbered classes from those cities, respectively, than those in the two preceding tables and to make all the necessary readjustments of their tariffs. These rates are a conservative reduction of the existing rates and, while it is believed they will go far to do away with the "undue prejudice" to which Central territory is now subjected, they are probably not so low as they might be made if fuller and more accurate data were accessible. If the rates by the Eastern Seaboard lines be taken as the standard of comparison, the rates in these tables will be found to make in the main due allowance for the estimated effect on those rates of water competition *via* the Atlantic. They are also higher than the proportions of the through rates from New York *via* Cincinnati to Chattanooga, Birmingham and Meridian, allowed for the hauls from Cincinnati to those points, and which were in effect for a long period of years; and they yield a rate per ton per mile largely in excess of the reported cost per ton per mile of freight on the roads from the Ohio south (and in other sections of the country) and much above the average of their receipts per ton per mile. (See tables in statement of facts.) They are, it seems scarcely necessary to add, prescribed as maximum rates and are not intended to be prohibitory of such lower rates as the carriers interested may find to be just and reasonable.

We are not unmindful that a compliance with the order in these cases may and probably will necessitate a readjustment of rates from Central territory to other points in Southern territory than those named, but as we took occasion to say in the case of the *Board of Trade of Troy* v. *Alabama M. R. Co.*, 4 Inters. Com. Rep. 348, 6 I. C. C. R. 1, "it cannot be held to be a valid objection to the correction of unlawful rates to one locality, that it involves a like correction to other localities."

Even pecuniary embarrassment of a road by reason of insufficient receipts from all sources is not a fact that will warrant making rates on a portion of its traffic unreasonably high for the accomplishment of a purpose such as is disclosed in these cases. Excessive rates on certain classes of traffic may be made the basis of proportionately low rates on other classes, and thus shippers of the former are taxed with burdens which in justice should be borne by the latter and without any addition to the general aggregate revenue of the carrier. It is believed, moreover, that the reduction in rates ordered in these cases will result in a corresponding increase in the tonnage of the roads in the traffic affected, and that the revenue therefrom will be augmented rather than lessened. This, at any rate, will be the natural tendency of the change.

POWER TO PRESCRIBE RATES

INTERSTATE COMMERCE COMMISSION v. CINCINNATI, N. O., & T. P. RY. CO. ETC.[1]

On May 29, 1894, the Interstate Commerce Commission entered an order, of which the following is a copy:

At a general session of the Interstate Commerce Commission held at its office in Washington, D.C., on the 29th day of May, A.D. 1894.

The Commission having found and decided that the rates complained of and set forth in said report and opinion as in force over roads operated by carriers defendant herein, and forming routes or connecting lines leading southerly from Chicago or Cincinnati to Knoxville, Tenn., Chattanooga, Tenn., Rome, Ga., Atlanta, Ga., Meridian, Miss., Birmingham, Ala., Anniston, Ala., and Selma, Ala., are unreasonable and unjust, and in violation of the provisions of the act to regulate commerce:

It is ordered and adjudged that the above-named defendants, engaged or participating in the transportation of freight articles enumerated in the Southern Railway & Steamship Association classification as articles of the first, second, third, fourth, fifth, or sixth class, do from and after the tenth

---

[1] "The Maximum Freight Rate" case. Decided by the Supreme Court of the United States, May 24, 1897. 167 U. S. 479. The historical setting and importance of this decision will be found in Ripley's Railroads: Rates and Regulation, p. 469.

day of July, 1894, wholly cease and desist and thenceforth abstain from charging, demanding, collecting, or receiving any greater aggregate rate or compensation per hundred pounds for the transportation of freight in any such class from Cincinnati, or from Chicago, to Knoxville, Tenn., Chattanooga, Tenn., Rome, Ga., Atlanta, Ga., Meridian, Miss., Birmingham, Ala., Anniston, Ala., or Selma, Ala., than is below specified in cents per hundred pounds under said numbered classes, respectively, and set opposite to said points of destination ; that is to say :

ON SHIPMENTS OF FREIGHT FROM CINCINNATI

To	CLASS 1 RATES PER 100 LBS.	CLASS 2 RATES PER 100 LBS.	CLASS 3 RATES PER 100 LBS.	CLASS 4 RATES PER 100 LBS.	CLASS 5 RATES PER 100 LBS.	CLASS 6 RATES PER 100 LBS.
	Cents	Cents	Cents	Cents	Cents	Cents
Knoxville . .	53	45	37	27	22	20
Chattanooga .	60	54	40	30	24	22
Rome . . .	75	64	54	44	34	24
Atlanta . . .	86	73	60	45	35	27
Meridian . .	114	98	80	62	49	38
Birmingham .	87	74	60	46	36	28
Anniston . .	86	73	60	45	35	27
Selma . . .	108	92	78	60	48	36

ON SHIPMENTS OF FREIGHT FROM CHICAGO

To						
Knoxville . .	93	79	62	44	37	32
Chattanooga .	100	88	65	47	39	34
Rome . . .	114	97	79	61	49	38
Atlanta . . .	127	107	85	62	50	39
Meridian . .	114	98	82	60	47	38
Birmingham .	111	95	72	52	44	34
Anniston . .	126	107	85	62	50	39
Selma . . .	128	112	89	66	53	38

And said defendants, and each of them, are also hereby notified and required to further readjust their tariffs of rates and charges so that from and after said 10th day of July, 1894, rates for the transportation of freight articles from Cincinnati and Chicago to southern points other than those hereinabove specified shall be in due and proper relation to rates put into effect by said defendants in compliance with the provisions of this order.

The railroad companies having failed to comply with the order, the Interstate Commerce Commission instituted this suit in the circuit court of the United States for the southern district of

Ohio to compel obedience thereto. The court, upon a hearing, entered a decree dismissing the bill (76 Fed. 183), from which decree an appeal was taken to the court of appeals, and that court, reciting the order, submits to us the following question: "Had the Interstate Commerce Commission jurisdictional power to make the order hereinbefore set forth; all proceedings preceding said order being due and regular, so far as procedure is concerned?"

Mr. Justice BREWER, after stating the facts in the foregoing language, delivered the opinion of the court.

In view of its importance, and the full arguments that have been presented, we have deemed it our duty to reëxamine the question in its entirety, and to determine what powers Congress has given to this Commission in respect to the matter of rates. The importance of the question cannot be overestimated. Billions of dollars are invested in railroad properties. Millions of passengers, as well as millions of tons of freight, are moved each year by the railroad companies, and this transportation is carried on by a multitude of corporations working in different parts of the country, and subjected to varying and diverse conditions.

Before the passage of the act it was generally believed that there were great abuses in railroad management and railroad transportation, and the grave question which Congress had to consider was how those abuses should be corrected, and what control should be taken of the business of such corporations. The present inquiry is limited to the question as to what it determined should be done with reference to the matter of rates. There were three obvious and dissimilar courses open for consideration. Congress might itself prescribe the rates, or it might commit to some subordinate tribunal this duty, or it might leave with the companies the right to fix rates, subject to regulations and restrictions, as well as to that rule which is as old as the existence of common carriers, to wit, that rates must be reasonable. There is nothing in the act fixing rates. Congress did not attempt to exercise that power, and, if we examine the legislative and public history of the day, it is apparent that there was no serious thought of doing so.

The question debated is whether it vested in the Commission the power and the duty to fix rates, and the fact that this is a debatable question, and has been most strenuously and earnestly debated, is very persuasive that it did not. The grant of such a power is never to be implied. The power itself is so vast and comprehensive, so largely affecting the rights of carrier and shipper, as well as indirectly all commercial transactions, the language by which the power is given had been so often used, and was so familiar to the legislative mind, and is capable of such definite and exact statement, that no just rule of construction would tolerate a grant of such power by mere implication. Administrative control over railroads through boards or commissions was no new thing. It had been resorted to in England and in many of the states of this Union. In England, while control had been given in respect to discrimination and undue preferences, no power had been given to prescribe a tariff of rates. In this country the practice has been varying. Notice the provisions in the legislation of different states. We quote the exact language, following some of the quotations with citations of cases in which the statute has been construed : [Abridged. — Ed.]

Alabama. Code 1886, p. 295, § 1130 : " Exercise a watchful and careful supervision over all tariffs and their operations, and revise the same, from time to time, as justice to the public and the railroads may require, and increase or reduce any of the rates, as experience and business operations may show to be just."

California. In the constitution going into effect January 1, 1880 (article 12, § 22) : " Said commissioners shall have the power, and it shall be their duty, to establish rates of charges for the transportation of passengers and freight by railroad or other transportation companies, and publish the same from time to time, with such changes as they may make."

Georgia. Code 1882, p. 159, § 719 : " Make reasonable and just rates of freight and passenger tariffs, to be observed by all railroad companies doing business in this state on the railroads thereof." Railroad v. Smith, 70 Ga. 694.

Illinois. St. 1878 (Underwood's Ed.) p. 114, § 93 : " To make, for each of the railroad corporations doing business in this state, as soon as practicable, a schedule of reasonable maximum rates of charges for the transportation of passengers and freights on cars on each of said railroads."

Minnesota. Laws 1887, c. 10, p. 55 : " In case the commission shall at any time find that any part of the tariffs of rates, fares, charges or classifications so filed and published as hereinbefore provided, are in any respect unequal or unreasonable, it shall have the power, and is hereby authorized and directed to compel any common carrier to change the same and adopt such rate, fare, charge or classification as said commission shall declare to be equal and reasonable." *State* v. *Chicago, St. P., M. & O. Ry. Co.*, 40 Minn. 267, 41 N. W. 1047.

New Hampshire. Laws 1883, p. 79, § 4 : " Fix tables of maximum charges for the transportation of passengers and freight upon the several railroads operating within this state, and shall change the same from time to time, as in the judgment of said board the public good may require ; and said rates shall be binding upon the respective railroads." Merrill v. Railroad Co., 63 N. H. 259.

On the other hand, in —

Kansas. Laws 1883, p. 186, § 11, reads :

No railroad company shall charge, demand or receive from any person, company or corporation, an unreasonable price for the transportation of persons or property, or for the hauling or storing of freight, or for the use of its cars, or for any privilege or service afforded by it in the transaction of its business as a railroad company. And upon complaint in writing, made to the board of railroad commissioners, that an unreasonable price has been charged, such board shall investigate said complaint, and if sustained shall make a certificate under their seal, setting forth what is a reasonable charge for the service rendered, which shall be *prima facie* evidence of the matters therein stated.

Section 18 authorized an inquiry upon the application of parties named in reference to freight tariffs, and an adjudication upon such inquiry as to the reasonable charge for such freights ; section 14 required a notice of the determination to be given to the railroad company, and a communication of a failure to comply with such determination in a report to the governor; and section 19 reads :

Any railroad company which shall violate any of the provisions of this Act shall forfeit for every such offense, to the person, company, or corporation aggrieved thereby, three times the actual damages sustained by the said party aggrieved, together with the costs of suit, and a reasonable attorney's fee, to be fixed by the court : and if an appeal be taken from the judgment, or any part thereof, it shall be the duty of the appellate court to include in the judgment an additional reasonable attorney's fee for services in appellate court or courts.

The effect of these provisions was to make the determination of the commission *prima facie* evidence of what were reasonable rates, and to subject the railroad company failing to respect such determination or to prove error therein to the large penalties prescribed in section 19.

Kentucky. The act of April 6, 1882, § 1 (Gen. St. p. 1021), provided that " if any railroad corporation shall wilfully charge, collect or receive more than a just and reasonable rate of toll or compensation for the transportation of passengers or freight in this state . . . it shall be guilty of extortion," etc. Further sections created a commission, and by section 19 the commissioners were authorized to hear and determine complaints under the first and second sections of this act, and upon such complaint and hearing file their award with the clerk of the circuit court, which might be traversed by any party dissatisfied, and the controversy thereafter submitted to the court for consideration and judgment.

Massachusetts. Pub. St. 1882, p. 603, § 14 : " The board shall have the general supervision of all the railroads and railways, and shall examine the same." By section 15, if it finds that any corporation has violated the provisions of the act, or any law of the commonwealth, it shall give notice thereof in writing, and if the violation shall continue after such notice shall present the facts to the Attorney-General, who shall take such proceedings thereon as he may deem expedient. By section 193 special authority is given to the board to revise the tariffs and fix rates for the transportation of milk. See *Littlefield* v. *Railroad Co.*, 158 Mass. 1, 32 N. E. 859.

*   *   *   *   *   *   *   *

The legislation of other states is referred to in the Fourth Annual Report of the Interstate Commerce Commission, Append. E., p. 243 *et seq*. It is true that some of these statutes were passed after the Interstate Commerce Act, but most were before, and they all show what phraseology has been deemed necessary whenever the intent has been to give to the Commissioners the legislative power of fixing rates.

It is one thing to inquire whether the rates which have been charged and collected are reasonable, — that is a judicial act; but an entirely different thing to prescribe rates which shall be charged in the future, — that is a legislative act. *Chicago, M. & St. P. Ry. Co.* v. *Minnesota*, 134 U. S. 418, 458, 10 Sup. Ct. 462, 702, etc.

It will be perceived that in this case the Interstate Commerce Commission assumed the right to prescribe rates which should control in the future, and their application to the court was for a mandamus to compel the companies to comply with their decision; that is, to abide by their legislative determination as to the maximum rates to be observed in the future. Now, no-where in the Interstate Commerce Act do we find words similar to those in the statute referred to, giving to the Commission power to " increase or reduce any of the rates "; " to establish rates of charges "; " to make and fix reasonable and just rates of freight and passenger tariffs "; " to make a schedule of reasonable maximum rates of charges"; " to fix tables of maximum charges"; to compel the carrier " to adopt such rate, charge or classification as said Commissioners shall declare to be equitable and reason-able." The power, therefore, is not expressly given. Whence then is it deduced? In the first section it is provided that " all charges . . . shall be reasonable and just; and every unjust and unreasonable charge for such service is prohibited and declared to be unlawful." Then follow sections prohibiting dis-crimination, undue preferences, higher charges for a short than for a long haul, and pooling, and also making provision for the preparation by the companies of schedules of rates, and requir-ing their publication. Section 11 creates the Interstate Commerce Commission. Section 12, as amended March 2, 1889 (25 Stat. 858), gives it authority to inquire into the management of the business of all common carriers, to demand full and complete information from them, and adds, "and the Commission is hereby authorized to execute and enforce the provisions of this act." And the argument is that, in enforcing and executing the pro-visions of the act, it is to execute and enforce the law as stated in the first section, which is that all charges shall be reasonable and just, and that every unjust and unreasonable charge is pro-hibited ; that it cannot enforce this mandate of the law without a determination of what are reasonable and just charges, and, as no other tribunal is created for such determination, therefore it must be implied that it is authorized to make the determination, and, having made it, apply to the courts for a mandamus to compel the enforcement of such determination. In other words, that though Congress has not, in terms, given the Commission the power to determine what are just and reasonable rates for the future, yet, as no other tribunal has been provided, it must have intended that the Commission should exercise the power. We do not think this argument can be sustained. If there were nothing else in the act than the first section, commanding reasonable rates, and the twelfth, empowering the Commission to execute and enforce the provisions of the act, we should be of the opinion that Congress did not intend to give to the Commission the power to prescribe any tariff, and determine what for the future should be reasonable and just rates. The power given is the power to execute and enforce, not to legislate. The power given is partly judicial, partly executive and administrative, but not legislative. Pertinent in this respect are these observations of counsel for the appellees :

Article 2, § 3, of the Constitution of the United States, ordains that the President " shall take care that the laws be faithfully executed." The act to regulate commerce is one of those laws. But it will not be argued that the president, by implication, possesses the power to make rates for carriers engaged in interstate commerce. . . .

The first section simply enacted the common-law requirement that all charges shall be reasonable and just. For more than a hundred years it has been the affirmative duty of the courts " to execute and enforce " the common-law requirement that " all charges shall be reasonable and just," and yet it has never been claimed that the courts, by implication, possessed the power to make rates for carriers.

But the power of fixing rates under the Interstate Commerce Act is not to be determined by any mere considerations of omission or implication. The act contemplates the fixing of rates, and recognizes the authority in which the power exists. Section 6 provides, etc. . . .

Finally, the section provides that, if any common carrier fails or neglects or refuses to file or publish its schedules as provided in the section, it may be subject to a writ of mandamus issued in the name of the people of the United States at the relation of the Commission. Now, but for this act it would be unquestioned that the carrier had the right to prescribe its tariff of rates and charges, subject to the limitation that such rates and charges should be reasonable. This section 6 recognizes that right, and provides for its continuance. It speaks of schedules showing rates and fares and charges which the common carrier "has established and which are in force." It does not say that the schedules thus prepared, and which are to be submitted to the Commission, are subject, in any way, to the latter's approval. Filing with the Commission and publication by posting in the various stations are all that is required, and are the only limitations placed on the carrier in respect to the fixing of its tariff. Not only is it thus plainly stated that the rates are those which the carrier shall establish, but the prohibitions upon change are limited in the case of an advance by 10 days' public notice, and on reduction by 3 days. Nothing is said about the concurrence or approval of the Commission, but they are to be made at the will of the carrier. Not only are there these provisions in reference to the tariff upon its own line; but, further, when two carriers shall unite in a joint tariff (and such union is nowhere made obligatory, but is simply permissive), the requirement is only that such joint tariff shall be filed with the Commission, and nothing but the kind and extent of publication thereof is left to the discretion of the Commission.

It will be perceived that the section contemplates a change in rates, either by increase or reduction, and provides the condition therefor; but of what significance is the grant of this privilege to the carrier, if the future rate has been prescribed by an order of the Commission, and compliance with that order enforced by a judgment of the court in mandamus? The very idea of an order prescribing rates for the future, and a judgment of the court directing compliance with that order, is one of permanence. Could anything be more absurd than to ask a judgment of the court in mandamus proceedings that the defendant comply with a certain order, unless it elects not to do so? The fact that the carrier is given the power to establish in the first instance, and the right to change, and the conditions of such change specified, is irresistible evidence that this action on the part of the carrier is not subordinate to, and dependent upon the judgment of, the Commission.

We have therefore these considerations presented: First. The power to prescribe a tariff of rates for carriage by a common carrier is a legislative, and not an administrative or judicial, function, and, having respect to the large amount of property invested in railroads, the various companies engaged therein, the thousands of miles of road, and the millions of tons of freight carried, the varying and diverse conditions attaching to such carriage, is a power of supreme delicacy and importance. Second. That Congress has transferred such a power to any administrative body is not to be presumed or implied from any doubtful and uncertain language. The words and phrases efficacious to make such a delegation of power are well understood, and have been frequently used, and, if Congress had intended to grant such a power to the Interstate Commerce Commission, it cannot be doubted that it would have used language open to no misconstruction, but clear and direct. Third. Incorporating into a statute the common-law obligation resting upon the carrier to make all its charges reasonable and just, and directing the Commission to execute and enforce the provisions of the act, does not by implication carry to the Commission, or invest it with the power to exercise, the legislative function of prescribing rates which shall control in the future. Fourth. Beyond the inference which irresistibly follows from the omission to grant in express terms to the Commission this power of fixing rates is the clear language of section 6, recognizing the right of the carrier to establish rates, to increase or reduce them, and prescribing the conditions upon which such increase or reduction may be made, and requiring, as the only conditions of its action — First, publication ; and, second, the filing of the tariff with the Commission. The grant to the Commission of the power to prescribe the form of the schedules, and to direct the place and manner of publication of joint rates, thus specifying the scope and limit of its functions in this respect, strengthens the conclusion that the power to prescribe rates or fix any tariff for the future is not among the powers granted to the Commission.

These considerations convince us that under the Interstate Commerce Act the Commission has no power to prescribe the tariff of rates which shall control in the future, and therefore cannot invoke a judgment in mandamus from the courts to enforce any such tariff by it prescribed.

But has the Commission no functions to perform in respect to the matter of rates, no power to make any inquiry in respect thereto? Unquestionably it has, and most important duties in respect to this matter. It is charged with the general duty of inquiring as to the management of the business of railroad companies, and to keep itself informed as to the manner in which the same is conducted, and has the right to compel complete and full information as to the manner in which such carriers are transacting their business. And, with this knowledge, it is charged with the duty of seeing that there is no violation of the long and short haul clause; that there is no discrimination between individual shippers, and that nothing is done, by rebate or any other device, to give preference to one as against another; that no undue preferences are given to one place or places or individual or class of individuals, but that in all things that equality of right, which is the great purpose of the Interstate Commerce Act, shall be secured to all shippers. It must also see that that publicity which is required by section 6 is observed by the railroad companies. Holding the railroad companies to strict compliance with all these statutory provisions, and enforcing obedience to all these provisions, tends, as observed by Commissioner Cooley in *Re Chicago, St. P. & K. C. Ry. Co.*, 2 Interst. Commerce Com. R. 231, 261, to both reasonableness and equality of rate, as contemplated by the Interstate Commerce Act. * * * *

Our conclusion, then, is that Congress has not conferred upon the Commission the legislative power of prescribing rates, either maximum or minimum or absolute. As it did not give the express power to the Commission, it did not intend to secure the same result indirectly by empowering that tribunal to determine what in reference to the past was reasonable and just, whether as maximum, minimum, or absolute, and then enable it to obtain from the courts a peremptory order that in the future the railroad companies should follow the rates thus determined to have been in the past reasonable and just.

The question certified must be answered in the negative, and it is so ordered.

Mr. Justice HARLAN dissented.

REASONABLE RATES

Receivers' and Shippers' Association of Cincinnati v. Interstate Commerce Commission, etc.[1]

CARLAND, *Judge* :

In this opinion, for the sake of brevity, the Cincinnati, New Orleans & Texas Pacific Railway Co. will be abbreviated C., N. O. & T. P.; The Interstate Commerce Commission will be abbreviated Commission; the Louisville & Nashville Railway Co. will be abbreviated L. & N.; and the Nashville, Chattanooga & St. Louis Railway Co. will be abbreviated N., C. & St. L.

Petitioners are firms, partnerships, and corporations engaged in various kinds of mercantile, commercial, industrial, and manufacturing pursuits in Hamilton County, Ohio, and manufacture and produce goods, wares, and merchandise, and sell annually large quantities thereof of great value, alleged in the bill to be several hundred thousand dollars, to purchasers located at Chattanooga, Tenn., which said goods, wares, and merchandise are enumerated in the freight tariffs and classifications governing the same of the respondent, C., N. O. & T. P. Said petitioners have invested in building up and maintaining their respective lines of business an amount exceeding the sum of $25,000,000.

The C., N. O. & T. P. is a corporation duly organized under the laws of the State of Ohio and is a common carrier engaged in the transportation of goods, wares, and merchandise by railroad from the city of Cincinnati, Ohio, to the city of Chattanooga, Tenn., the northern terminus of said C., N. O. & T. P. being at Cincinnati and the southern at Chattanooga.

On the 14th day of July, 1910, petitioners filed their bill of complaint in the Circuit Court of the United States for the Southern District of Ohio, Western Division, for the purpose of obtaining a judgment of that court setting aside and annulling

[1] United States Commerce Court ; decided July 20, 1911. For the significance of this decision, consult Ripley, Railroads: Rates and Regulation, p. 588.

an order of the Commission dated February 17, 1910, but in fact rendered May 24, 1910, and which order is in the following language:

This case being at issue upon complaint and answers on file, and having been duly heard and submitted by the parties, and full investigation of the matters and things involved having been had, and the Commission having on the date hereof made and filed a report containing its findings of fact and conclusions thereon, which said report is hereby referred to and made a part hereof, and having found that the present rates of defendant the Cincinnati, New Orleans & Texas Pacific Railway Co. (lessee of the Cincinnati Southern Railway) for the transportation of articles in the numbered classes of the Southern Classification from Cincinnati, Ohio, to Chattanooga, Tenn., are, to the extent that said rates exceed the rates named in paragraph 3 hereof, unjust and unreasonable.

2. It is ordered, That said defendant be, and it is hereby, notified and required to cease and desist, on or before the 15th day of July, 1910, and for a period of not less than two years thereafter abstain, from exacting its present rates for the transportation of articles in the numbered classes of the Southern Classification from Cincinnati, Ohio, to Chattanooga, Tenn.

3. It is further ordered, That said defendant be, and it is hereby, notified and required to establish, on or before the 15th day of July, 1910, and maintain in force thereafter during a period of not less than two years, rates for the transportation of articles in the numbered classes of the Southern Classification from Cincinnati, Ohio, to Chattanooga, Tenn., which shall not exceed the following, in cents per 100 pounds, to wit:

Class	1	2	3	4	5	6
Rate	70	60	53	44	38	29

The C., N. O. & T. P. and the Commission filed demurrers to the bill. Subsequently the case was transferred to this court under the provisions of section 6 of the act to create a Commerce Court and to amend the act entitled "An act to regulate commerce," and the cause has now been submitted for decision upon the bill and demurrers.

The bill of complaint is quite voluminous, consisting, exclusive of exhibits, of 66 printed pages. The material allegations, however, which in our judgment are necessary to be considered in order to dispose of the case may be stated briefly as follows:

In 1894 the Commission decided the cases of *Cincinnati Freight Bureau* v. *C., N. O. & T. P.*, and *Chicago Freight Bureau* v. *L. & N., et al* (6 I. C. C. Rep., 195).[1] These proceedings had been instituted by the commercial interests of Cincinnati and Chicago for the purpose of correcting an alleged discrimination in rates upon the numbered classes from points of origin in the Central West as compared with rates from points of origin in the East, to southern territory. The complaint of the Chicago Freight Bureau alleged that the rates for the transportation of freight from western to southern points upon the numbered classes from Cincinnati and other Ohio river crossings to southern points of destination were excessive, and that the rates from Chicago were even more excessive. Under this allegation the Commission held that it might inquire into the inherent reasonableness of these rates, and proceeded to dispose of the case upon that ground. The Commission held that the rates from Cincinnati were too high and should be materially reduced. The following are the rates then in effect from Cincinnati to Chattanooga and those ordered by the Commission, showing the reductions made:

Classes	1	2	3	4	5	6
Rates in effect	76	65	57	47	40	30
Reduced rates	60	54	40	30	24	22
Reductions	16	11	17	17	16	8

The order of the Commission, made in pursuance of this decision, was not complied with by the carriers, and the Commission thereupon instituted proceedings in the Circuit Court for the Southern District of Ohio to enforce obedience to its requirements. Such proceedings were had in that suit that the Supreme Court of the United States finally directed a dismissal of the bill of complaint upon the ground that the act to regulate commerce as it then stood conferred no authority upon the Commission to establish a rate for the future; that this order was in effect the fixing of a future rate and therefore without warrant of law, and void. (*I. C. C.* v. *C., N. O. & T. P.*, 167 U. S., 479.)

[1] Reprinted at head of this chapter.

When the interstate commerce law was amended in 1906 by giving to the Commission power to fix and establish a rate for the future, the Receivers & Shippers Association of Cincinnati commenced proceedings before the Commission and against the C., N. O. & T. P. and the Southern Railway Co. for the purpose of obtaining the benefit of the holding of the Commission in the former case. As a result of a hearing had by the Commission in the proceedings last mentioned, the order complained of in this action was made.

It is claimed by the petitioners that the maximum rate fixed by said order is much too high and is extortionate, so much so that the Commission in making the order violated the fifth amendment to the Constitution of the United States; which prohibits the taking of private property without due process of law or without just compensation. While said order of the Commission was in full force and unsuspended in any way, the C., N. O. & T. P. put into effect a schedule of rates for the transportation of freight between Cincinnati, Ohio, and Chattanooga, Tenn., in accordance with the maximum fixed by the Commission, and said rates are still in force.

In the report of the Commission, which is made a part of said order, it is found as follows:

If it is our duty to take this railroad by itself and to determine the reasonableness of these rates by reference to cost of construction, cost of maintenance, and profit upon the investment, we think the complainants have established their case and that these rates ought fairly to be reduced by as great an amount as was formerly found reasonable by this Commission.

This language of the report refers to the finding made by the Commission in 1894, and the reductions made then by the Commission appear in the table heretofore mentioned in this opinion.

The bill in this case also alleges that if the schedule of rates fixed by the Commission in 1894 had been in force or had been applied during the years 1903 to 1908, both inclusive, the yearly average net profit of the C., N. O. & T. P. would have been 40.66 per cent. It also appears from the bill of complaint that the city of Cincinnati owns the line of railroad between the city of Cincinnati, Ohio, and the city of Chattanooga, Tenn., which is commonly known as the Cincinnati Southern, and now and during the times mentioned in the bill operated by the C., N. O. & T. P. The road originally cost the city of Cincinnati $18,000,-000, and the city subsequently spent for terminal facilities $2,500,-000, making a total cost of the Cincinnati Southern to the city of Cincinnati of $20,500,000. The C., N. O. & T. P. leased this property, and is still leasing it, and the basis of rental returned to the city of Cincinnati prior to 1906 was 6 per cent, and 5 per cent subsequent to that date. The C., N. O. & T. P. owns its own equipment and never did have any interest in the Cincinnati Southern beyond the right to use the property under the terms of the leasehold. The capital stock of the C., N. O. & T. P. for the years 1903 to 1908, both inclusive, was $5,000,000, divided into $3,000,000 of common stock and $2,000,000 of preferred stock, and about the year 1908 it increased its capital stock by adding $500,000 of preferred stock, making its entire issued capital stock for 1908 $5,500,000. The value of the property of the C., N. O. & T. P. between the years 1903 and 1908, both inclusive, was $5,000,000, and after 1908 was $5,500,000, and was all the property of the C., N. O. & T. P. devoted to and employed in the public service and use and for the public convenience.

The C., N. O. & T. P. is a single-track railroad from Cincinnati to Chattanooga, a distance of 336 miles, without branches, and has an average gross earning per mile of $26,082.66. The L. & N. runs from Cincinnati to Louisville, and from Louisville to Nashville, the distance from Cincinnati to Louisville being 114 miles and the distance from Louisville to Nashville being 185.9 miles. The distance from Cincinnati to Nashville *via* the L. & N. is thus shown to be 299.9 miles. Nashville is connected with Chattanooga by the N., C. & St. L., the distance from Nashville to Chattanooga being 151 miles, making the distance from Cincinnati to Chattanooga, *via* the L. & N. from Cincinnati to Louisville and Louisville to Nashville, and from Nashville to Chattanooga over the N., C. & St. L., 450.9 miles. The direct haul from Cincinnati to Chattanooga *via* the C., N. O. & T. P. is thus 114.9 miles shorter than the indirect haul *via* the L. & N. and the N., C. &

St. L. by way of Louisville and Nashville. The average gross earnings, per mile, between Cincinnati and Chattanooga *via* the L. & N. and the N., C. & St. L. is $25,593.40.

In view of the finding of the Commission heretofore mentioned, it necessarily follows that its order ought to have followed its findings, unless the reasons stated by the Commission for not doing so are valid. In this connection it must be remembered, however, that the power to establish reasonable and just rates for the future for the transportation of freight by common carriers is vested by law in the Commission and no part thereof is vested in this Court, and this Court may not disturb the order complained of unless it can be clearly found that it conflicts with the provisions of the fifth amendment to the Constitution of the United States, providing the power conferred has been regularly exercised. The order of the Commission itself does not fix a schedule of rates to be put in effect by the C., N. O. & T. P., but simply fixes a maximum rate beyond which the railroad may not go. The railroad, however, upon the making of this order established the schedule of rates as high as the order would permit, and therefore it may be truly said that the schedule of rates put in effect by the railway company is the schedule of rates made by the Commission or at least authorized by it. All that this Court could do if it found the maximum schedule fixed by the Commission violated the constitutional rights of shippers over the C., N. O. & T. P. would be to set aside the order; but as the rates prescribed thereby have already gone into effect, and as this Court has no authority or power to establish rates or to order that any particular rate be put in effect, it necessarily results that the rates now in effect on the C., N. O. & T. P. would continue in effect unless changed by the carrier or the Commission. The carrier could change its rates if the order was set aside and even make them higher than they are now. The Commission could again investigate the matter and fix a new schedule of rates. So that it appears that all the shippers would gain in this litigation would be the vacation of the order, and if the court held that the rates permitted were so high as to be violative in a constitutional sense of the rights of the shippers then no doubt the Commission would not again establish such a high schedule of rates. But in any event if we should set aside the order on constitutional grounds the shippers would be obliged to go again to the Commission for relief. At first we were inclined to think that the result which would be obtained by a successful termination of this suit in behalf of the shippers would be so inconsequential as to render it unnecessary for this Court to take jurisdiction over the case, but upon further reflection it would seem that the shippers have the right to a judgment of this court as to whether or not the schedule of rates contained in the order complained of is so high as to be violative of the fifth amendment to the Constitution as to the difference between what the Commission found would be reasonable if they considered the C., N. O. & T. P. by itself and the maximum rates that were fixed. Then if the shippers again went before the Commission they would have the benefit of the judgment of this court upon that subject. And in that view we proceed to consider the question as to whether the reasons given by the Commission for not reducing the schedule of rates for the classes mentioned to the sums which the Commission found would be reasonable if the C., N. O. & T. P. should be considered by itself are valid.

It is claimed by the petitioners that the Commission, having found that the so-called 60-cent schedule would be reasonable for the C., N. O. & T. P. considered by itself, was bound to establish such schedule as the result of its finding, and that the Commission's establishing a higher schedule for the reasons mentioned in its report, while seemingly within its power to fix a reasonable rate, was really and in fact beyond its power, as the Commission had no right to take into consideration in fixing a higher schedule the matters which induced it to make the order which it did.

There are two questions which are presented to this court for decision: First. Are the reasons given by the Commission for the establishment of the schedule mentioned in the order valid, or are they so outside and beyond the power of the Commission to fix a reasonable rate as to come within the rule that prohibits the Commission from fixing a rate for reasons which the Commission is not authorized to consider? (*Southern Pacific Co.* v.

I. C. C., 219 U. S., 433.) Second. Is it shown, beyond reasonable question, by the present record that the schedule of rates contained in the order of the Commission complained of clearly violates the fifth amendment to the Constitution of the United States by taking the property of petitioners without due process of law or without just compensation if the taking is for a public purpose ?

It seems to have been decided in the case of *Board of Railroad Commissioners of the State of Kansas* v. *Symms Grocery Co. et al.*, 35 Pac., 217, that the shipper can not invoke these constitutional provisions for the reason that he is not obliged to ship ; that he may utilize the rate prescribed or he may not. We are not impressed with the soundness of this decision. The logical result of such a holding as applied to the facts in the present case would be equivalent to saying to the shipper, " You may pay an unconstitutional rate or go out of business " ; and we do not think that the protection of the Constitution is held on any such condition.

In stating the reasons which in the judgment of the Commission compelled it to take into account in fixing the schedule of rates which it did other considerations and other railroads than the C., N. O. & T. P., we can do no better than to quote from the report of the Commission, as follows:

The defendants also contend that these rates should be fixed not only with reference to the financial results and the financial necessities of the Cincinnati, New Orleans & Texas Pacific Co., but also with reference to other companies whose rates are necessarily affected by these; otherwise stated, the Commission should establish rates which are just and reasonable for the section in which they prevail; if a particular company is so situated that it can make a handsome profit under such rates, that is the good fortune of that company, just as it would be the misfortune of some other company if it could not show as favorable earnings.

The rate from Cincinnati and Louisville to Chattanooga has been the same for the last 28 years. The distance is substantially the same, and this relation in rates will undoubtedly be maintained in the future. Whatever reduction is made from Cincinnati will be met by corresponding reductions from other Ohio river crossings. Rates from Memphis to Chattanooga are lower by a fixed differential than from the Ohio river, and this relation would undoubtedly be preserved, and perhaps ought to be, since the distance is 300 miles as against 336 miles from Cincinnati.

In the original case the Commission ordered reductions to many other points besides Chattanooga. While Chattanooga is the only southern point of destination referred to in these complaints, it is frankly stated that the purpose is to obtain a general reduction to this southeastern territory; and no reason is apparent why, if the Commission adheres to its former decision in case of Chattanooga, it ought not to do the same in case of other localities in this territory. It will be remembered that in 1905 certain reductions were made from the Ohio river to Atlanta without any corresponding reductions to Chattanooga. Originally, the same rate had been made to Atlanta from Louisville as was made from Baltimore. After the opening of the Cincinnati Southern this same rate was applied from Cincinnati to Atlanta, and the rate from Cincinnati to Chattanooga was constructed by using the same rate per mile, although the distance was shorter. At the present time the rate per mile is greater in case of Chattanooga than in case of Atlanta. The defendants say that the present rate is constructed upon the proper basis, and that the reductions made to Atlanta could not be applied to Chattanooga without undoing what was accomplished at that time, for the following reasons:

The reductions of 1905 grew out of the claim upon the part of Atlanta that its rates from the north were too high in comparison with Birmingham and Montgomery. By that readjustment Atlanta was made the same as Montgomery and the difference between Atlanta and Birmingham reduced.

The distance from Memphis to Birmingham is 251 miles, from Memphis to Chattanooga 300 miles, from Cincinnati to Chattanooga 336 miles. The rate from Memphis to Chattanooga has always been somewhat less than that from Cincinnati, in recognition of the shorter distance, and the St. Louis & San Francisco Railway insists that the rate from Memphis to Birmingham shall not materially exceed the rate from Memphis to Chattanooga, which seems reasonable in view of the fact that the distance is 50 miles shorter. If, now, this rate from Cincinnati to Chattanooga is reduced, that will in all probability carry with it a reduction from Memphis to Chattanooga, which will involve a corresponding reduction from Memphis to Birmingham, and this will create the same discrimination out of which the reduction of 1905 came. This would mean a reopening of that contest.

It must also be remembered that any reduction from the north to Atlanta and corresponding territory would undoubtedly be followed by similar reductions from the east as was the case in 1905.

It is apparent, therefore, to make any considerable change in this rate from Cincinnati to Chattanooga will work a lowering in rates throughout this entire southern territory, or will produce a change in the relation of those rates which now seem to be adjusted upon a basis fairly satisfactory to that territory. How far are we at liberty to consider all this in fixing a reasonable rate over the Cincinnati, New Orleans & Texas Pacific? It should be noted that Chattanooga is not complaining of unfair treatment as compared with other southern points.

Some indignation was expressed by several witnesses upon the part of the city of Cincinnati because after that community had expended this enormous amount of money in the construction of the Cincinnati Southern Railroad that property was not more devoted to the interests of the city of Cincinnati. If that city, under proper legislative authority, had seen fit to operate its railroad, it might have established to Chattanooga whatever rates it saw fit, and if the results of municipal operation had been as favorable as the present, it could have materially reduced those rates and still obtained a fair return upon its investment. Such a reduction would have cheapened the cost of this freight to the dealer and probably in a degree to the customer, and so might have benefited the ultimate consuming public. It is doubtful if it would have benefited the interests of Cincinnati, since the rates established by it would have been met by carriers serving rival communities, and the relation of rates would have continued the same. However this may be, the city has parted with its right to operate this property, and the matter stands exactly as though this road had been built by private capital.

In the Matter of Proposed Advances in Freight Rates (9 I. C. C. Rep., 382) the Commission, having under consideration the rates on grain from Chicago to the Atlantic seaboard, announced that the interests of all competing lines must be considered in determining the reasonableness of those rates, and not merely that line which could handle the business the cheapest. In the *Spokane case* (15 I. C. C. Rep., 376) the same subject was considered and the same conclusion reached. The last affirmance of this doctrine is found in *Kindel* v. *N. Y., N. H. & H. R. R. Co.* (15 I. C. C. Rep., 555), in which the rule is stated by Clark, Commissioner, as follows:

" In the *Spokane case* (15 I. C. C. Rep., 376) we held that the reasonableness of a rate between two points, served by two or more carriers, could not be determined by consideration alone of that line which is shortest and most favorably situated as to operation, earnings, etc., but that the entire situation must be considered. . . .

" As before suggested, we can not, in determining competitive rates, select that railroad which is the shortest or most advantageously situated and limit the rate to what would allow that property fair earnings. We must consider the entire situation and determine a reasonable rate not merely with reference to the Union Pacific, but with reference to all lines serving these Colorado points by reasonably direct lines."

We have no doubt as to the correctness of this principle and believe it must be applied here within proper limits.

The Cincinnati Southern Railroad is a single trunk line without branches, running from Cincinnati to Chattanooga. The main line of the Louisville & Nashville extends from Cincinnati to Louisville, and from

Louisville to Nashville. Traffic from Louisville to Chattanooga passes through Nashville, and over the Nashville, Chattanooga & St. Louis to Chattanooga. For the year 1907 the gross earnings per mile of the Cincinnati Southern were, as already stated, over $26,000 per mile, those of the Louisville & Nashville about $11,000 per mile, and of the Nashville, Chattanooga & St. Louis less than $10,000 per mile. The same year the earnings of that portion of the line of the Louisville & Nashville between Cincinnati and Louisville were $25,000 per mile; between Louisville and Nashville $30,000 per mile; those of the Nashville, Chattanooga & St. Louis between Hickman and Chattanooga, a distance of 320 miles, over $20,000 per mile. Now, in adjusting the rates of the Louisville & Nashville, or the Nashville, Chattanooga & St. Louis, shall the Commission consider each section of the road by itself, or shall it establish a common rate for the whole?

Commission rates are usually the same for all lines, both main line and branches. It is fair that the main line should in a degree contribute to the support of the branch line, for the branch-line business when it reaches the main line is surplus traffic, from which a larger profit is made. It is in the public interest that rates shall be so adjusted that population and industries may freely diffuse themselves. It hardly seems proper to fix the rates upon the Cincinnati Southern, which is really a main line, without any reference to the branch lines which contribute to it.

This should be further borne in mind. Of the entire traffic handled by the Cincinnati, New Orleans and Texas Pacific in the year 1907 over two-thirds of the tonnage was delivered to it by its connections and most of it hauled as a through transaction from Cincinnati to Chattanooga or the reverse. Comparatively little traffic originates upon this railroad between these two termini. The present large earnings may be due to the fact that the Southern Railway is able to turn onto this road large amounts of traffic which it would exchange with some other railroad but for its interest in the Cincinnati Southern. If the city of Cincinnati were operating this property itself, it is by no means certain that the apparently undue profits of to-day might not be a deficit.

The complainants urge that the Cincinnati Southern is really a part of the Southern Railway system. If it were so considered the gross earnings per mile of the entire system would be less than those of either the Louisville & Nashville or the Nashville, Chattanooga & St. Louis.

If these rates are to be established with reference to other rates in the vicinity it becomes pertinent to inquire how the present rates compare with other rates for similar distances in the South. Extensive tables have been furnished by the defendants instituting such comparisons, and these tables have been to some extent criticized and replied to by the complainants.

It fairly appears that the rates now in effect from Cincinnati to Chattanooga upon the numbered classes are lower than similar rates prescribed by the railroad commissions of most States in the South. They are as low and usually lower than the interstate rates made by southern roads for similar distances.

The complainants call our attention to rates from Cincinnati to Nashville. The distance is 300 miles and the rates are materially lower than those from Cincinnati to Chattanooga, being, first class, 53 cents as against 76 cents, and sixth class, 23 cents as against 30 cents. But this Commission has found (*Chamber of Commerce of Chattanooga* v. *Southern Ry. Co.,* 10 I. C. C. Rep., 111), and the Federal courts have found (*East Tenn., Va. & Ga. Ry. Co.* v. *I. C. C.,* 181 U. S. I.), that water competition influences these rates to Nashville. The rate from Cincinnati to an intermediate point where there is no water competition is higher in proportion to distance than those to Chattanooga. Thus the first-class rate from Cincinnati to Gallatin, 20 miles north of Nashville, is 78 cents.

The complainant also refers to rates from Virginia cities to Atlanta which are less per ton-mile than those in question. But it is well understood that these rates are materially affected by water competition, and ordinarily the long-distance rate would be less per ton-mile than the rate for the shorter distance. If rates from Virginia cities south for distances of from 300 to 350 miles are examined, it will be found that they usually equal or exceed the Chattanooga rates.

The complainants urge that the volume of traffic in this territory has increased and is increasing, all of which should make for lower rates; and this is certainly true; but it must also be borne in mind that the cost of operation is advancing. In the past railways have been able to introduce various economies in the handling of their business, which have tended to offset the added cost of labor and supplies, so that the net result has been that the increase in the cost of transporting a ton of freight 1 mile has but slightly, if at all, increased. It is doubtful if in future similar economies can keep pace with advancing prices.

We hesitate at this time to make widespread and far-reaching reductions in rates where there is no special occasion for it and where the rates themselves are not clearly excessive.

It appears from the findings of the Commission that it has always refused in the consideration of the reasonableness of a rate or rates to consider only the particular carrier making the same by itself, but on the contrary has always considered the rates in a particular territory or the rates of other carriers to be affected by the change of the particular rate or rates in question; and we think it fair to say that so far as the Commission is concerned there has been a uniform policy, public policy if you please, because the Commission represents the United States in so far as it acts within the scope of its delegated authority in the establishment of reasonable and just rates, to the effect that it will not fix rates or determine their reasonableness solely upon a consideration of the particular carrier whose rates are directly involved. We think this court may take judicial knowledge of the fact that the interstate rates prescribed for the transportation of freight by common carrier must necessarily be more or less interdependent, or at least be so related to each other that the rate-making power will not simply, because it has the power, fix a rate upon a single line of railroads which will necessarily disorganize established and reasonable rates on other railroads in the same territory. All rates established in accordance with law are presumed to be just and reasonable. It is for this reason that the rates for the transportation of freight of other carriers in the same territory may be looked into as evidence of what should be a just and reasonable rate, providing conditions are similar. We can not as a court not vested with the power to fix rates say, beyond question, that the elements which the Commission took into consideration in fixing the schedule complained of were improper for the Commission to consider, and therefore can not conclude that the Commission based a schedule of rates upon improper grounds.

It was said by the Supreme Court in *Texas & Pacific Railway* v. *I. C. C.*, 162 U. S., 233,

that the purpose of the act is to promote and facilitate commerce by the adoption of regulations to make charges for transportation just and reasonable, and to forbid undue and unreasonable preferences or discriminations : that, in passing upon questions arising under the act, the tribunal appointed to enforce its provisions, whether the Commission or the courts, is empowered to fully consider all the circumstances and conditions that reasonably apply to the situation, and that, in the exercise of its jurisdiction, the tribunal may and should consider the legitimate interests as well of the carrying companies as of the traders and shippers. . . .

Under the second proposition we can not disturb the order of the Commission on the theory that it fixed rates so high as to be violative of the fifth amendment to the Constitution, unless it shall clearly appear to us that the constitutional rights of the shippers were invaded thereby. The fixing of the schedule of rates complained of was a legislative act.

Munn v. *Illinois*, 96 U. S., 113.

Peil v. *Chicago N. W. Ry. Co.*, 94 U. S., 164.

Express Cases, 117 U. S., 1.

C. M., etc., Ry. v. *Minnesota*, 134 U. S., 418.

Reagan v. *Farmers' Loan & T. Co.*, 154 U. S., 362.

St. L. & S. F. Ry. Co. v. *Gill*, 156 U. S., 649.

C., N. O. & T. P. Ry. Co. v. *I. C. C.*, 162 U. S., 184.

T. & P. Ry. v. *I. C. C.*, 162 U. S., 197.

I. C. C. v. *Cincinnati Ry. Co.*, 167 U. S., 479.

Railroad Commission Cases, 116 U. S., 307.

Smyth v. *Ames*, 169 U. S., 515.

Chord v. *L. & N. R. R. Co.*, 183 U. S., 483.

Alpers v. *City of San Francisco*, 32 Fed., 503.

So. Pac. Co. v. *R. R. Commissioners*, 78 Fed., 236.

New Orleans Water Works Co. v. *New Orleans*, 164 U. S., 471.

Atlantic Coast Line v. *North Carolina Corporation Com.*, 206 U. S., 1.

And while we are of the opinion that our power to review the order of the Commission fixing a schedule of rates is coextensive with the limits of the protecting shield of the Constitution, still it must clearly appear that such protection in some degree has been taken away. The Commission found that the rates complained of were not clearly excessive. Much less are we able to find that the rates authorized by the Commission in the order complained of and which were a reduction of the former rates are clearly excessive. In making this statement we are fully aware of the allegation of the bill as to the net earnings of the C., N. O. & T. P., and the whole case as to the excessive feature of the rates fixed by the Commission is almost entirely based upon the earnings of the C., N. O. & T. P. While earnings may be considered in the fixing of a reasonable rate to be charged by a carrier for the transportation of freight, rates necessarily can not be based upon earnings alone. This is made clearly to appear when we consider that a just and reasonable rate is one which is just to the carrier and to the shipper. It is a rate which yields to the carrier a fair return upon the value of the property employed in the public service, and it is a rate which is fair to the shipper for the service rendered; and when this rate is established if it results in large profits to the carrier the carrier is fortunate in its business, and if it results in a loss of earning power so that the business of the carrier is unprofitable the carrier is unfortunate. But the rate may not be lowered or raised merely upon the ground that the carrier is either making or losing money, providing always the rate is a reasonable and just rate. Indeed, it has been held that the earning power of the rate is one of the least considerations in fixing a just and reasonable rate.

Canada Northern R. R. Co. v. *International Bridge Co.*, L. R. 8 App. Cases, 723.

Board of Railroad Comm. v. *I. C. R. R. Co.*, 20 I. C. C. Rep., 181.

Being satisfied that the Commission did not err in taking into consideration the grounds they did in fixing their schedule of rates, and not being clearly satisfied that the rates themselves are so high as to violate the constitutional rights of the shippers, we are of the opinion that the bill must be dismissed.

And it is so ordered.

ARCHBALD, *Judge*, dissenting:

There can be no serious question as to the conclusion which would have been reached by the Commission had they confined themselves to the determination of what was a just and reasonable rate from Cincinnati to Chattanooga by the Cincinnati Southern, without regard to the effect upon other roads. This was gone into at length in 1894, and the 60-cent schedule, which is now contended for, sustained.[1] But as the law then stood there was no authority in the Commission to fix future rates, and its action was therefore held of no effect.[2] But even with the lapse of time and the change of conditions, the issue as is recognized by the Commission is the same, and the same conclusion

[1] Reprinted at head of this chapter.
[2] Decision reprinted in this chapter, *supra*.

would confessedly have been reached except as they were influenced by a regard for the necessities of other roads. "If it is our duty," says Commissioner Prouty in the report, "to take this railroad by itself and to determine the reasonableness of these rates, by reference to cost of construction, cost of maintenance, and profit upon the investment, we think the complainants have established their case, and that these rates ought fairly to be reduced by as great an amount as was formerly found reasonable by this Commission." Unfortunately, however, for the complainants this view did not prevail. It was contended by the railroad company that the rates should be fixed not only with reference to the final results to itself and its own financial necessities, but also with reference to other companies whose rates were necessarily affected thereby; or, in other words, that the Commission should establish rates which would be just and reasonable for the whole section of territory in issue, and that if a particular carrier was so situated that it could make a handsome profit it was to be recognized as a piece of good fortune with which the Commission was not to interfere. Adopting this view, which had also been followed in other cases (*in re* proposed advance in freight rates, 9 Inter. Com. Com. Rep., 382; *Spokane* v. *North Pac. R. R.*, 15 Inter. Com. Com. Rep., 376; *Kindel* v. *New York, New Haven & Hartford R. R.*, 15 Inter. Com. Com. Rep., 555), it was accordingly held that the reasonableness of the rate between points served by two or more lines could not be determined by reference to that line alone which was shortest and most favorably situated with respect to operation and earnings, and the rate limited thereby; but that the entire situation was to be considered, and a rate fixed which would be reasonable with respect to all the lines directly serving the points involved. That rates for similar distances on other lines similarly conditioned may be referred to, to assist in determining what is fair and reasonable in any case, is clear. And it is no doubt proper also to take into account the effect on rates upon freight moving to and from other points beyond those immediately in view. But that, in my judgment, is as far as it is permitted to go. There is no right, as I look at it, to consider the effect of the rate or rates to be established on those of other roads, between the same points, or to maintain such rates at a figure which is necessary to meet the needs of those roads. And so far as the order of the Commission was induced by any such idea, it can not be sustained.

If the Cincinnati Southern was the only line from Cincinnati to Chattanooga the rate, of course, so far as it was not a joint rate, would be fixed with reference to that road alone. And if it was a line that was costly to build, or that could not be economically run, this would operate to increase the rates, and the shipper would have to pay, to correspond. But, on the other hand, if the reverse of this was true, and the road was neither an expensive one to construct, maintain, or run, the shipper would clearly be entitled to the benefit of these conditions and to the lower rates necessarily to ensue. So, also, if this favored road was the first in the field, and other roads had come in after it was built, it certainly would not be contended that with the introduction of new and additional facilities the lower rates prevailing on the more favored line could be raised to meet the necessities of others not so well placed. It is not to be thought of that the construction of a second or third road should be made the basis for higher rates. The standard would be that of the original and most favored line. But what difference does it make whether the road which can afford the best rate is the first or the last to be built? It is the condition at the time the rate is fixed that controls. The shipper is entitled to the benefit of any advance in transportation facilities that may be made and is not to be tied down to the unprogressive and outdistanced past. The supposed advantage in competing lines between the same points becomes a detriment if rates are to be kept up to help the weakest road.

The Cincinnati Southern extends in a short and direct route due south from Cincinnati to Chattanooga without branches 336 miles. It was expensive to build, and the cost of operation and maintenance is high. But its net earnings are nevertheless large, amounting to some 44 per cent on the capital stock. The route between the same points by way of the Louisville & Nashville and the Nashville, Chattanooga & St. Louis roads is a third longer, or 450 miles, and both of these roads have more or less unremunerative branch lines. And yet the Commission have not only put the two routes on an equality, but have even considered the influence of unprofitable branches, which have to be taken care of, fixing a rate which shall be fair for the whole system, and not simply for the immediate section of road which is involved. This, in my judgment, they had no right to do. The shipper is entitled to a just and reasonable rate, having regard to the service which is to be rendered by the carrier that is to perform. And this service is largely to be measured by the facilities for economically rendering it, which are possessed by that particular road. It is not to be augmented or kept up, beyond what is fair and just, by the consideration of what some other road, not so favorably situated, may need.

The order of the Commission, being based upon mistaken and erroneous grounds, is therefore invalid and should be so declared. (*Southern Railway* v. *St. Louis Hay & Grain Co.*, 214 U. S., 297; *Inter. Com. Com.* v. *Stickney*, 215 U. S., 98; *Southern Pacific Railway* v. *Inter. Com. Com.*, 219 U. S., 833.) And the case should be thereupon remanded to the Commission in order that a rate may be fixed which shall be just and reasonable as respects the respondent carrier, by whom the services are to be performed. This does not take from the Commission the right to say what that rate shall be. Much less does it involve the determination of the rate by the Court. It merely disposes of the rate which has been mistakenly made, as preliminary to a new consideration of it by the Commission upon correct and proper grounds. (*Cin., N. O. & T. P. R. R.* v. *Inter. Com. Com.*, 162 U. S., 184, 238, 239; *Southern Railway* v. *St. Louis Hay & Grain Co.*, 214 U. S., 297.)

I therefore dissent from the judgment of the court, sustaining the demurrer and dismissing the bill.

MACK, *Judge:*

I concur in the above dissent.

VII

COMMERCIAL COMPETITION: RATES ON SALT

Railroad Commissioners of Kansas *v.* Atchison, Topeka & Santa Fé Railway [1]

PROUTY, *Chairman:*

This proceeding involves the relative distributive rates on salt from the Kansas as compared with the Michigan field into

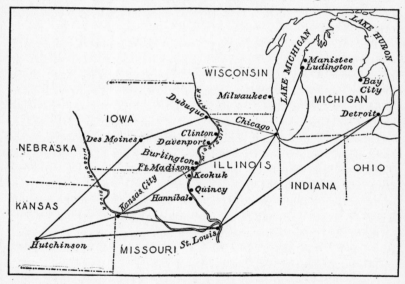

intermediate territory. The situation will be best understood by a glance at the accompanying map.

The Kansas salt field extends about 120 miles north and south by some 60 miles east and west. Hutchinson is situated near the

---

[1] Decided February 5, 1912. 22 I. C. C. Rep. 407–419. The original case, 5 *Idem*, 299, was reprinted in the first edition of Railway Problems, p. 190.

center of this field and may be selected as typical of the whole
field. Rates from all points of production in this field to the disputed territory are the same, there being therefore no competition
in the rate between different points of production in this field.

The Michigan field covers nearly the entire lower peninsula of
the state of Michigan, extensive salt works being located at Ludington, Manistee, Bay City, Port Huron, Detroit, Saginaw, and
some other points. This field is therefore more extensive than
the Kansas field. Rates at the present time are substantially the
same from all points in the Michigan field to the destinations in
controversy; but, owing to conditions of transportation, which
will be later referred to, there has been in the past active competition in rates between the Michigan points of production themselves, which has produced, at times, differences in those rates,
some vestiges of which still remain.

It will be seen by reference to the map that as salt moves from
the Kansas field east and northeast it meets salt moving from the
Michigan field in the opposite direction, the debatable ground
being, roughly speaking, between the Mississippi and the Missouri
rivers. The cost of producing salt in Kansas and Michigan is substantially the same. The quality of the salt is about the same,
although this record indicates that at the same price the Michigan salt sells somewhat more freely. Whether, therefore, this
intermediate territory shall be supplied from Kansas or Michigan
depends mainly upon the rate of transportation.

This proceeding is instituted by the Kansas railroad commission in the interest of the salt producers of that state, and the
complaint is:

1. That the rates from the Kansas field into this disputed
territory are unreasonable in and of themselves.

2. That these rates are unduly high in comparison with corresponding rates from the Michigan field.

Certain salt producers in Kansas have intervened in favor of
the prayer of the complainant, and certain producers in the Michigan field against it, so that the whole situation is before us.

In support of its contentions the complainant relies first
and largely upon the fact that under the present rates Kansas

producers are not only unable to increase their production, but can not even maintain that of recent years, while production in the rival Michigan field is increasing; and this phase of the case may be referred to before proceeding to a discussion of the rates themselves.

This record does not show in a very satisfactory way the relative production of these two fields, past and present. When this same matter was before the Commission in 1891 it appeared that production in the Kansas field was about 1,000,000 barrels annually, as compared with 4,000,000 barrels in the Michigan field, while it now appears that in 1909 the corresponding figures were 2,500,000 Kansas, 6,000,000 Michigan. If, therefore, we compare the present with 20 years ago the percentage of development has been in favor of Kansas.

It is said, however, that in 1891 the Kansas field was in its infancy, and this record indicates that for the last few years there has been little increase in the Kansas field, while Michigan production has shown a substantial advance. It is suggested that this is due, not to any undue advantage which Michigan enjoys into this territory, but rather to the fact that other sources of production have been developed to the south and west of Kansas, which have limited its market in those directions.

This Commission has often said that it can not require of carriers the establishment of rates which will guarantee to a shipper the profitable conduct of his business. The railway may not impose an unreasonable transportation charge merely because the business of the shipper is so profitable that he can pay it; nor, conversely, can the shipper demand that an unreasonably low charge shall be accorded him simply because the profits of his business have shrunk to a point where they are no longer sufficient.

The effect of a rate upon commercial conditions, whether an industry can exist under particular rates or a particular adjustment of rates, are matters of consequence, and facts tending to show these circumstances and conditions are always pertinent. But they are only a single factor in determining the fundamental question. A narrowing market, increased cost of production, overproduction, and many other considerations may render an industry unprofitable, without showing the freight rate to be unreasonable.

A reduction in the rate on salt from the Kansas field to these points in controversy would not increase to any appreciable extent the total amount of salt consumed, but a reduction from the Kansas field with no corresponding change from the Michigan field would throw the business to the complaining interests. The question is not what rate the traffic will bear, for the rate is already sufficiently low to move the traffic to its limit from either Kansas or Michigan, but is rather one of relative adjustment. Kansas shippers have a right to demand of these defendants who serve them rates which are first of all reasonable in and of themselves, and, next, rates which, in so far as these defendants can properly control the situation, are fairly adjusted with respect to these rival fields of production.

The inherent reasonableness of the rates in controversy will be first considered.

The original complaint directed attention especially to the rate from the Kansas field to St. Louis. That rate then was and now is 13½ cents per 100 pounds for a distance of approximately 500 miles. Is this unreasonable *per se?*

Salt is very desirable traffic from a transportation standpoint. It loads heavily, is not liable to loss or damage in transit, can be handled at the convenience of the carrier, and affords a uniform business. Its value is comparatively little, being from $1.50 to $2 per ton at the point of production. While not consumed as largely as coal, cement, brick, and similar commodities, and while therefore the freight rate is not so noticeable, it is an article of universal and necessary consumption. All these considerations call for a low rate of transportation, and have been repeatedly recognized by this Commission. It is also true that the ability of a particular producer to sell in a given market has depended largely upon the cost of transportation, and this in turn has operated to force down rates generally, so that salt rates in this territory, certainly, have been established by the voluntary action of the carriers at a low level. Notwithstanding, however, all these considerations which make for a low charge in the handling of this commodity, we are unable, upon any theory, to hold that a rate which pays only 5 mills per ton-mile is unreasonable in and of itself. While this record shows that lower rates have been maintained in the past under stress of competition and are in some cases being maintained to-day, and while if a carrier maintains a lower rate in favor of one locality, it may perhaps be required to accord similar treatment to some other locality, we can not hold that the maintenance of this rate is inherently unreasonable.

The rates established by the state commissions in the two states through which this transportation is mainly conducted are instructive. They can not be given for distances as great as that involved in the St. Louis rate, but for 400 miles they are: Missouri, 15½ cents; Kansas, 15½ cents.

While the attack of the complaint is mainly directed against the St. Louis rate, the intervening petitions put in issue rates from the Kansas field to Mississippi river crossings north of St. Louis, and these should also be referred to.

It will be noted from the map that Hutchinson lies nearly due west of St. Louis. Since the course of the Mississippi river is nearly north and south, it follows that the upper crossings are farther from the Kansas field in an air line than is St. Louis, and although the actual mileage from Hutchinson to some of the more northerly crossings is less than to St. Louis, the average from the entire Kansas field would ordinarily be greater. Having reference to distance, therefore, the rate to the upper crossings might well be somewhat higher than to St. Louis. Those rates are the same to Hannibal and Quincy, 15 cents to Keokuk and Fort Madison, and 18 cents to Burlington, Davenport, Clinton, and Dubuque. The distance from Hutchinson to Dubuque is 610 miles, as compared with 500 to St. Louis.

Considered as a whole, the increase to the upper crossings where it occurs seems to be fairly justified by an increase in distance over St. Louis, and we hold, with respect to all these Mississippi river rates, that they are not unreasonable *per se*. Considering the whole situation, they are perhaps sufficiently high, but can not be pronounced excessive.

This proceeding also puts in issue rates at interior points in Iowa and Missouri, and these rates are sometimes slightly higher than those to the Mississippi river, although the distance is somewhat less.

While the reasonableness of rates from the Kansas field to points west of the Mississippi river is put in issue, but little, if any, attention was directed to those rates. They are in many cases blanket rates, the same from both the Kansas and the Michigan fields, so that the same rate applies through a considerable variation in distance. It is quite probable that some of these rates might upon detailed examination be found excessive, but there is nothing in this record upon which we can base an intelligent opinion, nor do we feel called upon at this time to examine the rate from the Kansas field to each one of these numerous points. Without prejudice to the right to find upon fuller investigation that some of these charges may be excessive, we do not at this time find that the charge of unreasonableness is sustained in any of the cases covered by this complaint.

While the Kansas interests have alleged that these rates to the Mississippi river from the Kansas field are excessive and have insisted upon that claim, it is evident that this is not the real objective point. The Kansas producer is interested not in the absolute rate from his field to this intermediate territory, but in the relative rate made from his plant as compared with that from the plant of his Michigan competitor. As already suggested, a few cents more or less in the rate from the Kansas field does not increase or diminish the total amount of salt consumed, but it may absolutely determine whether that salt shall be produced in Kansas or in Michigan. The real purpose of this proceeding is to secure a readjustment of rates between these competing fields.

At the date when this complaint was filed rates upon package salt from Detroit to St. Louis were, for local consumption, $11\frac{1}{2}$ cents; when for beyond, $8\frac{1}{3}$ cents. There was also a rate on bulk salt of $7\frac{1}{2}$ cents. The distance from Detroit to St. Louis is almost exactly the same as from Hutchinson, from which the lowest available rate was $13\frac{1}{2}$ cents; and the Kansas producer insisted that if these rates were maintained from Detroit, then the rate from the Kansas field was too high and should be reduced. The St. Louis rate was made the principal point of attack, and we may properly inquire whether the rates in effect to this market from Detroit and from the Kansas field discriminate in favor of Detroit.

Since the filing of the complaint, rates from Detroit have been advanced and now are upon package salt 11½ cents local, 10 cents proportional; upon bulk salt 9 cents. Our discussion will be addressed to the present rates.

The defendants urge at the outset that whether the adjustment be proper or improper undue discrimination can not be affirmed, for the reason that the carriers which make the rate from the Kansas field are not the same as those which make that from Detroit. It is well understood that if the same carrier serving both Kansas and Detroit names a lower rate for substantially the same distance from Detroit than from Kansas, it must be prepared to justify that discrimination, but if carrier A serves St. Louis from the Kansas field, while carrier B serves that market from the Detroit field, then carrier A is not guilty of discrimination because it declines to meet the rate established by carrier B.

The answer of the complainants to this claim of the defendants is that the Wabash Railroad, which is the short line from Detroit to St. Louis, and which names the low rate between those points, also extends from Kansas City to St. Louis and joins in the rates from the Kansas field to the same market. They point to the previous decisions of this Commission in which we have held that a carrier which is party to a joint rate may be held responsible for that rate and for any discrimination which results from its maintenance.

Two questions would seem to be open to inquiry:

(*a*) Is the Wabash Railroad justified in naming its present rates from Detroit to St. Louis?

(*b*) Does that carrier, or can that carrier so control the rate from the Kansas field to St. Louis that it should be held answerable for the discrimination which results from a failure to reduce that rate to correspond with the Detroit rate?

It will be seen upon a reference to the map that the salt-producing points of Michigan are located mainly upon the water. They are, upon the western side of the peninsula, Manistee and Ludington upon Lake Michigan, and upon the eastern side, Bay City, Port Huron, Wyandotte, and Detroit upon Lake Huron. It was said in testimony that salt was produced in Michigan, in quantities, at but a single interior point, Saginaw, which lies in close proximity to the water.

The distance from Ludington and Manistee to Milwaukee and Chicago is from 100 to 150 miles. It appears from this record that salt has for many years been transported from these points of production by water to both Milwaukee and Chicago. Much of this transportation is in boats owned by the producers of the salt; but there is to-day, and for some time has been, a regular tariff of the Pere Marquette steamers naming a rate of $2\frac{1}{3}$ cents from both these producing points to Milwaukee and Chicago.

While it does not appear under what circumstances salt is carried from ports upon Lake Huron to Chicago and Milwaukee nor the cost of the transportation, it does appear that the salt produced at these Lake Huron ports moves mainly by water. The testimony shows that 80 per cent of all the salt manufactured in Michigan starts upon its journey by water, and it was said that 90 per cent of the salt going into this contested territory moved by lake and rail.

It can not, therefore, be doubted and must be assumed, that this Michigan salt can be laid down in Chicago or Milwaukee for $2\frac{1}{3}$ cents per 100 pounds. The cost of reaching any particular point of consumption can not exceed the rate from these two railroad centers plus $2\frac{1}{3}$ cents for the water carriage.

The distance from Chicago to St. Louis by the short line is 278 miles. Several different lines of railway connect these great commercial centers, and competition for business by these different routes is, and always has been, most active. It appears that the rate on salt from Chicago to East St. Louis was for a long time $6\frac{2}{3}$ cents per 100 pounds. The local rate on package salt is now 9 cents per 100 pounds, the rate on bulk salt the same.

Detroit is within the Michigan field. The quality of the salt produced at that point and the cost of production are substantially the same as at other points. The price at which that salt is sold can not exceed that obtained for salt produced at other Michigan plants. If Detroit salt is to find a market in St. Louis or upon the Mississippi river it must move there at no higher cost of transportation than obtains from other Michigan producing points.

The Wabash Railroad has upon its rails at Detroit extensive salt works. If it is to move any part of the product of that factory to St. Louis or other Mississippi river points it must make a rate fairly commensurate with that from the plants of its competitors, and this is precisely what the Wabash Railroad has attempted to do in the past and is attempting to do to-day. It insists that just as the Kansas field is treated as an entirety in the naming of rates, so shall the Michigan field be treated, and that Detroit is a part of that field.

The cost of transporting salt from Ludington or Manistee to Chicago is $2\frac{1}{3}$ cents per 100 pounds; from Chicago to St. Louis, 9 cents per 100 pounds, making a total cost of $11\frac{1}{3}$ cents. The present rate from Detroit is $11\frac{1}{2}$ cents. It is difficult to see how the Wabash road can maintain a higher rate from Detroit than it now does in view of the competition which it meets from the Michigan field by other lines of transportation. Nor can it be said that the present rate from Chicago is an unnatural or an abnormal one. That rate, considering the general level of rates obtaining in the respective territories, is not much if any lower than the present rates from the Kansas field to Kansas City — not as low as the $13\frac{1}{2}$-cent rate from that field to St. Louis.

Should the Wabash Railroad, under the circumstances of this case, be required to insist upon the maintenance of as low a rate from Hutchinson to St. Louis as it maintains from Detroit to St. Louis?

It may be questioned, to begin with, whether there is to-day any unreasonable disparity in the rates on package salt, which are $11\frac{1}{2}$ cents from Detroit as against $13\frac{1}{2}$ cents from Hutchinson.

While the rate from Detroit is less, although the distance is the same, it must be remembered that the general level of rates in the territory east of St. Louis is much lower than that in territory to the west. Indeed, this difference greatly exceeds the difference between these rates. For example, the first-class rate from Hutchinson to St. Louis is $1.19½, while that from Detroit is 46 cents. In official classification salt is classified as sixth-class, and the sixth-class rate from Detroit to St. Louis is 14 cents. That commodity is not rated in the western classification, but the lowest rate named from Hutchinson to St. Louis upon any class is 22 cents.

It has been recently held in *Sunflower Glass Co.* v. *A., T. & S. F. Ry. Co.*, 22 I. C. C. Rep., 391, that this difference in transportation conditions may justify a lower commodity rate, mile for mile, east than west of the Mississippi river. On the whole, we are inclined to the opinion that the difference between these rates on package salt from the east and from the west is no greater than it ought to be under all the circumstances.

The proportional rate of 10 cents applies upon traffic destined for points beyond St. Louis. This Commission has in several instances held that a proportional rate applying to through traffic might well be lower than the corresponding local rate, and we do not find in this instance any undue disparity.

The rate of 9 cents upon bulk salt is the same as that from Chicago and is not therefore justified by competitive conditions. This rate gives to Detroit a distinct advantage over other points in the Michigan field and over the Kansas field, to which it is not entitled. In our opinion, a corresponding rate from the Kansas field of 11 cents, with a minimum of 60,000 pounds, would be relatively fair, and such a rate would afford better business for the carriers than the present package rate, minimum 37,500 pounds.

Our conclusion is that in the main rates from Detroit to St. Louis do not unduly discriminate against the Kansas producer, but assuming that they do, can the Wabash Railroad be properly required to correct that discrimination? We do not think that it should be, for the reason that this carrier does not bear such a relation to the rates from Hutchinson to St. Louis that it should be properly held responsible for whatever discrimination may exist in the present relation.

The Wabash takes up this traffic at Kansas City. It can only engage in the transportation from the Kansas field in connection with some line operating to Kansas City from the west. Were the Wabash disposed to reduce the rate from the Kansas field to St. Louis it could only do so by sacrificing its own revenue from Kansas City to St. Louis to a sufficient extent to bring about the desired readjustment. The present rate to the Missouri river from the Kansas field is 10 cents, and the Wabash must, therefore, if it establishes a rate of $11\frac{1}{2}$ cents to St. Louis, accept for its transportation service from Kansas City $1\frac{1}{2}$ cents per 100 pounds.

The distance from Kansas City and Chicago, respectively, to St. Louis is almost exactly the same. The cost of bringing salt from the Kansas field to Kansas City is 10 cents per 100 pounds; the cost of bringing salt from the Michigan field to Chicago is $2\frac{1}{3}$ cents per 100 pounds. How, in this posture, can the Wabash Railroad, extending from both Chicago and Kansas City to St. Louis, be required to maintain from Chicago and Kansas City such rates as will make the through rate from the point of production the same? To do this that carrier must name a rate from Kansas City which is $7\frac{2}{3}$ cents per 100 pounds less than from Chicago, although upon every consideration the Chicago rate should be the lower.

There is, in our opinion, undue discrimination upon the part of the Wabash Railroad in maintaining the present rate of 9 cents upon bulk salt. That rate, which is the same as the present rate from Chicago, is not forced by legitimate competition upon the carrier, and the Wabash Railroad should either join in establishing a corresponding rate from the Kansas field or should advance its rate from Detroit.

As to all other rates there is no undue discrimination, and if there were the Wabash could hardly be called upon to remove the same, since, except as to this bulk-salt rate, it simply accepts a situation which it can not control. There is no similarity between this case and that presented in *Railroad Commission of Tenn.* v. *A. A. R. R. Co.*, 17 I. C. C. Rep., 418, for there the lines beyond the Ohio river absolutely dominated the situation, and the discrimination could not exist except by their voluntary action.

It has already been noted that the average distance from the Kansas field to the upper Mississippi river crossings is greater than to St. Louis. Upon the other hand, the distance from the Michigan field grows less as we proceed north from St. Louis. If the Kansas field is not entitled to meet the Michigan field upon an equality of rate at St. Louis, it is still less entitled to do so at Mississippi river points north of St. Louis. For example, the distance from Hutchinson to Dubuque, the most northerly of these crossings in controversy, is 610 miles, while the distance from Chicago is but 172 miles. Rates from the Kansas field increase, as has been already noted, from $13\frac{1}{2}$ cents at St. Louis to 18 cents at Dubuque. Rates from the Michigan field are $13\frac{1}{2}$ cents to all Mississippi river crossings north of St. Louis. Manifestly, if there is no undue discrimination at St. Louis none exists at the more northerly crossings.

This complaint also puts in issue the justice of the present adjustment with respect to a great number of points west of the Mississippi river, mostly in the states of Iowa and Missouri.

The competitive situation embraced in the present proceeding was presented to the Commission in *Anthony Salt Co.* v. *M. P. Ry. Co.*, 5 I. C. C. Rep., 299, the Kansas shippers being in that case, as at the present time, the complainants. It is impossible to tell from the report of that case exactly what the relation of rates complained of then was, but, clearly, it was much more favorable to Michigan than the present adjustment. The case shows, for example, that the rate from the Kansas field to St. Louis was $24\frac{1}{2}$ cents, while the rate from the Michigan field at that time was $10\frac{1}{2}$ cents. It seems fairly inferable from the statement of facts that under the then existing rates the Michigan producer met the Kansas producer upon a substantial equality at the Missouri river and had an advantage in the rate with respect to most territory east of that river.

While that complaint was dismissed, the controversy continued. Carriers serving the Kansas field were defendants to that proceeding and resisted the application of the complainants, but none the less it was and is manifestly in their interest to supply this territory between the Mississippi and Missouri rivers from Kansas. Kansas producers continued to insist upon a better rate, and rates were gradually reduced at all points. At St. Louis the cut was from 24½ cents to 13½ cents, at Fort Madison from 24½ cents to 15 cents. There were also advances from Michigan. The whole situation was a most troublesome one, leading to many disputes and to many unfortunate rate situations from the standpoint of the carriers. Frequent conferences were held, until finally the matter was laid at rest by the present adjustment.

This case does not clearly show the exact theory upon which that adjustment has been worked out, nor does there seem to have been any exact theory. Probably, in view of the conflicting interests and the great number of carriers involved, it would be impossible to apply any uniform rule. Generally stated, rates from Michigan in all cases are less to the Mississippi river, as, in our opinion, they properly should be. Soon after crossing that river a point is reached where the rate from Michigan and from Kansas becomes the same, and this relation is continued west, producing a blanket of considerable extent, beyond which the rate is in favor of Kansas.

We have examined a great number of these intermediate points. As must be the case with every blanket, instances are found upon the edges where the present adjustment is not altogether in accordance with the relative distances and is not probably the adjustment which would be established if that point alone were under consideration. In the very nature of things it would be almost impossible for us to look into each instance, nor have we attempted to do so. The matter has been long the subject of controversy; the settlement seems to have been honestly made, and without undertaking to approve the adjustment in detail and without expressing an opinion which would prevent a further examination of particular instances which may be called to our attention, we fail to find, on the whole, that this adjustment unduly discriminates against the interests of Kansas, which are represented by the complainants.

On the whole, we are satisfied that the present rates of freight are as favorable to the Kansas field as, all things considered, they should be, except that a rate applicable to the transportation of bulk salt from the Kansas field to St. Louis should be named to correspond with that established from Detroit.

The Wabash Railroad Company will be required to cease and desist from the discrimination now arising out of the maintenance from Detroit to St. Louis of the 9-cent rate upon bulk salt. Otherwise the complaint will be dismissed.

FOURTH SECTION APPLICATIONS

It has been already noted that rates from the Kansas field to some points west of the Mississippi river are slightly higher than those at the river crossings, and it therefore results that in some instances there is a violation of the fourth section. This is referred to in the complaint and the intervening petitions.

The case was originally heard in the fall of 1910, but was not argued or disposed of at that time for the reason that the parties indicated a desire to make certain rate changes which it was thought might remove the cause of complaint. In fact, the rates from Detroit to St. Louis were advanced, as already indicated, but this was not sufficient to satisfy the complainants, and the case was accordingly set down for further hearing in November, 1911.

No reference was made upon the first hearing to the violations of the fourth section. It was the purpose of the Commission to set down for investigation upon the same date with the last hearing the applications which had been filed by the defendants to this proceeding for leave to maintain the higher intermediate charge, but through error, only the Wabash Railroad Company was notified.

Upon the hearing the examiner called attention to the fact that the fourth-section applications of the defendants should have been assigned and the defendants were given an opportunity to introduce any testimony upon that point which they desired. Some of them availed themselves of this opportunity, and the subject is referred to in more or less detail in all the briefs which have been filed and was to some extent discussed upon the argument. It was, however, said by counsel for one or more of the defendants upon the argument that this matter ought not to be disposed of upon the present record, for the reason that other carriers not defendants to this proceeding were interested in these rates.

So far as appears the question presented under these fourth-section applications is an extremely simple one. Lines leading from Kansas in meeting competition upon the Mississippi river have made rates which they allege to be abnormally low, and for this reason they ask to maintain at intermediate points higher rates, which, they say, are reasonable. We have found that there is active competition upon the Mississippi river between these two salt fields and that the rates from both directions, especially from the Kansas field to these various Mississippi river crossings, are low, but we have not found, nor do we find, that they are so unreasonably low as to justify the charging of a higher rate at intermediate points.

Neither do we find that the competitive conditions which are alleged to justify the higher intermediate rates do, under all the circumstances of this case, afford such valid justification. Nor yet, while declining to condemn as unreasonable the intermediate rates, have we given to those rates such examination that we can pronounce them reasonable at this time.

Before we allow these defendants to depart from the mandate of the statute as expressed in the present fourth section we must be satisfied that the more distant rates are unduly low and that the departure from the fourth section is warranted by competitive conditions at the more distant point which do not exist at the intermediate point. In this case we fail to find that the long-distance rates are unreasonably low, and apparently the competition at the more distant point is of exactly the same sort as at the intermediate point.

If, therefore, these applications stood for disposition, we should deny the right to maintain the higher intermediate rates. So far as we can see, the facts are fully before the Commission, and nothing would be gained by another hearing; but if these defendants, or any of them, conceive that a further investigation should be held they may file with this Commission, on or before the 15th day of March, a statement asking for such further investigation and giving, briefly, the reasons why the present investigation has not been sufficient. If upon considering these statements ground for further investigation appears, the applications will be set down for hearing. Otherwise orders will be entered denying the applications as to these rates on salt, effective as of May 1, 1912.

VIII

RELATIVE RATES

THE EAU CLAIRE LUMBER CASE[1]

KNAPP, *Commissioner :*

*   *   *   *   *   *   *   *

1. The complainant, the Eau Claire Board of Trade, is an association of citizens and residents of the city of Eau Claire, Wisconsin, organized to promote the business interests of that city. The defendant railroad companies are severally common carriers engaged in the interstate transportation of lumber and other freight. The sources of supply of the west-bound lumber shipped over these roads are the forests of northern Michigan, Wisconsin and Minnesota ; and the main points from which such shipments are made are Minneapolis, Eau Claire, Winona, La Crosse, Oshkosh, Milwaukee and Chicago, and the following towns on the Mississippi river, south of La Crosse, to wit : Dubuque, Clinton, Lyons, Fulton, Moline, Rock Island, Davenport, Muscatine, Burlington, Keokuk, Hannibal and Louisiana. The market or distributing towns to which these shipments are made are for the most part the " Missouri river points," Sioux City, Omaha, Council Bluffs, St. Joseph and Kansas City.

2. No one of the defendant roads reaches all these points of production. From Eau Claire shipments of lumber are made to the Missouri river over the Chicago, Milwaukee & St. Paul, the Chicago, St. Paul, Minneapolis & Omaha, and the Wisconsin Central. The Chicago, Milwaukee & St. Paul road, (hereinafter designated the " Milwaukee,") has main lines as follows : from Chicago to Council Bluffs ; from Marion, Iowa, on said former

---

[1] Decided June 17, 1892. Interstate Commerce Commission Reports, Vol. V, pp. 264–298. For significant features of this case, consult Ripley's Railroads : Rates and Regulation. (Index.)

line, to Kansas City; from Oshkosh to Milwaukee; from Milwaukee to Sabula Junction; from Minneapolis *via* Wabasha to Sabula Junction, called the "river line;" from Minneapolis to Mason City, called the "Iowa & Minnesota line." Minneapolis, Winona and La Crosse are on the "river line," but Eau Claire is on a branch forty-eight miles in length connecting with that

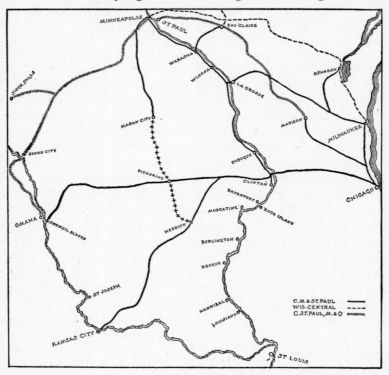

line at Wabasha. The Milwaukee road has an arrangement with the Iowa Central by which, in hauling from Eau Claire and Winona to Council Bluffs, it uses the latter road from Mason City to Pickering, a distance of 97 miles, and, in hauling to Kansas City, it uses the same road from Mason City to Hedrick, a distance of 167 miles. The distances *via* the Iowa Central are considerably less than those over the Milwaukee line proper.

The Chicago, St. Paul, Minneapolis & Omaha road (hereinafter styled the " Omaha ") has a line extending from Eau Claire through St. Paul and Minneapolis to Sioux City, Omaha, and Council Bluffs.   *   *   *   *   *

3. As above stated, the sources of supply of the lumber carried by these roads are the forests of Northern Minnesota, Wisconsin and Michigan. The Minnesota timber is manufactured into lumber largely at Minneapolis, and thence transported to market; the Michigan timber is manufactured into lumber in that state and carried by water to Milwaukee, Chicago and other lake ports ; the Wisconsin timber is manufactured extensively at Eau Claire, Winona, La Crosse and Oshkosh. Eau Claire and La Crosse are in western Wisconsin, the former about 75 miles by water from the Mississippi river, and the latter on its eastern bank ; Winona is in Minnesota, on the western bank of the Mississippi, and Oshkosh is on Lake Winnebago in eastern Wisconsin. Minneapolis is about 100 miles from Eau Claire ; Winona about 80 miles, and La Crosse about 108 miles. Eau Claire is situated at the junction of the Eau Claire and Chippewa rivers ; the Eau Claire is a branch of the Chippewa, and the latter empties into the Mississippi. Logs are floated down the Eau Claire and Chippewa rivers to Eau Claire, and thence on the Chippewa and Mississippi rivers to Winona and La Crosse, and also to Mississippi river points below. Logs are also floated down the Black river to La Crosse and other Mississippi river towns. A large part of the timber on the Eau Claire and Black rivers can be floated with about equal facility down either stream and taken to Winona and La Crosse on the one hand or Eau Claire on the other. Eau Claire, Winona, La Crosse and Oshkosh are small cities, each having from 18,000 to 20,000 inhabitants, while Minneapolis has about 150,000. These cities are all natural lumber markets ; they have large sawmills, and the manufacture, sale and shipment of lumber are conducted on a large scale at Minneapolis, and constitute the principal business of the other places. Eau Claire and all the cities of Wisconsin, Minnesota and the northern peninsula of Michigan, and also Mississippi river points engaged in the manufacture and

shipment of lumber to the Missouri river, may be said to be in competition in this business, but the most active competitors of Eau Claire are Winona and La Crosse. The principal distributing points for Eau Claire lumber are, and for 20 or 25 years have been, the Missouri river towns, which are also the principal markets for other shipping points both on the Mississippi river and in the interior. Eau Claire seems to be more rigidly confined than its competitors to the Missouri river market. Since 1884 when the Bogue award was made, southern yellow pine from the states of Georgia, the Carolinas, Southern Missouri, Arkansas and Texas, has come into competition with the white pine from Minnesota, Wisconsin and Michigan. This competition extends north to the southern line of Minnesota, and is strong in Missouri, Kansas, Nebraska and Iowa. The natural tendency of this competition is to reduce the price of the northern pine, and in that way affect transportation rates on the latter, but it does not appear to have an appreciable effect on the *relation* of rates on lumber between Eau Claire and its immediate competitors.   *   *   *

5. The Omaha road was built to Eau Claire in 1878 or 1879, and the Milwaukee road about 1882. Prior to the building of these roads, lumber produced at that place was rafted and then floated down the Chippewa and Mississippi to various towns on the latter river, from which it was distributed by rail to market destinations mainly in the west. These towns on the Mississippi have been engaged in this business since 1850 or 1852. After these roads were constructed, Eau Claire entered largely into the business of "piling, drying and manufacturing lumber" and shipping the same to market by rail. About half the cut at Eau Claire in 1890 was shipped in this way, and the other half was rafted to Mississippi river towns; and it is estimated that eighty per cent of the lumber rafted to points below Winona comes from the Chippewa river. Eau Claire appears to be adapted by location and in other respects for the manufacture and sale of lumber; it has a natural booming ground or place for the safe storage of logs, cheap transportation from the stump to the mills, proximity to the timber and locations suitable for mills and yards.

Being situated nearer the pine forests, the sources of timber supply, and at the confluence of two rivers which penetrate those forests, the Eau Claire and Chippewa, it appears to have natural advantages over its neighboring competitors. . . . After lumber is in the raft, the cost of its transportation by water down the Mississippi is less than for the same distance by rail; but, including the rafting and preceding expenses, the testimony is to the effect that lumber can be shipped from Eau Claire by rail direct to Missouri river markets at as little if not less, cost than it can be floated to Mississippi river points and thence transported by rail to those markets. The railway companies whose lines run from Chicago across the Mississippi to the Missouri river territory naturally desire that lumber be carried by water down the Mississippi to shipping points on that river, and be thence shipped over their roads to the Missouri river markets. The Omaha road is also interested in maintaining high lumber rates at Eau Claire, because of an agreement between that road and the purchasers of its timber lands in northwestern Wisconsin, by which those purchasers bound themselves to ship over its line the timber from such lands, (which is further from the Missouri river markets than Eau Claire timber), on condition of receiving the same rates as might be charged by that road on such shipments from Eau Claire.

6. The rates from Eau Claire and the other shipping points to the Missouri river markets are based on the rate from Chicago, being certain differentials over or under that rate, and the same rate is made from any one of the shipping points to all the Missouri river markets, although the distances to the latter vary materially. * * * * * *

In the early history of the lumber industry in this territory the principal points of competition were Chicago on the one hand, and St. Louis, Hannibal and Louisiana on the other. Chicago received its lumber from Michigan by way of the lake, and the other towns received theirs by way of the Mississippi. As railroads were built from time to time into the northern pineries, and numerous towns engaged in the manufacture of lumber, the conflict of rates increased and much uncertainty and

demoralization resulted. After several unsuccessful attempts
to adjust these differences, the railway companies finally submitted the matter to Mr. George M. Bogue, under an agreement
between them to abide by his arbitration. The decision rendered
by him, known as the " Bogue Award " was made May 26, 1884,
and is as follows:

AWARD OF THE ARBITRATOR AS TO THE DIFFERENTIALS WHICH SHALL GOVERN ON LUMBER TO MISSOURI RIVER POINTS

J. W. Midgley, Esq.,   Chicago, May 10, 1884.
    Chairman, etc., — Chicago.

Dear Sir : — The question as to what difference shall govern in rates
from the several shipping points on or east of the Mississippi river on
lumber destined to Missouri river points, referred to me for arbitration, has
had my careful consideration.   *   *   *   *   *

I am impressed with the idea that, instead of this question being settled
on the basis of the cost of lumber, the question at issue is, " What rate will
enable each line party to this arbitration to place its fair proportion of
lumber in the territory under consideration? for it is fair to assume that
no road will see its principal lumber points dismantled and dried up till all
efforts to retain their prominence have been exhausted; and, meantime, in
the effort to do this, a great deal of money will be wasted. It is no doubt
true that the roads reaching Chicago — which is the largest primary grain
and stock receiving point in the world — can in their return make rates on
lumber without loss, which would net a loss if applied to the roads reaching
the pineries direct; and it is doubtless true, also, that the actual cost of the
haul from Chicago does not greatly exceed the shorter haul from the Mississippi river; and so long as this is the case, it is natural to expect that the
Chicago roads will support the Chicago market.

This theory must not, however, be carried to the extreme, for if transportation costs anything, it certainly costs something for the haul from
Chicago to the Mississippi river ; and it is neither just nor politic for any
road to claim that the rate from the Mississippi river should be as much or
more than the Chicago rate, whatever may be the cost or the price at the
two markets.

While, therefore, it seems easily apparent that lumber can be sold at the
Mississippi river at as low, or lower, prices than at Chicago, it cannot be
safely argued that the same rate should be made for so much greater
distance.

After a most careful investigation of the subject in all its bearings, and
with a keen appreciation of the delicate and difficult duty confided to me,
I shall make the following award :   [Abridged. — ED.]

From St. Louis . . . .   6½ cents per cwt. less than Chicago
   "   La Crosse and Winona . .   1 cent   "   above   "
   "   Minneapolis and St. Paul . .   2 cents   "   "   "
   "   Menomonie (Wis.), Eau Claire
      and Chippewa Falls . . .   6½ cents   "   "   "

All of which is respectfully submitted.

George M. Bogue, Arbitrator.

7. To show the construction placed upon this award by railroad authorities and their understanding of the principle upon which it was based, we make the following extracts from the testimony: A. C. Bird, Traffic Manager of the " Milwaukee " road, stated that " the acknowledged principle of the award was that each company was entitled to all the lumber it could carry at reasonable rates — that is, rates that were *relatively fair as between the railroads*, and to put all the manufacturers on any one road on a fair equality with the manufacturers on another road, to the end that each road might thereby receive the benefit of its manufacturing industries; " and, again, that " primarily the object of the Bogue award was to place each line in a position to carry its fair share of the Missouri river lumber, and further to place each manufacturing locality upon an even footing with its competitors. . . . *If Eau Claire could produce lumber cheaper than Winona or La Crosse, then the latter points were to have a lower rate so as to enable them to compete.*"

This award appears to have been observed by the defendant roads since its date, May 26, 1884, except that from February 8, to June 20, 1888, the Milwaukee road had a four-cent differential in force on shipments from Eau Claire. . . . It is plain that if the rate from Eau Claire should be reduced, a corresponding reduction could be made by the roads leading from other lumber-producing and shipping points which would restore the present relation of rates between Eau Claire and such other points.

8. At the time the complaint was filed, July 7, 1890, the Chicago rate to Missouri river points was ten cents per hundred pounds. It has since been advanced to fifteen cents.

The following table shows the rates from the towns named therein to Missouri river points, with the " Bogue differentials " applied to the rates from Chicago of ten and fifteen cents, respectively; also the present rates as announced by the tariffs of the Western Freight Association: [Abridged. — ED.]

	RATES UNDER BOGUE DIFFERENTIALS		PRESENT RATES AS PER TARIFFS OF WESTERN FREIGHT ASSOCIATION
	Cents	Cents	Cents
Chicago	10	15	15
Minneapolis . . .	12	17	17
Eau Claire	16¼	21¼	21¼
Winona . . . . ;	11	16	16
La Crosse	11	16	16
Oshkosh	15½	20½	20½
Rock Island . . .	6¼	11¼	13
Burlington	5½	10½	11½
St. Louis	3½	8½	8½

While these rates are based on the Chicago rate, it appears that the building of large sawmills at other points, and the extension of railways into the timber regions of the northwest, have, to a large extent, withdrawn from Chicago the business of supplying lumber to western markets. Chicago, however, does as large a business as heretofore in supplying its local demand

DISTANCES BY SHORT LINES

FROM	To SIOUX CITY	To COUNCIL BLUFFS	To ST. JOSEPH	To KANSAS CITY
	Miles	Miles	Miles	Miles
Chicago . .	517	488	479	458
Eau Claire .	358	457	586	605
Winona . .	328	427	556	560
La Crosse .	356	443	546	540
Minneapolis .	263	362	491	531
Oshkosh . .	580	604	655	647
Rock Island .	416	317	319	337
Burlington .	355	291	273	341
St. Louis . .	511	412	307	277

and in shipping east. Lumber from Oshkosh is also shipped extensively through Chicago to the east; and it appears that the western shipments from both Chicago and Oshkosh are mainly the surplus remaining after eastern markets have been supplied. * * * * * *

10. As before stated, Minneapolis, Winona and La Crosse are on the main line of the Milwaukee road from Chicago to Minneapolis, while Eau Claire is 48 miles distant from the main line on a branch road from Wabasha. On an average there is a train and a half each way per day on this branch road, which is about one tenth of the business of the main line. This branch road is comparatively level, with no difficult grades, and the cost of " physical movement" of a train over it is not greater than over the main line. It appears, however, that a full train cannot always be made up on this branch line, and hence engines employed there cannot always be utilized to their full capacity. As a general rule the operating expenses per ton per mile are greater on branch than on main lines. Eau Claire is, however, on the main line of the Omaha road, and is reached by the Wisconsin Central and other roads hereinbefore named. Oshkosh is also on a branch of the Milwaukee road about 40 or 50 miles from the main line. It may be stated as in the nature of an admission that Mr. E. P. Ripley, Third Vice President of the Milwaukee road, testified that he knew of no " conditions that should make the rate higher from Eau Claire than from Oshkosh except that Eau Claire is nearer the lumber-producing territory and perhaps may be said to be able to pay more," and that " there are no dissimilar conditions existing at Winona, La Crosse and Minneapolis as compared with Eau Claire which would justify the charge of a higher rate per car per mile on lumber from Eau Claire to the Missouri river points than from the points first named, except that they are farther from the supply and it costs more to get the logs there." * * * *

11. The average weight of a car load of lumber being about 35,000 lbs., the total freight per car load to Missouri river points, under the Bogue differentials, is about $75.25 from Eau Claire ; from Winona and La Crosse about $56.00, from Minneapolis

about $59.50, from Chicago about $52.50 and from Oshkosh about $71.75, making the differences per car load against Eau Claire in favor of Winona and La Crosse about $19.25, in favor of Chicago about $22.75, in favor of Minneapolis about $15.75 and in favor of Oshkosh about $3.50. As is shown by the table of distances above given, the mileage from Eau Claire is somewhat greater than from Winona and La Crosse.

Eau Claire, Winona and La Crosse procure their lumber from practically the same region of country, but, as before stated, Eau Claire has natural advantages of location over the latter towns in being nearer the sources of supply. Under the system of differentials in force, timber can be and is hauled from points three or four miles west of Eau Claire across the Eau Claire river to Black river, a distance of seven miles, and carried by the latter to La Crosse. The differentials are important factors in making up the price lists on lumber from the several shipping points, and it is estimated that the difference in rates prevailing at Eau Claire, Winona and La Crosse has practically depreciated Eau Claire lumber, as compared with Winona and La Crosse lumber, about $300,000.00 each year since the Bogue award went into effect. It further appears that since the system of rates established by that award has been in force many mills in and about Eau Claire have gone out of business or been moved to other points, its population has decreased from about 22,000 to 18,000, and, as shown by the table heretofore given, the cut of lumber in the district including Eau Claire has fallen off from 454,544,723 feet in 1884 to 394,622,292 feet in 1890. From 1878, about the time the first railroad (the Omaha) was built to Eau Claire, the cut of lumber in the Eau Claire district had annually increased up to and including 1884. On the other hand, the cut of lumber at Winona increased from 90,630,550 feet in 1884 to 145,000,000 feet in 1890, and in the district including La Crosse it increased from 187,700,000 feet in 1884 to 243,195,583 feet in 1890. . . . After the Bogue award was put in effect, the shipment of lumber from Eau Claire over the Omaha road was substantially abandoned. The evidence is to the effect that, under the existing differential, Eau Claire cannot successfully compete with Winona and La Crosse in piling lumber and shipping it by rail to Missouri river markets.

12. About a year previous to the commencement of the present proceeding, a similar proceeding was begun in behalf of Eau Claire, but was subsequently discontinued at the request of the traffic manager of the Milwaukee road and the general freight agents of the Omaha and the Wisconsin Central. These railway officers substantially admitted that the 6½ cent differential was too high, and promised on the withdrawal of that proceeding to have the Eau Claire differential lowered if they could induce the other lumber roads to agree to it. At a meeting of railroad officials held for the consideration of this matter, the representatives of these roads voted for a reduction of the Eau Claire rate, but the proposition did not receive the support of the other roads, and was defeated.   *   *   *   *   *

Conclusions

The case presented by the complainant rests upon the general averment that rates on lumber from the city of Eau Claire to certain specified points on the Missouri river are unreasonable and oppressive in comparison with rates on the same article from Minneapolis, Oshkosh, La Crosse and Winona. The lower rates from Minneapolis and Oshkosh are not made the leading feature of this contention, the more distinct and special ground of complaint being the alleged disparity between Eau Claire and its immediate rivals, La Crosse and Winona. These three towns have considerable similarity in location, industries, population and distance from western centers of distribution, and they are active competitors with each other in the various lumber markets which they seek to supply. So far as has been made to appear, the west-bound rates on this commodity from La Crosse and Winona have at all times been the same; but since May, 1884, when the so-called "Bogue award" went into effect, the rate from Eau Claire has always been greater by five and one-half cents per hundred pounds, except for a period of about four months in the spring of 1888 when this excess was only three cents a hundred.

The first circumstance to arrest attention is the attitude of the Chicago, Milwaukee & St. Paul road. This carrier is the only defendant named in the original complaint, and the only one against which relief is now distinctly demanded. The great system of railways operated by this company embraces in its mileage lines which connect each of these three towns with the principal lumber markets on the Missouri river, and its alleged discrimination against Eau Claire is the essential grievance sought to be redressed in this proceeding. In the answers filed by this defendant there is no denial that the lumber rate from Eau Claire is out of proportion to the rate from La Crosse to Winona, nor is there any disclosure of facts concerning the location and business of these rival places, and its own relation to them as a common carrier, which are claimed to justify this disparity. No witness was produced upon the trial at the direct instance of this company, and the argument of its counsel at the final hearing was mainly confined to a statement of its position. If this position is correctly apprehended by us, the Milwaukee road virtually concedes that the existing rates on west-bound lumber discriminate against Eau Claire, and that it is entitled to lower charges on this article as compared with the competing towns of La Crosse and Winona. This admission is coupled with a professed willingness to make a substantial reduction in the Eau Claire rate, provided other defendant carriers engaged in transportation of lumber to Missouri river markets, from various producing points on their lines, will not make a corresponding reduction at those places to neutralize the effect of lower charges at Eau Claire. As evidence of its good faith in taking this position, the Milwaukee company shows that the reduced rate which it conceded to Eau Claire in 1888 was followed by equivalent reductions granted at once to those other towns by rival carriers, which rendered its own action in aid of Eau Claire wholly ineffectual, and claims that it was compelled to restore the present differential rather than continue a contest injurious to itself and of no benefit to that community. In effect, therefore, this defendant acknowledges that Eau Claire is unjustly treated, but alleges in extenuation that it is powerless to afford relief.

A brief examination of the findings discloses the reasons for this anomalous situation. At a number of places on the Mississippi south of La Crosse, the manufacture of lumber is extensively carried on, the timber from which it is produced being mainly obtained along the tributary streams north of that point. Each of these towns is connected with the Missouri river by one or more of the defendant railroads other than the Milwaukee. These towns compete in the same markets with the lumber-manufacturing districts nearer the timber supply, and they naturally desire to retain and develop an industry in which they are so largely interested. The railroads extending westerly from those places are equally anxious for the traffic which this industry supplies, and they appear to have some advantage over their northern competitors in shorter distances and greater aggregate tonnage. Any reduction, therefore, in the rate established at Eau Claire, which would tend to increase the output of lumber in that locality at the expense of lumber towns more remote from the forest sources, is deemed by those towns and the carriers identified with them inimical to their common interests, and meets, almost as a matter of course, their combined opposition. Under these circumstances it is obvious that the lumber-carrying roads which do not reach Eau Claire, and which are quite independent of the Milwaukee system, *have it in their power* to perpetuate the inequality of which that town complains by making a reduction in rates from other points equal to any reduction which the Milwaukee company may make at Eau Claire. This in substance is the excuse offered by the original defendant for maintaining rates on lumber shipments from Eau Claire which it admits to be relatively unjust, and its request that other carriers acting under the Bogue award be made parties to the proceeding was an indirect invitation to them to answer the accusation of the complainant.

So far as the defense interposed by these parties goes to the merits of the controversy, it rests ultimately upon two propositions. One is, that under the schedule of rates fixed by the Bogue arbitration Eau Claire is now paying less for the transportation in question then the lower Mississippi towns, *in*

proportion to their respective distances from the common markets;
the other is, that any interference with a system of charges which
numerous carriers have so long enforced, and to which the
lumber interests of so many towns have become adjusted, would
result in a demoralizing " rate war " between these competing
roads, and inflict injury upon other localities much greater than
any advantage which might accrue to Eau Claire.

The first of these positions is readily seen to be untenable.
The doctrine that transportation charges should be in proportion to the distances between different points, *where those distances are greatly dissimilar*, has never been advocated by the
railroads or recommended by the Commission. It may be the
rule to which tariff construction will some time approximate,
but there is no opportunity for its application under present
conditions. To fix the rate for a thousand miles at twice the
sum prescribed for half the distance would be most arbitrary and
intolerable. It does not follow, therefore, that Eau Claire should
pay $21\frac{1}{2}$ cents for a haul of 603 miles to Kansas City, because
Keokuk pays $11\frac{1}{2}$ cents for a haul of 213 miles to the same
place. The whole practice of rate making is opposed to the
principle of exact proportion, and even in theory there is little
reason for its adoption. But distance, nevertheless, is an ever-
present element in the problem of rates and not unfrequently
a controlling consideration. Where all the distances brought
into comparison are considerable, and the differences between
them relatively small, we should expect substantial similarity in
the respective rates, unless other modifying circumstances justified a disparity. It is doubtless true that the present adjustment
of charges gives Eau Claire a rate per ton per mile not greater
than the rate per mile from some of the shipping points on
the lower Mississippi; but how does that fact excuse inequality
between Eau Claire and places nearer by, whose competition is
much more active and direct? The rates now in force may be
relatively just as between Eau Claire and Davenport, and yet
seriously unequal as between Eau Claire and Winona. Every
locality in a producing region of such wide extent as the one in
question is more or less interested in the rates on a common

commodity from all other shipping places in that territory, but at the same time each of them is chiefly concerned with the rates from contiguous towns whose situation and facilities are not greatly unlike its own, and which are its actual and constant rivals in the same markets. It is, therefore, no sufficient answer to complainant's charge to show that the rate from Eau Claire is not proportionally higher than the rates from remote lumber towns in Missouri and Southern Iowa which only indirectly and casually compete with Eau Claire; nor does any suggestion come from the interveners in this case which seems to counteract the force of the admission made by Mr. E. P. Ripley, Third Vice President of the Milwaukee road, that "there are no dissimilar conditions existing at Winona, La Crosse and Minneapolis, as compared with Eau Claire, which would justify the charge of a higher rate per car per mile on lumber from Eau Claire to Missouri river points than from the points first named except that they are farther from the supply, and it costs more to get the logs there." This statement seems to us a confession of injustice to the shippers of Eau Claire, which is neither explained nor excused by any facts bearing legitimately upon the rates in question. The discrimination is admitted, and stands without adequate defense.

If rates from different points of shipment to common terminals could properly be fixed on the basis of mileage, there would be great persuasiveness in the argument of the learned counsel for the Atchison road, who contends that the relief, to which he virtually concedes Eau Claire is entitled, can be effectively secured only by increasing the rates from La Crosse and Winona. But charges for distances greatly dissimilar cannot be adjusted on that principle, and it furnishes no practical rule for establishing rates from different places unequally remote from the same destination. It may be that the rates from these northerly towns are generally too high in comparison with the rates from lower Mississippi points, but that question is not before us and we have no occasion to consider it in this proceeding. The distinct issue now presented is the relative reasonableness of the Eau Claire rate, and that must mainly be determined by comparing it with the rates from the neighboring towns, similar in size, situation and volume of competing traffic, and at approximately the same distance from common markets. Bearing in mind, also, that since this investigation was commenced all these rates have been advanced by an addition equal to fifty per cent of the rate upon which the others were based, viz., the ten-cent rate from Chicago to the Missouri river, we deem it quite unsuitable to attempt the correction of the inequality complained of by ordering a further advance in the rates from competing points in the vicinity of Eau Claire. For this reason it is unnecessary to discuss the power of the Commission, in dealing with discriminations between different localities, to require an increase in rates deemed relatively preferential.

The further general argument against a reduction of the Eau Claire differential does not persuade us that the present rate should be continued. This impression involves some consideration of the Bogue award as it affects the town making this complaint, and the consequences to be apprehended from lowering the lumber rate at that point. The most noticeable fact in this connection is that the results apparently experienced do not accord with the principle upon which that award avowedly proceeds. Mr. Bogue expressly declares the question to be, "What rate will enable each line party to this arbitration to place its fair proportion of lumber in the territory under consideration?" This appears to us equivalent to asking, "What rate will enable each town in this territory to place its fair proportion of lumber in the common markets?" for the arbitrator surely did not intend to imply that a " line " which, as compared with some rival road, gets its " fair proportion " of lumber tonnage, taking into account the aggregate shipments from all the towns which it serves, may so discriminate *between those towns* as to stimulate production at one and prevent it at the others. The Milwaukee road, for instance, may have a " fair proportion " of the lumber business under the present schedule, but that circumstance furnishes no reason for favoring La Crosse and Winona at the expense of Eau Claire. It could not have been the design of Mr. Bogue to equalize this traffic between the railroads without regard to the interests of competing localities, and his award does not appear to have been so interpreted by the carriers. What he evidently intended was that lumber should cost the producer approximately the same *when delivered at destination*, whether manufactured at one place or another. Increased charges for transportation were to offset advantages of location or other natural facilities for cheap production. In this way the tonnage was to be fairly divided between the roads, and the prosperity of all these towns secured by enabling them to compete on an even footing in the common markets. But the rate prescribed for Eau Claire hardly permitted a result consistent with this theory. As it seems to us, this town has been placed at a manifest disadvantage. So far from enjoying equal opportunity with its rivals, it appears to have been overweighted with a differential which has excluded it, to a great extent, from the field of competition. A number of its establishments have gone out of business, its industrial development has been checked and its population seriously diminished. While neighboring towns have been prosperous, Eau Claire has not held its own. These adverse consequences may not have been caused by the operation of the Bogue award, but no other explanation is suggested. Obviously, such an outcome was not designed, and the fact that it has occurred indicates an injustice to this locality which ought to be corrected.

We are not to be understood as indorsing the principle which governs that award. On the contrary we consider it radically unsound. That rates should be fixed in inverse proportion to the natural advantages of competing towns, with the view of equalizing "commercial conditions," as they are sometimes described, is a proposition unsupported by law and quite at variance with every consideration of justice. Each community is entitled to the benefits arising from its location and natural conditions, and any exaction of charges unreasonable in themselves or relatively unjust by which those benefits are neutralized or impaired, contravenes alike the provisions and the policy of the statute. There is no occasion for enlarging upon this point, as it is only incidentally involved in the discussion. Our chief object in commenting on the Bogue award in this connection is to draw attention to the fact that its declared purpose, so far as Eau Claire is concerned, has not been accomplished. Its effect upon that town has proved oppressive. Even if we could accept the theory upon which it is based, we should still be convinced that the rate fixed for Eau Claire was excessive, because its operation has prevented that town, as it seems to us, from retaining its " fair proportion " of the lumber business. As no such result was intended, the rate which produced it cannot be upheld by the rule adopted.   *   *   *   *   *

We are unable to discover how other localities can reasonably object to a more equitable rate for Eau Claire, and our belief is that apprehensions based on a reduction at that point are not well founded. Relatively lower charges may enable Eau Claire to increase its lumber production, but that this will result in serious injury to competing towns is an unwarranted assumption. Remote places on the lower Mississippi can scarcely be affected by the removal of inequalities between Eau Claire and its neighboring rivals, and the latter cannot justly complain because the former is accorded a rate fairly proportioned to their own. The relative volume of lumber shipments from La Crosse and Winona may be somewhat reduced by lower charges at Eau Claire, but any such effect will be attributable to natural advantages of which that town cannot justly be deprived. In short we see no reason why justice to Eau Claire should work injustice to any other community, much less result in the general disturbance of an established industry.

Nor will any such consequences follow a reduction of the Eau Claire differential as would justify other carriers in lowering their rates at competing points, for the purpose of preserving the co-relation of rates created by the Bogue arbitration. Undoubtedly those roads have it in their power to continue the present disparity, but we do not anticipate, and certainly cannot assume, that they will resort to such inconsiderate and arbitrary action in order to nullify the lawful order of this Commission. Even if we believed otherwise, it would still be our duty to render a decision in accordance with our convictions, and thus place the responsibility upon them, if they should attempt to defeat our ruling.

A further position was taken in this proceeding which is apart from the merits of the principal issue. The roads which were made parties at the request of the original defendant insist that no case has been made against them, and that the Commission has no authority to include them in any order based upon the complaint of Eau Claire. We are disposed to agree with this contention. The sole complaint in this case is discrimination, and Eau Claire is the sole complainant. It is not easy to see how any carrier can "discriminate" against a town which it does not reach, and in whose carrying trade it does not participate. None of the roads so brought into the case run to Eau Claire or engage, even indirectly, in the transportation of lumber from that point. Of what offense *against that town* can they be legally guilty? It would be quite absurd to charge a railroad with giving preference or advantage to a community which it does not serve, and it is equally illogical to say that it can prejudice or discriminate against such a community. All these terms imply comparison, and the basis of comparison is wanting unless the rates compared are made by the same carrier. These views are so fully concurred in by counsel for the respective parties that further argument is unsuitable. They lead to the conclusion that no order can properly be made in this proceeding against the roads which do not run to Eau Claire. This determination must also include the intervening manufacturers and dealers, who have obviously no standing in the case independent of the lines which extend from their respective localities. It does not follow that these roads will be legally free to reduce their rates at other points to correspond with any lower rate which may be fixed for Eau Claire. They have responded to the demand that they should defend the differential complained of, and they have endeavored to justify it by evidence and argument. They have presented their case and will be formally notified of our decision. While they are not legally connected with the rate claimed to be excessive, and not technically subject to an order for its correction, they will have no better right to render it ineffectual than they would have to openly disregard a direction clearly within the scope of our authority.

The attitude of the Omaha road is somewhat peculiar. It was not proceeded against originally, and the Milwaukee company did not ask to have it made a defendant. It voluntarily sought an opportunity to oppose the complainant, and was made a party on its own application. After engaging in the litigation with considerable vigor, it now earnestly asks to be exempted from any order reducing the Eau Claire differential. These circumstances might well justify us in denying this request, but we incline to the opinion that it should be granted. Measured by the lumber rates which it maintains at other places on its line, the Omaha road cannot be said to discriminate against Eau Claire, nor is it charged with enforcing rates at different points which are relatively unequal. For this reason much embarrassment might result to that company from an order requiring it to reduce its rate at the place in question, and as such an order is not demanded by the complainant or deemed necessary for the relief which it seeks, we are disposed to leave that carrier the option of accepting the Eau Claire rate prescribed for the Milwaukee company or going out of the Eau Claire business. No order, therefore, will be made against the Omaha road at this time, but the case will be held as against that company for such directions as may hereafter seem to be required.   *   *   *   *   *

We hold that the lumber rates in question discriminate against the shippers of Eau Claire, and that such discrimination is unjust and unlawful. The undue prejudice and disadvantage to which Eau Claire is thus subjected consists generally in the lower relative rates accorded to competing towns, especially those granted to La Crosse and Winona, and the complainant is entitled to an order correcting the inequality between these rival places.

The extent to which the Eau Claire differential should be reduced has been the subject of much deliberation. We have not considered it as an abstract proposition, based on mileage and cost of service, but have endeavored to make proper allowance for other existing circumstances and actual conditions. It is our desire to prescribe a rate which will be reasonably just to Eau Claire, and which the Milwaukee road will be fairly satisfied to accept. No mathematical rule has been followed and no particular theory applied, but that rate has been selected which, on the whole, best satisfies our judgment. To a certain extent our determination is arbitrary, but equally so is the fixing of a rate in the first instance. As the injustice which Eau Claire suffers arises mainly from the lower rates at La Crosse and Winona, the rate from the former should bear a fixed and permanent relation to the rates from the latter, independent of the Chicago rate upon which all the others are based under the Bogue arbitration. Taking everything into account, we think the rate from Eau Claire should not exceed the rate from La Crosse and Winona by more than 2 cents per hundred pounds, when the latter rate is not over 11 cents per hundred; and that such excess over the present rate of 16 cents from La Crosse and Winona should not be greater than $2\frac{1}{2}$ cents per hundred. Compared with the 16-cent rate now in force at these competing towns the rate thus fixed for Eau Claire will be higher by $8.75 per car; and the rate per car per mile and per ton per mile to the several Missouri river markets will still be considerably greater from Eau Claire than from La Crosse or Winona. All things considered, however, we believe that an addition of $2\frac{1}{2}$ cents to the present rate from those places will not be unjust to Eau Claire, and that a greater reduction in the differential now in force against that town should not at this time be required. If the operation of this rate fails to give equitable results, the complainant will not be debarred from making a further application for relief.   *   *   *

The order of the Commission is that from and after the tenth day of July, 1892, the Chicago, Milwaukee & St. Paul Railway Company cease and desist from charging, collecting, or receiving for or on account of lumber transported by it, in carload quantities, from Eau Claire, Wisconsin, to the various Missouri river points mentioned in this report, any greater sum or amount than two and one-half cents per hundred pounds more than shall or may from time to time be charged, collected or received by that company for the like transportation from the towns of La Crosse and Winona aforesaid.

IX

RELATIVE RATES

THE SAVANNAH NAVAL STORES CASE[1]

Facts

CLEMENTS, *Commissioner :*   *   *   *   *

1. The complainants are the Savannah Bureau of Freight
& Transportation, an association of business men of the city of
Savannah, Ga., organized to protect the transportation interests
of that city, and certain general merchants, naval-stores manufacturers and cotton shippers, most of whom are located along
the line of the Pensacola & Atlantic division of the Louisville
& Nashville Railroad. The defendant railroad and steamship
companies are severally common carriers and engaged in the
interstate transportation of freight articles. The lines of the
defendants, the Alabama Midland Railway Company, the Savannah, Florida & Western Railway Company and the Charleston
& Savannah Railway Company, are, with other lines of road,
operated by the " Plant System."

2. The Pensacola & Atlantic division of the Louisville &
Nashville Railroad System extends from Pensacola, Fla., to
River Junction, Fla., a distance of 161 miles. At River Junc-
tion it connects with the Savannah, Florida & Western Railway
for Savannah (Plant System), and also with the Florida Central
& Peninsular Railroad (Seaboard Air Line) for Jacksonville and
Savannah. The distance from River Junction to Savannah by
the former route is 259 miles, and by the latter route it is 347

---

[1] Decided January 8, 1900. Interstate Commerce Reports, Vol. VIII, pp. 376–
408. Sustained by the United States Circuit Court. 118 Fed. Rep. 613.

The main contention in this case related to rates on naval stores, turpentine
and rosin ; but inasmuch as the same principles involved are more simply and
briefly stated with reference to rates on cotton, that issue is mainly described
in this abstract. — ED.

miles. The distance from River Junction to Pensacola is 161 miles, and as Pensacola is distant from Mobile and New Orleans 104 miles and 245 miles, respectively, the distance from River Junction to Mobile and New Orleans is 265 miles and 406 miles, respectively.

The Pensacola & Atlantic division lies wholly within the State of Florida. It was built by the Pensacola & Atlantic Railroad Company with the assistance of the Louisville & Nashville Railroad Company, and subsequently purchased under a mortgage sale by the latter company. The State of Florida granted to the Pensacola & Atlantic Railroad Company 3,890,619 acres of land. This company had sold of said grant up to June 12, 1891, 668,590.05 acres for $552,330.50. The Louisville & Nashville Railroad Company from June 12, 1891, to April 30, 1897, sold 571,985.85 acres for $516,503.76. Some of the deeds, however, were

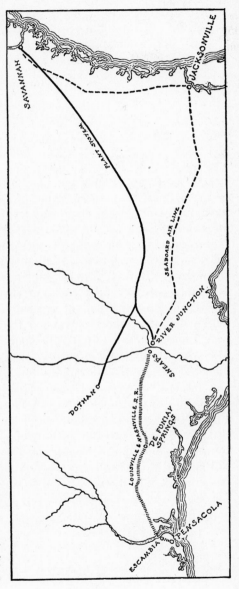

canceled, and the total net sales by both roads amounted on April 30, 1897, to 995,481.34 acres for $860,343.65.

According to a statement put in evidence for the defense, the Pensacola & Atlantic, considered as a distinct line, does not earn sufficient to pay operating expenses and interest on its fixed charges. It appears that the Louisville & Nashville has been operating the road since the beginning of the year 1885, and that it bought the property under foreclosure sale in May, 1891. The road is operated in connection with the other portions of this large system, and serves as a connection with the Plant System and Florida Central & Peninsular in Florida. The Louisville & Nashville Railroad Company is solvent and prosperous. It has increased its funded debt from $79,158,660 in 1895 to $110,693,660 in 1899, and during the fiscal year ended June 30, 1899, it paid its accruing funded debt obligations and declared a dividend of $3\frac{1}{2}$ per cent on its stock. The amount of stock outstanding was reported at $54,911,520.

3. West Florida, through which the Pensacola & Atlantic division runs, is very sparsely settled between Pensacola and River Junction, the termini of the road, there being, according to the census of 1890, no town on the line except the city of Pensacola, with a population of 1000 inhabitants. The volume of traffic originating along the road is comparatively small. The principal articles received for shipment are cotton, naval stores and lumber. Some wool and a few melons are also shipped. According to the census of 1890 Pensacola had a population of 11,750 inhabitants and Savannah a population of 43,189. Lumber from Pensacola & Atlantic stations is shipped principally to Pensacola, one of the largest markets for exporting lumber in sail vessels along the coast. Savannah, Ga., is the largest naval-stores market in the world, while Pensacola is a small market for rosin and turpentine, receiving these commodities principally from stations on the Louisville & Nashville system.

*   *   *   *   *   *   *   *

5. The Louisville & Nashville Railroad Company does not own or control any line of road entering Savannah. In the transportation of cotton or naval stores to Savannah from

Pensacola & Atlantic stations the interest of that company ends with the delivery to its connection, the Savannah, Florida & Western Railway Company or the Florida Central & Peninsular Railway Company, at River Junction. The only revenue it can receive from east-bound shipments is for the short haul to River Junction. The conditions are reversed on traffic going westward.

Most of the naval stores shipped from Pensacola & Atlantic stations westward are ultimately destined to interior points, such as Louisville, Cincinnati and Chicago, and on these shipments the Louisville & Nashville generally receives a long haul from Pensacola. The Louisville & Nashville therefore has a substantial interest in having this freight move west to or through Pensacola instead of east *via* River Junction to Savannah or other destinations, and its rates are made with a view of inducing such westward movement. Efforts to build up the naval-stores industry on the Pensacola & Atlantic division had failed until about two years prior to the filing of the complaint in this case. At that time the Pensacola naval-stores firm began business, and the Louisville & Nashville put in a lower schedule of rates from stations on that division, pursuant to an agreement it had made with the Pensacola firm. The rates to Savannah were not raised when the rates to Pensacola were reduced. A result of such action on the part of the railroad company has been to largely increase the volume of shipments of this class of traffic to Pensacola. The proportion of the total product of rosin and turpentine at the Pensacola & Atlantic stations which formerly went to Savannah has decreased under present rates, so that very little of either commodity is shipped to Savannah.

A former agent of the railroad company at a station on the Pensacola & Atlantic division testified that his salary was made to depend in some degree upon whether these shipments were sent west or east, that he received a larger commission when the traffic was destined west. There is evidence to the effect that shippers have had difficulty in ascertaining the rates in force on shipments to Savannah, and also that solid car loads of rosin or of turpentine were required when the destination was Savannah, while mixed car loads were permitted in the west-bound move-ment. These practices, if enforced, tend, as a matter of fact, to discriminate unjustly against shippers desiring to use the Savannah market.

* * * * * * * *

On a shipment of rosin from Sneads, Fla., to Savannah, the Louisville & Nashville would receive 15 cents per 100 pounds, or 75 cents per barrel of 500 pounds, for a haul of 6 miles to River Junction, while the connecting roads, the Savannah, Florida & Western or the Florida Central & Peninsular, would only receive $9\frac{1}{4}$ cents per 100 pounds, or $46\frac{1}{4}$ cents per barrel of 500 pounds, for the haul respectively of 259 miles or 347 miles from River Junction to Savannah. On a west-bound shipment of rosin from Sneads to Pensacola, a distance of 155 miles, the rate is $9\frac{1}{2}$ cents per 100 pounds, or $47\frac{1}{2}$ cents per barrel of 500 pounds, and from Bohemia to Pensacola, a distance of 6 miles, the rate is 5 cents per 100 pounds, or 25 cents per barrel of 500 pounds. From De Funiak Springs, which is about half-way between Pensacola and River Junction, the Louisville & Nashville receives for the transportation of rosin $7\frac{1}{2}$ cents per 100 pounds for the haul to Pensacola, and 15 cents per 100 pounds to River Junction, as its proportion of the through rate to Savannah.

Dothan, Ala., on the Plant System, and Cottondale, Fla., on the Pensacola & Atlantic division, are each about 294 miles from Savannah. The line of the Plant System runs from Dothan north of the Pensacola & Atlantic division of the Louisville & Nashville, and connects with the short branch to River Junction, about 65 miles from Dothan. The rate on rosin from Dothan by the Plant System to Savannah is 12 cents per 100 pounds, or about 8 mills per ton per mile. * * * *

9. There are, however, some other facts connected with the question. The Louisville & Nashville has made these rates with a view, not only of providing a market at Pensacola for naval stores shipped from its Pensacola & Atlantic division, but of encouraging the production of such commodities in that sec-tion; and it is a fact that the output at its Pensacola & Atlantic

stations is much greater than it was before the establishment of the present rates to Pensacola. The building up of the Pensacola market has benefited producers and dealers along this division. The present rates to Savannah were in effect before the Louisville & Nashville made these rates to Pensacola, and whatever wrong now exists has not been caused by changes in the Savannah rates, but by the relation in rates as between Pensacola and Savannah, which causes the great bulk of the traffic to go to Pensacola.

Another consideration is that the Louisville & Nashville by inducing this traffic to go to Pensacola is able to secure return local loading for cars which have been used to haul supplies from or through Pensacola to its Pensacola & Atlantic stations. It must also furnish cars for naval-stores shipments to Savannah, but it cannot rely upon those cars coming back with supplies for stations on that division. The car passes from its control at River Junction, and it may reach its line again at some point far distant from its Pensacola & Atlantic division. This might not be material with free interchange of cars carrying a large traffic to and from the Pensacola & Atlantic division, but it is of some importance in view of the present small volume of business which is done at points on that part of the Louisville & Nashville system.

It is urged by the Louisville & Nashville that these rates to Pensacola are applied in large degree on naval stores which are reshipped from Pensacola to points north, like Cincinnati and Louisville, and that it thereby gets a long haul which it could not obtain from shipments to Savannah. The rates to Pensacola are not necessarily the proportion which the Louisville & Nashville must take into account in fixing rates on shipments from the Pensacola & Atlantic stations to Louisville or Cincinnati. It can make low rates over its own line for the long haul to those points, with no other regard to the local rates to Pensacola than that the charge to Cincinnati or Louisville should not be less than the rate to Pensacola. It does in fact make through rates from its Pensacola & Atlantic stations *via* Pensacola to various points which are considerably less than the sum of rates to and from Pensacola. The Louisville & Nashville has in effect a special rate over its own line of 25 cents on turpentine from Pensacola to Evansville, Ind., a distance of 621 miles. This is no more than the share it exacts out of the through rate to Savannah from points on the Pensacola & Atlantic division for which it carries the turpentine no greater distance than 155 miles from Bohemia to River Junction, and its haul to River Junction may be as low as 6 miles. The Louisville & Nashville rates to Pensacola are intended to draw naval stores to that market for sale and subsequent reshipment, and the Louisville & Nashville secures the carriage of all shipments from Pensacola. The roads to Savannah make naval-stores rates low to Savannah, not for consumption there, but because it is a market, a point of concentration and reshipment, for such stores. A large part of the domestic shipments of this traffic from Savannah is shipped north by water, and the Plant System and Florida Central & Peninsular must share the rail shipments from Savannah with the other roads entering that city. The Louisville & Nashville can justly claim that its rates on naval stores to the near-by market of Pensacola from these Pensacola & Atlantic division stations, as compared with the through rate to Savannah, the much more distant market, should give some advantage to Pensacola, which it has contributed largely to build up as a concentrating point for these commodities.

*   *   *   *   *   *   *   *

11. Both upland and sea-island cotton are produced along the line of the Pensacola & Atlantic division, and about 10 per cent of the crop is of the long staple or sea-island variety. The sea-island grade is generally worth 3 or 4 cents a pound more than upland cotton. Most, if not all, of the sea-island cotton appears to go to Savannah. During the year 1896–97 the shipments of cotton from Pensacola & Atlantic stations to Savannah, New Orleans and Mobile were as follows: To Savannah, 4077 bales; to New Orleans, 3713 bales; to Mobile, 2021 bales. Pensacola is not a cotton market and practically no cotton is shipped to that point. The rate on cotton from Pensacola & Atlantic stations to Savannah at the time of complaint and at the date of the hearing in this case was $2.75 per bale, and the bale is estimated to weigh 500 pounds. This resulted in a rate of 55 cents per 100 pounds. The rate applied from all stations and had been in effect for a number of years. The Louisville & Nashville share of the $2.75 rate was $1.75 per bale for its haul to River Junction, while connecting roads only received $1.00. There are no compresses on the Pensacola & Atlantic division, and if the cotton was compressed by the carrier in transit it was done by the road east of River Junction. Notwithstanding the blanket-cotton rate from Pensacola & Atlantic stations to Savannah is challenged by the complaint in this case, that rate was increased by the defendants after the hearing from $2.75 to $3.30 per bale, and if for export the rate was still higher, $3.45 per bale. The special export rate was afterwards canceled, and the rate to Savannah for all purposes is now $3.30 per bale of 500 pounds. From most stations on the Pensacola & Atlantic division the rate to Pensacola was $1.50 per bale of 500 pounds. A few stations comparatively near Pensacola, including Galt City and Escambia, took rates of 26 and 27 cents, the former being the lowest rate to Pensacola. These rates were also in effect at the time of the hearing.

The rate on cotton from all Pensacola & Atlantic stations to Mobile was, at the time of the complaint, and still is, $2.00 per bale, and to New Orleans it was and still is $2.50 per bale. The rates to Mobile and New Orleans commence with Escambia, 10 miles from Pensacola, and include River Junction, 161 miles from Pensacola. The distance from Escambia to Mobile is 114 miles and to New Orleans 255 miles. From Sneads, 6 miles west of River Junction, these distances are 259 miles to Mobile and 400 miles to New Orleans. From Escambia to Savannah the distance is 410 miles, and the distance from Sneads to Savannah is 265 miles. From De Funiak Springs, a central point on the Pensacola & Atlantic division, the distance to Mobile is 183 miles and to New Orleans 324 miles. That point is distant from Savannah 341 miles. The Louisville & Nashville obtained $1.75 out of the former rate to Savannah, and it actually gets as much or more out of the higher rate now in force. It received that sum for the short haul to River Junction, and only charges 75 cents more for, in most cases, more than double the distance to New Orleans. From only three or four Pensacola & Atlantic stations near Pensacola is the distance to Mobile less than the distance to River Junction, and it is not understood that any cotton is sent from those stations near Pensacola. From De Funiak Springs the mileage is much greater to Mobile than to River Junction. The rate to Pensacola, Mobile and New Orleans does not include the cost of compression.

It was testified by the vice president of the Louisville & Nashville that having reached a basis of, say, 50 cents to 55 cents per 100 pounds on cotton, it has been found from experience that that is about the maximum rate which can be secured; and we find that to be the fact in this southern territory.

On account of risk of fire, bulk and loading expenses, cotton is not an attractive commodity to a carrier on a short haul of 50 miles or less. The rate to Savannah is a joint rate, while the rates to Mobile and New Orleans are only those of the Louisville & Nashville. The rate to New Orleans must be fixed with reference to the obtainable price in that large cotton market.   *

It is not found that the entire rate of $2.75 is excessive, unreasonable or unjust in itself or in comparison with the rate to Mobile or New Orleans; but we do find that the present rate of $3.30 per bale, equal to 3.8 cents per ton per mile for a haul of 341 miles, is excessive, and that the action of the Louisville & Nashville and its connections to Savannah in advancing the rate above the former existing charge of $2.75 per bale was altogether unreasonable and unjust.   *   *   *

Conclusions

*   *   *   *   *   *   *   *

We shall dispose of the cotton rate first. When the complaint was filed the rate was $2.75 per bale, of which the Louisville & Nashville obtained $1.75 for its short haul to River Junction. This rate was still in effect at the time of the hearing. It was testified for the defense that the rate of $2.75 per bale was reasonable, and the rate had been in force for a considerable period. It was also asserted by the same witness that a rate of 50 to 55 cents a hundred, equal to $2.50 and $2.75 per bale of 500 pounds, was about as high a rate as could be charged without prohibiting the shipment. Under that rate, of a given year's crop, about 4000 bales moved to Savannah, while the remainder, about 5700 bales, went to Mobile and New Orleans, but the quantity sent to Savannah included the sea-island variety, amounting to about 10 per cent of the total amount shipped from the Pensacola & Atlantic stations, and for which Savannah is the principal market. Sea-island cotton is more valuable than upland cotton, and it may be that it could stand a somewhat higher rate, but the amount produced and shipped from Pensacola & Atlantic stations is very small as compared with upland cotton, and the carriers in fixing their rates have not made any distinction between the two kinds. Some time after the hearing the carriers to Savannah made the rate from Pensacola & Atlantic stations $3.30 per bale. This was an increase of 55 cents. The rate of $3.30 per bale is still in force. No advance was made in the rate of $2.00 to Mobile, or in the rate of $2.50 to New Orleans. Under such a rate adjustment the cotton (except the sea-island) must go to Mobile or New Orleans, or the shipper to Savannah must bear the large additional expense occasioned by the advance of 55 cents per bale. In making this advance in rates the carriers acted unjustly and unreasonably to the producer and to the shipper of cotton carried from these Pensacola & Atlantic stations, and subjected them to unlawful prejudice. The carriers to Savannah, also, by so advancing the cotton rate to that city gave undue and unreasonable preference and advantage to Mobile and New Orleans and to dealers in cotton at and the traffic in cotton to those places; and they subjected Savannah and her cotton merchants and shipments of cotton to that market to wrongful prejudice and disadvantage. The whole advance was unlawful. It violated sections 1 and 3 of the Act; and any higher rate on uncompressed cotton from any of these Pensacola & Atlantic stations to Savannah than the former difference of 25 cents per bale above the rate in force from the same stations to New Orleans is unlawful under those sections.   *

The Louisville & Nashville insists that the near-by market of Pensacola is entitled to all of this great advantage.[1] It claims that the lower rates to Pensacola were necessary to create a market there for these stores, and, further, that the carriage to Pensacola is only part of its haul on the great majority of the shipments, while on shipments to Savannah it can only have the short haul to River Junction, where it must turn the traffic over to one of its connecting roads. Whatever difference in rates may have seemed necessary at the outset to create a demand in the Pensacola market, it is apparent now, after several years' trial, that the rates to Savannah as compared with the Pensacola rates give an unwarranted advantage to Pensacola. In endeavoring to build up a near-by market at Pensacola, and so furnish these products with a market in addition to the one existing at Savannah, the Louisville & Nashville was acting in the interest of producers of and dealers in naval stores on its Pensacola & Atlantic division. It went beyond this, however, and so controlled the adjustment of rates to the two markets as to give Pensacola a practical monopoly of the trade. A carrier cannot lawfully establish and maintain an adjustment of rates which in practice prevents shippers on its line from availing themselves of a principal market which they have long been using, and confers a substantial monopoly upon a new market in which, for reasons of its own, it has greater interest. That is what has been done in this case.

The further and perhaps chief ground relied upon to justify this abnormal relation in rates on traffic which is competitive mainly as between Savannah and Pensacola is that the present lower scale of rates to Pensacola is required to hold the traffic for long hauls on the Louisville & Nashville system. This company can and does make through rates on naval stores from its Pensacola & Atlantic division *via* Pensacola to numerous points. Its claim goes further than this, however. It also aims to compel shipments locally to Pensacola, that it may get the benefit

---

[1] The conclusions of the Commission as to rates on naval stores are so interwoven with those relating to cotton rates that they are reproduced in full. — ED.

of the reshipments from that point, and it has the only railroad entering that city. A shipment billed and transported to Pensacola for local delivery there constitutes a complete transaction, just as a shipment billed and transported for delivery in Savannah is a complete transaction. As between two transactions of this character the Louisville & Nashville may prefer itself in the matter of rates to the extent of its fair interest as a common carrier, but it can no more be permitted to create a monopoly in its west-bound movement as compared with the east-bound than Pensacola can be permitted as a new market to have a monopoly of the traffic, and so shut out the old market of Savannah. We hold, in other words, that when a carrier makes rates to two competing localities which give the one a practical monopoly over the other because it can secure reshipments from the favored locality and none from the other, it goes beyond serving its fair interest, and disregards the statutory requirement of relative equality as between persons, localities and particular descriptions of traffic.

Our ruling in *Colorado Fuel & Iron Co.* v. *Southern P. Co.*, 6 I. C. C. Rep. 488, bears upon this point. In that case the rate to San Francisco on iron articles produced at Pueblo, Colo., was prohibitive, while on iron shipped from Chicago to San Francisco the rate was low. The Southern Pacific was the delivering line in San Francisco on shipments from both Pueblo, and Chicago, but it would get a much longer haul on Chicago traffic sent over a circuitous route *via* New Orleans than it would on either Pueblo or Chicago traffic sent direct to San Francisco. The testimony tended to show that the Southern Pacific secured greater compensation if shipments came to San Francisco *via* New Orleans. The Commission held that inequality in the treatment of shippers, having no other justification than this end, was indefensible.

The Louisville & Nashville insists also that it is unusual for a carrier reaching a seaport on its own line to make joint rates with another carrier which will divert traffic originating on its road to a rival seaport. In the view we take of this contention, it is unnecessary to discuss whether this is or is not a railway practice. It is not understood that the complainants are here asking for an order which will so divert traffic from Pensacola as to place it at a disadvantage as compared with Savannah. If a railroad company cannot secure other than an unreasonably low share of the joint rate to a seaport on another road, it may be justified in declining to join in such a rate, especially when it can take the traffic to a seaport reached by its own road; but a carrier engaged in transportation over the through line finds no such justification when it is able to secure for itself a share of the joint rate which fully equals the rate established by it for purely local service over like distances on its own road. That is this case under the readjustment indicated by the findings.

We think that readjustment fully meets the objections to the complaint which are raised by the Louisville & Nashville Company. It still gives considerable advantage to Pensacola; it gives the Louisville & Nashville for the less service involved in the haul to River Junction on shipments to Savannah the same compensation that it obtains on purely local shipments carried for like distances to Pensacola, and on turpentine from the more easterly stations it gives more.

We hold that the present shares of the Louisville & Nashville in the through rates to Savannah are unreasonable and unjust, and that they operate to make the entire through rates unjust and unreasonable as compared with the rates charged by the Louisville & Nashville to Pensacola; that because of such excessive shares of the Louisville & Nashville in the through rates to Savannah such through rates do, as related to the rates to Pensacola, subject producers and shippers along the Pensacola & Atlantic division of the Louisville & Nashville Railroad to wrongful prejudice and disadvantage; that such through rates as related to the rates to Pensacola also subject Savannah, naval-stores dealers in Savannah, and the traffic in naval stores to that city, to undue and unreasonable prejudice and disadvantage, and they result in undue and unreasonable preference and advantage to Pensacola, dealers in naval stores in Pensacola, and the traffic in naval stores to that city. It results, therefore, that the present rates to Savannah are in violation of sections 1 and 3 of the Act.

The wrong and injustice so inflicted, and the unjust favoritism so resulting, would be remedied by charges on rosin and turpentine to Savannah which will embrace the proportions now and for several years accepted by the carriers east of River Junction, and also give the Louisville & Nashville for its hauls to River Junction its full local rates for approximately the same distances to Pensacola, with the exception that on turpentine from stations east of Mossy Head the rate to Savannah should exceed the rate from Sneads to Pensacola to the extent of 6 cents per hundred pounds, thereby giving the Louisville & Nashville on turpentine from such stations more than its local rate for the like distance to Pensacola.

We determine, therefore, that the rates on rosin and turpentine from these Pensacola & Atlantic stations to Savannah should bear the following definite relations to the rates on those commodities to Pensacola. The rate from any such station to Savannah is to be adjusted by adding to the local rate of the Louisville & Nashville for the distance to Pensacola which is nearest to the distance from that station to River Junction the present share accepted by the carriers to Savannah from River Junction. Provided, however, that from all stations east of Mossy Head the rates on turpentine to Savannah shall be determined by adding 6 cents to the rate fixed by the Louisville & Nashville from Sneads to Pensacola, the carriers east of River Junction accepting their present share from such stations east of Mossy Head. In the event that the defendant carriers operating east of River Junction should decline to accept their present proportions, any party may apply for a further or modified order. While the Louisville & Nashville share of the Savannah rate is held to be unreasonable, we base the remedy upon the relation of rates to the two competing markets. This will enable the Louisville & Nashville to increase the rates to Pensacola, or in conjunction with its connections east of River Junction reduce the rates to Savannah, or to use both means in conforming to the adjustment which appears to be required by the facts in this case; provided, of course, that the rates to Pensacola should not be made unreasonable.

Order will be issued in accordance with these conclusions.

X

RELATIVE RATES

The Chattanooga Case[1]

(Map at p. 154, supra)

KNAPP, *Chairman:*   *   *   *   *   *

The complaint relates to the rates of the defendants on the six numbered classes of traffic and on a large number of commodities from Boston, Providence, New York, Philadelphia, and Baltimore to Chattanooga and Nashville, respectively, both by the direct lines to Chattanooga and *via* Chattanooga to Nashville, and by the lines *via* Cincinnati to Chattanooga and *via* Cincinnati to Nashville, and it charges :

First, That the rates to Chattanooga are unjust and unreasonable in themselves, in violation of section 1 of the Act to regulate commerce, which requires all rate charges for any service rendered in the transportation of property or in connection therewith to be reasonable and just and prohibits and declares unlawful every unjust and unreasonable charge.

Second, That the rates to Chattanooga are higher than for the longer haul through Chattanooga and 151 miles on to Nashville, and are in violation of the provision of section 4 of the Act to regulate commerce which declares it to be unlawful for any common carrier subject to the provisions of the Act " to charge or receive any greater compensation in the aggregate for the transportation of a like kind of property under substantially similar circumstances and conditions, for a shorter than for a longer distance over the same line, in the same direction, the shorter being included within the longer distance."

---

[1] Originally decided March 12, 1904. Interstate Commerce Reports, Vol. X, pp. 111–147. Decision, originally rendered in favor of Chattanooga in 1892, was sustained by both the United States Circuit Court and the Circuit Court of Appeals; was then reversed by the Supreme Court (181 U. S. 29) under its interpretation of the law in the Alabama Midland case (*vide,* p. 378, *infra*), but without prejudice to the right of the Commission to reopen the case. This is the case as thus reopened. The dissenting opinion, herein reproduced, represents the claims of Chattanooga. Its larger significance is set forth in Ripley's Railroads : Rates and Regulation. (Index.) The special map on p. 229 will be found serviceable in the study of the case.

Third, That "the merchants and other business men of Chattanooga and Nashville, respectively, compete for business largely in the same territory; that the excesses of the Chattanooga rates over the Nashville rates amount in most, if not all, instances to a reasonable profit on the traffic and subject Chattanooga merchants to an undue or unreasonable prejudice or disadvantage in such competition and give Nashville an undue or unreasonable preference or advantage over Chattanooga in such competition, and that the rates in question to Chattanooga and Nashville are, therefore, in violation of section 3 of the Act to regulate commerce, which declares unlawful such undue or unreasonable prejudice or disadvantage and such undue preference or advantage."

It is alleged in the complaint that if there should be any difference in rates as between Chattanooga and Nashville, such difference should be made by making the Chattanooga rates lower than the Nashville rates, because, (1) of Chattanooga's greater proximity to the points of shipment, Boston, Providence, New York, Philadelphia and Baltimore; (2) of transportation by the Tennessee river to Chattanooga; and (3) of the greater number of rail lines which enter Chattanooga and compete for business from those cities to Chattanooga than enter Nashville and compete for such business to Nashville.   *   *

The defendants admit that the rates in question are higher for the shorter haul to Chattanooga than for the longer haul by 151 miles through Chattanooga to Nashville; that the rates are correctly set forth in the complaint and that they participate in those rates either as members of the lines to Chattanooga and through Chattanooga to Nashville, or as members of the lines through Cincinnati to Chattanooga and to Nashville, but they deny that those rates are in violation of either section 1, 3 or 4 of the law as charged in the complaint.

In justification of the lower rates from New York and other eastern seaboard cities to Nashville than to Chattanooga, it is alleged that those rates were primarily made by the Trunk Line roads through the Ohio river crossings, Cincinnati, Louisville and Evansville, "and are controlled by the following competitive circumstances and conditions: "

First, Water competition by the Hudson river, the St. Lawrence river, the Erie canal and the lakes, which fixes the rail rates from New York to

Chicago and to which latter rates, it is alleged, the rates from New York and other eastern seaboard cities to Cincinnati, Louisville and Evansville " are made to bear certain fixed relations."

Second, Water competition between Paducah and Evansville on the Ohio river, on the one hand, and Nashville on the Cumberland river, on the other, by means of boats on the Cumberland river which connect with boats on the Ohio river.

Third, Water competition from New York and the other eastern seaboard cities to Cincinnati, Louisville and Evansville by way of the ocean, the gulf and the Mississippi and Ohio rivers.

Fourth, Competition by ocean from New York and other eastern seaboard cities to Norfolk and Newport News, Virginia, and thence by the rail lines, the Norfolk & Western and the Chesapeake & Ohio railways, from those cities to Louisville, Cincinnati and Evansville.

It is alleged that the rates from said eastern seaboard cities to Cincinnati and Louisville having been fixed by these competitive circumstances and conditions, the rates from said eastern seaboard cities to Nashville cannot greatly exceed the rates to Cincinnati or Louisville added to the rates which can be obtained by steamboats from Cincinnati or Louisville over the Ohio and Cumberland rivers to Nashville, but that there is no effective open water route from the eastern seaboard cities to Chattanooga, nor from Cincinnati or Louisville to Chattanooga and the water competition which forces down the through rail rates from Cincinnati and Louisville, respectively, to Nashville, does not extend to Chattanooga.

It is further alleged that Nashville enjoys a position geographically which is not enjoyed by Chattanooga, being practically the center of a circle, of which Cincinnati, Louisville, Evansville, Cairo and Memphis may be regarded as points on the circumference, and that there is a large territory tributary to Cincinnati, Louisville, Evansville, Cairo and Memphis, south of the Ohio river, which is also tributary to Nashville, and the rate adjustment to Nashville relatively to the points specified above has been, is, and should be such as to enable it to do business in comparison with those cities.

The Southern Railway Company alleges in its answer that all rates from eastern seaboard cities to Chattanooga are fixed by the eastern lines and are made relative to the rates from those cities to Atlanta, Rome, Birmingham and Anniston, which cities compete directly with Chattanooga in territory common to those cities and to Chattanooga, and that this is the basis upon which the Chattanooga rates are made.

The Louisville & Nashville road denies that it is engaged in the transportation of traffic *through Chattanooga* to Nashville.

* * * * * * * *

It is also alleged in behalf of the defendants that the Chattanooga and Nashville rates are governed by different classifications; the Chattanooga rates by the Southern Classification and the Nashville rates by the Official Classification.

Facts

1. The defendants . . . are common carriers engaged as parts of through lines and under joint tariffs of rates in transporting traffic from New York and other eastern seaboard cities to Chattanooga and to Nashville.

2. The following table gives the rates in question from Boston, Providence and New York to Chattanooga and Nashville, respectively, on the six numbered classes in cents per hundred pounds, and also shows the excesses in cents per hundred pounds and per car loads of 30,000 pounds of the Chattanooga rates over the Nashville rates.

	1	2	3	4	5	6
Chattanooga	114	98	86	73	60	49
Nashville	91	78	60	42	36	31
Excess per 100 lbs. of Chattanooga rates	23	20	26	31	24	18
Excess per car load of 30,000 lbs. . .	$69	$60	$78	$93	$72	$54

The same excesses of the rates to Chattanooga over those to Nashville as are shown in the above table in rates from Boston, Providence and New York, exist under the rates from Philadelphia and Baltimore.

The following table [Abridged.— ED.] gives the rates in cents per hundred pounds from Boston, Providence and New York to Chattanooga and Nashville, respectively, and the excesses of the Chattanooga rates over the Nashville rates on car loads of 30,000 pounds on a few commodities. Those rates are given as illustrating the differences in rates in favor of Nashville on the entire list of commodities.

COMMODITY RATES

Canned goods Boston and New York to Chattanooga, C/L $0.48
Canned goods Boston and New York to Nashville 36
Difference on a car load of 30,000 pounds in favor of Nashville . . 36.00
Green coffee Boston and New York to Chattanooga, C/L 60
Green coffee Boston and New York to Nashville 36
Difference on a car load of 30,000 pounds in favor of Nashville . . 72.00
Agate ware Boston and New York to Chattanooga, C/L. 73
Agate ware Boston and New York to Nashville. 42
Difference on a car load of 30,000 pounds in favor of Nashville . . 93.00
Cartridges Boston and New York to Chattanooga, C/L 60
Cartridges Boston and New York to Nashville 42
Difference on a car load of 30,000 pounds in favor of Nashville . . 54.00

The same differences in rates in favor of Nashville as are shown in the above table in rates from Boston, Providence and New York, exist under the rates from Philadelphia and Baltimore.

The rates by all the lines to Chattanooga are the same and the rates by all the lines to Nashville are the same.

3. Chattanooga class rates are governed by the Southern Classification, and Nashville class rates by the Official. A large number of articles are in the same class in both classifications; there are some articles which are classed higher under the Official Classification than under the Southern, and some that are classed higher under the Southern Classification than under the Official; but even where articles are classed higher under the Official Classification than under the Southern, they still have lower rates under the Official Classification than under the Southern, because the Southern Classification rates are so much higher per class than the Official Classification rates. For example, the class 6 rate of the Southern Classification is higher than the class 4 rate of the Official Classification.

4. By the lines from New York and other eastern seaboard cities through Chattanooga, Huntsville is a longer-distance point than Chattanooga by 97 miles, Decatur by 122 miles, Tuscumbia by 165 miles, Sheffield by 170 miles, and Florence by 173 miles, but the rates to all these points are the same as the rates for the shorter haul to Chattanooga (map, p. 154). The testimony shows that these rates as applied to the longer hauls to these longer-distance points yield the carriers a remuneration in excess of operating expenses and fixed charges.

The rates for the haul from eastern seaboard cities through Chattanooga and 310 miles on to Memphis are lower than for the shorter haul to Chattanooga. For example, the class 1 rate from New York to Memphis is 100 cents as against a rate of 114 cents to Chattanooga. The testimony is that if this rate of 100 cents were applied to the shorter haul to Chattanooga "it would not be unremunerative." The Memphis rail rates are made with a view of meeting competition by the Mississippi river on which Memphis is located.

The rates from eastern seaboard cities by ocean to Norfolk and thence by rail to Evansville are lower than the rates to Chattanooga. For example, the class 1 rate by that route to Evansville is 73 cents per hundred pounds. The class 1 rate by that route to Chattanooga is $1.14, 41 cents higher than the Evansville rate. The testimony tends to show that the 73-cent rate as applied to the haul to Evansville is reasonably remunerative, and it is testified that the same rate as applied to the haul to Chattanooga "would yield more than the cost of transportation to Chattanooga."

5. The Chattanooga rates from eastern seaboard cities yield rates per ton per mile much greater than — in some instances more than double — the average receipts per ton per mile of the principal defendants, of roads throughout southern territory and of roads throughout the United States.

6. The rates in question from New York and other eastern seaboard cities to Chattanooga were established by the roads as members of the Southern Railway & Steamship Association,[1]

and are still with immaterial exceptions maintained as originally fixed. The Southern Railway & Steamship Association
ceased to exist under that name in about 1895, but it was succeeded by the Southern States Freight Association, which in
turn was succeeded, May 1, 1897, by the Southeastern Freight
Association. The existing association names rates and fixes
classifications through joint committees, each road having a
representative on the committee, and the rates are, as a rule,
concurred in and maintained as under the Southern Railway &
Steamship Association, although the succeeding association has
not the power, which the Southern Railway & Steamship Association had, of enforcing the maintenance of rates by fines. The
roads not belonging to the association conform to the association
rates. The Chattanooga rates as now fixed have been in force
more than 18 years and were established long before the Southern Railway & Steamship Association was dissolved.

7. In establishing rates from eastern seaboard cities to
Chattanooga, the Southern Railway & Steamship Association
grouped Chattanooga with the following cities and towns and
perhaps others, to wit: Dalton, Rome, Atlanta, Americus,
Athens, Columbus, Fort Gaines and Griffin, in the State of
Georgia; Huntsville, Decatur, Sheffield, Tuscumbia, Florence,
Gadsden, Oxford, Talladega, Anniston, Birmingham, Opelika,
Montgomery, Selma and Eufaula, in the State of Alabama and
Meridian, in the State of Mississippi. The sea and rail rates
to all these points are the same as to Chattanooga, although
many of them are longer-distance points from the east than
Chattanooga and the haul to them is through Chattanooga, for
example, Huntsville, Decatur, Florence, Tuscumbia and Sheffield. The sea and rail rates are the rates by ocean to Norfolk,
Pinner's Point, Charleston or Savannah and thence by rail, and
are the rates complained of in this case. The bulk of the traffic
to Chattanooga and the Chattanooga group comes by these sea
and rail lines and these sea and rail rates are applied to that
traffic. Of the cities and towns named above as belonging to the
Chattanooga group, Dalton, Rome, Atlanta, Americus, Athens,
Columbus, Griffin, Anniston, Gadsden, Oxford, Opelika and

Eufaula have higher all rail class rates than Chattanooga — their
all rail rates on the six numbered classes being as follows:

1	2	3	4	5	6
126	108	95	81	66	54

The all rail rates to the other points in the group are the
same as to Chattanooga.

It is claimed and the testimony is to the effect that a reduction in the rates to Chattanooga would necessitate a reduction
in the rates to all the points in the same group with Chattanooga, as without such reduction, Chattanooga would be given
an unjust advantage in rates over those points.

8. Nashville is situated on the Cumberland river and is
reached by the Louisville & Nashville road, the Nashville,
Chattanooga & St. Louis Railway and the Tennessee Central
Railroad.

Chattanooga is located on the Tennessee river and is reached
by the following nine originally independent railroads, to wit:
The Cincinnati Southern Railway; the Southern Railway; the
Georgia Division of the Southern Railway; the Western & Atlantic Railroad; the Chattanooga, Rome & Southern Railroad;
the Chattanooga Southern; the Alabama Great Southern; the
Memphis & Charleston Railroad; and the Nashville, Chattanooga & St. Louis Railway.

These nine roads are now operated by about four distinct
companies or systems.

9. In the former case the only lines involved were the direct
lines, all rail or sea and rail, to Chattanooga and through Chattanooga to Nashville, and the order of the Commission related
to rates over those lines alone. The lines involved under the
complaint in the present case are the lines from New York and
other eastern seaboard cities, either all rail, or sea and rail, *via*
Norfolk, Charleston or Savannah, to Chattanooga and through
Chattanooga to Nashville, and also the lines *via* Cincinnati to
Chattanooga and to Nashville.

The short all rail line from New York *via* Cincinnati to Nashville is made up of the Pennsylvania Railroad from New York to Cincinnati and the Louisville & Nashville road from Cincinnati to Nashville, and is 1058 miles in length.

The short all rail line from New York to Chattanooga is by the Pennsylvania Railroad from New York to Alexandria, the Southern Railway from Alexandria to Lynchburg, the Norfolk & Western Railway from Lynchburg to Bristol and the Southern Railway from Bristol to Chattanooga, and is 846 miles in length.

The excess of the distance by the above line *via* Cincinnati to Nashville over the above line to Chattanooga is 212 miles.

The short all rail line from New York *via* Chattanooga to Nashville is by the line above given to Chattanooga and thence over the Nashville, Chattanooga & St. Louis Railway 151 miles on to Nashville. By this line and by all lines through Chattanooga to Nashville, Nashville is the longer-distance point by 151 miles.   *   *   *   *   *   *   *

10. The Louisville & Nashville Railroad Company owns and operates the road from Evansville to Nashville and the road from Cincinnati through Louisville to Nashville, and is part of the short through line from New York and other eastern seaboard cities *via* Cincinnati to Nashville. It also operates jointly with the Atlantic Coast Line Railroad the road from Augusta to Atlanta, Georgia, and it owns a majority of the capital stock of the Nashville, Chattanooga & St. Louis Railway Company, which latter road, having leased the Western & Atlantic extending from Atlanta to Chattanooga, operates the line all the way from Atlanta through Chattanooga to Nashville.

The Louisville & Nashville road by virtue of its ownership of a majority of the stock of the Nashville, Chattanooga & St. Louis Railway, can name the entire board of directors and has the power to control the operations of the latter road. If competition of the Nashville, Chattanooga & St. Louis Railway Company with the Louisville & Nashville Railroad Company on traffic from the east to Nashville should for any reason become objectionable to the Louisville & Nashville road, it possesses the power to control or put an end to that competition.

The two roads, however, have separate and distinct corps of officers and employees and appear to be in active competition for traffic from eastern seaboard cities to Nashville. The Louisville & Nashville road has no interest, as stockholder or otherwise, in any railroad east of Augusta or in any ocean steamship company whose vessels ply from South Atlantic ports to New York and other eastern seaboard cities.[1]

The competition of the Nashville, Chattanooga & St. Louis Railway, as a member of the lines through Chattanooga to Nashville, with the Louisville & Nashville Railroad, as a member of the lines through Cincinnati to Nashville, for traffic from eastern seaboard cities to Nashville does not affect the rates to Nashville. The rates of the lines through Chattanooga and through Cincinnati are the same and have been the same as now for a long period of time. There is active competition between the two sets of lines for business, but *that competition is at the "established rates."* There has been no competition *affecting rates* since the rates were established by the Southern Railway & Steamship Association more than 18 years ago.   *

11. By steamboats operating on the Cumberland river and connecting with Ohio and Mississippi river boats, Nashville has water communication with Cincinnati, Louisville, Evansville, Brookport or Paducah, and Cairo.

The Cumberland river is navigable from 7½ to 10 months in the year, an average of about 8½ months. On shipments by the Ohio and Cumberland rivers from Cincinnati to Nashville, the traffic is transferred from the Ohio river boat to the Cumberland river boat at Evansville or Paducah.

The distance from Cincinnati to Nashville by the Ohio and Cumberland rivers is 690 miles and by all rail (the Louisville & Nashville road) 295 miles. From Evansville to Nashville by river the distance is 340 miles and by rail 154 miles. The time by boat from Cincinnati to Nashville is 6 days, and for the round trip 12 days. The time from Evansville to Nashville is 2½ days and for the round trip about 6 days.

---

[1] The Atlantic Coast Line has since then absorbed the entire Louisville and Nashville system. — ED.

There is no material amount of traffic from New York and other eastern seaboard cities which moves to Nashville by boat on the Cumberland river. There are no through rates published or agreed upon from eastern seaboard cities by rail to Cincinnati or Evansville and thence by river to Nashville, and there never have been such through rates. The boat lines from Cincinnati and from Evansville to Nashville have no published rates. The largest business done by boats on the Cumberland river from Ohio river points to Nashville is the grain business. The bulk of the traffic besides grain transported on the Cumberland river from Evansville to Nashville consists of buckets, brooms, sieves, wooden ware, molasses and glucose.

The rail lines have great advantages over the river lines and merchants much prefer the former. It is only when the rail rates are excessive or unreasonable that they resort to the river. And the goods and commodities shipped by Nashville merchants by river to Nashville are for the most part, if not entirely, traffic as to which time is not an element of importance. The risk by river is greater than by rail and river traffic from Cincinnati to Nashville is insured.

Since the advent of railways, the business of river lines on long through hauls has almost entirely ceased and, although the rail rates from Cincinnati, Louisville and Evansville to Nashville are much higher than the river rates, the railroads get all but an inconsiderable portion of the business.

Nashville merchants testify that they have the Cumberland river to rely upon for protection from excessive rates by rail and that a material increase in the present rail rates would force them to resort to a large extent to the river line.

Before the rail lines were completed to Nashville, traffic came from eastern seaboard cities by the Pennsylvania Railroad to Pittsburg and thence by the Ohio and Cumberland rivers to Nashville, but there were no through rates and no through billing.

The Nashville, Chattanooga & St. Louis road, connecting Chattanooga with Nashville, was completed in 1854, five years before the completion of the Louisville & Nashville road to

Nashville. The construction of the former road commenced at Nashville and extended east to Chattanooga. After it had been completed as far east as Stevenson, a point 38 miles from Chattanooga, rates were made from New York for the transportation of traffic *via* Charleston to Chattanooga, thence by the Tennessee river to Caperton's Landing, thence 4 miles by wagon to Stevenson and thence by rail to Nashville. The first through rates from the east to Nashville were made over this line through Chattanooga.

The testimony is that when the Nashville, Chattanooga & St. Louis road was completed from Nashville to Chattanooga the competition it met on traffic from the east to Nashville was that of the Cumberland river, and that when the Louisville & Nashville road was subsequently completed from Cincinnati to Nashville the Cumberland river competition was "transferred" to that road, and the Nashville, Chattanooga & St. Louis road had to meet the rates of that road thus influenced by Cumberland river competition.

The Cumberland river is stated by defendants' witnesses to be and to have been the controlling competitive force, or in the language of a witness, the "common enemy," which the rail lines from the east to Nashville have to meet; and that because of this competition by the Cumberland river the Nashville rates even before the completion of the roads to Nashville were lower than the Chattanooga rates. It is to be noted that at that time and until a comparatively recent period, the Tennessee river was not, as it now is by the completion of the canal through the Mussel Shoals referred to in the next subdivision of this report and opinion, opened up for continuous transportation from Chattanooga to the Ohio river.

Nevertheless, upon all the evidence in this case and our general knowledge of the situation, we are convinced and find that the rates accepted for the transportation of eastern merchandise to Nashville are not forced upon the carriers by water competition for that traffic. The competition which the lines *via Chattanooga* meet is distinctly the competition of the trunk lines and the Louisville & Nashville road whose northern termini

are at points on the Ohio river; it results from the fact that
the Trunk Line basis of rates was long ago extended to Nashville. In this connection we repeat the finding in the former
case, as follows:

The river rates are now considerably lower than the rail rates, and
more or less of the local traffic goes by water; but the through business
from Atlantic cities, saving the time, distance and cost of breaking bulk
at Cincinnati, would continue to go by rail, in our judgment, even if the
disparity between land and water rates were materially greater than it is
now. There might, of course, be such an advance in rail rates that shipments from the east would take the water route from Cincinnati. What
amount of difference would produce that result it is impossible to determine from the testimony; but we find that such difference might be substantially greater than it is at present without important effect upon the
railroad tonnage from the east, and that the through rate to Nashville is
in no sense controlled by water competition at that point, either actually
encountered or seriously apprehended.

12. By means of boats on the Tennessee river, Chattanooga
now has continuous water transportation from Chattanooga to
Paducah at the confluence of the Tennessee and Ohio rivers and
to Ohio and Mississippi river points, St. Louis, Cairo, Evansville, Louisville and Cincinnati. The Tennessee river is navigable from Chattanooga to the Ohio river from 8 to 10 months
during the year, an average of 9 months. The distance by the
Tennessee river from Paducah to Chattanooga is 464 miles
and it takes from 3 to 4 days for a boat to go from Paducah to
Chattanooga.

When the complaint in the former case before the Commission was filed, continuous transportation by the Tennessee river
from Chattanooga to Paducah and the Ohio river was interrupted by the Mussel Shoals. A canal was then being built by
the government through the shoals and it was opened in November, 1890. Since that time it has been maintained "in a
state of efficiency and readiness for use throughout the entire
year, and there has been a steady annual increase in the number of vessels passing through the canal." (Annual Report
upon Improvements of Tennessee river by the United States
Chief of Engineers for the year 1901, p. 466.)

The boats on the Tennessee river running from Chattanooga to Florence and Paducah have increased from 16 in 1890 to 54 in 1899, and the tonnage of traffic has increased from 78,820 tons in 1892 to 253,340 tons in 1899.

The bulk of the traffic from New York and other eastern seaboard cities to Chattanooga is shipped by ocean to Norfolk and thence by rail to Chattanooga, but shipment from those cities to Cincinnati or Paducah and thence by river to Chattanooga is practicable. Such shipments are made but not to any material extent in consequence of the great advantage of the direct all rail or rail and ocean lines *via* Norfolk to Chattanooga.

A large proportion of the business of boats on the Tennessee river originates in Chicago, St. Louis and Louisville and there is a considerable tonnage of traffic from Cincinnati and Evansville. Traffic from Cincinnati, Louisville and Evansville is transferred at Paducah.

In order to protect themselves from excessive rates by rail and to meet the discrimination in rates against Chattanooga and in favor of Nashville, the Chattanooga merchants have established a boat line on the Tennessee river operating between Chattanooga and Paducah and points on the Ohio river. The steamer Avalon of this line has a tonnage of 305 tons and from February 6 to July 4, 1901, it made 15 round trips through the Mussel Shoals to Paducah carrying 674 passengers and 3,557 tons of freight. This steamer also goes to Cairo.

The principal traffic transported on the Tennessee river consists of general merchandise, lumber, hay and grain, cotton and cotton seed, flour, peanuts, produce, fertilizers, live stock, logs and wood, railroad ties, staves, stone, sand and gravel.   *

13. Chattanooga is entitled to the benefit of low Trunk Line rates to Cincinnati and has it to practically the same extent as Nashville. The difference in rates between the two cities begins at Cincinnati and results from the higher rates charged by the Cincinnati, New Orleans & Texas Pacific road from Cincinnati to Chattanooga than are charged by the Louisville & Nashville road from Cincinnati to Nashville.

If the proportions of the Cincinnati, New Orleans & Texas Pacific road from Cincinnati to Chattanooga were reduced so as to make them not higher than the proportions of the Louisville & Nashville road from Cincinnati to Nashville, the Chattanooga rates would be about as high as, or not materially different from, the Nashville rates from the eastern seaboard cities. The distance by the Cincinnati, New Orleans & Texas Pacific road from Cincinnati to Chattanooga exceeds the distance by the Louisville & Nashville road from Cincinnati to Nashville by about 37 miles. It is testified that this "slight difference" in distance is immaterial and had nothing to do with fixing the rates.

Some traffic from the east comes to Chattanooga *via* Cincinnati, but the most of it comes, as before stated, *via* the Virginia ports, Norfolk and Newport News, and the direct short rail lines to Chattanooga.

There is no evidence that any traffic from the east comes to Chattanooga *via* Cincinnati and Nashville or *via* Evansville and Nashville.

14. Trunk Line territory *proper* lies east of the Mississippi and north of the Ohio and Potomac rivers and Southern territory is that east of the Mississippi and south of those rivers. Nashville, as well as Chattanooga, is in Southern territory, but Nashville is not as far removed from Trunk Line territory as Chattanooga. Nashville by the Louisville & Nashville road is 155 miles from Trunk Line territory at Evansville, 185 miles at Louisville and 301 miles at Cincinnati. Chattanooga by the Cincinnati, New Orleans & Texas Pacific Railway is 338 miles from Trunk Line territory at Cincinnati and by the Louisville & Nashville road *via* Nashville is 306 miles at Evansville.

Because of the greater density of population and greater volume of traffic in Trunk Line territory than in Southern territory, the rates charged by the Trunk Line roads can be and are made lower than in Southern territory.

The transportation by the Louisville & Nashville road of eastern traffic from Cincinnati to Nashville is through Southern territory, but the rates charged by that road for the portion of

the through haul from Cincinnati to Nashville are practically
extensions of Trunk Line rates, the rate per ton per mile under
those rates being about the same as the rate per ton per mile
under the Trunk Line rates from the east to Cincinnati. . . .
The through rates from New York and other eastern cities *via*
Cincinnati to Nashville are, in the language of the witnesses,
"*prorated* all the way to Nashville," while the through rates
via Cincinnati to Chattanooga are not prorated.

15. Nashville competes with Cincinnati, Louisville, Evansville, Paducah, Cairo and Memphis, in territory between Nashville and those cities. Cincinnati, Louisville and Evansville
are shorter-distance points than Nashville from eastern seaboard
cities by the direct rail or rail and water lines and their rates
are lower than the Nashville rates.

Any material advance in the Nashville rates would injure
Nashville in that competition and would also increase the river
business on the Cumberland river.

16. Nashville also competes with Chattanooga in territory
between Nashville and Chattanooga on the line of the Nashville,
Chattanooga & St. Louis Railway and in territory south and
west of Chattanooga in Tennessee, Georgia and Alabama on
the Memphis & Charleston, Alabama Great Southern, Western
& Atlantic and other roads.

On the line of the Nashville, Chattanooga & St. Louis Railway between Nashville and Chattanooga, Nashville has the advantage in rates over Chattanooga. The combinations of the
through rates on class 1 goods from New York, for example, to
Chattanooga with the local rates from Chattanooga to stations
on the Nashville, Chattanooga & St. Louis Railway between Chattanooga and Nashville, exceed to a material extent the combinations of the through rates to Nashville with the local rates
from Nashville to those stations, and Chattanooga merchants
testify that they cannot sell goods shipped from the east on
terms of equality in competition with Nashville merchants in
territory west of a point 30 miles from Chattanooga and 121
miles from Nashville on the Nashville, Chattanooga & St.
Louis Railway and that they are forced to sell at a much less

profit in that territory, if they sell at all, than Nashville merchants realize.

The Nashville merchants also have a material advantage in rates over Chattanooga merchants in territory west of Chattanooga on the Memphis & Charleston (now Southern) road and at a number of points on the roads south of Chattanooga in Georgia and Alabama much nearer to Chattanooga than to Nashville.

The testimony of a large number of Chattanooga merchants was taken, and it shows that the growth of Chattanooga and her mercantile business, particularly "jobbing business," have been greatly retarded by the materially higher rates from the east to Chattanooga than to Nashville.

At the time when the lower rates from the east to Nashville than to Chattanooga were established, Chattanooga was a small town with only one partially wholesale house, while Nashville had 12 or 13 wholesale houses. Nashville was then recognized as the distributing point for the section of country up to, if not including, Chattanooga. The situation in this respect has changed. It is conceded that Chattanooga is now entitled to recognition and treatment as a distributing center, that her "shipping facilities are superior to those of either Nashville or Knoxville" and that "taking into account the claims of those cities, the *legitimate* trade of Chattanooga covers a strip of territory extending northeast and southwest a distance of about 200 miles in length by about 125 miles in width."

At the same time, we are constrained to find, as a deduction from the foregoing and other facts appearing in the record, that the circumstances and conditions under which this eastern traffic is carried to Nashville are not substantially similar to the circumstances and conditions under which the same traffic is carried to Chattanooga. The lower rates to Nashville *via* the Ohio river gateways are not made or controlled by the lines operating *via* Chattanooga, and the latter are under compulsion to meet those rates or forego participation in the traffic from the eastern seaboard to Nashville.

Conclusions

The facts appearing in the present case are not materially different from those disclosed in the former proceeding.[1] While minor changes have taken place since the prior investigation, the salient features of the situation remain practically unaltered. It is clear now as it was then that the lower rates from eastern seaboard cities to Nashville than to Chattanooga give Nashville merchants, on traffic from these cities, an advantage over Chattanooga merchants in territory which may be said to be naturally tributary to Chattanooga; it is equally clear that this disparity in charges has its origin and alleged justification in differences of circumstances and conditions which have existed in substantially the same form for many years. In its practical aspects the problem has not been simplified by lapse of time, while the law from which the Commission derives its authority has meanwhile received repeated and binding construction. The theory upon which our former ruling was based has been declared unsound, and it is obviously our duty to test the facts presented in this case by the law as it has been interpreted for our guidance. If these facts do not show a violation of the regulating statute, as that statute has been construed, we should so decide, whatever appears to be the injustice suffered by Chattanooga, since the making of an order which would not be enforced by the courts would be useless and unwarranted.

In the light of various decisions of the Supreme Court, and as stated in the foregoing findings, we cannot seriously doubt that the traffic in question is carried to Nashville and Chattanooga, respectively, under substantially different circumstances and conditions. This being so, the action of the carriers in maintaining a higher rate for the shorter haul to Chattanooga cannot be regarded as unlawful under the fourth section of the act, or otherwise condemned merely because a lower rate is granted to Nashville. This question is now so well settled as not to be open to discussion.

[1] Cf. footnote, p. 266, *supra.*

We have no authority, even if we had the disposition, to require an advance of the Nashville rates. Those rates are the product of influences which have long been in potent operation. They are rates to which many and important commercial interests are adjusted and on which those interests are largely dependent. The testimony shows that Nashville had lower rates from the east than Chattanooga before the railroads were constructed between Cincinnati and Nashville and between Chattanooga and Nashville, and these lower rates to Nashville have ever since been in force. Their origin and continuance are attributed to the fact that Nashville is much nearer to Trunk Line territory than is Chattanooga, and to the fact of water competition by the Ohio and Cumberland rivers. Before the rail lines were extended to Nashville, traffic from eastern seaboard cities came by the Pennsylvania Railroad to Pittsburg and thence by the Ohio and Cumberland rivers to Nashville. When the Nashville, Chattanooga & St. Louis road was opened between Chattanooga and Nashville, which was prior to the completion of the Louisville & Nashville road from Cincinnati and Evansville to Nashville, the competition it met on traffic from the east to Nashville was that *via* the Cumberland and Ohio rivers; and when the Louisville & Nashville road was subsequently constructed from Cincinnati to Nashville, the evidence shows that the competition of the Cumberland and Ohio rivers was " transferred " to that road, and that the Nashville, Chattanooga & St. Louis road had then to meet the rates of the Louisville & Nashville road thus influenced by Cumberland and Ohio river competition.

It is virtually undisputed that Nashville rates from the east are the result of this competition, coupled with the interest of the Louisville & Nashville road to maintain the commercial importance of Nashville. The competition at Chattanooga, whether of carriers or commercial forces, has not been equally effective, as is evidenced by the fact that it has not reduced Chattanooga rates to the level of Nashville rates. In deciding the former case the Supreme Court said (*East Tennessee, V. & G. R. Co.* v. *Interstate Commerce Commission*, 181 U. S. 19, 45 L. ed. 726, 21 Sup. Ct. Rep. 516) :

Competition which is real and substantial and exercises a potential influence on rates to a particular point, brings into play the dissimilarity of circumstances and conditions prescribed by the statute, and justifies the lesser charge to the more distant and competitive point than to the nearer and noncompetitive point, and *this right is not destroyed by the mere fact that incidentally the lesser charge to the competitive point may seemingly give a preference to that point and the greater rate to the noncompetitive point may apparently engender a discrimination against it.*

The principle or rule here laid down would apply, and was evidently intended to apply, to a case where both points are competitive, but where competition has resulted in lower rates to the longer- than to the shorter-distance point.

It is further shown that Nashville competes with Cincinnati, Louisville, Evansville, Cairo and other Ohio river points in territory north and west of Nashville; that rates from the east to those Ohio river points are lower than to Nashville; that the present Nashville rates are necessary to enable Nashville to engage in this competition and were fixed, partly at least, with reference to that fact; that even under these rates Nashville is at a disadvantage in the greater part of that territory; and that, therefore, an increase of Nashville rates would place Nashville at quite as great a disadvantage in comparison with Ohio river points as Chattanooga is now under in comparison with Nashville. In a word, we regard it impracticable to relieve Chattanooga by advancing the Nashville rates.

The whole case, therefore, comes to the question of the reasonableness of the Chattanooga rates. While there is more or less evidence of a persuasive character, standing by itself, that these rates are unreasonably high, such as the fact that they are greater per ton mile than the average of roads in Southern territory and throughout the United States, and are the same as rates for longer hauls through Chattanooga to Sheffield, Tuscumbia, Florence and a few other points in the same territory, with other facts of similar import, the force of this evidence is materially modified, if not overcome, by the kindred fact that Chattanooga rates are no higher than rates to Atlanta, Rome, and a large number of other places with which Chattanooga is grouped.

It is frequently asserted, and with apparent reason, that Atlanta is the most strongly competitive point in the south, and it is situated somewhat nearer the eastern seaboard than Chattanooga. The rates to the Atlanta group are the basis upon which numerous rates are adjusted throughout an extensive area, and these rates are applied to a large volume of traffic. The Atlanta rates are the outgrowth of competition between a number of independent lines, and there is no proof that these rates are unreasonable, except such proof as appears in this case respecting the reasonableness of the same rates to Chattanooga. The fact that rates for the shorter haul to Chattanooga are higher than for the longer haul through Chattanooga to Nashville, or for the longer haul to Evansville, does not warrant the conclusion, under the decisions referred to, that the Chattanooga rates are unreasonable, because the rates to Nashville and Evansville are controlled by competitive forces which do not operate with like effect on rates to Chattanooga.

As above indicated, Chattanooga is " grouped," or classed for rate-making purposes, with Atlanta and some 23 other points in Georgia, Alabama and Mississippi, all of which take the same rates from the east. It is claimed by the defendent carriers, and there is no evidence to the contrary, that a reduction of the rates to Chattanooga would require a reduction in the rates to Atlanta and all other points taking the same rates ; that this in turn would require a corresponding reduction in rates to other localities outside the Atlanta and Chattanooga group ; and that, in short, the ultimate and necessary result would be a reduction in rates throughout the entire Southern territory, with a consequent loss of revenue which the roads serving that territory are unable to bear.

Whatever may be said of this contention, and we doubt whether it is well founded to the extent claimed; it seems clear that a reduction of the Chattanooga rates, without a like reduction in rates to Atlanta and the other points with which Chattanooga is grouped, would give Chattanooga an advantage to which that town is not shown to be entitled. In that case Atlanta and other distributing points would be in much the same position with reference to Chattanooga that Chattanooga is now with reference to Nashville. Moreover, so far as we can see, the facts in this case which are claimed to establish the unreasonableness of Chattanooga rates would apply with equal force to rates to Atlanta and other destinations. Nor is it otherwise suggested by complainant. Apparently, therefore, a ruling that Chattanooga rates are unreasonable, and so in violation of the first section of the act, would inferentially and in effect condemn as unlawful the rates to Atlanta and many other points of importance which have long had the same rates as Chattanooga.

Upon the facts now appearing we are not satisfied that such a ruling is warranted. There is much to induce belief that the Chattanooga rates are excessive, though to what extent it would be difficult to determine. It is quite apparent that these rates, to a considerable degree at least, operate to restrict the commercial activities of Chattanooga, particularly in its competition with Nashville; and there is little reason to doubt that the charges now imposed on this eastern traffic to Chattanooga should be materially reduced, if that can be done without injustice to the carriers and localities affected by a readjustment. While this is undoubtedly true, it does not follow that these rates are shown to be unreasonable within the meaning of the first section of the act; and this, it should be remembered, is the only question we have authority to decide.

It appears clear to us that the Chattanooga rates cannot be independently considered, even as respects their reasonableness. They are embraced in and connected with a system of equalized rates which have been applied for many years throughout an extensive region, and are closely related to rates in a still larger area comprising the greater part of what is known as Southern territory. To deal intelligently with a rate question of such magnitude and complexity seems to require a wider survey than this record permits. Impressed with this view, we feel justified in deferring a final judgment until the situation can be investigated in its larger relations and a more confident basis found than now appears for declaring that this comprehensive system of rates is unlawfully maintained. We do not find or decide that

these rates are reasonable; we only say that they are not shown
to be otherwise. Upon the facts now presented, and the law as
it has been interpreted, we are constrained to hold that no violation of the act has been established.

It follows that the complaint will be dismissed without
prejudice to any future investigation.

CLEMENTS, *Commissioner*, dissenting:

I do not agree with the conclusion of the Commission dismissing the complaint in this case because I believe, First, that
the rates to Chattanooga are shown to be unreasonable ; and,
Second, because I believe the adjustment and relation of rates
to Chattanooga and Nashville, respectively, are shown to be
unduly preferential to Nashville and prejudicial to Chattanooga.
The general tenor of the report seems to this effect although
relief to Chattanooga is denied, for the reasons therein stated.

It is said in the conclusions of the Commission that " there is
much to induce belief that the Chattanooga rates are excessive,
though to what extent it would be difficult to determine. It is
quite apparent that these rates, to a considerable degree at least,
operate to restrict the commercial activities of Chattanooga, particularly in its competition with Nashville ; and there is little
reason to doubt that the charges now imposed on this eastern
traffic to Chattanooga should be materially reduced, if that can
be done without injustice to the carriers and localities affected
by a readjustment."

The original complaint of Chattanooga was presented to the
Commission in April, 1890. In December, 1892, the Commission, after hearing the case, partially disposed of the same according to its interpretation at that time of the long and short
haul clause, requiring the carriers to cease and desist from
charging more to Chattanooga than to Nashville, unless upon
application, as provided by law, and upon hearing by the Commission, it should be shown that a greater charge for the shorter
distance was justified. In the report of the Commission at
that time it was said : " We entertain little doubt, therefore, that
equity between shipper and carrier requires some reduction in

the rates now enforced on Chattanooga traffic from Atlantic points, and are convinced of the necessity for such a reduction to secure relative justice between that town and Nashville. We refrain from further statement of the reasons which have induced this conclusion, as the amount to which the Chattanooga rate should be reduced will not now be decided."

Suit was begun by the Commission to enforce the order made at that time, which, having passed through the various stages of the several courts, was finally determined by the Supreme Court of the United States in 1901 adversely to the ruling of the Commission, which was as stated under the so-called long and short haul provision of the statute, subject to the right of the Commission to further investigate the matter and determine the questions involved according to law.

The present complaint is substantially a continuation of the former one, but was made and has been heard in the light of the interpretation of the law by the Supreme Court in respect to the so-called long and short haul rule, leaving for the determination of the Commission the questions: First, the alleged unreasonableness of the rates to Chattanooga, and, Second, the alleged undue and unreasonable discrimination in the adjustment of the rates to Chattanooga and Nashville, respectively. The ground upon which the Supreme Court overturned the order of the Commission in the former case was that it did not consider competition between rail carriers to Nashville and competition of markets affecting the rates to that place.

There are three material and important facts shown in this case which were not shown before the Commission in the former case; to wit, First, that transportation by water is quite as effective to Chattanooga now as to Nashville; Second, that all of the rates in question are the product of the concurrent or joint action of the carriers alleged to be in competition, though in fact not competing, as to the rates; but, on the contrary, establishing the same and maintaining them by a common understanding and coöperation in restraint of competition; Third, that the Louisville & Nashville Railroad Company controls the Nashville, Chattanooga & St. Louis Railway Company and its lines by the ownership of a majority of the stock of the latter company.

It is true that some of these facts were brought out in the case before the Court for the enforcement of the order of the Commission ; but the Supreme Court appears to have held that they could not be considered by the Court in upholding a decision by the Commission not based upon these facts but upon an erroneous interpretation of the long and short haul clause whereby material testimony had been excluded from its consideration.

In a pamphlet published jointly by the defendants, the Louisville & Nashville Railroad, the Nashville, Chattanooga & St. Louis Railway and the Southern Railway, entitled " Tennessee," there appears the following :

Chattanooga is the terminus of more leading railway lines and is reached by a larger number of competing systems than any other point in the South. Extending north to Cincinnati, a distance of 338 miles, is the Cincinnati Southern Railway, a part of the Cincinnati, New Orleans & Texas Pacific (Queen & Crescent) System, making connection at Burgen, Ky., for Louisville and the Northwest. Washington, New York, and the New England cities are reached by the Southern Railway, *via* Knoxville, Asheville, and Salisbury. Atlanta and the Southeastern Atlantic Coast and Gulf cities are reached from Chattanooga by two competing lines, the Western & Atlantic Railroad and the Georgia Division of the Southern Railway. Due south extends the Chattanooga, Rome & Southern Railroad, a distance of 140 miles to Carrolton, Ga. The Chattanooga Southern, another line extending southward from Chattanooga, has been completed to Gadsden, Ala., a distance of 91 miles with fair prospects of being extended farther south at an early date. To the southwest the Alabama Great Southern (Queen & Crescent) reaches Birmingham, Ala., and Meridian, Miss., the latter city being distant 295 miles from Chattanooga, and continuing from Meridian over the same system to New Orleans and Texas points. Due west extends the Memphis & Charleston Railroad to Memphis, 310 miles, and northwest, the Nashville, Chattanooga & St. Louis Railway reaches Nashville and cities of the Northwest and Southwest.

* * * Geographically, Chattanooga is so situated as to eventually become a jobbing market of more than ordinary importance. The numerous lines of railway radiating from Chattanooga like the spokes of a wheel and reaching every section of Tennessee and adjoining states, warrants this statement. Her rivals for the jobbing trade are Nashville, 151 miles to the northwest; Knoxville, 112 miles northeast; and Atlanta, 138 miles south. *Her shipping facilities, however, are superior to those of either of these cities, notably so in the cases of Nashville and Knoxville.* Taking into account the

claims of these cities, what might be termed *the "legitimate" trade of Chattanooga covers a strip of territory extending northeast and southwest, a distance of about 200 miles in length by 125 miles in width.*

These statements do not in my judgment exaggerate the advantageous natural position of Chattanooga. The confederated action of these carriers and others has greatly impaired the vigor of Chattanooga in this field.

The Commission finds that " the Chattanooga rates from eastern seaboard cities yield rates per ton per mile much greater than — in most instances more than double — the average receipts per ton per mile of the principal defendants, of roads throughout southern territory and of roads throughout the United States." " The rates in question from New York and other eastern seaboard cities to Chattanooga were established by the roads as members of the Southern Railway & Steamship Association, and are still with immaterial exceptions maintained as originally fixed."

The rates per ton per mile on the six numbered classes for the haul of 848 miles (short line distance) from New York to Chattanooga are as follows :

1	2	3	4	5	6
2.68 cents	2.31 cents	2.02 cents	1.72 cents	1.41 cents	1.15 cents

The average of the above rates per ton per mile to Chattanooga being 1.88 cents.

The revenue per ton per mile of the principal defendants named below, taken from their annual reports for the years ending June 30, 1900, and 1901, is shown in the following table :

	1900	1901
Southern Railway Company	.916 cents	.936 cents
Louisville & Nashville Railroad Company . .	.752 "	.772 "
Nashville, Chattanooga & St. L. Ry. Company	.887 "	.883 "
Cincinnati, N. O. & T. P. Ry. Company . .	.730 "	.745 "
Chesapeake & Ohio Railway Company . .	.343 "	.388 "
Georgia Railroad	1.135 "	1.097 "
Central of Georgia Railroad Company . . .	1.096 "	1.064 "
Norfolk & Western Railway Company . . .	.430 "	.461 "

RATES PER TON PER MILE FOR THE YEAR ENDING JUNE 30, 1900

Of roads in West Virginia, Virginia, North Carolina and
  South Carolina . . . . .595 cents
Of roads in Kentucky, Tennessee, Mississippi, Alabama,
  Georgia and Florida. . . . . .808 "
Of roads throughout United States . . . . .729 "

Illustrative of the discrimination of the present adjustment of rates against Chattanooga and in favor of Nashville the following table is inserted, showing combination of class 1 through rates from Boston and New York to Chattanooga and Nashville with local class 1 rates from Chattanooga and Nashville to intermediate stations on the Nashville, Chattanooga & St. Louis Railway, and distances from Chattanooga and Nashville to those stations:

To	DISTANCES FROM NASHVILLE	DISTANCES FROM CHATTANOOGA	NASHVILLE COMBINATION RATES	CHATTANOOGA COMBINATION RATES
Bolivar . . .	118 miles	33 miles	91 + 50 = 141	114 + 28 = 142
Bass	107 "	44 "	91 + 49 = 140	114 + 31 = 145
Sherwood . .	97 "	54 "	91 + 45 = 136	114 + 34 = 148
Cowan . . .	87 "	64 "	91 + 43 = 134	114 + 36 = 150
Estill Spring .	77 "	74 "	91 + 40 = 131	114 + 40 = 154
Normandy . .	62 "	89 "	91 + 35 = 126	114 + 43 = 157
Wartrace . .	55 "	96 "	91 + 34 = 125	114 + 46 = 160
Fosterville . .	46 "	105 "	91 + 31 = 122	114 + 50 = 164
Winsted . .	37 "	114 "	91 + 30 = 121	114 + 50 = 164
Florence . . .	26 "	125 "	91 + 22 = 113	114 + 50 = 164
Smyrna . . .	20 "	131 "	91 + 20 = 111	114 + 50 = 164
Kimbro . . .	13 "	137 "	91 + 15 = 106	114 + 50 = 164
Glencliffe . .	5 "	146 "	91 + 12 = 103	114 + 50 = 164

On all the other classes as well as class 1, the combinations are in favor of Nashville.

The following table gives the combination of class 1 rates from New York to Nashville and Chattanooga with the local rates from those points to certain stations in Tennessee, Mississippi and North Alabama; also distances from Chattanooga and Nashville to those stations:

To	DISTANCES FROM NASHVILLE	DISTANCES FROM CHATTANOOGA	NASHVILLE COMBINATION RATES	CHATTANOOGA COMBINATION RATES
Winchester, Tenn.	85 miles	72 miles	$1.33	$1.53
Stevenson, Ala. . .	113 "	38 "	1.41	1.44
Hollywood, Ala. .	126 "	51 "	1.46	1.55
Cowan, Tenn. . .	87 "	64 "	1.34	1.50
Gadsden, Ala. . .	210 "	92 "	1.63	1.71
Anniston, Ala. .	271 "	137 "	1.63	1.71
Huntsville, Ala. .	146 "	97 "	1.35	1.54
Meridian, Miss. .	360 "	296 "	1.74	1.91
Decatur, Ala. . .	121 "	122 "	1.35	1.54
Tuscumbia, Ala. .	134 "	165 "	1.35	1.64

Nashville, it will be perceived, has the advantage in rates over Chattanooga at all these stations, many of which are beyond Chattanooga from Nashville. For example, at Gadsen, Alabama, 210 miles from Nashville and 92 miles south from Chattanooga, the Chattanooga combination rate exceeds the Nashville combination rate by 8 cents.

The following table gives the excesses of what are termed the Nashville *combination distances* over the Chattanooga *combination distances* to the stations named in the preceding table and also the excesses of the Chattanooga combination rates over the Nashville combination rates in cents per hundred pounds and on car loads of 40,000 pounds. By combination distances is meant the distances from the point of shipment, New York in this instance, to Chattanooga and Nashville, respectively, added to the distances from those points to the stations named:

	EXCESSES OF NASHVILLE COMBINATION DISTANCES OVER CHATTANOOGA COMBINATION DISTANCES	EXCESSES OF CHATTANOOGA COMBINATION RATES OVER NASHVILLE COMBINATION RATES	
		In Cents per 100 Pounds	On Car Loads of 40,000 Pounds
Winchester . .	164 miles	20 cents	$80.00
Stevenson . . .	226 "	3 "	12.00
Hollywood . .	226 "	9 "	36.00
Cowan	174 "	16 "	64.00
Gadsden . . .	269 "	8 "	32.00
Anniston . . .	285 "	8 "	32.00
Huntsville . .	200 "	22 "	88.00
Meridian . . .	215 "	17 "	68.00
Decatur . . .	150 "	19 "	76.00
Tuscumbia . .	120 "	29 "	116.00

The shortest all rail line from New York to Chattanooga is *via* Alexandria, 846 miles ; that to Nashville is *via* Alexandria and through Chattanooga, 997 miles. It is shown that the greater part of the freight moving from the east to both Nashville and Chattanooga moves *via* Norfolk, sea and rail. Chattanooga, therefore, is materially nearer both the markets of production and shipment, and Norfolk, the point where for the most part the sea carriage ends and the rail haul begins. Nothing else appearing, it would seem clear upon this situation that Chattanooga should have even lower rates than Nashville. The reverse, however, is the fact, and this is, in large part, the cause of complaint. Upon what theory is this reverse order of rates — lower for the long haul to the more distant point — justified? The justification is put mainly upon the ground of Nashville's closer proximity to the territory north of the Ohio river where a lower scale of rates has been fixed by the associated carriers of that territory than by the associated carriers in Southern territory by practically the same methods and upon the ground that Nashville desires to meet in competition the cities on the Ohio river, and St. Louis in the region between these cities and Nashville.

The same theory that justifies and requires rates to Nashville which accomplish this purpose would seem from equal necessity to require a like adjustment of rates to Chattanooga to give her a fair chance in competition with Nashville in territory between that city and Chattanooga. But this has been utterly ignored in the framework of this adjustment of rates by the singleness of action of the associated carriers south of the Ohio river. Chattanooga is not only met in substantially all the regions between the two cities by Nashville with an overwhelming advantage to the latter, but is overreached by the advantages of the latter in rates to many important points south of Chattanooga. Not only is this true, as will be seen by the combination of rates on eastern traffic which as to Nashville passes through Chattanooga on through rates from the East and then out from Nashville in distribution by Nashville jobbers back through and around Chattanooga, but Chattanooga is, by the methods of rate making in vogue in this territory, grouped with a large number of other

places far to the south and west of her taking the same rates
under this so-called "equalized system," so that these places
have their natural disadvantages of location overcome by more
favorable rates to the detriment of Chattanooga, which is not
only nearer the points of production and shipment than most
of the places in this group but is also much nearer to the
Virginia cities, Ohio river points, and Nashville, all of which
enjoy the lower scale of official or Trunk Line rates and
classifications.

*　　*　　*　　*　　*　　*　　*　　*

In the argument of the case in court for the enforcement of
the previous order of the Commission counsel for the carriers
said: " The Louisville & Nashville Railroad is vitally interested
in maintaining the commercial importance of Nashville," and
urged there as in this case that rates to Nashville not higher
than at present are necessary " to enable Nashville to compete
with Cincinnati, Louisville and Evansville in the territory between Nashville and the Mississippi river." I repeat that like
reasoning would, upon the undisputed facts of this case, entitle
Chattanooga to such rates as would give her a fair chance in
competition with Nashville in the territory between the two
cities, and certainly in that south of Chattanooga. Nor can the
Louisville & Nashville Railroad, in the light of the testimony
in this case, disclaim responsibility in common with the other
carriers for the rates and adjustments in question. What concessions one to another these carriers have made from time to
time during the 18 or 20 years they have maintained these rates
and adjustments, and what compromises of the views and purposes of individual carriers in respect thereof, in disregard of
that equality of treatment to all which the law enjoins, have
been made in their conferences in order to avoid competition in
rates and secure the greatest net revenue to themselves, we do
not know. This can probably never be shown, for these things
are " done in a corner." But it is not probable that this adjustment and scale of rates could have remained intact, as shown,
for so long a period except by the substantial agreement of the
carriers in restraint of competition.

Chattanooga has been complaining of and protesting against these rates continuously for more than fourteen years. The foregoing facts and other testimony in the case indicate the extent and hurtfulness of the discrimination against that city; also the excessiveness of the rates to Chattanooga. The facts seem to me to be convincing that the complaint is well founded and that the rates should be condemned by an order to that effect.

XI

THE LONG AND SHORT HAUL CLAUSE [1]

THE ST. CLOUD, MINN., CASE .

(Vide map, p. 298)

PROUTY, *Commissioner :* * * * * *

The railroad of the defendant extends from Minneapolis and St. Paul in a northwesterly and northerly direction to Brainerd, Minn., thence easterly to Duluth, Minn., and Superior, Wis., the distance from St. Paul to Duluth being 241 miles. St. Cloud is upon the line of the defendant, 76 miles north of St. Paul. The defendant engages in the transportation of freight both ways between Duluth and St. Paul, through St. Cloud. Its rates from St. Paul to Duluth are less than those from St. Cloud to Duluth. In the opposite direction its rates from Duluth to St. Paul are less than those from Duluth to St. Cloud.

The two rates specifically referred to in the testimony are those upon flour from St. Paul and Minneapolis east, and those upon coal from Duluth and Superior west. The through rate on flour from St. Paul to New York *via* the defendant's line to Duluth, and thence by water and rail to New York, was, at the time of the hearing, $21\frac{1}{2}$ cents per hundred pounds. The defendant apparently published no through rate from St. Cloud to New York, but applied to such shipments its local rates from St. Cloud to Duluth or Superior, in combination with the through rate from those cities to New York. The local rate from St. Cloud was 12 cents, and the through rate from Duluth $16\frac{1}{2}$ cents, making the rate from St. Cloud to New York $28\frac{1}{2}$ cents. Flour from St. Paul to New York by the defendant's line

---

[1] Decided November 29, 1899. Interstate Commerce Reports, Vol. VIII, pp. 346–363. The Long and Short Haul Clause is discussed in Ripley's Railroads: Rates and Regulation, chap. xix.

passes through St. Cloud. It was conceded by the defendant
that its division of the through flour rate from St. Paul yielded
it about 5.375 cents per hundred pounds, as against 12 cents
per hundred pounds when the transportation was from St. Cloud.

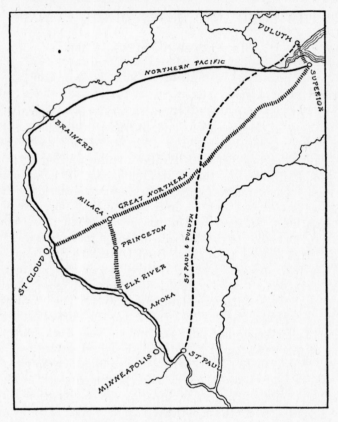

The rates on coal from Duluth to St. Cloud are, soft coal
$1.60 per ton, hard coal $2.00 per ton ; to St. Paul $1.25 per
ton for hard coal and 75 cents for soft coal. The transportation
in the latter case is through St. Cloud.

There are three lines of railroad, besides that of the defendant, connecting St. Paul and Minneapolis with Duluth and

Superior,—namely: the Chicago, St. Paul, Minneapolis & Omaha, distance 179 miles; the St. Paul & Duluth, 160 miles; the Great Northern, over the Eastern Minnesota, 169 miles. It was also said that the Great Northern had in process of construction a line by which the distance would be somewhat reduced. Large quantities of freight move between these points, and these three lines are active competitors for this traffic. The rail lines from St. Paul to Duluth in connection with water lines upon the Great Lakes furnish a means of communication between St. Paul and the northwest and the Atlantic seaboard and the east. Lines of railway leading south from St. Paul through Chicago and other points reach, by their connections, the eastern section of the country as well, and there is fierce competition between the lines leading south and the lines leading to Duluth and Superior, for business between the northwest and the seaboard.

In the making of their rates the three lines above mentioned between St. Paul and Duluth observe at the present time the rule of the fourth section; that is, they make no higher rate from or to the intermediate point than is made from or to the more distant point. Anoka, Elk River, Princeton and Milaca are situated upon the line of the Great Northern, and take the same rate as do St. Paul and Minneapolis. The line of the defendant runs through Anoka and Elk River, the former being 29 and the latter 41 miles from St. Paul, and the rates to and from these points by the defendant's line are the same as those to and from Minneapolis and St. Paul.

It has for some fifteen years been physically possible to transport freight between Duluth and St. Paul by the defendant's line in question; but in point of fact until April, 1889, the defendant did not publish a tariff by that route, owing apparently to the fact that it was much more circuitous than the others in use. During certain seasons of the year the defendant is compelled to haul in the transaction of its business empty cars from Duluth to St. Paul, and during other times of the year to haul empty cars from St. Paul to Duluth. Its traffic manager testified that his attention was called to this fact by the management, and that he was asked to provide, if possible, some freight for these empties, and that for this purpose, in the hope that some traffic might be obtained, especially flour from Minneapolis to the east and coal from Duluth to St. Paul, the rates in question were published. In the publication of these tariffs the defendant simply met those rates which were already in force by other lines. It appears that the other lines publish, either by some arrangement among themselves, or through some more comprehensive association, common tariffs ; for some reason they declined to publish the rates of the defendant upon these tariffs, and the defendant was compelled to and did print its own rate sheets. Rates to and from St. Cloud were, previous to the publication of this tariff, the same that they were afterwards ; nor were the rates at any of the points mentioned in any way changed by the putting in of the defendant's schedule. Whether rates between St. Paul and Duluth, and at other points taking those rates, have been influenced or affected since the publication of this schedule by the fact that the defendant has entered the field as a competitor, we cannot determine. The St. Paul rates are at the present time higher, and the discrimination against St. Cloud therefore less, than when the complaint was filed.

There are situated at or near St. Cloud three flouring mills besides that of the complaining company. That of the complainant has a capacity of 1000 barrels per day. The others are considerably smaller. The wheat which is ground at these mills is partly drawn from local territory, and is partly brought in from more distant points. The milling-in-transit privilege is available there upon the payment of an additional 2 cents per hundred pounds.

About one half of the flour ground at the mill of the complainant company is exported. It was said that the profit upon this flour was often not more than from 1 to 3 cents per barrel. It follows, therefore, that this mill cannot compete with Minneapolis and other points enjoying the same rate, if its flour costs the same price at the mill. It does not, for the reason that the mills at St. Cloud pay less for their wheat than do those at Minneapolis. It was said in testimony that the price at St. Cloud was usually about 6 cents per bushel below the Minneapolis price. A change in the rate on flour to the Atlantic seaboard works a corresponding change in the price which mills at St. Cloud can pay for local wheat. Princeton is situated some 25 miles east of St. Cloud. The Princeton miller enjoys the same rate as does Minneapolis, and he can and does pay the farmer for his wheat some 6 cents a bushel more than the miller at St. Cloud, with the result that intermediate territory between St. Cloud and Princeton delivers most of its wheat at Princeton rather than at St. Cloud.

Considerable testimony was introduced in behalf of the city of St. Cloud, tending to show that these freight rates were much to the disadvantage of that city as compared with Princeton, Elk River, and points in the vicinity taking the Minneapolis rate. This is of necessity true. All commodities coming by rail cost the retail merchant more at St. Cloud than at Princeton or Elk River. The expense of living is somewhat greater in that city. The difference in the freight rate upon heavy articles into which the rate enters as an important factor is sufficient to divert the business to Princeton and Elk River as against St. Cloud. We find, as a fact from the testimony, that business is so diverted, and that St. Cloud, owing to the circumstance that it pays the higher rate, is put to a disadvantage as compared with Milaca, Princeton, Anoka and Elk River. These findings refer to conditions existing at the time of the hearing.

The mill of the complaining company is situated upon the Great Northern Railroad, and can only be reached by the road of the defendant by the payment of a switching charge of $5.00 per car. The flour traffic of the complainant company, which is very large, seems to have been sent entirely over the Great Northern. Only two cars have ever been tendered the defendant for shipment by the company complainant, and these were tendered for the purpose of enabling it to establish its case in this proceeding. One of them was accepted and shipped to its eastern destination. The other was declined. The freight depots of the two roads are about equally accessible to the business portion of St. Cloud, although that of the defendant is situated across the river, in what is sometimes known as East St. Cloud.

No claim was made that the rates to and from St. Cloud were unreasonable of themselves, unless made so by comparison with the lower rates to and from the more distant points.

It did not definitely appear what amount of through traffic between St. Paul and Duluth had been carried by the defendant under its present tariff. The traffic manager of that company testified that in the month of July 7223 car loads of flour left Minneapolis for the east, that of this number his road carried but 73, and that in no month between the putting in of these rates and the date of the hearing in August had his line carried 2 per cent of the total out of Minneapolis. No statement was made as to traffic in the opposite direction, but it fairly appeared, from all that was said, that up to the date of the hearing the amount of through business done by the defendant had been insignificant.

The statute of Minnesota provides that no greater charge shall be made for the short than for the long haul, in the same direction, the less being included within the greater, without the permission of the Railroad Commission of that State. St. Paul and Duluth are both situated in the State of Minnesota, and the transportation between those points is therefore intrastate. When the defendant first determined to meet the rates of its competitors it did so by the publication of a tariff between St. Paul and Duluth, in which the rate between those points was made lower than the rate from local intermediate points. Either before the putting in of this tariff or after it had been published the defendant applied to the Railroad and Warehouse Commission of Minnesota for leave to make the lower rate between the more distant points, and this application was denied by that board. Thereupon the defendant published the through rates in question, claiming that these, being interstate, were beyond the jurisdiction of the State Commission.

Conclusions

Is the action of the defendant in charging more to and from St. Cloud, an intermediate point, than is charged to and from St. Paul, a more distant point, in violation of the fourth section?

The defendant affirms that it is not, for the reason that the transportation is not conducted "under substantially similar circumstances and conditions."

The only fact relied upon by the defendant to make out a dissimilarity of circumstances and conditions is competition between the four lines of railway connecting Duluth and St. Paul, of which the defendant is one. Water competition is not to be considered, for the reason that, while such competition is an important factor in determining the through rate between New York and St. Paul, of which the rate in question is a part, the rail lines from Duluth to St. Paul are links in the lake and rail route, and cannot, therefore, be heard to set up water competition in excuse of the rate which they themselves make in furtherance of that competition.

In its earliest decisions this Commission said that competition between carriers subject to the Act could only make out substantially dissimilar circumstances and conditions in rare and peculiar instances, and, afterwards, that such competition could not be shown in any instance for that purpose. This rule was applied by the Commission in many cases, and finally came before the Supreme Court of the United States for consideration in *Interstate Commerce Commission* v. *Alabama Midland R. Co.*, 168 U. S. 144, 42 L. ed. 414, 18 Sup. Ct. Rep. 45. That court declined to accept the construction of the Commission in this respect, and held that competition between railways subject to the Act should be considered in determining whether the circumstances and conditions were similar. The present case must, of course, be disposed of in accordance with that interpretation of the Act, and not in accordance with the views previously entertained and applied by this Commission.

It has been claimed by some, in reliance upon the above decision, and is perhaps the contention of the defendant in this case, that if actual bona fide railway competition is shown, that of itself creates the dissimilar circumstances and conditions necessary to except the defendant from the operation of the rule of the fourth section. That such was not the understanding of the Supreme Court is plainly asserted in the language of the opinion. On page 167, L. ed. 423, Sup. Ct. Rep. 49, it is said :

In order further to guard against any misapprehension of the scope of our decision it may be well to observe that we do not hold that the mere fact of competition, no matter what its character or extent, necessarily relieves the carrier from the restraints of the third and fourth sections, but only that these sections are not so stringent and imperative as to exclude in all cases the matter of competition from consideration in determining the questions of " undue or unreasonable preference or advantage," or what are " substantially similar circumstances and conditions." The competition may in some cases be such as, having due regard to the interests of the public and of the carrier, ought justly to have effect upon the rates, and in such cases there is no absolute rule which prevents the Commission or the courts from taking that matter into consideration.

It is apparent from the above quotation that what the court held was, not that competition between railways in and of itself created dissimilar circumstances and conditions, but that it was one factor which might be, and perhaps ought to be, taken into account in determining that question. The question is still largely one of fact, and is in each particular instance whether, in view of all the facts surrounding that individual instance, the circumstances and conditions are so dissimilar as to justify the greater charge for the shorter distance. In answering this question we are to consider the interests of all parties, the carrier as well as the public.

That in the case under consideration there is a discrimination, and a most grievous discrimination, owing to this disparity in rates, cannot be denied. The rate on flour from St. Cloud to market is 7 cents per hundred pounds more than from Minneapolis, Princeton or Elk River. This difference in the rate is often two or three times the profit which the miller makes in the grinding of his flour. A considerable part of the wheat which is ground at the mill of the complainant and at the other mills at or near the city of St. Cloud is local wheat. As a result of this difference in rate this wheat is worth some 6 cents a bushel less at St. Cloud than at Minneapolis or at Princeton or Elk River. This must mean a difference of fully $1 per acre in the net product of land in the vicinity of St. Cloud, as compared with similar land in the vicinity of Princeton or Elk River; and this difference in the productive value of the soil must produce a substantial difference in the value of the land itself, and in the prosperity of the owners of that land, if long continued.

The same thing is true in a less degree with reference to whatever St. Cloud consumes. Its anthracite coal must cost 75 cents per ton, and its bituminous coal 85 cents per ton, more than at St. Paul. The testimony shows that the difference in freight rate is so great that in articles of hardware of the coarser kinds the merchants of St. Cloud cannot compete with those of Princeton and Elk River. Whatever goes to the maintenance of life in that community, where the freight rate enters into the price, costs the consumer more than in these near-by communities. It is sometimes difficult to point out the direct and individual hardship of these freight-rate discriminations, although this could be done in the case under consideration, but their effect is none the less real; they are a perpetual tax upon the vitality of the community discriminated against, and sooner or later must produce a visible result.

The defendant earnestly insists, however, that while this discrimination may exist, it is in no sense responsible for it; that the discrimination was equally great before its rates between Duluth and St. Paul were put in, and that the putting in of those rates in no way aggravated that discrimination. It urges, therefore, that inasmuch as these rates do not in any respect injure the complaining company or the community of St. Cloud, while they do to some extent benefit the defendant, they ought not to be declared unlawful.

There is great force in this contention of the defendant. Having reference only to the moment when these rates were first published, its claim that the complainants were in no way prejudiced is probably a valid one. The rates from Minneapolis, Anoka, Elk River and Princeton were the same before as after. The local rates from St. Cloud to Duluth were the same. The mere act of the defendant in publishing its lower rates between the more distant points did not, therefore, produce or aggravate the discrimination with which the complainant is finding fault. But this question cannot be disposed of as of the instant when these rates were inaugurated. The condition which we are examining is a continuing one. By the putting in of those rates the defendant became a competitor for this traffic between Duluth and St. Paul, and from that moment became a factor in the determination of that through rate. Just what effect the defendant may have produced in the past upon those rates, to just what extent it may in the future influence those rates, is a thing which can never be exactly determined.

The defendant has the long line, and suggests that this fact creates a dissimilarity in circumstances and conditions which justifies it in disregarding the rule of the fourth section, while the short lines are bound by that rule. To this we cannot assent. Without deciding that cases may not arise in which difference in distance may justify the higher intermediate rate, we are of the opinion that such effect cannot be given to that circumstance in the present case. To permit this defendant to meet competition at the more distant point without the sacrifice of its intermediate rates, while its competitors were obliged in all cases to reduce their intermediate rates, would place those competitors at the mercy of this defendant. It carries but little of this through traffic. A reduction in the through rate has small effect upon its revenues, while it may bankrupt its rivals. If, however, a reduction of the through rate by the defendant carried with it a corresponding reduction of the intermediate rate the result to the defendant would be too serious to permit of unreasonable action.

The defendant urges that it does not ask to reduce the through rate; it simply asks to meet the rate already in effect. Since mere difference in the length of the defendant's line does not create substantial dissimilarity, we may assume, for the present discussion, that its line is no longer than that of its competitors. The case stands as it would if this defendant had on the first day of April completed and opened for business for the first time the shortest line between St. Paul and Duluth. It finds these rates in effect. It has had no voice in the making of them. It insists that they are unreasonably low, and it asks to be allowed to simply meet those rates without reference to its intermediate territory. In what essential respect would that case differ from the position of the defendant which is now under consideration? We repeat what has been already affirmed; this question cannot be determined as of any particular moment, but must be considered as a continuing condition. When this defendant comes into this field of competition, whether it be as the long line or as the short line, it comes subject to the same limitation as every other competitor.

Counsel for the defendant in his argument puts the two propositions together, namely the length of line and the mere meeting of the rate, as though the long line might simply meet the rate of its competitor while the short line could not do so. This involves a further suggestion that the long line has not the same voice in the determination of the rate as the short line. Such is not our observation as applied to circumstances like the present. Upon the contrary, the long line is much more likely to become a disturbing factor in rate situations than the short line. It is the circuitous route, in its struggle for business, which is most apt to reduce the published rate or to secretly depart from the open rate, thereby forcing reductions by the short line in its open tariffs. This defendant has been carrying 73 car loads of flour between these points, as against more than 1000 per month by each of its competitors. It will hardly rest permanently satisfied with that division of traffic. If its present traffic manager is disposed to do so, he is quite likely to be succeeded by some one who will not. It is not intended to suggest that the defendant will violate the law to obtain more of this freight, but all experience shows that in this competitive contest the presence and active participation of the long line exercises as potent an influence over the rate, in one way and another, as does the short line.

It has been said that each case depends upon its own circumstances. Why, it may be inquired, if this is so, should it not be determined in each case, as a controlling circumstance, which carrier is responsible for the low rate, those carriers which are not being permitted to meet such rate without reference to their intermediate territory. Why should not the defendant in this case be allowed to meet the rate of its competitors untrammeled by the fourth section until it is found as a fact that the defendant has done something more than merely meet these rates?

The practical answer to this would be that no such basis is a workable one. It cannot be satisfactorily determined, in the great majority of instances, which one of several competitors is responsible for a given reduction or a given advance in rates. The causes which lead to rate fluctuations are so intangible, often resting upon a suspicion more or less well founded, that any attempt to say in an individual case what those causes were would ordinarily be futile. We have often had occasion to examine this question, but in no one instance within our present recollection has it ever satisfactorily appeared which carrier actually determined the competitive rate.

It is equally clear that the statute never contemplated any such basis. To enforce such a rule would effectually stifle that competition which the Act to Regulate Commerce took pains to secure. If a carrier could only reduce its rates to a competitive point at the expense of its intermediate territory, while the competitors of that carrier might meet the reduction without corresponding reductions at intermediate points, no carrier would ever openly reduce such rates.

There would be more reason in the claim that flagrant or outrageous conduct of a competitor might create the necessary disparity, and possibly under the rule laid down by the Supreme Court instances of that nature might arise. This Commission held in *Re Chicago, St. P. & K. C. R. Co.*, 2 I. C. C. Rep. 231, 2 Inters. Com. Rep. 137, that the mere unreasonable reduction of a competitive rate at the more distant point would not have this effect. However this may be, it is enough to say that in the case under consideration there is no element of that sort. These four lines are all fairly competing for this traffic. No one has been guilty of any improper conduct in the establishment of the rate or in its methods of obtaining business.

It should be carefully noted that there are no special circumstances or conditions involved in this case. St. Cloud is no farther from Duluth by the line of the defendant than is St. Paul by the more direct lines. The traffic from St. Cloud and St. Paul is of the same character. There is nothing peculiar in the movement of that traffic. The attitude of the different competitors of the defendant, or of all those competitors taken together, is, so far as appears, perfectly fair. No reason can be assigned for permitting this defendant to disregard the fourth section in the handling of this competitive traffic which is not equally applicable to each of its competitors. If the fourth section may be disregarded in case of this railway competition, it is difficult to imagine a competitive condition in which it might not be equally disregarded.

The defendant suggests that, if the other competing lines between St. Paul and Duluth were to imitate its course by making the higher rate to and from the intermediate point, the discrimination against St. Cloud would thereby be removed, for the reason that Princeton, Anoka and Elk River, which now enjoy lower rates, would then be given substantially the same rate which St. Cloud now has. That might in point of fact remove the discriminations as to St. Cloud considered in reference to these three stations, but would it not create a discrimination against those stations in favor of more favored localities? Such a reduction of rates would reduce the price of wheat at Princeton 6 cents a bushel, and would correspondingly reduce the value of land tributary to Princeton. The same would be true of all intermediate territory between Minneapolis and Duluth. Wheat lands in the vicinity of Minneapolis, or even farther west than that city, would be worth more than those through which the products of these lands must pass upon their way to market.

The fact that whatever rule is applied to this defendant must be applied to its competitors has undoubtedly influenced us largely in the determination of this question. The three shorter lines now observe the rule of the fourth section, but they cannot be required or expected to do so if this defendant is permitted to disregard it. To allow all these lines to adopt the course now pursued by this defendant would be to create discrimination not now existing against all intermediate territory between St. Paul and Duluth. It would be to remove the main protection against exorbitant and discriminating interstate rates which that territory now has.

This defendant carries an insignificant amount of through business, and must derive therefrom an insignificant benefit. In order to obtain this benefit it introduces a practice which may demoralize the rate situation in that whole territory. We do not think, having due regard to its interest, as well as the interest of the public, that this ought to be permitted.

The other competing lines, aside from this defendant, observe the rule of the fourth section. When, therefore, the through rate is reduced, this operates to reduce the rate at points like Princeton, Anoka and Elk River, which are in competition with St. Cloud. To the extent, therefore, that this defendant is directly or indirectly responsible for the through rate, it is responsible for the discrimination against St. Cloud. The defendant by becoming a competitor for this through traffic has put itself in a position where it may control, and must, under ordinary circumstances, be held to control, the through rate equally with other competing lines. This being so, it must observe, in the carrying of this competitive traffic, the rule of the fourth section with reference to its intermediate stations, as do its rivals.

* * * * * * * *

In both those cases (Dallas and Savannah Freight Bureau)[1] no prejudice against the intermediate point was shown. In this case such prejudice does appear. Upon a view of the whole situation, it is our conclusion that the defendant carries this business from and to St. Paul, Minneapolis, Anoka and Elk River "under substantially similar circumstances and conditions" as exist in case of business to and from St. Cloud, and that the higher rates to St. Cloud are in violation of the fourth section.

It is said that the rate from St. Cloud is reasonable in and of itself. A rate can seldom be considered "in and of itself." It must be taken almost invariably in relation to and in connection

[1] Cf. p. 314, *infra*.

with other rates. The freight rates of this country, both upon
different commodities and between different localities, are largely
interdependent, and it is the fact that they do not bear a proper
relation to one another, rather than the fact that they are absolutely either too low or too high, which most often gives occasion for complaint, and which is the ground of complaint here.
A rate of 12 cents per hundred pounds on flour from St. Cloud
to Duluth may be reasonable when compared with a similar rate
from Minneapolis. When compared with a rate of $5\frac{1}{2}$ cents from
the latter place, it is certainly *prima facie* grossly unreasonable.
Minneapolis and St. Cloud are competitors in the milling business,
and when this defendant charges the St. Cloud miller 12 cents
per hundred pounds for transporting his flour from St. Cloud to
Duluth, while it charges the Minneapolis miller but $5\frac{1}{2}$ cents for
identically the same service plus an additional haul of 60 miles,
it is guilty of a discrimination against the St. Cloud shipper,
which is not justified by the circumstances of this case.

It should be noticed, moreover, that there is nothing in the
record to show that the rate of $21\frac{1}{2}$ cents on flour from St. Paul
to New York is an unreasonably low one, or that a similar rate
applied to St. Cloud would be unreasonably low. It is certainly
astonishing that so great a service can be rendered for so small
a sum, but, in comparison with similar rates at the same time
prevailing in other parts of the country, this one can hardly be
classed as extraordinary. The defendant compares its rates from
St. Cloud to Duluth and Superior with the distance tariffs of
various States and of various railroad companies, and asserts
from this comparison that they are unduly low; but this is hardly
the proper standard by which to estimate the rates of the defendant in question. The distance tariffs referred to are strictly local
tariffs. This rate under consideration is in effect a division of
the through rate from St. Cloud to New York, for this defendant
cannot treat traffic from St. Paul to New York as through, and
that from St. Cloud to New York as local. *Cincinnati, N. O. &
T. P. R. Co.* v. *Interstate Commerce Commission*, 162 U. S. 184,
40 L. ed. 935, 5 Inters. Com. Rep. 391, 16 Sup. Ct. Rep. 700.
While 12 cents may be an extravagantly low *local* rate as applied

to the distance and traffic in question, it is, when considered as a charge for a haul of 160 miles out of a total through haul of 1500 miles, an extravagantly high rate. We do not express, however, any opinion upon the reasonableness of the through rate or the propriety of the division which the defendant receives, since the latter question especially must depend upon conditions of which no information is afforded by the testimony.

It has been urged that the consequence of the conclusion at which we have arrived must be to compel the Northern Pacific Company to withdraw from this through business, and that as a result that company will lose the profit which might accrue from that traffic, without any benefit whatever to St. Cloud. Should the defendant elect to comply with our order by canceling its through. tariffs it cannot be affirmed that the community of St. Cloud has derived no advantage from such action. The injury to that community lies in the discrimination between it and other localities. That discrimination is intensified in proportion as the St. Paul rate is forced down below the St. Cloud rate. As already remarked, it is impossible to say what effect the competition of the Northern Pacific Company might produce upon this through rate, and therefore impossible to say to what extent St. Cloud is or is not benefited by its withdrawing from that competition.

If the Northern Pacific withdraws from this business it will certainly lose a certain amount of traffic. That traffic is insignificant, however, and it is handled under such conditions that the profit arising from it must be more insignificant still. Moreover, this traffic goes to a shorter line which can handle it at less expense. Wasteful competition by circuitous routes is to the disadvantage of railways as a whole, certainly of the country as a whole, for ultimately there must be some relation between rates and the actual cost of transportation. What the Northern Pacific loses here by the application of the long and short haul rule it probably gains somewhere else through the general observance of that same rule by other carriers.

Even if it were true that the defendant did lose without corresponding advantage at other points, that would be no controlling reason against our conclusion. The application of a beneficent general rule often works a certain hardship in individual cases. At the present time the rule of the fourth section is observed except in certain southern territory and in the making of transcontinental rates. The application of that section for which the defendant contends would permit throughout the whole country the making of higher rates to intermediate points, thereby disarranging business conditions and producing endless discriminations which do not now exist. We cannot feel that any such application was intended by the Act, nor that it should be permitted in due consideration of the interests of all parties concerned.

* * * * * * * *

XII

RELATIVE RATES [1]

THE SAVANNAH FERTILIZER CASE

PROUTY, *Commissioner:*

The Savannah Bureau of Freight and Transportation is an organization of the business men of Savannah, Ga., having in charge the transportation interests of that city. Certain fertilizer companies located at Savannah join with it in this complaint.

Savannah, Ga., Charleston, S.C., and Wilmington, N.C., are important centers for the distribution of commercial fertilizers. This complaint refers to the rates upon such commodities from these three cities to points in North Carolina, South Carolina, Georgia, Florida, and Alabama, and is in substance that the system by which these rates are made is vicious in principle, and that the rates, as made under that system, discriminate against Savannah in favor of Charleston and Wilmington, and are in violation of the fourth section. The facts are not for the most part in dispute, since they arise mainly upon the published tariffs of the defendants.

While it will be unnecessary to refer to all the instances cited in the pleadings and proofs, two or three cases will best state the nature of the complainants' contention. The rates given are, unless otherwise specified, those in force at the time the complaint and answers were filed.

The Charleston & Savannah Railway extends from Charleston to Savannah. At Savannah, it connects with the Savannah, Florida & Western Railway, which runs southerly to Jacksonville, Fla., and westerly across the southern portion of Georgia,

[1] Decided December 31, 1897. Interstate Commerce Reports, Vol. VII, pp. 458–489. This case is compared with other long-and-short-haul controversies in Ripley's Railroads: Rates and Regulation, p. 224.

to the Alabama State line, where it connects with the Alabama Midland Railway extending to Montgomery. These three lines of railway are operated under a common management by what

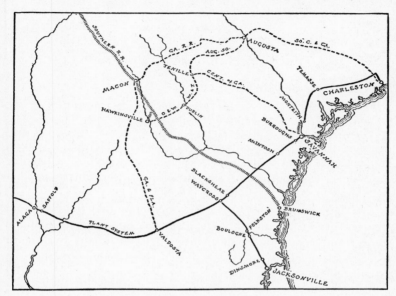

is known as the Plant System, and constitute in practical operation but one line of railroad.

The distance between Charleston and Savannah by this line is 115 miles. Monteith, Ga., is a station upon the Charleston & Savannah Railway, 101 miles from Charleston. Burroughs, McIntosh, Blackshear and Sparks are all stations in the State of Georgia upon the Savannah, Florida & Western Railway. The rate per ton of 2000 pounds and distance from Savannah to these stations is as follows :

To	Rate	Distance
Burroughs	$0.88	12 miles
McIntosh	1.10	31 "
Blackshear	1.71	87 "
Waycross	1.82	97 "

The rate and distance from Charleston to these various points is as follows:

To	RATE	DISTANCE
Monteith	$1.74	101 miles
Savannah	.80	115 "
Burroughs	1.38	127 "
McIntosh	1.60	146 "
Blackshear	1.71	202 "
Waycross	1.82	212 "

The complainants urge that a comparison of the rates and distances from Charleston and Savannah to those various points shows that the rates are made without any reference to distance or cost of transportation, and that they discriminate against Savannah.

The defendants insist, upon the other hand, that the rate from Charleston to Savannah is fixed by water competition, that the rates from Savannah to all points upon the Plant System in Georgia are made by the Georgia Railroad Commission, that the rates from Charleston to these same points are made by adding 50 cents to the Georgia Commission rate, and that this difference, in view of the low rate between Charleston and Savannah, is a reasonable one.

The rates between all points in the State of Georgia are fixed by the Railway Commission of that State. The facts as to water competition between Charleston and Savannah are stated upon another branch of this case.

As already stated, the Savannah, Florida & Western Railway extends from Savannah, Ga., to Jacksonville, Fla. The difference in rate between Charleston and Savannah to all points upon the line of that railway in the State of Georgia, not common points, is 50 cents in favor of Savannah. Folkston, Ga., is the last station in that State and is distant 245 miles from Charleston and 130 miles from Savannah, and the rate is $2.20 from Savannah and $2.70 from Charleston. Boulogne, Fla., is the next station beyond and 5 miles distant from Folkston. At Boulogne the difference in rate is but 24 cents per ton in favor of Savannah, while at Dinsmore, Fla., 30 miles south of Folkston, the rate is the same from both Charleston and Savannah, viz., $2.30 per ton.

Complainants say that if Savannah is entitled to an advantage of 50 cents in Georgia it is certainly entitled to the same advantage in Florida, and that the shrinkage in all instances, and the entire disappearance in many instances of any difference, is an unjust discrimination against Savannah in favor of its competitor Charleston. The defendant excuses this by saying that Jacksonville is an important ocean port, between which and Charleston and Savannah the rate is practically the same, and that in going south upon the Savannah, Florida & Western Railway it is necessary to lower the rate and diminish the difference as Jacksonville is approached. Since the water rate is the same from both Charleston and Savannah to Jacksonville the rail rate must also be the same, or substantially the same, to points which can be reached from Jacksonville.

We find that there is actual water competition between Charleston and Savannah and Jacksonville, and that the rates by water from Charleston and Savannah to Jacksonville upon commercial fertilizers are substantially the same. It did not appear how far from Jacksonville into the interior freight could be transported upon the ocean and rail rate as against all rail competition from Savannah. The rates to Florida points have been changed since the filing of the complaint, so that this alleged discrimination is to some extent removed.

The Savannah, Florida & Western Railway crosses the Chattahoochee river at Saffold, Ga., where it connects with the Alabama Midland Railway. Saffold is the last station in the State of Georgia. Alaga, 1 mile beyond, is the first station in the State of Alabama. The rate from Charleston via Savannah to Saffold, distant 384 miles, is $3.64 ; from Savannah to Saffold, distant 269 miles, $3.14, while the rate to Alaga from both Charleston and Savannah is the same, $3.25. This is true of all the stations upon the Alabama Midland Railway, the rate being the same from both Charleston and Savannah. These rates seem to have been changed also since the filing of the complaint, so that there is now a differential of 20 cents in favor of Savannah to points on the Alabama Midland in Alabama.

The complainants insist that this equalizing of the rate between Charleston and Savannah to points in Alabama, while the difference in distance remains the same, is an unjust discrimination against Savannah. The defendants reply that all stations upon the Alabama Midland Railway between Alaga and Montgomery are grouped, and that the rate is made by competition with other railway lines and other lines partly rail and partly water, operating through Montgomery; the rate from Pensacola, Fla., and Mobile, Ala., to Montgomery being $1.80, and from New Orleans, La., to Montgomery $3.00. These rates are correctly stated, but nothing appears as to the cost of fertilizers at Pensacola, Mobile or New Orleans; nor did it appear whether or not fertilizers were actually brought from these points to Montgomery.

The foregoing illustrations sufficiently indicate the manner in which it is alleged that the Plant System discriminates by these rates against the city of Savannah in favor of Charleston; but the complaint goes much further than this and attacks, not merely the rate of individual lines, but the entire scheme of rate making which, it is alleged, abolishes distance in favor of Charleston and Wilmington as against Savannah. The nature of this alleged discrimination appears from the following examples:

Valdosta, Ga., is situated upon the Savannah, Florida & Western Railway 158 miles from Savannah and 273 miles from Charleston, and this is the direct rail line between Charleston and Valdosta. Valdosta can, however, be reached from Charleston by another line made up of the South Carolina & Georgia Railway to Augusta, the Georgia Railroad from Augusta to Macon, and the Georgia Southern & Florida Railway from Macon to Valdosta. The distance by this route is 413 miles as against 273 miles by the direct route. It has already been said that to most points in the State of Georgia upon the Plant System there exists a difference in rate of 50 cents between Charleston and Savannah in favor of Savannah, but in the case of Valdosta the rate is the same, $2.48, and this is for the reason that the circuitous line from Charleston demands and obtains the right to make the same rate from Charleston to Valdosta as is made from Savannah to Valdosta.

Hawkinsville, Ga., is upon the Southern Railway between Brunswick, Ga., and Macon. It is also connected by lines of railway with both Charleston and Savannah. The route from Charleston is over the South Carolina & Georgia to Augusta, the Augusta Southern to Tennille, the Wrightsville & Tennille to Dublin, and the Oconee & Western from Dublin to Hawkinsville, a distance of 297 miles. The line between Savannah and Hawkinsville is by the Central of Georgia Railway to Tennille, the Wrightsville & Tennille to Dublin, and the Oconee & Western from Dublin to Hawkinsville, being the same route from Tennille. The rate from all three points is the same, although the distances are from Brunswick 160 miles, Savannah 211 miles, and Charleston 297 miles.

The complainants have referred to several instances as showing this kind of discrimination in favor especially of Charleston and Wilmington as appears from the following tables. By "one line" is meant one continuous line operated by one company, and by "two or more lines," that the line between the points named is made up of two or more independent roads.

To TENNILLE, GA.

FROM	DISTANCE	LINES
Savannah	134 miles	1
Charleston	221 "	2
Wilmington	354 "	3

Rate $2.31 per ton.

To DENMARK, S.C.

Savannah	90 miles	1
Charleston	81 "	1
Wilmington	213 "	1

Rate $2.60 per ton.

To Columbus, Ga.[1]

FROM	DISTANCE	LINES
Savannah	291 miles	1
Charleston	389 "	4
Wilmington	553 "	2

Rate $3.14 per ton.

To Troy, Ala.[1]

Savannah	360 miles	1
Charleston	475 "	1
Wilmington	687 "	2

Rate $3.50 per ton.

To Montgomery, Ala.[1]

Savannah	340 miles	1
Charleston	527 "	1
Wilmington	611 "	2

Rate $3.00 per ton.

The complainants say that these tables show that the rates complained of are made without any consistency, without any reference to distance, and that they uniformly discriminate against Savannah by admitting Charleston and Wilmington upon equal terms into that territory which is naturally tributary to Savannah.

The defendants do not deny that the rates are made upon the principle complained of, but they say that the principle is just, advantageous to the various localities which thereby enjoy the benefit of the competition, and that, whatever objection there may be to it, it is the only system which is possible under the peculiar circumstances which exist in this southern territory.

[1] Cf. map, p. 154, *supra.*

Exactly what this system is, and exactly the points of difference between the claims of the complainants and the defendants is well indicated by a graphic illustration produced upon the trial by counsel for the defendants, which was made an exhibit and is reproduced here.

Referring to the above outline, Wilmington, Charleston, Savannah and Brunswick are four points upon the seacoast. A, B, C, and D are four interior points. The heavy lines represent

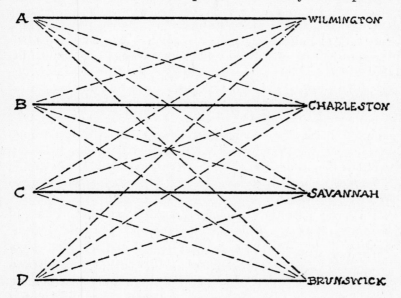

lines of railway connecting each one of these ocean ports with the corresponding interior point, and designate the shortest line of railway between such points. The dotted lines represent lines of railway between the several ocean ports and the interior points. Now, the complainants insist that the lowest rate should in all cases be made upon the shortest line; that is, Wilmington should have the lowest rate to A, Charleston to B, Savannah to C, and Brunswick to D. The defendants insist that when the rate has been made over the short line, as from Savannah to C., then Wilmington, Charleston and Brunswick are all entitled to the same rate to C, although the lines of communication are much longer.

To state the proposition with reference to some of the points actually in evidence in this case. Valdosta is 158 miles from Savannah by the Savannah, Florida & Western Railway. The rate upon fertilizers from Savannah to Valdosta is fixed by the Georgia Railway Commission. Now, the defendants say that when this rate is once fixed, if Charleston can reach the same point by a longer line, it is entitled to do so at the same rate, although that line is 413 miles in length and composed of three independent railroads as against 158 miles over one railroad.

So in the case of Hawkinsville. This station is situated upon the Southern Railway between Brunswick and Macon. The rate from Brunswick is fixed by the Georgia Commission. Now, when that rate has been determined, Charleston and Savannah, or rather the lines leading from Charleston, Savannah and Wilmington, insist that they are entitled to the same rate, although the distance from Brunswick to Hawkinsville is but 161 miles over one line as against 211 miles from Savannah over two lines, 297 miles from Charleston over four lines, and 430 miles from Wilmington over five lines.

It appears from the testimony that there are in the States of Kentucky, Virginia, Tennessee, Mississippi, Alabama, Georgia, Louisiana, North Carolina, South Carolina and Florida, 148 of these points to which the rates on fertilizers from Charleston, Savannah, Brunswick and Jacksonville are the same. The illustrations given in these findings of fact all show that Savannah loses the benefit of the less distance. There must be many of these common points to which the distance from Savannah is greater than from Charleston and in respect of which Savannah has the advantage over Charleston. No attempt has been made, however, upon the part of the defendants to show what these points are, nor whether, on the whole, Savannah is at an advantage or disadvantage under this system of rate making. Upon the other hand, the defendants claim that this is entirely immaterial, that these points have the right to the common rate provided that the primary, or determinative rate, which is usually the short-distance rate, is properly made ; and provided further that the long line can carry without loss at that rate.

We are unable to find that the short-distance rate in any case called to our attention discriminates against Savannah. In most cases that rate is the one made by the Railroad Commission of either Georgia or South Carolina. Neither can we find from the testimony that the long line in any case carries at a loss. Although the rate per ton per mile in some instances is low, the testimony of the defendants tends to prove that it is a remunerative rate, and there is nothing to show the contrary.

It does not appear that the Southern Railway & Steamship Association originated this system of "common points," but that it found the same already in existence and adopted it. For a long time Brunswick, Savannah, Port Royal and Charleston have entered upon equal terms this common-point territory. Wilmington did not formerly, but the lines leading from that city strenuously insisted upon their right to participate in the same rates, and in many instances exacted that right. Finally that question was submitted to the Board[1] of Arbitration of the Southern Railway & Steamship Association, and that Board published its award April 29, 1895, by which it was decided that the rates should be the same from Wilmington as from other South Atlantic ports to all points in this territory, excepting those upon and south of the Savannah & Western extension of the Central Railroad of Georgia from Savannah to Lyons and the Georgia & Alabama Railway in the State of Georgia. This award was accepted by the various lines interested and has since been acquiesced in.

The complainants put in evidence upon the trial certain tables of rates and distances which they claim show a discrimination against Savannah and in favor of Charleston. The first of these consists of two sets of tables, each made up of 33 stations. In the first set the stations selected are in the States of Georgia and Florida, and the tables show the distance, the rate per ton, and the rate per ton per mile from both Savannah and Charleston.

[1] *Vide*, p. 144, *supra*.

These averages are :

FROM	DISTANCE	RATE PER TON	RATE PER TON PER MILE
Savannah	190 miles	$2.47	$.013
Charleston . . .	284 "	2.79	.0098

The second set is made up of 33 stations in the States of North Carolina and South Carolina. The facts shown are the same and the averages are :

FROM	DISTANCE	RATE PER TON	RATE PER TON PER MILE
Savannah	176 miles	$2.87	$.0163
Charleston . . .	116 "	2.21	.0191

The complainants introduced another table made up of 74 stations, no one of which appears in the tables last referred to. These stations are situated in the States of Georgia, Alabama, Florida, and South Carolina. The average distance, rate per ton, and rate per ton per mile from Savannah and Charleston are as follows :

FROM	DISTANCE	RATE PER TON	RATE PER TON PER MILE
Savannah	156 miles	$2.25	$.02079
Charleston . . .	252 "	2.50	.01244

It may be observed in this connection that according to the testimony of the defendants only 10 per cent of the fertilizer and fertilizer rock carried to Valdosta during the year 1896 went by the Plant System. Assuming that the Plant System carried nothing from Charleston, this would mean that nine tenths of the fertilizer used in Valdosta was transported 413 miles instead of 158 miles.

The complaint incidentally charges that in the application of this system the carriers charge less for the longer haul to the competitive point than they charge to intermediate points upon the same line.   There seems to be a difference between a " common point," which is a point reached by two or more lines, and a "base point," which is a point at which competition has forced down the rates below those upon either side of it. The defendants admit that the rate is in many cases lower to the basing point than to intermediate points, and the complainants have called our attention specifically to the following instances in which the greater charge is made to the nearer point, when the transportation is over the same line, in the same direction at the same time.

1. The Charleston & Savannah Railway connects Charleston and Savannah. Going south from Charleston the rate to Monteith, Ga., is $1.74 and the distance 101 miles, while the rate to Savannah, 14 miles further, is $.80 per ton. So going from Savannah north towards Charleston the rates and distances to intermediate points are (cf. map, p. 315, *supra*):

To	Rate	Distance
Hardeeville	$1.20	24 miles
Yemassee	1.50	54 "
Jacksonboro	1.70	78 "
Drayton	2.00	103 "
Charleston	.80	115 "

The respondent Charleston & Savannah Railway Company alleges that these rates are justified by water competition between Charleston and Savannah. We find that there is such water competition which is of controlling force, and that the respondent could not, as against this competition, charge more than $.80 per ton, while the rates to intermediate points are substantially those fixed by the Railroad Commissions of Georgia and South Carolina. That the rates are not exactly the same going north as going south for the same distance is accounted for by the fact that the South Carolina Commission allows a higher rate upon fertilizers than the Georgia Commission.

2. The Charleston & Savannah Railway is the direct line between those two cities, but there is another somewhat longer line made up of the South Carolina & Georgia Railroad from Charleston to Denmark, and the Florida Central & Peninsular Railroad from Denmark to Savannah. These two defendants make a joint rate between Charleston and Savannah of $.80, the distance being 171 miles. Rincon, Meinhard and Wheat Hill are all stations upon the Florida Central & Peninsular Railroad in the State of Georgia, distant from Charleston respectively 153 miles, 161 miles and 167 miles, and the rate is in each case $2.30 per ton.

We have already found that water competition between Charleston and Savannah necessitates the rate of $.80. The rate of $2.30 to the intermediate points above referred to does not exceed that allowed by the State Commissions of Georgia and South Carolina.

*   *   *   *   *   *   *   *

4. As already stated, the long line between Charleston and Valdosta is composed of the South Carolina & Georgia Railroad from Charleston to Augusta, the Georgia Railroad from Augusta to Macon and the Georgia Southern & Florida Railway from Macon to Valdosta. These lines make a joint rate from Charleston to Valdosta of $2.48.

Thomson, Mayfield and Haddocks are stations upon the Georgia Railroad between Augusta and Macon. The South Carolina & Georgia Railroad and the Georgia Railroad make the following joint rates for the following distances to those points :

To	Rate	Distance
Thomson	$2.64	175 miles
Mayfield	2.64	198 "
Haddocks	2.64	244 "
Macon	2.64	263 "

Kathleen, Sycamore, Tifton and Sparks are stations upon the Georgia Southern & Florida Railway between Macon and

Valdosta. The South Carolina & Georgia Railroad, the Georgia Railroad and the Georgia Southern & Florida Railway make joint rates from Charleston to these stations as follows:

To	Rate	Distance
Kathleen	$3.32	288 miles
Sycamore	2.83	349 "
Tifton	2.53	367 "
Sparks	2.87	388 "
Valdosta	2.48	413 "

Of the above stations, Thomson, Mayfield, Haddocks, Kathleen, Sycamore and Sparks are noncompetitive stations, while Macon, Tifton and Valdosta are competitive points.

The defendants allege that the low rates at these competitive points are forced by railway competition, and that the rates to intermediate points are reasonable in and of themselves. We find that there is railway competition at the above-named competitive points, which undoubtedly *occasions* the low rates. That competition does not necessitate the low rates, except that it induces a number of carriers, all of whom are subject to the Act to Regulate Commerce, to fix them by voluntary agreement. The rates to intermediate points are not greater than those allowed by the State Railroad Commissions of Georgia and South Carolina, and in this sense they are reasonable " in and of themselves." The making of the lower rate to the more distant competitive point introduces, we think, a new element, and we are not prepared to find affirmatively that the higher intermediate rates in comparison with the lower competitive rates are reasonable either as matter of law or as matter of fact.

5. The line from Charleston to Hawkinsville is made up of the South Carolina & Georgia Railway to Augusta, the Augusta Southern from Augusta to Tennille, the Wrightsville & Tennille from Tennille to Dublin and the Oconee & Western from Dublin to Hawkinsville. The line from Savannah to Hawkinsville is composed of the Central of Georgia Railway from Savannah to Tennille, the Wrightsville & Tennille from Tennille to Dublin

and the Oconee & Western from Dublin to Hawkinsville, being the same line from Savannah to Hawkinsville and from Charleston to Hawkinsville both make a joint rate from those two cities to Hawkinsville of $2.53.

Hephzibah, Matthews and Warthen are upon the line of the Augusta Southern. The Augusta Southern and the South Carolina & Georgia maintain the following rates from Charleston to these stations:

To	Rate	Distance
Hephzibah	$2.94	153 miles
Matthews	3.10	169 "
Warthen	2.87	208 "

Wrightsville is upon the Wrightsville & Tennille Railroad between Tennille and Dublin. The South Carolina & Georgia Railroad, the Augusta Southern Railroad and the Wrightsville & Tennille Railroad make the following joint rates from Charleston:

To	Rate	Distance
Wrightsville	$2.92	238 miles
Dublin	3.12	257 "

Dexter is upon the Oconee & Western Railway between Dublin and Hawkinsville. The South Carolina & Georgia Railroad, the Augusta Southern Railroad, the Wrightsville & Tennille Railroad and the Oconee & Western Railway maintain the following joint rates from Charleston:

To	Rate	Distance
Dexter	$3.10	270 miles
Hawkinsville	2.53	297 "

The rate from Savannah to Tennille over the Central of Georgia Railway is $2.31 and the distance 134 miles. Between

Tennille and Hawkinsville and to Hawkinsville the Central of Georgia Railway, the Wrightsville & Tennille Railway and the Oconee & Western Railway maintain the same rates as above stated.

The defendants named in this paragraph offer the same justification as stated in the preceding paragraph, *viz.*, that Hawkinsville is a competitive point and that the rates to the intermediate stations named are reasonable.

We find that Hawkinsville is a competitive point, and that the rate from Brunswick to Hawkinsville is fixed by the Georgia Commission. Our finding as to the rates to the intermediate stations is the same as that in paragraph four.

*   *   *   *   *   *   *   *

Upon these findings to what relief, if any, are the complainants entitled?

The underlying cause of complaint is the system upon which these rates are made, and the most important question is whether that system is in violation of the Interstate Commerce Act in the respect complained of, and if so, whether the Commission has power to correct such violation.

The position of the complainants seems to be that certain territory is tributary to the city of Savannah and that Charleston must not be allowed to enter this territory upon equal terms as to freight rates. This really amounts to saying that the rate should be determined by the distance. It has often been said that distance is an important element in the making of rates, and it has been held that a carrier would not be *compelled* to disregard distance in order to place two localities upon commercial equality. *Commercial Club of Omaha* v. *Chicago, R. I. & P. R. Co.*, 6 I. C. C. Rep. 647; *Cincinnati Freight Bureau* v. *Cincinnati, N. O. & T. P. R. Co.*, 7 I. C. C. Rep. 180.

Upon the other hand, it often happens that distance is altogether disregarded, and it has been held that this may be proper within certain limits and under certain conditions. *Imperial Coal Co.* v. *Pittsburg & L. E. R. Co.*, 2 I. C. C. Rep. 618, 2 Inters. Com. Rep. 436. The proposition of the defendant is, however, that in this whole territory distance should be entirely obliterated. The mere fact that a town is situated at the junction of two railroads entitles that town to the same freight rate from Charleston and Savannah, no matter what the relative distance may be.

To put the question in a concrete form. Valdosta is 158 miles from Savannah and 413 miles from Charleston, yet the defendants claim that the rate from Savannah and Charleston should be the same. It is found that only 10 per cent of the fertilizer used in Valdosta during the year 1896 came from Savannah, the balance of it being brought from Charleston. Assuming that the cost of that article was the same at Savannah and Charleston, this would mean that nine tenths of all the fertilizer consumed in that vicinity was transported 413 miles while it might have been obtained by transporting it 158 miles. Now, the complainants say that this is wrong ; that manifestly it costs much more to transport fertilizer from Charleston than from Savannah, and that somebody in the end must pay for that species of foolishness, if it be allowed to continue. Upon the other hand, the defendants urge that this system gives Valdosta the benefit of competition in the markets of both Charleston and Savannah, and that so long as railroad companies are operated as private enterprises they may of right engage in any legitimate business which yields a profit.

Probably the true solution of this controversy is to be found in a mesne between the contentions of the two parties. It can hardly be said that a particular locality is entitled to describe about itself a circle and exclude its competitors from this area. Neither can it well be claimed that distance ought not to be a factor in the making of rates, and that a city is entitled to no benefit by reason of its advantageous position. The defendants themselves concede that there are limits beyond which this disregard of distance ought not to extend. Formerly Wilmington was not allowed to come into this common-point territory for the very reason that the distance was against that city. Finally that question was submitted to arbitration and the arbitrators determined that Wilmington might come into certain territory, but a line was established below which it could not go, and that city is to-day excluded from points south of this line solely on account of distance. However, we do not feel called upon to decide in this case whether the principle itself is right, nor whether the application of that principle is too extensive, for the reason that, if we determine that there is a wrong, we clearly have no power to correct that wrong.

Valdosta is reached by one line of railroad from Savannah and by an independent line of railroads from Charleston. The rate from Savannah to Valdosta is fixed by the Railroad Commission of Georgia. If the railroads constituting the line from Charleston to Valdosta see fit to make the same rate from Charleston as is made from Savannah we have no power to order them not to do so, for it has always been understood that the Commission had no authority to fix a minimum rate. *Re Chicago, St. P. & K. C. R. Co.*, 2 I. C. C. Rep. 231, 2 Inters. Com. Rep. 137.

If some point is taken to which both rates are interstate, like Montgomery, the result is still the same. Each line is an independent line and may fix its own rate wherever it pleases, and we have no power whatever over that rate when established. It is manifest that a wrong like that complained of in this case could not be corrected without authority to establish both the maximum and the minimum rate. And we can establish neither. *Interstate Commerce Commission* v. *Cincinnati, N. O. & T. P. R. Co.*, 167 U. S. 479, 42 L. ed. 243.

But if the Commission has no power to correct a discrimination of this sort where the rate from Savannah is made by one line and the rate from Charleston is made by another line, has it not power to correct it where the same line makes both rates, and ought it not to do so? The Plant System extends from Charleston through Savannah to Valdosta. The rate by that system from both Charleston and Savannah to Valdosta is the same, although the distance from Charleston is almost twice as great. Should not this apparent wrong to Savannah be righted?

If this rate stood alone and were voluntarily made by the Plant System, it would probably be a discrimination against Savannah which ought to be corrected. But under the circumstances it is difficult to see how it can be called an unjust discrimination or how it works to the injury of Savannah. The rate from Charleston to Valdosta is fixed by an independent line. The distance through Savannah is but 275 miles as against 413 miles by that line. Unless the Plant System makes the same rate as is made by the circuitous line it can do no business whatever. Under these circumstances we think it may properly meet the rate from Charleston which is made by the longer line, and that it does not, in making and maintaining this rate, unjustly discriminate against the city of Savannah. If the rate from Charleston to Valdosta were in any way subject to control, our judgment might be otherwise.

The complainants insist that even though the common-point system of rate making is consistent, nevertheless the defendants discriminate unduly against Savannah in the application of that system. They introduce certain tables which apparently show that Charleston has the benefit of a better rate into the territory of Savannah than Savannah has into the territory of Charleston. It is not clear that these tables fully sustain the contention of the complainants, since the average distances are not the same and the rate per ton per mile should not be the same for short as for long distances ; but assuming that they do show that Charleston has such an advantage, that may well follow from the system and not from its unfair application. If the common points to which Savannah and Charleston take the same rate are so located that upon the whole the distance is less from Savannah than from Charleston, then manifestly the result must be the one which the complainants say their tables demonstrate. In other words, the vice, if one is established, is that of the system, and not of its application ; and we have already said that we cannot correct that fault.

But the complainants say that there are instances in which there is a manifest discrimination against Savannah in the making of these rates. For instance, Charleston is 115 miles distant from Savannah. To all stations in Georgia, not common points, a difference in rate of 50 cents per ton in favor of Savannah is made by the Plant System. It is urged that this difference is too little in view of the difference in distance.

To this we cannot assent. It is found that water competition between Charleston and Savannah compels the making of a rate of 80 cents per ton between those two cities. If 80 cents is a proper local rate, 50 cents cannot be said to be an unfair difference in the through rate from Charleston *via* Savannah to Georgia points. Looking merely to the cost of service, the Plant System would probably make more money in transporting fertilizer from Charleston to Burroughs upon the through rate of $1.38 than in transporting the same article from Charleston to Savannah upon a local rate of 80 cents and from Savannah to Burroughs upon another local rate of 88 cents. The Charleston-Savannah rate is fixed by water competition ; the Savannah-Burroughs rate is fixed by law. These two rates being established, the through rate from Charleston to Burroughs is not an unreasonable one.

The difference in rate between Charleston and Savannah is maintained to all points, not common points, in the State of Georgia upon the Plant System, but when that line of railway crosses the southern boundary of Georgia and enters the State of Florida this difference begins to diminish and finally disappears altogether.

If not in some way accounted for this would be a manifest discrimination against Savannah ; but it is accounted for by the fact that the water rate on fertilizers from both Charleston and Savannah to Jacksonville, Fla., is the same, and must accordingly be the same at all intermediate points to which fertilizer can be brought *via* Jacksonville by ocean and rail as against the all rail line. Circumstances over which the Plant System has no control determine that the rate from Charleston and Savannah to these points shall be the same by other lines. This being so, we have already indicated that the Plant System may meet that rate.

Something of the same sort occurs upon the Plant System in the State of Alabama. That system is operated as a continuous line from Savannah to Montgomery, the portion of it which is in the State of Alabama and which extends from Alaga to Montgomery being known as the Alabama Midland Railway in

Alabama. Upon all stations on the Plant System in the State of Georgia, not common points, a difference of 50 cents per ton is made in favor of Savannah, but as soon as the Alabama State line is crossed this difference disappears, and at all stations between Alaga and Montgomery the rate from Charleston and Savannah is the same. This was the case when the answer of the Plant System was filed, but at the date of the hearing the rates had been revised and a differential of 20 cents per ton in favor of Savannah established. Nothing in this case appears to justify a different differential to most points upon the Plant System in Alabama from what it is in Georgia. There are common points upon that system in both Georgia and Alabama.

We are inclined to think that there are stations upon the Plant System in Florida, and also upon the line of the Florida Central & Peninsular Railroad in Florida to which a sufficient difference is not made in the rate from Charleston and Savannah, and that the same thing is probably true of stations upon the Alabama Midland Railway in Alabama; but we do not feel that our information is sufficiently definite to enable us to make any order in this respect.

We are satisfied that water competition through Jacksonville justifies the same rate from Charleston and Savannah to certain points in Florida, but we do not know to what points. We know that competition through Montgomery, and perhaps at other points upon the Alabama Midland, justifies a diminution in the difference in rate between Charleston and Savannah, but we do not know just how far. It appears that changes have been made in these rates since the filing of the complaint, which in some cases remove the ground for complaint. We think best, therefore, not to attempt to make any order in this particular, but to rely upon the defendants to adjust these rates in accordance with our suggestions, giving the complainants leave to apply for an order if this is not done.

The complaint incidentally charges the defendants with certain violations of the fourth section and the findings of fact state the instances which were called to our attention by the pleadings and proofs.

The charging by the Charleston & Savannah Railway of higher rates to intermediate points between Charleston and Savannah than the rate over the entire distance between those cities is justified by the existence of water competition; and this is also true of the line between the same cities composed of the South Carolina & Georgia and the Florida Central & Peninsular Railway Companies.

In all other instances the justification relied upon is the existence of railway competition between carriers subject to the Act to Regulate Commerce. The Commission has uniformly held up to the present time that this species of competition does not create the necessary dissimilarity of circumstances and conditions under that section, and such would have been its decision in this case upon the law as it was supposed to be when the findings of fact were prepared. Since then, however, the Supreme Court of the United States by its decision in the case, *Interstate Commerce Commission* v. *Alabama M. R. Co.* decided November 8, 1897, 168 U. S. 144, 42 L. ed.,[1] has determined that this view of the law is erroneous, and that railway competition may create such dissimilar circumstances and conditions as exempt the carrier from an observance of the long and short haul provision. Under this interpretation of the law as applied to the facts found in this case, we are of the opinion that the charging of the higher rate to the intermediate points, as set forth, is not obnoxious to the fourth section. The section declares that the carrier shall not make the higher charge to the nearer point under " substantially similar circumstances and conditions." If the conditions and circumstances are not substantially similar, then the section does not apply and the carrier is not bound to regard it in the making of its tariffs. The court has decided that railway competition, if it exists, must be considered. If, therefore, such competition does actually control the rate at the more distant point that rate is not made under the same circumstances and conditions as is the rate at the intermediate point and the higher rate is not prohibited by the fourth section.

[1] Cf. p. 378, *infra*.

Recurring now to the findings of fact, we see that in every case the rate by the longer line to the more distant point is not only controlled but absolutely fixed by competitive conditions. If the lines from Charleston to Valdosta have a right to compete at that point for traffic in commercial fertilizer, the rate which they make is determined by competition alone, and that rate is not in fact made under the same circumstances and conditions as are the rates to intermediate points, if such railway competition is to be taken into account. It is our opinion, therefore, that the higher intermediate rates involved in this case are not in violation of the fourth section.

XIII

JOINT THROUGH RATES AND PRORATING: JOBBING COMPETITION [1]

REPORT OF THE COMMISSION

CLARK, *Commissioner:*

Complainants are individuals, partnerships, and corporations engaged in jobbing trade at Kansas City and St. Joseph, Mo., and Omaha, Nebr., to which points they ship *via* the lines of the defendants large quantities of goods from the Atlantic seaboard, largely under class rates, and from which points they distribute such goods throughout a large territory to the southwest, west, and northwest and also to a comparatively small and limited territory east of the Missouri river.

In sale and distribution of their goods, complainants come in competition with jobbers located at Minneapolis and St. Paul, hereinafter referred to as the Twin Cities, and the complaint alleges unjust and unreasonable discrimination in favor of the Twin Cities and undue prejudice against Kansas City, St. Joseph, and Omaha, hereinafter referred to as the Missouri River Cities, due to and measured by the difference in the class rates from the Atlantic seaboard to the Twin Cities, as compared with like rates from same points to the Missouri River Cities.

In testimony, briefs, and argument complainants make a strong attack upon the long-established system of rate making under which rates to points west of the Mississippi river are made upon the basis of the rates to the Mississippi river crossings.

---

[1] *Burnham, Hanna, Munger Co.* v. *C., R. I. & P. Ry.*, etc. Decided June 24, 1908, by the Interstate Commerce Commission (14 I. C. C. Rep., 299) ; upheld by the United States Supreme Court, 1910. The legal significance of this case is discussed in Ripley's Railroads : Rates and Regulation, p. 542. Prorating will be treated in the volume on Finance and Organization. Jobbing rates and commercial competition are analyzed in the former volume (see Index).

As railroads were constructed into the undeveloped West and, for a time at least, had their western termini at the east bank of the Mississippi river, it seems natural that when the river was crossed, and rates were established to points beyond, they should be constructed by adding certain sums to the rates already established to the river, and as additional lines were built and additional railroad crossings over the Mississippi river were constructed, competition between carriers and localities naturally established common rates to the Mississippi river crossings, especially when applied to traffic going beyond.

As the West was further developed, this same condition and like results followed at the several crossings of the Missouri river, so that to-day the rates from the Mississippi river crossings to the Missouri river crossings, Kansas City to Omaha, inclusive, are the same, and from points east, to the Missouri River Cities, are the same *via* any of the Mississippi river crossings, East St. Louis to East Dubuque, inclusive.

Complaint alleges unreasonableness of the class rates from the Atlantic seaboard, and the defendants named in the complaint were the Chicago, Rock Island & Pacific Railway Company, the Chicago, Burlington & Quincy Railway Company, the Chicago, Milwaukee & St. Paul Railway Company, the Chicago & Northwestern Railway Company, and the Chicago Great Western Railway Company. All of these are carriers whose lines do not extend east of Chicago, and all of them have lines from Chicago, through the several Mississippi river crossings, to the Missouri River Cities. The defendants whose lines are east of Chicago were made defendants upon application of the Chicago & Northwestern Railway Company. It will, however, be seen that the complaint, the testimony, and the argument are all against the rates charged west of Chicago and the Mississippi river crossings.

The Sioux City Commercial Club intervened and supported the complainants' request, introducing and emphasizing, however, the view that whatever might be done for Omaha should likewise be done for Sioux City, and arguing that as Sioux City was also a Missouri river crossing it should be placed upon a parity with Omaha. The St. Paul Jobbers and Manufacturers'

Association, of St. Paul, and the Commercial Club of Minneapolis intervened and in substance joined with and supported the defendants. The Chicago Association of Commerce and the Merchants' Traffic Bureau and the Business Men's League of St. Louis appeared at the hearings on behalf of the commercial interests of their respective cities, offered evidence and were heard on brief and in oral argument in defense of the system of rate construction based upon the Mississippi river, and in opposition to a rate adjustment that would give the Missouri River Cities an advantage at the expense of Chicago and St. Louis.

Complainants allege that the class rates from the Atlantic seaboard, of which New York will be taken as representative, to the Missouri River Cities, to wit, in cents per 100 pounds,

1	2	3	4	5
147	120	93	68	57

are unjust and unreasonable; that they are unjustly discriminatory against the Missouri River Cities as compared with the class rates from New York to the Twin Cities, to wit, in cents per 100 pounds,

1	2	3	4	5
115	99	76	53	46

and they ask that the Commission establish from New York to the Missouri River Cities the following through class rates in cents per 100 pounds,

1	2	3	4	5
110	95.25	72.5	51.5	44

together with proportionate reductions from eastern producing points as shown in Western Trunk Line Tariff No. 786, I. C. C. No. 678, or such other rates as may be found just and reasonable.

Defendants, Chicago, Rock Island & Pacific Railway; Chicago, Burlington & Quincy Railway; Chicago, Milwaukee & St. Paul Railway; Chicago & Northwestern Railway, and Chicago Great Western Railway are parties to the tariff so referred to. It contains rates on classes and commodities from "Atlantic seaboard and points west thereof, east of the western termini of the trunk lines" to St. Paul, Minneapolis, etc., and the term "Atlantic seaboard" is used herein in that sense.

Defendants admit the correctness of the rates stated in the complaint, and the divisions thereof between the several carriers, and the distances *via* the various routes, but they deny that such rates are unjust and unreasonable, or unjustly discriminatory in comparison with the rates to the Twin Cities. Of the five original defendants, the Rock Island, the Northwestern, and the Great Western, allege justification for the lower rates to the Twin Cities on the ground of competition by water as well as of competition *via* the Canadian Pacific and the Minneapolis, St. Paul & Sault Ste. Marie Railway, hereinafter referred to as the Soo Line.

Of the numerous complainants only representatives of the dry goods interests appeared to give evidence at the hearings, with the exception of one wholesale grocer, introduced by the intervenor, Sioux City Commercial Club. The jobbers of Sioux City sell goods in northwestern Iowa, southwestern Minnesota, South Dakota, northern Nebraska, and a part of Wyoming. They come into competition with jobbers at Chicago, Omaha, the Twin Cities, and other intermediate jobbing points, their strongest competition being with Omaha on the south and the Twin Cities on the north.

With the exception of North Dakota, western and northwestern Minnesota, and Canada it may be said in general that the dry goods concerns in the Missouri River Cities compete in all the territory from the Missouri river to the Pacific Ocean and from the Canadian boundary to the Gulf, and in much of this territory they meet competition more or less keen from jobbers at Chicago, St. Louis, the Twin Cities, Denver, San Francisco, and various smaller jobbing points. In Montana, Washington, and common-points territory the Missouri River Cities jobbers meet strong competition from jobbers in the Twin Cities, New York, Chicago, St. Louis, and San Francisco; New York and the Twin Cities having an advantage in that territory of the difference between the rates from New York to the Missouri River Cities and from New York to the Twin Cities. In the West and Southwest the strongest competitors of the Missouri River Cities are New York, Chicago, and St. Louis. In Iowa, southeastern Dakota, and southwestern Minnesota the rates equalize at greater distances from the Twin Cities than from the Missouri River Cities.

While the Missouri River Cities jobbers are at a disadvantage as compared with the Twin Cities jobbers in Minnesota, North Dakota, northeastern South Dakota, and Canadian territory, the Twin Cities jobbers are at a like and apparently equal disadvantage in the territory immediately west and southwest of the Missouri River Cities and in the Black Hills district of South Dakota. There are points west of the Missouri river which can be reached by the jobber at St. Louis or at New York, under a combination rate based on St. Louis, cheaper than they can be reached by the Missouri river Cities jobbers under a combination rate based on the Missouri river, but the evidence seemed to show that in general this was where the application of a through rate at an intermediate point on the same line had that effect.

The record shows that 3 wholesale dry goods houses at Kansas City, 4 at St. Joseph, and 2 at Omaha do an aggregate annual business of about $40,000,000. They estimate that their inbound freight charges amount to about $3\frac{1}{4}$ per cent of the total sales; that their total expenses amount to 13 per cent of the total sales and that on an annual business of $5,000,000 the Twin Cities jobbers would have an advantage of approximately $40,000 over the jobbers at the Missouri River Cities by reason of the difference in freight rates. This estimate presumably assumes that the total of the year's sales is made in territory strictly competitive between the Missouri River Cities and the Twin Cities, and that it all moves under the first-class rate.

Complainants insist that the system of basing rates to the Missouri River Cities and points beyond the Mississippi river crossings is improper. Their expert testified that the Mississippi river basis should be abolished, but he did not think the Missouri river basis should be abolished because, in his opinion, the country west of the Missouri river had not developed sufficiently as yet to warrant that change.

As has been noted, the Missouri River Cities have a certain territory naturally tributary to them in which the Twin Cities are apparently unable to compete with them, but in certain other territory naturally tributary to the Twin Cities, the Twin Cities jobbers have an advantage over the Missouri River Cities jobbers, and this must necessarily be so as to all distributing centers if the cost of the service and the distance which goods are transported are to be given any consideration in determining transportation rates. It is not possible to place all commercial centers on an equality in the cost of transportation except by basing transportation charges upon the same principle that underlies the Government's charges for the transmission of mail matter.

It is therefore proper for us to here look into the question of not only what the rates are but upon what principles they are constructed, by what conditions they are controlled, and what would be the effect of important changes therein. Chicago is 912 miles and St. Louis is 1063 miles from New York, Kansas City is 280 miles northwest of St. Louis, St. Joseph is about 65 miles northwest of Kansas City, and Omaha is approximately 200 miles northwest of Kansas City. The short-line mileages from New York to the Missouri River Cities are *via* St. Louis to Kansas City, 1342 miles; to St. Joseph, 1390 miles; to Omaha, 1477 miles, and *via* Chicago to Kansas City, 1370 miles; to St. Joseph, 1382 miles, and to Omaha, 1405 miles. The short-line mileage from Chicago to Kansas City is 458 miles, to St. Joseph 470 miles, and to Omaha 492 miles. The short-line mileage from Chicago to Minneapolis is 420 miles and to St. Paul 409 miles. The average distances, however, between Chicago and the Missouri River Cities and between Chicago and the Twin Cities are approximately the same.

For a long time the rates from New York to points east of Chicago and to points between Chicago and the Mississippi river have been established on a percentage basis, the New York-Chicago rate being taken as 100 per cent. The rates from New York to points east of Chicago are fixed at certain percentages below the New York-Chicago rates and from New York to points beyond Chicago up to the Mississippi river crossings at certain percentages above the New York-Chicago rates.

Rates from New York to the Mississippi river crossings were fixed by the establishment of the New York-East St. Louis rate at 116 per cent of the New York-Chicago rate, and it will be seen that the mileage from New York to East St. Louis is substantially 116 per cent of the mileage from New York to Chicago. On January 1, 1908, the bridge tolls between East St. Louis and St. Louis were taken into the through rates and St. Louis, Mo., and East St. Louis, Ill., were placed upon the basis of 117 per cent of the New York-Chicago rates, which resulted in increasing the class rates 1 cent in each of the first three classes. The rates and divisions quoted herein, however, are those in effect at the time of the hearing of this case.

East St. Louis being a Mississippi river crossing, and the rates having been established at 116 per cent of the New York-Chicago rates, the rates from New York to all of the other Mississippi river crossings to and including East Dubuque, Ill., were fixed the same as to East St. Louis on traffic moving through them and to points beyond. This resulted in establishing class rates from New York to the several Mississippi river crossings, in cents per 100 pounds, as follows:

1	2	3	4	5
87	75	58	41	35

The local class rates under Western Classification applying from the several Mississippi river crossings on traffic moving through them from New York and destined to the Missouri River Cities were, in cents per 100 pounds:

1	2	3	4	5
60	45	35	27	22

It will, therefore, be seen that the through class rates from New York to the Missouri River Cities made by combination of the class rates to the Mississippi river crossings applicable on business beyond and the class rates from the Mississippi river crossings to the Missouri River Cities resulted in class rates in cents per 100 pounds as follows:

1	2	3	4	5
147	120	93	68	57

It should be understood that these rates apply on traffic moving *via* Chicago and that much of the traffic moving through the upper Mississippi river crossings moves *via* Chicago, and it should be remembered that the rates west of the Mississippi river crossings are not constructed upon percentages of the New York-Chicago rates, or upon any other percentage basis. They are the independently established class rates applying between the Mississippi river crossings and the Missouri river crossings and are made without reference to any methods employed in fixing the rates from the Atlantic seaboard to the Mississippi river crossings.

The local class rates from Chicago to the several Mississippi river crossings are on scales which range from 35.3 to 43.3 cents first class, and it will therefore be seen that the proportional rate from New York to the Mississippi river crossings applicable on business going west of the Mississippi is considerably less than the full combination of class rates on Chicago. The proportionals from New York to the Mississippi river crossings through Chicago are divided as follows:

Lines east of Chicago:

1	2	3	4	5
72.3	62.4	48.4	34.3	29.4

Lines west of Chicago:

1	2	3	4	5
14.7	12.6	9.6	6.7	5.6

In addition to the above division of the proportional rate up to the Mississippi river crossings the lines west of Chicago on business destined to the Missouri River Cities get their full class rate local giving them as earnings on this traffic for their service between Chicago and the Missouri River Cities the following, in cents per 100 pounds:

1	2	3	4	5
74.7	57.6	44.6	33.7	27.6

The through class rates from New York to the Twin Cities in cents per 100 pounds are divided as follows:

To the lines east of Chicago:

1	2	3	4	5
75	65	50	35	30

To the lines west of Chicago:

1	2	3	4	5
40	34	26	18	16

And it is thus seen that in this division the lines east of Chicago get their full New York-Chicago rates. The division going to the lines west of Chicago constitute a line of proportional rates applicable only upon through business, the local class rates between Chicago and the Twin Cities being established on a scale of 60 cents first class.

Complainants allege that the operating and transportation conditions between Chicago and the Missouri River Cities and between Chicago and the Twin Cities are not substantially different and in no sense justify the existing differences in rates.

As has been seen, the defendants allege the controlling influence of competition by water and *via* the Soo Line in the fixing of the Chicago-Twin Cities proportionals. Complainant argues that this claim is not possessed of any merit, and in support of that argument cites the fact that these Chicago-Twin Cities rates have been increased during the season of lake navigation and reduced at a time when navigation was closed. There is much conflict in the testimony as to the effect of the competition of the Soo Line and as to when that became a factor in the situation. Complainants went to great trouble to locate the facts, but a careful inquiry into the records of the Commission show that in some respects complainants' witnesses were mistaken on this point.

The reports of the Commission disclose that in 1886 there were class rates between Chicago and the Twin Cities, in cents per 100 pounds, as follows:

1	2	3	4	5
40	30	20	15	10

These rates were in effect at the time the Chicago, Burlington & Northern Railway (now Chicago, Burlington & Quincy Railway) began its operations in that year. From that time to June 4, 1888, these rates were sometimes higher and sometimes lower than above quoted. A short time prior to the date last mentioned, the Northwestern Association, made up of all the lines between Chicago and the Twin Cities, excepting the Chicago, Burlington & Northern, increased these rates to the basis of 60 cents first class. The Chicago, Burlington & Northern assented to the 60-cent scale, but claiming an alleged violation of the agreement it said:

Finding that many of our patrons would be discriminated against by the 60-cent scale, and owing to the extremely low rates from the seaboard prevailing by Lake Superior lines, we have decided the scale,

which was:

1	2	3	4	5
40	33	26	18	12½

At the same time the same carrier established all-rail proportional class rates, applicable only upon traffic originating at or
east of the western termini of the Trunk Lines, as follows:

1	2	3	4	5
31	22	23	17	11

In re C. St. P. & K. C. Ry., 2 I. C. C. Rep., 231.

The Minneapolis, St. Paul and Sault Ste. Marie Railway
Company completed its line from Sault Ste. Marie to Minneapolis
in January, 1888.

In July, 1889, all of the roads between Chicago and the Twin
Cities established the 60-cent scale between Chicago and the Twin
Cities on traffic from the Atlantic seaboard; on September 25 it
was again reduced to the 40-cent scale and remained there until
November, when the 60-cent scale was again restored. This
remained in effect until in February, 1890, when the 40-cent
scale was again adopted. It was raised to a 50-cent scale in
August and to the 60-cent scale in November of the same year.
This continued in force until January, 1897, when the Soo Line,
against the vigorous protests of the other lines, issued a tariff
which became effective in February, 1897, and which established
proportional class rates from Sault Ste. Marie to the Twin Cities
on all traffic originating south of Ogdensburg and east of Newport, Vt., when routed *via* the Soo Line, and on traffic originating
at or east of Pittsburg when routed *via* Mackinaw City destined
to Minneapolis and St. Paul in cents per 100 pounds as follows:

1	2	3	4	5
40	35	26	18	16

This line of differentials in connection with the Canadian
Pacific rates to Sault Ste. Marie materially reduced the through
class rates, and all of the lines between Chicago and the Twin
Cities followed this reduction in May of 1897. In June, 1899,
the Chicago-Twin Cities lines advanced these proportionals to a

50-cent scale and at a time when lake navigation was open. This
scale remained in effect until January, 1901, when it was again
reduced to the 40-cent scale at a time when navigation was
closed. It is thus seen that these carriers have made numerous,
persistent, and vigorous efforts to maintain proportional rates
between Chicago and the Twin Cities higher than the 40-cent
scale, and that they have been unable to do so.

The Canadian Pacific Despatch tariff referred to by defendants
as showing maintenance of a 40-cent scale by the Soo Line, at the
same time it was party to the tariffs fixing the 50-cent scale, taken
in connection with Boston & Maine Railroad's joint west-bound
tariff, show that class rates from Boston and points taking same
rate to the Twin Cities were established *via* the Canadian Pacific
Railway and the Soo Line, in cents per 100 pounds, as follows:

1	2	3	4	5
105	91	70	49	42

The Chicago-Twin Cities lines were named as parties to these
tariffs as well as the Soo Line, but it should be understood that
these rates applied *via* a differential line upon which the same
rates are now in effect.

With further reference to the influence of the water transportation upon the Chicago-Twin Cities proportionals, it is found
that the class rates from New York to Buffalo, in cents per
100 pounds, are:

1	2	3	4	5
39	33	28	19	16

And that the class rates from Duluth to the Twin Cities, in cents
per 100 pounds, are:

1	2	3	4	5
35	30	23	17	10

The through first-class rate New York to the Twin Cities is $1.15. The sum of the rail rates New York to Buffalo and Duluth to the Twin Cities on first class is 74 cents, leaving 41 cents that could be applied to the cost of transportation by water between Buffalo and Duluth. It seems safe to say that if the all-rail through rates were materially increased with any assurance that the increase would be maintained for a long period, there would be every inducement for the interested jobbers to arrange for independent water transportation from Buffalo to Duluth and avail themselves of the combination that could be so constructed. The lake-and-rail rate on first class New York to Duluth is 68 cents per 100 pounds, which added to the first-class rate Duluth to the Twin Cities of 35 cents makes a combination rate of $1.03 as compared with the all-rail rate *via* Chicago of $1.15. There are now in effect lake-and-rail rates from New York to the Twin Cities on a scale of 83 cents per 100 pounds on first class *via* Duluth.

The controlling influence of the water and Canadian competition over the rates from the seaboard to the Twin Cities is apparent, and it is also apparent that the defendant carriers west of Chicago must meet the force of that competition or refrain from participation in that business. Their local class rates from Chicago to the Twin Cities are on the basis of 60 cents first class, as compared with a 55-cent scale *via* lake and rail from Chicago to the Twin Cities *via* Gladstone and the Soo Line, and a 50-cent scale from Chicago to the Twin Cities *via* Duluth.

The joint through class rates from New York to the Twin Cities apply up to the Missouri river crossings on traffic from the Atlantic seaboard destined through them to Montana common points and to Spokane, Wash., and common points, as well as upon traffic through the Twin Cities to the same destinations. The locals from the Missouri river crossings and from the Twin Cities are added thereto to make up the combination through rates. The local class rates from the Twin Cities to Montana common points, and to Spokane, Wash., and common points, are the same as from the Missouri river crossings to the same destinations. This adjustment is forced by competition. If the lines *via* the Missouri river crossings did not make the same rates to Montana and Washington points that are available *via* the Twin Cities they could get none of that business.

The class rates from Chicago to Oklahoma City moving *via* Kansas City are on a scale of $1.50 per 100 pounds first class, of which the carriers between Chicago and Kansas City receive as their division 48 cents.

The class rates from Chicago to Texas common points applying *via* Kansas City are on a scale of $1.57 per 100 pounds first class, of which the carriers between Chicago and Kansas City receive 47.1 cents. The class rates from Chicago through Kansas City to El Paso, Tex., are on the scale of $1.69 per 100 pounds, first class, of which the carriers between Chicago and Kansas City receive as their division 47.1 cents. The distance from New York to the Missouri River Cities is substantially the same as from Chicago to El Paso.

On transcontinental traffic from the Atlantic seaboard to the Pacific coast terminals, carriers west of Chicago receive as their division of the class rates for the haul between Chicago and the Missouri river crossings on the first five classes, in cents per 100 pounds, the following:

1	2	3	4	5
33	28.50	24.75	22.50	19.50

From these divisions of through rates accepted by the carriers between Chicago and the Missouri river crossings and from the admission of the Chicago, Burlington and Quincy Railway Company in its answer that they give said carriers some profit, complainants argue that the rates charged from the Mississippi river crossings to the Missouri river crossings are unreasonably and unjustly high.

Defendants answer this by asserting that a low division of the through rate for a long haul is not fairly comparable with the local rate between the same points; that the through rates are not made or controlled by them; that they are frequently made in competition with water transportation to the Pacific coast terminals or to the Gulf ports, and that while none of them can be said to represent less than the actual cost of the service they can not be considered in and of themselves as remunerative and can not be fairly taken as a measure of their rates. Manifestly, a carrier may not properly or lawfully engage in transportation at a rate less than the cost of the service. So to do would place an improper and unlawful burden upon other traffic, but if a carrier elects to accept a low division of a through rate for a long haul rather than to stay out of that business it can not be held to have thereby committed itself to that division as a measure of the reasonableness of its other rates for transportation between the same points on business from or to different destinations or of a different character.

Complainants argue that the cost of transportation on eastern and western roads is about the same; that the average rate per ton per mile received by the western roads is greater than that received by the eastern roads, and that the conditions of transportation are so substantially similar that it would be entirely fair to project to the Missouri river the same rate per ton per mile that represents the rates from the Atlantic seaboard to the Mississippi river. There are, however, differences in the physical conditions. The density of population and of traffic is materially less west of the Mississippi river, and the cost of operation is greater, due among other things to higher wages and higher cost of fuel and other necessary supplies. It seems clear that the lines west of the Mississippi river are entitled to a somewhat higher charge than would be received for the same service on the lines east of the Mississippi river and it seems that the only question to be determined here is whether or not the class rates of the defendant carriers between the Mississippi river and the Missouri River Cities on business from the seaboard and destined to the Missouri River Cities are too high. It seems patent that any change in the rates east of the Mississippi river, even if warranted, would fail to accomplish what the complainants desire, because whatever of advantage accrued therefrom to the Missouri River

Cities would accrue to a like degree or extent to their principal competitive commercial centers, to wit, New York, Chicago, St. Louis, and the Twin Cities.

The average short-line distance between the nearest Mississippi river crossings and the individual Missouri River Cities is about 275 miles. The average distance between the Mississippi river crossings, *via* which the rates apply, and the Missouri River Cities is 325 miles. As has been before stated, the local class rates between the Mississippi and the Missouri river crossings are, in cents per 100 pounds:

1	2	3	4	5
60	45	35	27	22

And these are the rates that are added to the rates up to the Mississippi river crossings to make up the through rates from the Atlantic seaboard to the Missouri River Cities. Are these rates as so used, and the through rates resulting therefrom, unwarrantedly high or unduly discriminatory or unjustly prejudicial? Can they be changed without doing injustice elsewhere?

As has been seen, the first-class rate from the Atlantic seaboard to Chicago is 75 cents, and to the Mississippi river crossings is 87 cents. From Chicago to the Missouri river crossings the first-class rate is 80 cents, and from the Mississippi river to the Missouri river is 60 cents. The through first-class rate from the seaboard to the Missouri river is, therefore, $1.47; the combination on Chicago is $1.55 and on St. Louis is $1.47. The St. Louis jobbers can, so far as freight charges are concerned, purchase in the East and sell at all points east of the Missouri River Cities cheaper than can the jobbers in the Missouri River Cities, while at the same time the St. Louis dealers can sell in the Missouri River Cities themselves and at some points beyond them just as cheaply as can the dealers located in the Missouri River Cities. The Chicago dealer seems to have a handicap of 8 cents on the first-class rate as compared with St. Louis. This no doubt is due to the fact that direct lines from the seaboard to St. Louis, belonging to one system, make the rate to St. Louis.

The class rates from the Atlantic seaboard to Sioux City when made upon the Mississippi river combination through any crossing East Burlington to East Dubuque, inclusive, are the same as to Omaha. The combination on Chicago is the same to Sioux City as to the Missouri River Cities. The combination on Mississippi river crossings south of East Burlington is higher to Sioux City.

If the local class rates of defendants between the Mississippi and Missouri rivers were reduced, it would give the same degree of advantage to all the producing and distributing centers on and east of the Missouri river, and their relative advantages or disadvantages would not be changed, while a very serious inroad upon the revenues of the carriers would inevitably result, and at a time of industrial depression when it could not well be borne. Such a change would necessitate corresponding changes in the rates to and from intermediate points and would probably be reflected in changes in commodity rates as well. The local class rates between the rivers are high, but this is not the time to precipitate such a violent change as would follow an important reduction of them. The first-class rate from Buffalo to Chicago, about 540 miles, and from Pittsburg to Chicago, about 465 miles, is 45 cents. From Cincinnati to Chicago, 306 miles, it is 40 cents.

Complainants urge that defendant carriers west of Chicago and the Mississippi river crossings have, from their operations, accumulated enormous surpluses and that therefore they can not fairly present the plea of financial difficulty. Especial attention is called to the reports of the defendant, Chicago, Burlington & Quincy Railway Company, which show a surplus of nearly $42,000,000. The carrying of this item in reports is certainly misleading to those who are not otherwise acquainted with the true facts. This surplus is in no sense available cash or free surplus. The record in this case shows that it simply represents the amount of earnings that have been expended in past years for betterments and improvements in the road, and additions to its equipment.

An abundant share of the prosperity and development of the trans-Mississippi and trans-Missouri territories has come to the Missouri River Cities, from which this complaint comes, but the fact that they have prospered in the past as a result of rapid expansion and development of new territory may not be taken as conclusive evidence of the correctness or justness at this time of the rate adjustment that has prevailed in the past. We are not impressed with the view that the system of making rates on certain basing lines should be abolished. No system of rate making has been suggested as a substitute for it, except one based upon the postage-stamp theory, or one based strictly upon mileage. Either of these would create revolution in transportation affairs and chaos in commercial affairs that have been builded upon the system of rate making now in effect. It must not, however, be assumed that a basing line for rates may be established and be made an impassable barrier for through rates, or that cities or markets located at or upon such basing line have any inviolable possession of, or hold upon, the right to distribute traffic in or from the territory lying beyond. Development of natural resources, increase in population, growth of manufacturing or producing facilities, and increased traffic on railroads create changed conditions which may warrant changes in rates and in rate adjustments in order to afford just and reasonable opportunity for interchange of traffic between points of production and points of large consumption.

We can not agree with the argument that the rates from the Atlantic seaboard or from Chicago to the Missouri River Cities should be the same as or lower than rates from same points to the Twin Cities. As has been seen, the rates to the Twin Cities can not escape the influence of the water and Canadian competition.

As has been stated, the through rates from Atlantic seaboard territory to the Missouri River Cities are made by adding together the rates from points of origin to the Mississippi river crossings, using proportional rates when such are available, and the local class rates from the Mississippi river crossings to the Missouri River Cities. The through rates so established are, in our opinion, unreasonably high. This is so because those portions of the through rates which apply between the Mississippi river crossings and the Missouri River Cities are too high. These are defendants' "separately established rates" which are "applied to the through transportation," and, therefore, the through rates should be adjusted by reduction of those factors or parts thereof which are found to be unreasonable.

Out of consideration for long-established custom in rate construction and publication, involving different classifications, we refrain from establishing joint through rates, and, permitting the rates from Atlantic seaboard territory to the Mississippi river crossings to remain as at present, we conclude that the separately established rates of the defendants, Chicago, Rock Island & Pacific; Chicago, Burlington & Quincy; Chicago, Milwaukee & St. Paul; Chicago & Northwestern, and Chicago Great Western Railway companies, applied between the Mississippi river crossings and the Missouri River Cities to the through transportation of shipments moving under class rates and coming from the Atlantic seaboard, taking New York as representative, should be reduced to the following scale:

1	2	3	4	5
51	38	30	23	19

and that these rates should also be applied to the transportation of through shipments which move under class rates and which originated at points of origin specified on pages 3 and 4 of complainants' Exhibit A, same being the aforesaid Western Trunk Line Tariff No. 786, I. C. C. No 678, or at points taking the same rates.

These rates should also be applied on traffic from same points of origin destined to Sioux City, Iowa, when it moves through any of the Mississippi river crossings, East Burlington to East Dubuque, inclusive.

As to the other defendants, the complaint should be dismissed.

An order will be entered in accordance with these views.

XIV

THE SOUTHERN BASING POINT SYSTEM

THE ALABAMA MIDLAND CASE[1]

Long and Short Haul

CLEMENTS, *Commissioner :*

*   *   *   *   *   *   *   *

Troy is situated at the intersection of the roads of the Alabama Midland and the Georgia Central companies. Montgomery is at the terminus of the Alabama Midland, fifty-two miles northwest from Troy, and shipments to Montgomery over that road from New York, Baltimore and northeastern cities, and from the Atlantic seaports, Brunswick, Savannah, Charleston, West Point and Norfolk, and from Port Royal, S. C., and Gainesville, Ocala and Tampa, Fla., pass through Troy.

The Savannah, Florida & Western Railway and the Ocean Steamship Company, and the Savannah, Florida & Western Railway and Merchants & Miners Transportation Company, form with the Alabama Midland Railway two through lines, the former from New York and the latter from Baltimore, over which traffic is carried on through rates and through bills of lading to Troy and through Troy to Montgomery. The Georgia Central forms through lines in connection with the Ocean Steamship Company and Merchants & Miners Transportation Company to Troy and Montgomery from New York and Baltimore. The class rates in cents per hundred pounds, except class F, which is per bbl., over the above lines (sea and rail) from New York and Baltimore to Troy and Montgomery, respectively, are, as follows:

[1] Decided August 15, 1893. Interstate Commerce Reports, Vol. VI, pp. 3–35. Overruled by the Supreme Court, *vide*, p. 378, *infra*. Chapter XIII of Ripley's Railroads: Rates and Regulation describes the southern basing-point system as a type of long-and-short-haul problem. At p. 473 of the same work this case is treated in its legal aspects.

From E.B.Whitney Brief.

GULF OF MEXICO.

SEA AND RAIL

CLASS	FROM NEW YORK		FROM BALTIMORE	
	To Montgomery	To Troy	To Montgomery	To Troy
1	114	136	106	129
2	98	117	90	111
3	86	103	83	98
4	73	89	70	84
5	60	74	57	70
6	49	61	46	58
A	36	—	33	—
B	48	—	45	—
C	40	—	37	—
D	39	—	36	—
E	58	—	55	—
H	68	—	72	—
F (per bbl.) .	78	—	65	—

There are also published "all rail" rates *via* the "Great Southern Despatch" line, from New York and Baltimore to Troy and Montgomery. On this line traffic is carried from New York to Harrisburg over the Pennsylvania road, from Harrisburg to Hagerstown over the Cumberland Valley road, from Hagerstown to Bristol over the Norfolk & Western, and from Bristol to Chattanooga over the East Tennessee, Virginia & Georgia road. . . .[1]

The class rates in cents per hundred pounds (except class F, which is per bbl.) over the above-described "all rail" lines to Troy and Montgomery from New York and Baltimore, are as follows :

ALL RAIL

CLASS	FROM NEW YORK		FROM BALTIMORE	
	To Montgomery	To Troy	To Montgomery	To Troy
1	114	144	106	136
2	98	123	90	115
3	86	108	83	105
4	73	93	70	90
5	60	77	57	74
6	49	63	46	60
A	36	—	33	—
B	48	—	45	—
C	40	—	37	—
D	39	—	36	—
E	58	—	55	—
H	68	—	65	—
F (per bbl.) .	78	—	72	—

It appears that shipments of phosphate rock are made *via* the Alabama Midland, as the terminal road, to Troy and through Troy to Montgomery from Charleston and Port Royal, South Carolina, and from Gainesville and other points in Florida. The roads which connect, and constitute through lines, with the

---

[1] These routes are mapped in the able and elaborate argument of Judge (Ed.) Baxter before the Supreme Court. U. S. Sup. Court, October term, 1896, No. 563, pp. 39 *et seq.* — ED.

Alabama Midland, from those cities to Troy and Montgomery, are the following: . . .

The rates in cents per ton on phosphate rock from Port Royal, Charleston and Gainesville, to Troy and Montgomery, respectively, are as follows:

To	From Port Royal	From Charleston	From Gainesville
Troy	322	322	322
Montgomery . .	300	300	300

The following roads constitute through routes or lines in connection with Alabama Midland to the Atlantic seaports, Brunswick, Savannah, Charleston, West Point and Norfolk; to wit,   *   *   *   *   *   *   *   *

The rates in cents per hundred pounds on cotton from Troy and Montgomery respectively, to these ports are:

From	To Brunswick	To Savannah	To Charleston	To West Point	To Norfolk
Troy . . .	47	47	52	—	—
Montgomery	45	45	45	51	51

When the complaint was filed the cotton rate from Montgomery to Brunswick, Savannah and Charleston was 40 cts. per hundred pounds. It has since, as appears above, been raised to 45 cts. and the rate from Troy to Charleston has been raised to 52 cts.   *   *   *   *   *   *   *

None of the traffic involved in this case is carried by the Georgia Central either through Troy to Montgomery or through Montgomery to Troy. . . .

But as to the Alabama Midland and its connections constituting through lines, the case is different. Interstate traffic is carried over that road to Troy and through Troy on to Montgomery, and in the opposite direction, from Troy, and from Montgomery through Troy, the haul to and from Montgomery being 52 miles greater; and in respect to this traffic the proof shows departures from the rule of the Statute, (1) as to class goods shipped from New York, Baltimore and the East; (2) as to phosphate rock, shipped from Port Royal and Charleston, S. C., and Gainesville and other points of origin of such shipments in Florida; and (3) as to cotton shipped from Troy and from Montgomery to the Atlantic seaports, Brunswick, Savannah, Charleston, West Point and Norfolk. As will be seen from the tables given above, the "sea and rail" rates on class goods from Baltimore to Troy range from 12 cts. per hundred pounds on class 6 to 23 cts. on class 1 higher than those on such goods shipped through Troy to Montgomery, and from New York to Troy, from 12 cts. to 22 cts., and the "all rail" rates from Baltimore and New York to Troy, from 14 cts. to 30 cts. These class rates are applied to sugar and coffee, which are the heavy goods mostly shipped to Troy from the East, and also to dry goods, notions, and many other commodities. The rate on phosphate rock from Port Royal, Charleston, and Gainesville to Troy is 22 cts. per ton higher than that on such rock shipped through Troy to Montgomery, and on cotton the rate from Troy to the seaports, Brunswick and Savannah, is 2 cts. per hundred pounds and to Charleston 7 cts. per hundred higher than that from Montgomery *via* Troy.

Where substantial dissimilarity of circumstances and conditions is set up by defendant carriers in justification of departures from the "long and short haul" rule of the Statute, the burden is upon them to establish such dissimilarity. *Re Louisville & N. R. Co.*, 1 Inters. Com. Rep. 278, 1 I. C. C. Rep. 31; *Spartanburg Board of Trade* v. *Richmond & D. R. Co.*, 2 Inters. Com. Rep. 193, 2 I. C. C. Rep. 304. Water competition at Montgomery *via* the Alabama river, is adduced as a justification in the answer of the Alabama Midland and by some of the other defendants. In the case of *Re Louisville & N. R. Co.*, *supra*, it was held that "actual" water competition "of controlling force in respect to traffic important in amount" may constitute the dissimilar circumstances and conditions authorizing a departure from the general rule of the Statute. In the

case of *Harwell* v. *Columbus & W. R. Co.*, 1 Inters. Com. Rep.
631, 1 I. C. C. Rep. 236, the complaint alleged unjust discrimination against Opelika and in favor of Montgomery and Columbus. Water competition at Montgomery *via* the Alabama river
was (as in the present case) set up by way of justification. This
defense was not sustained and the Commission in overruling it
said, " the mere fact that a point is situated upon a navigable
stream does not of itself justify the lesser charge for the longer
haul to such point," and that, in order to justify such lesser
charge, the water competition must " *control the carriage of the
traffic on which the discrimination is made.*" In that case it is
further said, " The Commission is aware that an independent
and active line of steamers connects Montgomery with the Atlantic seaboard at Mobile," but that the fact " without more,"
that the " railroads have water competition and are compelled
to meet it," is not held to be " sufficient to justify the lesser
charge for the longer distance." Conceding that there is a line
of boats running between Montgomery and Mobile (of which
fact, however, there is no proof, in this case) that alone would
not be sufficient to justify the greater charge to Troy than to
Montgomery. . . . In the affidavit filed by counsel for the defendants is a statement that " *the business on the Alabama river*,
according to the report of the United States Engineer, for the
year, 1891, was 52,349 bales of cotton carried by boat and 44,500
tons of other freight." This statement . . . purports to give
the entire cotton and other business on the river for the year
named without stating the point or points at which it originated,
or the direction in which it was moved. How much of it went
from Montgomery or points above or below Montgomery *down*
the river towards Mobile, or from Mobile and points above that
city *up* the river to Montgomery does not appear. As showing
water competition of controlling force at Montgomery on traffic
to that city from New York, Baltimore and other northeastern
cities, or from the South Carolina and Florida phosphate beds,
or from Montgomery to the Atlantic seaports, Brunswick,
Charleston and Savannah, the statement is valueless. (This is
true, also, as to the traffic from St. Louis and from Louisville,

Cincinnati and other Ohio river points, hereinafter to be considered.) There are regular lines of ocean steamers from those ports to New York, Baltimore and other cities on the northeast coast, but there does not appear to be such line from Mobile, either to those cities or to any foreign port. The only witness questioned by counsel for the defendants as to the effect of water competition at Montgomery on shipments of cotton to the Atlantic ports testified that " the river competition plays no great part." An attempt was made to show that some shipments of phosphate rock had been made from the Florida points, Ocala and Tampa (the latter on the Gulf coast) *via* Mobile and the Alabama river to Montgomery, but the witness testified that he had never known such shipments to be made, that he himself had " tried to get a rate by that line to Montgomery and had been unable to get it," and that he thought it impracticable as " the goods would have to be transferred at Mobile to get to Montgomery and then would have to be hauled to the works." No attempt is made to establish substantial dissimilarity of circumstances and conditions at Montgomery on the ground of rail competition further than by proof of the fact that there are a number of railway lines running to and through that city connecting with different parts of the country. This alone, it is scarcely necessary to say, is not sufficient. *Re Louisville & N. R. Co.*, 1 Inters. Com. Rep. 278, 1 I. C. C. Rep. 31.

Our conclusion is that no justification has been shown for the departures, complained of and established by the proof, from the general rule of the 4th section of the Act to Regulate Commerce.

*   *   *   *   *   *   *   *

The main cause of complaint on the part of Troy, however, in connection with this system of making export rates, as disclosed by the evidence, is, that while its benefits are given by the roads composing the Southern Railway & Steamship Association to Montgomery and other favored localities on their lines, they are denied to Troy, and it is contended that this is an unjust discrimination against Troy. This contention is apart from and independent of the question, whether the system is itself lawful and justified as applied to Montgomery and other points. If it be lawful in itself, it cannot lawfully be so applied as to unduly favor one locality, to the prejudice of another. Both the Alabama Midland and the Georgia Central are members of the Southern Railway & Steamship Association, and Troy as well as Montgomery is located on those roads. The haul from Montgomery over the Georgia Central to the Atlantic ports named is about 10 miles longer than from Troy over that road, and the haul from Montgomery to those ports over the Alabama Midland is 52 miles longer than from Troy, and is also through Troy. The charge of the lesser rate from Montgomery than from Troy over the Georgia Central would seem to be a discrimination against Troy and over the Alabama Midland, also, a departure from the "long and short haul rule" of the Statute. The principal article of export shipped from Troy and Montgomery over these roads to the Atlantic is cotton. The cotton business of Troy is large, amounting in 1892 to 38,500 bales, aggregating in value $1,500,000, nearly a third of its total business of all kinds. No excuse is offered, and we are unable to conjecture any valid reason, why Troy is excluded from the benefit of the export system of rate making applied to Montgomery. The fluctuations in ocean rates at the southern ports and other matters set up by the southern carriers as rendering necessary or justifying this system, would seem to apply to shipments from Troy as well as from Montgomery.

It appears, as alleged in the complaint, that on shipments of cotton from Troy *via* Montgomery to New Orleans, the shipper is charged the full local rate to Montgomery both by the Alabama Midland and the Georgia Central. The local from Troy to Montgomery is 23 cts. per hundred pounds and the rate from Montgomery on is 45 cts., making a total through rate from Troy to New Orleans of 68 cts. The testimony is that under this rate Troy is debarred from shipping cotton *via* New Orleans for Europe and is left only the outlet *via* Savannah and other Atlantic ports, and that this is a disadvantage to Troy inasmuch as cotton shipped *via* New Orleans is classed "New Orleans cotton," which is valued at from $\frac{3}{16}$ to $\frac{1}{4}$ of a cent per pound higher than other cotton.

The haul from Troy to Montgomery may be made either over the Alabama Midland or *via* Union Springs over the lines of the Georgia Central and from Montgomery to New Orleans it is made over the Louisville & Nashville road.

In the case of *Harwell* v. *Columbus & W. R. Co.*, 1 Inters. Com. Rep. 631, 1 I. C. C. Rep. 236, cited in his brief by counsel for complainant, it was charged that through rates and through bills of lading were unjustly denied to Opelika on shipments of cotton *via* Montgomery to New Orleans, and the Commission held that such through rates and bills, being important facilities in the transportation of cotton and being given on other commodities and to other points similarly situated, should be given Opelika and that the refusal of the same in the absence of a valid excuse for such refusal was an unjust discrimination against Opelika. In the present case, however, it is neither alleged nor proven that through rates and billing are denied Troy on shipments of cotton *via* Montgomery to New Orleans, but that on the haul from Troy to Montgomery over either the Alabama Midland or the Georgia Central, the local rate between those points is charged and collected as a part of the through rate to New Orleans. The charge is in legal effect that the aggregate through rate thus arrived at is unjustly discriminatory against Troy. "While," as was said in the case of the *Railroad Com. of Florida* v. *Savannah, F. & W. R. Co.*, 3 Inters. Com. Rep. 688, 5 I. C. C. Rep. 13, "the complainant has no interest in the division the defendants may make between themselves of a through rate and that division does not determine what the charge to the public should be, yet 'it is not without significance in determining what are reasonable rates for the whole distance on the lines in question.'" See *Brady* v. *Pennsylvania R. Co.*, 2 Inters. Com. Rep. 78, 2 I. C. C. Rep. 131. The distance from Troy to Montgomery over the Alabama Midland (the short line) is 52 miles and from Montgomery to New Orleans over the Louisville & Nashville road, 320 miles. The rate of 23 cts. per hundred pounds from Troy to Montgomery is 4.42 mills per mile; the rate of 45 cts. from Montgomery to New Orleans is 1.40 mills per mile; the rate of 47 cts. from Troy to Savannah (359 miles) is 1.30 mills per mile; and the rate of 45 cts. from Montgomery to Savannah (411) miles is 1.09 mills per mile. There is, also, a through rate on cotton from Columbus, Ga., to New Orleans of 50 cts. per hundred pounds. The distance from Columbus to New Orleans over the Georgia Central *via* Union Springs to Montgomery and thence over the Louisville & Nashville road is 414 miles, and this rate of 50 cts. is 1.20 mills per mile. It thus appears that the rate of 23 cts. from Troy to Montgomery is, on a mileage basis, four times as large as that from Montgomery to Savannah and more than three times as large as the rates from Montgomery and from Columbus to New Orleans, and from Troy to Savannah. The aggregate through rate from Troy to New Orleans of 68 cts. yields 1.80 mills per mile.

Through rates, it is true, are not required to be made on a strictly mileage basis, but mileage is as a general rule an element of importance and "due regard to distance proportions should be observed in connection with the other considerations that are material in fixing transportation charges." *McMorran* v. *Grand Trunk R. Co. of Canada*, 2 Inters. Com. Rep. 604, 3 I. C. C. Rep. 252. The cost of the services in railway transportation is the expense of the two terminals and the intermediate haul. The terminal expenses remain the same without reference to the length of the haul. A local rate covers the expenses of *both* terminals, but a division of a through rate allotted to either of the terminal carriers of the through line can only embrace the expense of one terminal, and because of this difference in expense among other reasons, local rates are made as a general rule much higher in proportion to the length of haul than through rates or any division thereof. A local rate, which presumably is adopted as covering both the initial and final expenses of the haul, is *prima facie* excessive as part of a through rate over a through line composed of two or more carriers. The rate of 23 cts. from Troy to Montgomery is admitted to be the local between those points, which is charged on a haul originating at the former and ending at the latter and hence covers the expense to the carrier (either the Alabama Midland or the Georgia Central) at both terminals.

*   *   *   *   *   *   *   *

On the hauls from Montgomery to New Orleans, from Montgomery to Savannah, from Troy to Savannah and from Columbus to New Orleans, there are the expenses of both terminals as well as the haul from Troy to New Orleans. It cannot be assumed that on a haul from Troy to New Orleans the initial expenses at Troy are greater than at Montgomery on haul from that point to New Orleans or to Savannah, or at Columbus on haul from that point to New Orleans, or at Troy itself on a haul in the opposite direction to Savannah. No reason has been shown, and we can conceive of none, why a higher proportionate rate should be charged on cotton from Troy to New Orleans than from Montgomery, or from these other points on the several hauls mentioned. The disproportion, as we have seen, is attributable to the charge, as a part of the through rate to New Orleans, of the local from Troy to Montgomery, and the truth appears to be that this exaction of the local rate is an incident and in pursuance of what is termed the "trade center," or "basing," or "distributing point" system, which the Commission has more than once condemned as unjust discrimination and in violation of law, and which we will be called on to refer to more at length in connection with the class rates from Louisville, Cincinnati and St. Louis to Montgomery, Columbus and Troy, hereafter to be considered.

A rate from Troy to New Orleans based on the present mileage rate from Montgomery to that city would amount to 52.21 cts. As a general rule, however, while the aggregate through rate steadily increases as the distance increases, the rate per ton or hundredweight per mile decreases. Under this rule, the distance from Troy being 52 miles greater than from Montgomery, the rate per hundred pounds per mile from Troy, in the absence of exceptional conditions, should be slightly less than that from Montgomery. In view of this rule, and of the rate of 50 cts. from Columbus, a longer distance point by 42 miles than Troy, our conclusion is that the through rate on cotton from Troy *via* Montgomery to New Orleans should not exceed 50 cts. per hundred pounds.

The class rates in cents per hundred pounds (except class F, which is per bbl.) to Troy, Montgomery and Columbus from Louisville, Cincinnati and St. Louis, are given in the following table:

	CLASSES											
	1	2	3	4	5	6	A	B	C	D	E	H	F
From Louisville, Ky., to													per bbl.
Troy, Ala.	140	130	113	95	75½	62	45	50	37	32	69	59	66
Montgomery, Ala. . . .	98	92	78	63	52	41	28	31	24	20	48	33	40
Columbus, Ga.	107	92	81	68	56	46	28	36	29	25	50	55	50
From Cincinnati, O., to													
Troy, Ala.	150	140	123	103	82½	68	49	52	39	34	73	63	70
Montgomery, Ala. . . .	108	102	88	71	59	47	32	33	26	22	52	77	44
Columbus, Ga. . . .	117	102	91	76	63	52	32	38	31	23	54	59	54
From St. Louis, Mo., to													
Troy, Ala.	168	153	133	109	87½	72	52	58	44	37	77	69	80
Montgomery, Ala. . . .	126	115	98	77	64	51	35	39	31	25	56	43	54
Columbus, Ga.	135	115	101	82	68	56	35	44	36	30	58	65	64

The local class rates in cents per hundred pounds (except class F, which is per bbl.) from Montgomery and Columbus, respectively, to Troy, are as follows:

	CLASSES											
	1	2	3	4	5	6	A	B	C	D	E	H	F
													per bbl.
From Montgomery to Troy	49	46	40	33	27	21	19	21	16	15	27	33	32
From Columbus to Troy	58	55	48	39	31	24	22	24	19	17	31	39	38

It was testified at the hearing by Mr. Bashinsky, a witness for the complainant, that on goods shipped on through bills of lading from Louisville and the West to Troy, the Troy merchant is charged the full local rate from Montgomery to Troy, and the counsel for the Alabama Midland states in his brief, that "the through rate from Troy to any western market is made up by adding the local rate from Troy to Montgomery to the through rate from Montgomery to the West." From a comparison of the above local rates with the difference between the rates from Louisville and the other cities named to Montgomery and Troy, respectively, it will be found that this is true only as to rates on goods of class 6. The difference between the class 6 rate to Montgomery and that to Troy from all these points is 21 cts., which is the local rate on that class from Montgomery to Troy. On the other classes the local rate from Montgomery to Troy exceeds the proportion of the through rate between those points as follows:

	CLASSES												
	1	2	3	4	5	6	A	B	C	D	E	H	F
Excess of local rate over through	7	8	5	1	$3\frac{1}{2}$	—	2	2	3	3	6	7	6

The distance from Louisville to Montgomery over the Louisville & Nashville road is 490 miles and from Montgomery to Troy over the Alabama Midland, 52 miles. The following table shows the mileage rate on the different classes in mills per hundred pounds yielded by the through rate from Louisville to Montgomery and by the additional charge on through shipments from Louisville to Troy for the haul from Montgomery to Troy:

	CLASSES												
	1	2	3	4	5	6	A	B	C	D	E	H	F
Louisville to Montgomery	2	1.8	1.6	1.3	1.06	.83	.57	.63	.49	.40	.98	.67	.40
Montgomery to Troy . .	8	7.1	6.7	5.9	3.8	4	2.6	3.6	2.5	2.3	4	5	2.5

The testimony is that the Troy merchant gets the most of his heavy goods from the West. The class 6 (on which the through rate from Louisville, St. Louis & Cincinnati to Troy is made by the addition of the local from Montgomery to Troy) embraces sugar, coffee, flour, buckwheat, animal food, cement, axle and car grease, green hides, iron architecture, agricultural implements, nails, spikes, and many other heavy as well as light articles in constant demand, too numerous to be set forth here. Classes 4 and B on which the difference between the local rate and proportion of through rate from Montgomery to Troy as shown above is only 1 and 2 cents, are applied, the former, among numerous other articles, to machinery of all kinds, agricultural implements, earthenware, moldings, engines, castings, axes, cotton-seed-oil mills, dry hides, window glass, ale, beer, porter, canned beef and pork, canned fruit and potatoes; and the latter, among many other articles, to salted beef, pork and bacon. It seems probable, that the statement above referred to, made by the witness and counsel, that the through rate from Louisville and the west *via* Montgomery to Troy is made up of the rate to Montgomery plus the local on to Troy, is substantially true as to the goods constituting the bulk of the traffic from those points to Troy. When the mileage rate from Louisville (which point is taken as an illustration) to Montgomery, is compared with that from Montgomery on to Troy, it seems clear that the rate to Troy on all the classes is made from Montgomery as a "basing point." This comparison, it will appear from the table given above, shows that the proportion of the rate from Montgomery to Troy is from four to seven times as large per mile as that from Louisville to Montgomery.

The following table shows the sum of the rates on class goods from Louisville to Montgomery and Troy, respectively, plus the rates from those points on reshipment to Brundidge, Ozark, and Dothan:

IN CENTS PER 100 POUNDS, EXCEPT CLASS F, WHICH IS PER BARREL

FROM LOUISVILLE, KY., TO	CLASSES											
	1	2	3	4	5	6	A	B	C	D	E	F
Brundidge, Ala., reshipped from Montgomery, Ala. .	146	136	117	98	81	65	52	52	38	33	72	per bbl. 68
Brundidge, Ala., reshipped from Troy, Ala. . . .	168	154	135	115	93½	76	59	62	46	40	83	84
Ozark, Ala., reshipped from Montgomery	156	144	122	103	84	67	54	54	40	35	74	72
Ozark, Ala., reshipped from Troy, Ala.	176	161½	143	122	95½	80	59½	66	49	43	87	90
Dothan, Ala., reshipped from Montgomery	162	147	125	106	88	71	57	57	40	35	78	72
Dothan, Ala., reshipped from Troy, Ala.	188	174	152	130	104½	86	69	71	51	45	93	94

Brundidge, Ozark and Dothan are towns and stations on the Alabama Midland Railway, all east of Troy and shipments to them over that road from Montgomery pass through Troy. Brundidge is 17 miles from Troy and 69 from Montgomery; Ozark, 40 miles from Troy and 92 from Montgomery; and Dothan, 68 miles from Troy and 120 from Montgomery.

The sum of the rates from Louisville to Columbus and Troy, respectively, plus the rates on reshipments from those cities to Brantley, in cents per 100 lbs., except class F, which is per bbl., is as follows :

FROM LOUISVILLE TO	CLASSES											
	1	2	3	4	5	6	A	B	C	D	E	F
Brantley, Ala., reshipped from Columbus. . .	1.73	1.53	1.32	1.10	90	73	52	63	50	44	84	per bbl. 92
Brantley, Ala., reshipped from Troy	1.76	1.64	1.43	1.19	95½	78	60	66	50	44	89	92

Brantley is on the Georgia Central road 26 miles south of Troy and 111 miles from Columbus, and goods shipped from Columbus to Brantley over that road pass through Troy. A like disparity in rates on reshipments prevails as to points west of Troy on the Alabama Midland and north of Troy on the Georgia Central, the distances of which from Troy are much less than from either Montgomery or Columbus; and the situation in this respect is the same, when the shipments originate at Cincinnati, and other Ohio river points, and at St. Louis, as when they come from Louisville.

The fact that the sum of the rates from points of origin to points of destination, as shown in the above tables, on reshipment from Montgomery, Columbus and Troy, are greater in cases of such reshipments from Troy than from Montgomery and Columbus, is attributed by the complainant to alleged relatively unjust through rates to Troy as compared with those to Montgomery and Columbus. There is no allegation and no proof that the rates to Montgomery and Columbus are unreasonable in themselves. The through rate to Troy is, therefore, the object of attack.

The differences in rates as against Troy, it will be noted, are much smaller on reshipments from Columbus than on reshipments from Montgomery, and the local rates from Columbus to Troy are much greater than the difference between the through rates to Columbus and those to Troy. It is not shown that there are through rates from Louisville, St. Louis and Ohio river points *via* Columbus to Troy *based on the Columbus rate*, and the natural course of the traffic from those points to Troy appears to be *via* Montgomery. As before stated, the through rates to Troy are based on the Montgomery rates and in making them Montgomery is treated as a " trade center " or " basing " point and Troy as a local. This is conceded on the part of the defendants. The vice in the through rate to Troy, if any, arises from this fact and from the consequently greatly disproportionate charge for the haul from Montgomery to Troy, when compared with that from Louisville and the west to Montgomery.

The " trade center " or " basing point " system has been in many cases pronounced unlawful by this Commission. . . . In the Louisville & Nashville case, it is said in this connection, that the Act to Regulate Commerce " aims at equality of right and

privilege, not less between towns than between individuals, and
will no more sanction preferential rates for the purpose of per-
petuating distinctions than of creating them ; " and in the Martin
case, the Statute is declared to be one " enacted in the interest
of equality as between large and small interests," under which
" there can be no unjust discrimination in giving to large and
small towns relatively equal rates." It is further said in the latter
case, that " a fatal difficulty with the theory that a trade center
as such is entitled to specially favorable rates is found in the
fact, that it is in conflict with the spirit and purpose of the Act
to Regulate Commerce — one of the reasons for the passage of
which was, that by means of rebates and other contrivances,
large towns and heavy dealers secured advantages which gave
them a practical monopoly of markets and shut out the small
towns and small dealers." In a recent decision by the Supreme
Court of the United States in a case brought up from the U. S.
Circuit Court, for the District of Colorado (*Union Pac. R. Co.* v.
Goodridge, 149 U. S. 680, 37 L. ed. 896) Mr. Justice Brown, in
speaking of the purpose of the Colorado act under consideration
as being the same as to intrastate commerce as that of the Act to
Regulate Commerce as to interstate commerce, says very forcibly,
that it was designed " to cut up by the roots the entire system
of rebates and discriminations in favor of *particular localities*,
special enterprises, or favored corporations," and pertinently refers to the fact, that carriers being dependent upon the will of
the people for their corporate existence, are " bound to deal
fairly with the public, to extend them reasonable facilities for
the transportation of their persons and property, and to put all
their patrons *upon an absolute equality*." . . . The fact, therefore,
insisted upon by counsel for the roads as a matter of defense,
that Montgomery is a much larger city with more extensive
business interests than Troy, and is and has been treated by the
roads in making rates to Troy and other surrounding towns as
a " trade center " or " basing point," is no justification for discriminations in those rates in favor of Montgomery.

Water and rail competition at Montgomery are also set up as
justifying the disproportion in the rates in question as between

Troy and Montgomery. Here, as we have shown in connection with the violations of the long and short haul rule of the Statute, these defenses are not sustained by the proof. Water competition *via* the Alabama river, in order to control rates from St. Louis and Louisville, Cincinnati and other Ohio river points, on traffic from those cities stopping at Montgomery, must, it is obvious, grow out of transportation of such traffic *via* Mobile *up* the river to Montgomery. The carriage of goods by river from or *via* Montgomery to Mobile would be limited in its effect to rates to the latter city. Water transportation may be possible from localities on the Ohio and Mississippi rivers *via* those rivers to the gulf at New Orleans, on the gulf to the Alabama river at Mobile, and up that river to Montgomery, and the Mobile & Ohio Railroad carries freight from St. Louis to Mobile, which might be transported thence up the Alabama river to Montgomery. No competition by either of these routes is shown in this case on traffic from St. Louis or Ohio river points to Montgomery, and it does not seem probable that such competition of controlling force is likely to arise. That it does not now exist would appear to be indicated by the lower rates from St. Louis, Cincinnati and Louisville to Mobile than to Montgomery at present prevailing as shown in the following table:

RATES IN CENTS PER 100 POUNDS, EXCEPT CLASS F, WHICH IS PER BARREL

DISTANCES	FROM	CLASSES											
		1	2	3	4	5	6	A	B	C	D	E	H	F
644 miles *via* M. & O. 805 miles *via* L. & N.	St. Louis to Mobile . . .	90	75	65	50	40	35	25	25	25	20	28	25	45
625 miles *via* L. & N.	St. Louis to Montgomery .	126	115	98	77	64	51	35	39	31	25	56	43	54
669 miles *via* L. & N.	Louisville to Mobile . . .	90	75	65	50	40	35	25	25	25	20	28	25	45
490 miles *via* L. & N.	Louisville to Montgomery	98	92	78	63	52	41	28	31	24	20	48	33	40
779 miles *via* L. & N.	Cincinnati to Mobile. . .	98	83	73	54	44	39	28	27	27	22	31	28	49
600 miles *via* L. & N.	Cincinnati to Montgomery	108	102	88	71	59	47	32	33	26	22	52	37	44

Although over the lines of the Louisville & Nashville Company the distances from all three of the above cities to Mobile is 180 miles greater than to Montgomery, and the haul to Mobile is through Montgomery, the rates to the latter are materially higher than to the former. The higher rates to Montgomery than to Mobile shown in the above table seem inconsistent with the claim that the rates to Montgomery are controlled by water competition *via* Mobile up the Alabama river to Montgomery.

* * * * * * * * *

Our conclusion on this branch of the case is, that the through class rates from Louisville, St. Louis, Cincinnati and the West to Troy are relatively unjust to that city, when compared with those to Montgomery, and that this injustice arises from the practice of basing the Troy rates on the rates to Montgomery as a " trade center."

The question remains to be determined, what the rates to Troy shall be. In arriving at a conclusion on this point, no light is furnished by proof of cost of service or other matters proper to be considered in determining what rates are just and reasonable from the standpoint both of the carrier and shipper. If there is an expense incident to the continuation of the through haul to Troy, which calls for and justifies exceptional rates, the burden, as we have seen, is upon the carrier to show it. The roads, however, do not claim that there is anything in the nature of the service of transportation to Troy which justifies the disproportionate rates charged to that city, but base their defense of those rates on another and distinct ground (which we hold not to be established) namely, dissimilarity of circumstances and conditions resulting from water and rail competition at Montgomery. In the absence of proof of exceptional conditions, the transportation from Montgomery to Troy, including terminal expenses, will be presumed to be not more costly to the carrier than for like distances in the same or like territory. On examination we find, that the class rates from Louisville, Cincinnati and St. Louis and Ohio river points generally, are the same to Columbus, Eufaula and Opelika. The distances from Louisville and St. Louis to Columbus by the shortest available route (that *via* Birmingham and Opelika over the Columbus & Western road) are 9 miles greater and by the routes *via* Montgomery are about 42 miles greater than to Troy. The distance from Cincinnati to Columbus by the shortest route appears

to be about 14 miles less than to Troy. The distances to Eufaula
are greater than to Troy, and to Opelika they are somewhat
less. The distances from the cities named to Columbus and
Eufaula being on the average greater than to Troy and other
things being equal, the rate to Troy should, if anything, be
slightly less than to those cities. No substantial dissimilarity
of circumstances and conditions justifying a higher rate to Troy,
has been attempted to be shown. The class rates in cents per
hundred pounds (except class F, which is per bbl.) to Columbus,
Eufaula and Opelika, and to Troy, from Louisville, and the
excess of the Troy rates over those to Columbus, Eufaula and
Opelika are given in the following table:

	CLASSES												
	1	2	3	4	5	6	A	B	C	D	E	H	F
From Louisville to Columbus, Eufaula, and Opelika . .	107	92	81	68	56	46	28	36	29	25	50	55	per bbl. 50
From Louisville to Troy . .	140	130	113	95	75½	62	45	50	37	32	69	59	66
Excess of Troy rates . . .	33	38	32	27	19½	16	17	14	8	7	19	4	16

The excess of the Troy rate is the same under the rates from
Cincinnati and St. Louis.

*   *   *   *   *   *   *   *   *

Columbus and Eufaula are located in or are contiguous to
the territory in which Troy is situated, and the former, at least,
is in active competition with Troy for business in the country
immediately around Troy. We are of the opinion that the class
rates to Troy from Louisville, Cincinnati and St. Louis should
be at least as low as those above given to Columbus and Eufaula.

It is claimed on the part of the roads, that the establishment
of lower rates to Troy will disarrange and call for a readjustment of the rates to the localities around Troy in order to prevent unjust discrimination in favor of Troy and against such
localities. It appears from the tariffs on file with the Commission, that the through rates to these points around Troy are
made on the basis of the rates to Montgomery plus the local

rates from Montgomery on — in other words, that Montgomery is given the undue advantage of a "trade center" as against these points. This being the case, these rates now call for readjustment with a view of remedying the unjust discrimination thus appearing. The adjustment of the rates to these points so as to make them conform to the reduced rates which we have ordered for Troy, will tend to bring them in line with the law and do away with the unjust discrimination in favor of Montgomery already existing under them. It certainly cannot be held to be a valid objection to the correction of unlawful rates to one locality, that it involves a like correction as to other localities. Unjust discrimination as between localities or individuals cannot be essential to the business prosperity of the roads; on the contrary, we believe that in the end, if not immediately, their financial welfare would be promoted by the application in the matter of rate making of the principle of absolute fairness as between all interests, large and small, enjoined by the Statute. Rates should in the first instance be fixed upon a fairly remunerative basis and then so applied as to result in no undue advantage or disadvantage to any interest. It will devolve upon the roads to make whatever changes in rates to surrounding towns may be incidental to, and a necessary consequence of, compliance in good faith with our order in reference to the rates to Troy.

In pursuance of the conclusions arrived at in this case, it is ordered, that the roads participating in the traffic involved cease and desist, (1), from charging and collecting on class goods shipped from Louisville, St. Louis and Cincinnati to Troy a higher rate than is now charged and collected on such shipments to Columbus and Eufaula; (2), from charging and collecting on cotton shipped from Troy *via* Montgomery to New Orleans a higher through rate than 50 cts. per hundred pounds; (3), from charging and collecting on shipments of cotton from Troy for export *via* the Atlantic seaports, Brunswick, Savannah, Charleston, West Point and Norfolk, a higher rate to those ports than is charged and collected on such shipments from Montgomery; (4), from charging and collecting on cotton shipped from Troy to Brunswick, Savannah and Charleston, a higher rate than is charged and collected on such shipments from Montgomery through Troy to those ports; (5), from charging and collecting on class goods, shipped from New York, Baltimore, and the northeast, to Troy, a higher rate than is charged and collected on such shipments to Montgomery; and (6), from charging and collecting on phosphate rock shipped from the South Carolina and Florida fields to Troy a higher rate than is charged and collected on such shipments through Troy to Montgomery.

INTERSTATE COMMERCE COMMISSION
v.
ALABAMA MIDLAND RAILWAY CO., ET AL. [1]

Long and Short Haul

*   *   *   *   *   *   *   *

Whether competition between lines of transportation to Montgomery, Eufaula, and Columbus justifies the giving to those cities a preference or advantage in rates over Troy, and, if so, whether such a state of facts justifies a departure from equality of rates without authority from the Interstate Commerce Commission, under the proviso to the fourth section of the act, are questions of construction of the Statute, and are to be determined before we reach the question of fact in this case.

It is contended in the briefs filed on behalf of the Interstate Commission that the existence of rival lines of transportation, and consequently of competition for the traffic, are not facts to be considered by the Commission or by the courts when determining whether property transported over the same line is carried under " substantially similar circumstances and conditions," as that phrase is found in the fourth section of the act.

---

[1] Known as the " Alabama Midland " case, stated in the preceding chapter. Decided by the Supreme Court of the United States, November 8, 1897. 168 U. S. 144.

Such, evidently, was not the construction put upon this provision of the Statute by the Commission itself in the present case, for the record discloses that the Commission made some allowance for the alleged dissimilarity of circumstances and conditions, arising out of competition and situation, as affecting transportation to Montgomery and Troy, respectively, and that among the errors assigned is one complaining that the court erred in not holding that the rates prescribed by the Commission in its order made due allowance for such dissimilarity.

So, too, in case *In re Louisville & N. R. Co.*, 1 Inters. Commerce Com. R. 77, in discussing the long and short haul clause, it was said by the Commission, per Judge Cooley, that "it is impossible to resist the conclusion that in finally rejecting the 'long and short haul clause' of the House Bill, which prescribed an inflexible rule, not to be departed from in any case, and retaining in substance the fourth section as it had passed the senate, both houses understood that they were not adopting a measure of strict prohibition in respect to charging more for the shorter than for the longer distance, but that they were, instead, leaving the door open for exceptions in certain cases, and, among others, in cases where the circumstances and conditions of the traffic were affected by the element of competition, and where exceptions might be a necessity if the competition was to continue. And water competition was, beyond doubt, especially in view."

It is no doubt true that in a later case (*Railroad Commission of Georgia* v. *Clyde S. S. Co.*, 5 Inters. Commerce Com. R. 326) the Commission somewhat modified their holding in the Louisville & Nashville Railroad Company Case, just cited, by attempting to restrict the competition that it is allowable to consider to the cases of competition with water carriers, competition with foreign railroads, and competition with railroad lines wholly in a single state; but the principle that competition in such cases is to be considered is affirmed.

That competition is one of the most obvious and effective circumstances that make the conditions under which a long and short haul is performed substantially dissimilar, and as such must have been in the contemplation of Congress in the passage of the Act to Regulate Commerce, has been held by many of the circuit courts.   *   *   *   *   *   *

In order further to guard against any misapprehension of the scope of our decision, it may be well to observe that we do not hold that the mere fact of competition, no matter what its character or extent, necessarily relieves the carrier from the restraints of the third and fourth sections, but only that these sections are not so stringent and imperative as to exclude in all cases the matter of competition from consideration, in determining the questions of "undue or unreasonable preference or advantage," or what are "substantially similar circumstances and conditions." The competition may in some cases be such as, having due regard to the interests of the public and of the carrier, ought justly to have effect upon the rates, and in such cases there is no absolute rule which prevents the Commission or the courts from taking that matter into consideration.

It is further contended on behalf of the appellant that the courts below erred in holding, in effect, that competition of carrier with carrier, both subject to the Act to Regulate Commerce, will justify a departure from the rule of the fourth section of the act without authority from the Interstate Commerce Commission, under the proviso to that section.

In view of the conclusion hereinbefore reached, the proposition comes to this : That when circumstances and conditions are substantially dissimilar the railway companies can only avail themselves of such a situation by an application to the Commission.

The language of the proviso is as follows :

That upon application to the Commission appointed under the provisions of this act, such common carrier may, in special cases, after investigation by the Commission, be authorized to charge less for longer than shorter distances for the transportation of persons or property, and the Commission may from time to time prescribe the extent to which such designated common carrier may be relieved from the operation of this section of this act.

The claim now made for the Commission is that the only body which has the power to relieve railroad companies from the operation of the long and short haul clause on account of the existence of competition, or any other similar element which would make its application unfair, is the Commission itself, which is bound to consider the question, upon application by the railroad company, but whose decision is discretionary and unreviewable.

The first observation that occurs on this proposition is that there appears to be no allegation in the bill or petition raising such an issue. The gravamen of the complaint is that the defendant companies have continued to charge and collect a greater compensation for services rendered in transportation of property than is prescribed in the order of the Commission. It was not claimed that the defendants were precluded from showing in the courts that the difference of rates complained of was justified by dissimilarity of circumstances and conditions, by reason of not having applied to the Commission to be relieved from the operation of the fourth section.

Moreover, this view of the scope of the proviso to the fourth section does not appear to have ever been acted upon or enforced by the Commission. On the contrary, in the case of *In re Louis-ville & N. R. Co.* v. *Interstate Commerce Commission*, 1 Inters. Commerce Com. R. 57, the Commission, through Judge Cooley, said, in speaking of the effect of the introduction into the fourth section of the words, " under substantially similar circumstances and conditions," and of the meaning of the proviso :

That which the Act does not declare unlawful must remain lawful, if it was so before ; and that which it fails to forbid the carrier is left at liberty to do, without permission of any one. * * * The charging or receiving the greater compensation for the shorter than for the longer haul is seen to be forbidden only when both are under substantially similar circumstances and conditions; and therefore if in any case the carrier, without first obtaining an order of relief, shall depart from the general rule, its doing so will not alone convict it of illegality, since, if the circumstances and conditions of the two hauls are dissimilar, the Statute is not violated. * * * Beyond question, the carrier must judge for itself what are the "substantially similar circumstances and conditions" which preclude the special rate, rebate, or drawback which is made unlawful by the second section, since no tribunal is empowered to judge for it until after the carrier has acted, and then only for the purpose of determining whether its action constitutes a violation of law. The carrier judges on peril of the consequences, but the special rate, rebate, or drawback which it grants is not illegal when it turns out that the circumstances and conditions were not such as to forbid it; and, as Congress clearly intended this, it must also, when using the same words in the fourth section, have intended that the carrier whose privilege was in the same way limited by them should in the same way act upon its judgment of the limiting circumstances and conditions.

. . . We are unable to suppose that Congress intended, by the fourth section and the proviso thereto, to forbid common carriers, in cases where the circumstances and conditions are substantially dissimilar, from making different rates until and unless the Commission shall authorize them so to do. Much less do we think that it was the intention of Congress that the decision of the Commission, if applied to, could not be reviewed by the courts. The provisions of section 16 of the act, which authorize the court to "proceed to hear and determine the matter speedily as a court of equity, and without the formal pleadings and proceeding applicable to ordinary suits in equity, but in such manner as to do justice in the premises, and to this end, such court shall have power, if it think fit, to direct and prosecute in such mode and by such persons as it may appoint, all such inquiries as the court may think needful to enable it to form a just judgment in the matter of such petition," extend as well to an inquiry or proceeding under the fourth section as to those arising under the other sections of the act.

Upon these conclusions, that competition between rival routes is one of the matters which may lawfully be considered in making rates, and that substantial dissimilarity of circumstances and conditions may justify common carriers in charging greater compensation for the transportation of like kinds of property for a shorter than for a longer distance over the same line, we are brought to consider whether, upon the evidence in the present case, the courts below erred in dismissing the Interstate Commerce Commission's complaint.

*   *   *   *   *   *   *   *

The Circuit Court, after a consideration of the evidence, expressed its conclusion thus:

In any aspect of the case, it seems impossible to consider this complaint of the Board of Trade of Troy against the defendant railroad companies, particularly the Midland and Georgia Central Railroads, in the matter of the charges upon property transported on their roads to or from points east or west of Troy, as specified and complained of, obnoxious to the fourth or any other section of the Interstate Commerce Act. The conditions are not substantially the same, and the circumstances are dissimilar, so that the case is not within the Statute. The case made here is not the case as it was made before the Commission. New testimony has been taken, and the conclusion reached is that the bill is not sustained; that it should be dismissed; and it is so ordered. 69 Fed. 227.

The Circuit Court of Appeals, in affirming the decree of the Circuit Court, used the following language:

Only two railroads, the Alabama Midland and the Georgia Central, reach Troy. Each of these roads has connection with other lines, parties hereto, reaching all the long-distance markets mentioned in these proceedings. The Commission finds that no departure from the long and short haul rule of the fourth section of the Statute, as against Troy, as the shorter distance point, and in favor of Montgomery, as the longer distance point, appears to be chargeable to the Georgia Central. The rates in question, when separately considered, are not unreasonable or unjust. As a matter of business necessity, they are the same by each of the railroads that reach Troy. The Commission concludes that as related to the rates to Montgomery, Columbus, and Eufaula, the rates to and from Troy unjustly discriminate against Troy, and, in the case of the Alabama Midland, violate the long and short haul rule.

The volume of population and of business at Montgomery is many times larger than it is at Troy. There are many more railway lines running to and through Montgomery, connecting with all the distant markets. The Alabama river, open all the year, is capable, if need be, of bearing to Mobile on the sea, the burden of all the goods of every class that pass to or from Montgomery. The competition of the railway lines is not stifled, but is fully recognized, intelligently and honestly controlled and regulated, by the traffic association, in its schedule of rates. There is no suggestion in the evidence that the traffic managers who represent the carriers that are members of that association are incompetent, or under the bias of any personal preference for Montgomery or prejudice against Troy, that has led them, or is likely to lead them, to unjustly discriminate against Troy. When the rates to Montgomery were higher a few years ago than now, actual active water-line competition by the river came in, and the rates were reduced to the level of the lowest practical paying water rates; and the volume of carriage by the river is now comparatively small, but the controlling power of that water line remains in full force, and must ever remain in force as long as the river remains navigable to its present capacity. And this water line affects, to a degree less or more, all the shipments to or from Montgomery from or to all the long-distance markets. It would not take cotton from Montgomery to the South Atlantic ports for export, but it would take the cotton to the points of its ultimate destination, if the railroad rates to foreign marts through the Atlantic ports were not kept down to or below the level of profitable carriage by water from Montgomery through the port of Mobile. The volume of trade to be competed for, the number of carriers actually competing for it, a constantly open river present to take a large part of it whenever the railroad rates rise up to the mark of profitable water carriage, seem to us, as they did to the Circuit Court, to constitute circumstances and conditions at Montgomery substantially dissimilar from those existing at Troy, and to relieve the carriers from the charges preferred against them by its board of trade. We do not discuss the third and fourth contentions of the counsel for the appellant, further than to say that within the limits of the exercise of intelligent good faith in the conduct of their business, and subject to the two leading prohibitions that their charges shall not be unjust or unreasonable, and that they shall not unjustly discriminate so as to give undue preference or disadvantage to traffic or persons similarly circum-stanced, the Act to Regulate Commerce leaves common carriers, as they were at the common law, free to make special rates looking to the increase of their business, to classify their traffic, to adjust and apportion their rates so as to meet the necessities of commerce and of their own situation and relation to it, and generally to manage their important interests upon the same principles which are regarded as sound, and adopted, in other trades and pursuits. The carriers are better qualified to adjust such matters than any court or board of public administration, and, within the limitations suggested, it is safe and wise to leave to their traffic managers the adjusting of dissimilar circumstances and conditions to their business. 21 C. C. A. 51, 74 Fed. 715.

The last sentence in this extract is objected to by the Commission's counsel, as declaring that the determination of the extent to which discrimination is justified by circumstances and conditions should be left to the carriers. If so read, we should not be ready to adopt or approve such a position. But we understand the statement, read in the connection in which it occurs, to mean only that, when once a substantial dissimilarity of circumstances and conditions has been made to appear, the carriers are, from the nature of the question, better fitted to adjust their rates to suit such dissimilarity of circumstances and conditions than courts or commissions; and when we consider the difficulty, the practical impossibility, of a court or a commission taking into view the various and continually changing facts that bear upon the question, and intelligently regulating rates and charges accordingly, the observation objected to is manifestly just. But it does not mean that the action of the carriers, in fixing and adjusting the rates, in such instances, is not subject to revision by the Commission and the courts, when it is charged that such action has resulted in rates unjust or unreasonable, or in unjust discriminations and preferences.

* * * * * * * *

Coming at last to the questions of fact in this case, we encounter a large amount of conflicting evidence. It seems undeniable, as the effect of the evidence on both sides, that an actual dissimilarity of circumstances and conditions exists between the cities concerned, both as respects the volume of their respective trade, and the competition, affecting rates, occasioned by rival routes by land and water. Indeed, the Commission itself recognized such a state of facts, by making an allowance in the rates prescribed for dissimilarity resulting from competition; and it was contended on behalf of the commission, both in the courts below and in this court, that the competition did not justify the discriminations against Troy to the extent shown, and that the allowance made therefor by the Commission was a due allowance.

The issue is thus restricted to the question of the preponderance of the evidence on the respective sides of the controversy. We have read the evidence disclosed by the record, and have endeavored to weigh it with the aid of able and elaborate discussions by the respective counsel.

No useful purpose would be served by an attempt to formally state and analyze the evidence, but the result is that we are not convinced that the courts below erred in their estimate of the evidence, and that we perceive no error in the principles of law on which they proceeded in the application of the evidence.

The decree of the Circuit Court of Appeals is accordingly affirmed.

Mr. Justice HARLAN, dissenting:

I dissent from the opinion and judgment in this case. Taken in connection with other decisions defining the powers of the

Interstate Commerce Commission, the present decision, it seems to me, goes far to make that Commission a useless body, for all practical purposes, and to defeat many of the important objects designed to be accomplished by the various enactments of Congress relating to interstate commerce. The Commission was established to protect the public against the improper practices of transportation companies engaged in commerce among the several states. It has been left, it is true, with power to make reports and to issue protests. But it has been shorn, by judicial interpretation, of authority to do anything of an effective character. It is denied many of the powers which, in my judgment, were intended to be conferred upon it. Besides, the acts of Congress are now so construed as to place communities on the lines of interstate commerce at the mercy of competing railroad companies engaged in such commerce. The judgment in this case, if I do not misapprehend its scope and effect, proceeds upon the ground that railroad companies, when competitors for interstate business at certain points, may, in order to secure traffic for and at those points, establish rates that will enable them to accomplish that result, although such rates may discriminate against intermediate points. Under such an interpretation of the statutes in question, they may well be regarded as recognizing the authority of competing railroad companies engaged in interstate commerce — when their interests will be subserved thereby — to build up favored centers of population at the expense of the business of the country at large. I cannot believe that Congress intended any such result, nor do I think that its enactments, properly interpreted, would lead to such a result.

XV

THE SOUTHERN BASING POINT SYSTEM

THE DAWSON, GA., CASE[1]

PROUTY, *Commissioner :*

The complainant in this case is a mercantile organization representing the commercial interests of the city of Dawson, Ga. No question is made about its competency to prosecute this proceeding. The complaint is that freight rates now in force from New York and northeastern cities, from Cincinnati, Ohio, Nashville, Tenn., Chattanooga, Tenn., and New Orleans, La., to Eufaula, Ala., and Georgetown, Americus and Albany, Ga., as compared with those to Dawson, Ga., are in violation of the third section of the Act to Regulate Commerce, in that they work an undue preference against Dawson. . . .

The class rates from the points aboved named are as follows : [Abridged. — ED.]

RATES IN CENTS PER 100 POUNDS, EXCEPT CLASS F, WHICH IS
PER BARREL

	CLASSES												
	1	2	3	4	5	6	A	B	C	D	E	H	F
From New York, N.Y., to Dawson, Ga.,													
via sea and rail	131	111	98	83	69	56	46	55	42	40	67	78	81
" all rail	143	121	107	91	75	61	51	—	—	—	—	—	—

[1] Decided March 27, 1899. Interstate Commerce Reports, Vol. VIII, pp. 142–157. Other similar cases have been recently decided for Cordele, Ga. (*Ibid.*, Vol. VI, 343) ; Griffin, Ga. (*Ibid.*, Vol. VII, 225) ; Hampton, Fla. (*Ibid.*, Vol. VIII, 503) ; Wilmington, S.C. (*Ibid.*, Vol. IX, 118) ; and Tifton, Ga. (*Ibid.*, Vol. IX, 160).

RATES IN CENTS, ETC. (*continued*)

	1	2	3	4	5	6	A	B	C	D	E	H	F
							CLASSES						
From New York, N.Y., to													
Albany, Ga.,													
via sea and rail	109	96	83	70	59	48	34	47	35	34	52	60	68
" all rail	121	106	92	78	65	53	39	52	40	39	58	68	78
Americus, Ga.,													
via sea and rail	114	98	86	73	60	49	36	48	40	39	58	68	78
" all rail	126	108	95	81	66	54	41	53	45	44	64	76	88
Eufaula, Ala.,													
via sea and rail	114	98	86	73	60	49	36	48	40	39	58	68	78
" all rail	126	108	95	81	66	54	41	53	45	44	64	76	88
Georgetown, Ga.,													
via sea and rail	114	98	86	73	60	49	36	48	40	39	58	68	78
" all rail	126	108	95	81	66	54	41	53	45	44	64	76	88
From Cincinnati, Ohio, to													
Dawson, Ga.	139	121	107	91	75	60	42	51	37	33	69	73	66
Albany, Ga. . . . }	127	109	96	81	67	55	37	41	32	28	60	65	56
Americus, Ga. . . . }													
Eufaula, Ala.	117	102	91	76	63	52	31	39	32	28	54	59	56
Georgetown, Ga.	122	106	94	78	65	54	36	44	24½	29½	59	65	61
(Based on Eufaula.)													
From Nashville, Tenn., to													
Dawson, Ga.	104	91	82	69	57	47	34	43	30	26	54	60	52
Albany, Ga. . . . . }	92	79	71	59	49	42	29	33	25	21	45	47	42
Americus, Ga. . . . . }													
Eufaula, Ala.	72	62	56	46	38	33	20	29	23	19	35	37	38
Georgetown, Ga.	87	76	69	56	47	41	28	36	27½	22½	44	47	47
(Based on Eufaula.)													
From New Orleans, La., to													
Dawson, Ga.	135	117	103	87	71	56	38	47	34½	30	65	69	61½
Albany, Ga. . . . . }	123	105	92	77	63	51	33	37	28	24	56	61	48
Americus, Ga. . . . . }													
Eufaula, Ala.	103	88	77	64	52	42	24	33	26	22	46	51	44
Georgetown, Ga.	118	102	90	74	61	50	32	40	30½	25½	55	61	53
(Based on Eufaula.)													

The commodity rate on sugar from New Orleans is, per hundred pounds, to Eufaula, Americus and Albany 18 cents, to Dawson 31 cents.   *   *   *   *   *   *

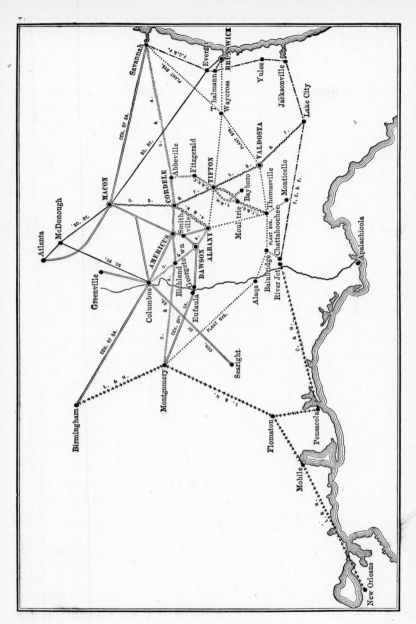

An examination of this map shows that the lines of the defendant Central of Georgia Railway Company reach Americus, Albany, Eufaula and Dawson, its outlying termini being, so to speak, Savannah upon the coast and Atlanta, Birmingham and Montgomery in the interior. The line of the defendant Georgia & Alabama Railway Company reaches Americus, Albany and Dawson, its termini being Savannah upon the coast and Montgomery in the interior. It also has a line extending from Columbus to Albany through Dawson, crossing the main line at Richland. The Plant System connects Albany with Brunswick upon the Atlantic seaboard.

Traffic from New York and other Atlantic cities may reach these different points, either all rail or by rail and ocean. The rate in the two cases is somewhat different, but one is supposed to be fairly the equivalent of the other. Traffic coming by ocean and rail would reach Savannah by water, from whence it might pass by either of the defendant lines to any one of the points in question, except Eufaula, which is only reached by the Central of Georgia Railway. Traffic coming all rail from the North would also ordinarily pass through Savannah, although it might reach these points through lines farther inland. The rate is the same by all routes. The distance from Savannah to these several points by the Central of Georgia Railway is —

To Americus	262 miles
To Dawson	289 "
To Eufaula	335 "
To Albany	298 "

Traffic passing over this line from Savannah would naturally, although not necessarily, pass through Americus and Dawson in reaching Eufaula, and through Americus in reaching Albany. The distance from Savannah by the Georgia & Alabama Railway is as follows:

To Americus	199 miles
To Dawson	253 "
To Albany	276 "

Traffic from Savannah to Albany by this line would pass through Dawson. The distance from Brunswick to Albany *via* the Plant System is 171 miles, and from Albany to Dawson by the Georgia & Alabama line 23 miles.

The short line all rail distance from New York is —

To Americus	1036 miles
To Dawson	1063 "
To Eufaula	1109 "
To Albany	1072 "

For the purposes of this inquiry Cincinnati, Nashville and Chattanooga may be treated as one group. Traffic from these points reaches the points in question through either Atlanta, Birmingham or Montgomery. The rate by all those gateways is the same and the difference in distance is not considerable. Traffic for all these points *via* the Central of Georgia Railway might come to that line at Atlanta, Birmingham or Montgomery. The Georgia & Alabama would ordinarily receive traffic for Americus, Dawson or Albany at Montgomery. The distance by that line from Montgomery is —

To Americus	141 miles
To Dawson	126 "
To Albany	162 "

Traffic from these points *via* Montgomery over this line would pass through Dawson in reaching Albany.   *   *   *

New Orleans freight reaches the points in question over the defendant lines ordinarily through Montgomery, although it might come through points north of Montgomery, but in that event the distance would be considerably increased. The short line distance from New Orleans is —

To Eufaula	401 miles
To Dawson	447 "
To Americus	462 "
To Albany	483 "

The rates from all the points in question to Americus, Albany and Eufaula are arbitrarily made; that is, these points are regarded as base points. The rate to Dawson is said to be the lowest combination, which is understood to mean the lowest through rate which can be made by adding the local rate from some base point to Dawson. It was further said in testimony that the lowest combination at the present time in most cases was that upon Eufaula.

Dawson is a town of from 2500 to 3000 inhabitants. It has one wholesale and some fifty-four retail establishments. Several important industries are located at that point.

Americus, Albany and Eufaula are all towns of from 5500 to 8000 inhabitants. They have from four to eight wholesale houses each, with industries of various kinds, two or three times as extensive as Dawson. The only two lines of railway at Americus are those of the defendants, and the same is true of Dawson. Albany has, in addition to the lines of the defendants, the Plant System from Brunswick upon the seacoast in. The only line at Eufaula and Georgetown is the defendant Central of Georgia Railway.   *   *   *   *   *   *

We find nothing in the commercial conditions existing at Eufaula, Americus and Albany which requires the defendants to give those towns better freight rates than Dawson or justifies them in so doing. Albany has in the Plant System an additional line of railway which is an aggressive competitor for business from New York and other Atlantic ports, and which might perhaps reasonably justify a somewhat better rate from such points.

Eufaula is situated upon the Chattahoochee river. The distance from Columbus to Eufaula is about 105 miles, from Eufaula to Alaga about 125 miles, and from Alaga to River Junction 50 miles. Some five or six different railways connect at Columbus. The Plant System, running from Brunswick through Alaga to Montgomery, crosses the river at Alaga, while the Louisville & Nashville touches it at River Junction, upon the west bank, and the Florida Central & Peninsular at Chattahoochee, upon the east bank. Counsel for the defendants stated upon the argument that he did not claim that traffic reached the points in question from points like New York or New Orleans by way of the ocean and the Chattahoochee river, but that he did claim that this river was navigable, and that there were in fact lines of steamboats upon it which brought into easy connection different towns upon the river itself.

It did not appear what the rate of freight was between Columbus and Eufaula, nor whether freight from the points in question was ever actually transported to Eufaula by way of Columbus and the river. Neither did it appear what the rate or the movement of freight was between Alaga, River Junction and Eufaula. The rates from New York, Cincinnati, and the other points in question are the same to Columbus and Eufaula, while to Alaga they are materially higher, being ordinarily somewhat higher than to Dawson. At River Junction and Chattahoochee, where rail competition again becomes possible, they are about the same as at Eufaula. No reason was given to account for the fact that river competition between Columbus and Eufaula could reduce the Eufaula rate to a level with the Columbus rate, while the same competition between Columbus, Eufaula, Alaga, and River Junction left the rates at Alaga materially above those at Eufaula, reducing them again at River Junction to the same level.

We find that there is no movement of freight, and no probability that any freight will be moved, from New York, Cincinnati, Nashville and New Orleans by water to Eufaula or any other point upon the Chattahoochee river, and that the lower rates to Eufaula are not justified by any such possible competition. There is communication for about ten months each year by steamboat between different points upon that river which affords actual means for the transportation of freight between such points.

The testimony shows this service to be about triweekly during the season of navigation. We find that this competition existing between Columbus and Eufaula does not necessitate the maintenance of the same rate at Eufaula as at Columbus. Just what relation between the Columbus and Eufaula rates that competition might establish, we have no means of determining. In our opinion it does not enter into the fixing of the present Eufaula rates.

Eufaula is situated upon the west bank of the Chattahoochee river. Georgetown is a small village just opposite Eufaula upon the east bank, and the rate to Georgetown is of necessity substantially the same as the Eufaula rate.   *   *   *

Formerly rates in the State of Georgia from Atlanta to Albany were lower than rates from Atlanta to Dawson. Upon complaint of the Dawson Board of Trade, the Railroad Commission of Georgia, on September 1, 1897, ordered an adjustment of these rates so that all rates from Atlanta and all rates which based upon Atlanta were made the same to Dawson and Albany. In accordance with this order the intrastate rates are now the same from Atlanta to these two points, but the interstate rates, which are made through Atlanta or which base upon Atlanta, as all these rates both from the East and from the West in effect do, still favor Albany as hereinbefore set forth.

Conclusions

It is plain that the rates under consideration create a preference against Dawson in favor of Albany, Americus and Eufaula. Americus is to the northeast, Albany to the southeast, and Eufaula to the west, of Dawson, thus surrounding it upon all sides. And yet, no matter from what point the traffic comes, whether from the North, the East, the South or the West, the rate to all these points is lower than to Dawson.

It is equally clear that this preference works to the disadvantage of Dawson as compared with Eufaula, Americus and Albany. This follows both from necessary inference and from actual testimony. The Dawson merchant, whether wholesale or retail, pays just so much more for his goods than his brother merchant in these surrounding towns, and this amount is in many cases a very considerable one. If he sells his goods to the consumer at the same price as does the merchant in Americus, Albany or Eufaula, he loses exactly so much, and is therefore prejudiced to exactly that extent. If, upon the other hand, he recoups himself for this difference in the freight rate by an increased price to his customer at or in the vicinity of Dawson, then that customer is injured to exactly the same extent.

It is found as a fact from the testimony in the case that it is impossible to do a wholesale business from Dawson in competition with any one of these three towns in territory which legitimately belongs to Dawson, and it is also found that in the development of that center these increased freight rates are a serious drawback.

The question then remains, Is this preference an undue one? Even if it does work to the disadvantage of Dawson, is it not justifiable?

The defendants insisted in their answers that so far as Eufaula was concerned these rates were justified by water competition upon the Chattahoochee river. The answers alleged, and some attempt was made to show by the testimony of witnesses, that commodities consumed at Eufaula were actually brought from New York, Cincinnati and New Orleans by ocean or river and ocean to the mouth of the Chattahoochee, and thence carried up that river to Eufaula and other points upon it. This claim was not, however, supported by the testimony, and was formally abandoned by counsel for defense upon the argument, who stated that he did not claim upon the evidence that freight was brought by ocean to the mouth of the Chattahoochee, and from thence carried up the river to these different points like Eufaula, but he did claim that the Chattahoochee river connected different lines of railway touching it at different points, and thereby brought these lines of railway into competition with each other. The Chattahoochee river is navigable during a portion of the year, and is at the present time navigated by several small steamboats, which afford communication between the various points upon that river from Columbus to Apalachicola. That river is crossed by several railroads at Columbus, by the Central of Georgia Railway at Eufaula, by the Plant System at Alaga, and is touched by the Louisville & Nashville at River Junction, and the Florida Central & Peninsular at Chattahoochee.

The only line of railroad reaching Eufaula is that of the defendant Central of Georgia Railway Company. There are, however, several lines at Columbus which create active competition at that point, and the contention of the defendants, as stated by counsel in his argument and in his printed brief, is, that inasmuch as these two points are connected by the river, higher rates cannot be maintained at Eufaula than are maintained at Columbus.

This contention has been examined and rejected in the findings of fact. Eufaula is 105 miles from Columbus. Its water connection with Columbus is by small steamers which pass it on their way to Apalachicola three times a week for ten months in the year. No through rate *via* Columbus and the river is maintained, nor does the case show that a pound of freight ever passed from New York, Chattanooga or New Orleans through Columbus and down the river to Eufaula. There is nothing in this situation which leads to the conviction that the rates at Eufaula are appreciably affected by this river competition, — especially when this same competition, operating in exactly the same way, produces no effect at Alaga or River Junction.

Very probably the Central of Georgia Company believes it good policy to make the low rate to Eufaula, thereby developing that town and stimulating the movement of freight to and from it; but might not the same policy result in an increased movement to Dawson, and at all events has not Dawson the right, under the Act to Regulate Commerce, to insist upon equal treatment?

The remaining alleged justification for this discrimination against Dawson is railway competition or the competition of markets acting through the railways. As already said, the Central of Georgia Railway is the only line reaching Eufaula and traffic whether from the East, the West or the North must enter that town over that line. Traffic from New Orleans to Dawson would pass by the short line through Eufaula, and this might justify a lower rate to Eufaula than to Dawson. The short line distance from Nashville and Cincinnati is through Chattanooga, and is less to Dawson than to Eufaula. It is difficult to see, therefore, how the higher rate to Dawson than to Eufaula from these points can be justified, and we hold that it is not.

In case of New York and corresponding eastern cities the discrimination is even more manifest. Traffic from these points, whether by rail or by ocean, ordinarily reaches Eufaula through Savannah. In passing from Savannah to Eufaula it would naturally pass through Dawson, and, by whatever route it went, the distance to Eufaula would be greater than to Dawson. The competition at Eufaula we have already referred to. At Dawson the Georgia & Alabama Railway is a direct competitor. We can see no possible reason why rates to Eufaula from New York and other eastern points should be lower than to Dawson, and we think that the maintenance of such rates is without justification, and is in violation of the third section.

Comparing, now, Americus and Albany with Dawson, we find that traffic from New York and eastern points reaches Americus and Dawson by the lines of both defendants through Savannah. The distance from Savannah to Americus is considerably less than to Dawson. While the distance to Albany by the lines of the defendants is as great as that to Dawson, the Plant System brings Albany nearer to the seacoast at Brunswick, and gives it an additional means of connection with New York, which would entitle it to as low a rate as Americus. We do not think, therefore, that it can be affirmed that under no circumstances should Americus and Albany receive a better rate from New York and the East than Dawson.

Traffic from Nashville, Cincinnati and Chattanooga might reach these three points over the lines of the defendants in various ways. The short line in all cases is through Chattanooga and Atlanta, and is somewhat less to Americus and somewhat greater to Albany than to Dawson. While as a transportation proposition this difference in distance is insignificant, we are not prepared to affirm that under no rate adjustment might the rates to Americus be less than those to Dawson, but we do hold that under no circumstances should the rate to Albany be lower than the rate to Dawson. In this we determine with reference to interstate rates what the Commission of Georgia has already established in respect to rates within the State.

Traffic from New Orleans for either of these three points passes by the short line through Birmingham, the distance to Americus and Albany being substantially the same, and that to Dawson somewhat less. We hold that there is no justification for a lower rate from New Orleans to either Americus or Albany than to Dawson.

It is urged that these rates have been made under stress of competition between eastern and western markets. It is said both the East and the West demand a rate which will entitle either section to sell in this territory.

But, first, is there any reason why the market of production should demand an equality which is not also accorded to the market of consumption? If New York and Chicago demand the same right to sell in both Eufaula and Americus, may not Dawson demand the same right to purchase in either market that Eufaula or Americus has?

Then, again, what eastern and western markets ask for is equal rights. They do not demand a higher rate to Dawson than to Americus. These defendants absolutely control the situation both at Dawson and at Americus. Now, if it be true that the rate must be the same to Americus from both the East and from the West, why, nevertheless, cannot that rate be somewhat raised from all directions and the Dawson rate correspondingly lowered? The discrimination of which Dawson complains would thereby be removed and the adjustment between eastern and western markets equally preserved.

The situation complained of in this case grows out of the system of basing points, which prevails in Southern territory. For the purpose of making rates into this territory certain points are selected to which an arbitrary rate is made, the rate to surrounding points being determined by adding to these arbitrary base rates the local rates. Americus, Albany and Eufaula are basing points, and by virtue of that circumstance enjoy the low rates in question. Dawson is not a basing point. Now, granting that the carrier may make lower rates to competitive points than are made to intermediate noncompetitive points, we think it clear that the carrier is not at liberty in the selection of these basing points to determine that this town shall have the benefit of the low rate and that town shall not, when the means of competition and the conditions surrounding that competition do not materially differ. Take as an illustration Americus and Dawson. The only two railroads serving these towns are the lines of the defendants. No water competition is involved. The distances from the markets in question to these two cities are substantially the same. Now, what reason is there for giving Americus a rate of 18 cents per hundred pounds on sugar from New Orleans, while Dawson pays a rate of 31 cents upon the same commodity?

It should be carefully noticed that the rate to Americus is an arbitrary rate. If that rate were fixed by adding to the competitive ocean rate between New York and Savannah the rate of the Georgia Railroad Commission, it might be said that the Americus rate was fixed by competition beyond the control of either of the defendants. Such is not, however, the case. The rate to Americus is less than the rate to points like Huntington, Leslie and De Soto upon the line of the Georgia & Alabama east of Americus. Why, then, is it that the rate to Americus is made lower than the surrounding rates and lower than the Dawson rate?

Counsel for the defendants stated upon the argument that it was owing to competition between the Central of Georgia and the Georgia & Alabama, and that the same competition did not operate at Dawson, although the same means of competition existed. He said that the rate to Americus was made by one line, and that the other line must accept that rate or refuse the business.

The city of Dawson, in its distress, asks of the Traffic Manager of the Central of Georgia Railway, " Why do you make the low rate to Americus and maintain the high rate to Dawson?" and the answer is, " I make the low rate to Americus because my competitor, the Georgia & Alabama Railway, over which I have no control, makes that rate, and I must either meet it or go out of the business. I do not make a corresponding rate to Dawson because my competitor, the Georgia & Alabama Railway, does not make such a rate." Thereupon the city of Dawson turns to the Traffic Manager of the Georgia & Alabama Railway, and inquires, " Why is it that you make the low rate to Americus while maintaining the high rate to Dawson?" and again the answer is, "I make the low rate to Americus because my competitor, the Central of Georgia Railway, over which I have no control, makes that rate, and I must meet it or refuse the business. I do not make the same rate to Dawson because my competitor, the Central of Georgia Railway, does not." This is

worse than Hindoo Mythology, according to which the earth
was supported upon the back of a tortoise, which in turn rested
on the back of an elephant. In that case the turtle at least
had something to stand upon.

Now, it is pretty apparent unless the traffic managers of these
lines can give some intelligent reason for making the low rate at
Americus and not at Dawson, the Act to Regulate Commerce,
which forbids an undue preference, is violated.

Counsel for the defendants, being pressed with this observation, said that in the present instance the justification for the
lower rate at Americus was found in the fact that Americus
was a larger trade center than Dawson, and therefore entitled to
a better rate.

By the Census of 1890 the population was:

Of Macon	22,746
Of Columbus	17,303
Of Montgomery	21,883
Of Americus	6,398
Of Albany	4,008
Of Eufaula	4,394
Of Dawson	2,284

Macon had six, Columbus three, Montgomery six, Albany
three, Americus two, Eufaula one, and Dawson two railroads.

Americus with 6000 inhabitants and two railways had the
same rate as Columbus with 17,000 inhabitants and three railways ; Albany with 4000 inhabitants and three railways obtained the same rates as Macon with 22,000 inhabitants and six
railways ; Eufaula with 4000 inhabitants and one railway obtained the same rates as Montgomery with 21,000 inhabitants
and six railways. Still, these defendants who make and participate in the aforesaid rate adjustments, insist that Dawson with
2000 inhabitants and two railways is not entitled to the same
rate as Americus with 6000 inhabitants and the same two railways. It should be observed that this discrimination is one
which fortifies itself from year to year, since the more favorable
freight rate increases every day the difference in population between Americus and Dawson. It was said upon the argument,
and not denied, that when the Georgia & Alabama Railway was

first completed between Americus and Savannah, Americus and Dawson did not differ materially in size.

It has been found as a matter of fact that there are no commercial or competitive conditions at Americus which entitle that city to a better rate than Dawson. Under some different adjustment of freight rates Americus might be entitled in some instances to a better rate than Dawson. So long as the present system of rate making is continued, we hold that Dawson should be given the same rate as Americus. We do not approve that system, but if the defendants put and continue it in force they cannot be heard to say that Dawson should not receive the same treatment as Americus.

In accordance with the foregoing views an order will be made directing :

First : That the Central of Georgia Railway Company cease and desist from maintaining higher rates from New York and other eastern points to Dawson than are maintained to Eufaula ;

Second : That both the defendants cease and desist from maintaining higher rates from Nashville, Cincinnati and Chattanooga to Dawson than to Albany ;

Third : That both the defendants cease and desist from maintaining higher rates from New Orleans to Dawson than to Americus or Albany ;

Fourth : That so long as the present system of rate making is adhered to, the defendants cease and desist from maintaining higher rates from any of the points in question to Dawson than are maintained to Americus.

XVI

RATES TO COMPETING LOCALITIES

The Danville, Va., Case[1]

PROUTY, *Commissioner*:

* * * * * * * *

The rates complained of are divided in the complaint into four groups. First, those to Danville from northern and eastern cities; second, rates on sugar, molasses, rice, and coffee from New Orleans to Danville; third, rates from certain western points to Danville; fourth, the rate on tobacco from Danville to western points.

1. Freight from northern and eastern cities may come to Danville either all rail or by rail and water. This case does not show to what extent all rail competition exists, but it fairly appears from the testimony that the great bulk of such traffic is brought by water to Norfolk, or to some point in that vicinity which may be conveniently designated as Norfolk, and is from thence carried by rail to its destination. Taking New York as a type of these cities, the class rates to Lynchburg and Danville are as follows:

RATES IN CENTS PER 100 POUNDS, EXCEPT CLASS F, WHICH IS PER BARREL

FROM NEW YORK TO	CLASSES												
	1	2	3	4	5	6	A	B	C	D	E	H	F
Lynchburg, Va., water and rail	54	47	38	25	22	18	18	22	18	18	22	25	36
Danville, Va., water and rail	66	58	47	33	29	24	24	27	24	22	29	33	46

[1] Decided February 17, 1900. Interstate Commerce Reports, Vol. VIII, pp. 409–442. Resumed in *Ibid.*, Vol. VIII, pp. 571–583. Finally disposed of in the Chattanooga decision. See Ripley's Railroads: Rates and Regulation, p. 483.

The map on the following page gives a general idea of the location of the points in question and the lines of transportation involved.

This traffic comes by boat to Norfolk. From Norfolk the Southern Railway leads directly to Danville, distance 205 miles. The short line from Norfolk to Lynchburg is by the Norfolk & Western 204 miles. The distance by the Chesapeake & Ohio is 231 miles. Lynchburg is upon the Southern road, 66 miles north of Danville, and a third route from Norfolk to Lynchburg is by the Southern to Danville 205 miles and from Danville to Lynchburg 66 miles, making 271 miles in all. Lynchburg is upon the main line of both the Chesapeake & Ohio and the Norfolk & Western.

There are three lines of railway leading north and east from Danville, which were formerly independent, but are now all controlled by the Southern. These are the Atlantic & Danville to Norfolk, the Richmond & Danville to Richmond, and the Lynchburg & Danville to Lynchburg.

* * * * * * * *

Rates from eastern cities to Richmond are much lower than to Lynchburg, due probably to the fact that Richmond has by the James river direct water communication with the Atlantic seaboard. All other rates appear to be uniformly the same to Norfolk, Richmond and Lynchburg, certainly to Richmond and Lynchburg. For the purpose of avoiding unnecessary repetition, only the rate to Lynchburg will be given.

2. The rates on sugar, molasses, rice, and coffee from New Orleans to Lynchburg and Danville are as follows:

FROM NEW ORLEANS TO	SUGAR	MOLASSES	COFFEE	RICE
Lynchburg	32	26	40	32
Danville	43	37	51	43

The Southern alone carries this traffic into Danville, but it may bring it either from the North *via* Lynchburg or from the South. The Chesapeake & Ohio, Norfolk & Western,

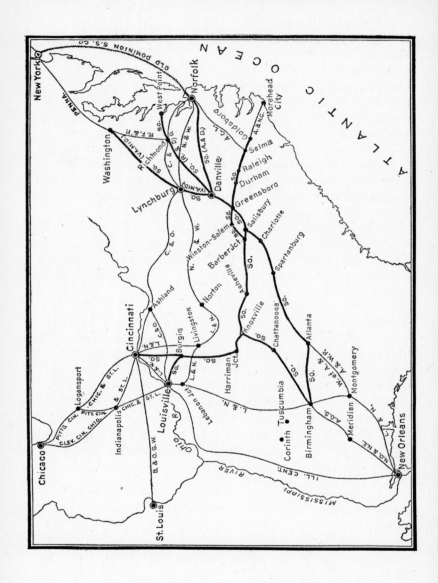

and Southern all compete for this same traffic to Lynchburg, Richmond, and Norfolk. Such traffic may leave New Orleans by various routes. It may reach the Southern road over either the Louisville & Nashville, the Queen & Crescent, or the Illinois Central, and it may also reach the Chesapeake & Ohio and Norfolk & Western over either of those lines. In going by the Southern to either Lynchburg or Richmond it passes through Danville, by whatever route it starts.

*   *   *   *   *   *   *   *

3. Rates from Cincinnati and Louisville are the same to Lynchburg and also to Danville. Those rates, together with the rates from Chicago and East St. Louis, are given below:

RATES IN CENTS PER 100 POUNDS, EXCEPT CLASS F, WHICH IS PER BARREL

	1	2	3	4	5	6	A	B	C	D	E	H	F	Grain	Flour	Packing-House Products
From Louisville, Ky., and Cincinnati, O., to																
Lynchburg, Va. . .	62	53½	40½	27½	23	18½	—	—	—	—	—	—	—	16	16	23
Danville, Va. . . .	68	56	45	33	28	21	19	22	22	21	30	30	—	21	22	22
From Chicago, Ill., to																
Lynchburg, Va. . .	72	62	47	32	27	22	—	—	—	—	—	—	—	19	19	27
Danville, Va. . . .	108	90	70	50	43	33	31	39	34	31	43	45	68	31	34	39
From East St. Louis, Ill., to																
Lynchburg, Va. . .	84	72½	55	37½	32	26	—	—	—	—	—	—	—	22½	22½	32
Danville, Va. . . .	106	89	70	50	43	33	28	39	34	29	43	45	68	29	34	39

The Southern Railway reaches in effect with its own iron Louisville and Cincinnati from Lynchburg and Danville. Traffic from either of these cities to Lynchburg by that route would necessarily pass through Danville. The Chesapeake & Ohio also reaches both Louisville and Cincinnati. The Norfolk & Western by its connections takes traffic from these two cities. The distances by the several routes are as follows:

From Cincinnati
  To Lynchburg
      via the Chesapeake & Ohio 474 miles;
      via the Norfolk & Western 510 miles;
      via the Southern 742 miles.

  To Danville
      via the Southern 676 miles.

From Louisville
  To Lynchburg
      via the Chesapeake & Ohio 537 miles;
      via the Norfolk & Western 551 miles;
      via the Southern 722 miles

  To Danville
      via the Southern 656 miles.

*　　*　　*　　*　　*　　*　　*　　*　　*

Traffic from Chicago, St. Louis and other parts of the West and Southwest passes through Cincinnati and Louisville, reaching those points by various lines. It might be expected that the same difference in rate would prevail between Lynchburg and Danville in case of traffic originating beyond and passing through Cincinnati and Louisville as in case of traffic originating at those cities, but an inspection of the rates above given shows that the discrimination against Danville is very decidedly greater with freight starting at St. Louis or Chicago than it is with the same freight when it originates at Louisville or Cincinnati. The reason for this will be stated later.

4. The rate on leaf tobacco from Danville to Louisville is 40 cents per hundred pounds, while the rate from Lynchburg and Richmond to the same point is 24 cents per hundred pounds. The Southern road makes this rate and carries this traffic from Richmond, Lynchburg and Danville, that from Richmond or Lynchburg passing through Danville *en route* for Louisville. Tobacco rates from Danville to other western destinations are correspondingly higher than those from Richmond and Lynchburg.

All the rates above referred to are made and participated in by the Southern Railway. In case of all those rates, no matter from what direction the traffic comes, it is carried through Danville to Lynchburg or Richmond. The complainants insist that by thus making the lower charge to the more distant point the defendant violates the 4th section and is also guilty of an unjust discrimination under the 3d section.

The defendant justifies the difference in rates between Danville upon the one hand and Richmond and Lynchburg on the other by showing the existence of competitive conditions at the two last-named points. The claim, briefly stated, seems to be this:

Baltimore is an important commercial center, and is so situated and has such railroad connections that it competes both in domestic business and as a port of export and import with other commercial centers upon the Atlantic seaboard, like New York, Philadelphia, etc. The lines of railway connecting these centers with the West are strong trunk lines, and are so situated that competition between them has been unusually active. The Erie Canal to New York has been and is an important factor in fixing the Baltimore rate, especially the export rate, which has generally been the same as the domestic rate. From all these causes it had resulted, previous to the construction of the Chesapeake & Ohio Railway, that the Baltimore rate from almost all directions was an extremely low one.

When the Chesapeake & Ohio Railway was completed from Cincinnati through to Richmond and Norfolk, these points were put into communication with the West in the same manner that Baltimore was by its lines of railway, and that company at once adopted the policy of making its rates from the West to Richmond and Norfolk the same as the Baltimore rate. This was probably done for two reasons: First, to enable Richmond and Norfolk to compete with Baltimore for the wholesale trade in intermediate territory; second, that the Chesapeake & Ohio might conduct through the port of Norfolk an export and import business.

After the passage of the Act to Regulate Commerce, the Chesapeake & Ohio, under its interpretation of the 4th section of that Act, applied no higher rate to intermediate points than was applied to Norfolk upon business moving east, and, in most cases, to Cincinnati upon business moving west; and this had the effect of giving intermediate points as low a rate as Norfolk or Cincinnati. The original line of the Chesapeake & Ohio did not pass through Lynchburg, but about 1886 it acquired a line of railway leading from Clifton Forge through Lynchburg to Richmond, and the effect of this was to give Lynchburg the Richmond rate.

Still later, when the Norfolk & Western Railway was completed through Lynchburg to Norfolk, that company was obliged to adopt those rates of the Chesapeake & Ohio to Richmond, Lynchburg and Norfolk which were then in effect. It also placed the same construction upon the 4th section which the Chesapeake & Ohio, together with most northern roads, had, and charged no more to the intermediate than to the distant point in either direction. This gave all stations upon the main line of the Norfolk & Western the same rate as Norfolk. The Southern came into this field of competition last of all. When that company determined to compete for this traffic it simply met the rates of the Chesapeake & Ohio and the Norfolk & Western which were already in effect, and this is all it has ever done. It has not reduced the Richmond or Lynchburg or Norfolk rate. It has not raised the Danville rate. It has in no way intensified the discrimination against Danville, but has simply left the situation where it found it. By entering this competitive field it did not injure Danville; to withdraw from it would not benefit Danville. The business is a source of some profit to the Southern Company; therefore that company should be allowed to continue in it.

The above is the claim of the Southern Railway Company defendant, as we understand it. The facts stated in that claim are for the most part correct. The Baltimore rate, owing to various competitive influences, was, previous to the construction of the Chesapeake & Ohio Railway, an extremely low rate. We find from the testimony in this case that the Chesapeake & Ohio determined to place Richmond and Norfolk upon an equality with Baltimore in the matter of rates, and that subsequently, upon the passage of the Interstate Commerce Act, it so interpreted the 4th section of that Act as to give to all intermediate points as low a rate as the more distant point. When the Norfolk & Western entered Richmond, Lynchburg and Norfolk it found this relation in rates in effect, and that relation has ever since been maintained. The Southern was the last competitor to enter this territory, and we find upon the testimony of Mr. Culp, its Traffic Manager, that the policy of that line has been to meet at Richmond, Lynchburg and Norfolk the rates made by other lines.

We do not find, as claimed by the Southern Railway, that the Baltimore rate has fixed the Richmond and Norfolk rate. Upon the other hand, these two rates have mutually interacted the one upon the other, and while the Baltimore rate has been subject to reductions by influences from the north as well as from the south, we think that the Norfolk rate may have operated to reduce the Baltimore rate quite as frequently as the reverse. Neither do we find, as claimed by this same defendant, that the Chesapeake & Ohio has been responsible all along for the Richmond, Lynchburg and Norfolk rates, and that the Norfolk & Western upon entering the field, and subsequently the Southern, have simply met those rates. These three lines of railway are in competition for this business, and there is no evidence which satisfies us that any one of them has been in the past, or will be in the future, entirely responsible for fluctuations in the competitive rates. * * * * * *

The Southern Railway Company was organized in July, 1894, for the purpose of effecting the consolidation of certain railway properties. As a result of that consolidation that company almost or quite from the first owned a through line from the Ohio river to Norfolk, as well as to Richmond and Lynchburg. Previous to this time the roads composing the Southern had not competed for western business to these three points, but the Southern decided at once to become such competitor, and has been since.

The lines of railway composing the Southern had, previous to the consolidation, formed a through route for the transportation of merchandise from New Orleans to Richmond, Lynchburg and Norfolk. It does not very clearly appear to what extent such lines north of Danville had engaged in traffic between northern cities and Lynchburg.

What has been said sufficiently states the competitive conditions existing at Richmond and Lynchburg as compared with Danville. There is, however, still another phase of this situation which should be especially referred to.

It has been already seen that the Chesapeake & Ohio, the Norfolk & Western, and Southern all compete for business from Louisville and Cincinnati to the three cities in question. It has been further noticed that the difference in rates on traffic originating north of the Ohio river is much greater than in case of traffic originating at Cincinnati & Louisville, although the competition between these rival lines is through Cincinnati & Louisville. The reason seems to be this:

In the making of rates between the West and the Atlantic seaboard the New York-Chicago rate is taken as a base. The rate from Chicago to Baltimore is a certain differential below that from Chicago to New York. Rates from various sections in the West to New York are a percentage of the Chicago rate. Thus, Louisville is a 100 per cent point, and the rate from there to New York or Baltimore is the same as Chicago. Cincinnati is an 87 per cent point, and the rate from Cincinnati would be 87 per cent of the rate from Chicago to Baltimore. Now, Richmond and Lynchburg take the Baltimore rate, and upon the rule above stated the rate from Cincinnati to Richmond and Lynchburg ought to be less than the rate from Louisville. It seems, however, that at some time in the past the lines leading from Louisville insisted upon making the same rate from that city as from Cincinnati. It further appears that the same lines, working probably through Southern territory, insisted that the Danville rate should approach quite nearly the Lynchburg rate on Louisville and Cincinnati business.

The rate from Chicago to Danville is made by adding to the Louisville and Cincinnati rate the local rate from Chicago to those cities; that is, traffic which has come from Chicago to Louisville pays exactly the same rate from Louisville to Danville as does traffic which originates at Louisville. The local first-class rate from Chicago to Louisville is 40 cents, which, added to the first-class rate from Louisville to Danville, makes a through rate of $1.08; but the rate from Chicago to Baltimore, first class, is 72 cents, and since Lynchburg takes the Baltimore rate the rate from Chicago to Lynchburg is also 72 cents. This rate of 72 cents is divided, from Chicago to the north bank of the Ohio river 23 cents, and from the river to Lynchburg 49 cents.

The testimony was that Danville merchants bought largely in the markets of Chicago and St. Louis, and but little in those of Cincinnati and Louisville, so that the Chicago and St. Louis rates are the ones which especially concern that city.

It will be seen from an examination of the foregoing facts that through rates to and from all directions, whether north, east, south, or west, are higher to Danville than to Richmond and Lynchburg. The complainants insist that this discrimination in favor of the two cities last named is most detrimental to the material interests of Danville.   *   *   *

It appears from the testimony that it has been possible to ship tobacco from Danville to Richmond, store it for a time at Richmond, and send it along to market upon the same rate that it could have been shipped from Danville itself in the first instance, although the first carriage from Danville to Richmond was by the Southern, and the final shipment from Richmond may have passed back through Danville over the same line.

The complainants insist that not only does this discrimination in freight rates cripple the business industries already located at Danville, but that it prevents the establishment of new industries at that point. . . .

The complainants further insist that, in addition to the specific injuries previously pointed out, the general effect is most baleful. This, as we have often remarked in previous cases, must also be true. The cost in Danville of everything into which the freight rate enters is more than in the favored localities, and unless there are some compensating circumstances the effect of this must be to decrease the value of property and to depress all kinds of business in that city.

Twenty years ago Danville was a town of some 3000 inhabitants. To-day it is a place of nearly 20,000. Most of this growth had taken place previous to the last ten years. In the whole period it has developed more than Lynchburg, but it is not at the present time as thriving as its rival. It will be remembered that Lynchburg only received the Richmond rate when the Chesapeake & Ohio obtained possession of the Richmond & Allegheny Railroad, about 1886. * * *

The Southern Railway was organized in 1894 for the purpose of consolidating certain railroad properties, and it has since its organization, from time to time, taken on additional properties. The lines which it now controls into Danville were originally built and operated by independent companies. . . . In 1886 or thereabouts the Richmond & Danville Company leased the Virginia Midland, which it continued to operate from then on until absorbed by the Southern. The complainants insist that previous to the lease of the Virginia Midland and while these roads were in competition for business, Danville enjoyed substantial equality in freight rates with Lynchburg and Richmond.

The Traffic Manager of the Southern Railway testified that he had been familiar with the rate situation in this vicinity since 1875, and that during that time rates had been uniformly higher to Danville than to either Richmond or Lynchburg. . . . Generally speaking the difference was greater than now exists in amount and perhaps equally great in percentage. Since 1887 the published rates to Danville have been higher by about the present degree than to Richmond and Lynchburg.

While this is true of the established rate, the testimony of numerous witnesses introduced by the complainants leaves as little doubt, and we find, that previous to 1886 the actual rate paid by Danville was not materially higher than that of its competitors, Lynchburg and Richmond. It is well understood that published rates previous to 1887 were not observed. Special rates, rebates, and all kinds of concessions to shippers were in those days the rule, not the exception; and we are satisfied that merchants at Danville then obtained much better rates in comparison with their competitors at Richmond and Lynchburg than they do to-day. It is not probable that these rates were in all cases equal. The average was probably higher, but the effect of any difference against Danville was not felt as it now is, for the reason that business is now transacted upon smaller margins than it then was. From about 1886, when there ceased to be effective competition, the rates were better maintained, and since then the business interests of Danville have suffered more from the effect of these discriminations.

The defendant Southern Railway insisted that, if compelled to reduce its rates at Danville, it must make corresponding reductions throughout its intermediate territory, and that the effect of this would be to seriously cripple its revenues. An examination of rates from the points in question to other points upon the lines of the Southern Railway reveals the fact that those rates are usually higher at the present time than the Danville rate. Rates from northern and eastern cities are considerably higher to Greensboro and Raleigh than to Danville, being first class from New York to Danville 66 cents, Raleigh 84 cents, and Greensboro 84 cents. The same is true of rates from New Orleans and from the West. Thus, the rate on molasses is 37 cents to Danville against 47 cents to Raleigh and 44 cents to Greensboro. The first-class rate from Chicago is $1.08 to Danville, and $1.33 to Raleigh and Greensboro. Flour from Chicago takes a rate of 19 cents to Lynchburg, 34 cents to Danville, and 43 cents to Raleigh and Greensboro. This is true with respect to rates from all directions in Southern Railway territory south and southwest of Danville. Traffic for Raleigh and Greensboro would not pass through Danville ordinarily, and need not in any event, but these towns are in the vicinity of Danville, and are in competition with that city in much the same way that Danville competes with Lynchburg; and there are many instances in which traffic from New Orleans and from the West bears a higher rate to points which are strictly intermediate than to Danville.

The rates of the Southern Railway are apparently adjusted largely upon the " basing point " system, which so generally prevails in territory south of the Ohio and east of the Mississippi rivers. This system has been often referred to and commented upon by the Commission, and need not be gone into here. As is well understood, the central idea of that system is the higher intermediate rate. There is nothing in this case to show what the effect upon the revenues of the Southern road would be if the rule contended for by the complainants were applied to all this intermediate territory, and those rates reduced to the level of Lynchburg and Richmond. It is certain, however, that such an application of the 4th section would result in a most sweeping reduction of rates, and would very seriously impair the income of the Southern Railway unless the volume of traffic was very materially increased; it might even go to the length stated by the Traffic Manager of that company, of entirely eliminating the profits accruing from the transaction of business in that territory. *　　*　　*　　*　　*　　*　　*

Conclusions

*　　*　　*　　*　　*　　*　　*　　*

As stated in the *St. Cloud Case*,[1] the question for this Commission is one of fact arising upon the whole situation. We are to consider the interest of the producing market, the consuming market and the carriers, and upon the whole to determine whether there is such a dissimilarity of circumstances and conditions as justifies the rates in question. In the case before us we have nothing to do with the market of production, for, so far as the testimony shows, there is no question as to what market should supply Lynchburg, Danville and the surrounding localities, nor what market should receive the products of these localities. It is simply a question of the avenues by which supplies shall be transported to and products carried from this territory, or, in other words, of competition between carriers serving the same markets.

We have held in complaints under the 4th section, that a case for the complainant was made out by the mere showing of the higher rate to the intermediate point, and that the defendant was thereupon required to justify these rates. In the present

[1] *Vide*, p. 297, *supra*.

instance the complainant has gone further, and has shown in the first instance the injurious effects which these discriminations inflict upon Danville. We may follow the same order, and inquire first whether Danville is actually injured, and to what extent, by the adjustment of rates which is complained of.

The testimony establishes as a matter of fact that the burden thereby imposed upon the complainants is a most serious one. The facts in this connection have been already stated and need not be repeated here. . . . The case appeals to us more strongly, perhaps, for the reason that Danville is a larger community than usually prefers complaints of this sort. It cannot be said to be a little village which has no right to expect to do business, for it is a city which in the past has done business and whose people desire to continue it. The complainants have clearly established the injurious effects which result to them from the obnoxious rates.

It does not follow from this alone that the rates in question are unjustifiable. Deserted warehouses and depreciated values are always sad objects to contemplate, but they often occur in the development of society; and if the avenues of commerce have so changed as to dry up the prosperity of this particular locality, the Interstate Commerce Law cannot grant relief, for that law, as has been often said, was not intended to hamper, but to promote, trade and commerce. We turn, therefore, to the justification of the defendant, for the purpose of ascertaining whether the hardship which is inflicted upon these complainants is, under all the circumstances, a reasonable one. As stated by the defendant that justification is this: Owing to competitive conditions the Baltimore rate from almost all directions is an extremely low one. When the Chesapeake & Ohio Railway was completed from Cincinnati to Norfolk the management of that property determined to put Richmond and Norfolk upon an equality with Baltimore. Subsequently, by the acquisition of the Richmond & Allegheny Railroad, Lynchburg came to be on the main line, and was given the benefit of the same rate. When the Norfolk & Western Railway was constructed to Lynchburg and Norfolk it found in effect and adopted this system of rate making. The Southern came last of all into the field of competition. It simply accepted the rates which it already found in effect at Lynchburg, Richmond and Norfolk. Its rate to Danville is a reasonable one. The rate to Lynchburg is unreasonably low, but yields to the Southern Company something above the actual cost of movement. By handling this traffic through Danville the rate to Danville is not changed. Danville is not therefore injured, and the Southern Railway is to an extent benefited.

The facts have been already stated in our findings of fact. The Baltimore rate is an extremely low one. The Chesapeake & Ohio did determine to put Richmond, Lynchburg and Norfolk upon the same basis with Baltimore. The Norfolk & Western did adopt the same policy. The Southern Railway did enter this competitive field last, and did at the outset meet the rates which it found in effect by the Chesapeake & Ohio and the Norfolk & Western. It is not true that the Baltimore rate has during all the time since the completion of the Chesapeake & Ohio determined the Richmond rate. Upon the contrary, the Baltimore and the Norfolk rate have mutually affected each other. Competition has at times forced down the Norfolk rate below that of Baltimore, and at times *vice versa*. The resulting rate has always been a low one as compared with other rates. It cannot be found as a fact that the Southern Railway has simply accepted the rates named by its competitors.

The argument urged by the defendant is not new. It is the theory upon which every traffic manager justifies in every case the making of the lower rate to the more distant point. If proof of the facts upon which that deduction rests were a sufficient justification, there are few, if any, violations of the 4th section which could not be justified.

That argument omits, however, one most important factor, namely, the interest of the public. This, as well as the interest of the carrier, must be considered. The Southern road insists in this case that Danville would not be benefited if it should withdraw from Richmond, Lynchburg and Norfolk business. But this cannot be affirmed. The desire to transact business at the more distant point is a continual inducement to the Southern road to obtain an equitable adjustment of rates between the intermediate and the more distant point. If the Southern can only do business at Lynchburg by procuring a just relation of rates between Lynchburg and Danville, it becomes for the interest of the Southern road to secure that adjustment of rates, and it will use all its enormous power to that end. To-day the Southern Railway constructs its Danville tariffs with reference to its own interest alone. An order requiring a proper relation of rates between Danville and Lynchburg as the condition of transacting business at Lynchburg compels that company to consider the interest of Danville as well as its own.   *   *

In considering this case it may be well to refer separately to the rates from each direction involved, and first the rates from New York.

The transportation from New York to Norfolk is the same whether traffic is destined to Lynchburg or Danville. The distance from Norfolk to Danville is 205 miles by the Atlantic & Danville Railway, which is the direct line. For the year ending June 30, 1899, that road was operated by an independent company, and during that year its gross receipts were $2083.97 per mile, and its operating expenses 71.11 per cent of its gross earnings. . . .

As a part of the Southern system that line will undoubtedly carry much more traffic from Norfolk to Danville than it did as an independent line. Still, it can hardly be said that the above divisions afford an excessive return for the service rendered. Whether the entire rate from New York be considered, or the rail division from Norfolk to Danville, the present rate can hardly be said to be extravagantly high; neither is it extravagantly low.

There are three lines of railway by which this traffic can reach the city of Danville: The Atlantic & Danville, from Norfolk, the Richmond & Danville from Richmond, and the Lynchburg & Danville from Lynchburg. Previous to the acquisition of the Atlantic & Danville by the Southern, that company, as we understand the testimony, carried traffic from Norfolk to Danville by a fourth route, which was from Norfolk to Greensboro,

270 miles, and from Greensboro to Danville, 48 miles. If these routes were all independent lines, and all competing bona fide without agreement among themselves, as to the Danville rate, we think the effect must be, and ought to be, to give Danville a rate not much above that of Lynchburg.

As we have already seen, the direct line from Norfolk to Lynchburg is by the Norfolk & Western, and the distance, 204 miles, is almost identical with the short line distance to Danville. Lynchburg is upon the main line of both the Norfolk & Western and the Chesapeake & Ohio, whose location is such, and the volume of whose traffic is such, that they can perhaps afford to carry freight at a lower price than the Danville lines. On the whole we are impressed that legitimate competitive conditions would entitle Lynchburg to a somewhat lower rate than Danville on traffic from the North.

We turn now to rates from New Orleans. It has been seen that the Norfolk & Western, the Chesapeake & Ohio, and the Southern all carry this traffic into Lynchburg. Such traffic generally leaves New Orleans by either the Illinois Central, the Queen & Crescent, or the Louisville & Nashville. There are, however, numerous intermediate routes over which such traffic may pass. All traffic delivered by the Southern necessarily passes through Danville and 66 miles beyond to Lynchburg. The shortest line from New Orleans to Lynchburg is *via* the Louisville & Nashville to Montgomery, the Atlanta & West Point to Atlanta and the Southern to Lynchburg, distance 971 miles. The distance by this line to Danville is 905 miles. The shortest line by the Norfolk & Western, of which the Southern is not a part, is from New Orleans to Norton, Va., *via* the Louisville & Nashville, and from Norton to Lynchburg *via* the Norfolk & Western, the distance here being 1265 miles. The shortest route by the Chesapeake & Ohio is 1326 miles, being from New Orleans over the Illinois Central to Louisville, and from there by the Chesapeake & Ohio. As will be seen by referring to the findings of fact there are several routes by which the distance is less than 1265 miles, in all of which the Southern is an important link.

Taking now, for the purposes of comparison, the short line *via* the Southern, the short line *via* the Norfolk & Western, and the short line *via* the Chesapeake & Ohio, we find that sugar in car loads is carried from New Orleans to Lynchburg at the following rates per ton per mile:

> *via* the Southern 6.59 mills;
> *via* the Norfolk & Western 4.91 mills;
> *via* the Chesapeake & Ohio 4.82 mills.

Upon the same traffic to Danville the Southern receives 9.49 mills.

Ordinarily the initial carrier makes the rate. In this case the Louisville & Nashville, Queen & Crescent, and Illinois Central, being the initial carriers, are without doubt largely responsible for the rate to Lynchburg, while the Southern, being the only carrier which enters Danville, can control the rate to that point. In fixing the rate the initial carrier would consult its own interest by obtaining as long a haul as possible. By the Norfolk & Western route, above referred to, the Louisville & Nashville obtains a haul of 1003 miles from New Orleans to Norton, while the Norfolk & Western has a haul of only 262 miles. Other things being equal, the Louisville & Nashville would carry New Orleans traffic for Lynchburg by this route. These competitive conditions, this bidding for business *via* the different lines entering Lynchburg, have undoubtedly tended to force down the Lynchburg rate.

While we are hardly prepared to say upon the testimony in this case that the rate from New Orleans to Danville upon sugar, molasses, coffee and rice is unreasonable when considered in and of itself, we are strongly of impression that it may be. We certainly do not find that it is reasonable, and in view of the rates in which the Southern road participates by various routes, and the rates which its competitors make upon this same traffic by other lines, those rates must be grossly unreasonable.

So far as the testimony shows, and so far as we have any understanding of the matter, here is no competition of contending markets. With respect to this traffic from New Orleans,

Lynchburg is upon no great thoroughfare which in its struggle for competitive business beyond gives to it an unduly low rate. There is nothing except the mere competition between several different lines of railway, and yet that competition has brought it about that merchandise is carried for the inhabitants and merchants of Lynchburg at an average rate per ton per mile of just about one half what the Southern receives for the same service when rendered for the inhabitants and merchants of Danville, but 66 miles distant, and that, too, although the Southern carries this traffic through Danville under exactly the same physical conditions for Lynchburg as when it is destined for Danville itself. We very much question whether in serving these two competitive localities competition between carriers should be allowed to have any such unreasonable and unjust effect as this.

Rates from the West to Danville and Lynchburg exhibit some peculiar features. It will be remembered that, treating the Cincinnati, New Orleans & Texas Pacific as a part of the Southern system, both the Chesapeake & Ohio and the Southern reach Louisville and Nashville over their own lines. The Norfolk & Western reaches both these points by its connections. These three lines, therefore, are competitors for traffic between Cincinnati and Louisville on the west, and Lynchburg and Danville on the east. By the Southern route traffic passes through Danville to Lynchburg; by the two other routes it passes through Lynchburg to Danville.

By referring to the findings of fact it will be seen that the distance by the Southern to Danville is considerably greater than by either the Norfolk & Western, or the Chesapeake & Ohio to Lynchburg. It will also be remembered that both the Norfolk & Western and the Chesapeake & Ohio transact a large through business both for export and domestic consumption *via* Lynchburg, and that Lynchburg takes the same rate which is granted to all this competitive business. An examination of the rates themselves in effect from Cincinnati and Louisville to Danville and Lynchburg, respectively, shows that there is no very extravagant difference in favor of Lynchburg upon class rates. The widest difference seems to be made upon grain and flour. We hardly think it can be said that the rates from these points to Danville are in the main unreasonably high when considered of themselves, if it is possible to measure a rate by any such standard.

Traffic from Chicago, St. Louis and other points similarly situated comes, or may come, to these three lines at either Cincinnati or Louisville, and the rate through either one of those points must determine the rate through all other points. The distance from points beyond Louisville and Cincinnati by these competitive lines is the same respectively as from those two cities, and the cost of movement is substantially the same whether the traffic originates at Louisville or Cincinnati, or whether it comes to these lines at those points. We might naturally expect, therefore, that the same difference in rate to Lynchburg and Danville would obtain in the case of traffic from beyond as in case of traffic which originates at Louisville or Cincinnati. Such is not, however, the fact. Traffic originating at Chicago, St. Louis, and all corresponding territory takes a much lower rate proportionately to Lynchburg than does Cincinnati and Louisville traffic. Thus, the first-class rate from Cincinnati is to Lynchburg 62 cents, to Danville 68 cents, a difference of but 6 cents per hundred pounds. From St. Louis the same class rate is to Lynchburg 84 cents, to Danville $1.06, a difference of 22 cents per hundred pounds. From Chicago the first-class rate to Lynchburg is 72 cents, while the corresponding rate to Danville is $1.08, a difference of 36 cents against Danville. In case of those commodities which are most consumed the difference is even more marked. Thus, the flour rate from Cincinnati to Lynchburg is 16 cents, and to Danville 22 cents per hundred, a difference of 6 cents; while from Chicago it is 19 cents to Lynchburg, and 34 cents to Danville, a difference of 15 cents. Since Danville desires to purchase largely in the markets of St. Louis, Chicago, and corresponding territory, it follows that these rates are the ones in which that community is particularly interested.

The reason for this discrimination has been fully stated in the findings of fact. It arises out of the rule that Lynchburg shall take the Baltimore rate. The Danville rate is in all cases made by adding the local rate from Chicago to the Ohio river to the Cincinnati or Louisville rate from the Ohio river, while the Lynchburg rate is determined by the Baltimore rate from the locality in question. On traffic from Chicago to Lynchburg the carrier from Chicago to the Ohio river receives 23 cents, and the carrier from the Ohio river to Lynchburg 49 cents. On the same traffic destined to Danville the carrier north of the Ohio river receives 40 cents, while the carrier from that river to Danville receives 68 cents. If the traffic, whether originating at Cincinnati or Louisville, reaches Danville *via* Lynchburg, the Southern exacts its full local rate of 36 cents. The divisions above stated are those of the first-class rate, but other rates are divided upon the same basis. Broadly stated, carriers from Chicago and St. Louis prorate upon business to all points on the Norfolk & Western Railroad. To all points in territory south of the Norfolk & Western Railroad there is no prorating, but each carrier receives the sum of its locals to and from the Ohio river.   *   *   *   *   *   *   *   *

This system of rate making into Southern territory by adding together the sums of the locals to and from the Ohio river is not before us as a general scheme in this case. We are only considering it with reference to the city of Danville, and with reference to that city we hold it to be utterly unreasonable. Danville is situated but 66 miles south of Lynchburg. It is in competition with Lynchburg. Now, these carriers have no right to put in effect a system of rates which prohibits the city of Danville from transacting business in competition with the city of Lynchburg. Whether or not they may make their rates into Southern territory in this manner is something about which we express no opinion, but if they desire to do that they must so adjust their rates in passing from Norfolk & Western to Southern territory as not to annihilate the city of Danville. They have no right to put that locality between the upper and nether millstone of these two schemes of rate making. Rates to Danville must be adjusted with relation to rates to competitive localities like Lynchburg, and the carriers from the point of origin to destination should prorate in these rates if they participate in either Lynchburg or Danville business.

Lynchburg is situated but 66 miles from Danville. Danville rates from most western territory and from New Orleans base upon Lynchburg; that is, they are made by adding to the Lynchburg rate the Southern local rate from Lynchburg to Danville. We do not think that the rate to Danville upon this through business from New Orleans or from the West ought to be constructed upon that basis. Whatever competitive conditions may be at Lynchburg, Danville to some extent should enjoy the benefit of those competitive conditions by reason of its proximity, for by reason of that same proximity it is thrown into competition with Lynchburg.

This traffic is in no sense local traffic, but is in every sense through traffic. There is no loading at Lynchburg, no billing at Lynchburg, no soliciting of traffic at Lynchburg. It is in fact a through shipment, and to some extent Danville should enjoy the benefit of that fact. We do not mean that the Southern Railway may not exact from the Norfolk & Western or the Chesapeake & Ohio a division upon this business when it moves by way of Lynchburg, which is equal to its full local rate. Perhaps it may do that in the protection of its own line. About that we are called upon to express, and we do express, no opinion. What we say is that in determining the Danville rate, the Southern Railway, which dominates that situation, must recognize the fact that this business is through business upon which Lynchburg, a competitor of Danville, enjoys a low through rate, and upon which Danville itself is entitled to a through rate.

If the various railroad properties leading from Danville north to the line of the Norfolk & Western and Chesapeake & Ohio were operated to-day by their original builders there would be three independent avenues by which these northern roads could obtain access to the city of Danville. These lines, however, have all been absorbed by one corporation. That corporation controls every line leading to the city of Danville, with the unimportant exception of the Danville & Western, and by virtue of that fact it is able to exact, as it does, its full local rate from Lynchburg to Danville.

As already remarked, the Southern Railway is the consolidation of numerous independent railroad properties. It has become through this process of growth a great railroad system embracing to-day a mileage of more than 6000 miles. In this operation properties which were worthless have been put together to form a valuable whole. The physical condition of those properties has been enormously improved. The facilities afforded to their patrons have been increased. The whole territory involved must be benefited by this amalgamation, so far as its physical service is concerned.

This enterprise is a perfectly legitimate one. The men who have conceived and executed it are entitled to a fair return upon the money which has been actually invested in it. They are entitled, in addition, to a reasonable profit upon the ability to conceive and execute a project of this sort. They have no right to exact a return upon an extravagant capitalization, but whatever has honestly and in good faith and reasonably gone into this enterprise should be protected.

On the other hand, the people in this territory are entitled to protection. The Southern Railway, by virtue of the fact that it has obtained possession of and now controls the avenues of communication by rail between the city of Danville and the outside world, has no right to deprive that community of the competitive advantages which the enterprise of its citizens in one way or another had secured, and upon the strength of which business conditions have grown up. It must recognize the geographical position and the commercial importance of the city of Danville.

We fully realize the serious consequences to the Southern Railway of any reduction in its Danville rate, or in corresponding rates to other points. Such reduction means a deduction from its net revenues. As applied to the volume of business handled at Danville alone, such reduction must be very considerable, — it cannot from the testimony in this case be determined just how considerable.

Upon the other hand we think that as an offset to this the Southern would obtain some additional revenue by virtue of the increased amount of business at Danville. The ability to do business at that point depends largely upon the freight rate. The amount of traffic handled in and out of Danville is determined by the volume of business transacted there, — by the prosperity of the community. Whether the Southern Railway shall reduce its rates to the city of Danville with the hope of thereby stimulating an additional flow of traffic is purely a question of policy with which this Commission has ordinarily nothing to do ; but when we are commanded to consider the interests of all parties, we must consider what the probable effect of our order will be upon the carrier interested. In this view we are bound to inquire what effect it will have upon the volume of traffic, and the consequent increase or decrease of revenue. Any development at Lynchburg is necessarily shared by the Southern with the Norfolk & Western and the Chesapeake & Ohio, whereas any corresponding development at Danville belongs to the Southern Railway Company alone. We feel that a reduction in the Danville rate might ultimately be for the advantage of this defendant.

Under our original interpretation of the 4th section the duty of this Commission in determining whether that section had been violated was a comparatively simple one. We were confined to inquiring whether competition between carriers not subject to the Act to Regulate Commerce influenced or controlled the rate at the more distant point. If it did, that created the dissimilar circumstances and conditions. Now, however, we are bidden to examine the whole situation, and to determine whether, taking all things into account, the conditions which surround that situation justify the charging of the higher rate at the intermediate point. It is impossible to apply to the solution of that question any definite rule. Each case has to be considered upon its own peculiar facts. It is difficult in every case to determine what ought to be done in justice to the public and to the carrier, and it is even more difficult to state the reasons for that determination. We have given this question the best attention we could. It is an extremely perplexing one, but it must be decided, and, without attempting to state the reasons more fully than has been already done, our conclusion is this :

We think that under all the circumstances and conditions the rate to Lynchburg may properly be somewhat lower than the rate to Danville. We do not think that the present difference in rates is justifiable; or, in other words, we do not think that the circumstances and conditions justify the rates now in force. It is our opinion that rates from northern and eastern cities to Danville and rates from New Orleans upon the commodities mentioned in the complaint to Danville should not exceed those to Lynchburg by more than 10 per cent, and that rates between Danville and the West should not exceed those between Lynchburg and the West by more than 15 per cent. This also applies to the rate on tobacco from Danville to Louisville. It may well be called outrageous to impose upon the chief industry of Danville a rate from Danville to Louisville 15 cents above the rate from Lynchburg to Louisville, when the difference in rates upon that class of merchandise in the reverse direction is only $2\frac{1}{2}$ cents.   *   *   *   *   *   *   *

[No order was issued by the Commission at its first hearing; but ten months later, in November, 1900, after a rehearing of the case, a new opinion was rendered, concluding as follows. — ED.]

The Southern Railway shows that in the year 1899 it earned nothing upon its $120,000,000 of common stock, and urges that any order of this Commission which depletes the revenues of that company deprives the owners of this stock of their property without due process of law.

This common stock was issued as a part of a reorganization scheme under which the Southern Railway Company came into existence. It does not appear that the persons to whom this stock was originally issued ever paid one dollar in actual value for it. It simply appears that the stock is outstanding. This is not enough. Something more is needed when a claim of this kind is set up than the mere fact of the existence and amount of capitalization. It does not rest in the whim of a reorganization committee in Wall Street to impose a perpetual tax upon that whole southern country. In the year 1899 the Southern Railway earned net about 4 per cent on $40,000 a mile of the mileage of its entire system. That system extends, as a rule, through sparsely populated territories; no difficult and expensive engineering feats were involved in its construction, nor has it in proportion to its extent many expensive terminals. It will hardly be claimed that the cost of reproducing that property in its present state would equal $40,000 a mile.

The Southern Railway is of great benefit to the territory which it serves, and the money invested in that enterprise is entitled to the most careful protection; but the property of the citizens of Danville is just as sacred as are the securities of that company. No order should be made by this Commission which will deprive it of a dollar in revenue to which it is justly entitled, but we find nothing in its financial condition, as shown by the testimony, to prohibit a change of rates which will reduce to a limited extent its receipts.

This is not a question of revenue altogether. It is a question, to an extent, of right and wrong. The beggar upon the street has no right to steal merely because he is hungry; nor has the Southern Railway a right to do an unlawful act simply because it needs revenue. The state of its revenues has a bearing upon the lawfulness of the act, but is not conclusive.

Railway managers are prone to assume that, in the adjustment of their rates, only the interest of their own properties must be considered. Mr. Culp was asked what weight he gave to the interest of the city of Danville, to its proximity to Lynchburg, to the fact that it was a competitor of Lynchburg, and his reply in effect was, none. This is neither just nor lawful. Railways are public servants and subject to public control. In the exercise of that control the public has enacted that they shall not unduly discriminate in favor of one locality against another, and that they shall not charge more for the short than for the long haul under similar circumstances and conditions. The Supreme Court has declared that in determining what are similar circumstances and conditions, and what is undue discrimination, reference must be had to the interest of all parties, not merely the railway. After considering all the circumstances and conditions in the present case we have sustained the complaint of the city of Danville, and have indicated in a general way those changes in rates which should be made. If upon an actual trial, in good faith, the effect of those changes upon the revenue of the Southern Railway should prove to be more serious than anticipated, we might modify the opinion already expressed, but there is nothing in the testimony presented upon this motion for rehearing which leads us to do so now, and the motion is denied.

No order will be made until December 31, 1900. If the Southern Railway signifies by that time its disposition to endeavor to make this readjustment, such further time will be allowed as may be reasonably necessary. Otherwise an order will then issue in the premises.

* * * * * * * *

XVII

TRANSCONTINENTAL FREIGHT RATES

THE ST. LOUIS BUSINESS MEN'S LEAGUE CASE[1]

PROUTY, *Commissioner:*

The Business Men's League of St. Louis, the complainant in this proceeding, is an incorporated body whose membership represents some two thousand persons, firms and corporations engaged in business in St. Louis and that vicinity. The complaint is that the defendant carriers unjustly discriminate by their tariff rates against St. Louis and other jobbing houses of the middle west, and it is alleged that this discrimination is effected in the following ways:

1. By making a lower rate to Pacific Coast terminals than to points upon the coast which are farther east, and through which traffic must pass in reaching the terminal points.

2. By making a blanket rate from all territory east of the Missouri river to Pacific Coast destinations.

3. By undue and unreasonable differences between car-load and less than car-load rates, by an unjust system of varied commodity rates, and by unreasonably refusing to permit shipment of mixed car loads.   *   *   *   *   *

The complaint puts in issue the system of rate making between the territory east of the Missouri river and Pacific Coast points; and in order to understand the questions raised it is necessary to state briefly what that system is. Only west-bound rates are involved.

Certain points upon the Pacific Coast, of which Los Angeles, San Francisco and Portland may be taken as illustrative

---

[1] Decided November 17, 1902. Interstate Commerce Reports, Vol. IX, pp. 318–372. In editing, the issues concerning mixed car loads as well as details of cost of less than car-load service have been omitted for simplification. These matters as well as transcontinental rates in general are discussed in Ripley's Railroads: Rates and Regulation. (Index.)

examples, are designated as " Pacific Coast terminals," and rates to these points are known as " terminal rates." There are " terminal class rates," the western classification being used. There are also " terminal commodity rates," and the great bulk of the traffic moves under such latter rates, over two thousand articles being named. Both class and commodity terminal rates are the same from a given eastern point to all Pacific Coast terminals.

Stations upon the direct line by which traffic from the east reaches a terminal are called " intermediate " points. Rates to such points are made by adding to the terminal rate the local rate from the terminal back to such intermediate point, whether the rate in question be class or commodity. Thus, Reno, Nevada, is upon the main line of the Central Pacific, 155 miles east of Sacramento, California, a terminal. The terminal rate on zinc slab from Chicago to Sacramento is, C. L. (Car Load) $.80 ; L. C. L. (Less than Car Load) $1.10. The local rate from Sacramento to Reno is C. L. $.78, L. C. L. $.87, making the rate from Chicago to Reno, C. L. $1.58, L. C. L. $1.98.

Class rates are named to intermediate points which serve as maxima to those points ; i.e., when the intermediate rate is less than the terminal plus the local back, the lower rate prevails. As an illustration of this we may take the rate on sheet zinc from Chicago to Reno. The terminal rate is higher than on zinc slab, being C. L. $1.25 and L. C. L. $1.75. Adding the local back from Sacramento we have a rate of C. L. $2.03 ; L. C. L. $2.62. But sheet zinc in less than car loads under the western classification is 4th class, and in car loads 5th class ; the intermediate class rates from Chicago to Reno are 4th class, $2.10 and 5th class $1.85. These rates apply as maxima, and therefore the rate on sheet zinc from Chicago to Reno is C. L. $1.85 and L. C. L. $2.10. The rate on zinc slab, which takes the same classification as sheet zinc, but a lower terminal rate, is made by the combination, while that on sheet zinc is limited by the intermediate class rate. There are also a few intermediate commodity rates which apply as maxima, and have the same effect in establishing the point to which the combination of the terminal and local back will apply.

It will be seen that under this system of rate making the rate upon the Pacific Coast increases as we proceed farther east, or as the distance decreases, until limited by the intermediate class or commodity rate. Rates are uniformly higher at the nearer intermediate point through which the traffic passes than at the more distant terminal. . . .

The complaint also attacked the method of rate making from territory east of the Missouri river to the Pacific Coast, and this point was earnestly pressed by the complainants. At the present time these rates are made upon what is known as the blanket system; that is, rates from all that territory are the same. The first-class rate for instance from St. Louis to San Francisco is $3 per hundred pounds and the same rate obtains from New York. . . . Commodity rates follow the same rule, and in general it may be stated that . . . all common points east of the Missouri river take the same rate to Pacific Coast terminals, and to those points which base upon Pacific Coast terminals. This so-called blanket system of rate making is vigorously attacked by the complainants, who insist that what are termed " graded " rates should obtain; that is, that the rate should increase toward the Atlantic seaboard; and as one reason for this, it is asserted that such graded rates were until recently in effect.

There is no means of determining exactly what these rates were previous to 1887, when carriers were first required by law to publish and file their tariffs. An examination of the first transcontinental tariff filed with the Commission shows that graded rates were then in effect. By that tariff the first-class rate was, from the Missouri river $4, from the Mississippi $4.50, from Chicago points $4.70; while east of Chicago rates were apparently made by combination upon Chicago. This tariff seems to have been in the nature of an experiment, and very frequent changes were made between that date and January 1, 1889, when a tariff was put into effect which continued substantially the same, so far at least as these gradations were concerned, down to 1894. By this tariff the following differentials or grades were made : from the Missouri to the Mississippi 20 cents; from the Mississippi to Chicago 20 cents; from

Chicago to Cincinnati 5 cents ; from Cincinnati to Pittsburg 5 cents ; and from Pittsburg to New York 20 cents. Under West-bound Tariff No. T 1, effective April 11, 1893, which continued in effect until the rate war of 1894, the first-class rate was as follows: from the Missouri River $3 ; from the Mississippi $3.20 ; from Chicago $3.40; from Cincinnati $3.45 ; from Pitts-burg $3.50, and from New York $3.70. The same principle was applied to commodity rates. . . . Previous to 1894 the principle of graded rates was uniformly recognized in transcon-tinental tariffs.

In the beginning of that year, owing to conditions which will be hereafter detailed,[1] a transcontinental rate war occurred which lasted actively for two years, and the effects of which continued for some time afterwards. One of the first results of this disturbance was to abolish the graded rate ; first as far east as Chicago, and later all the way to the Atlantic coast. Under the tariff of June 25, 1898, which is said to have restored trans-continental rates to a normal condition, this blanket system was retained.

The contention of the complainants in this respect is in favor of the middle west as against the Atlantic seaboard. Since St. Louis is more than one thousand miles nearer San Francisco than New York its business interests insist that it ought to be given the advantage of that difference in distance. The defend-ants justify the present tariff upon the ground of water com-petition, and the facts bearing upon that issue will be stated later. No particular industry is complaining. The testimony tended to show and we find that since 1894, when graded rates were first abolished and the blanket system put in effect, the middle west has been steadily gaining in its sales upon the Pa-cific Coast in comparison with the Atlantic seaboard. Pacific Coast jobbers now buy much more extensively in the middle west than they did five or ten years ago. Middle west jobbers sell more upon the Pacific Coast than they did formerly. It was said that at least 60 per cent of the goods consumed upon the Pacific Coast, which originate in the east, came from points

[1] P. 443, *infra.*

west of Buffalo and Pittsburg. This gain of the middle west in Pacific Coast business seems to be due mainly to the increase of manufacturing in that section, and in a measure to the fact that middle west jobbers and manufacturers have worked Pacific Coast territory with more vigor and persistence than their eastern competitors. It will be observed, moreover, in the subsequent statement of the case, that freight rates from 1894 to 1898 were such as to stimulate business from the middle west; and it should be still further noted that while the terminal rate is blanketed from the Missouri river, the " intermediate " class rates in all cases, and intermediate commodity rates in many instances, are still graded. The first-class intermediate rate to California points under the present tariff is : from the Missouri river $3.50, from the Mississippi $3.70, from Chicago $3.90 ; while from points east of Chicago the rate seems to be made by a combination upon Chicago. The effect of this is to give the Missouri river an advantage over the Mississippi and Chicago in all territory covered by the intermediate rate, and to virtually prohibit business from points east of Chicago in that territory.

The most serious complaint is addressed to the alleged discrimination against eastern jobbers in favor of Pacific Coast jobbers. By eastern jobbers are now meant all those located east of the Missouri river, although it does not appear that any considerable business is transacted by jobbing houses east of Chicago. The tariff complained of is that of June 25, 1898, and the above discrimination is alleged to be effected by making too wide a difference between car loads and less than car loads, and by applying a scheme of varied commodity rates which prevents the shipping of different articles of a similar character in the same package, and the combining of similar articles in car loads.

It is very difficult to state in a comprehensive way the extent of the difference in rates applicable to car-load and less than car-load shipments. The western classification places many articles in the 4th class when shipped in less than car loads, and in the 5th class when shipped in car loads. The difference between 4th and 5th class rates is 30 cents from the Missouri river and 25 cents from the Mississippi river and points east. It has already been stated that the great bulk of transcontinental traffic moves upon commodity rates. An examination of the west-bound commodity tariff shows that 2219 articles so move, of which 922 have both car-load and less than car-load rates; 835 take the same rate both car-load and less than car-load, while 462 are provided with car-load rates only. Of the 922 articles taking both car-load and less than car-load rates, the differential is in very many instances 50 cents per 100 pounds. There are 152 instances in which that difference is less and 29 in which it is greater than 50 cents. In case of the 462 articles which take only a car-load commodity rate, any less than car-load movement is under the class rate, and this produces a differential which is very much greater, being in some instances more than $3.00, in almost no instance less than $1.00 per 100 pounds, and making a less than car-load rate, which is in almost every instance more than double the car-load rate. It was said by several witnesses for the complainants that the differential would average 50 cents per 100 pounds. This was probably intended to refer to the traffic in which the witness was interested, and it seems probable that, as applied to the transportation involved in this proceeding, that may be a fair average. . . .

It is much more important to understand the manner in which these differentials discriminate against the eastern wholesaler, and the extent of that discrimination.

The great bulk of manufactured articles consumed upon the Pacific Coast is produced in the east. Whether these commodities are wholesaled by the Pacific Coast jobber or by the middle west jobber the shipment is ordinarily in car loads from the factory to the warehouse of the jobber and in less than car loads from thence to the retailer. Of rail shipments from eastern factories by Pacific Coast jobbers at least 90 per cent goes in car-load lots and a considerable portion of the balance are emergency orders which require quick delivery. Upon the other hand, testimony showed that the eastern jobber could distribute to the retailer in car loads only to a very limited extent. When it is remembered that the warehouse of the Pacific Coast jobber is located at a terminal point, and that the rate from the east to the intermediate point is made by adding the local from this terminal point back to the intermediate point, it will be seen that the wholesaler upon the Pacific Coast has the advantage of the wholesaler in the east by the difference between the car-load and less than car-load rate. This advantage is important just in proportion as the value of the goods per hundred pounds, or more properly the margin of profit per hundred pounds, is greater or less.

A concrete illustration will make this clear, and for that purpose we may take bar iron. The rate on this commodity from the east to Pacific Coast terminals is C. L. 75 cents, L. C. L. $1.25. Assume now some intermediate point to which the local rate from the terminal is 50 cents L. C. L. The Pacific Coast jobber pays in freight upon a hundred pounds of iron delivered to the retailer at that point 75 cents to his warehouse and 50 cents local, in all, $1.25 ; while his eastern competitor pays on the L. C. L. shipment from his warehouse $1.75. This gives the Pacific Coast jobber a clear advantage of 50 cents in the freight rate at all points which base upon the terminal point. The testimony of the complainants tended to show, nor was it denied by the defendants, that the profit to the jobber in the handling of bar iron is less than 50 cents per hundred pounds. Unless, therefore, there be some compensating advantage to the eastern jobber he is by this differential prohibited from wholesaling this commodity to retailers upon the Pacific Coast when his shipment from the east is in less than car loads.   *   *

What is true of bar iron is also true of most classes of heavy hardware, so called, which include most kinds of manufactured iron in its simpler forms, as sheet iron, corrugated iron, nails, pipe, horseshoes and in general any form of hardware where the cost of manufacture has not added very materially to the price of the raw material. It also appeared that the same thing was true of some of the more bulky articles among drugs and medicines, paints and oils, stationary supplies, wagon material, plumbers' supplies and some other lines, with respect to which the differential often exceeded and generally approximated the profit per hundred pounds to the wholesaler. The testimony of retailers upon the Pacific Coast was to the effect that after the putting in of the tariff of June 25, 1898, they were unable to buy many of the heavier articles from eastern jobbers. We think it appears, and we find, that with respect to many of the more bulky articles above named the differential is prohibitive against the eastern wholesaler.

While, however, this is true of many heavier articles, it is not true of the greater number of commodities in which the eastern wholesaler deals. In case of the higher priced commodities the profit per hundred pounds is much greater than the differential. When the tariff complained of took effect the Simmons Hardware Company determined to equalize the disadvantage which its customers incurred by making a freight allowance of 50 cents per hundred pounds. At first this allowance was paid upon all articles, but it soon became evident that there were certain articles which, including the freight allowance, were handled at actual loss, and that company very soon ceased to pay freight allowances upon these commodities. The vice president testified that these commodities were the fifteen following: Shot, bar lead, grindstones, nails, wire, rope, anvils, sheet zinc, sheet steel, horseshoes, sheet iron, staples, wire staples, small chains. Except so far as these articles can be shipped in car loads, either straight or combined, they cannot be wholesaled from the east upon the Pacific Coast. It was claimed that these heavier articles were usually staple commodities, and that the inability to handle them was a serious handicap upon the eastern jobber, since the retailer preferred to patronize that concern which could supply all his wants.   *   *   *   *   *   *   *

The jobbing business of the Pacific Coast is transacted under peculiar conditions. As already said, the supplies of the jobber are almost entirely drawn from the east and middle west. Jobbing houses are situated mainly upon the coast, and these supplies are therefore taken to the coast and from thence sent back into the interior. Owing to the method by which rates are made, it necessarily follows that the territory to which the coast jobber can distribute is limited. It has been seen that the "intermediate" rate limits the territory within which the rate to intermediate points is made by building up upon the terminal rate, and it is evident that as soon as this limit is passed going towards the east the Pacific Coast jobber is at a disadvantage in the freight rate. This limit is not the same with respect to all commodities. In case of sheet zinc, as we have already seen, it is but 155 miles, while in some few instances the combination extends back from the coast a thousand miles, possibly farther. Nor does the line of demarcation so fixed exactly correspond with the actual business limit, since the jobber can only operate in territory accessible to most of the articles in which he deals. The distance towards the east which is open to the jobber upon the Pacific Coast varies somewhat in different lines of merchandise, but generally speaking it is about the 115th meridian, some three or four hundred miles from the coast. It was claimed by the defendants, and not seriously denied by the complainants, that east of this line the territory was exclusively occupied by the eastern wholesaler, except in case of some few articles originating upon the Pacific Coast.

This scheme of rate making also limits the territory of the individual jobber upon the Pacific Coast north and south as well as east. Rates from eastern originating points are the same to all terminals. Rates to interior points are made by adding the local rate to the nearest terminal. It follows therefore that the jobber located at some terminal point like San Francisco, as he goes north or south, very soon enters the territory of some other terminal point, like Portland or Los Angeles, in which his local rate is greater than that of his competitor located at such terminal. The effect is to draw a series of circles with each terminal point as a center within the circumference of which the jobber located at the terminal point has the advantage of all others.

Not only does this confine the territory within which a particular Pacific Coast jobber can compete upon even terms with some other Pacific Coast jobber, but it also limits the territory north and south within which the Pacific Coast jobber has the advantage of his eastern competitor. Less than car-load rates from the east are the same to interior points no matter upon what terminal a particular point may base, and it soon happens, therefore, that the less than car-load rate to such point is lower than the rate arrived at by combining the car-load rate to the terminal point and the local rate from that point. Take San Francisco as an example. Nominally, rates to San Francisco are the same as to other Pacific Coast terminals. Owing to its superior shipping facilities as a seaport it probably enjoys some actual advantage in the matter of the rate. When, however, the jobber attempts to distribute from San Francisco, he finds all around him terminal points through which he must operate, Marysville distant upon the north 142 miles, Sacramento upon the east 90 miles, Stockton to the southeast 103 miles and San José to the south 50 miles. Now, the rate to almost any interior point outside this cordon of terminals is made by adding the local from these points, while the San Francisco jobber must pay the local from San Francisco itself. This operates to materially decrease the advantage which the San Francisco wholesaler would otherwise possess. But still further, if he attempts to go farther north he very soon reaches territory where the rate bases upon Portland and where his combined car-load and less than car-load is higher than the less than car-load rate from St. Louis. So if he attempts to proceed south he speedily comes to a point where the rate bases upon Los Angeles and where the combined rate is in favor of the middle west jobber. Canned goods were frequently referred to in the testimony. Taking this commodity as an illustration, we find that the car-load rate to San Francisco plus the local rate to Ashland, Ore., a distance of 431 miles, is $2.08, while the direct L. C. L. rate from the Missouri river, basing on Portland, is $2.00. At Mojave, California, 382 miles southeast, the combined car-load and less than car-load rate of the San Francisco jobber is $1.81, as against a direct L. C. L. rate from the Missouri river of $1.99.

These illustrations serve to show how, while this scheme of rate making favors the Pacific Coast jobber as a class, it limits the territory of the individual Pacific Coast jobber both as against his competitor upon the coast and as against his competitor in the east. While it appears that San Francisco jobbers do business over the whole Pacific Coast, it is done at a serious disadvantage beyond the limits of a comparatively narrow sphere ; indeed, one witness in behalf of the complainants expressed the opinion that the territory of the wholesaler upon the coast was so narrow that there was really no excuse for his existence.

The territory of jobbers east of the Missouri is of course limited against one another. It is not material here to discuss the extent of that limitation, since we are considering the competition between eastern jobbers as a whole and those upon the Pacific Coast. The fact that the rate from the warehouse of every wholesaler in the middle west to the store of each retailer upon the coast is the same, gives him an advantage over the individual Pacific Coast jobber outside the immediate " sphere " of the latter, which in a measure offsets the decided advantage of the Pacific Coast jobber within that sphere.

The effect of thus circumscribing the territory of the Pacific Coast jobber is to render the volume of his business comparatively small. That of all the houses with which he competes in the east is much more extensive. The two concerns most prominent in the prosecution of this proceeding were the Simmons Hardware Company of St. Louis and Hibbard, Spencer, Bartlett & Co. of Chicago; of which the former does business in all portions of the United States except New England, while the representative of the latter testified that the operation of his house was only limited by the confines of the earth. Jobbers upon the Pacific Coast earnestly insisted that these great establishments were not dependent upon that territory for any considerable part of their business, and that they used it as surplus territory in which they could afford to operate at a very small margin of profit. It also appeared that owing to the distance at which these houses upon the Pacific Coast were located from their base of supply, the amount of stock carried was very large in proportion to the volume of business done; and that the expense of transacting that business was greater than in the east.

Certain articles are produced upon the Pacific Coast, and certain others are imported from Europe and from eastern Asia, while still others manufactured in the eastern portion of the United States are sold at a delivered price. With respect to all these the Pacific Coast jobber has the advantage of his eastern rival. But it did not at all definitely appear what the extent of that advantage might be. We are inclined to think that if the Pacific Coast jobber had no advantage in the freight rate at which he could bring his merchandise from points of production and distribute it to points of consumption, he would find it extremely difficult to hold his own.

The principal contention of the Pacific Coast jobbers is that their location entitles them to such an advantage. The controlling factor in that location is the possibility of bringing in goods from the Atlantic seaboard and foreign countries by water. The effect of water competition is also the defense largely relied upon by the carriers in justification of their tariffs, and the facts in reference to it as applicable to each may be stated together.

Several of the jobbing houses whose representatives testified in this proceeding were established at Sacramento and San Francisco a half century ago. At that time the only means available for the transportation of merchandise from the Atlantic seaboard to their warehouses was by sailing vessel around Cape Horn, or through the Straits of Magellan. In 1854 the Panama railroad was constructed. By this route freight passes from New York to Colon by ship, from Colon to Panama, a distance of fifty miles, by rail, and from Panama to San Francisco by water. Upon this route steamers have been used instead of sailing vessels, the distance is much shorter, the time much quicker, the certainty of arrival much greater, and generally the advantages offered are much superior to those by sail around South America. It has from the first transacted a considerable amount of business between the two coasts.

The first transcontinental line of railroad was the Central Pacific in connection with the Union Pacific, and was opened for business in 1869. This line at once began to compete for transcontinental freight, with no great amount of success at first. It succeeded in carrying a portion of the higher class merchandise, but the great bulk of all commodities continued to move by water or by the Panama route. It was estimated that as late as 1878 not over 25 per cent of the total tonnage moved into California by rail. In that year, for the purpose of obtaining a larger share of this traffic, the rail line inaugurated what was known as the special contract system involving a contract between the railway and each individual shipper, by which the merchant agreed to patronize the railway exclusively, in consideration whereof the railway made certain special rates of freight. . . . This system was not popular at the outset, but before long every important jobbing house in San Francisco, with one exception, had made a contract of this kind. The effect was to very much increase the rail tonnage. It seems probable . . . that in 1884 when this plan finally went out of vogue, the percentage of rail tonnage had risen from 25 per cent to between 60 and 75 per cent.

In 1881 the Atchison, Topeka & Santa Fé Railway was built to a connection with the Southern Pacific at Deming, and in 1882 the Texas & Pacific connected with the same line at El Paso. In 1883 the Southern Pacific route from New Orleans was opened, and the same year saw the completion of the Rio Grande Western and the extension of the Santa Fé to Mojave. In the northwest the Northern Pacific was opened for traffic that year, and the completion of the Oregon Short Line the following year gave the Union Pacific an entrance into Portland. The multiplication of these transcontinental routes produced a corresponding diversity of interest, . . . the contract system was abandoned because the various lines could not agree among themselves upon the division of business and the maintenance of rates. To obviate this embarrassment the Transcontinental Association was organized, having for its purpose a pooling distribution of transcontinental traffic, or earnings, and the fixing and maintaining of transcontinental tariffs.   *   *

When the Central Pacific and Union Pacific began business as the first transcontinental railway line they found in the

Panama route their most troublesome competitor. For the purpose of controlling this competition these two lines and their connections in 1871 entered into a contract with the Pacific Mail Steamship Company, which then did the ocean carrying by the Panama route both from New York to Colon and from Panama to San Francisco, by which the railways leased and paid for the entire space in the steamships of the Pacific Mail Company which was devoted to California business. Under this contract the steamship company disposed of this space according to the direction of the railways, naming such rates, making such regulations and generally so conducting with respect to traffic as they directed. The policy of the railways was to offset the Panama route against the clipper ships. This contract was taken over by the Transcontinental Association when it was formed, and it continued in effect with some slight interruptions from 1871 until December 31, 1892. . . .

Previous to this time there had been in force a contract between the Pacific Mail Steamship Company and the Panama Railroad Company under which the steamship company acquired the exclusive use of the Panama railway for business moving between the Atlantic and Pacific Coasts. That contract expired about this same time, and the Pacific Mail declined to renew it upon the original terms in view of the expiration of its own contract with the transcontinental railways. In consequence the Panama Railroad Company put on a line of steamers of its own between New York and Colon known as the Columbia Steamship Company. Meantime the merchants of San Francisco had become dissatisfied with the treatment which they were receiving from the railways. They knew of the existence of contracts between the transcontinental lines and the Panama route, and regarded the whole arrangement in the light of a monopoly which extorted unreasonable rates and imposed unreasonable conditions. Learning that the contract between the Panama Railroad and the Pacific Mail was about to expire they proposed to put on a line of steamships between San Francisco and Panama, thus making, in connection with the Panama Railroad and its own steamships, an independent line from New York to San Francisco. In the execution of this plan the North American Navigation Company was organized by the merchants of San Francisco.

This route began operations in the year 1893, and attempted from the first to maintain a differential upon traffic moving between the Atlantic and Pacific Coasts which would deprive the railroads of a considerable share of the business previously handled by them. The result was a most bitter and reckless rate war during which there was an utter demoralization of rates and rate conditions. The San Francisco jobbers were upon the side of the ocean, and not only were rates abnormally reduced, but differentials were abolished, the right to ship in mixed car loads was extended, every inducement was held out to the jobber of the middle west to invade the territory of the Pacific Coast. The North American Navigation Company only operated about one year, but its vessels were taken over by the Panama Company and the competition itself continued in full force until the end of the year 1895.

This episode had been an expensive one for all parties concerned. It is in testimony that the merchants had put into the North American Navigation Company $350,000, which was entirely lost; and their indirect loss must have been greater still. They had seen their territory diminish, their profits grow less, their business decrease under the competition which had been fostered by rail rates from the east. The situation was not more satisfactory to the railways for they had sacrificed millions of dollars in revenue and were still receiving what they regarded as abnormally low rates. Both parties were therefore anxious for some sort of an accommodation. Representatives of the transcontinental lines upon the coast were instructed to mollify as far as possible Pacific Coast shippers and the shippers in their turn seem to have been anxious to meet this advance. In 1897 a communication was addressed to the railways by the jobbing interests upon the Pacific Coast stating in substance that rates ought to be readjusted in the interest of the coast jobber; that more rigid inspection rules should be enforced preventing their competitors in the middle west from obtaining fraudulent rates; and intimating that if this was done they would not object to an advance in rates and would find it for their interest largely to place shipments with railroads. . . . The result of this conference was the tariff of June 25, 1898, which is attacked in this proceeding.

The jobbers of the middle west vehemently insisted that in this tariff they had not received proper consideration, and a subsequent meeting was held at St. Paul in May, 1899, at which the matter was again gone into by the parties in interest, with the result that the Great Northern and the Northern Pacific companies modified in certain essential respects the tariff of the previous June by a supplement taking effect May 1, 1899, and known in this case as the St. Paul Supplement. This supplement reduced in some instances the differentials between car loads and less than car loads, and modified the varied commodity rates in the hardware schedule, and perhaps in some others.

The complainants insist that the tariff of June 25, 1898, was the result of an agreement between the railways and the jobbers of the Pacific Coast that tariffs should be adjusted in their favor, and that they in consideration would patronize the rail instead of the water; and that the effect of that agreement has been to largely destroy effective competition by water.

From 1871 until January 1, 1893, the Panama route was absolutely controlled with respect to Pacific Coast business in the United States by transcontinental lines, and there was during that period no competition with that line. For some years afterwards that competition was extremely active. It appears that finally the Pacific Mail became the steamer part of the line from Panama to San Francisco, while the Columbia Steamship Company continued to form the link between New York and Colon. To-day the agent of the Panama Company in New York makes the west-bound rates while the agent of the Pacific Mail at San Francisco controls the east-bound shipments. The tariffs west-bound are based upon the corresponding tariffs of the rail lines, being 20 per cent less on car loads and 30 per cent less on less than car loads. This apparently gives that route substantially the full capacity of its steamers in traffic. . . . While the testimony in this case fails to show any contract or understanding through which competition by the Panama route is limited it can hardly be said that at the present time that line affords much actual competition between the coasts.

With respect to competition by the all ocean route the matter has all along stood entirely otherwise. At first this was the only means of transportation for merchandise. As late as 1878 probably 75 per cent of the entire tonnage came in by sail. In 1884 this percentage had very much fallen, but still equaled 25 per cent. Since then there has been a further decline, the testimony showing that for the last ten years not more than 10 to 15 per cent has arrived in this way. But there is nothing in the case to show that any agreement has ever subsisted between rail lines and the route around South America as to any division of traffic, or any establishment of rates.

The principal witness as to the present state of water competition by all ocean routes was Mr. Jackson, representative of Flint, Dearborn & Co., of New York, managers of the principal line of clipper ships between the Atlantic and Pacific Coasts. . . . From his testimony it appeared that during the year 1898 there were shipped from New York to California, mainly San Francisco, by sailing vessels about 34,000 tons, and from Philadelphia about 6000 tons. Substantially the same tonnage had been forwarded the previous year, 1897. It also appeared that some other vessels were engaged in the same business between Philadelphia and San Francisco, and perhaps between New York and Pacific Coast points. Formerly the tonnage carried by these lines had been much greater than it was in those years. For some years previous to 1890 it had varied from 50,000 to 100,000 tons per annum. The rate war which broke out in 1894 diverted the tonnage from sail to rail, and the effect of this was continued after the close of those rate disturbances by the Spanish war, which rendered rates of insurance high and ships scarce. The outlook for the future was, however, said to be more promising.

Mr. Jackson . . . was also the treasurer of the American-Hawaiian Steamship Company, a corporation organized for the purpose of owning and operating a line of steamers between New York, San Francisco and Hawaii *via* the Straits of Magellan. He first testified in November, 1899, and at that time this company had placed orders for four steamers of 8500 tons each to be used in this service. It was said that these steamships would carry, beside the necessary coal, 7500 tons of freight, and would make the run from New York to San Francisco in about 60 days. It was expected that each steamer would make two trips per year, thus affording a capacity of 60,000 tons west-bound which it was believed could easily be obtained.

Subsequently, in December, 1900, Mr. Jackson again testified, and then stated that two of the steamers above referred to had already been delivered and put into service ; that the two others referred to in his former testimony would soon be ready for delivery, and that his company had within the year contracted for three larger steamers for this same service with a capacity of 15,000 tons each. He stated that this would give a total carrying capacity west-bound of about 126,000 tons per annum. . . .

Almost every article which moves from the east to the Pacific Coast has been at times actually carried by ocean. A list of the articles transported during the year 1898 was introduced and it embraced nearly every article of merchandise. The territory from which this route draws its freight is mostly that in the immediate vicinity of New York. Shipments have been taken from as far west as Chicago, and even St. Louis, but this is of rare occurrence. The great bulk of its traffic is from points east of Buffalo and Pittsburg.

In the making of rates by ocean no distinction as such is observed between car-load and less than car-load lots. Mr. Jackson testified that about three fourths of the tonnage forwarded by him was in lots exceeding 30,000 pounds and one fourth in lots less than that figure ; the range of the smaller lots being from 1000 to 20,000 pounds. While there is no less than car-load rate as such the amount charged per hundred pounds for smaller quantities is greater than that charged for larger quantities, the difference being from 10 to 30 cents per hundred pounds. Everything depends, however, upon the quantity offered for shipment and the state of the ship's contracts for the freight. Large quantities are often taken at very low figures. We are inclined to think that the ordinary difference made by water between car loads and less than car loads, while not a fixed sum, is considerably less than the difference prescribed by the tariff of June 25, 1898, upon rail shipments.

The witness objected to stating the exact rates at which merchandise had been carried by his line, but did give some illustrative examples; among others the following, in connection with which the rail rate is also given:

	WATER RATE	RAIL RATE	
		L. C. L.	C. L.
Bar iron	30 to 35¢	$1.25	$ .75
Grindstones	32½¢	1.90	.75
Soil pipe	35 to 40¢	1.90	.75
Radiators	40 to 45¢	2.20	1.30
Hardwood lumber . .	40 to 42¢	1.25	.75

It must be remembered that a water rate of a certain number of cents per hundred pounds is by no means equivalent in value to the shipper to a rail rate of the same amount. Several things must be taken into account in determining the relative desirability of the two rates. The item of marine insurance is important, and Mr. Jackson stated that this was by his sailing vessels about $1\frac{1}{2}$ per cent of the value of the commodity; the time occupied in transit and the consequent loss upon the investment is an item of consequence, the ordinary run from San Francisco being in the vicinity of 135 days. In addition to this is the liability to damage by salt water in case of many articles as well as the delay and uncertainty incident upon that means of transportation. No witness was prepared to state what rate by ocean was equivalent to a rate of $1 by rail; indeed the witnesses seemed to agree that it would be impossible to answer that question definitely since its answer must depend upon the commodity transported. One witness said that after everything had been taken into account he would still pay the railways on most commodities a rate 5 per cent higher than that by water.

A portion of the disadvantages attending transportation by water will be largely obviated through the use of steamers in place of sailing vessels. As just stated the ordinary time by sail from New York to San Francisco is estimated at 135 days, but the time actually consumed often greatly exceeds this, sometimes being as much as a whole year. This uncertainty as to date of arrival has been a serious objection to that method of carriage. The steamer is expected to make the run around South America in 60 days, and its arrival can probably be counted upon with more exactness than arrivals by rail. The item of insurance will also be much less with steamers than with sailing vessels as will the loss on the investment during the period of transit. It was said that with a canal across the Isthmus of Panama the trip from New York by the steamers now ordered could be made in about 20 days, and that doubtless if such a canal were constructed faster steamers would be put on which would make the trip in from 15 to 16 days.   *   *

The carrier must meet this water competition mainly with the car-load rate. Ninety per cent of the merchandise brought from the east to the Pacific Coast by Pacific Coast jobbers comes in car-load lots. The less than car-load shipments are often in the nature of emergency orders requiring quick delivery and not therefore susceptible of ocean carriage.   *   *   *

Conclusions

The complaint in this case attacks the system of rate making in vogue upon the Pacific Coast. What that system is appears in the findings of fact, and is well understood by all persons having an elementary knowledge of the situation. The rate from an eastern point like St. Louis is lowest to the so-called " terminal " upon the coast. Going east from the terminal point the rate increases until limited by the so-called " intermediate " rate. This produces a higher rate at the intermediate point through which the traffic passes to the terminal point and compels the St. Louis merchant, although nearer in distance, to pay more for the transportation of his merchandise. He insists that his rate to the nearer station ought to be no higher than to the more distant point.   *   *   *   *   *   *

The complaint also attacks the scheme of transcontinental rate making in force east of the Missouri river as applied to west-bound rates. That system differs radically from the method followed upon the Pacific Coast. While upon the Pacific Coast the rate is lowest to the terminal at the ocean and increases toward the interior, in the east the rate from the seaboard does not increase as we proceed inland, but remains the same. This produces what is known as the blanket system of rates. The first-class rate from New York to San Francisco is $3 and the same rate applies from St. Louis. Commodity rates follow the same rule so that generally speaking rates both class and com-modity to Pacific Coast terminals and points basing upon such terminals are the same from all points east of the Missouri river. This St. Louis declares to be unjust ; being one thousand miles nearer San Francisco than New York it insists that it should be given the benefit of that advantage in distance.

The higher rate to the interior point in California is justi-fied by the carriers upon the ground of water competition, the theory being this : Water competition between New York and San Francisco establishes a cheaper rate than could reasonably be exacted from the rail carrier. Merchandise at New York can be taken by water to San Francisco at the low water rate and thence carried by rail to an interior point for the water rate from New York to San Francisco plus the local rate from San Francisco to the interior point. If the rail carrier engages in this business it must meet the rate thus established by water at San Francisco, and by water and rail at the interior point. It is claimed that the carrier may at his election meet this compe-tition and make its rates accordingly. It may therefore charge to the interior point a rate higher than the terminal rate by the local back, until a point is reached at which the rate so formed is more than a reasonable rate. This right upon the part of the carrier may perhaps be subject to certain qualifications and limitations, but generally speaking this is the theory upon which certain rates upon the Pacific Coast, which have been declared not in violation of the Act to Regulate Commerce, are constructed.

Now in theory the converse of this proposition would be true when applied to the point of origin in the east. Water transportation fixes the rate from New York to San Francisco. Pittsburg is four hundred miles west of New York. A commodity can move from Pittsburg to San Francisco in two ways; it may go directly by rail, or it may go by rail from Pittsburg to New York and from thence to San Francisco by ship. If it goes by rail and ocean manifestly the rate should be higher from Pittsburg than from New York, although Pittsburg is nearer San Francisco, since carriage by that route involves the rail haul from Pittsburg to New York. Applying this principle of water competition in the east exactly as it has been applied upon the Pacific Coast, rates to terminal points from the east would be lowest from the Atlantic seaboard and would gradually increase toward the interior until some point was reached at which the rate so constructed equaled a reasonable rate by the direct rail route. If that theory of rate making which has been sanctioned by the Courts and by the Commission in some cases were applied to this territory east of the Missouri river the rate from St. Louis to San Francisco would be, not lower than that from New York, as the complainants insist, but higher, unless the direct rail rate from St. Louis to San Francisco ought reasonably to be less than the rate established from New York by water competition.

That the same system is not in force in both the east and the west is due to differing conditions in those sections. Upon the Pacific Coast the great cities and the strong commercial interests are located at the seaboard. There are no interior towns of sufficient strength to insist upon a change of this policy, and apparently there never can be so long as the present system continues in force. In the east this is otherwise. Formerly manufacturing was mainly done upon the Atlantic seaboard, but to-day great cities have grown up and great commercial enterprises have developed in the middle west, and these demand an entrance to the markets of the Pacific Coast in tones which cannot be disregarded.

Still more important is the situation of the carriers themselves. Those lines which distribute upon the Pacific Coast control the adjustment of rates into that section, and their interests are united to maintain the present system. Indeed it is declared that to reduce intermediate rates to a level with terminal rates would bankrupt these lines, and it certainly would have a most serious effect upon their revenues. In the east we find many important systems beginning at the Missouri river or in the middle west. It is for the interest of these systems that traffic should originate at the eastern termini of their respective lines. Not only do they obtain more for the transportation of traffic so originating than they obtain from their division upon traffic originating farther east, but they also build up the industries of that locality and therefore remove these from the sphere of water competition. Moreover the traffic which the eastern connections of the transcontinental lines carry farther east is insignificant in amount and in revenue returned in comparison with the whole amount of their traffic. From these various causes it has transpired that the low rate which water competition establishes from New York has been extended to all points east of the Missouri river.

The Commission in a very recent case has examined and passed upon this same question. *Kindel et al.* v. *Atchison, Topeka & Santa Fé Railway Co. et al.*, 8 I. C. C. Rep. 608.

In that case the city of Denver alleged that by virtue of its location it was entitled to a lower rate to Pacific Coast terminals than the rate from points on the Missouri river and east. When the complaint was brought most rates were higher from Denver than from the Missouri river. The only fact upon which Denver based that claim was its location; being one thousand miles nearer San Francisco than Chicago, and nearly two thousand miles nearer San Francisco than New York, it insisted that it was entitled to a better rate. The Commission held that this did not necessarily follow; that while Denver was nearer in geographical miles it was not of necessity nearer in transportation units. The actual cost of transporting merchandise from New York to San Francisco by water was probably materially less than the cost of carrying it by rail from Denver to San Francisco. We said that if these carriers extended the low water rate of New York west to the Missouri river they must carry it still farther to Denver, but that we could not affirm upon the mere score of distance that the rate from Denver should be lower. We are satisfied with the disposition of that question in that case, and it must control the case before us.

To avoid any misapprehension it should be said that we . . . do not decide in this case that circumstances and conditions might not be such as to require a lower rate from the nearer point. If in this case the industries of St. Louis and the middle west showed that they were, by this adjustment of tariffs, excluded from the markets of the Pacific Coast their complaint might merit different consideration. But such is not the fact; on the contrary it appears that in recent years under the influence of this rate the industries, both manufacturing and jobbing, of the middle west have made steady gains upon the Pacific Coast. To-day, of all commodities transported into that territory which originate east of the Missouri it is estimated that more than 60 per cent is from points west of Buffalo and Pittsburg. The only grounds upon which the complainants rest in support of this contention are the greater proximity of the middle west, and the fact that these graded rates were formerly in effect; neither of which entitle them to the relief asked for.

It should also be observed that nothing in this decision would in any way interfere with the right of the transcontinental lines to put in effect, if they saw fit, such a system of graded rates as the complainants ask for. Carriers may or may not at their option meet the low water rate from New York. It is for the manifest interest of those lines beginning at Chicago and points west to maintain lower rates from there than from the seaboard, and if in the future such rates are established they will not be in violation of the Act to Regulate Commerce.

That branch of the complaint most discussed both in testimony and upon the argument was the alleged discrimination by the tariff of June 25, 1898, against the jobber of the middle west in favor of the jobber upon the Pacific Coast. This discrimination is accomplished, according to the complainants, by too wide a differential between car loads and less than car loads, by the application of improper varied commodity rates and by the refusal to permit shipment in mixed car loads. Of these three things the differential was by far the most prominent.

The statement of facts shows that most traffic from the east to the Pacific Coast moves upon commodity rates. Of these rates nearly one half name for the same commodity a car-load and less than car-load rate; about one third apply in any quantity, making no distinction between car loads and less than car loads, while the remaining one sixth apply to car loads only, leaving the less than car-load shipments to move under the class rate. The differential between car loads and less than car loads is all the way from nothing to $1.50 per hundred pounds, perhaps in instances even greater. Many of the differentials are exactly 50 cents; the complaint alleges that this is the average differential and the case finds that this is approximately true. Are these differentials in violation of the Act to Regulate Commerce?

In determining this the first inquiry is, by what standard shall the propriety of a differential between car loads and less than car loads be estimated? The complainants urged that the differential was justified largely by difference in expense of handling traffic at terminals, and that this difference when ascertained ought to constitute the difference between car loads and less than car loads; that the differentials thus arrived at would be approximately a fixed quantity, not varying materially with the rate or with the distance. This proposition can hardly be assented to. It really assumes that the proper differential is determined by the difference in the cost of handling the two kinds of traffic. But it appears from the statement of fact that this difference in expense is not confined to terminal points. It costs appreciably more to haul less than car-load business than car-load. If, therefore, the reason for the standard suggested by the complainants is a valid one, the differential ought to increase with the distance, and therefore ordinarily with the rate.   *   *   *   *   *   *   *   *

In order to understand the claim of the defendants it is necessary to have clearly in mind the entire situation. Traffic transported from the east to the Pacific Coast at the present time is controlled either by jobbers in the middle west or by jobbers upon the Pacific Coast. The middle west jobbers send their merchandise almost entirely in less than car-load lots. In the very nature of the case that freight is not subject to ocean competition, and the carrier may safely disregard such competition in the making of these less than car-load rates which apply to that transportation.

The Pacific Coast jobber upon the other hand brings his supplies from the east to his warehouse almost entirely in large lots. It is found that 90 per cent of his entire rail traffic moves in car loads. Of the remaining 10 per cent a considerable part is in the nature of emergency orders, which require quick delivery and which could not therefore be transported by water. In order to obtain the business of the Pacific Coast jobber it is necessary that the rail carrier make an attractive car-load rate, the less than car-load being of comparatively little importance. There is a certain amount of less than car-load traffic which can and does move by water, as the statement of actual movements by clipper ship and the tariffs of the Panama route show; but broadly speaking the less than car-load business is, from its point of origin, not subject to water competition; the car-load freight is that for which the rail carrier mainly contends with the ocean; hence water competition tends to produce a wide difference between the car-load and less than car-load.

There is still another reason. The fact that business originating in the middle west almost of necessity moves by rail, immediately suggests the thought that it would be for the ultimate interest of those lines which begin in the middle west to make such rates as would enable all business to be done by that section. Up to the present time two causes have prevented this. First, it has been in the interest of certain lines, notably the Southern Pacific, that traffic should move from the Atlantic seaboard, and second, the Pacific Coast jobber has objected to being extinguished. His warehouse is by the sea, and if the rail line makes a rate which will not permit him to bring traffic by rail and do business against his eastern competitor he must and he will turn to the ocean for relief. This may be disastrous to him; it proved to be so when tried; but it is even more disastrous to the railway. For the purpose therefore of maintaining peace, and at the same time obtaining a large part of the business of the Pacific Coast jobber, the railroad aims to maintain a differential which will enable that jobber to do business.

We have next to consider the interest of the wholesaler upon the coast and in the middle west, and it is really the conflicting claims of these parties which lie at the bottom of this controversy. The jobber upon the Pacific Coast insists that he rests under certain disadvantages in comparison with his eastern rival which render it extremely difficult for him to maintain himself without some advantage in the freight rate, and that his natural advantage of location entitles him to this preference. The alleged disadvantages have been fully stated in the findings of fact. They mainly spring from the limited territory to which his operations are necessarily confined. Owing to the adjustment of freight rates he cannot operate in any event more than about three hundred miles to the east, and the same distance north or south brings him to a point where both his eastern rival and his local competitor have an advantage in the rate. The field which is open to him is narrow, estimated in square miles, and even narrower when estimated by the population which he can reach. From this it results that the volume of his sales is small and the expense of transacting business large in proportion; still further his location and the manner in which he obtains his supplies force him to carry a disproportionately large stock. The Pacific Coast jobber finds it extremely difficult to maintain himself against his eastern rival without some advantage in the transportation charge, and we have seen that his location upon the seaboard by opening two avenues of communication gives him a certain advantage in this respect.

Most of the limitations under which the jobber upon the Pacific Coast works do not attach to the jobber in the middle west who is competing upon the Pacific Coast. His territory is extensive and the volume of his sales large. He goes east to New England, south to the Gulf of Mexico, north to the Dominion line, west 1700 miles, and whether he does or does not cover this narrow strip west of the 115th meridian in no way affects his general prosperity or his continued existence. This is true not of every jobber in the middle west but of those great houses in whose interest this complaint is prosecuted.

The controversy has been conducted by the railways and the two sets of wholesalers already referred to, but it must not be decided with reference to their necessities or desires alone. There is another interest seldom represented upon these hearings, but always to be considered by this Commission, and that is the consumer. No adjustment of rates made in the interest of carriers or of wholesalers should be permitted if it antagonizes unduly the public welfare. Considering the question before us as an economic problem two things should be secured. First, these commodities should be brought to the consumer at the least possible expense. Second, in both transportation and distribution unfettered competition should be maintained, thereby securing to the consumer the benefits to which he is entitled.

The greater part of the supplies consumed upon the Pacific Coast originate twenty-five hundred miles from the point of consumption, and these supplies should be transported that twenty-five hundred miles in the cheapest manner. Waste is always expensive; if the railways are required to carry this merchandise in an extravagant manner that extravagance is finally borne by the public. We have seen that the actual cost of handling this traffic in less than car loads is 50 per cent greater than the cost of handling car loads. It seems probable, therefore, that the cheapest way in which these supplies can be taken across the continent and distributed to the consumer is by transporting them in solid car loads from the factory to the warehouse upon the Pacific Coast and thence distributing to the retailer in less than car loads, although the effect of this may be somewhat diminished by the back haul from the wholesaler to the interior point which is not performed to the same extent where goods are sent across the continent in less than car-load shipments directly to the store of the retailer. It would in our opinion be unfortunate from an economic standpoint to establish a condition which would require distribution entirely or mainly in less than car-load lots from the middle west.

It is urged however that this tariff in effect stifles competition, thereby increasing the price to the consumer. It is alleged that this is done in two ways, first, by discouraging water competition and thereby permitting the maintenance of too high a rate, second, by restricting the market in which the retailer can buy, thus increasing the price to him and his customer.

The rate war of 1894 originated in the desire of the merchants of San Francisco to obtain a lower freight rate. The means which they employed was ocean transportation, and in that contest the jobber of the Pacific Coast was upon the side of the ocean. As a matter of retaliation rail lines gave to the eastern jobber every facility for entering Pacific Coast territory. Not only was the general level of rates reduced but differentials were abolished and the privilege of mixing shipments increased.

The result as has been noted in the statement of facts was disastrous to both parties. The San Francisco jobber lost in territory and in profits; the railways suffered severely in the diminution of revenues. At the expiration of three years both parties were anxious for relief and were seeking some ground of compromise. This was the genesis of the meetings at Del Monte and Milwaukee, and it was to effectuate this purpose that the tariff of June 25, 1898, was promulgated. The railway desired to retain its business at higher rates; the jobber upon the coast desired to retain his territory and increase his profits. There can be no doubt that the railways understood that the jobbers would patronize their lines at the higher rate, and that the jobbers had given them so to understand. There was no definite agreement of this sort, nothing like that involved in the old special contract system. It was rather a result growing out of the mutual interest of both parties.

The practical interpretation of this understanding has been to enable the railways to retain just about the same proportion of traffic at materially better rates. The tonnage brought from the Atlantic to the Pacific Coast since June 25, 1898, has not differed greatly from that of two or three years before. It ought perhaps to have increased, for the Spanish war had dealt this traffic a severe blow both by increasing the rates of insurance and by decreasing the supply of ships, and with the close of that war this traffic might be expected to recover. Clearly it is likely to do so in the future. The tonnage moving during the present year will probably greatly surpass that of the last six or seven years and within two years to come will be greater than at any time since 1880. We find a disposition upon the part of the coast jobbers to patronize the ocean whenever a rate is offered which is decidedly advantageous. It must be remembered that the effect of the rate war of 1894 was to depress ocean as well as rail rates.

Rail lines could not probably increase their car-load rates, and if we were to order a reduction of these differentials that would result in a reduction of the less than car-load rate. Another result would be to compel the coast jobber to seek cheaper means of transportation which might finally lead to a further reduction of the car-load rate and to the same disturbances which have previously occurred. We have already said that the reasonableness of the less than car-load rates considered by themselves is not questioned. Ought we then to order this reduction? If the effect of the present tariff, owing to any understanding between the rail lines and the coast jobbers, was to extinguish or seriously cripple ocean competition it would be our plain duty to interfere; but in fact this competition seems to be in a prosperous state. If the effect were to maintain a scale of rates unreasonably high, our duty would be equally plain; but there is no suggestion that this is true of the present terminal rates. We are not unmindful of the fact that a reduction in the terminal rate works a corresponding reduction at all points which base upon that rate; nor do we overlook the fact, although there is no mention of it in this case, that the earnings of transcontinental lines indicate that some reduction in their rates might properly be made; but we are of the opinion that if any such

reduction is to take place it should be in the high and discriminating intermediate rate rather than in the already extremely
low terminal charge. Competition is not healthy when it becomes destructive to the competing parties. It was said upon
the argument that this present adjustment provided a state of
" equilibrium " under which both the rail and the water, the east
and the west could fairly compete. So far as the testimony
shows we are inclined to think that this is true of competition
by water.

It is said that this tariff is unlawful because it excludes the
jobber of the middle west from this territory, gives to the wholesaler upon the Pacific Coast a monopoly, restricts the market
in which the retailer can buy and thereby enhances the price to
the consumer. The territory of the Pacific Coast jobber is extremely limited, and he is inclined to insist that he should be
left in the peaceable possession of that territory; that the jobber of the middle west whose territory extends a thousand miles
to the east and seventeen hundred miles to the west ought not
to covet the narrow strip which lies beyond the 115th meridian.
We do not accede altogether to this view. The adjustment of
rates upon the Pacific Coast is such that it confines the local
jobber to certain spheres making them almost omnipotent within
those spheres; and for this reason competition from the east,
which under this same adjustment of rates, tends to diffuse
itself over the whole coast, is important. If there be no controlling reason to the contrary, rates should be so adjusted as
to permit the operation of the wholesaler from the middle west
throughout all this territory.   *   *   *   *

Viewing the case in this broad sense we find that these differentials are not abnormal when compared with others in different parts of this country at the present time ; that they are not
greater than those in effect under the west-bound transcontinental tariff of 1893, and not greatly disproportionate to the
actual difference in cost of service. Considering them with
respect to their bearing upon the parties immediately interested,
namely, the carriers and the two classes of jobbers, we find that
they conserve the interests of the carrier, that they give to the

jobber upon the Pacific Coast a measure of advantage to which he is perhaps entitled by his location, and which he must probably have if he is to continue to exist, while they permit the jobber of the middle west to transact a considerable amount of business in this territory at a reasonable profit. Viewed as an economic problem, the tariff fosters that method of distribution which is probably the cheapest upon the coast, and at the same time permits reasonable competition and thereby secures to the customer the full benefits of such competition. This situation is in some sense the outgrowth of past experience. It is satisfactory to most interests upon the Pacific Coast, and we are not disposed to find fault with the adjustment of rates as a whole.

While, however, we cannot condemn this tariff as a whole upon the grounds put forward by the complainants, we are of the opinion that many of its details are in violation of law. Over four hundred commodity rates apply to car loads only, leaving the movement of these commodities in less than car loads to be governed by the class rate. This produces a differential which even under the peculiar circumstances of this traffic is in many cases excessive, provided there be any commercial reason for a corresponding less than car-load rate. In some instances there is none. Coal, for example, moves usually in car loads and takes a low commodity rate. What little movement occurs in less than car-load lots is not competitive with car-load shipments, and may well be governed by the class rate, although the difference between the two would otherwise be undue. Many similar instances will readily occur, but we are impressed from an inspection of these schedules that there are still many other instances in which the difference is altogether too great.

It is impossible to fix any standard by which these differentials shall be determined, for the reason that circumstances often render the application of a greater differential proper in one case than in another. This record finds that many of the commodity rates show a differential of 50 cents per 100 pounds, and it is said that this may be termed the average differential; it further finds that the cost of handling this less than car-load traffic exceeds the cost of handling car-load traffic by about 50 per cent. We are inclined to think that a differential which is at once more than 50 cents per 100 pounds and more than 50 per cent of the car-load rate is *prima facie* excessive. We do not mean that every differential may lawfully equal this, nor yet that every differential which exceeds this is unlawful, but that a differential exceeding this requires special justification.

*   *   *   *   *   *   *   *   *

FIFER, *Commissioner*, dissenting :

I concur in the opinion to the extent of deeming it inadvisable to attempt, without further investigation, a settlement of the great questions involved in this continental situation.

The undisputed facts involve three propositions : the postage stamp or blanket rate for the whole eastern territory from the Atlantic Coast to the Missouri river ; the wide difference between the car-load and less than car-load rate on west-bound traffic, and, the system common to all, the western mountain territory of making the rates from the east to any intermediate point by adding to the through rate to any Pacific Coast terminal the local rate back to the intermediate point.

Concerning the first, while it may be conceded that the so-called blanket rate is too firmly established, and has proved in too many instances of a great utility and profit to both the road and its patrons to warrant me in denouncing it, yet I am firmly of opinion that, carried to the extent of above a thousand miles, as in this instance, on practically all the schedules, is such an exaggeration of the system as to work serious injustice to the jobbers of the middle west by robbing them of the natural advantages of geographical location to which they are as much entitled as are points located upon the Atlantic Coast, which for that very reason are favored by rates that are denied to those situated farther west.

For this reason it seems to me the only solution of the problem which will be fair to all parties is the graded rate, perhaps not in the proportions formerly in force ; but that, at least, recognizes the advantage of proximity to the western market which

Pittsburg enjoys over New York, Chicago over Pittsburg, and the Missouri river over Chicago.

There seems to me to be just ground for protest against the differentials between car-load and less than car-load rates. These differences have been within a comparatively late period so much increased as to lead to the inference, inevitable to me, that they have been established with deliberate intention to discourage less than car-load shipments. To what extent these differentials should be modified, if at all, must depend upon a wider inquiry and deeper investigation than we have been able to accomplish at this stage of the present case.

The system of rate making which establishes rates for intermediate points by a combination of the through rate to the coast terminal point and the local rate back to destination has much in its favor, as water competition is held to justify even unreasonably low through rates, and as the freight thus favored is secured by the railroads by a rate which is to prevent its carriage by water — all freight, in theory, is treated as if it reached the coast by water and takes its place thereafter as local freight east — instead of through freight west.

But there comes a situation and a locality when this theory of rate making must break down of its own weight, and with a blanket rate from the east reaching to the Missouri river, the short middle west haul, say from the Missouri river to Ogden, is out of all proportion to the haul from the Missouri river to New York, from New York to San Francisco by water and back by rail to Ogden. Upon its face such a condition carries suspicion, and it requires some explanation to justify a situation where a haul practically a thousand miles shorter at each end is higher than the through rate. Just how far the combination through rate with the local back may extend under these circumstances will depend upon where it meets a reasonable rate from the east, and on that question in this case the evidence is incomplete ; we having developed only enough to bring me to fear that the schedules in force are discriminating and unjust.

The opinion finds that the Pacific Coast jobber carries his business not farther east than the 115th meridian, or about 300 miles from the coast, and I am inclined to believe that the evidence fairly sustains that finding. But an examination of the tariffs on file in the office of the Commission shows that the zone of their operations may be much wider, the combination rate basing on Pacific Coast terminals extending as far east as 800 or more miles in numerous instances.

For many articles of hardware, such as axes and other edged tools, picks and mattocks, bar, rod and sheet iron and steel, billets, blooms, ingots and scrap iron, the combination rate extends east on the Southern Pacific Railroad (Ogden line) to various points from Millis, Wyo., 828 miles east of Sacramento, to Cheyenne, Wyo., 1239 miles east of Sacramento, except on picks and mattocks, on which the combination rate equals the intermediate rate at Rye Patch, Nev., 273 miles east of Sacramento. On the Southern Pacific (El Paso line) the combination rate extends east to various points from Strauss, N.M., 797 miles east of Los Angeles, to San Elizario, Tex., 833 miles east of Los Angeles, except on picks and mattocks on which the combination rate equals the intermediate rate at Montezuma, Ariz., 400 miles east of Los Angeles. On the Great Northern line the combination rate extends east to various points from Troy, Mont., 579 miles east of Portland, on picks and mattocks, to Wagner, Mont., 1042 miles east of Portland, on billets, blooms, etc. On the Northern Pacific the combination rate tends east to various points from Noxon, Mont., 662 miles east of Portland, on picks and mattocks, to Central Park, Mont., 1009 miles east of Portland, on billets, blooms, etc. On the Santa Fé System the combination rate extends east to various points from Amboy, Cal., 226 miles east of Los Angeles, on picks and mattocks, to Albuquerque, N.M., 889 miles east of Los Angeles, on billets, blooms, etc.

Thus it will be seen that while the business of the coast jobber may, through his own volition or methods of transacting business, be confined to territory lying west of the 115th meridian, there is nothing in existing tariffs that would in any way so limit his field of operations. So far as these rates are concerned, he can apparently do business as profitably as far east as the points named as he can in the territory lying between the 115th meridian and the Pacific Coast. It should be noted that the differences between the car-load and less than car-load rates complained of in this case serve, under this method of making rates to the intermediate point, to greatly enlarge the Pacific Coast jobber's sphere of operations, and that he will sooner or later take full advantage of the opportunity thus afforded is to be expected.

It seems to me necessary that in the further investigation to which the opinion in this case tends, the feature of reasonable rates for the whole so-called western mountain territory should be made a main issue that the inquiry may develop whether or not the zone of combination rates should not be narrowed to points nearer the coast, and thus remove not only a burden on our commerce but an apparent discrimination that invites criticism, even if justifiable.

The Nevada Railroad Commission Case [1]

LANE, *Commissioner :*

The highest main-line rates to be found in the United States are those from eastern points to stations in Nevada. For carrying a carload of first-class traffic containing 20,000 pounds from Omaha to Reno the Union Pacific-Southern Pacific line charges $858. If a like carload is carried 154 miles further, to Sacramento, the charge is but $600. The first-class rate to the more distant point, Sacramento, is $3 per 100 pounds, and to the nearer point, Reno, $4.29 per 100 pounds. If a like carload of freight originates at Denver, 500 miles west of Omaha, the same rates to Reno and Sacramento apply ; and if the freight originates at Boston, 1700 miles east of Omaha, the rates are the same. This interesting rate condition arises out of two simple facts: (1) The whole of the United States from Colorado common points to the Atlantic seaboard, barring a few of the southeastern

---

[1] Decided June 6, 1910. 19 Interstate Commerce Commission Report, 238. Transcontinental rates are discussed in Ripley's Railroads : Rates and Regulation, pp. 395, 610.

states, is one wide group or zone from which practically uniform rates to Pacific coast water points are made, and (2) the rates to Reno are based upon these blanket rates to coast cities, and amount to the sum of the rates to the coast plus the local rates back to point of destination.

This great zone, extending from the Rocky Mountains to the Atlantic, a distance of over 2000 miles, from which practically uniform rates are made to Pacific coast terminal cities, is probably without parallel in the railroad world, excepting for a similar eastward blanket extended to Pacific coast producing points. The zone in which the same rates apply on California citrus fruits, for instance, extends from Salt Lake City on the west to Portland, Me. It is manifest that the transcontinental railroads have made a near approximation to the postage-stamp system of rate making. Their policy has been to give to all eastern producing markets an opportunity to sell to the terminal cities upon a parity as to transportation charges and to give to Pacific coast producing points access to all eastern markets upon a like basis. To the great basin lying between the Rocky Mountains and the Sierra Nevadas the carriers have in a limited degree extended this same policy by making rates into Nevada base on the coast cities, and thus, the carriers say, they give to this territory the advantage of its proximity to the Pacific seaboard; that the rates to the latter are made low because of water competition between the Atlantic and Pacific ports — lower than would be justified were Sacramento and San Francisco not upon the water — and that Nevada rates would be still higher but for its nearness to the Pacific coast.

The State of Nevada, through its railroad commission, now comes asking that Nevada points be given the same rates as are now given to Pacific coast terminals, urging that these coast rates are not unreasonably low in themselves, and are not the product of any real water competition.

The complaint originally filed in this case made the Southern Pacific the sole defendant; the reasonableness of the rates from the east to Nevada were not attacked, excepting in so far as they are based on the rates to further western points, and include a back-haul charge. As the complaint then stood the petition was that this Commission should hold it to be unreasonable for the Southern Pacific, delivering freight at Reno and other points in Nevada, to charge for a back haul which is not in fact given, and that we should adjudge the rates to Sacramento to be reasonable as applied to the intermediate points. Later the complaint was amended by adding carriers east of Ogden forming a single through route from the Atlantic coast. So that the petition of Nevada now is that from all points upon this through route reasonable rates shall be fixed which shall not exceed those now applicable on shipments from such points to the more distant coast terminals. It is suggested by the complainant that we bring in other carriers as defendants, so that the entire eastern territory may be covered by our order. This we think unnecessary, assuming, as we do, that the conclusions here reached as to a through route from the east to the west will be adopted and established by other lines similarly situated.

CONSTRUCTION OF NEVADA RATES

To reach a clear understanding of the basis upon which Nevada rates in general are now fixed, it is necessary to bear primarily in mind the fact before referred to, that the carriers of the country have united in establishing a zone 2000 miles in width from which rates are practically uniform to what are known as "coast terminals." There are 152 of these coast terminals, 97 of which are in California. They are points more or less arbitrarily established by the carriers, but which are either upon inlets from the ocean or rivers running to such inlets, or are but slightly removed from such water points. The most prominent coast terminals are Seattle, Tacoma, Portland, Sacramento, San Jose, Stockton, Oakland, San Francisco, Los Angeles, and San Diego. To these coast terminals are extended what are known as "terminal rates" on westbound transcontinental traffic. These rates apply either from all of eastern defined territory or from separate groups therein. The shaded portion of the accompanying map indicates eastern defined territory and the groups into which it is divided. These groups are lettered from A to J. A is limited to New York City piers, and has to do only with shipments by steamship *via* Gulf ports; B covers New England territory; C, New York territory and the middle states, with New York City as the principal point; D, Chicago and adjacent territory; E, the Mississippi river, with St. Louis as the principal city; F, the Missouri river; G, Kansas; H, Oklahoma; I, Texas; and J, Colorado, with Denver as its central point.

Class rates. Coming, then, to the construction of the Nevada class rates, we find that the carriers have employed three methods of construction during the past two years. Prior to January 1, 1909, there existed a body of what were known as intermediate class rates to Reno from certain designated eastern points. These rates were, on first class —

From Chicago-Milwaukee common points $3.90
From Mississippi river common points 3.70
From Missouri river common points 3.50
From Colorado common points 3.00

An alternative clause gave Reno the right to the combination rate based on Sacramento whenever that should be lower. This indefinite method of stating rates the Commission condemned in a general ruling. The tariffs were then changed so as to cancel the alternative clause and the intermediate class rates and thus to make all Nevada rates base on Sacramento. This was the situation when the case was heard. Later, however, in June of last year, a third plan was adopted, and that now obtains, viz., to divide Nevada into two zones with Humboldt as the dividing point. Points west of Humboldt take the Sacramento combination. Points east of Humboldt take generally the Ogden combination. It is unnecessary herein to trace the history and the effect of these various changes in the method of rate basing. We shall deal with the rates to all Nevada points as joint rates. And inasmuch as rates on all ten classes were quoted by the carriers' tariffs from all eastern defined territory to coast terminals and therefore by combination to interior points, at the time when this proceeding was brought, we shall consider that our jurisdiction extends to the installation of such rates to all of such territory.

To ascertain the rate upon a shipment from New York to Reno
one looks in vain for any one tariff in which such rate is to be
found. By examination of the tariff of the Transcontinental
Freight Bureau, to which the Southern Pacific Company is a
party, this note is discovered:

Rates to intermediate points

When no specific rate is named to an intermediate point shown in Transcontinental Freight Bureau Circular No. 16–C (I. C. C. No. 864), supple-
ments thereto, or reissues thereof, rate to such an intermediate point will
be made by adding to the rate shown to the point designated herein as
" Terminal," which is nearest destination of shipment, the local rate from
nearest terminal point to destination.

Turning to Transcontinental Freight Bureau Circular No. 16–C
(the issue at the date at which this complaint was brought), we
find Reno named as an intermediate point, and that the nearest terminal to Reno is Sacramento, 154 miles west of Reno.
We find, then, by returning to the Transcontinental Freight
Bureau west-bound tariff, the rate applicable upon the shipment
to Sacramento. Then, having ascertained this from a tariff to
which all of the carriers from New York to Sacramento are parties,
we must next find the local rate from Sacramento to the destination of the freight, which is east of Sacramento. This local rate,
Sacramento to Reno, we find in a tariff to which the Southern
Pacific Company alone is a party. Thus we have, through a
maze of tariffs, at length discovered the rate from New York to
Reno, which is made up of a joint through rate to Sacramento
and a local rate of the Southern Pacific Company alone from
Sacramento back to Reno.

The all-rail class rates, in cents, per 100 pounds from eastern defined territory to coast terminals were, when this case was
brought, as follows:

	CLASSES									
	1	2	3	4	5	A	B	C	D	E
Groups B, C, D, E, F, G, H, and I	$3.00	$2.60	$2.20	$1.90	$1.65	$1.60	$1.25	$1.00	$1.00	$0.95
Group J	3.00	2.60	2.00	1.75	1.60	1.40	1.20	.95	.85	.80

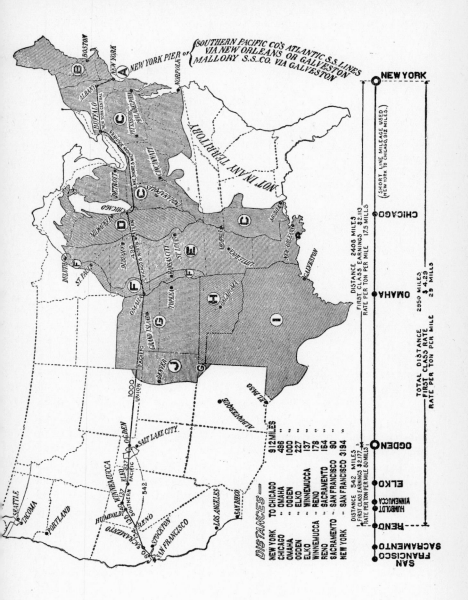

An examination of present tariffs will show that from New England and New York territories (Groups B and C) no class rates below fourth class are now extended. Prior to January 1, 1909, however, and at the time this complaint was brought, rates were given for the full 10 classes from these groups, and such rates upon the $3 scale are now given to coast terminals from Group A, the freight being carried from the New York City piers to New Orleans and Galveston by ocean carriers and thence by rail. It will also be seen that from Group J slightly lower rates are made on all classes below second class than are made from other groups. With these exceptions, however, the rates are uniform throughout the whole eastern defined territory as to classified freight.

The local rates on classes from Sacramento to Reno are as follows:

Class	1	2	3	4	5	A	B	C	D	E
Rate	129	112	102	87	78	78	24	23.5	25.5	25.5

The result of the combination on Sacramento is therefore to produce the following rates to Reno:

From Groups B, C, D, E, F, G, H, and I:

Class	1	2	3	4	5	A	B	C	D	E
Rate	429	373	322	277	243	238	159	$133\frac{1}{2}$	$125\frac{1}{2}$	$120\frac{1}{2}$

From Group J:

Class	1	2	3	4	5	A	B	C	D	E
Rate	429	373	302	262	238	218	154	$128\frac{1}{2}$	$110\frac{1}{2}$	$105\frac{1}{2}$

Rates to points east of Humboldt, such as Winnemucca and Elko, under the present method of making rates on the Ogden combination, vary as the rate from point of origin to Ogden.

The effect of this change in method of making rates may be illustrated briefly by the statement that the first-class rate to Reno from Chicago prior to January 1, 1909, was $3.90, whereas it is now $4.29; from Missouri river $3.50, and now $4.29. To Elko, on the other hand, the first-class rate from Chicago is now $4.27, as against a previous rate of $4.72½, when the rate based on Sacramento.

For many years the class rates to interior points, such as Reno, were no higher than to the terminals. On April 11, 1893, the practice of maintaining lower terminal rates was instituted. The first line of figures in the table below shows the Reno rates when this case was brought; the second line, the rates in 1892; and the third line, the difference, or the amount by which the rates have been increased.

To Reno from	CLASSES									
	1	2	3	4	5	A	B	C	D	E
Missouri river common points . .	429	373	322	277	243	238	159	133½	125½	120½
1892 rates	350	300	250	200	175	175	155	125	110	100
Difference	79	73	72	77	68	63	4	8½	15½	20½
Mississippi river common points .	429	373	322	277	243	238	159	133½	125½	120½
1892 rates	370	320	260	205	180	182	163	130	115	105
Difference	59	53	62	72	63	56	. . .	3½	10½	15½
Chicago common points	429	373	322	277	243	238	159	133½	125½	120½
1892 rates	390	340	270	210	185	190	170	135	120	110
Difference	39	33	52	67	58	48	. . .	. . .	5½	10½

Commodity rates. While there are many hundred commodity rates extended to coast terminals, there are but few given to intermediate points. On the following articles the commodity rates are the same to Utah and Nevada points as to Pacific coast terminals from Groups D, E, F, G, H, I, and J of eastern defined territory, which include all points from Chicago west:

Apples; bananas; beer, in wood; bones; broom corn; butter, butterine, oleomargarine, eggs, cheese, and dressed poultry; cars, street; barley, corn, rye, oats, and speltz, c. l. and l. c. l.; bran and shorts, c. l. and l. c. l.; brewer's grits, brewer's meal, corn

meal, corn chop or chop feed, chopped corn, cracked corn, and
hominy; buckwheat, c. l. and l. c. l.; wheat, c. l. and l. c. l.;
cooperage, cranberries; fertilizers, n. o. s.; household goods, c. l.
and l. c. l.; live stock; machinery, mining; mineral-water bottles,
returning; oil cake and oil-cake meal; onions; onion sets, l. c. l.;
packing-house products; pineapples; plaster, building; poultry,
alive; railway equipment; and staves and headings.

As to all but two or three of these commodities, the rates are
the same to Reno as to Sacramento from Chicago. That is to
say, the blanket rate made from all eastern defined territory to
coast terminals on these commodities is applied from Chicago
to Reno. There are a few other commodities upon which commodity rates are given to Reno which are somewhat higher than
the rates from Chicago to Sacramento, viz., automobiles, buggies,
carriages, wagons, vehicles, and coal, coke, and guano from certain far western points. From an examination of the tariffs it
appears that the transcontinental commodity rates — rates from
eastern defined territory to the coast terminals — are at the present time higher than they were ten years ago by a very considerable percentage and this regardless of the fact that the base of
supplies has been constantly moving westward, thereby narrowing
the distance between point of production and consumption.

VOLUME OF NEVADA TRAFFIC

Nevada is colloquially known as the "Sage Brush State," and
from the car window it presents the spectacle of an almost uninterrupted waste. Railroad men speak of it as a "bridge" —
unproductive territory across which freight must be carried to
reach points of consumption. The figures of the Southern Pacific
demonstrate, however, that while Nevada traffic may at one time
have been negligible such is no longer the case.

Some time before this proceeding was brought the Southern
Pacific Company, which is the lessee of the Central Pacific running from Ogden west into California, brought suit in the
United States circuit court for the district of Nevada attack-
ing certain rate schedules upon state traffic established by the

state commission. In support of its case the Southern Pacific Company filed an affidavit made by Mr. C. B. Seger, auditor of the Southern Pacific Company, showing the earnings of the Central Pacific on business wholly within the state, on business passing through the state, on business originating in and passing out of the state, and on business originating outside and having its destination in the state, for the fiscal year ending June 30, 1907. Mr. Seger said by way of explaining his figures:

The freight earnings accruing to and made by said Southern Pacific Company in Nevada, being the revenue itself, without reference to its disposition under any lease, agreement, or otherwise, are derived for the said fiscal year 1907 from through and local business, understanding by local business such as is strictly intrastate in character, picked up and laid down within the limits of the State of Nevada, and understanding by through business such as is interstate in character. Further differentiating, said interstate business consists, first, of business originating outside and coming into the state; second, of business originating in and passing out of the state; and, third, of business originating outside the state, having destination beyond the state, and, in relation to the state itself, simply passing through the state. The freight earnings for said fiscal year, and pertaining to the said business as above classified, are set forth under the appropriate heads, and are, in fact, as follows:

	REVENUE	PERCENTAGE OF TOTAL
Intrastate	$159,791.40	0.02
Originating outside and coming into the state . .	1,683,687.69	.20
Originating in and passing out of the state . . .	831,802.96	.10
	2,675,282.05	.32
Passing through the state	5,578,282.28	.68
Sum total	$8,253,564.33	1.00

Surprising as these figures are they apparently do not fully set forth the extent of Nevada business at this time, as is shown by an exhibit filed by the Southern Pacific Company in the present case, giving the business west of Ogden for the single month of February, 1909, which may be epitomized thus:

	REVENUE	PERCENT-AGE OF TOTAL	TONNAGE	PERCENT-AGE OF TOTAL
Intrastate	$29,001.00	0.03	4,715	0.04
Into and out of Nevada and Utah west of Ogden . . .	314,379.65	.38	64,367	.50
	343,380.65	.41	69,182	.54
Passing through the state . . .	495,128.37	.59	60,271	.46
Total for month of February, 1909	$838,509.02	1.00	130,453	1.00

Another most interesting showing is made by the Seger affi-davit as to passenger business on the Southern Pacific in the State of Nevada for the year 1907, the figures given being these :

	REVENUE	PERCENT-AGE
Intrastate	$286,235.65	10
Originating outside and coming into the state . .	357,511.55	13
Originating in and passing out of the state . . .	267,582.85	9
		— 22
		— 32
Passing through the state	1,962,915.33	68
Sum total	$2,874,245.38	100

The statement for the month of February, 1909, referred to above, sets forth very clearly not only the volume of business going into and out of Nevada and the earnings of the Southern Pacific thereon, but also gives a specific analysis of the sources of the traffic, showing the volume which comes into Nevada from the east and that which comes from California. Under " Question 2 " below will be found a statement of the freight received at Nevada and Utah points from points west of Calvada, which is a station directly on the California-Nevada state line. This table, however, should not mislead ; a considerable percentage of the traffic from California is traffic of eastern origin reshipped from California to Nevada. The table also includes coal and other commodities of very large tonnage (approximately one-half of the total in weight) coming from points west of eastern defined territory.

TERRITORIAL MOVEMENT	TOTAL	
	Tons	Southern Pacific Earnings
Gross total tonnage and earnings of the Southern Pacific Co. for the month of February, 1909 . .	913,302	$3,422,529.00
Question No. 1		
Freight *via* Ogden to California	37,886	320,220.55
Freight *via* Ogden from California	22,385	174,907.82
	60,271	$495,128.37
Question No. 2		
Freight *via* Ogden to points in Nevada and Utah . .	17,485	66,284.88
Freight received at Nevada and Utah points from points west of Calvada	16,823	144,965.00
Freight *via* Ogden from points in Nevada and Utah	18,381	33,462.77
Freight forwarded from points in Nevada and Utah to points west of Calvada	11,678	69,667.00
	64,367	$314,379.65
Question No. 3A		
Freight received in California, San Francisco and north, from all points in California, including interchange with connecting lines in California . . .	189,827	$365,168.00
Question No. 3B		
Freight picked up and laid down in Nevada and Utah and freight moving between Nevada and Utah —		
Nevada to Nevada	4,046	21,839.00
Utah to Utah	144	948.00
Utah to Nevada	499	5,122.00
Nevada to Utah	26	1,092.00
	4,715	$29,001.00

There was a time, doubtless, when Nevada traffic, save to the mines on its westernmost border, was but trifling. At present, however, it has a traffic, both freight and passenger, which is far too considerable to be overlooked under the rule *de minimis*. And it is to be remembered that the figures given apply to but one road, whereas a second is in operation across the state to the south, and a third is beginning operations on the north.

SOURCES OF EASTERN TRAFFIC

It is interesting in this connection to regard the point of origin of this eastern freight. The railroad commission of Nevada had access to the billing of all shipments reaching Reno, and from these compiled a series of statements which appear to show that the great body of Nevada traffic which comes directly from the east *via* Ogden originates west of the Indiana-Illinois state line.

From one exhibit it appears that of the 1,063,687 pounds of less-than-carload shipments originating in eastern defined territory and delivered at Reno during the months of January, February, March, and April, 1908, only 10 per cent originated at the Atlantic coast cities of New York, Boston, and Philadelphia, and only 25 per cent in Connecticut, District of Columbia, Maine, Maryland, Massachusetts, New Jersey, New York, Pennsylvania, and Virginia. This exhibit further shows that on the traffic moved the charges were $32,719.30; that if terminal rates had been applied charges would have been $21,956.24; and that the difference is $10,748.07. In other words, the charges on these shipments to Reno were 48.3 per cent higher than would have been the charges on the same shipments had they been carried over the mountains to Sacramento.

Another exhibit shows that of 21,000,000 pounds of carload freight, earning $278,000, moved from eastern defined territory into Reno, 9,500,000 pounds, earning $120,000, moved in at rates no higher than terminals. It further shows that only 4,500,000 pounds of the 21,000,000 originated east of Chicago. This exhibit shows, aside from the products carried to Reno at terminal rates, that the charges were, for the year 1908, $157,824.94; that the terminal charge would have been $99,679.90; and the difference, $58,524.40. In other words, the charges on carload shipments to Reno were 59 per cent higher than the charges on the same shipments would have been had they been carried to Sacramento.

Commissioner Thurtell estimated from the figures at his hand that the total receipts under present rates upon business brought into Reno *via* Ogden for the year 1908 amounted to

$454,343.69 and under terminal rates the revenue would have
been $363,865.23, a reduction of $90,478.46. The statement
also shows that the revenue to the Southern Pacific from this
business was $268,516.40 and would have been under termi-
nal rates $178,037.94, a reduction of $90,478.46, or about
33 per cent. Expressed in revenue the Southern Pacific on
the haul from Ogden to Reno earned $11.51 per ton, while if
terminal rates had been charged its earnings would have been
$7.63 per ton.

On the whole, the figures given in this case, which are the
most authoritative thus far presented to the Commission with
reference to the sources of westbound transcontinental traffic,
indicate that less than 25 per cent of the traffic into Reno from
the east originates east of Chicago, while 75 per cent originates
between Chicago and Denver. In other words, the needs of the
people on the west coast may be and are in great part supplied
from sources nearer home than the Atlantic seaboard.

The manufacturing center of the country has moved westward
and rates from the Atlantic seaboard that were once necessary
are now almost unused. It may be historically the fact, as the
carriers assert, that the transcontinental blanket rates given to
the Pacific coast cities were put in to meet water competition
from the Atlantic coast points, and that these rates were extended
westward from the Atlantic as matter of grace to western manufacturers and producers; to-day, however, it might well be said
that this blanket is extended not westward, but eastward, so as
to give the eastern manufacturer or jobber some opportunity to
reach the far western markets.

WATER COMPETITION

As we have seen, the rates are higher on almost all commodities from eastern producing points to Reno than on these same
commodities to Sacramento, the more distant point. Without
explanation this constitutes a violation of the long-and-short-haul
clause of the act. The carriers justify the lower rates to the more
distant point upon the ground of water competition. They say

carriers east of Ogden receive precisely the same earnings upon both shipments; but the Southern Pacific, west of Ogden, receives far more upon the Reno shipment than on the Sacramento shipment. This is illustrated in the following table:

FROM —	To —	RATE	EARNINGS EAST OF OGDEN	EARNINGS OF SOUTHERN PACIFIC COMPANY (WEST OF OGDEN)
		Cents	Cents	Cents
Group B, Boston	Sacramento	300	211.3	88.7
	Reno . . .	429	211.3	217.7
Group C, New York	Sacramento	300	211.3	88.7
	Reno . . .	429	211.3	217.7
Group D, including Chicago, etc.	Sacramento	300	181.9	118.1
	Reno . . .	429	181.0	248.0
Group E, including Mississippi river .	Sacramento	300	174.5	125.5
	Reno . . .	429	174.5	254.5
Group F, including Missouri river . .	Sacramento	300	159.3	140.7
	Reno . . .	429	159.3	269.7

Neither at the hearings nor in the argument did the carriers east of Ogden contend that their divisions of these rates were unreasonable. The Southern Pacific, however, the carrier which makes the last 700 miles of a 3100-mile haul, strenuously insists that its rates to the more distant points are compelled by water competition for the purpose of defending higher rates to intermediate points; while the carriers performing 2400 miles of that service appear to regard the rate as entirely reasonable. The line from New York to Sacramento and Reno constitutes a through route and in law the carriers engaging therein constitute one line. If the Sacramento rate is less than a reasonable rate and the result of competition then it would seem fair to assume that all of the carriers engaging in the transportation so consider it and would accordingly demand a lesser division than the division they would be justified in requiring out of the higher rate to the intermediate point. The fact remains, however, that for the 2400-mile haul from New York to Ogden the New York Central, the Lake Shore, the North Western, and the Union Pacific secure the same revenue out of the $3 rate to Sacramento that they do out of the $4.29 rate to Reno. This is graphically illustrated by the following diagram showing the division of the rate:

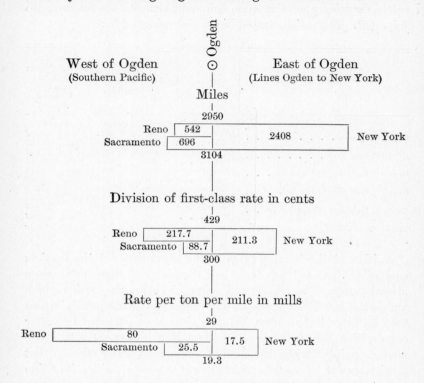

PRODUCTIVE FREIGHT TERRITORY

We have gone extensively into an investigation of the conditions surrounding this traffic and in anywise governing the basis upon which the rates to Nevada from the east should be governed. What has been said herein gives little more than a suggestion of the extent of the inquiry which has been made. We have, for instance, had reports made upon the financial condition of the carriers involved, and their ability to meet any reduction which the Commission might direct without serious impairment of their revenues, an interesting fact in this connection being this: During the past two years the operating revenues of the Southern Pacific Company's Pacific system have increased $8,000,000 while its operating expenses have decreased $5,000,000, thus producing an increased operating income of over $12,000,000, or a net increase of about $2000 per mile of road.

There appears in the record a compilation from the statistics of this Commission for the years 1898–1907 in which it is shown that in these ten years the carriers in the Pacific coast territory doubled their freight tonnage, which rose from 18,000,000 to 35,000,000 tons; almost doubled their gross revenue; their receipts per mile increased over 70 per cent; their receipts per ton per mile increased from 1.07 to 1.25, or about 20 per cent; while the relation of expenses to earnings remained practically constant at 62.50 per cent. These figures are for all the roads in the Pacific territory. But if we take the Central Pacific alone we find it third in the list of Pacific coast roads in tons carried and the highest of all in freight earnings per mile ($13,453 per mile in 1907). While it is one of three railroads in the West carrying over a million tons of freight per mile of road — the average for the United States — the earnings of the Central Pacific per mile are 65 per cent greater than the average for the United States and 100 per cent greater than the average of the roads west of Chicago.

Conclusions

The time has come, in our opinion, when the carriers west of the Rocky Mountains must treat the intermountain country upon a different basis from that which has hitherto obtained.

Nevada asks that she be given rates as low as those given to Sacramento. The full extent of this petition can not be granted. In making rates to Reno from a territory broader than the whole of continental Europe we have necessarily given consideration to existing rates to other intermediate points and to points upon the Pacific.

We are of opinion that the class rates to Reno, Winnemucca, and Elko, and other points in Nevada upon the main line of the Southern Pacific Company, from stations on the lines of the defendants between New York and Denver and other Colorado common points are unreasonable and unjust and that for the future no higher rates than those set forth below should be charged to Reno and points east thereof to, but not including, Winnemucca:

FROM —	CLASSES									
	1	2	3	4	5	A	B	C	D	E
Denver and other points in Group J[a]	$2.10	$1.82	$1.54	$1.33	$1.12	$1.12	$0.87	$0.70	$0.66	$0.60
Grand Island and other points in Group G[a]	2.30	2.00	1.68	1.45	1.22	1.22	.96	.76	.73	.65
Omaha and other points in Group F[a]	2.50	2.17	1.83	1.58	1.33	1.33	1.04	.83	.79	.71
Clinton and other points in Group E[a]	2.80	2.42	2.03	1.71	1.43	1.46	1.14	.91	.86	.78
Chicago and other points in Group D[a]	2.90	2.51	2.09	1.75	1.47	1.50	1.18	.94	.89	.80
Toledo and other Cincinnati-Detroit common points[b] . . .	3.05	2.63	2.19	1.81	1.52	1.56	1.23	.98	.92	.83
Buffalo and other Pittsburg-Buffalo common points[b] . . .	3.20	2.76	2.29	1.87	1.57	1.62	1.28	1.03	.96	.86
New York and common points[b] .	3.50	3.01	2.49	2.00	1.67	1.75	1.38	1.11	1.03	.93

[a] As designated in Transcontinental Freight Bureau Westbound Tariff 1–K, I.C.C. No. 920.
[b] As designated in Nor. Pac. No. 23,500, I.C.C. No. 3295.

And that for the future no higher rates than those set forth below should be charged to Winnemucca and points east thereof to the Nevada-Utah state line:

FROM —	CLASSES									
	1	2	3	4	5	A	B	C	D	E
Denver and other points in Group J[a]	$2.00	$1.72	$1.46	$1.26	$1.06	$1.06	$0.83	$0.67	$0.63	$0.57
Grand Island and other points in Group G[a]	2.19	1.90	1.60	1.38	1.16	1.16	.91	.72	.69	.62
Omaha and other points in Group F[a]	2.38	2.06	1.74	1.50	1.26	1.26	.99	.79	.75	.67
Clinton and other points in Group E[a]	2.66	2.30	1.93	1.62	1.36	1.39	1.08	.86	.82	.74
Chicago and other points in Group D[a]	2.75	2.38	1.99	1.66	1.40	1.43	1.07	.89	.85	.76
Toledo and other Cincinnati-Detroit common points[b] . . .	2.90	2.50	2.08	1.72	1.44	1.48	1.17	.93	.87	.79
Buffalo and other Pittsburg-Buffalo common points[b] . . .	3.04	2.62	2.18	1.78	1.49	1.44	1.22	.98	.91	.82
New York and common points[b] .	3.33	2.86	2.37	1.90	1.59	1.66	1.31	1.05	.98	.88

[a] As designated in Transcontinental Freight Bureau Westbound Tariff 1–K, I.C.C. No. 920.
[b] As designated in Nor. Pac. No. 23,500, I.C.C. No. 3295.

In directing the carriers to establish these class rates we have taken into consideration the fact that the general policy of the carriers is to make commodity rates somewhat lower than class rates on commodities, the movement of which is regarded as necessary to the development of mercantile interests and industries. There are at present, as we have seen, a considerable number of such commodity rates into Reno, but these are entirely insufficient to meet the needs of Nevada if she is to become in any way an independent business community. There is no foundation in the record in this case for the establishment of such commodity rates. The theory upon which the case was presented eliminated all other considerations excepting the claim that all rates extended to Sacramento were reasonable as to Reno and other Nevada points. The Nevada petition was tantamount to a request that under our legal authority to establish reasonable rates we should fix the same rate from Denver as from Boston. We do not so construe our authority as to permit this Commission to make rates upon such a basis. Without doubt the commodity rates made to the coast terminals are reasonable from a great portion of eastern defined territory, but a governmental authority may not exercise the latitude in fixing a rate blanket which the carriers themselves have here exercised.

In the *Spokane case*, 19 I. C. C. Rep. 162, some 600 commodity rates had been established voluntarily by the carriers, and the petition in that case was for the reduction of those rates to a reasonable figure. The carriers had made a special series of zones across the continent to meet the exigencies of the Spokane situation. In the case before us, however, no such favorable condition is presented. We have neither a schedule of commodity rates with which to deal as to which specific complaint is made, nor have the carriers so divided the continent into groups of originating territory, save in the sense that the transcontinental groups to the coast terminals, which are entirely different from those found in the *Spokane case, supra*, furnish a foundation for present combination rates to western Nevada.

In view of this situation we shall make no order as to commodity rates in this case at the present time, but shall direct the carriers to make a record of all shipments into Nevada from eastern defined territory during the months of July, August, and September, 1910, or during such other representative months as may be determined upon by the Commission after conference with the carriers, and furnish the Commission with a statement showing as to each shipment the following facts:

(1) The commodity; (2) the weight, carload or less than carload; (3) point of origin and the transcontinental territorial group in which the same is situated; (4) rate that would be applied under the tariffs in effect July 1, 1910; (5) the gross charges thereunder; (6) the rate applicable under the order made in this case; (7) the gross charges thereunder; (8) the rate that would be applied were the movement to Sacramento; (9) the gross charges thereunder.

The complainant will be ordered in this case, on or before October 1, 1910, to furnish to the Commission and to the defendant Southern Pacific Company a list of commodities upon which commodity rates are desired, together with an outline of the various territories or groups from which commodity rates should apply.

We are of the opinion that justice can not be done to Nevada unless Nevada points are put on a practical parity with points in eastern Washington and eastern Oregon, and a further hearing will, in due course, be held after the data here requested have been furnished by carriers and complainant.

XVIII

EXPORT AND DOMESTIC GRAIN RATES

ATLANTIC AND GULF COMPETITION [1]

PROUTY, *Commissioner :*

The purpose of this proceeding was the investigation of export rates upon grain and grain products. . . . The matters embraced were :

First. Relative domestic and export rates.

Second. Relative rates on grain and grain products for export.

Third. Publication of export tariffs upon grain and grain products.[2]

I

A domestic rate applies to traffic which is being transported for use in this country ; an export rate to traffic which is on its way to some foreign country.   *   *   *   *

An examination of the tariffs filed with the Commission since 1887 shows that until recently the published rates upon domestic and export traffic have ordinarily been the same. Taking Chicago as an example, no export rate appears until October 1, 1896. Upon that date, the domestic rate on corn being 20 cents to New York, an export rate of 15 cents was made which expired October 31, 1896. January 20, 1897, the domestic rate still being 20 cents, a 15-cent export rate was again put in and remained effective until September 6, 1897. No other export rate appears until February 1, 1899, when an export rate of $18\frac{1}{2}$ cents upon wheat and 16 cents upon corn was published, the domestic rates being 20 cents and $17\frac{1}{2}$ cents, respectively. April 17th this rate was reduced to 12 cents upon both wheat

---

[1] Decided August 7, 1899. Interstate Commerce Reports, Vol. VIII, pp. 214–276. The English practice is suggestively described at p. 754, *infra.* At p. 404 of Ripley's Railroads : Rates and Regulation the larger aspects of both import and export rates are discussed.

[2] This part of the case is omitted. — ED.

and corn, a domestic rate of 17 cents upon each commodity being made effective the following day.

From Minneapolis to the Atlantic seaboard the published rates upon all kinds of grain and the products of grain have been uniformly the same, that is, wheat, corn, and flour have always taken an identical rate. December 28, 1889, the domestic rate being $32\frac{1}{2}$ cents, an export rate of $30\frac{1}{2}$ cents was published which expired February 4, 1890. In one or two other instances export rates were in effect for short periods, but it was not until the present year that this became the rule. January 2, 1899, an export rate of 25 cents was made effective upon flour, the domestic rate upon grain and flour being $27\frac{1}{2}$ cents. This same export rate was, January 4, 1899, extended to grain and other grain products as well as flour. February 7th this rate was raised 1 cent to 26 cents. April 18th the domestic rate was reduced to $24\frac{1}{2}$ cents, and the export rate to 23 cents.

From the Mississippi river to New York no export rate is found until October 1, 1896, when a rate of 17 cents on corn was put in against a domestic rate of 25 cents. This export rate expired October 31, 1896. January 20, 1897, the domestic rate still being 23 cents, an export rate of 15 cents was applied to corn which remained in effect until September 6, 1897. February 1, 1899, a rate of $13\frac{1}{2}$ cents upon corn was made effective, the domestic rate being $20\frac{1}{2}$ cents. April 15th an export rate of 12 cents was made upon both wheat and corn, the domestic rate upon grain and grain products being established April 18th at $19\frac{1}{2}$ cents. Both domestic and export rates to other Atlantic cities are a certain differential above or below the New York rate, so that the history of the export rate to New York indicates its history to the entire Atlantic seaboard.

It would appear that export rates have been in effect to the Gulf ports for a longer time than to the North Atlantic ports. April 28, 1890, an export rate of 28 cents on corn from Kansas City to Galveston was established, the domestic rate being 48 cents, and this rate continued in effect until December 28, 1895. The domestic rate during that period fluctuated from 48 to 27 cents. December 28, 1895, an export rate of 27 cents was made upon corn against a domestic rate of 36 cents. July 21, 1896, this was reduced to 16 cents, and July 31 to 13 cents, the domestic rate being 35 cents. An export rate of 28 cents upon oats was made between these points July 20, 1891. The first export rate upon wheat was made February 16, 1896, and was 31 cents. From this time on the export wheat rate fluctuated, the lowest being 12 cents August 17, 1896. At the time of the hearing the rate on all kinds of grain for export was 10 cents. The domestic rate since June 5, 1896, has been 37 cents on wheat and 35 cents on corn. * * * *

It will be seen that lower rates upon export than upon domestic grain have for a considerable time prevailed through the Gulf ports, but that until quite recently no substantial difference has been made through North Atlantic ports, except in the case of Boston and Portland, which have taken the New York export rate, and of Montreal, which takes an export rate 1 cent below New York. The question now before us is whether these lower export rates are an unjust discrimination against consumers at points bearing the higher domestic rate, and so in violation of the 3d section of the Act to Regulate Commerce. This must depend upon the conditions under which export and domestic grain moves, and those conditions arise both at home and abroad.

Directing our attention first to wheat, and considering the world as a whole, we find that certain countries produce more wheat than they consume, while certain other countries consume more than they produce. The principal nations in the former class are the United States, the Dominion of Canada, Argentina, Russia, India, and Uruguay. * * * *

The United States always produces more wheat than it uses for domestic consumption, but the amount of this surplus differs greatly from year to year. The following table gives the amount of wheat exported from the different wheat-exporting countries averaged in periods of five years for the time indicated :

COUNTRIES	1881–1885	1886–1890	1891–1895
United States	122,157,043	115,788,774	171,731,480
Other countries . . .	115,690,816	134,484,937	179,646,922

The above table shows the exports from the United States of both wheat and flour reduced to bushels, and also from other countries, although the amount of flour exported from the United States is relatively much larger than it is from any other wheat-exporting nation. The exact statistics are not at hand to show exportations from other countries since 1895, but it sufficiently appears from the above statement what the relative position of the United States is as a wheat-exporting nation.

It is not material to state the wheat-consuming countries nor the amounts consumed by each. The United Kingdom and the European continent are the principal ones. It is sufficient to observe that all these principal grain markets are in direct communication with all wheat-producing countries. In Liverpool or Antwerp, American wheat comes into direct competition with foreign wheat from all these sources, and must be sold in competition with such wheat. It was said in testimony that the quality of American wheat was superior to that produced anywhere else, except in the Canadian Northwest, that this wheat was largely used by foreign millers to mix with inferior foreign grades, and that this sometimes created a demand for this particular quality of wheat which made the price higher than that of different grades of foreign wheat; but on the whole it must be true that the price of our American product is determined in these markets under the law of supply and demand in competition with all other wheat-producing nations. American wheat does not make the price abroad, although it may be the greatest single factor in the making of that price. To just what extent it does so operate must manifestly depend upon the amount available from different sources.

If the price of wheat in the foreign market is fixed by conditions outside the United States, that price of necessity determines the sum which can be realized in the foreign market for our American product. The cost of laying this wheat down in the foreign market is made up of two factors: the price paid the farmer who raises it, and the cost of transporting the grain from the grain fields to the foreign market. If the cost of transportation remains at all times the same, the price paid the farmer must

vary with the price abroad, and a reduction in the cost of transportation would benefit the farmer by exactly the amount of the
reduction. It was said by those familiar with the business that
the price at which our surplus can be sold determines the market
price of the entire product. It seems plain that this must be true
to a large extent. We are inclined to think, therefore, that there
might be, and at times probably are, market conditions abroad
which require the making of a low export rate for the purpose of
disposing of our surplus product, and that without such rate the
surplus product could not be moved, resulting in a demoralization
in price to the wheat producer. In that event the consumer would
get the benefit of the low price which the producer is compelled
to take, but it will hardly be claimed that, taking the people as
a whole, such fluctuations in price are desirable.

Market conditions in case of corn are somewhat different than
with wheat. In the sale of its corn in foreign markets the United
States has no serious competitor. Argentina exports corn in limited quantities, and considerable appears to come from southeastern Europe, but, taken altogether, the amount is insignificant in
comparison with that furnished by the United States. The corn
market of Chicago fixes the price throughout the world. In an
indirect fashion corn comes into competition with wheat both
abroad and in the United States. Wheat and corn are both capable of sustaining life, and the comparative expense at which
either article can be procured tends in a degree to determine the
amount of its consumption. The same is true of other grains.
It requires, however, a considerable difference in expense to overcome individual prejudices and habits in favor of a particular
article of food. The opinion of exporters examined upon the
hearing was that it would require a very substantial advance or
reduction in the freight rate to materially influence the export of
corn. We very much doubt whether market conditions abroad
require a low export corn rate, or whether such low rates produce a material effect in the movement of our surplus corn crop.
It is undoubtedly true that exporters in the United States are
often enabled to make sales by some concession in the freight rate
which they could not otherwise make, but in the making of those

sales they are probably competing with some other dealer in the United States who is exporting his corn by some different route. The lower rate is required, not to meet competition from other countries, but competition between transportation companies in this country.

While, however, we are of the opinion that low export rates, especially upon wheat, might be justified and required by market conditions abroad, we are not of the opinion that the particular rates under consideration are due directly or indirectly to such conditions. Many grain exporters were examined in the course of this investigation, many railroad men were asked to state the reasons for the wide difference between the export and domestic rate, and no one of them suggested that this had been brought about by conditions abroad. It was the universal opinion of grain dealers and the unanimous admission of railroad representatives that these rates were entirely due to competition between railways in America.

Grain which is grown east of the Rocky Mountains can ordinarily be exported either through the Atlantic ports or through the Gulf ports. The principal North Atlantic ports are Montreal, Portland, Boston, New York, Philadelphia, Baltimore, Norfolk, and Newport News, and the principal Gulf ports, Galveston and New Orleans. Grain grown to the west of the Rocky Mountains passes out through the Pacific ports.   *   *   *

The Pacific ports are not included in this investigation. Most of the grain exported through other ports is raised between a line drawn north and south through Chicago and the Rocky Mountains. All this territory is nearer in miles to the Gulf ports than the Atlantic ports. Owing to the geographical lines upon which our railway systems have been developed, export grain, until within a comparatively few years, has moved almost entirely through the Atlantic ports. These grain fields were first reached by roads from the East. Those roads have been strong and well equipped and have been able to control the greater part of this business. Within recent years, however, the lines leading to the South have become potential competitors for this traffic. Their physical condition has been greatly improved, expensive terminals have been constructed at New Orleans, and are being constructed at Galveston. Great sums have been expended by the government in improving the water approaches of these ports, until they now admit vessels of the largest tonnage. These railways, being in position to handle the traffic, and having a most important advantage in point of distance, now insist that a portion of the business belongs to them. The Illinois Central Railroad with its easy grades and unexcelled terminal facilities contends that the grain grown upon its own line, at least, should be exported by it. Lines leading south from Kansas City strenuously claim that grain should pass by their routes to the seaboard rather than go twice the distance to the Atlantic ports. Kansas City is distant from Galveston about 800 miles and from New York about 1400 miles. The whole country tributary to Kansas City, in which enormous quantities of wheat and corn are raised, is therefore much nearer the Gulf ports than the Atlantic ports. Testimony in this case showed that the grain exported through Galveston during the last two or three years had been hauled an average distance of from 700 to 1000 miles, while had it passed out by the Atlantic ports it must have been carried from 1400 to 1600 miles.

Plainly, this grain will pass out through that port by which it can reach its foreign destination most cheaply. The margin of profit in handling grain has been and is extremely small, and a slight difference in the freight rate, not more than one eighth to one fourth cent per bushel, determines the route which it will take. The ocean rate varies greatly from the same port, often fluctuating from day to day. It also varies between the different ports. The Gulf ports insist that they are under a very substantial and permanent disadvantage as compared with all the Atlantic ports, and especially Boston and New York, in that there are no regular lines of steamships from Galveston to foreign ports, and comparatively few from New Orleans. The volume of imports through these ports is extremely small, so that vessels coming there for cargoes must come mainly in ballast. From this and many other circumstances it results that the average of ocean rates from the Gulf ports to foreign markets is higher than from the North Atlantic ports. Upon this proposition the evidence in this case, and the evidence taken before the Commission in previous cases, leaves no question; but when the attempt is made to go a step further, and to determine what in cents per bushel, or per hundred pounds, represents the disadvantage attaching to the exportation of grain through these ports as compared with North Atlantic ports the problem is an exceedingly difficult one, and indeed one to which an exact answer is impossible. What is true of the Gulf ports as compared with the North Atlantic ports is true in a less degree of the North Atlantic ports in comparison with each other. Now the total rate must be the same by all the ports, and therefore the inland rate to the Gulf ports must be less than the corresponding inland rate to the North Atlantic ports, but just how much it is exceedingly difficult to say. From all this we conclude that competition between railways for a considerable portion of this export grain is most severe, both by reason of the number of competitors and the peculiar conditions under which the competition proceeds.

The first low export rates from the Mississippi river and Chicago were, by the admission of all parties, made to divert traffic from the Gulf ports to the eastern lines. It will be remembered that export rates were in effect from Kansas City to Galveston and New Orleans previous to this much lower than the ordinary domestic rates.

While Gulf competition was the cause of the low export rates from the Mississippi river to the Atlantic seaboard beginning October 1, 1896, that competition is not answerable for the extremely low rates which prevail at the present time, these being due to competition between carriers to different North Atlantic ports.

For many years previous to February 1, 1899, certain agreed differentials had existed in the rates from interior western points to the North Atlantic ports of export. On export traffic Boston and New York have taken the same rate, Philadelphia a rate 2 cents, and Baltimore, Norfolk and Newport News 3 cents per hundred pounds below New York. The lines leading to New York have long insisted that these differentials were too high as against that port, and in the month of January, 1899, an agreement was made by which they were to be reduced one half, leaving the rate to Philadelphia 1 cent and to Baltimore, Norfolk and Newport News 1½ cents per hundred pounds lower than to New York. Rates from St. Louis and Mississippi river crossings as far north as East Dubuque are the same. There was either in effect or in contemplation at the time of the making of the above agreement an export rate on corn from the Mississippi river of 15 cents to New York, 13 cents to Philadelphia and 12 cents to Baltimore, Norfolk and Newport News. The lines leading from St. Louis to Baltimore, Norfolk and Newport News insisted that the rate of 12 cents to these latter ports could not be advanced by reason of competition with the Gulf lines. It was therefore determined that the new differentials should be adjusted by reducing the rate to New York and Philadelphia. Accordingly, beginning February 1st, the rates were from the Mississippi river to New York 13½ cents, to Philadelphia 12½ cents, and to Baltimore, Norfolk and Newport News 12 cents.

Lines leading to the three latter points had always insisted that the original differentials did not unduly prefer those ports, and that under the modified differentials those ports would not obtain a fair share of the traffic. Some of these lines claimed that it was a part of the original arrangement by which the differentials were modified, that if an actual trial of the new differentials showed that lines leading to these ports did not obtain a fair share of the business the old differentials should be restored. These lines further insisted that the actual showing for the months of February and March demonstrated the correctness of their contention, and they accordingly published from St. Louis to these ports a rate of 10½ cents, being 3 cents below the New York rate. Thereupon lines leading to New York immediately met this by an export rate of 12 cents, thereby leaving the differential against that city at 1½ cents. In answer to this one line leading from St. Louis to Newport News published a rate of 9 cents upon corn, thus reëstablishing the 3-cent differential. Here the matter rested at the time of the hearing, this rate not having been met by either the Baltimore or New York lines.

Since the hearing other rates have been put in effect which will be stated hereafter.

It will be seen, therefore, that the first export rate from the Mississippi river was made to meet Gulf competition, and that subsequent reductions have been brought about entirely by competition between rail carriers leading to the North Atlantic ports. The recent low export rates to the Gulf have been made to meet these low rates east.

There seems to be certain territory from which it is conceded that grain ought to be exported by way of the Atlantic seaboard, and no attempt is made to divert it to the south. There may also be some regions from which eastern lines are willing to admit that grain ought to be exported through the Gulf, although if such regions do in fact exist their location was not very clearly developed upon this hearing. It is not our province to divide up this traffic nor apportion this territory; nor, if it were, is there evidence in this case which would enable us to do so. It is evident, and we find, that there is a large area from which this export business may properly be said to be competitive as between different ports, and that such competition does actually exist in a most intense degree; first, between the Gulf and the North Atlantic seaboard; secondly, as between different North Atlantic ports. This competition has produced the present export rates.

While, however, competition between rail carriers was responsible in the first instance for the present lower export rates, there is another factor which must have a most important bearing upon the maintenance of these rates. We refer to water competition.

Chicago is the most important grain market of the United States. The price of grain in that market probably controls the price throughout this country at least. Of all the corn which is sent from the West to the Atlantic seaboard the greater part passes through Chicago, or a Chicago junction. Of wheat the greater bulk seems to center at Duluth rather than Chicago, although Chicago handles large quantities.

Now it is possible to transport grain from Chicago to either Montreal or New York entirely by water. The same steamer which loads at a Chicago elevator can pass by way of the Great

Lakes, the St. Lawrence river and the Canadian canals to the
side of the ocean steamship at Montreal. Grain carried by lake
from Chicago to Buffalo can there be loaded into a canal boat
and taken through the Erie canal and the Hudson river to the
ship side in New York harbor. It did not appear very definitely
what the rate per hundred pounds by water from Chicago to
Montreal was, but the testimony leaves the impression that it
is between 8 and 9 cents per hundred pounds. Neither did it
appear exactly what the all water rate was from Chicago to
New York. . . .

We have already seen that export corn, being at Chicago, and
export wheat, being at Duluth, will reach the foreign port by
the cheapest route. Unless, therefore, the rail carrier makes
substantially the same route on this grain to New York as is
made by water lines the traffic will of necessity move by water,
and not by rail. Otherwise stated, no grain can be exported
from Chicago through New York by rail unless the rail rate is
practically the same as the water rate. There may be circumstances under which the rail carrier can obtain a slightly higher
rate, but the testimony shows, and the necessary conclusion from
the undisputed facts is, that no considerable difference can be
made in favor of rail transportation.

There was no testimony to show what the ocean rate from
Montreal to the foreign destination was, but it did appear in
this case, and has appeared in several previous cases, that the
ocean rate from New York is lower than from any other port
except Boston. It must follow, therefore, that all grain at Chicago, or which can be brought to Chicago, will be exported
through the port of New York unless carriers leading from
Chicago to the other ports make a rate as low or indeed lower
than is made to New York. The same remark applies to interior
points. Peoria, St. Louis and the lines leading from these cities
claim the right to participate in this export grain traffic, but this
they cannot do unless the rates from such interior points to the
port of export bear a certain relation to the Chicago rate, for the
grain can reach either Chicago or these points. A reduction
in the Chicago export rate necessarily forces a reduction in the

export rate from these interior points to the Atlantic seaboard; but we have already seen that the rate to the Atlantic seaboard and the rate to the Gulf must correspond if any business is to move through the Gulf. Hence the inevitable conclusion that the water rate from Chicago to New York and from Chicago to Montreal determines the export rate through all the ports of the United States to a large extent while that rate is available. Whatever has been said in reference to Chicago applies equally to Duluth, the lake rate from there being but a trifle higher than from Chicago.

Not only is water competition a controlling factor in theory, but in volume as well. The testimony upon this hearing was that nearly all the wheat which reached Duluth went from there by water. It appeared that in the year 1898, 127,000,000 bushels of corn passed through Chicago, and of this amount 97,000,000 bushels left that port by water. It was in evidence that one exporter during the year 1898 had sent 14,000,000 bushels of grain all water through the port of Montreal. Competition which actually carries such enormous quantities of traffic must be controlling in its effect.

It should be observed that these lake rates only apply during the period of navigation, which is ordinarily from the middle of April to the middle of December. During some five months in the year grain cannot be transported from Chicago by lake, but the effect of this water competition is not entirely confined to the period of navigation. Considerable quantities are accumulated during the closed season at different ports of export, as well as at Buffalo and other lake ports, to be sent forward after navigation closes. Upon the contrary, the elevators at Chicago, which are estimated to contain about 50,000,000 bushels, are emptied during the season of navigation, but as soon as navigation closes they begin to fill up with grain which is stored there in anticipation of the opening of the next season. Considerable quantities are also stored in vessels lying at Chicago and Duluth during the winter months. While, therefore, there is during nearly half the year no actual lake transportation, the water route in a degree controls even then the rail rate; it limits to an extent at all times the amount which the rail carrier can obtain from this traffic.

Water rates from Chicago to Montreal and New York apply to both export and domestic traffic, and no distinction appears to be made between the two kinds of traffic in case of the lake and rail rate.

A pertinent inquiry in all investigations of this sort is, Who is injured? In the present case, Whom does this difference between export and domestic rates harm? There are four different classes involved: the producer, the carrier, the domestic consumer and the foreign consumer. Many witnesses expressed the opinion that the producer had the benefit of the low rate. These statements were, however, merely expressions of opinion. No witness was able to say that the putting in of these rates had produced any actual effect upon the general market price of wheat and corn, and for the obvious reason that the elements which determine the market price of these commodities are so complex and so various and the prices themselves so fluctuate that it would be impossible to observe the connection if it existed. Whatever fact is found in reference to this must probably be by inference from other facts.

It appears plain that if the price of grain were absolutely fixed by the foreign market the American farmer would receive the entire benefit of the low rate. If grain cannot be sold for more than a certain price, and if that price is less than the market price in this country plus the established rate, then either the rate or the price in this country must be shrunk or the grain cannot find a foreign market. Upon the other hand, if the price of grain in the foreign market is determined by the American market, then the foreigner has the benefit of the low rate. The price which the American farmer receives is fixed by his home market, and the exporter can sell in the foreign country for that price plus the rate. When the rate is reduced, the price in the foreign market is correspondingly reduced. As an actual fact it is doubtless true that the price of grain, certainly wheat, abroad is fixed neither by the foreign nor by the American supply alone, but by the one acting upon the other.

Undoubtedly the American market has more to do with the price abroad at some times than at others, but it must always have something to do with that price, and the state of the foreign market must always act to some extent upon the American market. It is probable, therefore, that the producer and the foreign consumer obtain in varying degrees the benefit of the low export rate upon wheat. In view of the almost unanimous testimony that market conditions abroad have not required the recent low export rate, and that the volume of exports has not been stimulated by those rates, we are inclined to think that from these particular reductions in rate the American producer has derived no special benefit. The carrier has lost and the foreign consumer has gained.

There was no claim in this case that the present domestic rates were too high. If the American consumer suffers from the low export rate it must be from the necessary consequences which result from such an adjustment of rates. We cannot find specifically from the testimony in this case that the American consumer in the East is injured.

Whatever injurious effect is capable of being perceived is much more likely to result between different sections in the West, and arises, not from the principle of the lower export rate, but from the application of that rate.

Nearly all these low export rates are what are termed proportional rates. They do not apply to traffic originating at the point from which they are made effective, but only to traffic which has already paid the local rate up to that point. The 12-cent rate from the Mississippi river to New York cannot be used for the transportation of grain grown upon the east bank of that river, but only applies to grain grown to the west, and which has already been transported from some point farther west up to that river. It is evident that the application of this rate to the Mississippi, without the putting in of corresponding rates at points east, must have affected the price of grain grown west of that river as compared with the price of that grown east. The export rate from Chicago and from the Mississippi river is nominally the same. If it were actually the same, wheat would be worth exactly as much at the Mississippi as it is at Chicago for export. The testimony tended to show that the putting in of this low proportional rate did actually increase the price of grain at the Mississippi river in comparison with the Chicago price.   *   *   *   *   *   *

It may happen and in many cases does happen, that, by the application of these so-called proportional rates, grain from the more distant point obtains transportation to Chicago or to the Gulf at a less rate than grain from the intermediate fields through which the transportation passes. We held in the investigation as to these export rates last April that this created, as against such intermediate points, an undue preference. *In the Matter of Export Rates from Points East and West of the Mississippi River*, 8 I. C. C. Rep. 185. We now repeat that finding.

*   *   *   *   *   *   *   *

The carriers insist that while now, for the first time, a systematic difference is made in the published tariff between export and domestic rates, there has in fact always been such a difference in the actual rate. It is undoubtedly true that as to competitive traffic the published rate has been largely departed from in the past. This export traffic is highly competitive. It moves in large lots and is handled by comparatively few individuals. The idea has been more or less prevalent that the provisions of the Act to Regulate Commerce did not refer to export traffic. For these and other reasons export business has been peculiarly open to the manipulation of rates.

The testimony of representatives of carriers familiar with rates actually paid was to the effect that there had been in the past as wide a difference between the published rate and the actual rate upon export business as exists to-day in the published tariffs. We have no doubt that there has been in the past a difference between the published and actual rates. This difference has existed in the case of both export and domestic traffic. It has probably been greater in the case of export business, but how great we cannot definitely find.

Carriers also claim that they are justified in making a lower rate on export than on domestic business by the fact that the cost of service is less to them. This export business moves in large lots, often in train loads, from a single point of origin to a single destination. Large cars can be used and these cars can be loaded to their full capacity. For these and other reasons they urge that the cost of handling this traffic is less than in case of domestic. We are inclined to think that there may be some difference in the cost of service, but we cannot from any testimony in this case express an opinion as to the amount of such difference. * * * * * *

II

The second branch of this case refers to the relative rates upon grain and the products of grain. While the order instituting the investigation includes the products of both corn and wheat, the manufacturers of corn products did not appear and were not heard, nor were any complaints received from that class until after the close of this hearing. The only product of grain which was fully represented upon the hearing was flour. It seems, moreover, that flour is the only grain product which is exported in very large quantities, and that is the only subject accordingly to which this discussion will be directed.

From the time the Act to Regulate Commerce took effect until February 1, 1899, railway carriers have, with the exception of a short period in 1891, published the same rate upon export wheat and flour. Different rates upon these commodities have been made in certain parts of the United States, but those rates have never been applied to export traffic. February 1, 1899, carriers leading to the Atlantic seaboard published an export rate upon wheat from Chicago to New York of $18\frac{1}{2}$ cents. The domestic rate was then 20 cents and the rate upon flour was the same. These rates were not changed, and the rate upon export flour was thus $1\frac{1}{2}$ cents per hundred pounds higher than the rate upon export wheat. Subsequently the rate upon wheat was further reduced to 12 cents, the domestic rate upon wheat and the rate upon flour being established at 17 cents. Generally speaking the rate upon both domestic and export flour is the same as the rate upon domestic wheat, so that the difference between export wheat and export flour is represented by the difference between domestic wheat and export wheat. These rates have already been given, and need not be repeated here.

The statement that no distinction is made between domestic and export flour is subject to one most important exception. Flour from Minneapolis, the largest milling center in the United States, when for export takes a rate $1\frac{1}{2}$ cents per hundred pounds below the corresponding domestic rate by both rail and lake and rail routes, and this same difference obtains in the case of certain other milling points in the Northwest whose rates are governed by the Minneapolis tariff. This distinction does not apply in the case of Milwaukee, nor at any point south of a line drawn through Milwaukee east and west.   *   *   *

The milling interests of Minneapolis and other points which now enjoy an export rate did not appear upon this hearing, but practically all other sections of the country in which flour is ground for export were represented before us, protesting against the difference in rates upon export wheat and flour. These milling interests may be properly divided into the seaboard and the interior millers, and while the difference in rate, when actually paid, apparently affects both these classes in substantially the same way, their claims may be stated separately.

American millers compete in foreign markets with one another, but the testimony shows that their most serious competitor is the foreign miller. Most wheat purchased by wheat-consuming countries is exported before being ground. Russia and Canada grind a small amount of their surplus wheat, but the United States is the only nation which exports any very considerable amount of flour.

Considering the seaboard miller as compared with the English miller who grinds American wheat, both must derive their supply of the raw material from the same source. The American miller at New York pays the domestic rate, which is from the Mississippi river $19\frac{1}{2}$ cents per hundred pounds, while the English miller transports his wheat from the same point to New York at the rate of 12 cents per hundred pounds. Clearly, therefore, the Englishman has an advantage by reason of this difference in freight rate over the American of $7\frac{1}{2}$ cents per hundred.

It also costs the American miller more to transport his product across the ocean than it does the English miller to transport his wheat; but this is a matter with which we are not concerned. Plainly the American miller at New York pays, if he pays the published domestic rate, $7\frac{1}{2}$ cents per hundred pounds more than the Englishman in bringing his wheat to the seaboard, and is therefore placed at a disadvantage to just that amount.

While this must be so if the seaboard miller actually pays the published rail rate, it is not plain to us that at the present time he does pay that rate. During the period of navigation, practically all wheat moves to the east by lake and rail, and upon this traffic the rate is the same whether for export or domestic consumption. Apparently it costs the New York miller to-day exactly the same to get his wheat to New York that it costs the English miller. This would not be so during the period of closed navigation, since it seems that almost one half the grain actually received by the New York Central during the months of March and April last was billed and carried upon the domestic rate.

While the representatives of the seaboard millers stated that these rates seriously discriminated against them, their testimony did not show any considerable diminution in exports from these mills. The profit was said to be less both upon export and domestic flour than it had formerly been, but the relative amount which was exported continued to be about the same.

Chicago may be taken as a type of the interior milling situation, and to illustrate this situation we may select one Chicago mill. This mill had a capacity of about 1500 barrels a day. The wheat which it ground was entirely spring wheat and came from beyond the Mississippi river. In its export business it was in competition with the English miller who obtained his wheat from the same fields. The rate paid by the Chicago mill from the Mississippi river to Chicago was 5 cents per hundred pounds. That paid by the English miller upon the same wheat from the Mississippi river to Chicago was 1.8 cents per hundred pounds. From Chicago to New York the Chicago miller paid upon his manufactured product 17 cents while the English miller paid upon his raw product 10.2 cents, making a total difference in cost at New York against the Chicago miller of 10 cents per hundred pounds.

The Chicago miller could obtain the benefit of the through rate from the Mississippi river to New York under the milling-in-transit privilege by the payment of an added $1\frac{1}{2}$ cents per hundred pounds, but he could not apply this to the export rate. The domestic rate from the Mississippi river to New York was $19\frac{1}{2}$ cents per hundred pounds, which, with the added $1\frac{1}{2}$ cents for the milling-in-transit privilege, makes a total through rate of 21 cents compared with a rate of 12 cents to the English miller. It is probable that the discrimination would be rather less against the American who was grinding winter wheat, but not materially less. A statement filed by the representatives of the Milwaukee millers shows by many illustrations drawn from actual rates a discrimination of from 4 to 11 cents per hundred pounds.

Considerable testimony was given as to the margin of profit in the manufacture of flour. This must of course vary at different times and under different conditions, but the testimony fairly showed that from 1 to 2 cents per hundred pounds was at the present time a fair profit, and as great a profit as had been realized recently upon export flour. The testimony upon the whole tended to show that the profit on flour sold abroad was rather less than that upon flour consumed at home. The primary object of the flouring mill is usually to grind for home consumption, the foreign market being resorted to as a means of disposing of that portion of the product which cannot be marketed at home.

Minneapolis and the northwest generally, where the lower export rate upon flour prevails, did not complain. The seaboard miller insisted that his margin of profit had been reduced by this discrimination, but the volume of business was apparently about the same. Upon the other hand, Milwaukee, Chicago, St. Louis and corresponding territory not only showed a diminution in profits, but a very marked decrease in the volume of export business. It was said by these millers that January 1st they were largely oversold for export, and that for this reason they sent abroad during the early months of the current year considerable quantities of flour, but that they were unable to sell at the present prices and were largely out of the export trade. It is our conclusion and finding that the adjustment of rates is largely responsible for this. The northwestern miller enjoys a relatively better export rate. The seaboard miller can buy his grain during a large portion of the year upon the same terms as the foreign miller. Against the interior miller all these causes combine with the effect that he must be largely or entirely driven from the export trade.

The carriers justify the difference in rates in part at least upon the ground of difference in the cost of service. It was urged by them that for several reasons the transportation of export wheat is more profitable at the same rate than the transportation of flour for export, and that there ought to be a difference, although some thought that the present difference was too wide. They urge that it is a universal rule that the manufactured product pays a higher rate than the raw material; that flour is much more valuable than wheat; that it is more liable to damage than wheat; that wheat moves in larger volume, so that not merely car loads, but whole train loads are embraced in one shipment; that the cars can be, and in fact are, loaded more heavily with wheat than with flour. It is also said that the rate includes a delivery over the ship side in case of flour, and at the ship side in case of wheat.

The millers deny most of the above allegations, and say that if the movement of wheat is in larger volume at times, that of flour is much steadier, and that it is for the interest of the carrier to build up industries which bring other traffic in turn.

It is undoubtedly true that the raw material commonly takes a lower rate than the manufactured product, and for this there is usually a substantial reason in the character of the two commodities; but this is not by any means a universal rule, and the uniform practice of carriers for years has been to make the same rate upon export wheat and flour.

Export flour is probably on the whole somewhat more valuable than wheat, although when it is remembered that the cheaper grades of flour are usually exported it is questionable whether the difference in value is material. *   *   *   *

From all this we conclude that the actual cost of handling export flour somewhat exceeds that of handling wheat, but just how much cannot be determined with certainty. We do not think that the excess would be more than from 1 to 2 cents per hundred pounds.

The carriers also justify their rates upon the ground of water competition. It has already been seen that this species of competition between Chicago and the seaboard forces down the grain rate to a point much below the ordinary rail tariff. The same thing is true, although not to the same extent, of the transportation of flour. It is not only possible to carry flour from Chicago and Duluth to the Atlantic seaboard by all water routes, as well as by lake and rail routes, but considerable quantities of it are so transported. In 1898 nearly one fourth of all the flour leaving Chicago for the entire year went from that port by water. This for the most part is carried to some lake port like Buffalo, and from thence to the seaboard by rail, but it may be taken all water to Montreal or New York as in case of grain, and the possible rail route determines what the rail portion of the haul can exact in the case of flour, as it does in the case of grain.

When, however, the effect of this competition upon the rate is examined, we find that the lake or the lake and rail rate is not as low as the corresponding rate upon wheat. The reason seems to be that equal facilities do not exist for the carrying of flour by lake as for the carrying of grain. Boats which engage in this traffic upon the Great Lakes are either line boats or wild boats. Line boats ply between certain stated points like Buffalo and Chicago at frequent intervals, and are in all cases under the control of some railroad company in connection with which they are operated. Wild boats, on the other hand, ply between different points, sometimes starting from one port and sometimes from another. Line boats are equipped for the carriage of flour and other package freight, while wild boats as a rule are not. Flour is never carried by these wild boats, — at least such was the testimony, — but always goes by the regular lines. In consequence the rate upon flour can be better maintained than that upon wheat. The ruling rate by lake upon flour from Chicago to New

York in recent years has been from 11 to 15 cents as against a rate of from 8 to 10 cents upon wheat. The present lake and rail rate on flour is 14 cents per hundred pounds, and it was said that this rate was maintained. The present domestic rail rate is 17 cents, and under these rates the carriage of flour from Chicago for export was said to be pretty evenly divided between all rail and lake and rail. From this it would appear that the difference between all rail and lake and rail which can be secured in case of flour is somewhat greater than in case of wheat. The differential in favor of the lake lines in former years has usually been 5 cents per hundred pounds, instead of the present differential of 3 cents, and this was one ground of complaint by the millers. In the past the demoralization has been so general that the published rate has offered very little criterion of the actual rate. If the present differential were 5 cents in favor of lake lines the rate on lake and rail flour would be 12 cents, and the millers claim that the railroads take advantage of the fact that they control these regular lines to unduly raise the lake and rail rate on flour. There is probably something to this, since it appears that these regular lines which carry flour are all under the influence of railways leading from the lake ports to the Atlantic seaboard; but we think and find that lake competition fairly fixes the rate on flour at from 2 to 4 cents per hundred pounds above the wheat rate. Subject to this difference the effect of water competition upon export flour is exactly the same as upon export wheat, and that effect need not be restated here.   *   *   *   *

Conclusions

1. The first question presented for determination is, Does the Interstate Commerce Act, as a matter of law, prohibit the charging of an export and a domestic rate upon the same traffic to the same point? This question has recently been decided by the Commission in the negative in the case, *Kemble* v. *Boston & Albany R. Co.*, 8 I. C. C. Rep. 110. Since, however, the reasons upon which that decision rested have a certain bearing upon the questions of fact involved in this matter they may be briefly restated here.   *   *   *   *   *   *   *   *

January 29, 1891, a decision was announced in the case, *New York Bd. of Trade & Transportation* v. *Pennsylvania R. Co.*, 4 I. C. C. Rep. 447, 3 Inters. Com. Rep. 417, in which the matter of import rates was considered. The complaint was that carriers leading from New York to Chicago and the West were transporting freight which arrived from foreign destinations from New York to interior points at a less rate than was charged for the transportation of similar freight to the same interior points when such freight originated at New York. Many companies were made parties to this proceeding, and the case, in its original form, was intended to embrace practically all ports of entry upon the eastern seaboard and the Gulf. The conclusion reached was that the rate charged by the rail carrier from the port of entry to the inland destination must in all cases be the same upon merchandise originating at such port of entry as upon merchandise coming to that port from a foreign country. The Commission made this decision, however, not as question of fact, but as matter of law. Its holding was that the effect of the Act to Regulate Commerce extended no further than the boundaries of the United States; that the Commission had no power to consider conditions existing without the United States; that when traffic arrived at a port within the United States from a foreign country it was not proper to inquire from whence it came, but it must be treated in all respects as though it was domestic traffic originating at the port of entry.

The *Import Rate Case, Texas & P. R. Co.* v. *Interstate Commerce Commission*, 162 U. S. 197, 40 L. ed. 940, 5 Inters. Com. Rep. 405, was an attempt upon the part of the Commission to enforce its order in this last-named proceeding. The Texas & Pacific Railway Company, with its connections, was engaged in the transportation of merchandise from Liverpool, England, to San Francisco, Cal. This merchandise was taken upon a through rate, came by water from Liverpool to New Orleans, and by rail from New Orleans to San Francisco. This entire through rate was often much less than the rate on corresponding articles from New Orleans to San Francisco, and the division of the rail carrier was of course very much less than its domestic rate for a

corresponding service. For example, one of the articles so transported was dry goods; the rate on dry goods by this line from
Liverpool to San Francisco was 107 cents per hundred pounds,
while the rate from New Orleans to San Francisco over the same
rail line was 374 cents per hundred pounds. The defendants
justified the rate from Liverpool upon the ground that water
competition by various routes between Liverpool and San Francisco compelled them to charge this rate if they obtained any
portion of the business.

The rule laid down by the Commission, and which was contended for by the Commission, in that case would have compelled
the carrier to charge the same rate from New Orleans to San
Francisco upon import as upon domestic merchandise, and would
have excluded all consideration of conditions existing abroad.
The Supreme Court refused to concur in this construction of the
Interstate Commerce Act, holding that in case of imported traffic
as well as of traffic originating within the United States the Commission should have reference to all conditions, whether at home or
abroad, which bore upon the reasonableness of the rate adjustment.
It held that the Act to Regulate Commerce did not prescribe a
hard and fast rule which required that imported merchandise
should be taken from the port of entry at the same rate which
was applied to domestic merchandise originating at that point.
The exact point decided was that carriers were not, as a matter
of law, prohibited from participating in a through rate from a
foreign destination to an interior point, of which the division
received by the inland carrier was less than its rate for a similar
service in the transportation of domestic merchandise between
the same points. This decision must apply equally to export
traffic, and upon its authority we are constrained to hold that, as
matter of law, the Interstate Commerce Act does not prohibit a
rail carrier from making a through rate from a point within the
United States to a foreign destination, of which its division shall
be less than the amount charged for the corresponding transportation of domestic merchandise to the port of export.   *   *

Carriers in some quarters seem to assume that the *Import Rate
Case* above referred to in effect withdrew import and export

traffic from the purview of this Commission. Such is not at all the result of that decision. It rather enlarged the power of this body over that species of traffic, for while it was held that there was no rule like that contended for by the Commission it was also held that conditions abroad as well as at home should be considered, and that the interests of all classes, and not of a single class, should be taken into account. It is still a question of fact whether rates upon export or import traffic, as well as those upon domestic traffic, are in contravention of the provisions of the Act to Regulate Commerce.

The question for our consideration is therefore one of fact, and seems to be, upon this branch of the case, whether the present adjustment of export and domestic rates discriminates against the domestic consumer and in favor of the foreign consumer. What reason is there why the foreigner who eats our wheat should have it transported from the Mississippi river to New York for 12 cents a hundred pounds, while the American is obliged to pay $19\frac{1}{2}$ cents for the same service ?

The Supreme Court in the *Import Rate Case* has laid down the rule which should guide this Commission in the determination of that question. It is not every discrimination which is forbidden by the Act to Regulate Commerce, but only unjustifiable discriminations ; and the court holds that in determining whether a discrimination is in fact unjustifiable the interests of all parties involved must be considered. The parties involved in this case are the producer of the grain, the domestic consumer and the inland carrier; we are not concerned with the foreign consumer. Now, taking all these classes together, is the discrimination against the seaboard consumer an unjust one ?

The railways insist that it is a matter of no consequence to the eastern consumer what rate is charged the foreigner, provided the domestic rate is a reasonable one, and there is no pretense in this case that domestic rates are not sufficiently low. To this proposition we cannot fully assent. In the first place the foreigner is to an extent in competition with the American. Both are engaged in the production of articles sold in the same market, either abroad or in the United States. If the Englishman can procure the necessities of life cheaper than his American competitor, that gives him the advantage. A few cents per hundred pounds in the price of his flour would not be, of itself, a matter of great consequence, but the same sort of a preference applied to all articles which enter into his daily support, as well as to the product of his labor, may determine whether he or the American can manufacture for our own market even.

Again, railway rates are in amount interdependent the one upon the other. The railway is entitled to earn a fair return upon its investment. If the proposition is made to reduce the rate, one important factor in the determination of that question is the total amount of earnings. If the rate is too low upon one article, in the end other articles pay too high a rate. Unless there is some good reason for the distinction, the rate to the American ought not to be higher than to the foreigner. If our carriers, in the absence of any constraining reason, can transport corn from the Mississippi river to New York for 12 cents per hundred pounds for export, that of itself shows that a rate of $19\frac{1}{2}$ cents to the domestic consumer is unreasonable. Conditions may justify the existence of a lower rate for export than for domestic use, but in the absence of such conditions we cannot concur in the idea that any permanent system of rates which renders a service for the foreigner at a less price than is paid by the American can be just to the American; nor would we permit the continuance of such a system if we had the power to prevent it. From the standpoint of the eastern consumer the difference in rate of itself creates a discrimination which is undue, unless justifiable in the interest of the producer or the carrier.

How stands the interest of the producer; in other words, to what extent is the western farmer benefited by these low export rates?

The United States produces every year a certain quantity of wheat. Of that quantity the greater part is consumed by our own people, but a very large surplus still remains which must be disposed of abroad. This surplus is sold to foreign countries in competition with wheat from other parts of the world, and it must be sold at the price obtainable in the foreign market. While at times that price may be practically fixed by the United States, and while at all times it is influenced by the price here, still it must be admitted that ordinarily the foreign market is not entirely determined by our own market.

It has already been said, in the findings of fact, that our wheat must be delivered abroad at the market price there. If the foreign price is less than our market price plus the ordinary cost of transportation, either the price here or the price of transportation must be reduced. Witnesses of experience in this respect gave it as their opinion that market conditions abroad frequently require a low rate in order to dispose of our surplus product ; that the price of our surplus wheat establishes the market price in this country, and that, therefore, at times a low rate was of distinct benefit to the farmer, and indeed was necessary to prevent the demoralization of prices.

Conditions with reference to corn are apparently somewhat different. The corn market of the United States controls that of the world. The price at which our corn can be sold abroad has something to do with the amount which will be taken by foreign countries, but so does a lower price upon the eastern seaboard stimulate the consumption of corn. It is probable, and this was the testimony of exporters, that the difference in rate has little influence upon the volume of corn exportation.

Our conclusion is that a low export rate is sometimes necessary to dispose of our surplus wheat, and that in a much less degree it may promote the movement abroad of our surplus corn ; that to the extent that it does operate to move our surplus grain it is of distinct benefit to the producer, and that his interest would outweigh that of the American consumer, and would justify a moderate difference in the rate. The price of the surplus within certain limits, seems to fix the price of the whole, and in the disorganization of prices from a glut in the market the producer loses more than the consumer gains. The ability to dispose of an actual surplus is a sort of safety valve which steadies the whole situation. It must be observed, too, that in applying this low rate to our surplus product the railway does precisely what the miller does and what every other manufacturer is likely to do. The foreigner can buy American flour and almost every article of American manufacture cheaper than the American can at the mill or the factory. It is equally apparent that whether market conditions abroad do justify the lower export rate is a very delicate question to deal with, and one which had better be left to the law of supply and demand so far as it can.

An examination of this question from the point of view of the eastern consumer and the western producer leads to the conclusion that the low export rate is an unjust discrimination against the former unless it is required to move our surplus grain, in which event it is within some limits proper; that this Commission ought not to interfere unless it clearly appears that the difference is unduly great, or that no conditions abroad require it.

In the present case those facts did clearly appear. It appeared beyond all question that the low export rate in force at the time of the hearing had not resulted from any market conditions abroad. The witnesses were almost unanimous in the opinion that these rates had not been required by such conditions, and that they did not stimulate the export of our grain. It was practically conceded by the carriers that the rates were abnormally low, and that they had resulted entirely from competition between rail carriers themselves. If this is true, then it seems plain that the American producer has derived no substantial benefit from these rates; that the American carrier has lost enormously by them, and that the foreigner alone has had the benefit of them. The discrimination against the eastern consumer is not justified unless there is something in the interests of the carrier which excuses it.

* * * * * * * *

The cause of these low export rates has been fully stated in the findings of fact. The carriers themselves with one voice affirm that they were entirely the result of competition between American railways, first between the eastern lines and the Gulf lines, afterward between the different eastern lines. Since January 1st export rates on grain have been reduced in many cases almost one half; at these reduced rates enormous quantities of traffic have moved; no market conditions abroad required these reductions, and the American producer has not been materially benefited by them; our railways have sacrificed millions of dollars without producing any real effect upon the flow of traffic, for the relative rate has remained about the same and the low rate has not increased the total volume. This depletion in revenue has been a donation to the foreigner.

It is impossible more strongly to emphasize the folly of this whole proceeding than by the mere statement of it; and yet in just what way does it violate the Act to Regulate Commerce? The purpose of that Act was to foster railway competition. The highest judicial authority has declared that competition between railways may be a reason for making a lower charge to the more distant point. We have found that this traffic is not only the legitimate subject of competition, but that the competition for it must be conducted under such circumstances as to render it peculiarly active and difficult to control. To agree upon these differentials to the different ports might be a criminal act. Apparently there is no method by which these questions can be settled except by a resort to such measures.

The real question is whether, in this warfare, domestic as well as export rates ought not to be reduced; whether the American as well as the foreigner ought not to have the benefit of this competition. We should be inclined to take this view of the matter, and to make some order which would at least limit the extent to which export might be lower than domestic rates, were it not for two circumstances.

First: Assuming that the basis of export and domestic rates ought to be the same, we think there may be cases where a difference may properly exist. Of this Boston is a good illustration.

The through rate from Chicago to Liverpool must be the same by all the ports. The ocean rate from Boston to Liverpool is the same as from New York; therefore, unless the inland rate from Chicago to Boston is the same as that from Chicago to New York export traffic will move through New York, not through Boston. These circumstances have induced the railways serving these two ports to agree for the last thirty years that the export rate to Boston and New York from the West might be the same. It is difficult to see how this agreement can, in its operation, be treated as unjust or as in violation of the Act to Regulate Commerce. This Commission has twice decided that the Boston domestic rate may properly be higher than the New York domestic rate. We must assume, therefore, that the domestic rates to these two sections are properly adjusted, and that no discrimination is made against New England by charging the higher rate. The rate to the foreigner is fixed by that through New York, and therefore the making of the same rate *via* Boston does not discriminate in his favor as against the New England consumer. The commercial interests of Boston do not complain of the export rate. Under these circumstances, why should not New England carriers be permitted to engage in this export traffic?

It may be that if these carriers could be compelled, by an order of this Commission, to make the same domestic and export rates they would as a consequence reduce the domestic rate rather than surrender the export traffic, and that consequently Boston and perhaps some other New England territory would obtain the benefit of a lower domestic rate. They might, upon the other hand, prefer to surrender the export business rather than reduce the domestic rate; but the question before us is not what the carriers could be compelled to do, but what should they in fairness be required to do.

What is true of the rate to Boston is equally true of the export rate to Portland and Montreal; it is perhaps even more true of export rates to the Gulf ports. Taking effect July 1, 1899, the local export rate on wheat from Kansas City to Galveston is 19 cents, the proportional export rate 15 cents, and the local domestic rate 37 cents. Through rates *via* Kansas City undoubtedly make the ordinary domestic rate from Kansas City somewhat less than 37 cents, but the relation is probably pretty well indicated by the local export rate compared with the local domestic rate. We have here a domestic rate almost twice as great as the export rate. Without expressing any opinion as to the propriety of as wide a difference, or as to the reasonableness of the domestic rate, it seems evident, or extremely probable, that these lines may with propriety in competition for this export business make a lower charge upon export than upon domestic traffic.

Now if an order were to be made that domestic and export rates should under all circumstances be the same, it might result, and probably would result, in either driving out of business those lines where two rates may with propriety exist, or at all events in unjustly depleting the revenues of those lines. It would give to those lines in whose tariffs the difference is least an undue advantage over other lines in this competitive struggle. Before making any order which would not work injustice in the premises, it would be necessary to determine in each case by how much the domestic rate might properly exceed the export rate, if at all, and compel the observance of this relation. To do this would require us to determine what the differentials between these ports should be, and what reasonable domestic rates to these ports should be, and we certainly cannot undertake to do this upon the testimony before us.

The second circumstance which deters us from attempting to interfere is the existence of water competition. These rates were made before the opening of navigation, and were not probably influenced by that element; but we must dispose of the case with some reference to conditions as they now exist, and water competition is at the present time a factor which cannot be ignored.

By referring to the findings of fact it will be seen that Chicago and Duluth are the two points through which the greatest quantity of wheat and corn passes on its way to the seaboard. From both these points communication with the seaboard can be had by water. The greater part of the grain which leaves these cities for the east moves by water, and it cannot be questioned that the water rate to New York determines the rail or the water and rail rate to that same point. This Commission has always held that water competition, if it in fact exists, is an important circumstance in determining what rates may be justly charged by the rail carrier. The reasons for that have often been stated, and need not be repeated here. The water carrier is not subject to the provisions of the Act to Regulate Commerce; it publishes no rates; it may change its rates from day to day or from hour to hour; it can carry certain commodities at a lower rate probably than can be profitably made by rail. We have therefore been inclined to hold that competition of this kind might be met by the rail carrier without in all cases a corresponding reduction at points not affected by such competition. There is no invariable rule of this sort, nor can it be said that interior and intermediate points ought not to receive any benefit from water competition, but neither can it be affirmed that the carrier should in no case be allowed to meet such competition except at the expense of its interior and intermediate territory. Such a requirement would often be unjust to the carrier and of no benefit to interior points.

In this case the export rate to New York is absolutely fixed by water competition, although, as we have seen, the low export rates were first fixed without reference to such competition. The export rate to New York of necessity fixes that rate through every other port. This being true we are not inclined to say, so far as the export rate is actually controlled by water competition, and while it is so controlled, that carriers must at all points reduce correspondingly their domestic rates. The rate from Chicago to New York is a base rate. Thousands of other rates are a percentage of, or a differential above or below, that rate. A change in that rate automatically works a change in all these other rates. If the carriers prefer to leave the New York domestic rate higher than the export rate by reason of these many dependent rates, we should hardly be justified in interfering unless some specific injustice in some particular case was called to our attention.

Of course no business actually moves during the period of navigation between Chicago and New York upon the domestic rail rate so long as that rate is materially higher than the water rate. Grain to New York can move by water at the same rate both for export and domestic consumption, and the two rates must be practically the same to that point. Furthermore, the New York domestic rate of necessity to an important degree influences other domestic rates upon the seaboard. The Philadelphia miller cannot pay 5 cents per hundred pounds above the New York miller. Carriers apparently meet this condition by lake and rail rates which are much lower than the domestic rail rate, and which apply to both domestic and export traffic as a

rule. Under the operation of these tariffs most of the eastern
seaboard has the benefit of the low export rate, but we assume
that there is some substantial reason why carriers do not reduce
all rail domestic rates accordingly.

An examination of the tariffs in effect at the time of the
hearing, as well as those at present in effect, shows that the difference between export and domestic rates is the least through
the ports of New York, Philadelphia, Baltimore, Norfolk and
Newport News. The published rates both at present and in the
past show that the relation between the domestic and export
rate through these ports is about the same; if there were but
one rate at New York there would probably be no occasion for
but one through all these ports.

Our conclusion upon this branch of the case is that market
conditions sometimes in case of wheat, seldom in case of corn,
justify an export rate lower than the domestic through the port
of New York; and that water competition may have the same
effect. Ordinarily, during the period of closed navigation the
export and domestic rate should be the same through that
port, and the Atlantic ports above mentioned. Lower export
rates may perhaps with propriety be made through other ports,
thereby enabling lines leading to them to compete for this export
business. Such an adjustment of rates would be to the advantage of the carrier, just to the American consumer, and equally
so to the producer. With the opening of navigation water competition introduces a new element which may necessitate, in the
fair interest of the carriers, two rates at New York and consequently at all other ports. The problem is primarily one for the
carriers rather than this Commission, and we do not think at the
present time any interference on our part would contribute to
its solution.   *   *   *   *   *   *   *

III

The element of direct injury which was absent in the first
branch of this case is abundantly present in the second branch.
The complaint is that discrimination in the freight rate exists

against the milling industry in certain sections of the United States, and the miller makes oath that these freight rates have destroyed or are fast destroying his export business. We have found that this is in a measure true of Milwaukee, Chicago, St. Louis and corresponding territory in the middle west ; in all this territory millers are being excluded from the export trade ; and we have further found that this apparently results from the improper adjustment of freight rates. In part this improper adjustment consists in giving to certain sections better rates on flour in comparison with the complaining territory than have been previously enjoyed, and in part in creating an unreasonable difference in the rate upon wheat and flour. This being so, to what relief, if any, are the millers entitled?   *   *

The main complaint of the millers is directed to the difference in rates between export wheat and flour. The findings of fact fully state the case, and from them it clearly appears that a discrimination, and a most grievous one, does exist. It needs no argument to show that, when the entire margin of profit to the American miller in the grinding of export flour does not exceed from 1 to 3 cents per hundred pounds, a difference in the freight rate in favor of the English miller amounting to from 4 to 11 cents per hundred pounds is, other things being equal, prohibitive. The serious question is whether that discrimination is justifiable.   *   *   *   *   *   *   *

The carriers insist that the difference in rate is justified first, by water competition, and secondly by additional cost of service.

Water competition certainly limits during the period of navigation, and to a degree before the opening and after the close of navigation, the rates upon wheat and flour. Both the published and actual water rate on wheat has been lower than upon flour ; we have found from 2 to 4 cents lower.

This water competition for seven months of the year is not only possible but actual. Of all the traffic leaving Chicago by regular line boats during the period of navigation, 30 per cent is said to be flour and the balance grain and other commodities. It has already been said that water competition may to an extent be properly met by the rail rate. The water line does actually fix these relative rates on wheat and flour, and we think the carriers are justified by that competition in making, to a degree at least, the same difference which is thereby created. The millers urge with force that the rail carriers, by virtue of their control over the line boats by which alone flour is transported, unduly exaggerate the difference in rate between wheat and flour; but the fact still remains that water competition does create a substantial difference in those rates.

We have also found that to a limited extent the cost of service is greater in the transportation of export flour than in that of export wheat, and for this reason under the circumstances of this case we think that a slightly higher rate on flour than on wheat for export is justifiable. This is especially true in view of the fact that the flour rate includes the delivery on shipboard while the wheat rate does not. The rate from Chicago to New York upon flour puts the flour on board the vessel, whereas to put export wheat on shipboard an additional charge of about $1\frac{1}{8}$ cents per bushel is made.   *   *   *   *   *

It should perhaps be noticed that, although the rate upon flour has been confessedly higher than upon wheat for many years, the exportation of flour has steadily increased, being 3,947,333 barrels in 1878 and 15,349,943 barrels in 1898. The increase for the last six years has not, however, been marked, and exportations since 1894 have actually declined, having been in that year 16,859,533 barrels.

This Commission is of the opinion that public policy and good railway policy alike require the same rate upon export wheat and flour. Such rates tend to develop both the industries of the United States and the traffic of the railways. We are not, however, here settling national or railroad policy. We are simply administering the Act to Regulate Commerce; and in view of all conditions as we find them, we do not feel that charging a somewhat higher rate on flour than on wheat for export is in violation of that statute. We do think that the published difference is too wide, and that the rate upon flour for export ought not to exceed that upon wheat by more than 2 cents per hundred pounds.   *   *   *   *   *   *   *

XIX

FREIGHT CLASSIFICATION

The Hatters' Furs Case [1]

PROUTY, *Commissioner:*

The complainant is engaged in the manufacture of hats under the title of the Pioneer Hat Works at Wabash, Indiana, and his complaint is that "hatters' furs" and "fur scraps and cuttings" are wrongly classified, the present classification of both these commodities being double first class, while he insists that hatters' furs should be classified as first class and fur scraps and cuttings as second class. . . .

Hatters' furs is a trade name applicable to the various kinds of fur used in the manufacture of hats. These furs, as sold to the manufacturer and presented for transportation, are sheared from the skin, and packed in paper bags containing three or five pounds each, which are then assembled in wooden cases, 100 bags to the case. The case thus weighs from three to five hundred pounds and is in size about 36″ x 36″ x 40″, containing some 30 cu. ft.   *   *   *   *   *   *

The complainant testified that rabbit fur was the sort mostly used by him in the manufacture of hats, although he used to some extent nutria, and that the value of the furs which he used was from $ .40 to $2.50 per pound. The complainant makes a medium grade of fur hats. More of the higher priced furs would probably enter into the manufacture of hats of a higher grade. These furs, nutria and beaver, average in price as high as $6 per pound, and the price list show that the best grade of beaver has at times listed at $15 per pound; but it is fairly

[1] Decided November 21, 1901. Interstate Commerce Reports, Vol. IX, pp. 79–86.

inferable from the testimony that rabbit fur is the kind mainly used in the manufacture of fur hats of all grades, the more expensive sorts of fur being used only in comparatively small quantities. The testimony is not sufficiently definite to justify an exact finding, but we think it fairly appears, and find, that the average value of hatters' furs would be from $1 to $2 per pound, the great bulk of that commodity presented for transportation being within these limits.

The term fur scraps and cuttings seems to include the waste produced in working up fur pelts for various purposes. It embraces not only the waste from the preparation of hatters' furs but also the pieces which are left in the manufacture of fur garments. These fur scraps are purchased by fur brokers, by whom they are assorted into different grades and sold to different persons for various uses at widely different prices. The complainant testified that the fur scraps and cuttings used in the manufacture of hats were worth from $2\frac{1}{2}$ to 40 cents per pound. The pieces of fur which would also be embraced under the same title are often worth much more than this, sometimes as high as $1.50 per pound.

It is extremely difficult to fix any fair average value, but we are inclined to think that the great bulk of fur scraps and cuttings offered for transportation could not exceed in value 50 cents per pound, and that the average would not equal this. Fur scraps and cuttings are transported in cases, bags or bales weighing from 450 to 500 pounds. The proportion between bulk and weight is about the same as with hatters' furs.

Manufactured hats are classified first class and the complainant insisted that this was a discrimination against the raw material.

Upon this point testimony was given by both parties as to comparative value and desirability from a traffic standpoint of the raw material and the finished product.

Hatters' furs are put through three processes in preparation for use in the manufacture of hats and shrink about two ounces in the pound. Fur scraps and cuttings pass through from twelve to eighteen processes and only from 10 to $33\frac{1}{3}$ per cent in weight of usable fur is obtained. In the manufacture of the hat itself the average is still further shrunk.

Hats are shipped in cases weighing about sixty pounds to the case and are from two to three times more bulky than hatters' furs or fur scraps and cuttings. The complainant also insisted that they were much more valuable by the pound. This was denied by the defendants who claimed that the average value of all hats was less by the pound than the average value of hatters' furs.

Hats other than straw are sometimes made of other material besides fur, but the complainant testified that the proportion of fur hats to other hats would be fifty to one. Caps are made of cloth. The average value of fur hats per pound must greatly exceed the average value of the hatters' furs which enter into their construction, and without doubt this is true of all hats other than straw. It would be unprofitable to hazard a guess as to whether this might or might not be the case if straw hats were included.

The complainant further insisted that hatters' furs and fur scraps and cuttings were a more desirable kind of traffic than hats and caps for the reason that they were less liable to loss or damage in transit. From the very nature of the articles it is almost impossible that hatters' furs or fur scraps and cuttings should be stolen. They are not combustible and not easily injured by water or by jamming; and any injury from these causes would be confined to what was actually injured. Upon the contrary a hat is ready to wear and this is an inducement to abstract one from a case. Injury to a small part of a hat spoils the entire article. The complainant testified that in the whole course of his business he had never made a claim for damage to hatters' furs or fur scraps in transit while he had frequently had occasion to do so in case of hats.

The complainant is the only manufacturer of hats located in the West. All his competitors are upon the Atlantic seaboard in near proximity to New York. Most of these hatters' furs are imported and are distributed from the port of New York. The complainant claims that by reason of the higher rate upon raw material than upon the manufactured product he is placed at a disadvantage in comparison with the eastern manufacturer.

The market of the complainant is the whole United States west of Pittsburg and in all that territory he competes with the eastern manufacturer. The exact points in the East at which these competitors are located did not appear, and it is not therefore possible to make any exact comparison of rates; but generally speaking the rate from these eastern points is that of Boston or New York. There is considerable territory, like the Pacific Coast, to which rates upon hats are the same from the Atlantic seaboard as from Wabash, and in nearly all territory the sum of the rates, upon the same class, from New York to Wabash and from Wabash to the point of consumption is considerably greater than the rate from New York to the last-named destination.

Some question was raised as to the amount of complainant's shipments per year. Mr. Gill, Chairman of the Official Classification Committee, stated that a compilation of these shipments had been made and that they aggregated about 150,000 pounds per year. The rate from New York to Wabash is 72 cents, first class, and $1.44 double first class. If, therefore, the complainant is right in his contention as to what the correct classification should be he is damaged to the extent of something more than $1000 annually upon the statement of the defendants.

The complainant also urged that the classification in question created undue prejudice against his commodities as compared with dry goods, boots and shoes and many other articles classified as first class.

About 250 articles are classified as double first class by the Official Classification. Generally speaking, such articles offer some special reason for the classification, like unusual bulk, extraordinary risk, or something of that nature. An examination of the entire list fails to disclose a single commodity which affords as desirable traffic as the one under consideration, and in only three or four instances is there any approach to this. Something like 1500 articles are classified as first class. We have examined this list and our conclusion is that but very few of them are as desirable freight as hatters' furs and fur scraps and cuttings, and that none of them are more so.

No special reasons were shown why these two commodities should pay a higher rate than other similar commodities.

Conclusions

Upon these facts the complainant contends that the present classification of hatters' furs and fur scraps and cuttings is in violation of the Act to Regulate Commerce. His position is that in the forming of a classification a proper relation between different articles should be preserved and that when these articles under consideration are compared with others analogous from a transportation standpoint it appears that this present classification is too high.

To this the defendant replies that one commodity should not be compared with another unless the two are competitive; hatters' furs cannot therefore be tested by dry goods or boots and shoes. Mr. Gill, Chairman of the Official Classification Committee, speaking both as a witness and as counsel for the defendants, asserts that the main element in the determination of a classification is "value of service" or "what the traffic will bear."

There is undoubtedly much, we do not find it necessary to now inquire how much, truth in this contention of Mr. Gill; but it cannot be admitted that those are the only considerations to be observed. It has been repeatedly claimed by carriers and repeatedly held by the Commission that in the forming of a classification bulk, value, liability to damage, and similar elements affecting the desirability of the traffic should be considered, and that analogous articles should ordinarily be placed in the same class. *Warner* v. *New York C. & H. R. R. Co.*, 4 I. C. C. Rep. 32, 3 Inters. Com. Rep. 74; *Harvard Co.* v. *Pennsylvania Co.*, 4 I. C. C. Rep. 212, 3 Inters. Com. Rep. 257; *Page* v. *Delaware, L. & W. R. Co.*, 6 I. C. C. Rep. 548. Manifestly in determining what freight rates shall be borne by different commodities an attempt should be made to obtain a fair relation between those commodities, and a classification which utterly ignores all considerations of this kind or which utterly fails to give due weight to such considerations is unjust and unreasonable.

The present case falls within this rule. Here are two commodities, not bulky, offered for transportation in packages of convenient size, of not great value, and with practically no liability to loss or damage in transit. It has been found that hardly an article among all those in first class is so desirable traffic as they are, and still these commodities are classified as double first class. In our opinion this is unlawful. They should not be classified higher than first class. We should be inclined to say that fur scraps and cuttings must not be rated higher than second class were it not for the claim of the defendants that this would lead to fraud in the billing of furs as fur scraps.

There is another ground upon which the same conclusion must be reached. Mr. Gill himself admits that when two articles are competitive no preference should be shown in the freight rate. Hatters' fur, the raw material, does compete in a way with hats, the finished product, and we do not think that, under the circumstances of this case, the rate upon the raw material ought to be greater than that upon the finished product.

The complainant is located at Wabash, Ind., and is the only manufacturer of hats west of the Atlantic seaboard. Most of his competitors are in the immediate vicinity of New York from whence supplies of hatters' furs and fur scraps and cuttings are almost entirely drawn. For the purpose of noting the effect upon the complainant, let us assume that his competitor is located in New York itself.

The complainant pays upon his raw material double first class, and that raw material shrinks about one half in process of manufacture. His competitor pays upon the finished product first class or just one half the rate paid by the complainant upon the raw material. The item of freight, therefore, costs the complainant at his factory three or four times what it costs his competitor in laying down the same hat at that point.

The complainant sells exclusively in territory west of Pittsburg and the defendants urge that he has an advantage over his competitors in freights by reason of closer proximity to the market. But a moment's consideration will show that at points other than Wabash the discrimination is even greater than at the

complainant's factory. In some at least of this competitive territory rates from the Atlantic seaboard and Wabash are the
same, so that the complainant pays freight upon the raw material in addition to the same rate as the eastern manufacturer
upon the finished hat. In none of this competitive territory
probably is the rate from the east as great as the rate to Wabash
plus the rate from Wabash to the point of consumption.

In determining the relative amounts paid upon the raw material and the finished product we have disregarded the weight of
the cases. This is somewhat more in the case of hats than hatters' furs, but there is no definite testimony upon this point.

The defendants say that the complainant is the only person
who is finding fault with this classification. Were this true,
and without apparent reason, it would be no ground for denying
him the relief to which he is entitled ; but here the reason is sufficiently obvious since the discrimination is to the advantage of
every other manufacturer as against the complainant.

Neither is this a case, as the defendants intimate, where the
matter is of so slight consequence that it should not be inquired
into nor redressed. The law has a maxim that it will not concern itself with trifles and this perhaps ought to be all the more
true of traffic conditions where there can be no exact rule; but in
the case before us the excess paid by the complainants according
to the statement of the defendants amounts to $1000 a year, which
can hardly be called a trifle to the complainant, however it might
be with the defendants. We think the present adjustment between the raw material and the finished product is unjust and
unduly prejudicial to the complainant and that this should be
corrected.   *   *   *   *   *   *   *

The fixing of a classification determines the relation of rates,
not the rate itself. If we transfer these two commodities from
double first class to first class, we do not thereby determine the
rate under which they shall move in the future. The revenues
of the defendants are not necessarily diminished since they may
advance rates applicable to these classes. In *Danville* v. *South-*
ern R. Co., 8 I. C. C. Rep. 409, the right of determining the
relation in rates which should exist between two localities was

exercised and the same principle must apply to the relation between two commodities. In that case it was said that the authority was not clear, but having exercised it then, and believing that a plain distinction exists between fixing a rate and determining a relation in rates, we shall continue to do so until the Supreme Court of the United States has held otherwise.

* * * * * * * *

XX

HOW THE STATES MAKE INTERSTATE RATES [1]

THE widespread efforts of state legislatures and railroad commissions within the past two years to reduce railroad rates have presented many interesting phases to public observation. The extent and severity of the proposed reductions, the novel expedients adopted to prevent or to make difficult a review of the state action in the federal courts, the resulting conflict of judicial authority and the recent decision of the Supreme Court of the United States holding these expedients unconstitutional have kept the movement constantly in the public mind. Out of the many questions which discussion of the situation has evolved none are more interesting or important than those relating to the effect of state-made rates upon rates for interstate transportation. It is the purpose of this article not to show that the rate-making power of the states should be diminished or destroyed, or that this object, if desirable, can or cannot be accomplished under the federal constitution, but merely to state and to illustrate the proposition that, in fact, the states *do* make interstate rates.

The great movements of traffic in this country are eastward and westward. The volume of the westward movement has always been high-class merchandise, — dry goods, wearing apparel, groceries, hardware, and like articles. Formerly this was all produced in the East or imported through Atlantic ports; it is only within recent years that the larger cities in the West have become manufacturing centers.

When the evolution of our rate fabric began New York, Boston, Philadelphia, and Baltimore were the bases of supply.

[1] By Robert Mather. A paper prepared for the American Academy of Political Science, and published in its *Annals*, 1908. By permission. Much of the matter and all the maps for this article were prepared by Mr. Theodore Brent, of the Traffic Department, Rock Island-Frisco Lines, Chicago.

Chicago, St. Louis, St. Paul, Omaha, and Kansas City owe their development as trade centers primarily to strategic location at the head of navigation, or at points where the trans-continental trails left the watercourses for the West, Northwest, and Southwest. They commenced as outfitting points for prospectors and settlers; their business was that of distributing through the new western country the articles of commerce manufactured in or imported through the East; and that still constitutes a large part of their trade.

When railroads found their way to Chicago and St. Louis their rates were fixed largely by the water competition which met them on their arrival. Gradually railroads were constructed westward from these points and, as they reached common territory, the force of competition began to be felt. Intense rivalry developed between the distributing houses of Chicago and St. Louis, and pressure was brought to bear upon the railroads, both East and West, to keep the rate fabric so adjusted that goods, stored in and distributed from either city, might be laid down at any of the Missouri river points at substantially the same freight cost. The class rates from New York to Chicago thus became the basis of measurement for all class rates. The St. Louis rate was a fixed per cent higher, approximating the difference in the cost of reaching that point by water. The rates between the Mississippi river and Chicago on the one hand and the Missouri river on the other were fixed not at what would be a reasonable rate for the distance, but at what it was necessary to maintain in order that St. Louis and the lines leading through St. Louis might compete with Chicago for the expanding business of Kansas City, Atchison, St. Joseph, and Omaha.

In the territory west of the Missouri river the same process has been repeated, and rates are maintained in such relation not only that Kansas City, St. Joseph, and Omaha may compete with each other, but that goods distributed from St. Louis and Chicago, as well as from the eastern cities, may be handled through either Kansas City, St. Joseph, or Omaha and laid down at the several consuming points at practically the same freight cost. In the Northwest this same competitive adjustment is maintained between Chicago, Duluth, Minneapolis, and St. Paul. In the Southwest, Chicago, St. Louis, and Kansas City must be kept on an even keel, and when Texas is reached, the whole adjustment is modified to meet the competition of coastwise steamers plying from New York to Galveston. To Colorado and Utah, the routes through all these gateways are kept in constant adjustment, and the rates so arranged that Denver and Pueblo are enabled to do a distributing business.

What is true of westbound merchandise is equally true of the movement to the East of the great staples raised in the West. The grain territory is so divided and rates are so made that grain may move freely to the Mississippi river, the Lakes, and the Gulf, through the great storage centers of Minneapolis, Duluth, Chicago, St. Louis, Omaha, and Kansas City. In like manner live-stock rates are so arranged that the traffic may move freely to the rival packing centers of Kansas City, St. Joseph, Omaha, St. Paul, Chicago, and St. Louis.

These rate relations are not the work of the traffic departments of the railroads. They do not exist by virtue of acts of legislatures or of orders of commissions. They are the resultants of the commercial growth of the country. Trade is established along these lines; industries and communities are founded on the basis of these adjustments, and their existence and prosperity depend upon the continuance of these rate relations. They are the controlling facts in all rate disputes — more stubborn than distance and as immovable as mountains.

There is hardly a rate on any article of commerce but feels the force of these competitive conditions. They absolutely dictate the traffic policy of the railroads operating in the territory affected by them. The carrier makes no rates that are not effectively molded by these conditions, and the rate-making power of the Interstate Commerce Commission itself cannot ignore them. The only rate-regulating body that makes rates without reference to these commercial conditions is the legislature or the railroad commission of a single state. Its field of operations includes but a fraction of the territory whose traffic is controlled by these conditions; contains but few of the larger distributing centers which compete for that traffic; and is usually circumscribed, either wholly or in part, by imaginary boundaries fixed without regard to factors which exercise controlling influence upon the trend of traffic and of rates. The influence of lakes, of rivers and canals, the competition of rival markets, the relation between manufacturer and dealer, and other like forces that, in the making of rates, confront the traffic officer of an interstate railroad and the Interstate Commerce Commission itself, enter but slightly, if at all, into the calculations of the state. In every case, in the exercise of its rate-making power, distance is the one factor given serious consideration; and the result of its labors is invariably the production of a distance tariff.

This state distance tariff, is, on its face, a simple and a harmless thing. The right of the state to make it and to change it at its will seems to be amply buttressed by the conceded principle of law that the power of Congress over interstate commerce leaves untouched the power of the states to regulate their purely internal commerce. And no simpler or less obnoxious method of exercising that power would seem possible than to prescribe the rates at which traffic shall move from point to point within the state.

But when the traffic officer of an interstate railroad comes to apply this state distance tariff, made for state use on purely local considerations, to the traffic that actually moves over his rails, he finds that he cannot confine its influence to traffic within the state, and that, against his will and without his action, it readjusts his rates into and out of and through the state, and determines his revenue on traffic that never traverses the borders of the state. This is illustrated by the action of the following states:

Missouri and Iowa

Missouri has a far-reaching control over interstate rates by reason of the situation of the state at the point of least distance between the Mississippi river — the basing line for rates from the East — and the Missouri river, the base line for rates to the West.

There are three factors which go to make up the rates from
the East to the western territory, — whether or not they are
published as through rates, — namely, the rate from the seaboard to the Mississippi river or Chicago; the rate from the
latter base line to the Missouri river; and the rate west of the
Missouri river. Reduce the rate between the Mississippi river
and the Missouri river and you reduce the rates on all business
either locally or through or beyond these base lines.

The first-class rate between the Mississippi and Missouri rivers
practically determines the interstate rates on all classified articles

moving between the
East and West. It is
at present 60 cents
per 100 pounds, this
being the figure fixed
by the Missouri Rail-
road and Warehouse
Commission as a rea-
sonable maximum rate
for the short-line haul
of approximately 200
miles across the state
from the Mississippi
to the Missouri — the
distance from Hanni-
bal to St. Joseph being 196 miles, and from Hannibal to Kansas
City, 199 miles. Note the chart.

Though this rate is based on the distance of 200 miles, competitive conditions outside the state apply it at once to all hauls
across the state, no matter what their distance. The short line
from St. Louis to St. Joseph is 302 miles, and lines operating
between those cities would be privileged, under the commission's
maximum scale, to charge 74 cents, first class. The short line
between St. Louis and Kansas City is 277 miles, for which distance the commission's scale is 71 cents, first class. But here
considerations enter which are entirely outside the horizon of the
Missouri commission. The rates from New York to Hannibal

and St. Louis are the same. There are routes leading from New York to St. Joseph and Kansas City, through both Hannibal and St. Louis. Kansas City and St. Joseph compete in the same trade territory, and the rates to both points from New York must be kept the same through all gateways. Consequently the commission's maximum rate for the shortest distance becomes the rate between all four crossings.

Thus the element of distance even between points within the state is immediately modified by outside forces, controlling with the carriers, but which exerted no influence upon the commission when it fixed the nominal measure of the rates.

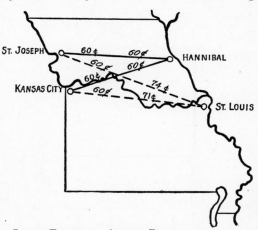

ITALIC FIGURES = ACTUAL RATES
ROMAN FIGURES = MISSOURI MAXIMUM RATES

Just north of Missouri lies the State of Iowa. To the untutored mind there would seem to be no reason why traffic of the same class should move within the State of Iowa for a less charge than within the State of Missouri. Yet the maximum charge under the Iowa distance tariff for hauling first-class merchandise 200 miles is 40 cents, as against 60 cents fixed by the Missouri tariff. The railroads in Iowa must haul the same class of merchandise 350 miles to be entitled to charge 60 cents; but, significantly enough, the 350 miles measure the distance in Iowa between the Mississippi and Missouri rivers, so that the rate between the two base lines is the same in both states. Should Missouri adopt the Iowa scale, the Missouri rate from the Mississippi river to the Missouri river, between all the points in Missouri that we have been considering, would, for the reasons already given, at once become 40 cents, regardless of distance.

The effect within the State of Missouri, however, is only the beginning. The rate between the Mississippi and Missouri rivers being, as previously explained, one of three factors of a through adjustment from points of production in the East; the rates from the East to all Mississippi river crossings being the same ; there being competitive routes from the East to all Missouri river points passing through all of these Mississippi river crossings ; and the merchants and manufacturers in the Mississippi river cities maintaining trade relations with all of the Missouri river cities and with the territory reached through them ; it follows that the rate between Dubuque, Iowa, and Kansas City, Missouri, cannot be higher than the rate between Dubuque and Council Bluffs (both points within the state of Iowa) ; nor can the rate between St. Louis, Missouri, and Omaha,

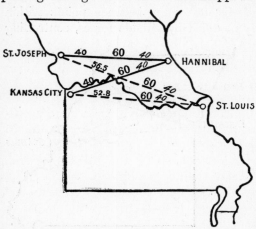

SMALL ROMAN FIGURES = RATES PERMISSIBLE, BASED ON ACTUAL MILEAGE, IOWA SCALE APPLIED IN MISSOURI.
ITALIC FIGURES = RATES CARRIERS WOULD ACTUALLY BE FORCED TO CHARGE BY REASON OF OUTSIDE FORCES
LARGE ROMAN FIGURES = PRESENT RATES

Nebraska, be higher than the rate between St. Louis and Kansas City or between St. Louis and St. Joseph (movements wholly within the State of Missouri).

Thus from the act of the Missouri commission in reducing its distance tariff from 60 cents to 40 cents for 200 miles, the following results directly flow :

(*a*) The local *Missouri* rate from points on the Mississippi river to points on the Missouri river, regardless of mileage, is reduced from 60 cents to 40 cents ;

(*b*) The local *Iowa* rate from points on the Mississippi river to points on the Missouri river (say Clinton to Council Bluffs, 350 miles) is reduced from 60 cents to 40 cents;

(*c*) The *interstate* rate from points on the Mississippi river in Missouri to points on the Missouri river in Iowa or Nebraska (say St. Louis to Council Bluffs or Omaha) is reduced;

(*d*) The *interstate* rate from points on the Missouri river in Missouri to points on the Mississippi river in Iowa (say Kansas City to Davenport) is reduced.

Not only this, but this Missouri commission rate for 200 miles fixes the maximum rate which the Missouri Pacific Railway may charge for its haul of 488 miles between St. Louis and Omaha, through Missouri, Kansas, and Nebraska; and in like manner the rate of the Illinois Central Railroad for its haul of 703 miles between the same points, through the States of Missouri, Illinois, and Iowa. See the map [p. 538].

Thus, within the territory inclosed by the Illinois Central, Missouri Pacific, and Rock Island as outlined on the map, any reduction made by the Missouri commission in the class rates for the 200-mile distance between Hannibal, Missouri, and Kansas City, Missouri, has the effect of bringing all rates to the level so fixed, not only between the crossings themselves but, with very slight exceptions, between all intermediate points.

This, again, is but a preliminary glimpse at the inevitable results of this action of the Missouri State Commission.

The first-class rate from Chicago to the Missouri river has for many years been 20 cents per 100 pounds higher than the rate from the Mississippi river. The competitive adjustment would require that there be no greater difference under the new scale. Indeed, the rates from the seaboard to Chicago and the Mississippi river remaining as at present, it is doubtful if Chicago and the routes through Chicago could compete should the present arbitrary difference be maintained under the reduced adjustment. The present rate of 80 cents, first class, from Chicago, is one-third higher than the rate from the Mississippi to the Missouri river. It is probable that not more than one-third greater would

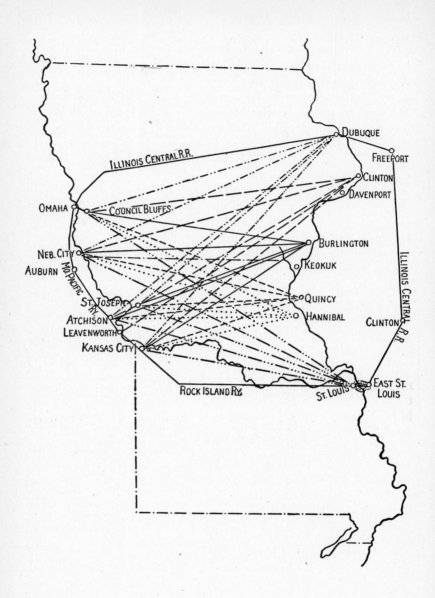

be practicable under the lowered scale, which would make the first-class rate from Chicago 54 cents per 100 pounds.

Peoria must be maintained at one half the difference between Chicago and the Mississippi river. Milwaukee must be kept on the same rate basis as Chicago. The rates from Minneapolis and St. Paul must be kept the same as Chicago to the Upper Missouri river crossings (Omaha, Council Bluffs, and Nebraska City), and 5 cents higher than Chicago to the lower crossings (St. Joseph, Atchison, Leavenworth, and Kansas City). Duluth takes fixed arbitraries above St. Paul. The intervening territory in Wisconsin, between Milwaukee and St. Paul, is built on arbitraries over either Chicago, Milwaukee, or St. Paul, and would call for readjustment accordingly. From Memphis, Tennessee, not higher than Chicago rates can be maintained to Lower Missouri river crossings, and to the upper crossings the first-class rate from Memphis cannot be more than two cents higher than Chicago. To Sioux City the rate from Chicago, St. Louis, and Peoria must be kept the same as from Chicago to Omaha. The first-class rate from Memphis to Sioux City is to-day 30 cents higher, and from Minneapolis and St. Paul 20 cents less, than from Chicago to Sioux City, and the same percentage relation must be maintained on the lower scale.

The immediate result, then, of the fixing by the Missouri commission of a maximum charge of 40 cents, first class, for the distance of 200 miles between Hannibal, Missouri, and Kansas City, Missouri, is to fix the rates for all routes shown on the map [p. 540] of what is termed Western Trunk Line territory.

The foregoing outline illustrates only the adjustment of first-class rates. In Western Classification territory there are five numbered and five lettered classes, and the other classes all bear a certain percentage relation to the first-class rates. This is true to the extent that any considerable reduction in the rate on first class involves necessary proportionate reductions in the rates on other classes, the severity of any such reduction lessening, of course, as the rates themselves grow less; but the rates on all classes must go down if one goes down, so that the same fixed relation between the classes may be maintained on the lower as on the higher basis.

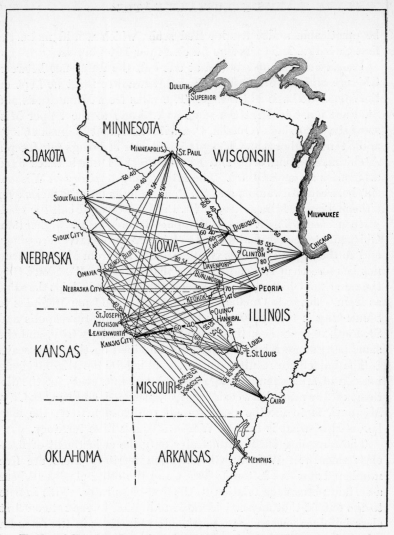

The broad line indicates the short-line distance of 199 miles across the state of Missouri between Hannibal and Kansas City which measures and controls all western rates.

Left-hand figures indicate present rates.

Right-hand figures indicate approximately the rates which would result were the Missouri commission to prescribe the Iowa scale as the maximum which may be charged in the State of Missouri.

Similarly, the outline only illustrates the change in the adjustment between the principal basing points in Western Trunk Line territory. But around these basing points are grouped all the adjacent cities and towns; so that an adjustment once reduced from Chicago, or Peoria, or the Mississippi river to the Upper or Lower Missouri river points, a corresponding reduction results from all points, both of origin and of destination, held common with these basing points. So the reductions become automatic, covering all interstate movements throughout the whole territory pictured in the outline.

The illustration thus far deals only with the change in rates on business which may be termed purely local to the territory immediately embraced in the illustration; that is, business which has both origin and destination within the territory. We have not yet touched upon that volume of eastern business to the Missouri river cities, to St. Paul and Duluth, and to the territory beyond as far west as the states of Utah, Idaho, and Montana, or to the southwest, including the State of Texas and territory of New Mexico. Yet the rates on this business are quite as vitally involved. The competitive adjustment between Chicago, Peoria, Memphis, the Mississippi river, and the head of the Lakes, as previously described, was originally evolved and has since been maintained in a measure to permit this merchandise to move freely by all routes to this trans-Missouri, northwestern and southwestern territory. Whenever the western factors of the through rates to this territory are reduced, the rates on such through business fall simultaneously with the rates on the local business.

Merchandise for this western territory moves from the East by every conceivable route. Every all-rail line and every conceivable combination of rail lines publish the rates. During lake navigation daily boats carry this merchandise to Chicago, Milwaukee, and the head of the Lakes. It is handled by steamer in connection with rail lines from every South Atlantic port from Norfolk to Jacksonville. There is a steamer load dispatched daily from New York and given to the rail lines at the port of Galveston, Texas. The rate fixed by the authority of the state of Missouri, between Hannibal and Kansas City, and based on purely local considerations, has its leveling effect upon the rates on every pound of this vast traffic. The next map shows the ultimate reach of the rate-making power of Missouri.

It is true that the illustration has proceeded thus far on the assumption that Missouri might make a reduction in its existing class rates, and not on the fact that such reduction has been made. But Iowa has precisely the same control over interstate adjustments that the illustration demonstrates Missouri to have, and as matter of fact east-and-west class rates are what they are to-day because Iowa some years ago prescribed 60 cents as the maximum charge, first class, for the haul within its borders between the Mississippi and the Missouri rivers. The Iowa distance tariff of 1887 actually measures to-day the revenues of the interstate railroads on all interstate freight passing into or out of or beyond that state.

Besides, Missouri has actually made radical reductions in other rates that illustrate as well the principle of our contention. The legislature of 1905 ordered drastic reductions of rates on grain, flour, lime, salt, cement, stucco, lumber, agricultural implements, furniture, wagons, and live stock, and the legislature of 1907 added stone, gravel, and other commodities. The rates have not been published, as the constitutionality of the legislation is in question before the courts; but if the state's right to order the reductions is finally established, the interstate rates on these bulk commodities, which constitute a large percentage of the carload tonnage of all western carriers, will come down with them.

The reductions which will result in rates on grain will illustrate. The short-line distance rate between the Missouri and Mississippi rivers will be reduced from 13 cents per 100 pounds, on wheat, and 12 cents per 100 pounds on corn and other grain, to $8\frac{1}{2}$ cents per 100 pounds on all grain. The state's action also calls for a reduction of $\frac{1}{2}$ cent per 100 pounds in the proportional rate on wheat between Kansas City and Hannibal. This proportional rate of 9 cents is the rate applied on all wheat coming from beyond the Missouri river, and, as in the case of the class rates, it is the pivotal rate in the whole adjustment. If the legislature's

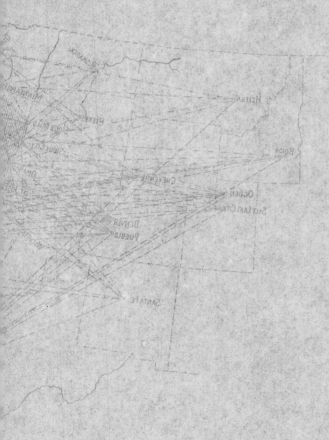

The shaded field indicates the territory immediately affected
controlling distance of 190 miles between the Mississippi river and
If the controlling factor in Western Trunk Line territory be
business falls automatically in proportion.
The water lines indicate the principal through rates operate
automatically with any fluctuation in the all-rail rates.

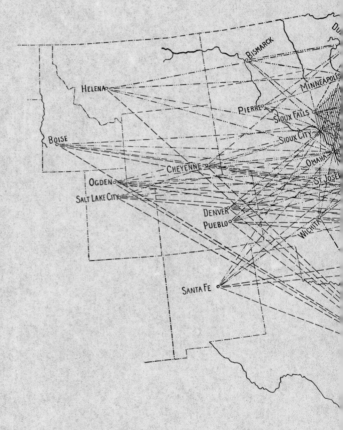

The shaded field indicates the territory immediately affected
controlling distance of 199 miles between the Mississippi river and

If the controlling factor in Western Trunk Line territory be
business falls automatically in proportion.

The water lines indicate the principal through rates operate
automatically with any fluctuation in the all-rail rates.

action is finally upheld, a readjustment of the whole rate fabric on western grain will result. There is no more sensitive adjustment in existence than the grain rates. No single part of any of the through rates can be disturbed without disturbing the revenue on a large part of the whole movement.

Competition and market conditions require that the rates on grain from the States of Kansas and Nebraska shall be so adjusted that the grain raised in those states can move eastward freely through either of the primary markets at the Missouri river, Kansas City, or Omaha. When these markets are reached, not alone the grain markets of the United States, but the foreign markets as well must be open to the producer, so that the Nebraska or Kansas producer may have the benefit of the best prevailing market price of the world to-day; and the adjustment must be maintained from day to day so that the large grain buyers may take the surplus grain into elevator storage, not only at the Missouri river, but at the large storage points at the Mississippi river, the Ohio river, the Lake ports, the milling centers, and the Atlantic and Gulf seaboard, with the full assurance that when the demand makes eastern or southern shipment desirable he will have a parity of rates in either direction through any market. If the reduced rates are finally enforced, the material reductions within the state will be insignificant compared with the automatic reductions in the interstate adjustment which must follow. The same reduction must be made from Omaha, not only to St. Louis but to the other Mississippi river crossings; to Peoria and Chicago, the gateways to the Central States; to Louisville, Evansville, Cairo, and Memphis, the market points for all the southeastern states; to Little Rock, Texarkana, Fort Worth, Dallas, and Shreveport, the principal market gateways for the States of Arkansas, Louisiana, and Texas; and to Minneapolis, the largest of the milling centers. Any reduction in the rate to the Mississippi river and Chicago means just that much reduction in the revenue on grain moving to Boston, New York, Philadelphia, Baltimore, and Newport News for export, as these rates are all made on the Mississippi river combination. And when these rates go down, a similar reduction is forced in the rate to Pensacola, Florida, Mobile, Alabama, New Orleans, Louisiana, and Port Arthur and Galveston, Texas, for export.

It has never been found feasible to carry local and proportional rates on the same basis, and there is therefore the probability of further reduction in the proportional basis. To what figure the proportional rate on wheat across Missouri might fall as the result of carrying a local rate of 8½ cents is, of course, problematical. The rates up to this time have always been maintained about four cents lower than the local rates. The accompanying chart only illustrates the direct reductions in the existing proportional rates.

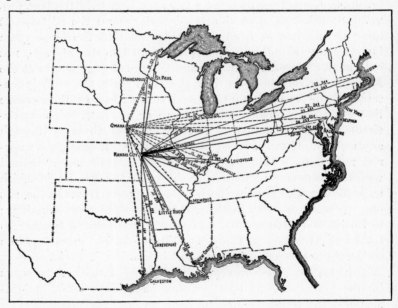

Reduction in the wheat and flour rate adjustment immediately resulting from reduction in the state mileage rates ordered by the Missouri legislature.

The broad line indicates the controlling distance of 199 miles between the Missouri and Mississippi river basing points.

LEFT-HAND FIGURES = PRESENT PROPORTIONAL RATES

RIGHT-HAND FIGURES = REDUCED RATES MADE NECESSARY BY REDUCTION IN RATE FROM KANSAS CITY TO HANNIBAL

KANSAS AND NEBRASKA

During the year 1907 the Railroad Commission of Kansas forced a reduction of 15 per cent in the existing rates on grain within the state. A reduction in grain rates always applies as well on flour, meal, and other grain products. The Nebraska Commission forced a 15 per cent reduction in state rates, not only on grain and grain products, but on live stock, coal, lumber and fruits, and vegetables.

Kansas and Nebraska do not consume a hundredth part of what they produce, and the great bulk of the commodities consumed within these states is produced outside of them. The freight destined from points of origin within either state and moving under the state's mileage rates to points of consumption within the state, is as nothing to that which moves to points beyond the state. That is to say, nearly all the traffic of both the states is interstate, and subject to the influence of the competitive interstate rate adjustments.

The products of Kansas and Nebraska find their primary markets (Kansas City, Kansas, and Omaha, Nebraska) on the Missouri river at the extreme eastern boundary of the state, and the state regulation fixes the rate at which the product is hauled from points of production to these primary markets, no matter what the ultimate destination of the product may be. As a result, the 15 per cent reductions in the grain rates required by both state commissions have called for a flat reduction of just that amount in all interstate rates, and a corresponding shrinkage in railroad revenues on practically all of the grain raised in both the states.

A contingent result is a horizontal reduction in the rates on Oklahoma grain. The Choctaw line of the Rock Island operates in Oklahoma under a charter which provides that its rates in that state must not be higher than they are in the states from which it enters Oklahoma. The line enters Oklahoma from Kansas, as well as from Arkansas, and the charter provision required an immediate adjustment of the Oklahoma rates on the Kansas scale. With the Oklahoma rates on the Kansas basis it was found impossible to maintain the adjustment formerly prevailing from points in southern Oklahoma to points in Texas, and a readjustment there was necessary. Similar reductions of the rates to Arkansas points will be required.

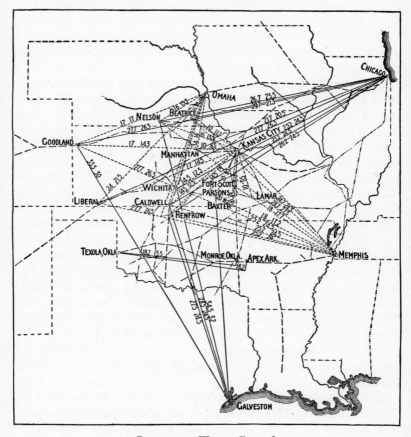

CHANGES IN WHEAT RATES [1]

Left-hand figures are former rates.
Right-hand figures are rates forced by Commission's reductions.

[1] Necessitated by the 15 per cent reduction ordered by the Kansas and Nebraska Commissions on their intrastate rates. Other grains and grain products are similarly affected. Every point is affected like the few here shown.

This situation clearly illustrates the interdependence of state and interstate rates. The chart on page 546 will give a partial illustration of the situation. It can, of course, picture the effect only at a few points. The reductions are general, affecting every point.

TEXAS

In Texas, state regulation of rates is deliberately designed to control the rates on interstate business both into and out of the state. There is, from the standpoint of the state, excellent reason for this policy; for, aside from its timber and a portion of its grain, little which Texas produces is consumed within the state, and the bulk of the food stuffs, wearing apparel, and manufactured articles which its citizens consume or use are imported from other states.

The State Commission has always conceived it to be to the state's interest to link its fortunes with the coastwise steamship lines rather than with the all-rail carriers reaching the state through its northern gateways. Consequently the Commission has made the port of Galveston the radiating point in its adjustment. The class rates from the eastern seaboard have always been made the exact combination of the steamship rates from New York, Boston, Philadelphia, and Baltimore to the port of Galveston, plus the Commission's local rates thence to every point in the state. This has forced the rail carriers to group all the producing territory west of seaboard territory, and to maintain a relative adjustment calculated to permit these territories to market their products in Texas in competition with the rates from the seaboard fixed for the rail carriers both in and outside the state by the Texas Commission and the steamship lines.

It necessarily follows that whenever the Texas Commission reduces a rate from Galveston the revenue of the state carrier on all Texas business originating at the Atlantic seaboard is lowered, and the interstate carriers are compelled to make corresponding reductions from every other basing point. The immediate effect of a reduction of 5 cents in the Commission's first-class rate from Galveston to Waco is outlined in the following chart.

Texas is above all a cotton-growing state. The wealth of its farming communities and the business of its cities is founded on the production and marketing of this staple. The revenues of the carriers within the state are largely dependent upon the movement of the cotton crop. Texas produces one quarter of

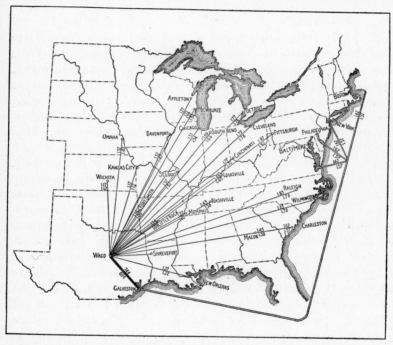

This chart shows the reduction in interstate rates which would follow a reduction of five cents in the Texas Railroad Commission's first-class rate from Galveston to Waco. (The rates shown apply only from the basing points. All other towns group around these and the reduction from all is the same as from the basing point.)

UPPER FIGURES = RATES AT PRESENT IN EFFECT

LOWER FIGURES = RATES WHICH WOULD APPLY FOLLOWING THE ABOVE-MENTIONED REDUCTION

all the cotton grown within the United States. It has, however, no cotton-spinning industry worthy the name. Probably 99 per cent of the cotton grown in the state is sent to New England and southeastern spinning points and to foreign countries. The revenues of the carriers on all this interstate and foreign cotton freight are absolutely dependent upon the rates fixed by the Railroad Commission of Texas to the port of Galveston.

Three years since, the Commission ordered a reduction in cotton rates of 5 cents per 100 pounds, or $1 per ton. The movement from Texas to interstate and foreign destinations in the fiscal year ending June 30, 1906, was a million and a half tons. The direct result to interstate carriers from this one act of the Commission has been an annual shrinkage in their revenues of something like a million and a half of dollars.

A cardinal principle in the three principal classification territories is that valuable commodities such as dry goods, notions, boots and shoes, hats, etc., shall take first-class rates, whether the goods are shipped in carloads or in less than carload quantities. There is no voluntary variation from this in any interstate adjustment. The principle has frequently been reviewed without disapproval by the Interstate Commerce Commission. The Texas Commission, however, has taken the opposite view, and in its state classification has fixed Class "A" basis on these commodities when shipped in carload quantities. This action on their part has no force or effect so far as concerns state traffic. None of these commodities are manufactured within the state, and no house in the state jobs them in carload quantities. The State Commission's action does, however, reduce the interstate rate on these commodities from New York to interior Texas towns 37 cents per 100 pounds in carload lots.

That the Texas Commission exercises its rate-making powers with deliberate intent to control the interstate rates for the benefit of its industries appears from the following illustration.

The Rock Island has a line running southwest from the State of Kansas, passing diagonally across the Panhandle of Texas into New Mexico and on to El Paso. There are large salt industries on this line at Hutchinson, Kansas, and in the year 1905 the Rock Island, being asked to establish a reasonable rate from Hutchinson into its Panhandle towns, published an average rate of 19½ cents. The average distance is about 300 miles. There are salt plants of considerable importance at Grand Saline, Salt

City and Colorado, Texas, and under the State Commission's orders, the Rock Island, in connection with other lines, had in effect an average rate of 20½ cents per 100 pounds from these

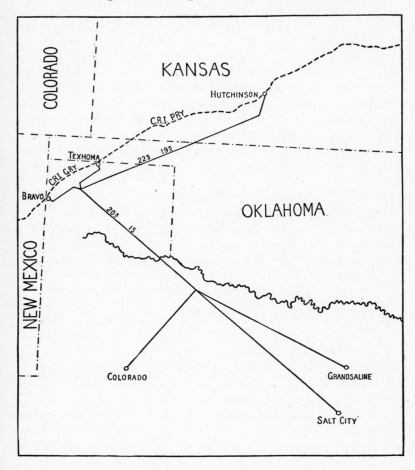

state salt plants to the Panhandle towns. The average haul to these points is from Grand Saline, 525 miles ; from Colorado, 660; and Salt City, Texas, 690 miles. When the Rock Island's interstate rate came to the attention of the Texas Commission, it ordered the Rock Island's Texas line to nonconcur in the reduction, threatening that if the interstate rate were allowed to stay in, they would compel the state carriers to haul salt from these state plants to the Panhandle points for 15 cents per 100 pounds. Needless to say, the interstate rate was withdrawn, and it remains to-day at the Texas maximum rate of $22\frac{1}{2}$ cents. The map on page 550 illustrates the situation.

ILLINOIS

Recent reductions in class rates in Illinois have forced reductions of the interstate rates between St. Louis, Hannibal, Quincy, Keokuk, Davenport, and Dubuque, and will eventually force similar reductions in rates between intermediate local points either wholly interstate or wholly within other states than Illinois.

ARKANSAS

The Arkansas Commission has prescribed a full line of class and commodity rates which produce an effect on all the rates on merchandise brought into the state from points beyond, similar to the results of the Texas Commission's regulation of the rates in that state.

MINNESOTA

The Minnesota Commission has fixed a scale of class rates within the state which recently required the leveling down of all rates from Minneapolis, St. Paul, and Duluth to Iowa and Dakota points. It was with respect to this situation that Judge Lochren said in the case before him involving the validity of these rates :

It would seem to be very difficult to avoid . . . the conclusion that these rates fixed in respect to Minnesota do necessarily and directly affect interstate commerce. . . . I have no doubt that Congress might very properly, under the constitutional provision giving it the entire power of control over interstate commerce, assume control of the avenues of interstate commerce, of the railroads which are engaged in interstate commerce, and of all rates which are collected by those railroads, whether within the states or without the states, because the matter of those rates would affect these avenues of interstate commerce, and might affect their ability to continue as avenues of interstate commerce.

And as to this argument, urged before the Supreme Court in the Minnesota rate case, recently decided, the opinion of Mr. Justice Peckham says:

Still another Federal question is urged growing out of the assertion that the laws are, by their necessary effect, an interference with and a regulation of interstate commerce, the grounds for which assertion it is not now necessary to enlarge upon. The question is not, at any rate, frivolous.

XXI

THE NORTHERN SECURITIES COMPANY [1]

THE certificate of incorporation of the Northern Securities Company was signed by the three incorporators and acknowledged in the state of New Jersey on the twelfth of November, 1901. During the three days immediately following, resolutions were adopted by the newly organized company, authorizing the purchase of any shares that might be tendered to the company, under specified conditions and terms. Power to do so was expressly granted in the charter. " The objects for which the corporation is formed are : To acquire by purchase, subscription, or otherwise, and to hold as investment, any bonds or other securities or evidences of indebtedness. . . . To purchase, hold, sell, assign, transfer, mortgage, pledge, or otherwise dispose of, any bonds or other securities or evidences of indebtedness created or issued by any other corporation. . . . To purchase, hold, etc., shares of capital stock of any other corporation . . . and, while owner of such stock, to exercise all the rights, powers, and privileges of ownership, including the right to vote thereon. . . ." The nature of these powers, with respect to the signs of indebtedness of other corporations, has caused the company to be commonly described as a holding company.

This particular idea of a holding company antedates the Northern Securities Company by seven or eight years; and, in a larger sense, the principle involved in the holding company has found at least partial expression in the organization of railway companies for half a century. The voting trust may also be regarded as an antecedent of the modern holding company,

[1] From "A History of the Northern Securities Case," *Bulletin of the University of Wisconsin*, No. 142, July, 1906, pp. 225–241. Elaborate footnote references are omitted. The problems of railroad combination both economic and legal are discussed in Ripley's Railroads : Finance and Organization. — ED.

and the causes which have produced the one are analogous to those which have produced the other. The process of metamorphosis between the voting trust and the holding company does not appear to be either long or complex.

Both the remote and the immediate causes of the organization of the Northern Securities Company were partly personal and partly economic. They were personal in so far as the Securities Company was the outgrowth of a desire on the part of certain men to perpetuate a certain policy. They were economic in that the execution of certain large, almost empire-building plans could be promoted, in the estimation of its founders, by the company. The founders of the company, through years of effort, had become accustomed to associate their railway properties with a certain economic policy. And thus the personal and the economic causes of the organization of the company practically become merged into one, namely, the desire to insure uninterrupted progress in the building of a great system of transportation. The existence of other causes, like the desire to suppress competition, to inflate values, has been alleged. An examination of these will be taken up later.

The original idea of the Securities Company was that it should embrace the ownership of about one third of the Great Northern stock. A small number of the Great Northern stockholders, not to exceed eleven out of about 1800, felt that they were getting along in years. One of them was eighty-six, another eighty-two, and several of them past seventy years of age; and they desired to work together as they had done for more than twenty years. Some of these stockholders lived in foreign countries. Their powers and privileges had to be exercised by their legal representative. This might continue to work satisfactorily as long as the old circle of associates remained unbroken; but a number of them felt that a more permanent arrangement would be preferable. A close corporation, embracing six or eight men, was suggested, to which others objected because such an arrangement would violate the principle of equality which had always prevailed among Great Northern stockholders. As soon as the idea of exclusiveness had been abandoned and an inclusive organization decided upon, " the question came up : Why not put in the Northern Pacific? That is the way it occurred." This, in substance, is the manner in which President J. J. Hill summarizes what has been alluded to above as the " personal " element in the organization of the Securities Company. And to place at the head of the new company the guiding spirit and constructive genius of that group of men at once made the Securities Company doubly a matter of "moral control," of " fortification," and of " strength." In the words of a colleague, who is familiar with the territory through which the Great Northern railway runs, that road is " regarded as a personality. People know that there is some one whom they can see and talk to. If other means fail, they know they can go to see ' Jim' Hill about it, and he will give them a fair hearing." From the threefold point of view of public policy, of personality, and of business, the actual course of the organization represents the best that could have been done.

The desire to secure a permanent basis for the interchange of commodities between great producing sections of the United States and of the Orient may be characterized as the largest economic cause of the organization of the Securities Company. The Great Northern and the Northern Pacific railways had lived in comparative peace with each other for twenty years. Both had maintained joint rates with other roads like the Burlington. The Burlington taps the principal live-stock markets, important cotton, coal and mineral areas of the United States. The unified control and management of these three great systems of railways — Great Northern, Northern Pacific, and Burlington — makes it possible to secure a sufficient variety and quantity of freight to make systematic back loading a certainty. Back loading, together with a steady flow of freight large enough to insure the economical utilization of motive power and car capacity, results in a general economy of operation which makes rates that would bankrupt numerous other roads remunerative to the systems embraced in the Securities Company. Such a flow of freight had been developed on the basis of joint rate agreements with railways and agreements with steamship lines.

The value of the railway properties concerned, as well as the continued prosperity of the commercial and industrial interests served by them, depended largely upon the permanency and security of the arrangements which had begun to crystallize with the turn of the century, and to which the opening of the Orient promised to bring still greater returns. However, joint rates may be withdrawn at any time, and it was thought too hazardous to build up a great business " extending across the continent and even across the ocean on the basis that to-morrow the rate might be changed or the party with whom we were working to reach the different points of production or consumption had some other interest or some greater interest elsewhere. It was necessary in doing this that we should have some reasonable expectation that we could control the permanency of the rate and that we would be able to reach the markets. In other words, if the man producing lumber on the coast, or cattle on the ranches, or ore in the mines, could not find a market for it and if we could not take it to a market that would enable him to sell his stuff for a profit, he would have to stop producing it. That was the line we worked upon, and that was the reason we felt called upon to put ourselves in a position where we could control access to the markets."   *   *   *   *   *

A glance at a railway map of the territory west of the Mississippi reveals the importance and strength of the Burlington system. West of the Missouri river it lies in the very lap of the Union Pacific, while east of that river it forms a great bridge, with its terminal pier in Chicago. The Northwestern, St. Paul and Burlington systems largely complement each other in the great manufacturing, agricultural and mineral regions of the greater northwest. In relation to the Great Northern and Northern Pacific, the Burlington is like the point and moldboard of a plow, the beam and handles of which are constituted by the former systems. The Burlington connects Chicago with St. Louis, Kansas City, Omaha, Denver, St. Paul and Minneapolis, and numerous smaller but important cities, which, taken collectively, represent the manufacture and sale of every staple commodity and the raw materials therefor.

An alliance with a system possessing the tactical and physical advantages of the Burlington could not be otherwise than a source of strength and profit to the party making such an alliance.

For many years the Great Northern and Northern Pacific had been contemplating direct connection with Chicago. The usual alternatives of the construction of a new line or the lease or purchase of an existing one, presented themselves. The former would result in unnecessary duplication and waste; the latter only was deemed expedient. The improved financial condition of the Northern Pacific and the dissolution of the voting trust planned for January 1, 1901, made the year 1900 propitious for the execution of the long-cherished plans for an eastward extension. At least five different lines were within the range of possibility. These were: the Wisconsin Central; Chicago & Northwestern; Chicago, Milwaukee & St. Paul; Chicago, Burlington & Quincy; and the Chicago Great Western. To what extent each of these great lines figured as possibilities in the minds of the Great Northern and Northern Pacific, and the relative degrees of desirability which were attached to each by them, does not appear in the testimony, although the statement may be positively made that more than two of these railways were made the subject of correspondence and probably, also, of tentative solicitation.

The preferences of J. J. Hill and J. P. Morgan, with respect to the particular line to be acquired as an eastward extension, do not appear to have coincided, when an extraneous factor appeared, which probably added the force of circumstances to Hill's preference. It appears that during the "fall of 1900 or early winter of 1901" the Union Pacific interests purchased in the market some $8,000,000 or $9,000,000 out of $108,000,000 or $109,000,000 of the Burlington stock. Much of the Burlington stock had been held for many years by people who had inherited it, and it was found impossible to secure control of the property through purchases in the open market. This episode in the stock-market hastened the completion of negotiations which probably had been begun before that time. The two northern transcontinental lines were not inclined to permit a rival interest to wrest from them this much-coveted property without leaving a single stone unturned. The testimony does not show a direct causal connection between the attempt of the Union Pacific interests to purchase the Burlington in the open market and the negotiations of Hill for the same property, although more than mere coincidence probably existed. Negotiations were opened by Hill with the executive committee of the board of directors of the Burlington system about Christmas, 1900, or January 1, 1901. Prior to this date no negotiations had taken place. " The actual negotiations commenced about or after the middle of January, 1901." Early in March, 1901, E. H. Harriman and Jacob H. Schiff, acting for themselves, or for the Union Pacific, or for interests friendly to the Union Pacific, requested to be allowed to join with the Great Northern and Northern Pacific in the purchase of the Burlington. This request was refused. At that time the Union Pacific interests no longer owned the eight or nine millions of Burlington stock which had been purchased during the preceding fall or winter, but they now desired to secure a half interest in the final purchase. A month later the Burlington sale was consummated. The two northern roads had made the offer which the Burlington directors had specified beforehand as satisfactory to Hill, and nearly all the Burlington shareholders accepted it. The Great Northern and Northern Pacific each received one half of the $108,-000,000 of capital stock of the Burlington at $200 per share, payable in joint collateral four per cent, long-time bonds of the two companies, for the payment of which the acquired 96.79 per cent of the stock of the old Burlington Company was pledged as collateral security. These two companies had now become joint owners of all the Burlington stock, and, as such, they had the right thereafter to exercise all the rights and privileges of shareholders, including the right to elect the board of directors. The purchase of the Burlington stock by the two companies in equal parts, it was thought, would serve each of them as well as if it were the sole owner of such stock, while such a purchase might have been beyond the financial means of either company by itself. "The evidence is therefore uncontradicted and conclusive that the Great Northern and Northern Pacific companies each purchased an equal number of shares of the Burlington stock as the best means and for the sole purpose of reaching the best markets for the products of the territory along the lines, and of securing connections which would furnish the largest amount of traffic for their respective roads, increase the trade and interchange of commodities between the regions traversed by the Burlington lines and their connections and the regions traversed or reached by the Great Northern and Northern Pacific lines, and by their connecting lines of shipping on the Pacific Ocean, and as the best if not the only means of furnishing an indispensable supply of fuel for their own use and for the inhabitants of the country traversed by their lines. These connections and the interchange of traffic thereby secured were deemed to be and are indispensable to the maintenance of their business, local as well as interstate, and to the development of the country served by their respective lines, and of like advantage to the Burlington lines and the country served by them, and strengthen each company in its competition with European carriers, for the trade and commerce of the Orient."

During the very days when the Burlington transaction was being perfected, the men who had been refused what they regarded an equitable share in that purchase elaborated plans which were calculated to vanquish their enemies and elevate the Union Pacific interests to a position of supremacy in transcontinental traffic. These stirring events led a cosmopolitan editor to invent a parable of fishes in which the bass had swallowed the minnow, and the pike swallowed the bass. In this instance, however, the bass, armed with retirement fins, compelled the pike to spew him out.

The total outstanding capital stock of the Northern Pacific was $155,000,000 of which $80,000,000 was common and $75,-000,000 preferred. During April and early in May, 1901, the Union Pacific interests acquired $78,000,000 of this stock, — $41,000,000 preferred and $37,000,000 common — with the view of controlling the Northern Pacific railway, with its half

interest in the Burlington system.   Such a movement appears to
have been anticipated.   " It was a common story at one time."
Individuals representing the Great Northern and Northern
Pacific interests, becoming apprehensive, increased their holdings in the Northern Pacific by purchasing about $15,000,000
of common stock in the market.   Short selling of Northern
Pacific stock and the scramble to cover, when it was discovered
that only a limited supply was to be had, drove the price of
Northern Pacific common stock up to about $1000 per share.
This was the climax of a series of events which culminated in
the stock-exchange crisis of May 9, 1901.   " The markets of the
world were convulsed, the equilibrium of the financial world
shaken, and many speculative interests in a critical condition."
On May 1, 1901, when the so-called " raid " upon Northern
Pacific stock became known, J. J. Hill and his associates, who
had been in possession of large blocks of Northern Pacific stock
from the time of the reorganization of the company, were holding from $18,000,000 to $20,000,000, par value, of common
stock ; and J. P. Morgan & Co. were holding some $7,000,000 or
$8,000,000.   Together, May 1, 1901, these individuals lacked
the dramatic $15,000,000 of common stock, which, when they
had acquired it, gave them a majority of some $3,000,000 par
value, of the $80,000,000 of common stock, when the " show
down of hands " occurred after May 9.   Although the Union
Pacific interests represented by E. H. Harriman and Winslow
S. Pearce, as trustees for the Oregon Short Line, held a majority
of $1,000,000 of the total amount of stock, their majority lay in
the preferred shares which could be retired on any 1st of January prior to 1917, — that is, before the present owners could
get an opportunity of exercising the authority which was assumed to reside in them, and which would give them the coveted
control.   This is why the pike did not swallow the bass.   To the
country at large and to Wall Street these events appeared like
a duel between giants, but one who appears to have been a
leading participant in the duel, on the losing side, asserted that
he never was in a contest, nor did he and his associates lose
money.

According to the by-laws of the Northern Pacific Company, the annual election of its board of directors by the stockholders occurs in October, and under the distribution of stock existing after May 9, 1901, the Union Pacific interests could have controlled this election, and thus prevented the retirement of the preferred stock on January 1, 1902, which would legislate them out of control. Both the preferred and the common stock could vote under the conditions existing on May 9, 1901. A postponement of the annual meeting from October till after January 1, 1902, was frequently thought of and advised by counsel. It could have been done. This potential power of retiring the Northern Pacific preferred stock before the same could be voted, residing in the Northern Pacific Board of Directors, appears to have generated a conciliatory attitude on the part of the representatives of Union Pacific interests, and negotiations for the purchase of such shares were successfully carried through by J. P. Morgan & Co. Direct testimony admitting this causal connection does not exist, but the admitted facts make it appear highly probable. To be sure, the retirement of the preferred stock had been thought of long before, and the right to do so on any 1st of January between 1896 and 1917 was expressly reserved; yet up to 1901, when this plan was finally consummated, no plan had been devised for the retirement of that stock. The interested parties agreed not to wait until October, but to act at once, in order to establish permanent peace and " to show that there was no hostility." The detailed movements following the 9th of May do not appear clearly from the evidence, but the results of what took place are indicated in the bulletin published on June 1st. " It is officially announced that an understanding has been reached between the Northern Pacific and the Union Pacific interests, under which the composition of the Northern Pacific board will be left in the hands of J. P. Morgan. Certain names have already been suggested, not now to be made public, which will especially be recognized as representative of the common interests. It is asserted that complete and permanent harmony will result under the plan adopted between all interests involved." This " understanding " had been incorporated in the Arbitration Agreement of May 31, 1901, which the bulletin just quoted announced to the public, and which gave "every important interest its representative." In it the "vitality and vigor of the peace policy established between the railroads" found definite expression. It showed "that they were acting under what we know as a community of interest principle, and that we were not going to have that battle in Wall Street. There was not going to be people standing up there fighting each other." Had this battle in Wall Street been fought to the last ditch and the Union Pacific interests triumphed, the measure of the injury done to the Great Northern and Northern Pacific would have been destruction, in the judgment of those who are responsible for the administration of these properties, — destruction in the sense that the properties would have been incapacitated from doing what it was intended they should do and what they were quite able to do in building up a great interstate and Oriental traffic, unless they had all gone into a single combination. "With the Northern Pacific as a half owner in the shares of the Burlington and responsibility for one half of the purchase price of these shares, the transfers of the shares of the Northern Pacific or the control of the Northern Pacific to an interest that was adverse or an interest that had greater investments in other directions, the control being in the hands of companies whose interests would be injured by the growth and development of this country would, of course, put the Great Northern in a position where it would be almost helpless, because we would be, as it were, fenced out of the territory south which produces the tonnage we want to take west and which consumes the tonnage we want to bring east, and the Great Northern would be in a position where it would have to make a hard fight — either survive or perish, or else sell out to the other interests. The latter would be the most businesslike proceeding." With the view of preventing the possibility of future "raids" upon the Great Northern and Northern Pacific stock and of fortifying these two roads and their connections in their competitive struggle with "the Suez Canal and the high seas and the entire world," the idea of a permanent holding company was invented. It has been persistently denied that the desire to restrain competition among the constituent companies had anything to do with the organization of the Northern Securities Company.   *   *   *

The organization of a holding company having been determined, it was necessary to decide upon the form and contents of a charter, or articles of incorporation, and the state in which the incorporation should take place. The general nature of the contents of such a charter had been discussed practically as long as the idea of a holding company had been entertained by the men interested in the matter; namely, for something like seven or eight years. The specific nature of such a charter for this particular company was not made the object of study until after the Arbitration Agreement of May 31, 1901. About this time several men began an examination of the laws of a number of states for the purpose of discovering a suitable charter and of deciding upon the state in which the company should be incorporated. The decision with reference to the place of incorporation was not made until a few days before the company was actually incorporated. The general aim in searching for a charter and a state "was to have beyond any question the power to purchase, own and hold and dispose of corporate securities on a large scale." Between June and October several different sketches of articles of incorporation were made and submitted to seven or eight men. These men were scattered so that no formal meeting for the consideration of the articles was ever held. The sketch referred to left blank the name of the corporation, the name of the state in which it was to be incorporated, and the amount of the capital stock. "There was practically no change in the substance of it from the beginning." Among the earliest efforts was a search for a special charter granted by the territory of Minnesota prior to the adoption of the constitution of 1858. "A large number of special charters that were passed when Minnesota was a territory have been very much sought after and extensively used by railroads that have since been built, by financial institutions of various kinds and business corporations." The old enactments were glanced through with a view of seeing if there was anything that would meet the desires and purposes of the contemplated organization, because " under our constitution all charters antedating the admission of the state into the union became fixed legislative contracts." Such a special, territorial charter could, however, not be found ; nor could a later charter suitable for the occasion be discovered. Hence, recourse was had to the general incorporation laws of Minnesota, New York, New Jersey, and probably also of West Virginia. The Minnesota statutes were regarded as too " new in that class of corporations. There are no large business corporations incorporated under the laws of the state of Minnesota ; she never has had any. There has been no occasion to put powers that are given by her general statutes to such organizations under judicial question." Furthermore, her own citizens, it was asserted, go to other states for the incorporation of enterprises of any magnitude. Whether West Virginia was any more than mentioned in this connection does not appear. As between the statutes of New York and New Jersey, the choice fell upon the latter because they had been in force a good many years and were regarded as " thoroughly well settled." Those of New York, on the other hand, while they were quite similar to those of New Jersey, and " had evidently been passed with a view of enlarging her legislation to put it on a parity with New Jersey," were of very recent origin, and had not been construed by the courts. In this connection, reference may be made to a pamphlet entitled "Advantages of the General Corporation Act of New Jersey," published without reference to the Securities Company, in which the author of it points out that since 1846 the policy of New Jersey towards capital has been that of " liberality." The changes introduced in the law since then have made it " simpler, more liberal and less burdensome." Since 1896, when the law was again revised and codified, its salient features have been simplicity of organization and management, freedom from undue publicity in the private affairs of the company, and facility of dissolution.

The charter, which was finally taken out in the state of New Jersey, is in many respects similar to the charters of other great corporations. It has many points in common with the charters of the United States Steel Corporation, and the Standard Oil Company, except that the Northern Securities charter does not grant the omnibus powers conferred by the others. The Standard Oil Company and the United States Steel Corporation can engage in practically every conceivable kind of enterprise, while the Northern Securities charter limits the company to the acquisition of valuable paper held by domestic and foreign corporations, exercising the rights of property over the same, aiding corporations whose paper is thus held, and acquiring and holding the necessary real and personal property. The amount of the capital stock with which the corporation began business was thirty thousand dollars, while the total authorized capital stock of the corporation is four hundred million dollars. The customary officers and committees are provided for and the usual powers conferred upon them. A board of fifteen directors was elected, six of whom represented Northern Pacific interests; four, the Great Northern, not counting the president; three, the Union Pacific; and two, unclassified. The composition of the board on the community of interest plan was one of the points of attack subsequently pursued by the state and federal authorities. Such an arrangement had numerous precedents, however. Chauncey M. Depew is an officer or director of fifty-six transportation companies; W. K. Vanderbilt of fifty-one; Geo. J. Gould of thirty-five; E. V. Rossiter of thirty-one; E. H. Harriman of twenty-eight; Charles F. Cox of twenty-seven; D. S. Lamont of twenty-four; J. P. Morgan of twenty-three, and so on through a list of more than a hundred names.

Much testimony was elicited with respect to the capitalization and the ratio at which the Northern Pacific and Great Northern shares were exchanged for Northern Securities stock. It seems that the capitalization of $400,000,000 was fixed at that figure in order to cover approximately the combined capital stock of the Northern Pacific and Great Northern at an agreed price apparently based upon earning capacity. The par value of the outstanding capital stock of the Great Northern was $123,880,400 and that of the Northern Pacific amounted to $155,000,000. The Northern Securities Company purchased about seventy-six per cent of the former and ninety-six per cent of the latter, on the basis of $115 per share of $100 of Northern Pacific and $180 per share of $100 of the Great Northern. The purchase of the stock of the two railway companies by means of the shares of the Securities Company was effected by and through the stockholders as such. An offer to make the purchase was conveyed to the Great Northern stockholders in a circular letter. This circular called forth numerous inquiries, in response to which President Hill sent out a letter setting forth the purposes of the company and suggesting that " the offer of the Securities Company is one that Great Northern shareholders can accept with profit and advantage to themselves." It was the expressed wish of the leading stockholders of the Great Northern that all of them should be dealt with on a basis of absolute equality, irrespective of the amount of their holdings. This appears to have been done. In case of the Northern Pacific no circular letter appears to have been sent out to stockholders; nor were the same rules of equality applied to them, for the Union Pacific interests received a cash premium of $8,915,629 in the exchange of their Northern Pacific holdings on the agreed basis for $82,492,871 par value of the Northern Securities stock. It also seems that the promoters of the Northern Securities Company had an understanding with the holders of at least a majority of the common stock of the Northern Pacific Railway Company that they would exchange that stock for the stock of the Northern Securities Company as soon as organized ; and also an agreement that the preferred stock of the Northern Pacific should be retired on the first day of January following.[1]

BALTHASAR H. MEYER

[1] Practically the full text of the decision of the United States Supreme Court, declaring the Northern Securities Company illegal, is reprinted in our Trusts, Pools, and Corporations, pp. 322–382. The corporation is now in process of dissolution. — ED.

XXII

THE DECISION ON THE UNION PACIFIC MERGER [1]

EVER since the decision in the Northern Securities case dissolving the merger of the Hill lines, it has seemed probable that an attempt would be made to break up the equally powerful Harriman system in the Southwest. It is true that the facts in the two instances were not altogether the same. The component parts of the Harriman lines were not competitors before their union in any such obvious way as the Great Northern and Northern Pacific had been, while the combination of the Union and Southern Pacific was not accomplished through a holding company formed for the purpose, but came about through a stock purchase by a genuine operating company. Doubtless for these reasons prosecution was postponed until less equivocal cases had been disposed of. The delay had the advantage, as matters turned out, of allowing a prior investigation by the Interstate Commerce Commission; so that the Government was enabled to incorporate in its record a large amount of evidence presented in January and February, 1907, without the expense of taking the testimony itself.[2]

The suit for dissolution under the Sherman law was finally brought by the United States before the Circuit Court for the District of Utah. The Government named as defendants the Union Pacific and its subsidiary companies, the Southern Pacific, the Santa Fé, the San Pedro, Los Angeles, and Salt Lake, the

[1] From the *Quarterly Journal of Economics*, Vol. XXVII, 1913, pp. 295–328. The legal aspects of combination and the financial history of the Harriman system will be outlined in Ripley's Railroads: Finance and Organization. (In preparation.)

[2] References, unless otherwise stated, are to the record submitted to the Supreme Court. The testimony and exhibits in the Merger case fill thirteen volumes and constitute an important addition to the source material on railroad transportation.

Northern Pacific, the Great Northern; certain individuals, — Edward H. Harriman, Jacob H. Schiff, Otto H. Kahn, James Stillman, Henry H. Rogers, Henry C. Frick, and William A. Clark; and the Farmers' Loan and Trust Company, the depositary of the San Pedro shares under the trust agreement of 1902. It asked decrees forbidding the Union Pacific, Oregon Short Line, and Oregon Railroad and Navigation Companies from voting shares of the other companies named in the petition, and also decrees enjoining these other companies from recognizing any shares which the Union Pacific and its subsidiaries might happen to hold. Briefs were filed by P. F. Dunne and N. H. Loomis for the Union Pacific and its subsidiaries and for the Southern Pacific. A separate brief was submitted for Mr. Frick, and a memorandum in behalf of Messrs. Stillman, Schiff, and Kahn. The Government's case was directed by Frank B. Kellogg and Cordenio A. Severance, with the Attorney General's assistance in the preparation of the brief. All of these gentlemen had been employed before in prosecutions under the Sherman law, and Messrs. Kellogg and Severance had tried the case against the Southern Pacific in the Circuit Court. Mr. Severance, however, bore the burden of examining and cross-examining witnesses in the case at bar, and was the best informed, as he was perhaps the ablest, of the Government counsel.

The original report of the Interstate Commerce Commission had dealt with the Harriman lines as a great combination of competing railroads.[1] The Circuit Court rendered its decision on June 24, 1911, and contrary to general expectation this proved unqualifiedly adverse to the Government's contentions. The case turned on the question of competition. Two judges ruled that the Union Pacific and the Southern Pacific were connecting and only incidentally competing lines.[2] Judge Hook filed a dissenting opinion. Appeal was taken to the Supreme Court in October of the same year.

The facts in the case seem reasonably clear. The so-called Harriman group of railroads in 1912 comprised a mileage of

---

[1] 12 I. C. C. Rep. 277.   [2] 188 Fed. Rep. 102.

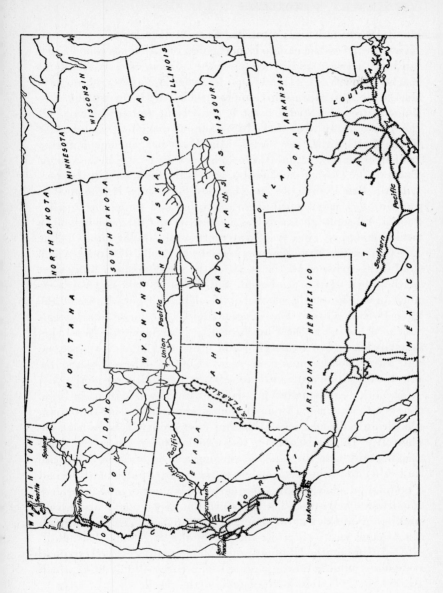

about 18,500 miles. It stretched from Omaha, Kansas City, and New Orleans on the east to Los Angeles, San Francisco, and Portland on the west, and by means of the Morgan Steamship Line it reached New York. In addition it owned a majority of stock in the Pacific Mail Steamship Company, which carries freight and passengers from the Pacific coast to the Orient and to Panama. Of the total mileage west of the Mississippi-Missouri river and south of the Northern Pacific Railroad the Harriman management controlled 19 per cent. Finally, through stock ownership in the Illinois Central, the Chicago and Alton, and other lines, and by contract with the San Pedro, Los Angeles, and Salt Lake, it possessed in varying degree influence over connecting and competing roads.

The different parts of the system were held together by a rather complex system of intercorporate stockholdings. The keystone of the structure was the Union Pacific Railroad, which held in its treasury all the stock of the Oregon Short Line, most of the stock of the St. Joseph and Grand Island, and considerable quantities of the shares of the Illinois Central and of the Chicago and Alton. The Oregon Short Line in its turn owned half of the stock of the San Pedro, Los Angeles, and Salt Lake, substantially all of the stock of the Oregon-Washington Railroad and Navigation Company, 46 per cent of the shares of the Southern Pacific Company, and interests in the Baltimore and Ohio, New York Central, Chicago and Northwestern, and other lines. The Southern Pacific Company, most important of all the Union Pacific subsidiaries, was a holding company, which owned substantially all the stock of the Central Pacific, the Southern Pacific Railroad, the Galveston, Harrisburg, and San Antonio and other roads in the Southwest, the Southern Pacific Railroad Company of Mexico, the Oregon and California, and other less important companies. The Southern Pacific Company also leased and operated the Central Pacific, the Southern Pacific Railroad, the Oregon and California, and the Southern Pacific Coast Railway. Including the Illinois Central the securities of the Harriman companies outstanding aggregated some $2,600,000,000, of which $1,650,000,000 were in the hands of the public.

Three periods may be segregated in the growth of the system.

The shares which the Union Pacific possessed in the capital of the Oregon Short Line, the holdings of the Short Line in the Oregon-Washington Railroad and Navigation Company, and the holdings of the Southern Pacific Company in the railroads of the Southwest and in the Central Pacific represented the normal growth of the Pacific railways which had been chartered in 1862 and 1864. The construction of the Short Line was undertaken by Union Pacific interests in order to secure a connection with the Pacific coast, and was financed in return for the stock of the company and a portion of its bonds. The Oregon Railway and Navigation Company [1] was purchased for the same reason, under the very nose of the Northern Pacific. In like manner, the parties which originally built the Central Pacific constructed additional track southward along the Californian coast, and then east through Arizona, New Mexico, and Texas. As a pure matter of convenience they organized different companies as they went along, and finally welded all together by means of stock control. It was in the second period that the control of the Salt Lake Company by the Union Pacific and Oregon Short Line was secured, and then also that the Union Pacific bought its holdings in the Southern Pacific. About the same time shares were purchased in the Northern Pacific which were later sold again. The third period began with the dissolution of the Northern Securities Company and represents the result of reinvestment of the sums secured from the sale of Northern Pacific and Great Northern stock. Among other securities certain shares in the Santa Fé were obtained. For the purposes in hand we have to deal mainly with the second group of purchases, as these, with the addition of the Santa Fé operation, were the basis of the Government suit. The characteristic feature of the earlier and later development was the acquisition of connecting lines; only in the middle period, if at all, was competition suppressed.

It is a matter of common knowledge that as late as 1901 the Union and Southern Pacific companies were entirely independent. Of the original builders of the Southern Pacific, Hopkins had

[1] Later expanded into the Oregon-Washington Railroad and Navigation Company.

died in 1878, Crocker in 1888, and Stanford in 1893; but until
August, 1900, Mr. Collis P. Huntington, then holding $37\frac{1}{2}$ per
cent of all the Southern Pacific stock outstanding, refused to
compromise in any way his company's separate existence. The
record shows that proposals were made to him. The Union
Pacific, dependent on the Southern Pacific for direct connection
with San Francisco, and fearful lest at Mr. Huntington's death
his stock should fall into unfriendly hands, offered to purchase
his shares, or failing this to conclude a permanent alliance. To
this offer Mr. Huntington remained indifferent. Huntington
died, however, in August, 1900, leaving his Southern Pacific
stock to his widow and nephew in the proportion of two-thirds
and one-third respectively; and both, as had been anticipated,
proved willing to dispose of their holdings. Negotiations were
carried to completion in February, 1901. 475,000 shares were
purchased from the Huntingtons and from Edwin Hawley, the
late financier's most intimate business associate, while enough was
secured from other parties through Kuhn, Loeb and Company
to make an aggregate of 677,700 shares, at an average price of
50.6146. Market quotations were then in the neighborhood of
45 per cent. On February 4, Kuhn, Loeb and Company engaged
to deliver to the Union Pacific one month later 72,300 additional shares at the same price, plus 4 per cent interest from
February 11, bringing the company's holdings up to 750,000
shares. This, in Mr. Harriman's opinion, was sufficient for control. A year or two later an attempt to force the Southern
Pacific to pay in dividends earnings which its managers thought
should be expended in improvements led the Union Pacific to
acquire still another 150,000 shares. In January, 1910, purchases
were renewed for the last time, in view of pending legislation in
Congress which promised to make the possession of an absolute
majority of Southern Pacific stock desirable; but these purchases
ceased after 74,000 shares had been obtained, and 50,000 shares
were subsequently sold. This concluded the episode. On June 30,
1911, the Union Pacific through the Oregon Short Line owned
1,266,500 shares of Southern Pacific common, or 46 per cent of
all outstanding — sufficient to give undisputed control.

It was stoutly maintained by Mr. Kahn, of Kuhn, Loeb and Company, that the desire to control the Southern Pacific line from San Francisco to El Paso was not a motive in the transactions described. The necessity of buying the Sunset Route, he said, was considered an obstacle and a deterring feature. If a way could have been found to secure the Central Pacific alone, it would have been preferred at the time. The possible reduction of competition was not even considered at any of the meetings of the Executive Committee at which the subject was brought up. The same was true of the acquisition of the boat lines to the Orient, the business to Colorado and Utah points, and other minor phases.[1] Speaking of the Southern Pacific, Mr. Kahn declared:

> We knew it would require a great deal of money to be spent on it, we knew it added thousands of miles to the burden of administration and management. We were very anxious that the Union Pacific should receive as much of the administrative ability and of the railroad genius of Mr. Harriman as it was possible for him to give it, and we were rather disinclined to put upon him any more burden than was necessary to the best development of the Union Pacific; and therefore we, individually, felt that if the Southern Pacific could be separated, keeping only the Central Pacific and the north and south lines in California, and getting rid of the southern part of the Southern Pacific, we would be getting rid of a nuisance.[2]

Some plausibility was given to this contention by Mr. Gould's later admission that he had requested a half interest in the Southern Pacific purchase, and had told Mr. Harriman that if the Union Pacific did not take the stock he would take it himself for his roads.[3] At this time the Gould lines ended at Ogden, and the control by them of the Central Pacific would have been disastrous to Union Pacific interests. There was also talk of possible construction to Ogden by the Burlington or the Chicago and Northwestern. No proof of intent is now possible. One can only surmise that Mr. Harriman was unlikely to have overlooked the great extension of his power in the Southwest which acquisition of the Sunset Route was bound to bring, whatever might have been true of the bankers who were supporting him.

[1] Pp. 4713–4714 Kahn.   [2] P. 4731 Kahn.   [3] Pp. 4952–4957 Gould.

A few years after the Southern Pacific purchase, the San Pedro, Los Angeles, and Salt Lake was brought into the fold. This line runs from Salt Lake City southwesterly to Los Angeles, cutting three or four hundred miles from the route *via* Sacramento, and giving to the Union Pacific yet another independent outlet to the coast. It appears that the project had been originally planned by Union Pacific interests and over a million dollars spent; but that the plans had been interrupted by the Union Pacific bankruptcy and had not been resumed until 1898.[1] In that year the Oregon Short Line made a contract with a man named Eccles and his associates, who engaged to form a company and to build a railroad along the old grade for some seventy-five or eighty-five miles. Under this contract sixty-six miles were built,[2] when construction ceased. About 1900 the matter was taken up by parties in Los Angeles, and Senator Clark became interested.[3] Land for a terminal was applied for in Salt Lake City and support asked for on the ground that the new line would be independent of the Southern Pacific.[4] By June, 1901, the San Pedro Company had raised $2,501,600, had obtained in the neighborhood of one hundred acres of land in Los Angeles favorably situated for terminals, and through the Los Angeles Terminal Railway Company had acquired about three miles of water front on the Bay of San Pedro, California.[5] One hundred and ten miles of the proposed main line from Los Angeles toward Salt Lake had been surveyed, ninety miles located, and right of way for thirty miles secured.[6] These vigorous efforts led to renewed activity on the part of the Union Pacific system, although the original reasons for construction had lost force after its consolidation with the Southern Pacific lines. An option on the Eccles mileage (Utah and Pacific Company) was taken up, forty-two miles were built on towards Caliente, surveys were made towards Los Angeles, and litigation was begun with the Clark interests over the right of way through certain narrow passes through which both roads, if constructed, would have to run. It was from

---

[1] P. 2435 Eccles.
[2] Pp. 2435 *et seq.* Eccles.
[3] Pp. 3282 *et seq.* Gibben.

[4] P. 2460 Love.
[5] Pp. 3278–3279 Clark.
[6] P. 3280 Clark.

the beginning evident that two railroads through this district would not pay,[1] and the San Pedro Company came to terms. In July, 1902, the Clark people sold to the Harriman lines an undivided half interest in the enterprise and agreed to the trusteeing of all the stock for ten years. Directors were to be equally divided between the two parties and various traffic and other agreements effectually prevented independent action as to rates.

The abortive attempt to control the Northern Pacific in 1901 needs only a bare reference.[2] It had no result except to provide the Union Pacific abundantly with funds that could be used in future expansion. It should be remarked, however, that an interest in the Santa Fé was acquired in 1906, at a time of active rivalry between Santa Fé and Southern Pacific interests. The Santa Fé was then and still is the only road connecting San Francisco and Chicago by its own rails (except for a few miles in California where Southern Pacific tracks are used), and the only one of importance apart from the Harriman lines that penetrates the Southwest. In 1901 projects for Santa Fé extension in Arizona were under discussion. The company had just bought the stock and second mortgage bonds of the Santa Fé, Prescott, and Phoenix, a road running from Ash Fork on the Santa Fé main line south and southeast through Prescott to Phoenix. The county was not a rich one, but it had mineral possibilities, and expected a considerable agricultural development through irrigation. The president of the last-named company was one Frank Murphy, whom Mr. Morawetz, chairman of the executive committee of the Santa Fé, characterized as an enthusiastic son of Arizona.[3] Mr. Murphy was anxious that the Phoenix road should be extended south to Benson, where connection could be made with the El Paso and Southwestern and a direct and independent outlet secured to the Gulf over this road and the Texas and Pacific from El Paso. It is obvious that this was of great importance to the Santa Fé, Prescott, and Phoenix so long as it remained independent. To the Santa Fé

---

[1] P. 2569 Kearns.

[2] *Vide* Chapter XXI, *supra*, and Ripley, Railroads : Finance and Organization. — ED.

[3] P. 1139 Morawetz.

it was less vital. Traffic which could be taken on Atchison rails clear to Chicago was scarce likely to be given to another road at Benson, and although part of the proposed road might have been used in a new low-grade route through Southern Arizona and New Mexico to Deming — a route parallel with the Santa Fé's existing line and about one hundred and fifty miles longer — the construction of this route was not immediately in prospect. For these reasons, and because the local business of the extension did not look attractive, Mr. Morawetz refused to undertake it.[1] Mr. Murphy promptly organized a new company, the Phoenix and Eastern, made surveys, secured rights of way, and negotiated for a trackage contract with the El Paso and Southwestern.[2] Seeing that the road was to be built, the Santa Fé decided that it had better build it itself, and arranged in 1902 for construction as far as Dudleyville, half-way.[3] Shortly after surveys were made for an eastern extension from Dudleyville toward the Santa Fé tracks at Deming, and a new road was incorporated to build through the Gila canyon.[4]

The construction south of Phoenix the Southern Pacific regarded as an invasion of its territory. Harriman graders occupied a canyon above the line of the Phoenix and Eastern and proceeded to blast down rocks upon their rival's right of way.[5] The next step was to ask the Santa Fé to sell to the Southern Pacific the constructed part of the Phoenix and Eastern, and to retire from the country in which it lay.[6] Mr. Morawetz was not unwilling to make the sale. He seized the opportunity, however, to secure certain advantages in northern California. In the summer of 1902, as he explained in his testimony, the Atchison had concluded that it would be desirable to extend its system north of San Francisco Bay. Negotiations were begun for the purchase of the stock of the California and Northwestern, but this stock was sold to Southern Pacific interests before the Atchison purchase was completed.[7] Thereupon the Atchison bought the stock of a short line running out of Eureka, about one hundred miles

[1] P. 1133 Morawetz.   [4] P. 5069 Murphy.   [6] P. 1134 Morawetz.
[2] P. 1162 Douglas.   [5] P. 1025 Murphy.   [7] P. 1134 Morawetz.
[3] P. 1133 Morawetz.

north of San Francisco. This railroad did a considerable passenger business and handled a good deal of lumber, but connected with San Francisco only by boat.[1] It was intended to build south to San Francisco,[2] but the construction would have been expensive, and the volume of business probably insufficient to support both a Southern Pacific and a Santa Fé line. The dispute in Arizona gave Mr. Morawetz the idea of attaching to his consent to sell the Phoenix and Eastern (at cost and interest) the conditions that Mr. Harriman sell him at the same time a half interest in the coast lines north of San Francisco Bay. Mr. Harriman at first refused,[3] but later agreed. As part of the same arrangement the Southern Pacific agreed to have built a low-grade line between Phoenix and Deming and the Santa Fé a line between Phoenix and Mojave — each company to have trackage rights over the other's road on mutually satisfactory terms upon request.[4]

It was while the relations between the Santa Fé and the Southern Pacific were thus subjects of dispute that Mr. Harriman informed Mr. Morawetz that he and some of his associates (Wm. Rockefeller, H. H. Rogers, Jas. Stillman, and Kuhn, Loeb and Company)[5] had purchased 300,000 shares of Atchison stock and desired representation on the Board of Directors. He called attention to the general desirability of establishing a better relationship between railroads, and offered Mr. Morawetz a place on the executive committee of the Southern Pacific; but stated that the stock referred to had been bought as a private investment. Mr. Morawetz declined to consider a change in the directorate until the differences between the Santa Fé and the Harriman lines should have been adjusted. By February, 1905, an agreement had been reached, and Messrs. Rogers and Frick were elected to the Atchison Board.[6] The bulk of the holdings of Mr. Harriman and his associates had been sold by the latter part of 1906, but by this time the Oregon Short Line had purchased 100,000 Atchison shares; and Rogers and Frick retained their positions. The stock owned by the Oregon Short Line was finally sold in 1909.[7]

[1] P. 509 Payson.
[2] P. 512 Payson.
[3] P. 1136 Morawetz.

[4] P. 974 Deming.
[5] P. 1105 Schiff.

[6] P. 1138 Morawetz.
[7] P. 4722 Kahn.

These were the bare facts on which the Government was to base its charge of violation of the law. They raised, it will be observed, three questions. (1) Was there competition between the companies named before the incidents occurred which were mentioned in the complaint? (2) Did these transactions do away with competition, assuming that it had existed? (3) If there had been competition, and it had ceased, was its suppression brought about by illegal means? Unless all three questions could be answered in the affirmative, the Government's case would fail. In the eyes of Mr. Wickersham and his associates the facts cited constituted cumulative evidence of a conspiracy to restrain and monopolize interstate and foreign commerce, carried through by competing railroads and by certain stockholders therein. On the other hand, the defendants interpreted the facts as isolated transactions, each justified by the special circumstances of the case, and totally devoid in intent and result of any semblance of restraint of trade or attempted monopoly.

In analyzing the evidence presented, we may first direct our attention to the matter which the Government offered as proof of the existence of competition between the Southern and the Union Pacific railroads, including with the latter the Oregon Short Line and Oregon Railroad and Navigation Companies. This evidence was vital, and was given more attention in briefs and testimony than any other portion of the case. The material was divided into seven parts:

1. Competition as to traffic between the Atlantic seaboard and the Pacific coast. The Government examined no less than seventy witnesses — shippers, Southern Pacific employees and ex-employees, and representatives of independent railroad lines. Among those who testified were Mr. Hawley, for nineteen years eastern agent of the Southern Pacific and after that a financier of prominence; Messrs. Stubbs, Spence, and Munroe of the traffic department of the Southern Pacific; Mr. Paul Morton, one time president of the Equitable Life Assurance Company, Mr. Jeffery, president of the Denver and Rio Grande, and Mr. Hannaford, in charge of traffic on the Northern Pacific. Substantially all of these witnesses testified that traffic from the

Atlantic seaboard could move to the Pacific coast either *via*
the Morgan Steamship line to New Orleans and thence over the
Sunset Route of the Southern Pacific to San Francisco, or *via*
the trunk lines and their connections to Omaha, thence over the
Union Pacific to Ogden and over the Central Pacific to the coast.
Although the Southern Pacific was interested in both of these
routes, yet it secured all the revenue from freight moving *via* the
Sunset Route and only 30.1 per cent of the total revenue from
freight delivered to it by the Union Pacific at Ogden. In consequence, it used its best efforts to influence freight to travel by the
southern line. The Government showed by the evidence of shippers
that freight was actually solicited in competition between the two
Pacific companies. The Southern Pacific, it appeared, took traffic
at New York rates from as far west as Buffalo and Pittsburg,
not including those cities, and from as far south as Norfolk.[1] Not
only this, but the Union Pacific was not altogether restricted to
the route *via* Ogden. By diverting freight at Granger and sending
it north to Portland over the Oregon Short Line and the Oregon
Railroad and Navigation Company, it could affect the transcontinental rate in two ways. In the first place, it was physically
possible for traffic to move from Portland to San Francisco by
boat ; and in the second place, a mere reduction in the rate to
Portland compelled a cut to every Pacific terminal point in order
to maintain these different cities in the same relative position for
the distribution of eastern goods. As Mr. Stubbs expressed it :
" Let the rate be cut on the Great Northern, and it goes down
to the Gulf of California." [2]

Mention may also be made in this connection of the route *via*
the Isthmus of Panama, in which the Southern Pacific had an
interest by virtue of its control of a steamship line from San
Francisco to Panama. The business was not large, but in so far
as any moved this way it was in competition with the rail lines
via Ogden.

2. Competition as to traffic between points in the interior of
the country and the Pacific coast. Much the same was true of
the traffic from points between Buffalo and Pittsburg and the

[1] P. 841 Hawley.   [2] P. 2005 Stubbs.

Mississippi river that held for the business from further east.
It was plainly impracticable to send them through New York,
but goods could move to the Gulf and thence *via* the Sunset
Route to California, or they could go by way of Ogden. The
Illinois Central was the most important road in this territory, and
Mr. Fish, its president, testified that the Union Pacific and the
Sunset Route competed for traffic originating anywhere in Illinois
Central territory as actively as any two roads that were in the
business.[1] Rates were the same either way, the competition being
in service and solicitation.[2]

3. Competition as to traffic between the Atlantic seaboard and
Colorado and Utah common points. A good many sheep wintered
in the desert west of Salt Lake, and in the spring moved to the
summer ranges in Idaho where they were sheared. The railroad
near which the shearing took place secured the outbound wool,
and for this reason the Union Pacific, Southern Pacific, and Rio
Grande Western offered every attraction possible to influence the
movement of the flocks. The Union Pacific, for instance, at one
time paid a head tax which Wyoming levied on all sheep brought
into that state.[3] The Oregon Short Line purchased salt on behalf
of the sheep owners, carried it to Idaho, and only collected back
the purchase price at the time the salt was delivered.[4] In the
same way there was competition in respect to cattle and horses
which wintered in southern Idaho and northern Nevada and
moved east in the spring.[5] In return for the wool, cattle, hides,
etc., shipped east, there were brought in shipments of miscellaneous merchandise, dry goods, machinery, and the like. When the
Union Pacific handled the business it moved from New York to
Norfolk or Newport News, thence by rail to Omaha and over the
Union Pacific lines to destination. When the Southern Pacific
took it, the freight went by Southern Pacific steamers to New
Orleans or Galveston, and thence over railroads controlled by
the company to Fort Worth, Texas, where it was given to connecting lines for delivery at destination. The rate was the same

[1] Pp. 1109–1110 Fish.   [3] P. 2391 Babcock.
[2] P. 2189 Stubbs.   [4] P. 2491 Love.
                [5] P. 2661 McBride.

either way, but the rivalry between soliciting agencies was intense.[1]

4. Competition as to traffic between Portland and Utah and Colorado common points, including certain points in Nevada. Portland enjoys a fairly direct route over the Oregon Railroad and Navigation Company's tracks to Huntington, and from there over the Oregon Short Line to Granger, a few miles east of Ogden. The Southern Pacific runs south from Portland to Roseville, near Sacramento, and thence east through California, Nevada, and Utah to Ogden. The distance over the one route is 945.3 miles and over the other 1487.3. The Roseville route has nearly twice the rise and fall of the Huntington road, while the curvature also is greater. A calculation by Mr. Kruttschnitt estimated that the direct-line haul was equivalent to 3498 miles of straight level track, but that the haul *via* Roseville was equivalent to 6164 such miles.[2] The evidence nevertheless showed that some business, especially lumber, had moved the long way around before 1901. Traffic also had moved *via* the Oregon Short Line and Central Pacific to points as far west of Ogden as Wells, Nevada. How much all this amounted to was not clearly shown — at best it was probably not a great deal. After the consolidation of the Union Pacific and Southern Pacific in 1902 the Shasta Route took out its through rates with the Oregon Railroad and Navigation Company, and withdrew from the competition.

5. Competition as to traffic between San Francisco and Portland. Some of the business between these towns used the same Southern Pacific rails through Oregon and California that were traversed by business going to Utah and Nevada. About two-thirds of it, however, came by water.[3] Mr. Stubbs, traffic director of the Harriman lines, testified as follows:

The steamship service between San Francisco and Portland is better than the rail service, with this single exception — that the rail service is daily while the steamship service is probably only once in five days. The points of delivery and taking at San Francisco and at Portland favor the steamship line. In the early opening of the Shasta Route, we had some

---

[1] Pp. 2358–2371 McCarthy.   [2] P. 4141 Kruttschnitt.

[3] Pp. 3953–3954 Stubbs.

ambition to load our trains north-bound, and made some attempts to get
the business, but found that we absolutely could not take the business as
against the steamship lines, but besides this, is the fact that there were
outside competitors with the Oregon Railroad and Navigation; other steamship lines, and steam schooners, that made the rates not only unremunerative, but they were unstable; so, after several attempts to join in that
business, we quit.[1]

The evidence showed clearly that for perhaps one and a half
years after 1894, the railroad and steamship lines competed
actively for the local coast-wise business, both freight and passenger. Rates fell to $1.00 a ton by water and $1.50 a ton by
rail for the 653 miles between San Francisco and Portland.[2]
Passenger fares were $2.50 and $5.00 on the boat,[3] and $5.00
and $10.00 by rail. The boat rate included meals and berth, for
which the regular charge was $6.00, so that it was actually
cheaper to pay fare than to ride on a pass. After the war was
over a differential was put in of 6 cents a 100 pounds L.C.L.
and 3 cents a 100 pounds C.L. between the steamers and the rail
lines [4] — all this before 1901. Competition in service continued,[5]
and large sums are still spent in advertising.[6]

6. Competition for traffic between San Francisco and points
in Montana, Idaho, etc. Wine, dried fruit, sugar, beans, and
other California products distributed from San Francisco could
pass north to Portland and Seattle *via* the Shasta Route or by
boat, and could go from there east over the Oregon Railroad and
Navigation and Oregon Short Line, over the Great Northern,
or over the Northern Pacific. Or it could go east from San Francisco by the Central Pacific to Ogden, and thence north over the
Oregon Short Line into Montana and Idaho. The business was
not large, but it was competed for actively.

7. Competition as to traffic between various ports in the
Orient and points east of the Missouri river in the United
States. The Southern Pacific Company bought a majority of the
stock of the Pacific Mail in the fall of 1902,[7] and used the ships
of that company for traffic from San Francisco to Yokohama,

[1] P. 3935 Stubbs.   [4] P. 2666 Ward.   [6] P. 3980 Stubbs.
[2] P. 2901 Connor.   [5] Pp. 2757–2758 Hurlburt.   [7] P. 1666 Schwerin.
[3] P. 2632 O'Reilly.

Kobe, Nagasaki, Shanghai, Hong Kong, and sometimes Amoy.[1] The greater part of the business moved *via* the Union and Central Pacific; some of it went west over the Sunset Route — in all, the rail lines west of the Missouri earned $63,382.86 on Oriental traffic moving through San Francisco in October, 1906.[2] On the other hand, the Oregon Railroad and Navigation Company owned all the stock of the Portland and Asiatic Company, running between Portland and substantially the same ports of call that the Pacific Mail reached in China and Japan. This company was the successor of three lines which in turn had failed to make the business through Portland pay,[3] and seems to have been established to assist the Oregon Railroad and Navigation in competition for the export business in grain and flour.[4] Ninety per cent of the traffic was westbound.[5] Of course the steamship company was eager for traffic, and competed in connection with the Oregon Railroad and Navigation, Oregon Short Line, and Union Pacific with the route formed by the Central Pacific and the Union Pacific, at least prior to 1901.

The voluminous evidence thus summarized showed that active competition had existed of almost every conceivable kind. There had been competition of parallel routes between the same termini, of parallel or roundabout routes between different termini, of roundabout routes entirely controlled by the competing lines, of routes in which the Union and Southern Pacific were links only in chains of connecting and independent roads, and finally there had been competition in cases where one competitor had to rely upon the other for a greater or less proportion of the haul.

There were certain considerations, nevertheless, which weakened the Government's case. Although the carriers had competed, yet counsel were able to show only in sporadic instances that rates had been cut. The most important through business which the Union Pacific had possessed had been the transcontinental traffic to and from the Pacific coast, and the connection with which it had interchanged most business was the Southern

[1] P. 1657 Schwerin.
[2] P. 1872 Stubbs, Exhibit 119.
[5] Pp. 4851–4852, *Ibid.*

[3] P. 4850 Campbell.
[4] P. 4851, *Ibid.*

Pacific. Now the Rio Grande Western reached as far west as
Ogden, and it was at all times possible for the Southern Pacific
to divert traffic this way. In consequence the Union Pacific had
not dared to push competition very far. The Oregon Short Line
and the Oregon Railroad and Navigation Company had remained
practically unused for transcontinental business. Mr. Munroe,
freight traffic manager of the Union Pacific, connected with
the traffic department of that company since 1882, testified that
the use of it would have been suicidal. Mr. Stubbs declared that
in all his experience he had never known any business to be
worked into or from California *via* the Portland gateway.[1] Even
had the route been resorted to, movement by it would have been
roundabout and difficult, and freight would have been necessarily distributed by the Southern Pacific from San Francisco.
Restricted, therefore, to interchange with the Central Pacific at
Ogden, the Union Pacific was unable to quote any through rates
except with the consent of the very company which it was its
interest to fight. Putting to one side the transcontinental business, the competitive traffic remaining was not large. Counsel
for the carriers characterized it as incidental and insignificant,
while the Government did not allege that the earnings on it
exceeded three or four million dollars.

A somewhat different situation appears when we pass from
the relations between the Southern Pacific and the Union Pacific
to the evidence touching the other railroads named in the complaint. It was undisputed that the Santa Fé, Great Northern,
and Northern Pacific had competed directly with the Central,
Union, and Southern Pacific. But this was not the whole story.
In the Salt Lake case there had been rivalry in construction
rather than in operation. Mr. Clark had desired to build a railroad; the Union Pacific had threatened to parallel it. There
was no rate-cutting, for there were no rates; but the pressure
of imminent financial loss had been as strong as though a rate
war had been well begun. *Mutatis mutandis*, the same was
true of a part of the dealings between Mr. Harriman and the
Santa Fé. The exchange of a right to buy a half interest in the

[1] P. 3906 Stubbs.

Northwestern Pacific for the privilege of buying a road in New Mexico had put an end to projects of building which would have involved considerable extension and great loss in profits. The position of the two parties to the suit in respect to these operations was confused. The Government was disposed to term them attempts at monopoly and to distinguish them on this ground from competition in rates or service. Counsel for the carriers referred to them as independent bargains which benefited the parties that made them and did not injure the public. It is difficult nevertheless to see why the negotiations in both the Santa Fé and the San Pedro cases were not forms of competition, bearing the same relation to rate conflicts that the strategy of a military campaign bears to the tactics of a battle. Nor is this disproved by the fact that the logical result of the conflict was consolidation; for this is true of any sort of competition whatsoever.

The second step in the Government's proof was the establishment of the fact that the consolidations which it charged had lessened competition. Mr. Wickersham had no difficulty in proving that the Union Pacific and Southern Pacific had consolidated the greater part of their soliciting agencies. The same officials were shown to be in general charge of traffic and operation on both roads. Business which formerly had been sought by the Sunset Route and the Harriman lines in competition was now routed so as to produce the most revenue for the system as a whole. So far as the San Pedro, Los Angeles, and Salt Lake Railroad was concerned, a traffic agreement had been entered into in 1902 which was a curiosity in railroad literature. The company had agreed to take no corporate action without the approval of Mr. Harriman. It was not to extend its lines north of the parallel of Salt Lake City; traffic was to be interchanged on a preferential basis with the Oregon Short Line and Union Pacific; the Salt Lake Company was to adopt Southern Pacific rates for its local traffic, and was to allow the Union Pacific and the Short Line to make through rates in both directions to and from points on its road.[1] In short, the Salt Lake road bound

[1] Pleadings, Exhibit A, pp. 24–27.

itself hand and foot. As for the Northern Pacific, the Northern Securities Company had been dissolved in 1905 and the old status of competition restored; but the Santa Fé was operating its lines in Northern California alternately with the Southern Pacific, and competitive construction in the Southwest had ceased. Besides this, an agreement had been entered into between the Southern Pacific and the Santa Fé dividing the citrus fruit traffic from Southern California, and another according to which cargoes from the Orient entering the port of San Francisco on steamships of the Pacific Mail were apportioned roughly in the proportion that the two railroads furnished outbound freight. Possibly because of this last-named arrangement, the Santa Fé had ceased to operate its line of steamships from San Diego.

The reply of the carriers on these points was technical. They urged, in the first place, quoting from *Whitwell* v. *Continental Tobacco Company*,[1] that "an attempt to monopolize a part of interstate commerce which promotes or but indirectly restricts competition therein, while its main purpose and chief effect are to increase the trade and foster the business of those who make it, was not intended to be made, and was not made, illegal by the second section." . . . The validity of this defense depended, of course, upon the acceptance of the assertion that only incidental restriction of competition had occurred,[2] and on proof that the merger of the Pacific railroads had, in fact, increased trade. Counsel put Mr. Kruttschnitt, chief operating official of the Harriman lines, on the stand, and drew from him a detailed and impressive list of the betterments and additions made since 1901, including the general statement that the Union and Southern Pacific together had spent $374,124,697.40 for these purposes in the eight years ending June 30, 1909. It was not a necessary conclusion that these expenditures had improved service or lowered rates; but the railroad officials testified positively that they had had such an effect, and the contrary was not satisfactorily established.

[1] 125 Fed. Rep. 458.
[2] Pp. 175 ff., Brief.

In the second place, the railroads maintained that, as a matter of law, ownership by one railroad of another's stock did not constitute control unless a clear majority were held. Control, said counsel, is a matter of *power*. A minority may direct the operation of a railroad because the majority has confidence in it; but this is lawful. The Southern Pacific stockholders had confidence in Mr. Harriman and his associates, but they could have superseded them at any time. The argument deserved and was given little weight. Unless courts are to shut their eyes to the facts in their interpretation of the law, they must recognize that under any ordinary circumstances less than a majority of the stock of a company will enable the holder to determine its policy. The indifference of a certain proportion of stockholders, the fact that the officers of the company alone have access to the stock list, the regularity with which a substantial number of proxies may be had for the asking, all work to the same result. This was, in fact, admitted by the defendants' own witnesses.

This left as a final step in the argument the charge that the Union Pacific had employed an illegal method in suppressing competition. The situation was not free from difficulty. The carriers maintained that the essential transaction complained of had been a purchase of stock. This, they contended, was a matter subject only to State legislation. The acquisition or disposition of property is not commercial intercourse.

If any citizen should step into a broker's office on Broadway, New York, buy some stock in the Pennsylvania Railroad, pay for it, put the certificates in his pocket, and walk out, would he, or the broker, or the broker's principal, be engaged in commercial intercourse between nations and parts of nations? . . . Would a State corporation buying those certificates be in any different situation from an individual purchaser, if the State of its domicile had endowed it with corporate power to buy stock?[1]

But even though purchases of stock were subject to Federal law they would violate no provisions of the Sherman Act. A purchase or sale is not a contract in restraint of trade, — for a contract is executory, implying something yet to be done; while a sale is

[1] Brief, Dunne, pp. 219–220.

executed, completed when made and because it is made. Nor is a contract in restraint of trade necessarily unlawful. It must be undue, that is, not entered into with the legitimate purpose of reasonably forwarding personal interest and developing trade. The same may be said of an attempt to monopolize. Every act of competition tends to drive competitors out of business, but competition is legal, in the absence of fraud or duress. It follows that an individual may buy out a competitor, and then another competitor, and so on, and a corporation may do the same thing. "It is evident," said Mr. Dunne's brief, — "*fraudulent, intimidating, coercive, and other like wrongful and unlawful* methods apart — that here we touch a fundamental principle of the freedom to buy and sell, of the legal right of the individual in respect to his own property." [1]

The case, as thus made up, was docketed on the Supreme Court calendar on October 9, 1911, and on the same day a transcript of the record was filed. On the following day, a motion to advance was submitted to the court; the motion was granted on October 23, and the case was assigned for hearing. Arguments were heard on April 19, 22, and 23, and the decision was handed down on December 2, a year and three weeks after proceedings had been begun before the final court of appeal.[2]

The opinion of the Supreme Court was remarkable for its brevity, for the sweeping terms in which the law was laid down, and none the less for the exceptions in practice which it countenanced. As was to be expected, the main emphasis was laid upon the facts. Was there or was there not such competition between the parts of the Southern Pacific system that combination between them would tend to monopoly and thus be in violation of the law? "To compete," said the Court, "is to strive for something which another is actively seeking and wishes to gain." Did the Southern Pacific before 1901 strive for anything which the Union Pacific was actively seeking? To state the case in these terms was to compel the answer.

[1] Brief, p. 285.
[2] No. 446. October Term, 1912. *U. S.* v. *The U. P. R. R. Co.* et. al.

The Southern Pacific, through its agents, advertisements and literature had undertaken to obtain transportation for its "Sunset" or southern route across the continent while the Union Pacific had endeavored in the same territory to have freight shipped by way of its own and connecting lines, thus securing for itself about 1000 miles of the haul to the coast. . . .

Competition between two such systems consists not only in making rates, which, so far as the shipper was concerned, the proof shows were by agreement fixed at the same figure whichever route was used . . . but includes the character of the service rendered, the accommodation of the shipper in handling and caring for freight, and the prompt recognition and adjustment of the shipper's claims. Advantages in these respects were the subjects of representation and the basis of solicitation by many active, opposing agencies. The maintenance of these by the rival companies promoted their business and increased their revenues. The inducements to maintain these points of advantage — low rates, superiority of service and accommodation — did not remain the same in the hands of a single dominating and common ownership as it was when they were the subject of active promotion by competing owners whose success depended upon their accomplishment.

The Court replied to the suggestion that the traffic competed for was infinitesimal with the remark that though relatively small it amounted in the aggregate to many millions of dollars. To the argument that though physically able the Union Pacific had never dared to compete with the Southern Pacific because of its dependency upon the latter for direct connection with the Pacific coast, it answered, first, that it would have been detrimental to the Southern Pacific to have declined an arrangement for the carriage of freight received from the Union Pacific, and second, that the terms of the Pacific Railroad Acts of 1862 and 1864 forbade any discrimination in favor of the Denver and Rio Grande at Ogden.

Granted that substantial competition had existed before 1901 the conclusion that this competition had been restrained by the purchase on the part of the Union Pacific system of stock of the Southern Pacific Company, and that this restraint had been in violation of law followed unfailingly.

The consolidation of two great competing systems of railroads engaged in interstate commerce by a transfer to one of a dominating stock interest in the other created a combination which restrains interstate commerce

within the meaning of the statute because, in destroying or greatly abridg-
ing the free operation of competition theretofore existing, it tends to higher
rates. It directly tends to less activity in furnishing the public with prompt
adjustment of the demands of patrons for losses. . . .

The contention that a consolidation by stock purchase was not
subject to Federal regulation the court brushed aside.

Nor do we think it can make any difference that instead of resorting
to a holding company, as was done in the Northern Securities case, the
controlling interest in the stock of one corporation is transferred to the
other. The domination and control, and the power to suppress competition,
are acquired in the one case no less than in the other, and the resulting
mischief, at which the statute was aimed, is equally effective whichever
form is adopted.

On the other hand the Court dismissed the complaint against
the Atchison, Topeka, and Santa Fé arising out of transactions
in Arizona discussed in connection with the Government's case.
It also refused to take action in the matter of the San Pedro,
Los Angeles, and Salt Lake. The Circuit Court had not believed that the Salt Lake road was naturally competitive with
the Union or Southern Pacific, and had been able to find in the
agreement with the Union Pacific only a laudable purpose to
adjust differences and to construct a line of railroad between
two points which would serve their joint interests as well as
those of the public. The Santa Fé matter had been thrown out
on technical grounds. In neither case did the Supreme Court
see fit to disturb the conclusion of the court below.

The only point of general interest in this decision is the
Court's attitude toward the facts. The questions of law raised
had been sufficiently covered in the Standard Oil and Tobacco
decisions, and received merely brief, though emphatic re-assertion.
It should be well understood now even by the legal profession
that the ordinary property rights of the individual are limited
by the Sherman Act, and cannot be pleaded as a defense against
it. As the law stands, the only way of bringing about a material
unification of interest between two railroads which are competing
in interstate business appears to be the purchase by a natural person of control of each, and the importance of this is limited by

the fact that individuals have but restricted means, and die in
the end in spite of the best of care.

Several interesting observations, however, are suggested by
the facts. This case is the first in which a thorough-going attempt
has been made to trace the competitive relations between two
great adjoining railroad systems. The result is likely to surprise
the general public as it becomes known. Very little of the competition between the Union and the Southern Pacific systems, it
appears, was the direct struggle between parallel roads so familiar
in early railroad history. The record abundantly shows that the
Southern Pacific dominated its connection at Ogden by its ability
to divert eastbound traffic at that point to the Denver and Rio
Grande. The Court's statement that the Pacific Railroad Acts
obliged the Central Pacific to afford equal advantages and facilities as to "rates, time and transportation" to all connections at
Ogden may be accepted as an authoritative though unexpected
interpretation of the law; but it is too much to believe that the
mere systematic diversion of unrouted traffic would not have involved a loss to the Union Pacific that no traffic manager would
have suffered except under extraordinary circumstances. On the
other hand, the more remote differences in interest appeared in
practically every corner of the United States. It was shown that
business from any point east of Omaha and New Orleans could
make use of either the Union Pacific or the Southern Pacific, as
the shipper desired, for stations in almost every state west of
those cities. Nor was this the most striking fact brought out.
Traffic from New York to Colorado moved *via* Southern Pacific
steamers to New Orleans or Galveston, thence over railroads controlled by the Southern Pacific to Fort Worth, and from Fort
Worth to destination it went over lines in which the Huntington
carriers had no interest. Galveston is located very nearly on the
meridian of Kansas City, and only that portion of the haul from
New York by the southern route which lay west of Galveston,
lay in any way parallel to it. Nevertheless, every single fraction
of the southern route competed, in the sense in which the Supreme
Court used the term, with every part of every other conceivable
route which connected the two terminal points. For example, the

New York, Ontario, and Western operated between New York and Buffalo. It delivered business to the Wabash, which in turn gave it to the Union Pacific, or Rock Island, or Burlington, at Kansas City. It follows that the New York, Ontario, and Western was a competitor of the lines between Fort Worth and Denver, although distant from them 1250 miles as the crow flies and connected by no lines over which it had control. In the same way, the Atchison, Topeka, and Santa Fé, running north from Fort Worth, competed with the Old Dominion Steamship Company, plying between New York and Norfolk, and the Chicago and Northwestern between Chicago and Omaha competed with the Louisville and Nashville between River Junction and New Orleans. Where one railroad formed part of two routes, it could even be a competitor of itself, as the Pennsylvania from Pittsburg to Chicago and from Pittsburg to St. Louis.

In view of this very broad conception of the nature of competition in rates and service, it is curious that the Supreme Court failed to recognize the existence of the "financial" or "diplomatic" competition which has been continuously in existence between the western groups of roads, a competition no whit less important than that upon which the Court laid stress. This took such forms as the threat of new construction, the readiness to divert traffic in one section to secure favors in another, or the purchase of huge blocks of a competitor's securities as a demonstration of financial strength. It is not to be supposed, of course, that this sort of struggle is limited to western lines. Great railroads are like great nations, in that open warfare is the crudest weapon which they employ. The larger the company the more important the influence which it can exert in indirect ways. It takes a good deal of credulity to believe anything other than that the Clark interests undertook the construction of an independent railroad between Los Angeles and Salt Lake, which the Harriman people contrived to dominate in order to forestall competition which might have ensued. The story of the relations between the Santa Fé and the Southern Pacific likewise is full of illustrations of the larger kind of competition. Similar facts appear in the recent New Haven-Grand Trunk negotiations, or in the agreements between the Hill and Harriman lines in the Northwest. Indeed, the most serious objection to big business merely because it is big is to be found in the growth of the financial power of the single units. Sooner or later the courts will have to recognize the problem.

Another point of interest is suggested by the fact that this merger case is the first in which dissolution will provide evidence of the effect upon operating efficiency of the division of a great business into two or more parts. The information was not available in the case of the Standard Oil and American Tobacco companies because they were not public service corporations. It was not useful in the Northern Securities case because the units in that merger were not closely enough combined. But for the Harriman lines we shall have detailed sets of records, prepared on a uniform basis and open to all under the Interstate Commerce Law, and relating to a company which has made a more systematic attempt to secure the full economies of large-scale production than any other in the United States. Thus at the present time purchases for the whole system are made by the Director of Purchases, Mr. Thorne. Standards in construction and operation have been established after consideration and discussion by the officers from general superintendent up. The best brains in the accounting department have worked in harmony for improvements in method. By means of a car pool the Harriman equipment is utilized wherever the local demand is greatest. A carefully planned course of instruction offers to promising employees the best general railroad training in the country, while every effort is made by correspondence instruction to encourage thought and develop interest among subordinates. If the greater decentralization resulting from splitting the system in two compensates for the loss in efficiency in other ways, an important precedent will have been created. Some at least among the members of the organization itself expect this to be the result. A contrary opinion is indicated by a decline in the price of Union Pacific common stock, after the decision, of 19 points in ten days. It is, of course, to be remembered that many of the achievements of the old administration will be enjoyed as a legacy by the new; so that conclusions cannot safely be drawn until after the lapse of several years.

In conclusion, a word may be said about the nature of the decree. The Supreme Court had no decree of the lower court before it, since the Government suit had been dismissed by that tribunal. It confined itself, therefore, to general instructions to the Court below. These were in brief:

> The decree to be entered in the District Court shall provide an injunction against the right to vote the stock while in the ownership or control of the Union Pacific Company, or any corporation owned by it or while held by any corporation or person for the Union Pacific Company, and forbid any transfer or deposit thereof in such wise as to continue its control, and shall provide an injunction against the payment of dividends upon such stock while thus held, except to a receiver to be appointed by the District Court to collect and hold such dividends until disposed of by the decree of the Court.

Plans were to be presented to the District Court within three months, failing which the said Court should proceed by receivership and sale if necessary. Nothing in the Supreme Court's instructions was to be construed as preventing the Union Pacific from retaining the Central Pacific connection from Ogden to San Francisco, if desired. A later ruling has held that a distribution or sale of Southern Pacific shares now held by the Oregon Short Line to the stockholders of the Union Pacific will not satisfy the law. Arrangements for the purchase of the Central Pacific stock by the Union Pacific or one of its subsidiaries can readily be made, provided that the Central Pacific stock collateral bonds, secured by the stock of the same company, are paid off. With the Central Pacific would go the lines of ferries connecting Oakland with San Francisco. The Southern Pacific stock itself is pledged under the Oregon Short Line refunding 4's to the extent of $108,000,000; but under the terms of the mortgage, the company is entitled to withdraw any particular collateral on deposit at the rate at which bonds were originally issued against the same, provided that securities of railroads or car companies be substituted. The Union Pacific owned $244,073,200 of unpledged stock and bonds of companies within the system at the date of its last annual report, so the requirements of the indenture can be easily complied with.[1]

STUART DAGGETT

[1] The later history of the dissolution may be briefly outlined. A first plan to distribute the Union Pacific's entire holdings of 1,266,500 shares of Southern Pacific's common stock among its own shareholders *gratis* was vetoed by the Supreme Court on the very proper ground that it would leave control in exactly the same hands as before, except that such control would be exercised through the medium of private persons, — dominant stockholders of the Union Pacific. Farcical proceedings in apparent dissolution like those of the Standard Oil Company were thus forestalled. A second plan likewise came to grief through refusal of the California Railroad Commission to give its assent to essential details. This plan proposed : first, a sale of its Southern Pacific stock, under privileged conditions, to all shareholders *both* of the Union Pacific and Southern Pacific companies, except, of course, to the Union Pacific or the Oregon Short Line Company ; and secondly, with funds thus acquired, an outright purchase by the Union Pacific from the Southern Pacific of the Central Pacific link. This would give the Union Pacific its long-desired access over its own rails to the coast — this having been the motive for taking over the Southern Pacific in first instance. But the California Commission insisted upon open and actual competition at all points.

A third plan was then evolved, quite different in principle. All the Southern Pacific shares were to be distributed *pro rata* among the Union Pacific stockholders, as by the first plan, but such disposition was to be coupled with disfranchisement for all purposes of control, of all holders of 1000 shares or over. A trustee was to issue certificates of interest upon deposit of all Southern Pacific shares held by the Union Pacific, which were to carry no voting rights while so held, and which should be exchangeable for actual Southern Pacific shares only on affidavit that the applicant for exchange held less than 1000 shares. This plan would exclude 368 other private shareholders from further increase of their holdings, and would thus appear to have been of doubtful legality.

The final plan adopted in July was entirely different in many ways. It aimed to dissolve another similar control by the Pennsylvania Railroad of a competing line, by substituting in each case control or at least a dominant interest in merely a connecting line. The Pennsylvania exchanged 212,737 preferred shares at $80 and 212,736 common shares at par of the Baltimore and Ohio Railroad with the Union Pacific system for its 382,924 shares of the Southern Pacific at par. This left the Union Pacific with a balance of 883,576 shares of Southern Pacific stock, which balance it was authorized by the court to distribute to the extent of 27 per cent of their then holdings among the other general shareholders of its own company. The expedient of issuance of certificates of interest by a trustee to be exchanged for actual stock upon affidavit that purchase was made in good faith on his own behalf independently of the Union Pacific interests, was borrowed from the preceding plan. The price of such privileged subscription was to be sufficiently favorable to insure the success of the distribution. This plan, it will be observed, differed from the first two in that it left the

Central Pacific link to the coast still in the hands of the Southern Pacific. But this feature, held by the outgoing administration as essential, was not emphasized by the new Democratic Attorney-General; and as for the Union Pacific, it was deemed that a traffic alliance with the Central Pacific providing for a through route and most-favored treatment as to facilities for interchange — guaranteed in any event by the significant clause upon the subject in the Hepburn law of 1906 — would in some ways be preferable to ownership. It would be more elastic and would, moreover, as a detail of interstate commerce be free from interference by the railroad commissions of the states concerned. Such a traffic agreement would also insure to the Union Pacific a due share of eastbound business, which otherwise, had it purchased the Central Pacific, the Southern Pacific might choose to route entirely over its own long line. Thus, at this writing, the dissolution promised by 1916, — the ultimate time allowed by the judicial decree, — to be brought to a successful close. — Ed.

XXIII

REASONABLE RATES [1]

STATES may fix local rates for public service, but decisions
of the United States Supreme Court have swept away the
power of states to make their rates conclusive.

This result has been reached gradually through a line of decisions under the Fourteenth Amendment.

In the earliest cases of rate regulation under the amendment
the court declined to review the reasonableness of rates fixed
by states, holding this to be purely a legislative question.
Later the court decided to review the extent of rate regulation,
but held that rates which permitted some, though only a slight,
return on the property devoted to a public service were legal.
Finally a position has been reached where rates fixed by states
are held invalid unless they permit as large profits as the
court thinks the public service ought to yield. In this way
the power to determine what are reasonable rates for public
service has been transferred from state legislatures to the
Supreme Court.

The first case in which the extent of state regulation of rates
for public service was brought before the Supreme Court for review, after adoption of the Fourteenth Amendment, was *Munn*
v. *Illinois*,[2] decided in 1876. This case involved the validity
of an Illinois statute that fixed a maximum rate for storing
grain in elevators at Chicago. Munn, having been convicted
and fined in the state courts for violation of the statute, appealed to the United States courts on the ground that enforcement of the rate provided by the statute would take his property

[1] From the *Journal of Political Economy*, December, 1903, pp. 79–97. The
same subject is much elaborated in *Publications of the American Economic Association*, 3d series, Vol. VII, 1906, pp. 24–82.   [2] 94 U. S. 113.

without due process of law and violate the Fourteenth Amendment. In the course of an opinion upholding the validity of the statute, Chief Justice Waite said, speaking for the court:

It is insisted, however, that the owner of property is entitled to a reasonable compensation for its use, even though it be clothed with a public interest, and that what is reasonable is a judicial and not a legislative question.

As has already been shown, the practice has been otherwise. In countries where the common law prevails, it has been customary from time immemorial for the legislature to declare what shall be reasonable compensation under such circumstances, or, perhaps more properly speaking, to fix a maximum beyond which any charge made would be unreasonable. . . . The controlling fact is the power to regulate at all. If that exists, the right to establish the maximum of charge, as one of the means of regulation, is implied.

From these statements it is perfectly clear that the question as to the right of those engaged in a public calling to have a judicial review of rates fixed by a legislature was squarely presented to the court in this case. It is equally clear that in the opinion of the court no such right existed.

Of the nine Supreme Court Justices, two, Field and Strong, dissented from the decision in *Munn* v. *Illinois*. The dissenting opinion was prepared by Justice Field and concurred in by Justice Strong. This dissent went on the broad ground that the storage of grain is not a public business or one for which a legislature has the power to fix rates. Nowhere in the dissenting opinion is it contended that in a public business where a legislature has the right to fix rates the amount or reasonableness of these rates can be reviewed by the court. On the contrary, Judge Field said in the course of his opinion:

If it be admitted that the legislature has any control over the compensation, the extent of that compensation becomes a mere matter of legislative discretion. . . . The several instances mentioned by counsel in the argument, and by the court in its opinion, in which legislation has fixed the compensation which parties may receive for the use of their property and services, do not militate against the views I have expressed of the power of the state over the property of the citizen. They were mostly cases of public ferries, bridges, and turnpikes, of wharfingers, hackmen, and draymen, and of interest on money. In all these cases, except that of interest on money, which I shall presently notice, there was some special privilege granted by the state or municipality; and no one, I suppose, has ever contended that the state had not a right to prescribe the conditions upon which such privilege should be enjoyed.

At the October term of the Supreme Court, in 1876, when the opinion in *Munn* v. *Illinois* was delivered, cases involving the validity of railway rates fixed by the legislatures of Iowa, Minnesota, and Wisconsin were also decided. Several of these cases involved the power of legislatures to fix conclusively the rates for public service under the Fourteenth Amendment, and in each case the court affirmed this power.

In *Chicago, Burlington & Quincy Railway Co.* v. *Iowa*,[1] maximum rates fixed for transportation by a statute of that state were contested on the ground, among others, that the rates fixed would take property of the railway without due process of law. Replying to this contention the court in an opinion upholding the statute said through Chief Justice Waite:

In the absence of any legislative regulation upon the subject, the courts must decide for it, as they do for private persons, when controversies arise, what is reasonable. But when the legislature steps in and prescribes a maximum of charge, it operates upon this corporation the same as it does upon individuals engaged in a similar business.

In other words, the court decided that due process of law was satisfied when rates for public service were fixed by the legislature.

The next case, *Peik* v. *Chicago & North-Western Railway Co.*,[2] was brought to restrain the enforcement of a law of Wisconsin that fixed maximum rates for passengers and freight. It was contended on the part of the railway security holders that the rates named in the statute would destroy the value of their securities, that the railway was entitled to collect reasonable compensation for its services, and that reasonable compensation was a question for the court and not for the legislature. Chief Justice Waite again delivered the opinion of the court, in which it was said, upholding the statute:

In *Munn* v. *Illinois*, *supra*, p. 113, and *Chicago, Burlington & Quincy Railroad Co.* v. *Iowa*, *supra*, p. 155, we decided that the state may limit the

[1] 94 U. S. 155.   [2] 94 U. S. 164.

amount of charges by railroad companies for fares and freights, unless restrained by some contract in the charter, even though their income may have been pledged as security for the payment of obligations incurred upon the faith of the charter. So far this case is disposed of by those decisions. . . . As to the claim that the courts must decide what is reasonable, and not the legislature. This is not new to this case. It has been fully considered in *Munn* v. *Illinois*. Where property has been clothed with a public interest, the legislature may fix a limit to that which shall in law be reasonable for its use. This limit binds the courts as well as the people. If it has been improperly fixed, the legislature, not the courts, must be appealed to for the change.

In *Chicago, Milwaukee & St. Paul Railroad Co.* v. *Ackley* [1] the court said, speaking through Chief Justice Waite:

The only question presented by this record is whether a railroad company in Wisconsin can recover for the transportation of property more than the maximum fixed by the act of March 11, 1874, by showing that the amount charged was no more than a reasonable compensation for the services rendered. . . . But for goods actually carried, the limit of the recovery is that prescribed by the statute.

Two cases [2] involving railway rates under a statute of Minnesota followed those just considered, and the court in brief opinions stated that they were covered by the rulings already made.

In *Stone* v. *Wisconsin*,[3] which was decided in favor of a state statute fixing rates, the only question not covered by *Chicago, etc., Railway Co.* v. *Ackley*, according to the court, related to the construction of a certain charter.

Justices Field and Strong dissented in each of the above railway cases, but gave no opinion until *Stone* v. *Wisconsin* was reached, when Justice Field prepared an opinion in which Justice Strong concurred. In this opinion the dissent to this entire group of railway cases was put on the ground that the railway charters were contracts with the legislatures, which should protect the companies from state regulation of rates.

Besides Chief Justice Waite, the celebrated group of cases headed by *Munn* v. *Illinois* was supported by Justices Clifford, Hunt, Bradley, Swayne, Davis, and Miller. The assertion by these judges of the power of states to fix conclusive rates for

[1] 94 U. S. 179.   [2] 94 U. S. 180.   [3] 94 U. S. 181.

public service seems to have been as emphatic as any believer in local self-government could desire.

The doctrine of the Granger Cases, that a state may fix conclusive rates for local public service was reaffirmed in the case of *Ruggles* v. *Illinois*,[1] where the validity of a law of that state providing a maximum fare per mile on railways was called in question. In the course of its opinion sustaining the law the Supreme Court said:

> This implies that, in the absence of direct legislation on the subject, the power of the directors over the rates is subject only to the common-law limitation of reasonableness, for in the absence of a statute, or other appropriate indication of the legislative will, the common law forms part of the laws of the state to which the corporate by-laws must conform. But since, in the absence of some restraining contract, the state may establish a maximum of rates to be charged by railroad companies for the transportation of persons and property, it follows that, when a maximum is so established, that fixed by the directors must conform to its requirements, otherwise the by-laws will be repugnant to the laws.

Seven judges supported the majority opinion in this case, and two judges, Field and Harlan, delivered separate concurring opinions. Judge Harlan held that the charter of the railway in question was a contract that gave it the right to collect reasonable rates, but that the rates fixed by statute were not shown to be unreasonable. Judge Field held that the statutory rates had not been shown unreasonable, but did not state why he thought that they were bound to be reasonable.

By 1885 a fundamental change had taken place in the position of a portion of the court on the question of state power over rates for public service. This change was brought out by the case of *Stone* v. *Farmers' Loan & Trust Co.*,[2] where an effort was made to enjoin the enforcement of rates under a Mississippi statute. The court through Chief Justice Waite affirmed the power of the state to fix rates and upheld the statute, but added:

> From what has been said, it is not to be inferred that this power of limitation or regulation is itself without limit. This power to regulate is not a

---

[1] 108 U. S. 526. [2] 116 U. S. 307.

power to destroy, and limitation is not the equivalent of confiscation. Under pretense of regulating fares and freights, the state cannot require a railroad corporation to carry persons or property without reward ; neither can it do that which in law amounts to a taking of private property for public use without just compensation, or without due process of law. What would have this effect we need not now say, because no tariff has yet been fixed by the commission, and the statute of Mississippi expressly provides "that in all trials of cases brought for a violation of any tariff of charges, as fixed by the commission, it may be shown in defense that such tariff so fixed is unjust."

Thus was the underlying principle of the Granger Cases as to reasonable rates brought in question. Unlimited power of regulation like that affirmed in those cases may certainly be used to destroy and did in fact destroy much of the value of railway securities under the Granger Acts. It was said of the United States Bank by Chief Justice Marshall in *M'Culloch* v. *State of Maryland* : [1]

That the power of taxing it by the states may be exercised so as to destroy it, is too obvious to be denied.

The tax imposed by Congress on note issues of state banks after the close of the Civil War in the exercise of its power to regulate the currency, and upheld in *Veazie Bank* v. *Fenno*,[2] certainly destroyed these issues completely. Of course, if the power to regulate is itself regulated by some other and higher power, the former may be held within any desired limits. The above quotation from the opinion in *Stone* v. *Farmers' Loan & Trust Co.*[3] must mean, therefore, an assertion by the court of its power to review rates fixed by a state. Even the Granger Cases never decided that a railway must continue in business against its will under rates fixed by a state; it was open to the railway to go out of business. Neither did the Granger Cases decide that the property used in a public service might be taken without due process of law, but rather that state regulation of rates for such service was due process of law. The power asserted by the court in the case under consideration must therefore relate to the review of the reasonableness or justice

[1] 4 Wheaton, 316.   [2] 8 Wall. 533.   [3] 116 U. S. 307.

of rates fixed by a state. This meaning is made clear by the statement that:

> What would have this effect we need not now say, because no tariff has yet been fixed by the commission. . . .

The opinion in the case under consideration was delivered by Chief Justice Waite who spoke in the Granger Cases, and was also supported by Justices Bradley, Miller, Woods, Matthews, and Gray, of whom Bradley and Miller took part in the Granger Cases. Justices Harlan and Field dissented, and Blatchford did not sit. The dissent of Harlan, J., went on the ground that the railway charters were contracts that permitted the companies to fix their own rates unless they were shown to be unreasonable.

In *Dow* v. *Beidelman*[1] a statute of Arkansas that fixed a maximum fare of three cents per mile on railroads in that state was upheld by a unanimous court. It was shown in this case that the rates fixed by statute, on the basis of the existing traffic, would yield a net yearly income of less than 1.5 per cent on the original cost of the road and only a little more than 2 per cent on the bonded debt. The evidence did not show, however, how much the then owners of the railway had paid for it. Justice Gray said in delivering the opinion of the court:

> Without any proof of the sum invested by the reorganized corporation or its trustees, the court has no means, if it would under any circumstances have the power, of determining that the rate of three cents a mile fixed by the legislature is unreasonable.

The dictum above quoted from *Stone* v. *Farmers' Loan & Trust Co.*,[2] as to limitations on the power of states to fix conclusive rates, was repeated with approval in the case under consideration.

In neither of these two cases was it open to members of the court who did not assent to this dictum, but who did agree with the decision, to dissent from the opinion, because the principle of the dictum was not acted on in either decision. The later of these two cases was decided by eight judges, Chief Justice Waite having died at Washington, March 23, 1888.

[1] 125 U. S. 680. [2] 116 U. S. 307.

In *Chicago, Milwaukee & St. Paul Railroad Co.* v. *Minnesota*,[1] the dicta put forth in previous cases that the reasonableness of rates fixed by a state is subject to review by the courts, was established by the force of a judicial decision. This case arose under a statute of Minnesota which authorized a commission to fix transportation rates. The commission reduced the rate for carrying milk between certain points from 3 cents to 2.5 cents per gallon, and the Minnesota courts refused to admit evidence offered by the railway that the latter rate was unreasonable, holding that under the statute the findings of the commission were conclusive. From this decision the railway appealed to the Federal court on the ground that the denial of a judicial hearing as to the reasonableness of the rates would deprive it of property without due process of law. Mr. Justice Blatchford delivered the opinion of the court, holding the Minnesota statute void because it made the rates fixed by the commission conclusive. In the course of this opinion the court said:

> The question of the reasonableness of a rate of charge for transportation by a railroad company, involving, as it does, the element of reasonableness, both as regards the company and as regards the public, is eminently a question for judicial investigation, requiring due process of law for its determination. If the company is deprived of the power of charging reasonable rates for the use of its property, and such deprivation takes place in the absence of an investigation by judicial machinery, it is deprived of the lawful use of its property, and thus, in substance and effect, of the property itself, without due process of law, and in violation of the Constitution of the United States ; and in so far as it is thus deprived, while other persons are permitted to receive reasonable profits upon their invested capital, the company is deprived of the equal protection of the laws.

Dissent from some of the judges who decided the Granger Cases was now due. This dissent could not properly have been delivered in the earlier cases where the power of the court to review rates fixed by a state had been asserted, because those assertions were mere dicta and were not involved in the decisions of the cases where they occurred.

In the course of a long dissenting opinion, concurred in by Justices Gray and Lamar, Justice Bradley said:

[1] 134 U. S. 418.

I cannot agree to the decision of the court in this case. It practically overrules *Munn* v. *Illinois*, 94 U. S. 113, and the several railroad cases that were decided at the same time. The governing principle of those cases was that the regulation and settlement of the fares of railroads and other public accommodations is a legislative prerogative and not a judicial one. This is a principle which I regard as of great importance. When a railroad company is chartered, it is for the purpose of performing a duty which belongs to the state itself. It is chartered as an agent of the state for furnishing public accommodation. The state might build its railroads if it saw fit. It is its duty and its prerogative to provide means of intercommunication between one part of its territory and another. And this duty is devolved upon the legislative department. If the legislature commissions private parties, whether corporations or individuals, to perform this duty, it is its prerogative to fix the fares and freights which they may charge for their services. . . . But it is said that all charges should be reasonable, and that none but reasonable charges can be exacted ; and it is urged that what is a reasonable charge is a judicial question. On the contrary, it is preëminently a legislative one, involving considerations of policy as well as of remuneration ; and is usually determined by the legislature, by fixing a maximum of charges in the charter of the company, or afterwards, if its hands are not tied by contract. If this maximum is not exceeded, the courts cannot interfere. . . . Thus, the legislature either fixes the charges at rates which it deems reasonable, or merely declares that they shall be reasonable ; and it is only in the latter case, where what is reasonable is left open, that the courts have jurisdiction of the subject. I repeat : when the legislature declares that the charges shall be reasonable, or, which is the same thing, allows the common-law rule to that effect to prevail, and leaves the matter there ; then resort may be had to the courts to inquire judicially whether the charges are reasonable. Then, and not till then, is it a judicial question. But the legislature has the right, and it is its prerogative, if it chooses to exercise it, to declare what is reasonable.

This is just where I differ from the majority of the court. They say in effect, if not in terms, that the final tribunal of arbitrament is the judiciary ; I say it is the legislature. I hold that it is a legislative question, not a judicial one, unless the legislature or the law (which is the same thing) has made it judicial, by prescribing the rule that the charges shall be reasonable, and leaving it there. It is always a delicate thing for the courts to make an issue with the legislative department of the government, and they should never do so if it is possible to avoid it. By the decision now made we declare, in effect, that the judiciary, and not the legislature, is the final arbiter in the regulation of fares and freights of railroads and the charges of other public accommodations. It is an assumption of authority on the part of the judiciary which, it seems to me, with all due deference to the judgment of my brethren, it has no right to make. . . . It is complained that the decisions of the board are final and without appeal. So are the decisions of the courts in matters within their jurisdiction. There must be a final tribunal somewhere for deciding every question in the world. Injustice may take place in all tribunals. All human institutions are imperfect — courts as well as commissions and legislatures. Whatever tribunal has jurisdiction, its decisions are final and conclusive unless an appeal is given therefrom. The important question always is, what is the lawful tribunal for the particular case? In my judgment, in the present case, the proper tribunal was the legislature, or the board of commissioners which it created for that purpose. . . . It may be that our legislatures are invested with too much power, open, as they are, to influences so dangerous to the interests of individuals, corporations, and society. But such is the constitution of our republican form of government; and we are bound to abide by it until it can be corrected in a legitimate way. If our legislatures become too arbitrary in the exercise of their powers, the people have always a remedy in their hands; they may at any time restrain them by constitutional limitations.

This strong dissent, in 1889, gives a glimpse of the conflict that had been going on in the Supreme Court since the decision of the Granger Cases, in 1876. As far as can be seen from the line of decisions noted, only two of the seven judges who decided those cases ever receded from the position there taken that the court could not review the reasonableness of rates fixed by a legislature. Of these two judges, Waite indicated his change of view by the dictum above quoted from *Stone* v. *Farmers' Loan & Trust Co.*, and Miller concurred in the majority decision of the Minnesota case just considered, by a separate opinion.

As new judges came on to the Supreme Bench, the support given by the court to the principles of the Granger Cases grew less. In *Chicago, etc., Railway Co.* v. *Minnesota*[1] the scales were turned and five justices — Fuller, Field, Harlan, Blatchford, and Brewer — supported the majority opinion. Of the nine judges who sat in the Granger Cases only Justices Field, Miller, and Bradley remained to take part in the case last decided, and of these three Justice Bradley alone adhered to the fundamental doctrine of the earlier decisions.

By *Chicago, etc., Railway Co.* v. *Minnesota*[2] the Granger Cases were in large measure overruled. Due process of law was no

[1] 134 U. S. 418.   [2] 134 U. S. 418.

longer to be found in rates fixed by states, but in decisions of the court as to what was reasonable. Under this decision the states may exercise as much or as little control over rates as the court sees fit to permit. In *Munn* v. *Illinois* [1] the court said:

> The controlling fact is the power to regulate at all. If that exists, the right to establish the maximum of charge, as one of the means of regulation, is implied.

With equal force it may be said that assertion by the court of authority to review the reasonableness of rates fixed by legislatures opened the way for a great reduction in state powers. Since 1889, when the paramount authority of the court was established by a judicial decision, suits to invalidate rates fixed by legislatures have multiplied and decisions have borne with increasing severity on state powers.

In *Budd* v. *New York*, decided in 1892, the validity of a statute of that state was contested on the ground that rates fixed by it for elevating and storing grain were not within the state power to make and were unreasonable. Mr. Justice Blatchford in delivering the opinion of the court, supported the power of the state to regulate the business of storing grain and said:

> In the case before us, the records do not show that the charges fixed by the statute are unreasonable, or that property has been taken without due process of law, or that there has been any denial of the equal protection of the laws; even if under any circumstances we could determine that the maximum rate fixed by the legislature was unreasonable.

It was also said in this opinion, referring to *Chicago, etc., Railway Co.* v. *Minnesota:*

> What was said in the opinion in 134 U. S., as to the question of the reasonableness of the rate of charge being one for judicial investigation, had no reference to a case where the rates are prescribed directly by the legislature.

This statement was *obiter dicta*, pure and simple, as the rates in *Budd* v. *New York* were not shown to be unreasonable, was in direct conflict with the language of the Minnesota case and

[1] 94 U. S. 113.

no support for it can be found in later decisions. Moreover, the three dissenting judges in the Minnesota case certainly understood the decision there to apply to rates fixed directly by a legislature as well as to those fixed by a commission. It is to be noted that the Minnesota statute itself, as construed by the Supreme Court of that state, was declared invalid by the United States Supreme Court, and not merely the rates fixed under the statute. This statute evidently failed because it denied the right of the courts to investigate the reasonableness of rates fixed under it.

As to reasonable rates *Budd* v. *New York* [1] simply shows that their unreasonableness must be proved before the court will hold them void on that ground. Justices Brewer, Field, and Brown dissented in this case.

Brass v. *North Dakota* [2] involved the validity of a statute of that state that fixed rates for storing grain. The case turned on the power of the legislature to fix rates at all, rather than on the reasonableness of the rates actually fixed. The court upheld the statute, and said in its opinion, delivered by Justice Shiras :

We are limited by this record to the questions whether the legislature of North Dakota in regulating by a general law the business and charges of public warehousemen engaged in elevating and storing grain for profit, denies to the plaintiff in error the equal protection of the laws or deprives him of his property without due process of law, and whether such statutory regulations amount to a regulation of commerce between the states.

Justices Brewer, Field, Jackson, and White dissented, leaving only Fuller, C. J., and Justices Harlan, Gray, Brown, and Shiras to decide the case.

In *Chicago & Grand Trunk Railway* v. *Wellman*,[3] decided a few months earlier than *Budd* v. *New York*, the court upheld a law of Michigan regulating railway rates, and said :

The legislature has power to fix rates, and the extent of judicial interference is protection against unreasonable rates. . . . Surely before the courts are called upon to adjudge an act of the legislature fixing the maximum passenger rates for railroad companies to be unconstitutional, on the ground that its enforcement would prevent stockholders from receiving any

---

[1] 143 U. S. 517.   [2] 153 U. S. 391.   [3] 143 U. S. 339.

dividends on their investments, or the bondholders any interest on their loans, they should be fully advised as to what is done with the receipts and earnings of the company; for if so advised, it might clearly appear that a prudent and honest management would, within the rates prescribed, secure to the bondholders their interest, and to the stockholders reasonable dividends.

The opinion delivered by Justice Brewer in this case clearly upholds the doctrine of *Chicago, etc., Railway Co.* v. *Minnesota*, that the court has power to review the reasonableness of rates fixed by a legislature.

Reagan v. *Farmers' Loan & Trust Co.*[1] furnished another application of the same doctrine by restraining the railway commission of Texas from enforcing rates fixed under a statute of that state. The statute provided that rates fixed under it were to be deemed reasonable until finally found otherwise in a direct action, but enforcement of the rates fixed was enjoined before their reasonableness was determined by evidence, in spite of the language of the statute. In the opinion of the court, delivered by Justice Brewer, affirming the preliminary injunction and holding the rates unreasonable and void, it was said:

Is there anything which detracts from the force of the general allegation that these rates are unjust and unreasonable? This clearly appears. The cost of this railroad property was $40,000,000 ; it cannot be replaced to-day for less than $25,000,000. There are $15,000,000 of mortgage bonds outstanding against it, and nearly $10,000,000 of stock. These bonds and stock represent money invested in the construction of this road. The owners of the stock have never received a dollar's worth of dividends in return for their investment. The road was thrown into the hands of a receiver for default in payment of the interest on the bonds. The earnings for the last three years prior to the establishment of these rates were insufficient to pay the operating expenses and the interest on the bonds. In order to make good the deficiency in interest the stockholders have put their hands in their pockets and advanced over a million of dollars. The supplies for the road have been purchased at as cheap a rate as possible. The officers and employees have been paid no more than is necessary to secure men of the skill and knowledge requisite to suitable operation of the road. By the voluntary action of the company the rate in cents per ton per mile has decreased in ten years from 2.03 to 1.30. The actual reduction by virtue of this tariff in the receipts during the six or eight months that it has been

[1] 154 U. S. 362.

enforced amounts to over $150,000. Can it be that a tariff which under these circumstances has worked such results to the parties whose money built this road is other than unjust or unreasonable?

It may be suggested that the decision in this case rested on the provision of the Texas statute that suits might be brought to determine the reasonableness of rates fixed by the commission. This view cannot be maintained, however, because the statute expressly provided that rates so fixed should be deemed reasonable until finally found otherwise in an action brought by the dissatisfied party, and that in such actions " the burden of proof shall rest upon the plaintiff, who must show by clear and satisfactory evidence that the rates, regulations (etc.), complained of are unreasonable and unjust." The case in which the injunction restraining the commission from enforcing the rates in question was granted came up to the Supreme Court on demurrer by the commissioners and the Attorney-General to the complaint of the Trust Company, so that there was no hearing on the merits as the statute required. In deciding the case the court went on the broad ground that it had power to determine whether rates fixed by states were reasonable. This was shown by the statement in the course of the opinion

that no legislation of a State, as to the mode of proceeding in its own courts, can abridge or modify the powers existing in the Federal courts sitting as courts of equity.

And also that there could be

no doubt of their power and duty to inquire whether a body of rates prescribed by a legislature or a commission is unjust and unreasonable, and such as to work a practical destruction to rights of property, and if found so to be, to restrain its operation.

The court modified the force of its decision by the statement that

It is unnecessary to decide, and we do not wish to be understood as laying down as an absolute rule, that in every case a failure to produce some profit to those who have invested their money in the building of a road is conclusive that the tariff is unjust and unreasonable. . . . There may be circumstances which would justify such a tariff ; there may have been extravagance and needless expenditure of money ; there may be waste in the management of the road ; enormous salaries, unjust discrimination as between individual shippers, resulting in general loss. The construction may have been at a time when material and labor were at the highest price, so that the actual cost far exceeds the present value ; the road may have been unwisely built, in localities where there is no sufficient business to sustain a road. Doubtless, too, there are many other matters affecting the rights of the community in which the road is built as well as the rights of those who have built the road.

Evidently this case decides only that under the circumstances stated a road is entitled to earn interest on its bonds and something for its stockholders, besides paying necessary operating expenses. How much the return to stockholders may be is not decided. As no evidence was taken, it does not appear how the court knew that the failure of the road to earn " some profit " was not due to some of the " matters " named above.

In the case just considered and also in that of *St. Louis & San Francisco Railway* v. *Gill*,[1] decided during the same year, 1894, there was no dissent, but the entire court concurred in the opinion. These two cases present interesting comparisons, as the railway company in each sought protection from a law for the regulation of rates, and each alleged in its pleadings that the rates fixed for transportation would yield no profit on the invested capital, and each case was decided on demurrer.

The case of *St. Louis & Santa Fé Railway* v. *Gill* came up under a law of Arkansas, passed in 1887, that fixed a maximum rate of three cents per mile for the transportation of passengers on railroads of that state, and named a penalty of $300 payable to any passenger from whom an overcharge was exacted. Gill was charged five cents per mile and obtained a verdict in the state courts against the railway for the amount of the penalty. The railway took the case to the Supreme Court on the ground that the rate fixed by statute would result in a taking of its property without due process of law. Proof was offered for the railway that on the branch where Gill was charged five cents per mile the actual cost to the railway was 3.3 cents per mile

[1] 156 U. S. 649.

for each passenger carried ; that this branch line had never earned more than 1 per cent annually above actual operating expenses on the capital stock that had been paid in cash and invested in this line. These offers of proof were not accepted, and the demurrer of Gill to the pleadings of the railway was sustained by the court in an opinion sustaining the validity of the rates fixed by the Arkansas law. The opinion, delivered by Justice Shiras, took occasion to assert the power claimed in previous cases, by saying:

This court has declared, in several cases, that there is a remedy in the courts for relief against legislation establishing a tariff of rates which is so unreasonable as to practically destroy the value of property of companies engaged in the carrying business, and that especially may the courts of the United States treat such a question as a judicial one, and hold such acts of legislation to be in conflict with the Constitution of the United States, as depriving the companies of their property without due process of law, and as depriving them of the equal protection of the laws.

The line of railway on which Gill was charged five cents per mile, and to which the offers of proof seemed to refer, extended from the northern boundary of Arkansas to Fayetteville in that state, and had formerly been owned by a separate company. Referring to these circumstances the court said :

In this state of facts we agree with the views of the supreme court of Arkansas, as disclosed in the opinion contained in the record, and which were to the effect that the correct test was as to the effect of the act on the defendant's entire line, and not upon that part which was formerly a part of one of the consolidating roads ; the company cannot claim the right to earn a net profit from every mile, section, or other part into which the road might be divided.

Finally came the important statement that

Even if the evidence could be understood as applicable to the entire line in Arkansas, there was no finding of the facts necessary to justify the courts in overthrowing the statutory rates as unreasonable, but that, on the contrary, the company's case depended on allegations admitted by the demurrer of a party who, in no adequate sense, represented the public.

This case seems to represent an effort of the court to stay the tendency of former decisions toward the destruction of state power in the regulation of rates. It is hard to see why the rates on a distinct line of railway should not be regulated according to the investment and expense of operation on that line, even though the line in question forms only a part of a large consolidated system.

The demurrer by a private litigant as a barrier to judicial annulment of rates fixed by legislatures did not stand the test of the next case on the subject that came before the court, namely, *Covington, etc., Turnpike Co.* v. *Sandford*.[1] By an act of the Kentucky legislature in 1890 the rate of toll that might be charged on the turnpike owned by the company just named was reduced. Sandford obtained an injunction in the state courts which required the turnpike company to charge no more than the statutory rate of toll. From this injunction the company sought relief in the Supreme Court on the ground that the reduction in rates would take its property without due process of law. In the decision of the Supreme Court, prepared by Justice Harlan, it was said that the answer of the company

alleged that the receipt for the several preceding years had not admitted of dividends greater than 4 per cent on the par value of the company's stock ; that the act of 1890 reduced the tolls 50 per cent below those allowed by the act of 1865 ; and that such reduction would so diminish the income of the company that it could not maintain its road, meet its ordinary expenses, and earn any dividends whatever for stockholders.

These allegations were sufficiently full as to the facts necessary to be pleaded, and fairly raised for judicial determination the question — assuming the facts stated to be true — whether the act of 1890 was in derogation of the company's constitutional rights. It made a *prima facie* case of the invalidity of that statute.

This opinion reversed the action of the Kentucky courts which granted the injunction, though no evidence was before the court that the allegations of the company in its pleadings were true. Sandford acted in this case simply as a private person who wished to use the turnpike, and the admissions of his demurrer to the pleadings of the company were held sufficient ground on which to overturn the statute. The previous decision

[1] 164 U. S. 578.

in the Gill case that a statute cannot be held invalid on the demurrer of a private person was thus overruled. Admitting the statements in the pleadings of the company in this Sandford case to be true, the case simply follows the rule previously laid down that rates cannot be reduced to a point where they allow no return on the investment above operating expenses. This case, decided in 1896, was concurred in by the entire court. Though not required for the decision of the case, it was stated in the course of the opinion that

It cannot be said that a corporation is entitled, as of right, and without reference to the interests of the public, to realize a given per cent upon its capital stock. When the question arises whether the legislature has exceeded its constitutional power in prescribing rates to be charged by a corporation controlling a public highway, stockholders are not the only persons whose rights or interests are to be considered. . . . If a corporation cannot maintain such a highway and earn dividends for stockholders, it is a misfortune for it and them which the constitution does not require to be remedied by imposing unjust burdens upon the public.

These dicta indicate that there might be instances due to unwise investments, or perhaps to competition, where a corporation would not be protected in a right to earn any return on its investment.

The next case to come before the court involving the reasonableness of rates fixed by state authority was that of *Smyth* v. *Ames*, decided in 1898.[1] A notable difference between this case and those that had preceded it lay in the fact that the decision of the court was based on evidence taken at the trial as to the investments and earnings of the railways involved, instead of on allegations or admissions of parties to the suit. The case arose under a Nebraska statute of 1893, that prescribed rates for the transporation of freight on railways in that state, by a prayer on the part of persons interested in these railways for an injunction to prevent enforcement of these rates. In a unanimous opinion, delivered by Justice Harlan, the court said:

We hold, however, that the basis of all calculations as to the reasonableness of rates to be charged by a corporation maintaining a highway under

[1] 169 U. S. 466.

legislative sanction must be the fair value of the property being used by it
for the convenience of the public. And in order to ascertain that value,
the original cost of construction, the amount expended in permanent improvements, the amount and market value of its bonds and stock, the present as compared with the original cost of construction, the probable earning
capacity of the property under particular rates prescribed by statute, and
the sum required to meet operating expenses, are all matters for consideration, and are to be given such weight as may be just and right in such case.

We do not say that there may not be other matters to be regarded in
estimating the value of the property. What the company is entitled to
ask is a fair return upon the value of that which it employs for the public
convenience. On the other hand, what the public is entitled to demand is
that no more be exacted from it for the use of a public highway than the
services rendered by it are reasonably worth. But even upon this basis,
and determining the probable effect of the act of 1893 by ascertaining what
could have been its effect if it had been in operation during the three years
immediately preceding its passage, we perceive no ground on the record
for reversing the decree of the circuit court. On the contrary, we are of
opinion that as to most of the companies in question there would have been,
under such rates as were established by the act of 1893, an actual loss in
each of the years ending June 30, 1891, 1892, and 1893; and that, in the
exceptional cases above stated, when two of the companies would have
earned something above operating expenses, in particular years, the receipts or gains, above operating expenses, would have been too small to
affect the general conclusion that the act, if enforced, would have deprived
each of the railroad companies involved in these suits of the just compensation secured to them by the Constitution.

The injunction confirmed by the court in this case enjoined
the Nebraska Board of Transportation and the Attorney-General
of the state from taking any steps to enforce the rates fixed by
the act of 1893. It should be noted that the court based its
decision on the income that would have been derived from the
local freight actually carried by the railways during the fiscal
years of 1891, 1892, and 1893, ending June 30, at the rates
prescribed by the act which took effect August 1, 1893. This
takes no account of the fact that a decrease in rates may be followed by an increase in traffic, especially as to heavy farm produce which it may not pay to move at all if the freight is more
than a very moderate figure.

The most important rule laid down by the case is that the
basis of calculations as to reasonable rates of a corporation " must

be the fair value of the property being used by it for the convenience of the public."

This statement with others in the opinion, appears to limit "fair value" to that of the physical property and to exclude franchise valuations. Unless the value of the physical property employed in a public service and the actual cost of performing that service are to be taken as the basis of rate calculations, the amount of rates would appear to depend mainly on the arbitrary opinion of the company or legislature making them. Though the majority of the railways in Nebraska could have made nothing on their investments under the rates prescribed by the act of 1893, as the court understood the evidence, yet the opinion states that two companies could have earned "something" above operating expenses. Reference to the evidence on which the court relied, and which was repeated in the opinion, shows that this something amounted to 1.99, 4.06, 6.84 and 10.63 per cent annually on the values of the railways. Unless the court thought that this rate of net earnings was so small as to amount to a taking of property without due process, it does not appear why the Nebraska act was unconstitutional as to the roads making this rate. According to dicta in the Sandford case above cited, an act might be constitutional as to some roads and unconstitutional as to the others.

A still later case in the Supreme Court, that of *Cotting* v. *Goddard*, decided in 1901, goes farther than any of the foregoing in its limitation of state powers. This case arose under a Kansas statute of 1897 that fixed charges for handling live stock at stock yards where more than a certain amount of business was done, and affected the yards at Kansas City. Petitions were filed asking that the Attorney-General of Kansas be restrained from enforcing the statute as to these yards, and, after hearings in which evidence was taken as to the value of the yards and the annual earnings, the injunction was granted. In the course of the unanimous opinion of the court, delivered by Justice Brewer, it was said:

If the rates prescribed by the Kansas statute for yarding and feeding stock had been in force during the year 1896, the income of the stock-yards company would have been reduced that year $300,651.77, leaving a net income of $289,916.96. This would have yielded a return of 5.3 per cent on the value of the property used for stock-yard purposes, as fixed by the master.

The actual net income of the company during 1896, as found by the master and the court below, was $590,558.73, and the value of its property in the stock yards was $5,388,003.25, so that its net income during that year amounted to nearly 11 per cent on its investment. After pointing out the liability of a person engaged in the operation of public stock yards to some legislative regulation, the court proceeded to define the limits of such regulation, and said :

> The question is not how much he makes out of his volume of business, but whether in each particular transaction the charge is an unreasonable exaction for the services rendered. He has a right to do business. He has a right to charge for each separate service that which is reasonable compensation therefor, and the legislature may not deny him such reasonable compensation, and may not interfere simply because out of the multitude of his transactions the amount of his profits is large.

These reasons for the decision of the court are negative in character. They tell us that it matters not that profits are large if rates are only reasonable. But what are reasonable rates? How are they to be determined if considerations as to investments and profits are put aside? If reasonable rates do not imply reasonable profits, where is the amount of charge to stop short of what the person receiving the service can be induced to pay?

A quarter of a century has transferred the test of reasonable rates from the opinions of state legislatures to the opinion of the Supreme Court. In the Granger Cases the court denied its right to interfere with local rates fixed by legislatures, even when these rates were so low as to destroy all profits. This doctrine, after various adverse dicta, was fully repudiated by the case of *Chicago, etc., Railway Co.* v. *Minnesota*, decided in 1889, thirteen years after the Granger Cases. From that date to 1896, when *Covington, etc.*, v. *Sandford* was decided, the court went no farther than to hold that legislative rates must afford some income above operating expenses. Another step was taken the following year, when the court held in *Smyth* v. *Ames* that rates which permitted a net profit of as much as 10.63 per cent on one road, but nothing on others, could not be enforced as to either.

Finally, in 1901 comes the decision, in *Cotting* v. *Goddard*, that rates which yield a profit of 10.9 per cent on the investment are not unreasonable, and that rates which would reduce this profit to 5.3 per cent are unconstitutional.

ALTON D. ADAMS

XXIV

THE DOCTRINE OF JUDICIAL REVIEW [1]

WE are now to undertake an investigation of the influence which the doctrine of judicial review has exerted on our American system of railroad control, in order to discover whether it has strengthened or weakened the efficiency of that control. In this inquiry we shall consider, first, its effect on the state's power to reduce rates; second, its effect on the state's power to enforce the rates it has established; and third, its effect, as a resultant of the other two, upon the spirit and ideas of railroad commissions.

Before coming to these precise questions, however, we shall do well to reflect for a moment upon the spirit of the law which has shaped the doctrine of judicial review, and which directs its application; for it will serve to illumine our entire discussion of this subject to recall at the outset the general attitude of the law and of the courts in all cases which involve both public and private interests. The attitude of the courts is determined by the fact that they are charged with the duty of interpreting and applying a law in which the individualistic spirit of the age has been firmly crystallized. In our modern régime the *individual* is the central figure. His importance, his dignity, his sanctity, his rights, and his liberties are everywhere recognized. His use of a free ballot is supposed to guard civil rights and to shape aright the course of government; his pursuit of his individual self-interest is supposed to secure industrial justice and welfare; his freedom of conscience, of thought, of will, and of action is not to be lightly infringed. "All men are created free and equal," says our Declaration of Independence, " and are endowed

---

[1] From "Railroad Rate Control," by Harrison Standish Smalley, Ph.D., *Publications of the American Economic Association*, 3d series, Vol. VII, 1906, pp. 83–110.

by their Creator with certain inalienable rights. . . . *To secure these rights, governments are established among men.*" The only limitation upon them is that they shall not, in their exercise, encroach upon the equal rights of other individuals.

It is true that this is a theory which has been gradually losing its hold both upon the minds and upon the hearts of men. So pernicious have been some of its results, especially in the world of industry, that the inquiry now is whether it has not passed the zenith of its usefulness, and whether it is not now necessary to modify it by an assertion of the social duties and responsibilities of individuals, and accordingly, by the enactment of laws restricting the individual for the general good. In this inquiry different minds have pursued different courses, have gone different lengths, and have, of course, reached different conclusions. Socialists would have us abandon the theory of individualism entirely and substitute therefor a theory of social duty, to be applied by the state. Long since, more conservative minds suggested factory legislation. Some thirty years ago, the consensus of public opinion demanded regulation of railroads for the public good. To-day there is agitation for municipal ownership, trust regulation, and other limitations upon private enterprise. This view is not intended to be complete. Its purpose is merely to recall the fundamental theory upon which our society is based, and some of the modifications of it which have been urged by many from time to time.

But while observing the gradual departure from the theory of individualism in industrial economics we must always remember that the law under which we live grew up with the growth of the individualistic theory and has received its stamp. The history of the English law is a record of the successful struggle of the individual, first for recognition, and then for supremacy. Indeed our law is permeated, saturated, with the theory of individual rights. Two centuries ago English law had been shaped to that theory, while in our country it no less lies at the basis of our law; and its dignity has been recognized in the bills of rights of our state constitutions, and in most of the Amendments to the Federal Constitution. Such limitations as the state may impose on private rights are regarded as exceptions to the general rule, repugnant to the spirit and genius of the law, and therefore to be confined within strict bounds. Moreover — and this is a point of deep significance — for almost all purposes the law considers those artificial persons, corporations, as individuals entitled to the legal rights and privileges of natural persons.

This is the law which our courts are established to interpret and apply. " The primary duty of the courts," said Mr. Justice Brewer, in deciding *Railway Co.* v. *Dey*, " is the protection of the rights of persons and property." [1] And again, speaking for the Supreme Court in the Wellman case, he said, " the protection of vested rights of property is a supreme duty of the courts." [2] This duty, it must be admitted, has not been neglected. In railroad rate cases its demands have been faithfully obeyed.

Such being the character of the law in which our judges are trained, and such being the acknowledged duty of the courts in its application, it is but natural that the professional sympathies of judges should all be with the railroads. Not that the judges, as *men*, are callous to the abuses which for a third of a century have irritated the general public, sometimes beyond the point of endurance ; but nevertheless, as *judges*, they must apply a law which is in thorough sympathy with private persons, their property and rights, and which knows almost nothing of the " public welfare " except as it is to be secured through the assertion and maintenance of individual rights. If it be true, as is sometimes stated, that judges are disposed to subordinate the public weal to individual advantage, it is because they have entered fully into the spirit of a system of law which allows no other course.

In the light of these general observations, let us proceed to inquire the effect of the doctrine of judicial review, as developed and applied under our legal system, and first to notice the manner in which it has affected the power of the states to reduce rates.

Low rates are not, of course, the only ideal of railroad regulation. Doubtless the most important thing is *proportion*, that

[1] 35 Federal Reports, 872.   [2] 143 United States, 346.

is, a proper adjustment of rates as among the various commodities and the various localities. But given this adjustment, the lower rates are, the better. There can be no doubt that the public interest demands that, so long as the due proportion is not disturbed, rates shall be as low as possible. A commission, therefore, being charged with the duty of advancing the public welfare, must require reductions in railroad schedules which are too high to be in accord with the public interest. And the efficiency of a commission must depend in no small measure on its ability to accomplish the reductions which are demanded by considerations of public utility. Now how great is its ability in this regard?

Clearly, if its action in the matter of rates were final and binding upon the companies, its power of lowering rates would be absolute. There would be no obstacle to prevent it from meeting in the most complete manner the requirements of the industrial situation. We have seen, however, that its rates are subject to review by the courts, and the consequence of judicial review has been to seriously impair a commissioner's power to reduce rates. While it is impossible to measure with exactness the extent to which this power is impaired, it is possible to see that the limitation placed upon the commissions' activity in this particular is very great. And in order that this may clearly appear, let us consider at length three reasons why the doctrine of judicial review, as practically applied by the courts, stands in the way of public reduction of rates. These reasons may be stated as follows:

I. The doctrine fixes an improper limit beyond which reduction of rates cannot be carried.

II. The methods employed by the Supreme Court in determining the effect of rates on earnings are such as to make that effect seem more disastrous than is the fact.

III. The principles recognized by the Court in determining reasonableness of income are unduly favorable to the railroads, and afford no adequate protection to the interests of the public.

These propositions we shall take up in order.

I. The first limitation upon the state's power to reduce rates is found in that part of the doctrine of judicial review which requires that rates shall be high enough to permit the railroad company to secure reasonable earnings. A state cannot lower rates so as to reduce earnings below that point without making adequate compensation to the company for all earnings, below the point of reasonableness, which are so taken. For to take any part of a railroad's "fair returns" is to deprive of property, — an act which, under the Fourteenth Amendment, must be accompanied with proper reimbursement.

This phase of the doctrine of judicial review is certainly subject to criticism, and the criticism touches a point so vital as to call in question the entire doctrine. The vulnerable point is the distinction made between earnings above the point of reasonableness, and earnings below that point. In effect the Court declares that above that point earnings are not property; but below it they are property; for the state may freely appropriate earnings above that point without violating the constitutional provision protecting property, though to take any below that point is declared to be a violation of it. This distinction is ingenious, and in making it the Court has perhaps saved from annihilation the state's right of rate control, but whatever merit may be claimed for it on that account, it may be admitted that it is a distinction which is artificial and which cannot be supported by reason. For, if income from property is itself property at all, surely all income must be property. To divide income into two parts — "property" and "not-property" — giving one part the protection of the constitution, and leaving the other defenseless, is an extraordinary proceeding. No one has ever thought of making a similar division in the case of any other kind of property. If the state were condemning a person's lot, it would not divide the lot into two parts and say: "one of these parts is property, and for it you may have compensation; but the other is not property, and for it, therefore, no payment will be made." Such a proceeding is unheard of, even in the case of property belonging to a quasi-public corporation. It cannot be imagined that the state, in taking any such property, would divide it into two parts and say: "one of these parts is property, and for it compensation will be made, but no payment will be made for the other because it is not property, since you are a quasi-public corporation and, your property being devoted to a public use, a part of it has ceased to be property "! But the absurdity is more clearly seen when such a distinction is applied, not to real estate or equipment but to the income of railroads. Suppose the state were to seek in the treasury of a railroad company the earnings it had received from the operation of its road, and were to attempt to appropriate those earnings. There is not the least doubt that if the appropriation were permitted at all, the courts would require the state to reimburse the company for every cent of the earnings taken. The wildest stretch of the imagination cannot picture the courts saying to the state : " a part of these earnings are reasonable, and hence are property, and if you take them you must recompense the company ; but the rest of the earnings are not property, because not reasonable, and you can have them for nothing." Yet this is just what the Supreme Court has said in regard to depriving a railroad of its income through the agency of low rates. The distinction is clearly without warrant and must be given a place among the pure fictions of the law.

It is evident from the absurdity of this distinction, which the Court has found it necessary to maintain in order to prevent judicial review from practically denying the established legislative power of rate control, that somewhere in the reasoning of the Court there is an error which is fundamental and which vitiates the whole process. That error, it is believed, consists in the actual, though not professed, transfer of rate regulation from the basis of the police power, where it has always been held to rest, to the basis of the eminent domain. While continuing to insist *in words* that rate control is an exercise of the police power, the Court has *in fact* treated it as if it were a phase of the power of eminent domain. The Court has apparently looked upon it as a means whereby the state may take property (in the form of income) for public use, and has consequently subjected it to the ordinary rules of eminent domain, requiring just compensation for property appropriated. It is because of this change of base that the Court has been driven to the dilemma of holding either that all income is property, which practically denies the ancient legislative right of control, or else that none of it is property, and hence that all of it is beyond constitutional protection, which the judicial mind is unwilling to concede. From this dilemma our jurists have extricated themselves by advancing the extraordinary idea that a part of income is property and a part is not. But they would have saved themselves from getting into the dilemma, and so would have spared themselves the necessity of resorting to this untenable fiction, had they actually continued to regard rate control in the light of their own repeated assertions, as a phase of the police power. For viewed as a part of the police power, rate regulation is, of course, not subject to the rules applying to the condemnation of property. It is the exercise of an entirely different sovereign power, subject to entirely different rules and restraints. If the court should really so regard it, there would be no question of appropriation or compensation to consider, no inquiry as to the effect of rates on earnings would have to be made, and hence no classification of income.

But, it may be objected, though rate regulation is a part of the police power, is it not true that in its exercise the income of the railroad may be decreased, which would amount to a deprivation of property, income being regarded as property? True; — from the control of rates many consequences may flow, and among other results, the income of a company may be reduced. But that is a consequence which also flows from other police regulations which the state may adopt. Railroad rate control is not peculiar in that regard. Yet no one thinks of subjecting other police regulations to the rules of eminent domain. Thus the legislature may pass laws requiring railroads to put in cattle guards at highway crossings, or to equip each passenger car with an ax, saw, and hammer, or with drinking water, or to substitute, within a given time, automatic couplers of a certain type for the couplers in use. Any of these requirements would necessitate an expenditure of money and consequently would reduce the net income of the company by increasing expenses while the improvements were being installed. In effect, if one wishes to think of it in this way, it amounts to an appropriation of property for a public purpose. A portion of the income, instead of being devoted to paying operating expenses, or interest on bonds, or dividends on stock, must be expended in a manner required for the benefit of the public. Thus income is affected just as truly — though in a somewhat different way — through these measures as through rate control. A railroad company may be deprived of income just as truly through police regulations requiring an expenditure of money for the public welfare as through those requiring a reduction in rates.

Nevertheless a railroad company is not permitted to object to ordinary police regulations on the ground that its "reasonable income" is threatened. A case can be imagined where a railroad could show that its existing income was no more than reasonable, and where the courts would so hold. In such a case to enforce a law requiring the installation of new couplers or other equipment would so increase the expenses of the company that the income would no longer be reasonable. Its existing income being just barely a reasonable one, to require expenditures from it for the public good would be in effect to deprive the company of a part of its reasonable income. But could the company demand compensation for the sum so taken? Of course not. In passing upon police regulations a court does not consider their incidental effect on earnings. It makes no difference whether the road can earn a reasonable income under them or not. A company in the last stages of insolvency is just as subject to them as the most prosperous of roads.[1]

---

[1] It should be noted that the validity of a police regulation is not a matter which is personal to certain individuals within the class affected, but rather is a quality of the regulation itself. A factory act applying to factories of a certain class is never valid as to some and void as to others. Its validity is determined on its own merits, irrespective of its financial effect on certain factories, and if it is held to be a valid exercise of the police power, it is binding on all the persons coming within its terms. Yet a general schedule of railroad rates may, under the present judicial doctrine, be held void as to one road but binding upon another, perhaps a competing line. This unfortunate consequence is, of course, a result of bringing into rate cases the rules of eminent domain, instead of judging rates on their merits, as a police measure designed to promote the public welfare.

In short the state is permitted through police regulation to appropriate earnings for the public benefit without any obligation, under the Constitution, to provide compensation. But the police power differs from eminent domain in that the appropriation of property is not direct, but is incidental and resultant. The direct and immediate effect of a police regulation is always the establishment of some condition or method or other regulation which the public safety or welfare or comfort demands. And its indirect or consequent effect on income is not regarded as a deprivation of property such as is contemplated in the law of eminent domain. There is no valid reason why an exception to this rule should be made in the case of that form of police regulation called rate control. It is a perfectly legitimate exercise of the police power and should certainly be treated in the same way as other police regulations, — at least it should not be subjected to more stringent restraints.

Two objections to this view of the case might conceivably be raised, neither of which, however, it is believed, is well taken. In the first place it may be said that there is a difference between rate control and other forms of police regulation, in that the latter are of real benefit to the company. The railroad is in possession of equipment which proves of decided advantage to it. For example, its automatic couplers and cattle guards decrease accidents, with their losses of property and subsequent damage suits, while passenger car equipment encourages patronage by the greater security and comfort offered to travelers. But two replies may be made to this objection. One is that public regulation of rates also is of advantage to the company. It does away with lawsuits to recover damages for overcharge, for a company is never guilty of extortion so long as it keeps within the maximum fixed by the state. Moreover, it tends to increase the popular favor in which the roads are held and to encourage traffic. The development of industry resulting from efficient public regulation is in itself of great advantage to the roads. But while this answer to the objection can be made, a better one, and one fully sufficient, is this: that the benefit which a police regulation confers on the road is *not* the reason why the courts do not subject the regulation to the law of eminent domain. The reason is simply that it is not an exercise of that power. The second possible objection is that a regulation of rates necessarily affects income ; but that in the case of other police laws the company may recoup whatever expense is involved, by raising its rates and so increasing its earnings. The reply to this objection is that a company is not able thus to manipulate its earnings. It is at many points subject to competition, and so is not, commercially speaking, free to raise its rates. And an increase of rates at any point might simply have the effect of decreasing traffic, so that earnings would be but slightly increased, if at all. Moreover, it may be that the state has prescribed rates and they are in force, so that the company is without legal power to raise its rates, and thus without the means wherewith even to try to recoup the expense forced upon it. Even here the attitude of the courts is just the same. A railroad cannot claim exemption from police regulations because it is unable to make up the expense through the manipulation of its rates.

We conclude, therefore, that since rate control is an exercise of the police power and not of the eminent domain, it should not be subjected to the law of eminent domain; that accordingly the test of its validity should not be, as is now held by the courts, its effect on the income of the company.

Does this mean that the legislative power of rate control is absolute and without limit? No. It simply means that the legislature is subject to the same limitations that it is in exercising other forms of the police power. In other words, the validity of rate control is to be determined just as the validity of other police regulations is determined. The same test that is applied to them should be applied to it. The question upon which the validity of a cattle-guard, or automatic-coupler, or drinking-water law hangs — or, for that matter, a factory act, or sanitary legislation, or an inspection law — is whether a sufficient public interest demands the law. Upon that same question should the validity of rate regulation depend. It should be a question of public welfare. And therefore just as a court sometimes sets aside a police law because its enactment is not justified by the public advantage to be secured through its operation, so rates made by public authority might be set aside on the same grounds. But this is vastly different from saying that their effect on earnings should be the conclusive test in determining their validity.[1]

If the view of the matter here suggested were to command acceptance, judicial review would be transformed. Instead of being what it now is, it would become a judicial investigation designed to apply to rate control the same test which is judicially applied to other police regulations. And beyond a doubt this would result in giving to legislatures and commissions much greater freedom of action in rate matters than they enjoy under the present doctrine. The full measure of their proper authority, of which they have been largely deprived by the courts, would be restored to them. And that it is their proper authority is made more evident by the following consideration. A state may, of course, and frequently does employ the police power to control private persons in matters of private concern. In such cases, as has been said, the regulation stands or falls according to whether the public interest, welfare, safety, health, morals, comfort, or, sometimes, even convenience, demand it. If that is the only limitation placed upon the legislature in its control of private persons in their management of private matters, surely no more stringent limitation should be placed on it in its regulation of the management of public business by quasi-public corporations. Indeed there is evidently much ground on which to contend that legislative authority should be even more extensive over public than over private business. It would certainly seem that the government should have more control over property devoted to public use than over property retained for purely private use. It is not an immoderate suggestion, therefore, that the authority in the first case should be barely equal with that in the second.

---

[1] Of course it is perfectly conceivable that the effect of rates on earnings might be *one* of the points considered by a court. It might be made a question whether the public interest demanded certain rates, if they reduced income so much that bare operating expenses could not be paid, for in that case the road might have to suspend operation. But even if the effect of rates were so considered, the limitation on legislative action would be decidedly different from what it is at the present time.

That a broader governmental power over rates would render more precarious the earnings from railroad properties is evident, but that, of course, is simply one of the hazards which one must contemplate in going beyond the boundaries of private enterprise, into the uncertain field of public activities. A forcible judicial expression of this idea may be found in the words of Mr. Justice Brewer, uttered *obiter*, in *Cotting* v. *Kansas City Stock Yards Company*.[1] In entering a public business, said he, a person "expresses his willingness to do the work of the state, aware that the state in the discharge of its public duties is not guided solely by a question of profit. It may rightfully determine that the particular service is of such importance to the public that it may be conducted at a pecuniary loss, having in view a larger general interest. At any rate, it does not perform its services with the single idea of profit. Its thought is the general public welfare. . . . Is there not force in the suggestion that as the state may do the work without profit, if he voluntarily undertakes to act for the state he must submit to a like determination as to the paramount interests of the public?"

In this connection it is instructive to notice that in other ways persons embarking in a public business must assume the risk of losing much or even all of their investments. Such dangers exist, — have been permitted by the courts to exist even since the adoption of the Fourteenth Amendment. Thus, it has been held that a state may grant a franchise to one railroad to parallel an already existing road. The value of the older property may be impaired by competition with the new road, yet it is held that the owners have no vested rights which can prevent its construction and operation. So also the value of a turnpike may be practically annihilated by the state through a franchise permitting a parallel railroad. Yet it has been held that the Fourteenth Amendment does not command just compensation in any sense which would require the state to compensate the turnpike company for the property so taken.[2] When

[1] 183 U. S. 93.

[2] For further illustrations, see Cooley's Principles of Constitutional Law, 3d ed., p. 370.

the public welfare demands more efficient means of transportation, the owners of existing roads must expect to suffer ; and the courts, aside from declining to relieve them, have not even claimed that any one but the legislature should be the final judge of the public necessity of the new improvement. A power such as this is one which properly belongs to the state to enable it to deal with property devoted to a public use in a manner conducive to the welfare of the community, and one of which the state has been deprived, so far as rate regulation is concerned by the doctrine of judicial review.

We thus conclude the discussion of our first reason why the doctrine of judicial review has seriously impaired the legislative power to reduce rates. It has fixed a limit beyond which reduction cannot be carried, and that limit is an improper one. By basing rate regulation on eminent domain rather than on the police power, it has prevented the legislatures and commissions from exercising the authority that is their right, and has thus subjected them to a serious restraint.

II. But this is not the only reason why the judicial doctrine has impaired the power of the state to reduce rates. The present judicial limit on legislative action is, as we have seen, the point of " reasonable income." But while the Court has repeatedly declared that this is the proper limit, it has, nevertheless, adopted principles and methods in the trial of rate cases which do not permit a state to fix rates so as to reduce income even to the point of reasonableness. In other words, the Court employs principles and methods which unduly favor the railroad and unduly restrict the state ; and thus the legislature cannot exercise even the limited authority which the Court has in general terms allowed it. Rates may be made which will not actually reduce the income below the point of reasonableness, yet the Court may hold that they will — so erroneous is the way in which it determines that point. In the further elucidation of this contention, let us consider the methods by which the Court determines the effect of rates on earnings. We shall see that those methods inevitably make that effect appear more favorable to the railroads than is really the case.

As we have already seen,[1] the Court begins with the rule that the effect of rates upon earnings shall be determined on the basis of *past* business. That is, the judicial estimate of earning capacity of the road under the new rates is arrived at on the assumption that the rates will neither increase nor decrease the traffic, but that the traffic will remain the same that it was for a period of time prior to the establishment of the rates.

Extraordinary as this assumption is, it is one which, as we have seen from our review of the cases, the courts have repeatedly recognized as legitimate. It need hardly be said that in this matter the courts have failed to take into consideration one of the most fundamental charactistics of the railroad business. For it is a matter of general knowledge that, usually, a reduction in rates results in an increase of business. At this stage of the railroad controversy no argument is needed to prove this contention, nothing beyond a mere appeal to those general facts of which all are cognizant. Curiously enough it was even admitted, with innocent frankness, by Mr. Carter, of counsel for the railroads in *Smyth* v. *Ames*. In arguing that there are sufficient protections against the danger of extortion, he said, " Moderate charges yield more profit by the greatly increased business they draw. A sound policy, perfectly well known to railroad managers, advises them that it is better to tempt and draw out a large traffic by low prices than to try to make a large profit on a small business." [2]

In spite of this universally accepted fact, however, the courts have definitely settled that the effect of lower rates may properly, for judicial purposes, be determined on the assumption that increase of business will not result from the decrease in rates. It must, of course, be admitted that compensating circumstances may occasionally prevent an increase in traffic, but such an occurrence is out of the ordinary. The rule remains that a reduction in rates, other conditions remaining the same, always tends to augment the volume of business. For the courts, then, to proceed upon the assumption which it does, is to unduly favor the railroads. It enables them to make a

----

[1] P. 58 of original monograph.   [2] 169 U. S. 506.

stronger case than they could were the correct assumption to be made. Upon this principle the judicial view must always be that rates will more seriously affect the earnings of the companies than would be true in nineteen cases out of twenty. As a matter of fact, to put the rates in operation might not reduce either gross or net earnings at all, or might reduce them but slightly. Yet, in contemplation of the courts, earnings would be diminished exactly in proportion to the reduction in the rates.

Of course it may be urged that this is the only definite test which the courts can apply; that to attempt to estimate the probable increase in traffic resulting from a decrease in rates would involve the courts in speculations in which they could never have the guidance of reliable principles.[1] Let this be granted as true; let it be conceded that the courts can find no other test. Nevertheless that fact does not make the test a good one, nor one adequate to the needs of rate cases, nor does it affect the fact that the test gives to the railroads an undue advantage as against the public.

No more favorable is the view which must be taken of the next step in the procedure of the Court. After declaring that the effect of rates upon earnings must be decided on the basis of past business, the Court goes on to hold that that effect must further be determined by applying to past earnings the percentage of reduction in the rates.[2]

If the effect of the new rates upon earnings were to be determined at all on the basis of past business, it would seem that the correct method of arriving at the result would be to apply freight rates to past tonnage, and passenger rates to past passenger traffic. This would give the maximum earnings which could be secured by the railroad under the new rates, on the condition, assumed by the courts, that traffic would continue

---

[1] It is said that it cannot be determined in advance what the effect of the reduction of rates will be. Oftentimes it increases business, and who can say that it will not in the present cases so increase the volume of business as to make it remunerative, even more than at present? But speculations as to the future are not guides for judicial actions; courts determine rights upon existing facts. — Mr. Justice Brewer in *Chicago, etc., Ry. Co.* v. *Dey*, 35 Fed. Rep. 881.

[2] P. 58 of original monograph.

unchanged. Instead of this method, however, the courts determine the percentage of reduction made by the new rates in the rates in force, and then assume that future earnings will equal past earnings reduced in the same proportion. For example : Suppose that past earnings were $1,000,000, and that the new rates are 80 per cent of the old rates. It is assumed by the courts that earning capacity under the new rates will be $800,000.

Now, here, again, is an assumption which gives the railroads a distinct advantage in suits involving rates. For the basis of the whole process is the reduction made by the new rates in the old schedules. Yet the old schedules, of course, contain only the *nominal* rates established by the railroad. As a matter of fact, in very many cases, the *actual* rates charged are lower than those named in the schedules. Discriminations, rebates, drawbacks, preferential advantages, all awarded, usually, under the veil of secrecy, are not yet, unfortunately, things of the past. The past earnings of the company, therefore, have been derived, not by charging the rates fixed in the schedules, but by charging rates which average considerably less than those scheduled. When the courts, then, compare the new rates with the old *nominal* ones, they discover a percentage of reduction greater than the percentage of reduction made by the new rates in the old *actual* ones. The assumption, therefore, that the earning capacity of the road will be reduced in proportion to the greater percentage, is clearly wrong. It makes the company's criminal practices a source of advantage to it, and of disadvantage to the public, in the trial of rate cases.

For example, let us make the same assumption, made above, that past earnings were $1,000,000, and that the new rates are 80 per cent of the old nominal rates. In such a case the courts hold that the maximum earning capacity of the road under the new rates will be $800,000.

Suppose that the nominal rate per mile was $.01; the new rate is, then, $.008. Now, it is evident, from the merest knowledge of railroad practices, that the earnings of $1,000,000 were not secured by charging an average of $.01 for each of 1,000,000 ton miles. As a matter of fact, the actual average rate charged was less then $.01. It might have been $.009, or $.008, or $.007, or even less. But in order to deal generously with the railroad, let us assume for the moment that it was as high as $.009. Then, the earnings of $1,000,000 were secured by charging $.009 for each of 111,111,111 ton miles. The actual traffic, therefore, being 111,111,111 ton miles, to put in force a rate of $.008 would give an earning capacity of $888,888.88. This, indeed, is less than the former earnings, but, on the other hand, it is over $88,000 greater than the earning capacity which the Court assumes the railroad would possess under an $.008 rate.

Now let us alter our last assumption, and suppose that the actual average rate which earned the receipts of $1,000,000 was low, say $.007. Then the $1,000,000 were earned by charging $.007 for each of 142,857,142 ton miles. But to apply to that tonnage a rate of $.008 would give an earning capacity of $1,142,857. This is greater by $142,857 than the old earnings, and is $342,857 greater than the earning capacity reached by the processes of the Court.

Thus it appears that the earning capacity determined by the courts is always less than that which the railroad will actually possess under the new rates. Furthermore, it appears that the earning capacity of the road under the new rates, if it will abstain from discrimination, may even exceed the actual amount of earnings received under the old rates.

This practice of the courts, then, is always unfair to the new rates, since it makes out their effect upon earning capacity to be more disastrous than it will be, except in the purely hypothetical case of a road which has not deviated from its nominal rates. As an item in a test of reasonableness, it is, therefore, clearly inadequate, and unduly favorable to the railroads. Under this practice, the more flagrant a company's violations are of the laws against discriminations, the more complete is its immunity from public regulation of its rates. In any event, a railroad is able to make out before the Court a stronger case than it has in fact.

True, in the Reagan cases, it was laid down that a railroad's right to profitable compensation is limited, *inter alia*, when it has indulged in "unjust discriminations resulting in general loss." [1] Accordingly the way is opened for the state to attempt to prove the unjust discriminations of which the road has been guilty. But satisfactory evidence upon such matters is, of course, almost impossible to get; and even were it secured, it is not certain to what extent and in what way the courts would make use of it. So far as the question of the effect of rates upon earning capacity is concerned, no fair or correct result can be secured by the method now employed by the courts. As said above, if past business is to be the basis of the calculation at all, the correct method would seem to be the application of the new rates to past tonnage, or past passenger traffic. Without discussing this point farther, however, it is sufficient for our present purposes to note that the method now employed by the Court may often result in the suspension of rates which, while looking toward the public welfare, are not really calculated to impair the earning capacity of the railroads, to say nothing of reducing it to the point of "reasonable returns."

III. Beyond this, however, it may be urged that the judicial conception of "reasonable income" is not adequate. At least it may fairly be said that the principles which the Court has laid down as the controlling considerations in determining reasonableness of income have so far proven unduly favorable to the railroads, and have not, as yet, given proper expression to the interests of the public. Let us recall what these principles are. Briefly stated, the Court has held [2] that a railroad's earnings must be sufficient, in general, to pay all expenses including interest on bonds, and yield a reasonable dividend upon stock, but that the reasonableness of the dividend, and, indeed, a railroad's right to any dividend at all, is dependent upon a large number of considerations. These considerations, we have also seen, may be grouped into four classes — one pertaining to the base upon which the rate of profit shall be reckoned, the second to the management of the road, another to the rights of the public, and the fourth to the industrial condition of the community.[3] The enunciation of these limitations upon a railroad's right to

---

[1] P. 74 of original monograph.   [2] *Ibid.*, p. 70.   [3] *Ibid.*, p. 72.

compensation is a most interesting feature of rate cases. At first blush it might seem that they are admirably calculated to aid in restoring the proper balance between the public and private interests. Yet it cannot escape observation that almost all of them are simply *obiter dicta*, and investigation shows that the Court has often forgotten them, either in determining procedure or in deciding special cases.

A few instances of this kind will serve both to explain and to enforce the point. In the Reagan cases is laid down the doctrine that the failure of rates to yield profitable compensation is not conclusive of reasonableness when, *inter alia*, the railroad has indulged in unjust discriminations resulting in general loss. And yet, as has just been seen, the Court has employed a method of determining the effect of new rates, which enables a railroad to take refuge under the very shelter of its own discriminations, and from that safe retreat, protected by the strong bulwark of the law, to defy legislatures and commissions. Again, the Reagan cases also recognized a limitation when a road was unwisely built, in districts where there is not sufficient business to sustain a road. Yet such was the case with almost all, if not all, of the roads involved *in those very cases*. The International & Great Northern had never been able to pay the interest on its bonds, and had been in a receiver's hands for three years. Of two other roads the Court speaks as follows:

The St. Louis Southwestern Railway Company is called by counsel for defendants, in their brief, "a reorganized bankrupt concern." It would seem to be a railroad *which was unwisely built, and one whose operating expenses have always exceeded its earnings*. Counsel says that "it is familiarly known as a 'teazer,' and, if it ever passes beyond this interesting but unprofitable stage, even its friends will be surprised." We are not advised and we can hardly be expected to take judicial notice of what is meant by the term "teazer," but *it is clearly disclosed by the record* that this was an unprofitable road. . . . The Tyler Southwestern Railway Company has a short road of ninety miles, and also appears to be a "reorganized bankrupt concern," and one whose road has been operated with constant loss.[1]

Here are cases which clearly, by the admission of the Court, come under the general limitation expressed in the body of the

[1] 154 U. S. 403.

opinion. Yet the limitation was entirely ignored. After making the statement quoted above, the Court continued, "it will not do to hold that, because the roads have been operating in the past at a loss to the owners, it is just and reasonable to so reduce the rates as to increase the amount of that loss." Here, then, one who has read, a few pages back in the opinion, the general rule laid down by the Court, finds the hopes aroused by it most rudely dashed.

Further evidence may be found of the Court's tendency to ignore the limitations upon a railroad's right to profitable rates. It is worth while mentioning that the Court in the Reagan cases specifically denied two claims which were allowed in general terms in later cases. The Covington case limits the railroad's right when competition of parallel lines so diminishes business as to make profitable rates exorbitant, and the last Minnesota case further limits that right when the industrial condition of the country is such that profitable rates would be exorbitant. Yet in the Reagan cases the Attorney-General showed that there were four lines in competition with the International & Great Northern, reducing its share of the traffic; alleged that there had recently been a commercial depression; and offered evidence to show that the price of products was so low that rates would have to be lower than those charged by the railroads in order to permit the farmers to market their produce with any profit. All this was not gladly received by the Court, as tending to support the rates which are "presumed to be reasonable." On the other hand it was summarily dismissed, and given no weight whatever in the case. We are accordingly left in grave doubt as to whether the Court meant much if anything by its later dicta in the Covington and the last Minnesota cases. At any rate, it is evident that the play of the Court's sympathy for individual as opposed to public rights, operates to seriously limit the limitations, as it were, which it has recognized upon the rights of the railroads. The view of the railroad industry which has been taken by the Court since the Granger cases requires the limitations to be stated; but the predilections of the judges create a tendency to disregard them. As statesmen, or publicists, the judges might recognize the full force and importance of those limitations ; but as *lawyers or judges*, they almost inevitably forget them.

It is true that as yet the Court has not been put to a severe test, and consequently it is not clear to just what extent it will go. For, up to the present time, counsel for the states have shown comparatively slight disposition to urge upon the Court the limitations it has recognized, or to introduce evidence in such matters. The Court by its repeated declaration and affirmation of its dicta, has offered an opportunity the significance of which has apparently not been fully appreciated by the representatives of the public. But the treatment which those dicta have received in the cases where they have been urged, as we have just seen, forbids any very sanguine hope that they hold much promise of better things for public control.

But it is not only because the Court tends to ignore in special cases the rules it has laid down in general terms, that they are not available for the cause of the public welfare. A further reason is that many of the limitations upon the rights of the railroads are so vague in character, and involve considerations so difficult to establish, that the public can derive little advantage from them. One illustration of this fact is to be found in the limitation which is recognized to exist when the management of the road has not been prudent and honest. But how difficult must it always be for state officers to secure satisfactory evidence upon such a point ! The secrecy which enshrouds many railroad operations and the possibility of manipulating accounts make difficult even the discovery of imprudence and dishonesty, to say nothing of securing evidence which will be satisfactory at law.

Again, the courts have, in general terms, given recognition to the rights of the public. In the Gill case the Court was hesitant to declare rates unreasonable when, among other things, the claims of the railroad were admitted in the demurrer of a party who in no adequate sense represented the public. In the Reagan cases it was said that the right of the road to compensation is limited, among other things, by " matters affecting the rights of the community in which the road is built."[1] And in the Covington and Smyth cases, it was stated that the rights of the public are not to be ignored, that rates must not be more than the services are worth to the public, that, in short, rates must be just to the public as well as to the railroad.[2] But what are the "rights of the community," or the "rights of the public," and how are they to be established? How is it to be determined what a railroad's services are worth to the public? How, indeed, is it to be discovered what rate is just to the public as well as to the railroad? And, when the interests of the public and of the railroad clash, which is to prevail? It need hardly be stated, in view of the preceding discussion, what the coloring is which must necessarily prevail in the Court's answers to these questions. The rights of the public are indeed difficult to establish. Generally speaking, the public has rights, which must not be invaded by the railroads. But specifically, what rights? To be exempt from the high rates necessary to compensate a railroad for losses due to its discriminations, or necessary to make profitable a road unwisely built, or necessary to sustain as many competing roads as may chance to divide the traffic? We have seen what answers the Court has given to these questions. The vague "rights" of the public have vanished with the appearance of a practical test.

But there is still another "limitation" upon the right of the railroad to compensation, namely, the industrial condition of the community, which is too vague and general to mean much in practice. Here again, it may be asked, how is the industrial condition of the community to be established at law, and just what "industrial condition" will justify a reduction of a road's earning capacity? Is it not inevitable that counsel for the state should find it difficult to secure satisfactory evidence in such a matter? The limitation is in general terms. In specific cases how much would it amount to? Probably not much. The only points ever argued by the states have, as we have already seen,[3] been summarily rejected by the Court.

[1] 154 U. S. 402.
[2] 164 U. S. 596–598; 169 U. S. 544–547. And see also 173 U. S. 754–756.
[3] P. 106 of original monograph.

The fact unfortunately seems to be that the euphonious generalities in which the Court has bound up the industrial welfare of the American commonwealths are more beautiful for contemplation than they are efficacious in use. To discover the practical meaning which is embodied in them, and to obtain recognition of it by the courts, is one of the difficult problems which now confronts the commissions, and one in the performance of which the attitude of the judiciary up to the present time gives little encouragement.

In these three ways, then — by placing an improper limitation on the legislative power to reduce earnings through regulation of rates, by employing erroneous methods in determining the effect of rates on earnings, and by setting up inadequate standards of reasonableness in earnings — has the Court practically destroyed the state's power of rate reduction. The doctrine of judicial review is therefore of great importance in the development of the railroad problem. But, more than that, it is of significance as a notable triumph achieved by the principle of individual interest over that of the public welfare. Under whatever constitutional pressure the courts may have been in announcing the doctrine, it is felt that it is a movement against the current of the times, and that it must result, in part, in deepening the conviction already growing in the minds of men, that the proper balance between the public and the private interests in industrial action has been much disturbed, and should be speedily restored.

HARRISON STANDISH SMALLEY

XXV

THE MINNESOTA RATE CASE, 1913 [1]

Mr. Justice HUGHES delivered the opinion of the court:

These suits were brought by stockholders of the Northern Pacific Railway Company, the Great Northern Railway Company, and the Minneapolis & St. Louis Railroad Company, respectively, to restrain the enforcement of two orders of the Railroad & Warehouse Commission of the state of Minnesota, and two acts of the legislature of that state, prescribing maximum charges for transportation of freight and passengers, and to prevent the adoption or maintenance of these rates by the railroad companies. In addition to the companies, the attorney general of the state, the members of the Railroad & Warehouse Commission, and also, in the cases of the Northern Pacific and Great Northern Companies, certain representative shippers, were made defendants.

The orders and acts, which, by their terms related solely to charges for intrastate transportation, were as follows:

(1) The commission's order of September 6, 1906, effective November 15, 1906, fixing the maximum class rates for general merchandise.

(2) The act approved April 4, 1907, to take effect May 1, 1907, prescribing 2 cents a mile as the maximum fare for passengers, except for those under twelve years of age, for whom the maximum rate was to be 1 cent a mile. Laws of 1907, chap. 176.

(3) The act approved April 18, 1907, to take effect June 1, 1907, fixing maximum commodity rates for carload lots of specified weights. Laws of 1907, chap. 232.

[1] 33 Supreme Court Reporter, p. 729. The conflict of Federal and State authority is discussed in Ripley's Railroads: Rates and Regulation, chap. xx, leading up to this decision, not then rendered. The inter-related cases have been only in part decided, but follow the same general line of argument, differing only in detail.

(4) The commission's order of May 3, 1907, effective June 3, 1907, establishing maximum "in-rates" for designated commodities in carload lots from St. Paul, Minneapolis, Minnesota Transfer, and Duluth to certain distributing centers. No complaint is made of this order in the case of the Minneapolis & St. Louis Railroad Company.

In 1905, the legislature of Minnesota had adopted a joint resolution directing the commission "to undertake the work of securing a readjustment of the existing freight rates in this state, which will give a more uniform system of rates throughout the state, and a uniform scale of percentages which each class rate shall bear to the first class, the readjustment to secure a substantial reduction in the existing merchandise rates." Laws of 1905, chap. 350. Pursuant to this direction, the commission conducted a prolonged investigation. Public hearings were held extending over several months, in which the railroad companies took an active part, submitting a large amount of testimony with respect to the matters involved. The commission found the existing class rates for general merchandise to be unreasonable, and by the order of September 6, 1906, above-mentioned, established a new schedule of lower maximum rates. These rates were applied to the classes shown by the so-called "Western Classification" between stations in the state. This was a classification, by which articles were arranged in groups with reference to their general character, value, and the cost of transportation, and with modifications made from time to time, it had long been used by common carriers in the West and Northwest as a basis for rates, the commodities of each class taking the same rate under like conditions. In Minnesota, however, a large number of commodities, amounting to several hundred, had, by the intervention of the commission, been removed from this classification by the application of special rates, known as "commodity rates," or reduced in class so that the Western Classification in operation in that state was very materially different from that in general use as a basis of rates in other states.

The schedule of rates set forth in the order of September 6 was such that each rate for each class bore an exact relation to each other rate. The plan of the schedule was this: For first-class merchandise an allowance of 11.02 cents per cwt. was made for terminal charges, and, in addition, there was permitted a hauling charge of .98 of a cent for each 5 miles up to 200 miles, for each 10 miles over 200 miles up to 400 miles, and for each 20 miles over 400 miles up to 500 miles. For other classes, the rates were a fixed per centum of the corresponding rates for the first class. These rates were maximum terminal rates; that is, they related to transportation to or from certain important stations called terminal or distributing stations. Between stations neither of which is so designated, the rates of the schedule might be increased by 5 per centum.

The railway companies complied with this order and the class rates were put into effect on November 15, 1906.

The commission also had under consideration a reduction in the commodity rates, at which certain commodities such as grain, coal, lumber, and live stock were moved in carload lots. Because of the agitation with respect to these charges, the railroad companies voluntarily reduced their rates about 10 per cent on grain (September 1, 1906) and coal (October 22, 1906). The commission, however, on December 14, 1906, ordered a further reduction in the commodity rates. The railroad companies brought suit in the circuit court of the United States, and obtained a temporary injunction restraining the enforcement of this order. Thereupon the legislature passed the act above-mentioned, approved April 18, 1907, which established a new schedule of maximum commodity rates in all respects like that fixed by the commission, save that the reduction was not so great. The act grouped the various commodities which it embraced in several classes, for which different rates were prescribed. There was no fixed percentage relation between the classes, and no regular rate of progression of the various charges with increasing distance. In other respects the method of making the schedules was similar to that adopted in the order of September 6, 1906, the hauling charge decreasing as the mileage increases.

The remaining action with respect to freight rates was taken by the commission in the order of May 3, 1907, for the purpose of securing more favorable in-rates to a number of minor jobbing centers. It applied to certain commodities, such as groceries in carload lots, and was supplemental to the order of September 6, 1906, being intended to re-establish the relation which had previously existed between the in-rates to these distributing points and the general schedule of class rates.

The railroad companies obeyed this order of May 3, 1907, as they had that of September 6, 1906, and they also put into effect the passenger rate of 2 cents a mile. They were about to adopt the commodity rates fixed by the act of April 18, 1907, when these suits were brought and a temporary injunction restrained them from taking that course. The other rates, that is, the class rates, special in-rates, and the passenger rates were permitted to remain in force pending the suits.

The complainants assailed the acts and orders upon the grounds (1) that they amounted to an unconstitutional interference with interstate commerce, (2) that they were confiscatory, and (3) that the penalties imposed for their violation were so severe as to result in a denial of the equal protection of the laws and a deprivation of property without due process of law. The jurisdiction of the circuit court was sustained in *Ex parte* Young, 209 U. S. 123, 52 L. ed. 714, 13 L.R.A. (N.S.) 932, 28 Sup. Ct. Rep. 441, 14 Ann. Cas. 764, where it was also held that the penal provisions of the acts, operating to preclude a fair opportunity to test their validity, were unconstitutional on their face. The circuit court then referred the suits to a special master, who took the evidence and made an elaborate report sustaining the complainants' contentions. His findings were confirmed by the court, and decrees were entered accordingly, adjudging the acts and orders (with the exception, in the case of the Minneapolis & St. Louis Railroad Company, of the order of May 3, 1907) to be void, and permanently enjoining the enforcement of the prescribed rates, freight and passenger, and their adoption or maintenance by the railroad companies. 184 Fed. 765.

From these decrees, the attorney general of the state and the members of the Railroad & Warehouse Commission prosecute these appeals.

The penal provisions being separable . . . the question of the validity of the acts and orders fixing maximum rates is presented in two distinct aspects: (1) with respect to their effect on interstate commerce, and (2) as to their alleged confiscatory character.

First. As to interference with interstate commerce.

None of the acts and orders prescribes rates for goods or persons moving in interstate commerce. By their terms, they apply solely to commerce that is internal. Despite this obvious purport, it has been found below that the inevitable effect of the state's requirements for intrastate transportation was to impose a direct burden upon interstate commerce, and to create unjust discriminations between localities in Minnesota and those in adjoining states; and hence, that they must fall, as repugnant to the commerce clause and to the action of Congress under it. To support its conclusion, the circuit court presents an impressive array of facts drawn from the approved findings of the master. 184 Fed. 775–792. Without giving all the details they embrace, these findings may be summarized as follows:

I. The railroad property of each of the three companies constitutes a single system. On June 30, 1906, the Northern Pacific Railway Company (a Wisconsin corporation) operated 7,695 miles of track, of which 1,625 miles were in Minnesota. The Great Northern Railway Company (a Minnesota corporation) at the same time operated 8,528 miles of track, of which ·2,779 miles were in Minnesota. Their lines extend westerly from Superior, Wisconsin, and Duluth, Minnesota, and from St. Paul and Minneapolis, through the states of Minnesota, North Dakota, Montana, Idaho, Washington, and Oregon, to the Pacific coast. The Minneapolis & St. Louis Railroad Company (also a Minnesota corporation) operated 1,028 miles of track running from St. Paul and Minneapolis westerly and southerly to points in South Dakota and Iowa. In the case of each company, the movement of interstate and local traffic takes place at the same time, on the same rails, with the same employees, and largely by means of the same trains and cars. There has never been a separation, and it is impracticable, in the exercise of fair economy, to make a separation, between the interstate and intrastate business in the case either of freight or of passengers. By far the larger part of the traffic is interstate. In the year 1906 the freight business of the Northern Pacific Company, local to Minnesota, was 2.67 per cent of its entire freight business, and 12.33 per cent of its freight business touching the state, and its passenger business local to the state was 5.79 per cent of its entire passenger business, and 67.21 per cent of its passenger business touching the state.

The conditions attending the transportation of passengers and freight are substantially the same for like distances within those portions of the states of Wisconsin, Minnesota, North Dakota, and South Dakota reached by the lines of these companies, whether the transportation is interstate or wholly intrastate. Prior to the acts and orders in question, the companies had maintained rates which were relatively fair, and not discriminatory as between interstate and intrastate business; and it is concluded that any substantial change in the basis of rates thus established, due only to the fact that the transportation was interstate or was local to a state, and any substantial difference in rates as between the two sorts of traffic, would constitute unjust discrimination in fact.

II. The state line of Minnesota on the east and west runs between cities which are in close proximity. Superior, Wisconsin, and Duluth, Minnesota, are side by side at the extremity of Lake Superior. Opposite one another, on the western boundary of the state, lie Grand Forks, North Dakota, and East Grand Forks, Minnesota; Fargo, North Dakota, and Moorhead, Minnesota; and Wahpeton, North Dakota, and Breckenridge, Minnesota. The cities in each pair ship and receive, to and from the same localities, the same kinds of freight. The railroad companies have always put each on a parity with the other in the matter of rates, and if there were a substantial difference it would cause serious injury to the commerce of the city having the higher rate. If the Northern Pacific Company failed to maintain as low rates on traffic in and out of Superior as on that to and from Duluth, its power to transact interstate business between Superior and points in Minnesota would be seriously impaired and the value of its property in Superior would be depreciated.

The maximum class rates fixed by the order of September 6, 1906, were from 20 per cent to 25 per cent lower than those theretofore maintained by the Northern Pacific and Great Northern Companies for transportation in Wisconsin, Minnesota, and North Dakota, whether such transportation was local to one of these states or was interstate between any two of them. When the Northern Pacific Company, pursuant to this order, installed the new intrastate rates, it reduced its interstate rates between Superior and points in Minnesota to an exact parity with its rates from Duluth. Reduction was also made in the rates between both Duluth and Superior and the above-mentioned points on the western boundary, so as to put the border cities in North Dakota on an equal basis with the neighboring cities in Minnesota. This reduction was substantial; and, had it not been made, the places adjoining the boundary, but outside the state, could not have competed with those within. Although the Northern Pacific Company thereby suffered a substantial loss in revenue from its interstate business, it had the choice of submitting to that loss or suffering substantial destruction of its interstate commerce to these border localities in articles covered by the orders. At the same time, the Great Northern Company made similar reductions, although, in its case, the transportation between Duluth and points in Minnesota was interstate, — its line passing through Wisconsin. The reason for these reductions was to preserve the relation in rates from Duluth which had always existed between localities on the Great Northern line and those similarly situated on the line of the Northern Pacific, and to meet the reduced rates on the latter.

III. Moorhead, Minnesota, Fargo and Bismarck, North Dakota, Billings and Butte, Montana, are so-called jobbing centers. Rates had always been accorded to them by the Northern Pacific Company which would allow them to compete with their nearest neighbors and with St. Paul, Minneapolis, and Duluth. The order of September 6, 1906, as supplemented by that of May 3, 1907, substantially reduced carload rates from the eastern terminals to Moorhead. This reduction would have given Moorhead an advantage in territory accessible to its jobbing industry not

only as against Fargo, unless carload rates to Fargo were similarly reduced, but also as against Duluth, St. Paul, and Minneapolis unless less-than-carload rates from these places to points
accessible to Moorhead, which included a considerable territory
in North Dakota, were proportionately reduced. If Fargo were
protected as against Moorhead, it would have an advantage over
Bismarck in territory common to them both, and an advantage
over the eastern terminals in territory common to them and to
Fargo, unless carload rates from the eastern terminals to Bismarck and less-than-carload rates from those terminals to the
territory accessible to Fargo were correspondingly reduced; and
so on from distributing point to distributing point.

IV. Every rate comprehends two terminal charges, the initial
and the final, and a haulage charge. It is declared to be a cardinal principle of rate-making that a rate for a longer distance
should be proportionately smaller than one for a shorter distance;
for even if the haulage charge in the former case were the same
per mile, the rate per ton per mile should be less for the longer
haul, as the terminal charges would be spread over a greater
distance. A comparison disclosed that the rates established by
the order of September 6, 1906, and maintained by the Northern
Pacific Company between St. Paul and Moorhead, were in general substantially less than the proportion of the interstate rates
maintained by the company to various points in North Dakota
and Montana, based on the mileage in Minnesota as compared
to that of the entire haul. Maintaining such a relation of rates
involves, it is found, substantial and unjust discrimination in
fact against the interstate localities.

V. After the installation by the Great Northern and Northern
Pacific Companies of the rates prescribed by the order of September 6, 1906, it appeared that the sum of the local rates from St.
Paul to Moorhead and from Moorhead to many points in North
Dakota was less than the interstate rates theretofore maintained
from St. Paul to these points. Both companies thereupon established rates from St. Paul to the North Dakota points as a rule no
greater than the sum of the locals on Moorhead, but substantially
lower in general than the interstate rates in force when the order

took effect. Maintaining interstate rates from St. Paul to North Dakota localities substantially greater than the sum of the locals based on the state line would have caused unjust discrimination in fact. The actual reason for the reduction in the interstate rates was to prevent transhipment at Moorhead in order to take advantage of the lower sum of the locals, and to retain on its line traffic which might reach Moorhead over other lines by reason of competition, and, as to less-than-carload lots, to enable jobbers in the Twin Cities and Duluth to compete with those in Moorhead and Fargo in territory which otherwise the latter would have exclusively occupied by reason of their closer proximity.

VI. It is further held to be one of the fundamental dogmas of rate-making that the haulage charge per mile should not increase with increasing distance if the conditions be the same. Under the progressive decrease in the haulage charge within the state, provided by the order of September 6, 1906, 100 pounds of merchandise transported by the Northern Pacific from St. Paul to Moorhead, 248 miles, would have been hauled for 48 miles, at the rate of .98 cents per 10 miles, when Moorhead is reached. If the same haulage charge of .98 cents per 10 miles were applied for the remaining distance to Spokane, 1510 miles from St. Paul (which is said to be taken as a fair example merely to illustrate the principle), it would produce a rate from St. Paul to Spokane on first-class merchandise of $1.79 per cwt. The Interstate Commerce Commission in the Spokane rate case fixed the reasonable rate on first-class merchandise from St. Paul to Spokane of $2.50 per cwt. Maintaining this rate and the state schedule in Minnesota at the same time necessarily involves the raising of the per mile haulage charge after the Minnesota state line has been crossed, or the charge of a higher rate within Minnesota for its mileage proportion of long-haul interstate business than for business local to the state which is carried under the same conditions, and hence is found to result in unjust discrimination in fact against localities west of the Minnesota line.

VII. For more than twenty-five years the Northern Pacific Company has maintained an equal basis of rates on merchandise between its eastern and western terminals, respectively, and

Butte, Montana, and between its eastern and western terminals, respectively, and localities intermediate between them and Butte. Other railroads reaching Butte have, during the same time, maintained like rates to Butte from Sioux City, Omaha, St. Joseph and Kansas City on the east, and from San Francisco, Sacramento, and Los Angeles on the west. Butte has been as the hub of a wheel with spokes representing equal rates to these various cities. Industries, it is said, have been born and have grown in reliance upon this parity of rates. Intermediate points have had rates fixed in proportion to the Butte rates. Competition of markets and of carriers has brought this about. The Northern Pacific Company cannot maintain the state rates between its eastern terminals and Moorhead, and at the same time its interstate rates from its eastern terminals to Butte, without substantial discrimination in fact against Butte or localities intermediate between its eastern terminals and Butte. If it lowers its rates from its eastern terminals to Butte and intermediate stations to such an extent as to obviate this discrimination, it must, to preserve the relation which has always existed, lower to a like extent its rates from its western terminals to Butte and intermediate stations. Consequently, it is found that if the Northern Pacific Company maintains the commission-made rates between its eastern terminals and Moorhead, it must either substantially discriminate in fact, or destroy the general relation of rates which has existed for many years in the territory between the Missouri river and the Pacific coast.

VIII. Prior to the taking effect of the order of September 6, 1906, the Great Northern and Northern Pacific Companies had established joint through rates in connection with other carriers from all localities east or south of Minnesota to all points in Minnesota west of St. Paul and Minneapolis. After the rates prescribed by this order were installed, the sum of the locals on St. Paul from all localities south and east of Minnesota to points in Minnesota west of St. Paul and Minneapolis was substantially less than the then-existing interstate rates for the through haul to such western points. To avoid the resulting discrimination in favor of St. Paul, the companies withdrew the existing interstate rates, and established a new tariff no higher than the sum of the locals on St. Paul.

IX. Further illustrations are given of inequalities resulting from the reduced Minnesota rates as compared with rates for like transportation under similar conditions into adjoining states; as, for example, from Moorhead easterly to Minnesota points and westerly into North Dakota, and also of the effects produced in the application of the state rates by reason of the difference in the distances from St. Paul at which the state line is reached on similar hauls over different lines. As the schedule of September 6, 1906, prescribes a fixed relation between rates for different distances and different classes, the conclusion is that if the rule must be adhered to in Minnesota, it cannot be departed from substantially because of the intervention of a state line at one distance or another without involving unjust discrimination in fact.

It is found further that while, after the order of September 6, 1906, became effective, both the Great Northern and the Northern Pacific Companies reduced certain interstate rates, as already mentioned, the reduction was not to such extent as to remedy the discrimination resulting from the fact that in most cases the general basis of rates within Minnesota was substantially lower than that maintained in North Dakota or upon traffic crossing the state line.

X. The similarity in the conditions of interstate and intrastate transportation is found also with respect to the commodities for which rates were prescribed by the act of April 18, 1907 (chap. 232). The main lines and branches of the Northern Pacific and Great Northern Companies within Minnesota and North Dakota, with the exception of certain limited tracts, lie within grain fields, and grain is shipped in substantial quantities from nearly all stations in these fields to Duluth, Minneapolis, and Superior. Shipments of coal originate at the head of the Lakes, — that is, at Duluth or Superior, — and find their destination at all localities served by the companies in Minnesota and eastern North Dakota. Shipments of lumber originate at Duluth, Cloquet, Little Falls, and other places in Minnesota, and are destined to points throughout Minnesota and North Dakota. Shipments of live stock are made in Minnesota, South Dakota, and eastern Montana and go to South St. Paul or Chicago. So far as the conditions of transportation are concerned, it matters not, as to commodities moving eastwardly, whether the shipment is made in Montana, North Dakota, or Minnesota, or the transportation ends in Minnesota or in Wisconsin; and, as to commodities moving westwardly, whether the shipments are from Minnesota points or from Superior, or whether they find their destination in Minnesota or in North Dakota. The conclusion is that to maintain the commodity rates for transportation wholly within Minnesota simultaneously with the interstate rates now in force would involve unjust discrimination and would seriously impair the interstate business of the companies, to avoid which it would be necessary to reduce the basis of the interstate rates to a substantial parity with that prescribed by the state law. It is also stated that if the rates fixed by chapter 232 of the Laws of 1907 should become effective, the rate on shipments of wheat, with milling-in-transit privileges, from points in Minnesota *via* Minneapolis to Chicago, would be automatically reduced, and that unless all interstate rates between Minnesota points and Chicago *via* interior mill towns with similar privileges should be correspondingly reduced, Minneapolis would have a substantial advantage over such towns in its interstate rates.

XI. Prior to the act of 1907, fixing the rate of 2 cents a mile, the general basis of rates for passengers (of twelve years of age or over) between any two points on the Northern Pacific system had been for some years 3 cents a mile. After the new state rate had been installed, the sum of the locals between Moorhead and other Minnesota points and Moorhead and points westerly thereof was less than the then-existing through interstate rates. The passenger fare act took effect May 1, 1907, and in the first month thereafter the revenue for passengers on the Northern Pacific line between Moorhead and other Minnesota points increased 647 per cent over that of the corresponding month of the preceding year, while, eliminating Moorhead business, the revenue for passenger business within the state decreased 2 per cent. In

June, 1907, the second month, there were sold by the Northern Pacific Company, 4,037 tickets between St. Paul or Minneapolis, on the one hand, and Moorhead or East Grand Forks on the other, as compared with only 172 such tickets in the corresponding month of the year before; and in June, 1907, there were sold only 173 tickets between St. Paul or Minneapolis, and Grand Forks and Fargo, as compared with 984 such tickets in the corresponding month of the previous year. In May and June, 1906, only one cash full fare was collected on a train from Moorhead to St. Paul or Minneapolis. In those months in 1907 there were 1,168 cash full fares and 82 cash half fares so collected. Hence, it is said, the necessary, immediate, and direct effect of the law was to deprive the Northern Pacific Company of a substantial amount of its interstate passenger business through Moorhead.

Notwithstanding the facility with which interstate passengers could avoid the discrimination against them by making two contracts with the company, it is found that discrimination in fact still existed against the interstate passenger who, applying for a through ticket, did not know that the sum of the locals on Moorhead was less than the through rate, against the passenger with a trunk which he could not check through unless on a through ticket, and against a passenger who was compelled to use a sleeping car. The Northern Pacific Company shortly remedied this discrimination by reducing all its interstate fares for passenger transportation through Moorhead to an amount no greater than the sum of the locals over Moorhead. Before this reduction Wisconsin had fixed the maximum passenger fare at 2 cents a mile, and North Dakota at $2\frac{1}{2}$ cents a mile. The rates thereafter established by the Northern Pacific Company between St. Paul, for example, and points in North Dakota and beyond, and by the Northern Pacific Company jointly with other companies for transportation between points easterly of Minnesota and points on the line of the Northern Pacific, were in general less than the previous rates by approximately 1 cent per mile for the mileage in Wisconsin and Minnesota, and by $\frac{1}{2}$ cent per mile for the mileage in North Dakota. It is concluded that these reductions were compelled to avoid unjust discrimination, and in order that the companies might transact interstate passenger business freely and without impairment of volume.

There are added various hypothetical calculations of the losses which would have been sustained if the basis prescribed by the state acts and orders had been applied to the interstate business and to local business in other states. We shall have occasion later to refer to the actual results of the business of the railroad companies during the time that the rates fixed by the acts and orders (with the exception of the commodity rates) were in force, and to the effect upon revenue which the adoption of the commodity rates would have had.

The foregoing findings, as stated by the master, were made "without regard to the justness or otherwise in fact of the interstate rates so affected by such local rates." The determination of the reasonableness of the interstate rates was not deemed to be within the province of the court.

The appellants do not concede the correctness of the findings in their full scope, and insist upon qualifications. They deny that the evidence justified the finding that the companies had maintained " an equable, that is, relatively fair, basis of rates " prior to the acts and orders in question. The general or comprehensive system of interdependent and fairly related rates, each so equitably adjusted to the others that any local change must of necessity throw the whole out of balance, is declared to exist only in imagination, — to be a fiction constructed in disregard of the facts of rate-making, and without attention to the inconsistencies shown by the schedules which had been in force. The actual reductions in interstate rates, which followed upon the adoption of the state tariffs, were made, it is urged, in rates voluntarily established by the companies themselves which had not been declared to be reasonable by competent authority, and in any case furnish no standard by which the validity of the action of the state, in the control of its internal affairs, should be judged. The appellants say that the local rates in Minnesota were incongruous and unreasonable; that frequent changes in the interest of favored shippers had been made through the filing of temporary intrastate tariffs until the practice was stopped by a statute of 1905 (chap. 176), forbidding changes without the consent of the commission; that with respect to grain and live stock, the principal agricultural products of the state, the companies maintained an "inharmonious jumble of arbitrary rates"; and that the acts and orders in question were designed to correct inequalities in the intrastate tariffs, and to prescribe charges which, upon thorough investigation and after public hearings in which the companies participated, were found to be reasonable and were brought into suitable relation with each other by means of a scientific plan. And it is denied that unjust discrimination as against localities without the state can be predicated of the establishment of reasonable state rates.

It is also insisted that the prescribed intrastate freight rates were not in general lower than the existing interstate rates. Reference is made to the long-distance traffic, which, it is said, was moved within the state on proportionals of long-haul rates which were much below the local rates fixed by the state. It is pointed out that the master found, in passing upon the question whether the rates were confiscatory, that the gross revenue which was derived from the interstate freight business during the fiscal year ending June 30, 1908 (when all the rates in question were in force save the commodity rates), was greater per ton-mile than that derived in the same period from the interstate business within the state, being in the case of the Northern Pacific Company in the ratio of 1.4387 to 1, and in that of the Great Northern Company of 2.02894 to 1. The appellants also contest the validity of the argument based on a hypothetical extension beyond the state line of the "rate of progression" for additional distance which had been prescribed by the state solely with reference to internal traffic, and they submit illustrations of incongruities which they contend would be shown by a similar extension of the rate of progression disclosed by the former intrastate tariffs of the companies. Again, it is urged that the extent of the reductions attributable to the 2-cent fare law may not be estimated properly by a comparison with the former maximum rate of 3 cents a mile. Various rates had been in force less than the maximum allowed. For the six years prior to the 2-cent fare law the average rate per passenger per mile for intrastate transportation in Minnesota, on the Northern Pacific line, had ranged from 2.299 cents in 1901 to 2.435 cents in 1905, 2.406 cents in 1906, and 2.197 cents in 1907;[1] and during the same time the average rate per passenger per mile for interstate transportation in Minnesota varied from 2.075 cents in 1901, 2.027 cents in 1905, 1.949 cents in 1906, and 1.981 cents in 1907.[1] In the fiscal year ending June 30, 1908, with the 2-cent fare law in force the average rate per passenger per mile in Minnesota was 1.930 cents for intrastate and 1.928 cents for interstate carriage.

It is conceded, however, that the schedules fixed for intrastate transportation "necessarily disturbed the equilibrium theretofore existing between the rates on the two classes of business" (state and interstate) "on the boundary lines." This applies to the rates to and from the cities situated on opposite sides of the Red River of the North, the boundary between Minnesota and North Dakota, and to and from Duluth and Superior on the eastern boundary. The reduction of the state rates brought them below the level of the interstate rates in those instances in which formerly both had been maintained on a parity. So, also, whatever may be said as to the nonexistence of a general or comprehensive system of equitably adjusted rates, it is clear that there are competitive areas crossed by the state line of Minnesota, and that the state's requirements altered the existing relation between state and interstate rates as to places within these zones of competition, and not merely as to the cities on the boundary of the state.

The situation is not peculiar to Minnesota. The same question has been presented by the appeals, now before the court, which involve the validity of intrastate tariffs fixed by Missouri, Arkansas, Kentucky, and Oregon. Differences in particular facts appear, but they cannot be regarded as controlling. A scheme of state rates framed to avoid discrimination between localities within the state, and to provide an harmonious system for intrastate transportation throughout the state, naturally would embrace those places within the state which are on or near the state's

---

[1] The 2-cent fare law was in force for two months of the fiscal year ending June 30, 1907.

boundaries; and when these are included in a general reduction
of intrastate rates, there is, of course, a change in the relation
of rates as theretofore existing to points adjacent to, but across,
the state line. Kansas City, Kansas, and Kansas City, Missouri;
East St. Louis, Illinois, and St. Louis, Missouri; Omaha, Nebraska,
and Council Bluffs, Iowa; Cincinnati, Ohio, and Covington and
Newport, Kentucky; and many other places throughout the country which might be mentioned, present substantially the same
conditions as those here appearing with respect to localities on
the boundaries of Minnesota. It is also a matter of common
knowledge that competition takes but little account of state
lines, and in every part of the land competitive districts embrace
points in different states.

With appreciation of the gravity of the controversy, the railroad commissioners of eight states [1] have filed their brief as
amici curiæ, in support of the appeals, stating that, if the doctrine of the court below were accepted, the regulation by the
states of rates for intrastate transportation would be practically
destroyed. They say that "there is practically no movement of
traffic between two towns within a state that does not come into
competition with some interstate haul," and that "if the disturbance of the existing relation between competitive state and
interstate rates is the correct criterion, no reduction can be made
in state rates without interfering with interstate commerce."
The governors of three states, pursuant to a resolution of a conference of the governors of all the states, have also presented,
by leave of the court, their argument in defense of the position
taken by Minnesota. They do not seek "to belittle the effect
of the action of Minnesota on the business between the places"
named in the findings, but they are convinced that if the principle announced by the circuit court is upheld, it can be made to
apply by a showing of similar facts in virtually every state.
Insisting that, under their reserved power, "the right of the
states to regulate their own commerce is as clear and broad as
that of Congress to regulate interstate commerce," they assail

[1] Nebraska, Iowa, Kansas, South Dakota, North Dakota, Oklahoma, Missouri,
and Texas.

the decision below, not upon the ground that it incorrectly sets forth conditions in Minnesota and adjoining states, but for what they consider to be " its plain disregard of the provisions of the Federal Constitution, which establish the relations between the nation and the states." " The operation of these provisions," they maintain, " was not made to depend on geography or convenience or competition. They cannot apply in one state and not in another, according to circumstances as they may be found by the courts, because they are vital principles which constitute the very structure of our dual form of government."

The controversy thus arises from opposing conceptions of the fundamental law, and of the scope and effect of Federal legislation, rather than from differences with respect to the salient facts.

For the purpose of the present inquiry, the rates fixed by the state must be assumed to be reasonable rates so far as intrastate traffic is concerned; that is, they must be rates which the state in the exercise of its legislative judgment, could constitutionally fix for intrastate transportation separately considered. If the state rates are not of this character, — a question to be dealt with later, — they cannot be sustained in any event; but, assuming them to be otherwise valid, the decree below, with respect to the present branch of the case, rests upon two grounds: (1) That the action of the state imposes a direct burden upon interstate commerce; and (2) that it is in conflict with the provisions of the act to regulate commerce.

These grounds are distinct. If a state enactment imposes a *direct burden* upon interstate commerce, it must fall regardless of Federal legislation. The point of such an objection is not that Congress has acted, but that the state has directly restrained that which, in the absence of Federal regulation, should be free. If the acts of Minnesota constitute a direct burden upon interstate commerce, they would be invalid without regard to the exercise of Federal authority touching the interstate rates said to be affected. On the other hand, if the state, in the absence of Federal legislation, would have had the power to prescribe the rates here assailed, the question remains whether its action is void as being repugnant to the statute which Congress has enacted.

Prior to the passage of the act to regulate commerce, carriers fixed their interstate rates free from the actual exertion of Federal control; and under that act, as it stood until the amendment of June 29, 1906 [34 Stat. at L. 584, chap. 3591, U. S. Comp. Stat. Supp. 1911, p. 1288], the Interstate Commerce Commission had no power to prescribe interstate rates. *Interstate Commerce Commission* v. *Cincinnati, N. O. & T. P. R. Co.* 167 U. S. 479, 511, 42 L. ed. 243, 257, 17 Sup. Ct. Rep. 896.[1] The states, however, had long exercised the power to establish maximum rates for intrastate transportation. Was this power, apart from Federal action, subject to the limitation that the state could not fix intrastate rates, reasonable as such, generally throughout the state, but only as to such places and in such circumstances that the interstate business of the carriers would not be thereby affected? That is, was the state debarred from fixing reasonable rates on traffic, wholly internal, as to all state points so situated that, as a practical consequence, the carriers would have to reduce the rates they had made to competing points without the state, in order to maintain the volume of their interstate business, or to continue the parity of rates, or the relation between rates as it had previously existed? Was the state, in prescribing a general tariff of reasonable intrastate rates otherwise within its authority bound not to go below a minimum standard established by the interstate rates made by the carriers within competitive districts? If the state power, independently of Federal legislation, is thus limited, the inquiry need proceed no further. Otherwise it must be determined whether Congress has so acted as to create such a restriction upon the state authority theretofore existing.

(1) The general principles governing the exercise of state authority when interstate commerce is affected are well established. The power of Congress to regulate commerce among the several states is supreme and plenary. It is "complete in itself, may be exercised to its utmost extent, and acknowledges no limitations, other than are prescribed in the Constitution." *Gibbons* v. *Ogden*, 9 Wheat. 1, 196, 6 L. ed. 23, 70. The conviction of its necessity sprang from the disastrous experiences under the

---

[1] P. 187, *supra*, and Ripley's Railroads: Rates and Regulation.

Confederation, when the states vied in discriminatory measures against each other. In order to end these evils, the grant in the Constitution conferred upon Congress an authority at all times adequate to secure the freedom of interstate commercial intercourse from state control, and to provide effective regulation of that intercourse as the national interest may demand. The words "among the several states" distinguish between the commerce which concerns more states than one, and that commerce which is confined within one state and does not affect other states. "The genius and character of the whole government," said Chief Justice Marshall, "seems to be, that its action is to be applied to all the external concerns of the nation, and to those internal concerns which affect the states generally; but not to those which are completely within a particular state, which do not affect other states, and with which it is not necessary to interfere, for the purpose of executing some of the general powers of the government. The completely internal commerce of a state, then, may be considered as reserved for the state itself." *Id.* p. 195. This reservation to the states manifestly is only of that authority which is consistent with, and not opposed to, the grant to Congress. There is no room in our scheme of government for the assertion of state power in hostility to the authorized exercise of Federal power. The authority of Congress extends to every part of interstate commerce, and to every instrumentality or agency by which it is carried on; and the full control by Congress of the subjects committed to its regulation is not to be denied or thwarted by the commingling of interstate and intrastate operations. This is not to say that the nation may deal with the internal concerns of the state, as such, but that the execution by Congress of its constitutional power to regulate interstate commerce is not limited by the fact that intrastate transactions may have become so interwoven therewith that the effective government of the former incidentally controls the latter. This conclusion necessarily results from the supremacy of the national power within its appointed sphere. . . .

The grant in the Constitution of its own force, that is, without action by Congress, established the essential immunity of interstate commercial intercourse from the direct control of the states with respect to those subjects embraced within the grant which are of such a nature as to demand that, if regulated at all, their regulation should be prescribed by a single authority. It has repeatedly been declared by this court that as to those subjects which require a general system or uniformity of regulation, the power of Congress is exclusive. In other matters, admitting of diversity of treatment according to the special requirements of local conditions, the states may act within their respective jurisdictions until Congress sees fit to act; and, when Congress does act, the exercise of its authority overrides all conflicting state legislation. . . .

The principle which determines this classification underlies the doctrine that the states cannot, under any guise, impose direct burdens upon interstate commerce. For this is but to hold that the states are not permitted directly to regulate or restrain that which, from its nature, should be under the control of the one authority, and be free from restriction, save as it is governed in the manner that the national legislature constitutionally ordains.

Thus, the states cannot tax interstate commerce, either by laying the tax upon the business which constitutes such commerce or the privilege of engaging in it, or upon the receipts, as such, derived from it. . . .

They have no power to prohibit interstate trade in legitimate articles of commerce . . . or to discriminate against the products of other states . . . or to exclude from the limits of the state corporations or others engaged in interstate commerce, or to fetter by conditions their right to carry it on . . . or to prescribe the rates to be charged for transportation from one state to another, or to subject the operations of carriers in the course of such transportation to requirements that are unreasonable or pass beyond the bounds of suitable local protection. . . .

But within these limitations there necessarily remains to the states until Congress acts, a wide range for the permissible exercise of power appropriate to their territorial jurisdiction although interstate commerce may be affected. It extends to those matters of a local nature as to which it is impossible to derive from the constitutional grant an intention that they should go uncontrolled pending Federal intervention. Thus, there are certain subjects having the most obvious and direct relation to interstate commerce, which nevertheless, with the acquiescence of Congress, have been controlled by state legislation from the foundation of the government because of the necessity that they should not remain unregulated, and that their regulation should be adapted to varying local exigencies; hence, the absence of regulation by Congress in such matters has not imported that there should be no restriction, but rather that the states should continue to supply the needed rules until Congress should decide to supersede them. Further, it is competent for a state to govern its internal commerce, to provide local improvements, to create and regulate local facilities, to adopt protective measures of a reasonable character in the interest of the health, safety, morals, and welfare of its people, although interstate commerce may incidentally or indirectly be involved. Our system of government is a practical adjustment by which the national authority as conferred by the Constitution is maintained in its full scope without unnecessary loss of local efficiency. Where the subject is peculiarly one of local concern, and from its nature belongs to the class with which the state appropriately deals in making reasonable provision for local needs, it cannot be regarded as left to the unrestrained will of individuals because Congress has not acted, although it may have such a relation to interstate commerce as to be within the reach of the Federal power. In such case, Congress must be the judge of the necessity of Federal action. Its paramount authority always enables it to intervene at its discretion for the complete and effective government of that which has been committed to its care, and, for this purpose and to this extent, in response to a conviction of national need, to displace local laws by substituting laws of its own. The successful working of our constitutional system has thus been made possible.

The leading illustrations may be noted. Immediately upon the adoption of the Constitution, Congress recognized the propriety of local action with respect to pilotage, in view of the local necessities of navigation. . . . It was sixty years before provision for Federal license of pilots was made (act of August 30, 1852, chap. 106, 10 Stat. at L. 61), and even then port pilots were not included. . . .

A state is entitled to protect its coasts, to improve its harbors, bays, and streams, and to construct dams and bridges across navigable rivers within its limits, unless there is conflict with some act of Congress. Plainly, in the case of dams and bridges, interference with the accustomed right of navigation may result. But this exercise of the important power to provide local improvements has not been regarded as constituting such a direct burden upon intercourse or interchange of traffic as to be repugnant to the Federal authority in its dormant state. . . .

While the state may not impose a duty of tonnage . . . it may regulate wharfage charges and exact tolls for the use of artificial facilities provided under its authority. The subject is one under state control, where Congress has not acted, although the payment is required of those engaged in interstate or foreign commerce. . . .

Quarantine regulations are essential measures of protection which the states are free to adopt when they do not come into conflict with Federal action. In view of the need of conforming such measures to local conditions, Congress from the beginning has been content to leave the matter for the most part, notwithstanding its vast importance, to the states, and has repeatedly acquiesced in the enforcement of state laws. . . .

State inspection laws and statutes designed to safeguard the inhabitants of a state from fraud and imposition are valid when reasonable in their requirements, and not in conflict with Federal rules, although they may affect interstate commerce in their relation to articles prepared for export, or by including incidentally those brought into the state and held for sale in the original imported packages. . . .

*　　*　　*　　*　　*　　*　　*　　*

. . . It has also been held that the state has the power to forbid the consolidation of state railroad corporations with competing lines although both may be interstate carriers, and the prohibition may have a far-reaching effect upon interstate commerce. . . .

Again, it is manifest that when the legislation of the state is limited to internal commerce to such degree that it does not include even incidentally the subjects of interstate commerce, it is not rendered invalid because it may affect the latter commerce indirectly. In the intimacy of commercial relations, much that is done in the superintendence of local matters may have an indirect bearing upon interstate commerce. The development of local resources and the extension of local facilities may have a very important effect upon communities less favored, and to an appreciable degree alter the course of trade. The freedom of local trade may stimulate interstate commerce, while restrictive measures within the police power of the state, enacted exclusively with respect to internal business, as distinguished from interstate traffic, may in their reflex or indirect influence diminish the latter and reduce the volume of articles transported into or out of the state. . . .

Within the state power, then, in the words of Chief Justice Marshall, is

that immense mass of legislation which embraces everything within the territory of a state, not surrendered to the general government; all which can be most advantageously exercised by the states themselves. Inspection laws, quarantine laws, health laws of every description, as well as laws for regulating the internal commerce of a state, and those which respect turnpike roads, ferries, etc., are component parts of this mass. No direct general power over these objects is granted to Congress: and, consequently, they remain subject to state legislation. If the legislative power of the Union can reach them, it must be for national purposes, or is clearly incidental to some power which is expressly given. *Gibbons* v. *Ogden,* 9 Wheat. 203, 204, 6 L. ed. 71, 72.

And whenever, as to such matters, under these established principles, Congress may be entitled to act, by virtue of its power to secure the complete government of interstate commerce, the state power nevertheless continues until Congress does act and by its valid interposition limits the exercise of the local authority.

(2) These principles apply to the authority of the state to prescribe reasonable maximum rates for intrastate transportation.

State regulation of railroad rates began with railroad transportation. The railroads were chartered by the states, and from the outset, in many charters, maximum rates for freight or passengers, or both, were prescribed. Frequently — and this became the more general practice — the board of directors was permitted to fix charges in its discretion, — an authority which, in numerous instances, was made subject to a limitation upon the amount of net earnings. In several states maximum rates were also established, or the power to alter rates was expressly reserved, by general laws. In 1853, the state of New York fixed the maximum fare for way passengers on the railroads forming the line of the New York Central at 2 cents a mile (Laws of 1853, chap. 76, § 7), and this rate extending to Buffalo and Suspension Bridge, on the boundary of the state, has continued to the present day (Consol. Laws [N. Y.] chap. 49, § 57). As a rule the restrictions imposed by the early legislation were far from onerous, but they are significant in the assertion of the right of control. More potent than these provisions, in the actual effect upon railroad tariffs, was the state canal. It is a matter of common knowledge that the traffic on the trunk lines from the Atlantic seaboard to the West was developed in competition with the Erie canal, built, maintained, and regulated by the state of New York to promote its commerce.

The authority of the state to limit by legislation the charges of common carriers within its borders was not confined to the power to impose limitations in connection with grants of corporate privileges. In view of the nature of their business, they were held subject to legislative control as to the amount of their charges unless they were protected by their contract with the state. . . . The question was presented by acts of the legislatures of Illinois, Iowa, Wisconsin, and Minnesota, passed in the years 1871 and 1874, in response to a general movement for a reduction of rates. The section of the country in which the demand arose was to a large degree homogeneous and one in which the flow of commerce was only slightly concerned with state lines. But resort was had to the states for relief. In the Munn Case, the court had before it the statute of Illinois governing the grain warehouses in Chicago. Through these elevators, located with the river harbor on the one side and the railway tracks on the other, it was necessary, according to the course of trade, for the product of seven or eight states of the West to pass on its way to the states on the Atlantic coast. In addition to the denial of any legislative authority to limit charges it was urged that the act was repugnant to the exclusive power of Congress to regulate interstate commerce. The court answered that the business was carried on exclusively within the limits of the state of Illinois, that its regulation was a thing of domestic concern, and that "certainly, until Congress acts in reference to their interstate relations, the state may exercise all the powers of government over them, even though in so doing it may indirectly operate upon commerce outside its immediate jurisdiction." In the decision of the railroad cases, above cited, the same opinion was expressed. The language of the court, however, went further than to sustain the state law with respect to rates for purely intrastate carriage. Thus, the act of Wisconsin covered traffic which started within the state and was destined to points outside, and this was treated as being within the state power (*Peik* v. *Chicago & N. W. R. Co.* 94 U. S. 164, 177, 178, 24 L. ed. 97–99), a view which was later repudiated (*Wabash, St. L. & P. R. Co.* v. *Illinois*, 118 U. S. 557, 30 L. ed. 244, 1 Inters. Com. Rep. 31, 7 Sup. Ct. Rep. 4).

It became a frequent practice for the states to create commissions, as agencies of state supervision and regulation, and in many instances the rate-making power was conferred upon these bodies. A summary of such legislation is given in *Interstate Commerce Commission* v. *Cincinnati N. O. & T. P. R. Co.* 167 U. S. 479, 495, 496, 42 L. ed. 243, 251, 252, 17 Sup. Ct. Rep. 896. One of these state laws, that of Mississippi, passed in 1884, came under review in *Stone* v. *Farmers' Loan & Trust Co.* 116 U. S. 307, 29 L. ed. 636, 6 Sup. Ct. Rep. 334, 388, 1191. The suit was brought to enjoin the railroad commission from enforcing the statute against the Mobile & Ohio Railroad Company. It had been incorporated in the states of Alabama, Mississippi, Tennessee, and Kentucky, for the purpose of constructing a railroad from Mobile to some point near the mouth of the Ohio river, where it would connect with another railroad, thus forming a continuous line of interstate communication between the Gulf of Mexico and the Great Lakes. The commission as yet had not acted. Sustaining the state power to fix rates upon the traffic wholly internal, the court directed the dismissal of the bill. The state, said the court, "may beyond all question, by the settled rule of decision in this court, regulate freights and fares for business done exclusively within the state, and it would seem to be a matter of domestic concern to prevent the company from discriminating against persons and places in Mississippi." In the same case, it was declared that the power of regulation was not a power to confiscate ; and that under pretense of regulating fares and freights, the states could not " require a railroad corporation to carry persons or property without reward," or do that which in law amounted " to a taking of private property for public use without just compensation, or without due process of law." *Id.* p. 331.

In *Wabash St. L. & P. R. Co.* v. *Illinois, supra,* it was finally determined that the authority of the state did not extend to the regulation of charges for interstate transportation. There the state statute was aimed at discrimination. It was said to have been violated by the railroad company in the case of shipments from points within Illinois to the city of New York. The state court had construed the statute to be binding as to that part of the interstate haul which was within the state, although inoperative beyond the boundary. So applied, this court held the act to be invalid.

But no doubt was entertained of the state's authority to regulate rates for transportation that was wholly intrastate. And, in illustrating the extent of state power (118 U. S. p. 564), the court selected transportation across the state from Cairo to Chicago and from Chicago to Alton, all boundary points constituting important centers of commerce — the one on Lake Michigan, and the others at the confluence of the Mississippi and Ohio rivers, and of the Mississippi and Missouri rivers, respectively. After reviewing decisions holding state laws to be ineffective which imposed a direct burden upon interstate commerce . . . the court emphasized the distinction with respect to the operation of the statute upon domestic transactions, saying:

Of the justice or propriety of the principle which lies at the foundation of the Illinois statute it is not the province of this court to speak. As restricted to a transportation which begins and ends within the limits of the state, it may be very just and equitable, and it certainly is the province of the state legislature to determine that question. *Id.* p. 577.

The doctrine was thus fully established that the state could not prescribe interstate rates, but could fix reasonable intrastate rates throughout its territory. The extension of railroad facilities has been accompanied at every step by the assertion of this authority on the part of the states and its invariable recognition by this court. It has never been doubted that the state could, if it saw fit, build its own highways, canals and railroads. *Baltimore & O. R. Co.* v. *Maryland*, 21 Wall. 456, 470, 471, 22 L. ed. 678, 683, 684. It could build railroads traversing the entire state, and thus join its border cities and commercial centers by new highways of internal intercourse, to be always available upon reasonable terms. Such provision for local traffic might indeed alter relative advantages in competition, and, by virtue of economic forces, those engaged in interstate trade and transportation might find it necessary to make readjustments extending from market to market through a wide sphere of influence; but such action of the state would not for that reason be regarded as creating a direct restraint upon interstate commerce, and as thus transcending the state power. Similarly, the authority of the state to prescribe what shall be reasonable charges of common carriers for interstate transportation, unless it be limited by the exertion of the constitutional power of Congress, is state-wide. As a power appropriate to the territorial jurisdiction of the state, it is not confined to a part of the state, but extends throughout the state, — to its cities adjacent to its boundaries as well as to those in the interior of the state. To say that this power exists, but that it may be exercised only in prescribing rates that are on an equal or higher basis than those that are fixed by the carrier for interstate transportation, is to maintain the power in name while denying it in fact. It is to assert that the exercise of the legislative judgment in determining what shall be the carrier's charge for the intrastate service is itself subject to the carrier's will. But this state-wide authority controls the carrier, and is not controlled by it; and the idea that the power of the state to fix reasonable rates for its internal traffic is limited by the mere action of the carrier in laying an interstate rate to places across the state's border is foreign to our jurisprudence.

If this authority of the state be restricted, it must be by virtue of the paramount power of Congress over interstate commerce and its instruments; and, in view of the nature of the subject, a limitation may not be implied because of a dormant Federal power; that is, one which has not been exerted, but can only be found in the actual exercise of Federal control in such measure as to exclude this action by the state which otherwise would clearly be within its province.

(3) When Congress, in the year 1887, enacted the act to regulate commerce (24 Stat. at L. 379, chap. 104, U. S. Comp. Stat. Supp. 1911, p. 1284), it was acquainted with the course of the development of railroad transportation and with the exercise by the states of the rate-making power. An elaborate report had been made to the Senate by a committee authorized to investigate the subject of railroad regulation, in which the nature and extent of state legislation, including the commission plan, were fully reviewed (Senate Report 46, submitted January 6, 1886, 49th Congress, 1st session). And it was the fact that beyond the bounds of state control there lay a vast field of unregulated activity in the conduct of interstate transportation which was found to be the chief cause of the demand for Federal action.

Congress carefully defined the scope of its regulation, and expressly provided that it was not to extend to purely intrastate traffic. In the 1st section of the act to regulate commerce there was inserted the following proviso:

Provided, however, That the provisions of this act shall not apply to the transportation of passengers or property, or to the receiving, delivering, storage, or handling of property, wholly within one state, and not shipped to or from a foreign country, from or to any state or territory as aforesaid.

When in the year 1906 (act of June 29, 1906, chap. 3591, 34 Stat. at L. 584, U. S. Comp. Stat. Supp. 1911, p. 1288), Congress amended the act so as to confer upon the Federal commission power to prescribe maximum interstate rates, the proviso in § 1 was reënacted. Again, in 1910, when the act was extended to embrace telegraph, telephone, and cable companies engaged in interstate business, the proviso was once more reenacted, with an additional clause so as to exclude intrastate messages from the operation of the statute. (Act of June 18, 1910, chap. 309, 36 Stat. at L. 545 [U. S. Comp. Stat. Supp. 1911, p. 1285].) The proviso in its present form reads:

> Provided, however, That the provisions of this act shall not apply to the transportation of passengers or property, or to the receiving, delivering, storage, or handling of property wholly within one state, and not shipped to or from a foreign country, from or to any state or territory as aforesaid, nor shall they apply to the transmission of messages by telephone, telegraph, or cable wholly within one state, and not transmitted to or from a foreign country, from or to any state or territory, as aforesaid.

There was thus excluded from the provisions of the act that transportation which was "wholly within one state," with the specified qualification where its subject was going to or coming from a foreign country.

It is urged, however, that the words of the proviso are susceptible of a construction which would permit the provisions of § 3 of the act, prohibiting carriers from giving an undue or unreasonable preference or advantage to any locality, to apply to unreasonable discrimination between localities in different states, as well when arising from an intrastate rate as compared with an interstate rate as when due to interstate rates exclusively. If it be assumed that the statute should be so construed (and it is not necessary now to decide the point), it would inevitably follow that the controlling principle governing the enforcement of the act should be applied to such cases as might thereby be brought within its purview; and the question whether the carrier, in such a case, was giving an undue or unreasonable preference or advantage to one locality as against another, or subjecting any locality to an undue or unreasonable prejudice or disadvantage, would be primarily for the investigation and determination of the Interstate Commerce Commission, and not for the courts. The dominating purpose of the statute was to secure conformity to the prescribed standards through the examination and appreciation of the complex facts of transportation by the body created for that purpose ; and, as this court has repeatedly held, it would be destructive of the system of regulation defined by the statute if the court, without the preliminary action of the Commission, were to undertake to pass upon the administrative questions which the statute has primarily confided to it. . . . In the present case there has been no finding by the Interstate Commerce Commission of unjust discrimination violative of the act ; and no action of that body is before us for review.

The question we have now before us, essentially, is whether, after the passage of the interstate commerce act, and its amendment, the state continued to possess the state-wide authority which it formerly enjoyed to prescribe reasonable rates for its exclusively internal traffic. That, as it plainly appears, was the nature of the action taken by Minnesota, and the attack, however phrased, upon the rates here involved as an interference with interstate commerce, is in substance a denial of that authority.

Having regard to the terms of the Federal statute, the familiar range of state action at the time it was enacted, the continued exercise of state authority in the same manner and to the same extent after its enactment, and the decisions of this court, recognizing and upholding this authority, we find no foundation for the proposition that the act to regulate commerce contemplated interference therewith.

Congress did not undertake to say that the intrastate rates of interstate carriers should be reasonable, or to invest its administrative agency with authority to determine their reasonableness. Neither by the original act nor by its amendment did Congress seek to establish a unified control over interstate and intrastate rates ; it did not set up a standard for interstate rates, or prescribe, or authorize the commission to prescribe, either maximum or minimum rates for intrastate traffic. It cannot be supposed that Congress sought to accomplish by indirection that which it expressly disclaimed, or attempted to override the accustomed authority of the states without the provision of a substitute. On the contrary, the fixing of reasonable rates for intrastate transportation was left where it had been found; that is, with the states and the agencies created by the states to deal with that subject. *Missouri P. R. Co.* v. *Larabee Flour Mills Co.* 211 U. S. 612, 620, 621, 53 L. ed. 352, 359, 360, 29 Sup. Ct. Rep. 214.

How clear was the purpose not to occupy the field thus left to the exercise of state power is shown by the clause uniformly inserted in the numerous acts passed by Congress to authorize the construction of railways across the Indian territory. This clause, while fixing a maximum passenger rate, made the laws of an adjoining state (in some cases Arkansas, in others Texas, and in others Kansas) applicable to the freight rates to be charged within the territory; and while the right to regulate rates on the authorized line of railroad was reserved to Congress until a state government should be established, it was expressly provided that, when established, the state should be entitled to fix rates for intrastate transportation, — the right remaining with Congress to prescribe rates for such transportation as should be interstate. Within a month after the act to regulate commerce was enacted, two acts were passed by Congress for this purpose with respect to railways extending across the territory from the Texas to the Kansas boundary. The provision — in both cases in identical language, save that the one referred to the laws of Texas and the other to the laws of Kansas — was as follows (act of February 24, 1887, chap. 254, § 4, 24 Stat. at L. 420; act of March 2, 1887, chap. 319, § 4, 24 Stat. at L. 447):

Sec. 4. That said railroad company shall not charge the inhabitants of said territory a greater rate of freight than the rate authorized by the laws of the state of Texas for services or transportation of the same kind: Provided, That passenger rates on said railway shall not exceed three cents per mile. Congress hereby reserves the right to regulate the charges for freight and passengers on said railway, and messages on said telegraph and telephone lines, *until a state government or governments shall exist in said territory within the limits of which said railway, or a part thereof, shall be located; and then such state government or governments shall be authorized to fix and regulate the cost of transportation of persons and freights within their respective limits by said railway;* but Congress expressly reserves the right to fix and regulate at all times the cost of such transportation by said railway or said company whenever such transportation shall extend from one state into another, or shall extend into more than one state: Provided,

however, That the rate of such transportation of passengers, local or interstate, shall not exceed the rate above expressed: And provided further,
That said railway company shall carry the mail at such prices as Congress
may by law provide; and until such rate is fixed by law, the Postmaster
General may fix the rate of compensation.

The same provision is found in similar statutes passed in almost
every year from 1884 to 1902, and relating to lines intended to
serve as highways of interstate communication. When Oklahoma
became a state, the laws of other states which were referred to
in these various acts ceased to be operative within its limits, and
by virtue of its statehood and with the direct sanction of Congress, it became authorized to prescribe reasonable maximum
rates for intrastate transportation throughout its extent. . . .

The decisions of this court since the passage of the act to
regulate commerce have uniformly recognized that it was competent for the state fix such rates, applicable throughout its territory. If it be said that, in the contests that have been waged
over state laws during the past twenty-five years, the question
of interference with interstate commerce by the establishment of
state-wide rates for intrastate traffic has seldom been raised, this
fact itself attests the common conception of the scope of state
authority. And the decisions recognizing and defining the state
power wholly refute the contention that the making of such
rates either constitutes a direct burden upon the interstate
commerce or is repugnant to the Federal statute.

In *Dow* v. *Beidelman*, 125 U. S. 680, 31 L. ed. 841, 2 Inters.
Com. Rep. 56, 8 Sup. Ct. Rep. 1028, the statute of Arkansas,
enacted in April, 1887, which established 3 cents a mile as the
maximum fare for carrying passengers within the state on railroads over 75 miles in length, was sustained against the objection
of the owners of the Memphis & Little Rock Railroad, who
attacked the act as confiscatory and arbitrary in its classification.
The same statute was again upheld in *St. Louis & S. F. R. Co.*
v. *Gill*, 156 U. S. 649, 39 L. ed. 567, 15 Sup. Ct. Rep. 484. In
Chicago, M. & St. P. R. Co. v. *Minnesota*, 134 U. S. 418, 33 L.
ed. 970, 3 Inters. Com. Rep. 209, 10 Sup. Ct. Rep. 462, 702,
the statute of that state (1887) creating a commission with

power to prescribe intrastate rates was adjudged to be invalid, but this was upon the ground that the act as construed by the state court made the rates published by the commission final and conclusive, and precluded any judicial inqury whether they were reasonable. In *Chicago & G. T. R. Co.* v. *Wellman,* 143 U. S. 339, 36 L. ed. 176, 12 Sup. Ct. Rep. 400, the act of the legislature of Michigan (1889), fixing the maximum fare for passengers within the state at 2 cents a mile in the case of companies whose gross earnings exceeded $3,000 a mile, was unsuccessfully assailed as confiscatory, and no contention was advanced that such an act, operating throughout the state, was an unwarrantable interference with interstate commerce.

In *Reagan* v. *Farmers' Loan & Trust Co.* 154 U. S. 362, 38 L. ed. 1014, 4 Inters. Com. Rep. 560, 14 Sup. Ct. Rep. 1047, the trustee of a railroad mortgage attacked the statute of Texas (1891), which established a railroad commission with authority to regulate tariffs, and the order of the commission providing a schedule of classified rates for the transportation of goods within the state. The challenge was of the tariff as a whole, and the inquiry was whether the body of rates was unreasonable, and such as to work a practical destruction of rights of property. Viewed in this aspect, the court, upon the allegations admitted by demurrer, held the action of the commission to be beyond its constitutional power, and affirmed the decree of the circuit court, enjoining the rates. The decree, however, was reversed so far as it restrained the commission from discharging the duties imposed by the statute, and from proceeding to prescribe reasonable rates and regulations. A further question was presented in *Reagan* v. *Mercantile Trust Co.* 154 U. S. 413, 38 L. ed. 1028, 4 Inters. Com. Rep. 575, 14 Sup. Ct. Rep. 1060, in respect to the same statute and order as applied to the Texas & Pacific Railway Company, which had been organized under the laws of the United States (16 Stat. at L. 573, chap. 122), and operated its road not only within that state, but also for several hundred miles outside. It was insisted that this company was " not subject to the control of the state, even as to rates for transportation wholly within the state," the argument being that it was not within the state power to limit the Federal franchise to collect tolls. But the court held that the act of Congress did not go to the extent asserted, but left the company, as to its intrastate business, subject to state authority.

The effect of intrastate rates upon interstate rates was urged in *Smyth* v. *Ames*, 169 U. S. 466, 42 L. ed. 819, 18 Sup. Ct. Rep. 418, and in the cases decided therewith. These suits were brought by stockholders of the Union Pacific Railway Company, the Chicago & Northwestern Railroad Company, and the Chicago, Burlington & Quincy Railroad Company, to enjoin the enforcement of the act of the legislature of Nebraska, passed in 1893. This was a comprehensive statute, classifying the freight transported from any point in Nebraska to any other point in that state, and prescribing tables of maximum rates. The companies affected were interstate carriers engaged in a vast commerce, only a small portion of which was wholly local to the state. On the eastern boundary lay Omaha, a city of large importance in interstate trade, situated on the Missouri river, with Council Bluffs, in the state of Iowa, directly opposite. The point was distinctly made in the circuit court that the statute interfered with interstate commerce because, first, it established a classification of freights different from that which prevailed west of Chicago, and second, by reducing local rates it necessarily reduced rates on interstate business. Mr. Justice Brewer, who tried the cases, overruled these objections, holding that neither the convenience of the carriers nor the consequences of competition with respect to interstate rates could be pleaded " in restraint of the otherwise undeniable power of the state." *Ames* v. *Union P. R. Co.*, 64 Fed. 165, 171, 172. Having disposed of this contention, the court considered the question of the reasonableness of the rates, and reached the conclusion that they were invalid because they amounted to a deprivation of the carriers' rights of property. On appeal to this court, the counsel for the appellees directed attention to the conditions of transportation in Nebraska. It was argued that the local traffic was carried over the same tracks, in the same trains, and often in the same cars with the interstate traffic ; that to separate the cost of carrying the one sort of traffic from that of the other was a "manifest impossibility"; and that it was a necessary consequence of existing conditions that, if Nebraska controlled the local rates, it, at the same time, controlled the interstate rates. But this contention was not sustained, and the affirmance of the decree was placed upon the distinct ground that the rates were confiscatory. It was ruled that the reasonableness of intrastate rates was to be determined by considering the intrastate business separately. In answer to the suggestion that the conditions of business might have changed for the better since the decrees, the court called attention to the proviso in the decrees intended to meet such a case, adding that if the circuit court found that conditions were such as to permit the application of the state rates without depriving the carriers of just compensation, it would " be its duty to discharge the injunction " and to make whatever order was necessary "to remove any obstruction placed by the decrees in these cases in the way of the enforcement of the statute." 169 U. S. 550; see *Smyth* v. *Ames*, 171 U. S. 361, 365, 43 L. ed. 197, 198, 18 Sup. Ct. Rep. 888.

In that one of the Smyth cases which was brought by the stockholders of the Union Pacific Railway Company, not only was the case presented of a trunk line crossing the state with a relatively small proportion of business local to Nebraska, but the company had been formed by a consolidation of several companies by authority of Congress, one of them being the Union Pacific Railroad Company, incorporated by the act of July 1, 1862, chap. 120, 12 Stat. at L. 489. By this act (§ 18, p. 497), it was expressly provided that Congress might reduce the rates of fare if unreasonable, and might fix the same by law whenever the net earnings of the entire road and telegraph should exceed a certain amount. But this language, while showing that Congress intended to reserve the power to prevent unreasonable exactions, was not deemed to be equivalent to a declaration that the states through which the road might be constructed should not regulate rates for intrastate transportation. The court said:

It cannot be doubted that the making of rates for transportation by railroad corporations along public highways, between points wholly within the limits of a state, is a subject primarily within the control of that state. . . .

Congress not having exerted this power, we do not think that the national character of the corporation constructing the Union Pacific Railroad stands in the way of a state prescribing rates for transporting property on that road wholly between points within its territory. Until Congress, in the exercise either of the power specifically reserved by the 18th section of the act of 1862, or its power under the general reservation made of authority to add to, alter, amend, or repeal that act, prescribes rates to be charged by the railroad company, it remains with the states through which the road passes to fix rates for transportation beginning and ending within their respective limits. 169 U. S. 521, 522.

It is plain that had the intrastate rates, established by the comprehensive statute of Nebraska, not been found to be confiscatory, they would have been sustained in their application to all intrastate traffic notwithstanding the reserved power of Congress over the Union Pacific line, and despite the argument based upon the interdependence of interstate and intrastate rates.

The cases of *Louisville & N. R. Co.* v. *Kentucky*, 183 U. S. 503, 46 L. ed. 298, 22 Sup. Ct. Rep. 95, and *Louisville & N. R. Co.* v. *Eubank*, 184 U. S. 27, 46 L. ed. 416, 22 Sup. Ct. Rep. 277, concerned the validity of the long and short haul provision of the Constitution of Kentucky, adopted in 1891. In the first case, violation was charged with respect to the transportation of coal from Altamont to Lebanon, an intermediate station, as compared with charges for transportation from Altamont to Elizabethtown and Louisville, all places being within Kentucky. The difference in rate was justified by the company on the ground that at Louisville the coal hauled from Altamont came into competition with that brought down the Ohio river, and at Elizabethtown with western Kentucky coal brought there by the Illinois Central Railroad. The contention that the state provision operated as an interference with interstate commerce was presented and overruled, the court saying:

It is plain that the provision in question does not in terms embrace the case of interstate traffic. It is restricted in its regulation to those who own or operate a railroad within the state, and the long and short distances mentioned are evidently distances upon the railroad line within the state. The particular case before us is one involving only the transportation of coal from one point in the state of Kentucky to another by a corporation of that state. It may be that the enforcement of the state regulation forbidding discrimination in rates in the case of articles of a like kind, carried for different distances over the same line, may somewhat affect commerce generally; but we have frequently held that such a result is too remote and indirect to be regarded as an interference with interstate commerce; that the interference with the commercial power of the general government to be unlawful must be direct, and not the merely incidental effect of enforcing the police powers of a state. 183 U. S. 518, 519.

In the Eubank case, which had been argued before the first case was decided, it appeared that the state court had construed the same provision of the Kentucky Constitution as embracing a long haul from a place outside to one within the state (Nashville and Louisville), and a shorter haul on the same line and in the same direction between points within the state. The court held that, so construed, the provision was invalid, as being a regulation of interstate commerce, because it linked the interstate rate to the rate for the shorter haul, and thus the interstate charge was directly controlled by the state law. 184 U. S. 41, 43. The authority of the former decision upholding the state law, as applied to places all of which were within the state, was in no way impaired, and the court fully recognized the power of the state to prescribe maximum charges for intrastate traffic although carried over an interstate road to points on the state line. *Id.* 33, 42.

The case of *Minneapolis & St. L. R. Co.* v. *Minnesota*, 186 U. S. 257, 46 L. ed. 1151, 22 Sup. Ct. Rep. 900, involved shipments of hard coal in carload lots from Duluth, Minnesota, to points in the southern and western portion of that state. The Railroad & Warehouse Commission of Minnesota, in 1899, prescribed a joint rate to be observed by the St. Paul & Duluth Railroad Company, the Minneapolis & St. Louis Railroad Company, and other carriers. The state court directed the issue of a writ of mandamus to compel compliance with the order. It was objected that the act under which the order was made was unconstitutional so far as it assumed to establish joint through rates over the lines of independent connecting railroads, and to divide joint earnings, and that the tariff as fixed was not compensatory. This court affirmed the judgment. In *Alabama & V. R. Co.* v. *Mississippi R. Commission*, 203 U. S. 496, 51 L. ed.

289, 27 Sup. Ct. Rep. 163, the company made what it called a "rebilling rate" on grain shipped from Vicksburg to Meridian, Mississippi, which was applicable only in case of shipments received at Vicksburg over the Shreveport line. It gave, however, to such shippers an option for a specified time to send other grain from Vicksburg instead, and thus it was in fact a local rate. To end this discrimination, the state commission, in 1903, fixed the same rate for all grain products shipped from Vicksburg to Meridian. It was urged that the effect of the order would be to force the plaintiff to enter into joint through interstate tariffs and divisions with all lines reaching Vicksburg by rail or river, whether it desired such arrangements or not. The court sustained the order, holding that it was competent for the state to enforce equality as to local transportation, and that this equality could not be defeated "in respect to any local shipments by arrangements made with or to favor outside companies."

In *Northern P. R. Co.* v. *North Dakota*, 216 U. S. 579, 54 L. ed. 624, 30 Sup. Ct. Rep. 423, the attorney general of North Dakota charged the company with continuous violation of a law fixing rates for the carriage of coal within the state (North Dakota, Laws of 1907, chap. 51), and asked for an injunction. It appears by the record that in its return to the rule to show cause in the state court, the company alleged that the statute was void because repugnant to the commerce clause, and also that the rate fixed thereby was confiscatory. In support of the last contention the return set forth that the maximum rates for carrying coal which the company was allowed to charge under the act in question were greatly lower than the rates for similar service fixed by Minnesota for that state (reference being made to chapter 232 of the Laws of 1907, the commodity rate act now in question), and those fixed by the railroad commissions of Illinois and Iowa, respectively; and that the conditions existing in North Dakota made it impossible to transport coal at a less rate than in the states named. The contention that the act violated the interstate commerce clause was said by the supreme court of the state to be based upon the assumption that state regulation of local rates on interstate lines amounted to an interference with interstate commerce. In view of the decisions of this court, the last question was not considered open to debate. *State ex. rel. McCue* v. *Northern P. R. Co.* 19 N. D. 45, 55, 25 L.R.A. (N.S.) 1001, 120 N. W. 869. This ruling was not challenged by the argument for the plaintiff in error here, and the question as to interference with interstate commerce was treated as removed from the case by the holding of the state court that the rates applied only to transportation within the state. 216 U. S. 580.

To suppose, however, from a review of these decisions, that the exercise of this acknowledged power of the state may be permitted to create an irreconcilable conflict with the authority of the nation, or that, through an equipoise of powers, an effective control of interstate commerce is rendered impossible, is to overlook the dominant operation of the Constitution, which, creating a nation, equipped it with an authority, supreme and plenary, to control national commerce, and to prevent that control, exercised in the wisdom of Congress, from being obstructed or destroyed by any opposing action. But, as we said at the outset, our system of government is a practical adjustment by which the national authority, as conferred by the Constitution, is maintained in its full scope without unnecessary loss of local efficiency. It thus clearly appears that, under the established principles governing state action, the state of Minnesota did not transcend the limits of its authority in prescribing the rates here involved, assuming them to be reasonable intrastate rates. It exercised an authority appropriate to its territorial jurisdiction, and not opposed to any action thus far taken by Congress.

The interblending of operations in the conduct of interstate and local business by interstate carriers is strongly pressed upon our attention. It is urged that the same right of way, terminals, rails, bridges, and stations are provided for both classes of traffic; that the proportion of each sort of business varies from year to year, and, indeed, from day to-day ; that no division of the plant, no apportionment of it between interstate and local traffic, can be made to-day, which will hold to-morrow ; that terminals, facilities, and connections in one state aid the carrier's entire business, and are an element of value with respect to the whole property and the business in other states; that securities are issued against the entire line of the carrier and cannot be divided by states; that tariffs should be made with a view to all the traffic of the road, and should be fair as between through and short-haul business; and that, in substance, no regulation of rates can be just which does not take into consideration the whole field of the carrier's operations, irrespective of state lines. The force of these contentions is emphasized in these cases, and in others of like nature, by the extreme difficulty and intricacy of the calculations which must be made in the effort to establish a segregation of intrastate business for the purpose of determining the return to which the carrier is properly entitled therefrom.

But these considerations are for the practical judgment of Congress in determining the extent of the regulation necessary under existing conditions of transportation to conserve and promote the interests of interstate commerce. If the situation has become such, by reason of the interblending of the interstate and intrastate operations of interstate carriers, that adequate regulation of their interstate rates cannot be maintained without imposing requirements with respect to their intrastate rates which substantially affect the former, it is for Congress to determine, within the limits of its constitutional authority over interstate commerce and its instruments the measure of the regulation it should supply. It is the function of this court to interpret and apply the law already enacted, but not, under the guise of construction, to provide a more comprehensive scheme of regulation than Congress has decided upon. Nor, in the absence of Federal action, may we deny effect to the laws of the state enacted within the field which it is entitled to occupy until its authority is limited through the exertion by Congress of its paramount constitutional power.

Second. Are the state's acts and orders confiscatory?

The rate-making power is a legislative power and necessarily implies a range of legislative discretion. We do not sit as a board of revision to substitute our judgment for that of the legislature, or of the commission lawfully constituted by it, as to matters within the province of either. *San Diego Land & Town Co.* v. *Jasper*, 189 U. S. 439, 446, 47 L. ed. 892, 896, 23 Sup. Ct. Rep. 571. The case falls within a well-defined category. Here we have a general schedule of rates, involving the profitableness of the intrastate operations of the carrier, taken as a whole, and the inquiry is whether the state has overstepped the constitutional limit by making the rates so unreasonably low that the carriers are deprived of their property without due process of law, and denied the equal protection of the laws.

The property of the railroad corporation has been devoted to a public use. There is always the obligation springing from the nature of the business in which it is engaged — which private exigency may not be permitted to ignore — that there shall not be an exorbitant charge for the service rendered. But the state has not seen fit to undertake the service itself ; and the private property embarked in it is not placed at the mercy of legislative caprice. It rests secure under the constitutional protection which extends not merely to the title, but to the right to receive just compensation for the service given to the public. . . .

In determining whether that right has been denied, each case must rest upon its special facts. But the general principles which are applicable in a case of this character have been set forth in the decisions.

(1) The basis of calculation is the "fair value of the property" used for the convenience of the public. . . . "What the company is entitled to demand, in order that it may have just compensation, is a fair return upon the reasonable value of the property at the time it is being used for the public."

(2) The ascertainment of that value is not controlled by artificial rules. It is not a matter of formulas, but there must be a reasonable judgment, having its basis in a proper consideration of all relevant facts. The scope of the inquiry was thus broadly described in *Smyth* v. *Ames* (169 U. S. 546, 547) :

In order to ascertain that value, the original cost of construction, the amount expended in permanent improvements, the amount and market value of its bonds and stock, the present, as compared with the original, cost of construction, the probable earning capacity of the property under particular rates prescribed by statute, and the sum required to meet operating expenses, are all matters for consideration, and are to be given such weight as may be just and right in each case. We do not say that there may not be other matters to be regarded in estimating the value of the property. What the company is entitled to ask is a fair return upon the value of that which it employs for the public convenience. On the other hand, what the public is entitled to demand is that no more be exacted from it for the use of a public highway than the services rendered by it are reasonably worth.

(3) Where the business of the carrier is both interstate and intrastate, the question whether a scheme of maximum rates fixed by the state for intrastate transportation affords a fair return must be determined by considering separately the value of the property employed in the intrastate business and the compensation allowed in that business under the rates prescribed. This was also ruled in the Smyth Case (*id.* p. 541). The reason, as there stated, is that the state cannot justify unreasonably low rates for domestic transportation, considered alone, upon the ground that the carrier is earning large profits on its interstate business, and, on the other hand, the carrier cannot justify unreasonably high rates on domestic business because only in that way is it able to meet losses on its interstate business.

In the present cases the necessity of this segregation of the domestic business in determining values and results of operation was recognized by both parties. Voluminous testimony was taken before the master, and numerous exhibits containing data and calculations were submitted for the purpose of showing their respective estimates of the value of the entire property of the carriers in Minnesota, the amount of income and expense in that state, their theories of apportionment between the interstate and intrastate business, and their contentions as to the net return for intrastate transportation under the state rates. The multitude of facts which are involved makes it impossible here to present a comprehensive review, even in a summary way. We must be content with a statement of the salient points, and deal only with those matters which, after a careful consideration of the entire record, we regard as controlling our decision.

In each of the three cases (save in certain particulars with respect to that of the Minneapolis & St. Louis Railroad Company) the method adopted by the master was as follows:

The period taken for the purpose of testing the sufficiency of the rates was the fiscal year ending June 30, 1908. During this period, all the rates in question, freight and passenger, were actually in force, with the exception of the commodity rates prescribed by the act of April 18, 1907, which had been enjoined. The amount of the reduction in the intrastate revenue which would have been caused by the application of the commodity rates is shown.

The master found the present value of the entire property of the carrier, used in the public service in the state of Minnesota. This valuation was as of June 30, 1908, and was made on the basis of the cost of reproduction new. The master also made findings as to the original cost of construction, and as to the present value on the basis of cost of reproduction new, of the entire system of the carrier. The estimated value of the railroad property within the state was divided between the freight and passenger business upon the relation of the gross revenue derived from each. The part of the total value which was thus assigned to the freight business within the state was then divided between the interstate and intrastate freight business on the basis of gross revenue; and a similar division was made between the interstate and intrastate business of the property value assigned to the passenger department. In this way the master found the value of the property used in intrastate transportation, freight and passenger, upon which he computed the net return received by the carrier.

There was no substantial dispute as to the amount of the entire revenue assignable to the state or as to its division between interstate and intrastate business, as an examination of the transactions in which the revenue was obtained permitted the making of the requisite apportionments with reasonable certainty.

The master also ascertained the total expense incurred by the carrier within the state. This expense was first divided between freight and passenger business. Those items of cost which were directly incurred in each sort of business, and not common to both, were directly assigned; and such items were found to cover about 60 per cent of all expenses. The remaining items, those of common expense, were divided between the freight and passenger business upon the relation, as to most of them, of revenue train-miles, and as to the others, of revenue engine-miles.

Having thus ascertained the share of the expense within the state of the freight and passenger departments respectively, it remained to divide that share, in each case, between the interstate and intrastate business. This apportionment was made, in the case of freight expense, upon what was termed an "equated ton-mile basis"; and in the case of passenger expense upon an "equated passenger-mile basis." That is to say, the master concluded that the cost per ton mile of doing the intrastate freight business was at least two and one-half times the cost per ton mile of the interstate freight business, and hence he divided the total freight expense according to the relation of the interstate and intrastate ton miles after the latter had been increased two and one-half times. In the case of the passenger expense, he concluded that the cost per passenger-mile in the intrastate business was at least 15 per cent greater than that in the interstate business, and the total passenger expense was divided upon the relation of passenger-miles after increasing the intrastate passenger-miles 15 per cent.[1] By the use of equalizing factors,

---

[1] The method is illustrated from the following extract from the findings in the Northern Pacific Case:

EQUATED TON-MILE BASIS

Freight—On basis of 1 intrastate ton mile costing as much as 2.5 interstate ton miles

	Actual	Equated	Proportion	Operating Exps.
Intrastate ton miles . . .	$130,580,988 \times 2.5 =$	$326,452,470 =$	25.362%	$1,355,273.82
Interstate ton miles . . .	$960,709,494 \times 1.0 =$	$960,709,494 =$	74.638%	3,988,444.43
	1,091,290,482	$1,287,161,964 = 100.\%$		$5,343,718.25

EQUATED PASSENGER-MILE BASIS

Passenger—On basis of 100 intrastate passenger miles costing as much as 115 interstate passenger miles

	Actual	Equated	Proportion	Operating Exps.
Intrastate passenger miles .	$52,317,140 \times 1.15 =$	$60,164,711 =$	37.347%	$863,325.18
Interstate passenger miles .	$100,931,180 \times 1.00 =$	$100,931,180 =$	62.653%	1,448,306.77
	153,248,320	$161,095,891 = 100.\%$		$2,311,631.95

the same result was obtained upon what was called an "equated revenue basis." [1]

The net profits of the interstate and intrastate businesses, respectively, passenger and freight, were then found by deducting the apportioned share of expense from the apportioned share of revenue, and the rate per cent of the net profit upon the rate value assigned to each sort of business was computed. The master concluded that the returns from intrastate transportation were unreasonably low, and hence that the rates in question were confiscatory.

The validity of the result depends upon the estimates of the value of the property within the state and the apportionments both of value and of expense between interstate and intrastate operations.

[1] Equated Revenue Basis. — In the case of the Northern Pacific Company it was found that the relation of freight revenue per ton per mile derived from the intrastate business, as compared with the interstate business, was as 1.4387 is to 1.0000. The relation of cost per ton per mile in the intrastate business in proportion to revenue, to the cost per ton per mile in interstate business in proportion to revenue, was then found to be as 1.7377 is to 1.0000, as follows:

$$\frac{250}{100} \div \frac{1.4387}{1.0000} = \frac{1.7377}{1.0000}$$

The actual intrastate freight revenue was multiplied by 1.7377 to obtain the equated revenue, and thus the same percentages were obtained as on the equated ton-mile basis, as follows:

EQUATED REVENUE BASIS. FREIGHT

	Actual Revenue	Equated Revenue
Intrastate	$1,555,342.92 × 1.7377 =	$2,702,719.39 = 25.362%
Interstate	7,953,734.41 × 1. =	7,953,734.41 = 74.638%
		$10,656,453.80 = 100.%

The relation of revenue per passenger mile, intrastate and interstate, was found to be as 1.0092 is to 1.0000 ; and thus, the relation of cost per passenger mile in relation to revenue was as 1.1395 is to 1.0000. The division was then made as follows:

EQUATED REVENUE BASIS. PASSENGER

	Actual Revenue	Equated Revenue
Intrastate	$1,015,150.34 × 1.1395 =	$1,156,763.81 = 37.347%
Interstate	1,940,718.17 × 1. =	1,940,718.17 = 62.653%
		$3,097,481.98 = 100.%

It will be convenient to take up the three cases separately:

1. *Northern Pacific Railway Company.* The par value, April 30, 1908, of the stock of this company, was found to be $215,539,-634.99, and of the bonds, $190,256,577.66; total, $405,796,-392.65. (Included in this statement of capital stock is the sum of $60,539,634.99 received to April 30, 1908, upon subscriptions to new capital stock [$95,000,000] authorized by stockholders' resolution January 7, 1907.)

These securities and their value in the market rest upon the entire property of the company. They include assets of considerable value (for example, the stock of the Northwestern Improvement Company, owning extensive coal lands), which, however, do not form part of what may be called the operating property of the company, or that devoted to the public service, upon which the fair return is to be calculated (15 Inters. Com. Rep. 376, 397, 407). Referring to the market value of the securities, the master said: " Assets and property not devoted to public service have not been valued, and as they are a large element in stock valuation it follows that value of bonds and stocks is wholly unreliable and cannot be used in these cases as an element in determining the value of operating property, or as a basis for rate-making." In this view the master was undoubtedly right.

Much evidence was produced before the master for the purpose of showing the actual cost of construction and equipment of .the entire railroad system from the beginning down to April 30, 1908. This, the master states, could be shown only by the corporate books and records; and in the early history of the original company these are somewhat obscure and uncertain, and, by reason of lapse of time, could not be verified by other proof. The total investment cost of the railroad system of the Northern Pacific thus shown was. $369,252,755. This included certain items which the master held not to be properly allowable as a part of the cost, and after their deduction the cost was found to be $312,243,555. Of this investment cost, it appears from the evidence submitted by the company's comptroller that the sum of $128,184,985.82 was expended for construction and equipment, and for improvements and betterments, during the period from September 1, 1896, to April 30, 1908. The master found that the Minnesota track mileage is substantially 21 per cent of the track mileage of the whole system [1] and that if the cost were proportioned accordingly, the amount assignable to the state of the entire cost of construction and equipment, as stated, would be $65,571,462.

The master, however, and the court below, in confirming his findings, held that rates were not to be predicated upon the original investment.

Taking, as the basis, the cost of reproduction new, the master found the value of the entire railroad system or operating property of this company to be $452,666,489.[2] The value of that portion of the system which was in the state of Minnesota was separately found, on the same basis, to be $90,204,545. It was upon this estimate of the value of the property in the state, as apportioned between the interstate and intrastate business, that the master computed the rate of return.

The total net profits of the company for the fiscal year ending June 30, 1908, from its Minnesota business (interstate and intrastate), was found to be $5,431,514.56. This was equal to 6.021 per cent on the entire estimated value of the property. This showing of the results of the entire business at once directs attention to the importance of the methods adopted in making apportionments; but before considering these, the question is presented as to the soundness of the underlying estimate of value. May it be accepted as a basis for a finding that the rates are confiscatory?

---

[1] The master found that the total track mileage of the system was 7695.80 and that the track mileage in Minnesota was 1625.20. In both cases spurs, yards, and sidings were included. In Minnesota, as shown by the company's statement, the "passing, side, and industry tracks" amounted to 512.41 miles, leaving for the single track, and second and third main track, miles, a total of 1112.79 miles.

[2] This estimate did not include the interest of the Northern Pacific in the Spokane, Portland & Seattle Railroad which was under construction, or the Big Forks & International Falls Railway, or the Minnesota & International Railway, or in certain lines in Manitoba, under lease, which were found not to be part of the operating system.

Values. The items entering into the valuation are set forth in the margin.[1]

[1] Valuation — Northern Pacific :

1. Lands for right of way, yards and terminals	$21,024,562
2. Grading, clearing, and grubbing	12,331,541
3. Protection work, rip-rap, retaining walls	374,091
4. Tunnels	253,250
5. Cross ties and switch ties	3,657,576
6. Ballast	1,960,969
7. Rails	5,645,307
8. Track fastenings	727,228
9. Switches, frogs, and railroad crossings	303,717
10. Track laying and surfacing	1,600,591
11. Bridges, trestles, and culverts	3,586,063
12. Track and bridge tools	28,073
13. Fences, cattle guards, and signs	471,609
14. Stockyards and appurtenances	37,098
15. Water stations	436,489
16. Coal stations	120,039
17. Stations, buildings, and fixtures	920,423
18. Miscellaneous buildings	1,054,874
19. Steam and electric power plants, gas plants	196,338
20. General repair shops	1,162,934
21. Shop machinery and tools	529,322
22. Engine houses, turntables, and cinder pits	1,026,346
23. Track scales	38,520
24. Docks and wharves	768,306
25. 26. } Interlocking plants and other signal apparatus	114,430
27. 28. } Telegraph and telephone lines	285,145
28½. General office furniture	73,654
29. Solidification of roadbed. (Absorbed in above.)	
Total 1 to 28	$58,728,685
30. Engineering, superintendence, legal expenses, 4½ per cent 1 to 28	2,785,036
31. Locomotives	3,454,040
32. Passenger equipment	1,349,829
33. Freight car equipment	7,519,722
34. Miscellaneous equipment	372,477
35. Marine equipment (none)	
Total items 1 to 34	$74,209,789
36. Freight on construction material — absorbed.	
37. Contingencies, 5 per cent 1 to 34	3,710,479
38. Stores and supplies in Minnesota	2,658,976
39. Interest during construction, 4 per cent, 2½ years, items 1 to 36	7,420,957
40. Interest in terminal properties, St. Paul depot, Duluth depot, Minnesota transfer	2,204,344
	$90,204,545

The first item is:

"Lands for right of way, yards, and terminals, $21,024,562."

This is for the bare land, without structures or improvements of any sort, as the entire cost of reproduction in building the road and erecting all the existing structures is covered in other items. The master states that the amount thus allowed for land is made up as follows:

Terminal properties, St. Paul appraisement of Read, Watson & Taylor, as modified by railroad company $7,645,100.24
Add 5 per cent for the cost of acquisition and consequential damages 382,255.01
Property acquired after appraisement 328,725.69
Minneapolis appraisement of Elwood, Barney, and Ridgeway, as modified by railway company 4,027,616.17
Add 5 per cent for acquisition and consequential damages . . 201,380.80
Property acquired after appraisement 227,737.26
Duluth, appraisement of Stryker, Mendenhall, and Little . . 3,602,443.43
Add 25 per cent for railway value, cost of acquisition, and consequential damages 900,610.85
Total value of terminals 17,315,869.45
Lands outside of terminals 3,708,693.45
Grand total 21,024,562.90

The appellants insist that no more than $9,498,099.27 should have been allowed.

It is contended that the valuation was made upon a wrong theory; that it is a speculative estimate of "cost of reproduction"; that it is largely in excess of the market value of adjacent or similarly situated property; that it does not represent the present value, in any true sense, but constitutes a conjecture as to the amount which the railway company would have to pay to acquire its right of way, yards, and terminals, on an assumption, itself inadmissible, that, while the railroad did not exist, all other conditions, with respect to the agricultural and industrial development of the state, and the location, population, and activities of towns, villages, and cities, were as they now are.

We may first consider the basis for the finding with respect to the "lands outside terminals," — that is, the right of way and station grounds, etc., outside the three cities.

(a) *Lands outside terminals.* The complainants' witness was Mr. Cooper, the land commissioner of the company, who has charge of the land grants for its entire system, of its right of way and land purchases, and has had a wide experience in connection with land values along the lines of the railway. In the latter part of 1906, the state notified the company to report the value of its properties, requiring a statement in one column of the "market value," and in another column, of the "value for railway purposes." Mr. Cooper was instructed to prepare the valuation for this report. From the information he received in special inquiries, and his own knowledge, and following what he understood to be the instructions from the state, he set down under the heading of "market value," not the market value in the proper sense of that term, but what in his judgment it would cost the railroad company to acquire the land. This included an excess which he estimated the company would have to pay over the market value of contiguous and similar property if it were called upon to undertake such a reproduction of its right of way. It did not, however, embrace an allowance for payments which might have to be made for improvements that possibly might be found upon the property in such case, or for the consequential or severance damages which might possibly have to be met, or for the expense of acquisition. These supposed additional outlays he undertook to estimate. For this purpose he increased the "market value" as stated (in the case of agricultural lands generally multiplying it by three), and thus reached the amount set down as the "value for railway purposes." As it serves clearly to illustrate the theory upon which the land valuations were made, we make the following excerpts from Mr. Cooper's testimony:

The Master. When you speak of value, you mean cost of purchase?

Witness. Cost of purchase; we are using the word "value" somewhat wrongly, as we are talking along here. It is the cost of purchasing that property to-day.

* * * * * * * *

Witness. The word "value" does n't seem to me to fit this case, because all the time we are figuring on the cost of reproducing this property, and our instructions from the state use the word "reproduce." Now, if a railroad company could buy property at what is generally considered its value, the word "value" would fit in all right, but there is this excess which a railroad company has to pay beyond what is generally accepted as its value which increases the cost of reproducing a railroad property.

Q. And this excess which you now speak of is included in your market values as reported to the state and used in your testimony?

A. That is right. . . .

Q. . . . Well, now, does the term "market value" as you have used it in making this report to the state and in your testimony here have the same meaning, or is it used in the same sense with reference to the values you have fixed and reported to the state for properties on the right of way outside of the terminals and outside of the larger cities?

A. Oh, yes.

Q. As in the cities here?

A. Yes; the same rule was applied all through in the Minnesota valuations.

*   *   *   *   *   *   *   *

Q. Therefore, your judgment as to the value of the railroad property is always that it is higher than the value of contiguous property?

A. Yes, yes, that is true. . . .

Q. So that, in every case, what you call the market value is the value of contiguous or similarly situated property, with an additional amount which a railroad company is ordinarily compelled to pay?

A. That is right. . . .

Q. You have put into the market value the excess which a railroad company pays for land?

A. That is correct.

Q. Then, when you multiply that by 3, you are multiplying by 3 one of the elements going to make up excessive cost to a railroad company?

A. That is right. . . .

Q. And you are unable to state how much upon the average you have added to the true or normal market value, to allow for the additional amount which the railroad company would have to pay upon the hypothesis that it is now compelled to purchase the land?

A. That is correct.

Q. And then having determined to your satisfaction at what figure or sum you would place the market value of this property to the railroad company, as you have described, you have added another sum for severance damage, cost of improvements unnecessary to the company, easements in abutting property, and general expenses?

A. That is correct.

Q. And you have determined that, in agricultural communities, this second addition is shown by the use of the multiple 3?

A. I think the multiple of 3 is too low, and I so testified in this case When you are going through a highly cultivated country I think the multiplier of 3 is not enough.

Q. But that is what you used for the purpose of the right of way value of land through the agricultural communities?

A. That is right, in this state.

Q. And in the cities, in the three large terminals, you have added to what you describe as the market value of the lands to the railroad company, ascertained as described by you already, the amount necessary to produce the difference shown in your testimony between the market value of the terminals and the right of way value?

A. That is right.

Q. And while you are able to show, and we can ascertain from an inspection of your testimony, the amount of the difference between the market value to the railroad company, as you have described, and the right of way value, and, in the rural communities or agricultural districts, the difference between the market value to you and the right of way value, there is nothing in any of your exhibits which will show, nor are you now prepared to state, the difference in what might be termed the normal, true, ordinary market value of the lands to the ordinary individual, and the sum which you have fixed as the market value to the railroad company if it were now compelled to purchase.

A. That is correct.

The " market value " of the lands (outside of the three cities) thus fixed and reported to the state was $2,008,491.50, and the increased amount estimated, in the manner stated, which was reported as the " value for railway purposes " was $4,944,924.60. The latter amount was submitted by the complainants in this case as the value of the lands. The master thought that the complainants' witness used too large a multiplier, and allowed 75 per cent of the amount thus claimed, or $3,708,693.45, stating that this was determined upon as the " fair reproduction value of the property." This allowance, it will be observed, was about $1,700,000 in excess of Mr. Cooper's estimate of " market value " as that term was used in making the report.

(b) *Terminal properties.* This term is used to designate the lands for the right of way, yards, and terminals in St. Paul, Minneapolis, and Duluth. The total original cost of these lands to the company (according to its statement based on the best information obtainable), including purchases to April 30, 1908,

was $4,527,228.76. The master allowed as their value, apart
from the improvements made by the company, which, as we have
said, were embraced in the other items of reproduction cost, the
sum of $17,315,869.45.

In preparing the valuation for the report to the state, Mr.
Cooper employed real estate men in each of the cities to make
an appraisement. He instructed them, as he testifies, "to make a
conservative report of the cost of reproducing the properties
owned by the company in each of their respective cities." They
divided the property into districts and reported their estimate of
units of value, as, for example, by the square foot. Mr. Cooper
took these reports, discussed their valuations with the appraisers,
and, aided by his own knowledge, formed an independent judgment, in no case increasing and in some instances (with respect
to certain St. Paul and Minneapolis property) reducing the appraisers' values. He then set forth under the heading "market
value," in the report to the state, as described in the testimony
we have quoted, his estimate of what it would cost the company
to purchase these lands, exclusive of improvements that might
be upon them, severance and consequential damages and expenses incident to acquisition. The amounts he thus fixed were
as follows: for the property in St. Paul $7,645,100.24; in Min-
neapolis, $4,027,616.17; in Duluth, $3,555,593.93. In the case
of the St. Paul and Minneapolis properties the amounts are precisely those adopted by the master in his findings, and to this he
adds 5 per cent to cover cost of acquisition and consequential
damages. The master was of the opinion that the appraisers of
these properties were "fully impressed with their value for railroad purposes" and that their appraisement as verified by them
before him and modified by the railway company "is a generous
valuation, and should be accepted as full railroad value of the terminal properties," and it was so accepted with the addition above
stated. With respect to the Duluth property, where the appraisement appears to have rested upon the ordinary values of real
estate, the master sets forth as the appraised value, $3,602,443.43,
to which he adds 25 per cent, or $900,610.85, "for railway
value, cost of acquisition, and consequential damages."

In reviewing the findings, the court below reached the conclusion that

the master in effect found that the cost of reproduction and the present value of the lands for the terminals in the three great cities, including therein all cost of acquisition, consequential damages, and value for railroad use which he allowed, was only about 30 per cent more than the normal value of the lands in sales between private parties. He found the value of the lands outside the terminals to be only twice their normal value.

From our examination of the evidence we are unable to conclude that the excess stated may be thus limited. What is termed the normal value does not satisfactorily appear. It further will be observed — from the summary of valuations we have set forth in the margin [1] — that the amount thus allowed in item 1 for lands, yards, and terminals, both in and out of the three cities ($21,024,562), was included in the total on which $4\frac{1}{2}$ per cent was allowed in item 30 for "engineering, superintendence, legal expenses," and again was included in the total on which 5 per cent was allowed in item 37 for "contingencies," and, in addition, was included in the total on which 10 per cent was allowed in item 39 for "interest during construction."

These are the results of the endeavor to apply the cost-of-reproduction method in determining the value of the right of way. It is at once apparent that, so far as the estimate rests upon a supposed compulsory feature of the acquisition, it cannot be sustained. It is said that the company would be compelled to pay more than what is the normal market value of property in transactions between private parties; that it would lack the freedom they enjoy, and, in view of its needs, it would have to give a higher price. It is also said that this price would be in excess of the present market value of contiguous or similarly situated property. It might well be asked, who shall describe the conditions that would exist, or the exigencies of the hypothetical owners of the property, on the assumption that the railroad were removed? But, aside from this, it is impossible to assume, in making a judicial finding of what it would cost to acquire the property, that the company would be compelled

[1] See note, p. 690.

to pay more than its fair market value. It is equipped with the governmental power of eminent domain. In view of its public purpose, it has been granted this privilege in order to prevent advantage being taken of its necessities. It would be free to stand upon its legal rights, and it cannot be supposed that they would be disregarded.

It is urged that, in this view, the company would be bound to pay the "railway value" of the property. But, supposing the railroad to be obliterated and the lands to be held by others, the owner of each parcel would be entitled to receive, on its condemnation, its *fair market value* for all its available uses and purposes. *United States* v. *Chandler-Dunbar Water Power Co.*, decided May 26, 1913 [229 U. S. —, ante, 667, 33 Sup. Ct. Rep. 667]. If, in the case of any such owner, his property had a peculiar value or special adaptation for railroad purposes, that would be an element to be considered. *Mississippi & R. River Boom Co.* v. *Patterson*, 98 U. S. 403, 25 L. ed. 206; *Shoemaker* v. *United States*, 147 U. S. 282, 37 L. ed. 170, 13 Sup. Ct. Rep. 361; *United States* v. *Chandler-Dunbar Water Power Co.*, *supra*. But still the inquiry would be as to the fair market value of the property; as to what the owner had lost, and not what the taker had gained. *Boston Chamber of Commerce* v. *Boston*, 217 U. S. 189, 195, 54 L. ed. 725, 727, 30 Sup. Ct. Rep. 459. The owner would not be entitled to demand payment of the amount which the property might be deemed worth to the company; or of an enhanced value by virtue of the purpose for which it was taken; or of an increase over its fair market value, by reason of any added value supposed to result from its combination with tracts acquired from others, so as to make it a part of a continuous railroad right of way held in one ownership. *United States* v. *Chandler-Dunbar Water Power Co.* and *Boston Chamber of Commerce* v. *Boston*, *supra*. There is no evidence before us from which the amount which would properly be allowable in such condemnation proceedings can be ascertained.

Moreover, it is manifest that an attempt to estimate what would be the actual cost of acquiring the right of way if the railroad were not there is to indulge in mere speculation. The

railroad has long been established; to it have been linked
the activities of agriculture, industry, and trade. Communities
have long been dependent upon its service, and their growth
and development have been conditioned upon the facilities it
has provided. The uses of property in the communities which
it serves are to a large degree determined by it. The values of
property along its line largely depend upon its existence. It is
an integral part of the communal life. The assumption of its
nonexistence, and at the same time that the values that rest
upon it remain unchanged, is impossible and cannot be entertained. The conditions of ownership of the property and the
amounts which would have to be paid in acquiring the right of
way, supposing the railroad to be removed, are wholly beyond
reach of any process of rational determination. The cost-of-
reproduction method is of service in ascertaining the present
value of the plant, when it is reasonably applied and when the
cost of reproducing the property may be ascertained with a
proper degree of certainty. But it does not justify the acceptance of results which depend upon mere conjecture. It is fundamental that the judicial power to declare legislative action
invalid upon constitutional grounds is to be exercised only in
clear cases. The constitutional invalidity must be manifest, and
if it rests upon disputed questions of fact, the invalidating
facts must be proved. And this is true of asserted value as of
other facts.

The evidence in these cases demonstrates that the appraisements of the St. Paul and Minneapolis properties which were
accepted by the master were in substance appraisals of what
was considered to be the peculiar value of the railroad right of
way. Efforts to express the results in the terms of a theory
of cost of reproduction fail, as naturally they must, to alter or
obscure the essential character of the work undertaken and
performed. Presented with an impossible hypothesis, and endeavoring to conform to it, the appraisers — men of ability and
experience — were manifestly seeking to give their best judg-
ments as to what the railroad right of way was worth. And
doubtless it was believed that it might cost even more to acquire

the property, if one attempted to buy into the cities as they now exist, and all the difficulties that might be imagined as incident to such a "reproduction" were considered. The railroad right of way was conceived to be a property *sui generis*, "a large body of land in a continuous ownership," representing one of the "highest uses" of property, and possessing an exceptional value. The estimates before us, as approved by the master, with his increase of 25 per cent in the case of the Duluth property, must be taken to be estimates of the "railway value" of the land; and whether or not this is conceived of as paid to other owners upon a hypothetical reacquisition of the property is not controlling when we come to the substantial question to be decided.

That question is whether, in determining the fair present value of the property of the railroad company as a basis of its charges to the public, it is entitled to a valuation of its right of way not only in excess of the amount invested in it, but also in excess of the market value of contiguous and similarly situated property. For the purpose of making rates, is its land devoted to the public use to be treated (irrespective of improvements) not only as increasing in value by reason of the activities and general prosperity of the community, but as constantly outstripping in this increase, all neighboring lands of like character, devoted to other uses? If rates laid by competent authority, state or national, are otherwise just and reasonable, are they to be held to be unconstitutional and void because they do not permit a return upon an increment so calculated?

It is clear that in ascertaining the present value we are not limited to the consideration of the amount of the actual investment. If that has been reckless or improvident, losses may be sustained which the community does not underwrite. As the company may not be protected in its actual investment, if the value of its property be plainly less, so the making of a just return for the use of the property involves the recognition of its fair value if it be more than its cost. The property is held in private ownership, and it is that property, and not the original cost of it, of which the owner may not be deprived without due process of law. But still it is property employed in a public calling, subject to governmental regulation, and while, under the guise of such regulation, it may not be confiscated, it is equally true that there is attached to its use the condition that charges to the public shall not be unreasonable. And where the inquiry is as to the fair value of the property, in order to determine the reasonableness of the return allowed by the rate-making power, it is not admissible to attribute to the property owned by the carriers a speculative increment of value, over the amount invested in it and beyond the value of similar property owned by others, solely by reason of the fact that it is used in the public service. That would be to disregard the essential conditions of the public use, and to make the public use destructive of the public right.

The increase sought for "railway value" in these cases is an increment over all outlays of the carrier and over the values of similar land in the vicinity. It is an increment which cannot be referred to any known criterion, but must rest on a mere expression of judgment which finds no proper test or standard in the transactions of the business world. It is an increment which, in the last analysis, must rest on an estimate of the value of the railroad use as compared with other business uses; it involves an appreciation of the returns from rates (when rates themselves are in dispute) and a sweeping generalization embracing substantially all the activities of the community. For an allowance of this character there is no warrant.

Assuming that the company is entitled to a reasonable share in the general prosperity of the communities which it serves, and thus to attribute to its property an increase in value, still the increase so allowed, apart from any improvements it may make, cannot properly extend beyond the fair average of the normal market value of land in the vicinity having a similar character. Otherwise we enter the realm of mere conjecture. We therefore hold that it was error to base the estimates of value of the right of way, yards, and terminals upon the so-called "railway value" of the property. The company would certainly have no ground of complaint if it were allowed a value for these lands equal to the fair average market value of similar land in the vicinity, without additions by the use of multipliers, or otherwise, to cover hypothetical outlays. The allowances made below for conjectural cost of acquisition and consequential damages must be disapproved; and, in this view, we also think it was error to add to the amount taken as the present value of the lands the further sums, calculated on that value, which were embraced in the items of "engineering, superintendence, legal expenses," "contingencies," and "interest during construction."

By reason of the nature of the estimates, and the points to which the testimony was addressed, the amount of the fair value of the company's land cannot be satisfactorily determined from the evidence, but it sufficiently appears, for the reasons we have stated, that the amounts found were largely excessive.

Finding this defect in the proof, it is not necessary to consider the objections which relate to the sources from which the property was derived or its mode of acquisition, or those which are urged to the inclusion of certain lands which it is said were not actually used as a part of the plant; and we express no opinion upon the merits of these contentions.

The property other than land, as the detailed statement shows, embraced all items of construction, including roadbed, bridges, tunnels, etc., structures of every sort, and all appliances and equipment. The cost of reproduction new was ascertained by reference to the prices for such work and property. In view of the range of the questions we have been called upon to consider, we shall not extend this opinion for the purpose of reviewing this estimate, or of passing upon exceptions to various items in it, as their disposition would not affect the result.

The master allowed the cost of reproduction new without deduction for depreciation. It was not denied that there was depreciation in fact. As the master said, "everything on and above the roadbed depreciates from wear and weather stress. The life of a tie is from eight to ten years only. Structures become antiquated, inadequate, and more or less dilapidated. Ballast requires renewal, tools and machinery wear out, cars, locomotives, and equipment, as time goes on, are worn out or discarded for newer types." But it was found that this depreciation was more than offset by appreciation; that "the roadbed was constantly increasing in value"; that it "becomes solidified, embankments and slopes or excavations become settled and stable and so the better resist the effects of rains and frost"; that it "becomes adjusted to surface drainage, and the adjustment is made permanent by concrete structures and rip-rap"; and that in other ways, a roadbed long in use "is far more valuable than one newly constructed." It was said that "a large part of the depreciation is taken care of by constant repairs, renewals, additions, and replacements, a sufficient sum being annually set aside and devoted to this purpose, so that this, with the application of roadbed and adaptation to the needs of the country and of the public served, together with working capital . . . fully offsets all depreciation and renders the physical properties of the road not less valuable than their cost of reproduction new." And in a further statement upon the point, the "knowledge derived from experience" and "readiness to serve" were mentioned as additional offsets.

We cannot approve this disposition of the matter of depreciation. It appears that the master allowed, in the cost of reproduction, the sum of $1,613,612 for adaptation and solidification of roadbed, this being included in the item of grading, and being the estimate of the engineer of the state commission of the proper amount to be allowed. It is also to be noted that the depreciation in question is not that which has been overcome by repairs and replacements, but is the actual existing depreciation in the plant as compared with the new one. It would seem to be inevitable that in many parts of the plant there should be such depreciation, as, for example, in old structures and equipment remaining on hand. And when an estimate of value is made on the basis of reproduction new, the extent of existing depreciation should be shown and deducted. This apparently was done in the statement submitted by this company to the Interstate Commerce Commission in the Spokane Rate Case in connection with an estimate of the cost of reproduction of the entire system as of March, 1907. See 15 Inters. Com. Rep. 395, 396. In the present case, it appears that the engineer of the state commission estimated the depreciation in the property at between eight and nine million dollars. If there are items entering into the estimate of cost which should be credited with appreciation, this also should appear, so that instead of a broad comparison there should be specific findings showing the items which enter into the account of physical valuation on both sides.

It must be remembered that we are concerned with a charge of confiscation of property by the denial of a fair return for its use; and to determine the truth of the charge there is sought to be ascertained the present value of the property. The realization of the benefits of property must always depend in large degree on the ability and sagacity of those who employ it; but the appraisement is of an instrument of public service, as property, not of the skill of the users. And when particular physical items are estimated as worth so much new, if in fact they be depreciated, this amount should be found and allowed for. If this is not done, the physical valuation is manifestly incomplete. And it must be regarded as incomplete in this case. *Knoxville* v. *Knoxville Water Co.* 212 U. S. 1, 10, 53 L. ed. 371, 378, 29 Sup. Ct. Rep. 148.

Apportionment of values. As the rate of net return from the entire Minnesota business (interstate and intrastate) during the test year was 6.021 per cent on a valuation of $90,204,545, and would be greater if computed upon a less value, we are brought to the question whether the methods of apportionment adopted are so clearly appropriate and accurate as to require a finding of confiscation of property used in the intrastate business.

The apportionment of the value of the property, as found, between the interstate and intrastate business, was made upon the basis of the gross revenue derived from each. This is a simple method, easily applied, and for that reason has been repeatedly used. It has not, however, been approved by this court, and its correctness is now challenged. Doubtless, there may be cases where the facts would show confiscation so convincingly in any event, after full allowance for possible errors in computation, as to make negligible questions arising from the use of particular methods. But this case is not of that character.

In support of this method, it is said that a division of the value of the property according to gross earnings is a division according to the "value of the use," and therefore proper. But it would seem to be clear that the value of the use is not shown by *gross* earnings. The gross earnings may be consumed by expenses, leaving little or no profit. If, for example, the intrastate rates were so far reduced as to leave no net profits, and the only profitable business was the interstate business, it certainly could not be said that the value of the use was measured by the gross revenue.

It is not asserted that the relation of expense to revenue is the same in both businesses; on the contrary, it is insisted that it is widely different. The master found that the revenue per ton-mile in the intrastate business, as compared with the revenue per ton-mile in the interstate business, was as 1.4387 to 1.0000. And, on his assumption as to the extra cost of doing the intrastate business, he reached the conclusion that the cost per ton-mile in proportion to the revenue per ton-mile in the intrastate business, as compared with the interstate business, was as 1.7377 to 1.0000. It is contended, according to the computations, that only a little over 10 per cent of the entire net revenue of the test year ($5,431,514.66) was made in the intrastate business, and that 90 per cent thereof was made in the interstate business; but approximately 21 per cent of the total value of the property was assigned to the intrastate business.

If the property is to be divided according to the value of the use, it is plain that the gross-earnings method is not an accurate measure of that value.

In *Chicago, M. & St. P. R. Co.* v. *Tompkins*, 176 U. S. 167, 44 L. ed. 417, 20 Sup. Ct. Rep. 336, the court below had found the value of the plaintiffs' property in South Dakota to be $10,000,000, and had divided it between the interstate and intrastate business, according to the gross receipts from each. Mr. Justice Brewer, in delivering the opinion of the court, after referring to the result reached, said:

Such a result indicates that there is something wrong in the process by which the conclusion is reached. That there was, can be made apparent by further computations, and in them we will take even numbers as more easy of comprehension. Suppose the total value of the property in South Dakota was $10,000,000, and the total receipts both from interstate and local business were $1,000,000, one half from each. Then, according to the method pursued by the trial court, the value of the property used in earning local receipts would be $5,000,000, and the per cent of receipts to value would be 10 per cent. The interstate receipts being unchanged, let the local receipts by a proposed schedule be reduced to one fifth of what they had been, so that instead of receiving $500,000 the company only receives $100,000. The total receipts for interstate and local business being then $600,000, the valuation of $10,000,000, divided between the two, would give to the property engaged in earning interstate receipts in round numbers $8,333,000, and to that engaged in earning local receipts $1,667,000. But if $1,667,000 worth of property earns $100,000, it earns 6 per cent. In other words, although the actual receipts from local business are only one fifth of what they were, the earning capacity is three fifths of what it was. And turning to the other side of the problem, it appears that if the value of the property engaged in interstate business is to be taken as $8,333,000, and it earned $500,000, its earning capacity was the same as that employed in local business — 6 per cent. So that although the rates for interstate business be undisturbed, the process by which the trial court reached its conclusion discloses the same reduction in the earning capacity of the property employed in interstate business as in that employed in local business, in which the rates are reduced. *Id.*, pp. 176, 177.

The value of the use, as measured by return, cannot be made the criterion when the return itself is in question. If the return, as formerly allowed, be taken as the basis, then the validity of the state's reduction would have to be tested by the very rates which the state denounced as exorbitant. And, if the return as permitted under the new rates be taken, then the state's action itself reduces the amount of value upon which the fairness of the return is to be computed.

When rates are in controversy, it would seem to be necessary to find a basis for a division of the total value of the property independently of revenue, and this must be found in the use that is made of the property. That is, there should be assigned to each business that proportion of the total value of the property which will correspond to the extent of its employment in that business. It is said that this is extremely difficult; in particular, because of the necessity for making a division between the passenger and freight business, and the obvious lack of correspondence between ton-miles and passenger-miles. It does not appear, however, that these are the only units available for such a division; and it would seem that, after assigning to the passenger and freight departments, respectively, the property exclusively used in each, comparable use-units might be found which would afford the basis for a reasonable division with respect to property used in common. It is suggested that other methods of calculation would be equally unfavorable to the state rates, but this we cannot assume.

It is sufficient to say that the method here adopted is not of a character to justify the court in basing upon it a finding that the rates are confiscatory.

Apportionment of expenses. As already stated, it was held in dividing the freight operating expenses, that the cost of doing the intrastate freight business was two and one-half times that of doing the interstate freight business. That is to say, the division of expenses was made according to ton-miles, interstate and intrastate, after the intrastate ton-miles had been increased two and one-half times.

The substantial question is whether the proof established this extra cost with that degree of certainty which is requisite to support a decree invalidating the state rates.

It appeared that the cost of intrastate business was not kept separately or set up in the accounts or statistics of the company.

The president of the company testified as to his judgment in the matter, which was based, in the absence of such accounts, upon the general facts of operation. His testimony was supported by that of other eminent railroad men, who testified in the Great Northern and Minneapolis and St. Louis cases. The elements entering into the greater expense of doing intrastate business were defined to be: that the average haul was shorter, being (in the case of the Northern Pacific) 104.52 miles for intrastate transportation as against 485.3 miles for interstate transportation; that the state business had to be handled twice at terminals; that the local short-haul business used most valuable terminal facilities in order to obtain its proper handling from the larger distributing centers, and used those facilities to a greater extent for the tons handled than did the longer through business; that the amount of clerical and warehouse labor in connection with the local business was much greater than in the case of the long-haul through business; that the chances of damage were greater in the short-haul business because of the greater number of individual transactions; that in the short-haul business there was an excess of equipment for loading and unloading; that local or way freight trains were "loaded lighter"; that the wear and tear on the local trains was greater because of frequent stopping and starting; that there was increased switching, resulting in greater damage to equipment and tracks; that the local train was generally on the road more hours than a through train, and therefore consumed more coal; that in the smaller stations the amount of shifting was large; that many of the local trains carried passengers, involving two stops at each station, one for passengers and the other for the local freight work; that the manner of operation of local trains increased the chances of injury to employees; that the short-haul business moved irregularly and spasmodically, and that its facilities were worked at their full capacity only for limited periods.

From these considerations, which were elaborated in the testimony, the witness reached the conclusion that the "so-called local short-haul intrastate business costs anywhere from three to six or seven times as much as the so-called long-haul through interstate business." In the Great Northern Case, the witnesses expressed the opinion that the extra cost of intrastate freight was three or four times greater than that of the interstate freight. One witness said that it would be from four to six times. These estimates, it is understood, had relation to the cost per ton mile.

The appellants do not dispute that business carried for short distances on local trains is more expensive than the handling of other business, but it is insisted that this is due solely to the different train service that it receives. It is said that all through trains start from divisional points and run from one end of the division to the other without stop; that the local trains are made up of cars carrying business destined for points intermediate the termini of the division, and take up all traffic originating at the intermediate stations; that the word " local," as applied to these trains, is not synonymous with intrastate, but that the local trains carry a large part of the interstate traffic, both in receiving and distributing it; and that by far the greater part of the extra cost of the local train service is properly chargeable to interstate business. It is also insisted that so far as this extra expense can be charged to interstate business, it is adequately met by the additional revenue of that business, which per ton mile, as compared with the interstate business, is as 1.4387 to 1.0000.

To establish these propositions, and to meet the testimony of the complainants' witnesses, the appellants introduced an elaborate series of calculations, made by a professional accountant, which were deduced from the results of an extended examination of the records of the companies. The witness made computations as to the character of the freight on each road, dividing it between through and local freight upon each operating division, and then subdividing it between intrastate and interstate freight. It is contended by the appellants that these calculations are sufficient to show that in the case of the Northern Pacific, about 91 per cent of the freight on through trains was interstate and about 9 per cent intrastate, and that on the local trains the interstate freight amounted to 68.67 per cent, and the intrastate, 31.33 per cent. Calculations of this witness were also introduced, showing his division of the total expenses between the passenger and freight business, and then in each department between the interstate and intrastate business; and by means of these, it was estimated that, under the rates in question (assuming them to have been applied to the business of the fiscal year ending June 30, 1907, to which the calculations were directed), the net profits on the intrastate business as a whole would have been slightly more than 6 per cent upon an amount equal to the share of property value attributed to that business by the master's estimate and apportionment of total value.

These computations are assailed by the appellees as inaccurate and as based upon erroneous estimates. We shall not go into the details, and, for the present purpose, we may assume that the appellees are right in their criticism.

Our conclusions may be briefly stated. The statements of the complainants' witnesses as to the extra cost of interstate business, while entitled to respect as expressions of opinion, manifestly involve wide and difficult generalizations. They embrace, without the aid of statistical information derived from appropriate tests and submitted to careful analysis, a general estimate of all the conditions of transportation, and an effort to express in the terms of a definite relation, or ratio, what clearly could be accurately arrived at only by prolonged and minute investigation of particular facts with respect to the actual traffic as it was being carried over the line. The extra cost, as estimated by these witnesses, is predicated not simply of haulage charges, but of all the outlays of the freight service, including the share of the expenses for maintenance of way and equipment assigned to the freight department. And the ratio, to be accurately stated, must also express the results of a suitable discrimination between the interstate and intrastate traffic on through and local trains respectively, and of an attribution of the proper share of the extra cost of local train service to the interstate traffic that uses it. The wide range of the estimates of extra cost, from three to six or seven times that of the interstate business per ton mile, shows both the difficulty and the lack of certainty in passing judgment.

We are of opinion that, on an issue of this character, involving the constitutional validity of state action, general estimates of the sort here submitted, with respect to a subject so intricate and important, should not be accepted as adequate proof to sustain a finding of confiscation. While accounts have not been kept so as to show the relative cost of interstate and intrastate business, giving particulars of the traffic handled on through and local trains, and presenting *data* from which such extra cost as there may be, of intrastate business, may be suitably determined, it would appear to have been not impracticable to have had such accounts kept or statistics prepared, at least during test periods, properly selected. It may be said that this would have been a very difficult matter, but the company, having assailed the constitutionality of the state acts and orders, was bound to establish its case, and it was not entitled to rest on expressions of judgment when it had it in its power to present accurate *data* which would permit the court to draw the right conclusion.

We need not separately review the findings with respect to the division of passenger expenses, as the same considerations are involved, with the distinction, however, that the extra cost attributed to the intrastate business is relatively small as compared with that charged to intrastate freight. And, in view of the conclusions reached on the controlling questions we have considered, we express no opinion with respect to the method adopted in dividing expenses between the passenger and freight departments.

For the purpose of determining whether the rates permit a fair return, the results of the entire intrastate business must be taken into account. During the test year the entire revenue, as found, from the intrastate business, passenger and freight, amounted to $2,897,912.26. All the rates in question were in force save the commodity rates, and it is further found that the loss that would have accrued in intrastate commodity business, by the application of the commodity rates which were under injunction, would have amounted to $21,493.67.

As neither the share of the expenses properly attributable to the intrastate business, nor the value of the property employed in it, was satisfactorily shown, and hence it did not appear upon the facts proved that a fair return had been denied to the company, we are of the opinion that the complainant failed to sustain his bill.

2. *Great Northern Railway Company.* The master found that at the time this suit was brought the par value of the stock of the company was $149,577,500, and of bonds, $83,119,939; total, $232,697,439. On June 30, 1908, the par value of the stock was $209,962,750, and of bonds, $97,955,939.39; total, $307,918,689.39. The property upon which these securities and their value in the market are based includes, it is found, a very considerable amount not devoted to the public service.

The balance sheet of the company of June 30, 1908, showed the book valuation of the entire system employed in the public service to amount to $319,681,815. The master held that various items were included which were not properly allowable as a part of the cost, and deducting these, there remained as the book-showing of the total amount expended in construction and equipment, $295,401,213. The Minnesota track mileage was found to be practically 32.59 per cent of the total mileage, and upon this basis, the amount assignable to the state of the total cost, as stated, amounted to $96,271,255.

The master found that the cost of reproduction new of the entire system was $457,121,469.[1] The value of the portion of the system in Minnesota was separately found, on the basis of reproduction new, to be $138,425,291. The net profits of the company during the test year from its Minnesota business, interstate and intrastate, were $8,180,025.11, equal to 5.909 per cent upon this estimated value.

The items entering into the estimate are the same in character as those set forth in the estimate of the value of the property of the Northern Pacific Company.[2]

Included in this reproduction cost was an allowance, for " lands for right of way, yards, and terminals," of $25,172,650.80, as follows:

St. Paul, appraisement of Read, Watson, and Taylor	$6,433,348.00
Add 5 per cent for cost of acquisition and consequential damages .	321,667.40
Minneapolis, appraisement of Elwood, Barney, and Ridgeway .	11,619,765.00
Add 5 per cent for cost of acquisition and consequential damages .	580,968.15
Duluth, appraisement of Stryker, Mendenhall, and Little . .	713,280.00
Add 25 per cent for railroad value, cost of acquisition, and consequential damages	178,320.00
Total value of terminals	19,847,366.55
Lands outside of terminals	5,325,284.25
Grand total	25,172,650.80

The appraisements thus referred to, adopted by the master with the additions stated, were made by the appraisers in the three cities who were employed in the case of the Northern Pacific company. The valuations were made at the same time, and upon the same basis, as the corresponding valuations in that case, and are open to the same objections. In the company's estimate of the value of the lands outside these cities, the amount

---

[1] This did not include the interest of the company in the Spokane, Portland, & Seattle Railroad, or lines under construction. [2] See p. 691.

stated as the market value was largely increased to obtain the
"right of way value "; with respect to lands in agricultural sections, the "market value" was generally multiplied by 3; and
of the total amount of the estimate of the company the master
allowed 75 per cent, as in the Northern Pacific Case.

In addition, $4\frac{1}{2}$ per cent of the aggregate land values, as
found, was allowed in the item for "engineering, superintendence, legal expenses," and the further allowance of 16 per cent
of these land values was made in the item of "interest during
construction " (4 per cent for four years).

In the physical valuation estimated on the basis of the cost of
reproduction new, the master made no deduction for depreciation,
while, on the other hand, there was included under the item
of grading the sum of $3,219,642 for adaptation and solidifica-
tion of roadbed. The engineer of the state commission estimated
the depreciation in the property at approximately $13,000,000.

What has already been said in the case of the Northern Pacific
Company with respect to estimates of value, the apportionment
of value, the testimony as to the extra cost of doing the intra·
state business, and the division of expenses between interstate
and intrastate business, is equally applicable here.[1] In these
respects there is no material distinction between the two cases,
and the same conclusion must be reached in both.

3. *Minneapolis & St. Louis Railroad Company.* This case presents distinct considerations. The lines of this company consist
of about 1028 miles of track, of which 396 miles are operated
under lease or trackage rights. Of its owned mileage (632 miles)
approximately 60 per cent is in the state of Minnesota. The
master thus describes it:

It runs south from the inland cities of St. Paul and Minneapolis to Des
Moines, with a branch to Storm Lake, Iowa, and a branch to the South
Dakota grain fields. Along its entire line it comes in sharp competition

---

[1] The total revenue received by the Great Northern during the fiscal year
1908, from its intrastate business, passenger and freight, was $4,641,829.58 ; and
it was found that the loss that would have been sustained by the application of
the enjoined commodity rates to the intrastate commodity traffic would have
amounted to $87,261.43.

with strong intersecting railroad lines, and while, as before stated, it subserves a useful public purpose and is operated in response to public demand, it can be maintained only by the exercise of the highest economy and watchfulness in its operation, and to succeed must be given greater latitude than is necessary with respect to the more favorably located and prosperous lines of railway.

The less favorable situation of the road is fully recognized by the appellants, who object to its being regarded as affording a fair test of the sufficiency of the rates. They say that its " total mileage and the geographical location " are such " that it cannot be taken as typical of the railway situation in Minnesota "; and they insist that " the important and material questions are raised by the showing made in the Northern Pacific and Great Northern Cases." And the appellees, on their part, assert that " it cannot be seriously contended that the rates complained of are sufficient to yield any reasonable return on a proportionate value of the property used in the conduct of the business covered by the rates "; that the net income of the road " from all sources is scarcely sufficient to pay interest on its outstanding bonds "; that " the value of the property is greatly in excess of the par value of the bonds "; and that, as it seems to the appellees, " this company must earn more money or go into the hands of a receiver, within a comparatively short time."

The main facts are: The par value in 1908, of its stock and bonds, was $30,011,800, divided as follows: stock, $10,000,000 (preferred, $4,000,000, common $6,000,000); bonds $20,011,800. It appeared that no dividends had been paid on the common stock since 1904. The annual interest charges amounted to $952,583.

The book cost of its property, after deducting items disallowed by the master, was $28,574,225; and this, if divided according to mileage, would give to Minnesota as its share, $17,127,390. The mileage basis of division, however, fails to take account of the fact that the property in Minnesota has a greater relative value.

The master found the total value of the property in Minnesota on the basis of the cost of reproduction new to be $21,608,464.

In this estimate there was included the sum of $5,999,397.90 for lands, yards, and terminals. Of this amount $4,556,298 was allowed for the lands in Minneapolis on the estimate of the same appraisers who had been employed in that city by the other companies; and to this the master added 5 per cent. The lands outside these terminals were valued at $1,215,285.

The net earnings of the entire system after paying only operating expenses and taxes, from 1903 to 1909, were found to be as follows: 1903, $1,398,895.30; 1904, $1,229,524.49; 1905, $1,277,870.96; 1906, $1,511,961.99; 1907, $1,419,822.54; 1908, $1,220,862.21; 1909, $1,286,494.08.

The net earning of the company on all its business in Minnesota, interstate and intrastate (involving any use of the property valued as stated), after paying only operating expenses and taxes, were, during the same period: 1903, $1,222,941.77; 1904, $1,052,478.74; 1905, $1,054,853.35; 1906, $1,109,260.56; 1907, $895,977.66; 1908, $742,377.46; 1909, $794,472.58. The reference in each case is to the fiscal year ending on June 30.

It thus appears that the net return from the entire Minnesota business in 1907 was about 4.14 per cent on the estimated value of the property ($21,608,464) in Minnesota; in 1908, less than 3.5 per cent; and in 1909, less than 3.7 per cent.

The master made his computations, with respect to the return permitted under the rates in question, upon the operations of the fiscal year ending June 30, 1907. The class rates had been effective from November 15, 1906, and the passenger fare act from May 1, 1907. It was estimated by the master that the additional loss, which would have accrued in the interstate business if these rates had been in force during the entire fiscal year ending June 30, 1907, and if, in addition, the commodity rate act, which was enjoined, had been applied to the intrastate traffic of that year, would have amounted to $131,358, thus making a very serious reduction in a return already inadequate; and his conclusion was that the rates in question were plainly confiscatory.

It is not necessary here to reproduce the computations, as we are satisfied, after a careful examination of the evidence, that while the methods of estimating value, and of apportionment, which have been disapproved in the discussion of the cases of the other companies, are subject to the same objections in this case, so far as they have been employed, the margin of error which may be imputed to them is not sufficiently great to change the result. The net return from the entire business in Minnesota, interstate and intrastate, fell to $742,000 in the fiscal year ending June 30, 1908, and it is plain that the latter amount would have been largely reduced had the commodity rate act been enforced. In view of the actual results of the business in the state, and the clearly established facts with respect to the conditions of traffic upon this road, the conclusion cannot be escaped that the rates prescribed by the acts and orders of Minnesota would not permit a fair return to this company.

Without approving, therefore, the methods of calculation which have been adopted, but recognizing the peculiar situation of this road, and the undoubted effect of the rates in question upon its revenues, we are of the opinion that the decree, so far as it rests upon the confiscatory character of the rates as applied to this company, should be affirmed. In the desire, however, to prevent the possibility that the decree may operate injuriously in the future, we shall modify it by providing that the members of the Railroad & Warehouse Commission, and the attorney general of the state, may apply at any time to the court, by bill or otherwise, as they may be advised, for a further order or decree, whenever it shall appear that, by reason of a change in circumstances, the rates fixed by the State's acts and orders are sufficient to yield to the company reasonable compensation for the services rendered.

The decrees in Numbers 291 and 292 are reversed and the cases remanded with directions to dismiss the bills respectively without prejudice.

The decree in Number 293 is modified as stated in the opinion, and, as modified, is affirmed.

Mr. Justice McKenna concurs in the result.

XXVI

THE REGULATION OF RAILWAY RATES UNDER THE FOURTEENTH AMENDMENT [1]

I

In 1873 the Supreme Court of the United States, in the first decision [2] that involved the construction of the Fourteenth Amendment, limited its application in a way that must have surprised both those who had advocated and those who had opposed its adoption on the floor of Congress. The court held that the privileges and immunities of citizens of the United States protected by the amendment were not the general privileges and immunities of citizens, but only those special privileges and immunities that belonged to citizens of the United States as such, — the right to come to the seat of government, to assert claims against the national government, to transact business with it, to seek its protection, to share its offices, to have free access to its seaports, subtreasuries, land offices, and the courts of justice of the several states, to demand its care and protection over life, liberty, and property when on the high seas or in the jurisdiction of a foreign government, to assemble and petition for redress of grievances, and to have the writ of habeas corpus; to use the navigable waters of the United States, and to enjoy all rights secured by treaty with foreign nations, to change citizenship from

---

[1] From the *Quarterly Journal of Economics*, 1912, pp. 389–424.

[2] Slaughter House Cases, 16 Wallace, 36.

It may not be amiss to quote the language of that part of the first section of the Fourteenth Amendment which is here under consideration:

No state shall make or enforce any law which shall abridge the privileges or immunities of citizens of the United States ; nor shall any state deprive any person of life, liberty, or property without due process of law; nor deny to any person within its jurisdiction the equal protection of the laws.

The reader need hardly be reminded that this Amendment was made after the Civil War, being ratified in 1868.

716

one state to another with the same rights as other citizens of that state. Important as these rights are, they are not the ordinary everyday rights that closely affect the citizen. For these he was left to the protection of the states. Though the actual decision related only to one clause of the amendment, the opinion of Mr. Justice Miller, who spoke for the court, intimated strongly that the clause forbidding the states to deprive any person of life, liberty, and property without due process of law, and to deny to any person within its jurisdiction the equal protection of the laws, was intended to protect against unjust discrimination the negro race only.

Three years later, however, in the Granger cases [1] (1876) it was taken for granted that the scope of the latter clause of the amendment was broader, and that it protected not merely those of the negro race, but all persons. The court in fact followed the dissenting opinions of Justices Field and Bradley, not the dictum of the prevailing opinion of Justice Miller.

The Granger cases settled the authority of the state legislatures to control the charges of a business affected with a public interest. Some of the language used by the court went far in denying any right of the court to interfere. It was said distinctly that though the power conceded to the legislature was liable to be abused, the people must resort for protection against abuses to the polls and not to the courts. It was conceded that under some circumstances, but not under all, statutory regulations might deprive the owner of his property without due process of law; but it was held that the amendment did not change the law; "it simply prevents the States from doing that which will operate as such a deprivation."

The question of rates seemed by these decisions determined to be a legislative, not a judicial question. Six years later [2] the court held that a railroad company whose board of directors was by the charter authorized to establish rates could not as against

<hr>

[1] *Munn* v. *Illinois*, 94 U. S. 113 (1877). *Chicago, B. & Q. R.R. Co.* v. *Iowa*, 94 U. S. 155. *Peik* v. *Chicago and N.W. Railway Co.*, *Lawrence* v. *Same*, 94 U. S. 164. *Chicago, M. & St. C. R.R. Co.* v. *Ackley*, 94 U. S. 179. *Winona & St. Peter R.R. Co.* v. *Blake*, 94 U. S. 180. *Stone* v. *Wisconsin*, 94 U. S. 181.

[2] *Ruggles* v. *Illinois*, 108 U. S. 526 (1883).

a general law of the state exact more than three cents per mile
per passenger. The reasoning was put on a narrow basis, involving only the construction of the charter. The power granted
was to determine the rates by by-laws; the power to pass by-
laws was limited to such as were not repugnant to the laws of
the state, and hence it was held that the by-laws could not fix
a greater rate than was permitted by the general legislation;
"grants of immunity from legitimate control," said the Chief
Justice, "are never to be presumed."

The states soon began to avail themselves of the power to
control business affected with a public interest. The first important case concerning the limitation of their powers arose in California.[1] It decided that the rates of a water company might be
fixed by a county board in which the water company was not
represented, although the charter of the company provided for
its representation. The court expressly reserved the question
what might be done in case the municipal authorities did not
exercise an honest judgment or fixed a price manifestly unreasonable. Two years later,[2] it was decided that railroad charges
might be fixed by a Railroad Commission, although charters
provided that the companies themselves might fix the tolls and
charges. The legislature of Mississippi, by legislation subsequent
to the charters, created a Railroad Commission with power to
revise rates and increase or reduce them as experience and business operation might show to be just. It was argued that the
legislature by the provision in the charters had surrendered the
power of control over fares and freights. It was conceded that
the rates must by the rule of the common law be reasonable,
and the court held that the state was left free to act on the subject of reasonableness within the limits of its general authority
as circumstances might require. "The right to fix reasonable
charges has been granted," said Chief Justice Waite, "but the
power of declaring what shall be deemed reasonable has not
been surrendered. If there had been an intention of surrender-
ing this power, it would have been easy to say so; not having

[1] *Spring Valley Water Works* v. *Schottler*, 110 U. S. 347 (1884).
[2] Railroad Commission Cases, 116 U. S. 307 (1886).

said so, the conclusive presumption is there was no such intention." The court, however, was careful to guard against an inference that the power of regulation was without limit. "The power to regulate," it was said, "is not a power to destroy, and limitation is not the equivalent of confiscation. Under pretense of regulating fares and freights, the State cannot require a railroad corporation to carry persons or property without reward; neither can it do that which in law amounts to a taking of private property for public use without just compensation, or without due process of law."

The statute was held not to be in conflict with the due process clause and the equal protection clause of the Fourteenth Amendment. "General statutes fixing maximum rates," it was said, "do not necessarily deprive the railroad company of its property contrary to the amendment." The importance of the qualifying word "necessarily" appeared in subsequent decisions when it was held that such statutes might sometimes be void. The decisions thus far were in favor of public control, and against review by the courts.

II

Four years later, in the Minnesota Rate Cases,[1] the court took a position hard to reconcile with what was said in *Munn* v. *Illinois* and the succeeding cases. The Minnesota Commission had ordered a reduction of rates for transportation of milk from three cents to two and a half cents a gallon; and for switching cars from $1.25 and $1.50 per car to $1.00 per car. The railroads resisted and, upon application to the state courts, a mandamus was issued to put in force the rates fixed by the commission. The Supreme Court reversed this action. Justice Blatchford rested the reversal upon the fact that the decision of the railroad commission was made a finality under Minnesota law; he said that the commission could not be regarded as clothed with judicial functions or possessing the machinery of a court of justice. "The question of the reasonableness of a rate of charge for

[1] *Chicago, M. & St. P. Railway Co.* v. *Minnesota*, 134 U. S. 418 (1890). *Minneapolis Eastern Railway Co.* v. *Minnesota*, 134 U. S. 467 (1890).

transportation by a railroad company, involving as it does the element of reasonableness both as regards the company and as regards the public, is eminently a question for judicial investigation, requiring due process of law for its determination. If the company is deprived of the power of charging reasonable rates for the use of its property, and such deprivation takes place in the absence of an investigation by judicial machinery, it is deprived of the lawful use of its property and thus in substance and effect, of the property itself, without due process of law and in violation of the law of the Constitution of the United States; and in so far as it is thus deprived, while other persons are permitted to receive reasonable profits upon their invested capital, the company is deprived of the equal protection of the laws."

The court seemed by this language to decide that the question of rates was always a judicial question, and not, as had been held before and has been held since, a legislative question; that it could therefore be settled by a judicial tribunal only; that if a railroad company was not allowed to charge reasonable rates, its constitutional rights were violated; and that it was entitled to reasonable profits in the same sense as other persons not engaged in a public calling. It is difficult to see how the right to profit as individuals not engaged in a public calling can be consistent with the right of the state to regulate the rates of those engaged in such a calling. The opinion, carried to its logical conclusion, would substitute the courts for the commission as final arbiter; and in effect would throw the whole burden of rate making upon the judicial machinery. No wonder the opinion did not command the unanimous voice of the court. Justice Miller concurred in the result, but upon the ground that the commission had applied to the courts to enforce their order; that in substance this was asking the courts to determine that the order was reasonable, and hence the court had the right and duty to inquire into the reasonableness of the tariff of rates.

Justice Bradley, speaking for himself and Justices Gray and Lamar, dissented. He pointed out that the decision practically overruled *Munn* v. *Illinois* and the railroad cases decided with it; that the question of the reasonableness of a charge, so far from being a judicial question, was preëminently a legislative one involving considerations of policy as well as of remuneration; that in practice it had usually been determined by the legislature by fixing a maximum in the charter of the company or afterwards if there were no binding contract; that the question only became judicial when the legislature enacted simply that rates should be reasonable, thus necessarily submitting the question what was in fact reasonable to the judicial tribunals; but that the legislature might itself or by its commission fix the rates; and that for that purpose their decision was final, unless they so acted as to deprive parties of their property without due process of law; but that a mere difference of judgment as to amount between the commission and the companies without any indication of intent on the part of the commission to do injustice, did not amount to a deprivation of property. The real difference between Justice Blatchford and Justice Bradley was as to the question presented in a rate case. According to the former it was: "is the rate a reasonable one, and such as would afford the same profit as could be realized by one not subject to regulation?" According to the latter it was: "is the rate so unreasonable as to be arbitrary and amount to confiscation of property rather than mere regulation of a rate?" The difference is striking and fundamental. If the legislature had the right to regulate rates, as had been settled in the Granger cases, then the property of the railroads was qualified by that public right, and there could be no deprivation of such qualified property as long as the legislature confined itself to fair regulation and did not undertake to confiscate under the guise of regulation. The view of the minority has finally prevailed.[1]

Justice Bradley in the course of his opinion took occasion to speak of the relations between the courts and the legislature. His words are worth quoting:

It is always a delicate thing for the courts to make an issue with the legislative department of the government, and they should never do so if it is possible to avoid it. By the decision now made we declare, in effect, that the judiciary, and not the legislature is the final arbiter in the regulation

[1] *Atlantic Coast Line* v. *No. Car. Corp. Comm.*, 206 U. S. 1 (1907).

of fares and freights of railroads and the charges of other public accommodations. It is an assumption of authority on the part of the judiciary, which, it seems to me, with all due deference to the judgment of my brethren, it has no right to make.

The decision of the Court in the Minnesota Rate cases, it was further pointed out, gave a new extension to the meaning of the words "due process of law." Justice Blatchford's language must mean that due process of law requires judicial procedure "with the forms and machinery," to quote his language, "provided by the wisdom of successive ages for the investigation judicially of the truth of a matter in controversy." Long before this decision the court had held in an elaborate opinion by Mr. Justice Curtis [1] that the same words in the Fifth Amendment did not necessarily imply a regular proceeding in a court of justice or after the manner of such courts; and this view had been adopted and applied in the construction of the Fourteenth Amendment. The difficulty of Mr. Justice Blatchford's view becomes apparent if it is applied to the taking of the property of the citizen by taxation, by assessments for public improvements, or by administrative measures under the police power; or to restraint of the person made necessary by our immigration laws. "In judging what is due process of law," said Mr. Justice Bradley, "respect must be had to the cause and object of the taking, whether under the taxing power, the power of eminent domain, or the power of assessment for local improvements, or none of these: and if found to be suitable or admissible in the special case, it will be adjudged to be due process of law; but if found to be arbitrary, oppressive and unjust, it may be declared to be not 'due process of law.'"

The decision in the Minnesota Rate case inevitably led to repeated efforts to secure review by the courts of rates fixed by statute or the orders of public commissions.

After an unsuccessful effort by a friendly litigation to have a particular rate declared unreasonable,[2] the question next arose in the great case of *Reagan* v. *Farmers' Loan & Trust Co.*,[3]

---

[1] *Murray's Lessee* v. *Hoboken Land and Improvement Co.*, 18 How. 272 (1856).
[2] *Chicago & Grand Trunk Railway Co.* v. *Wellman*, 143 U. S. 339 (1892).
[3] 154 U. S. 362 (1894).

noteworthy because it was the first successful effort to enjoin the enforcement of rates fixed by a commission.

The question was squarely raised, for the defendant denied the power of the court to entertain the inquiry at all, and insisted that the fixing of rates for carriage by a public carrier was a matter wholly within the power of the legislative department of the government and beyond examination by the courts. To this the court through Mr. Justice Brewer answered:

The province of the courts is not changed, nor the limit of judicial inquiry altered, because the legislature instead of the carrier prescribes the rates. The courts are not authorized to revise or change the body of rates imposed by a legislature or a commission; they do not determine whether one rate is preferable to another, or what under all circumstances would be fair and reasonable as between the carriers and the shippers; they do not engage in any mere administrative work; but still there can be no doubt of their power and duty to inquire whether a body of rates prescribed by a legislature or a commission is unjust and unreasonable, and such as to work a practical destruction to rights of property, and if found so to be, to restrain its operation.

The complainants challenged the tariff as a whole and the court's inquiry was limited to its effect as a whole. The facts were thus stated by the court:

The cost of this railroad property was $40,000,000; it cannot be replaced to-day for less than $25,000,000. There are $15,000,000 of mortgage bonds outstanding against it, and nearly $10,000,000 of stock. These bonds and stock represent money invested in the construction of this road. The owners of the stock have never received a dollar's worth of dividends in return for their investment. The road was thrown into the hands of a receiver for default in payment of the interest on the bonds. The earnings for the last three years prior to the establishment of these rates were insufficient to pay the operating expenses and the interest on the bonds. In order to make good the deficiency in interest the stockholders have put their hands in their pockets and advanced over a million of dollars. The supplies for the road have been purchased at as cheap a rate as possible. The officers and employees have been paid no more than is necessary to secure men of the skill and knowledge requisite to suitable operation of the road. . . . The actual reduction by virtue of this tariff in the receipts during the six or eight months that it has been enforced amounts to over $150,000.

Upon these facts the Court said:

A general averment in a bill that a tariff as established is unjust and unreasonable, is supported by the admitted facts that the road cost far more than the amount of the stock and bonds outstanding; that such stock and bonds represent money invested in its construction; that there has been no waste or mismanagement in the construction or operation; that supplies and labor have been purchased at the lowest possible price consistent with the successful operation of the road; that the rates voluntarily fixed by the company have been for ten years steadily decreasing until the aggregate decrease has been more than fifty per cent; that under the rates thus voluntarily established, the stock, which represents two-fifths of the value, has never received anything in the way of dividends, and that for the last three years the earnings above operating expenses have been insufficient to pay the interest on the bonded debt, and that the proposed tariff, as enforced, will so diminish the earnings that they will not be able to pay one-half the interest on the bonded debt above the operating expenses; and that such an averment so supported, will, in the absence of any satisfactory showing to the contrary, sustain a finding that the proposed tariff is unjust and unreasonable, and a decree reversing it being put in force.

In deciding whether a tariff is so unreasonable and unjust as practically to destroy the value of the carrier's property, it is of course essential to fix the standard or principle upon which that value is to be determined. Upon this question the Reagan case is indecisive. Some of the language suggests that cost of the property is the proper measure of its value; other language, cost of replacement; and still other language, present value. The question was left for discussion in the later cases.

The Reagan case had dealt with the effect of the tariff of rates as a whole. Similar questions arose in *St. Louis and San Francisco Railway* v. *Gill*,[1] where it was decided that the correct test was the effect of the rates on the whole line of the carrier's road, and not the effect upon that portion which was formerly a part of one of the consolidating roads; that a company cannot claim the right to earn a net profit for every mile of road, nor attack as unjust a regulation which fixes a rate at which some part would be unremunerative; that the earnings of the entire line must be estimated as against all its legitimate expenses

[1] 156 U. S. 649 (1895).

under the operation of the act within the limits of the state. The last qualification presents a new difficulty, — that of severing a railroad into parts divided by the imaginary state lines. The later effort to segregate intrastate and interstate business has led to difficult problems still in process of solution. The Gill case was a suit for a penalty, and the court in referring to Justice Miller's statement in the Minnesota Rate cases that the rates were binding until judicially determined to be void, added that in cases where the legislature itself fixed the rates, a bill in equity was impracticable because there was no public functionary or commission which could be made to respond, and the companies, if they were to have any relief, must have the right to raise the question by way of defense to an action for penalties. This remark was unnecessary to the decision, since the result of the case on the facts was against the carrier. The remedy by injunction to restrain legal officers of the state from prosecuting, came later.

The same principle that applies to the case of a carrier, applies also to a turnpike company. In *Covington, etc., Turnpike Company* v. *Sandford*,[1] the Court held that the facts that the tolls for several years prior to 1890 had not admitted of dividends greater than 4 per cent on the par value of the stock ; that the proposed reduction would so diminish the income of the company that it could not maintain its road, meet its ordinary expenses, and earn any dividends whatever for stockholders, showed that the constitutional rights of the turnpike company were violated. Justice Harlan was careful to say that a mere failure of the rates to suffice to earn four per cent on the stock would not justify holding the rates to be void. "It cannot be said," he added, "that a corporation is entitled, as of right, and without reference to the interests of the public, to realize a given per cent upon its capital stock. . . . The public cannot properly be subjected to unreasonable rates in order simply that stockholders may earn dividends." In dealing with the question how the reasonableness of rates was to be ascertained, the court was not very satisfactory. The inquiry was said to involve a consideration of the

[1] 164 U. S. 578 (1896).

right of the public to use the road on paying reasonable tolls,
and also of the reasonable cost of maintaining the road in good
condition for public use, and the amount that may have been
really and necessarily invested in the enterprise. It was held
that there might be other circumstances, not then necessary to
state; that each case must depend upon its special facts; and
justice might require different rates for different roads. In short,
the opinion merely holds that rates must be reasonable and fair
both to the public and the company and must not be so low as
practically to deprive the company of its property. No standard
was fixed, and the case decided only that the particular rates
infringed the constitutional provision. The language of the court
indicates that it is the actual and necessary investment of the
company that is to be considered. This seems to mean the
actual necessary cost as distinguished from cost of replacement
or present value.

The results reached up to this point may be thus summarized.
State enactments or regulations establishing rates that will not
permit of the carrier earning such compensation as under all the
circumstances is just to it and the public, infringe the provisions
of the Fourteenth Amendment; and the question whether rates
are so unreasonably low as to deprive the carrier of its property
cannot be conclusively determined by the legislative authority
of the state, but may be the subject of judicial inquiry.

III

These general principles do not go far to solve the question
in a particular case. The decision in the Nebraska Maximum
Rate cases [1] took a further step. It was contended on behalf of
the state that the compensation to be allowed the carrier after
payment of operating expenses was purely a question of public
policy to be determined by the legislature and not by the courts.
"It cannot be successfully contended," said counsel for the state,
" that so long as the rate fixed pays something above operating
expenses to the corporation for the carrying of property, it

---

[1] *Smyth* v *Ames*. *Smyth* v. *Smith*. *Smyth* v. *Higginson*, 169 U. S. 466 (1898).

amounts to the taking either of the use or of the property." "It must follow then, that, so long as the rate fixed by the law will pay the operating expenses when economically administered, and something in addition thereto, the power of the court ends, and the extent to which rates must produce profits is one of political policy." In short, the contention was that the right of property in a railroad consisted in the title and possession and the privilege to operate it economically, with the right to such additional compensation, however small, as the legislature chose to allow from time to time. The successful maintenance of this proposition would plainly have ended the control of the courts over the subject. It went to the very root of the matter. It might logically be contended that a property right that was subject to legislative regulation, as settled by the Granger cases, was not taken away when the legislature did in fact regulate; but it was nevertheless true that the power to regulate was not a power to destroy. The case involved really a definition of the word "property" as applied to a common carrier; and in view of the earlier decisions, the Court very naturally answered the contention of counsel by saying:

The idea that any legislature, State or Federal, can conclusively determine for the people and for the courts that what it enacts in the form of law, or what it authorizes its agents to do, is consistent with the fundamental law, is in opposition to the theory of our institutions. The duty rests upon all courts, Federal and State, when their jurisdiction is properly invoked, to see to it that no right secured by the supreme law of the land is impaired or destroyed by legislation. This function and duty of the judiciary distinguishes the American system from all other systems of government. The perpetuity of our institutions and the liberty which is enjoyed under them depend, in no small degree, upon the power given the judiciary to declare null and void all legislation that is clearly repugnant to the supreme law of the land.

The definition of "property" becomes, therefore, in the last resort a matter for the courts.

The Nebraska case involved also the question of rates within a state over railroads extending through other states. It was said that rates reasonable in Iowa might be unreasonable in Nebraska since the density of population, and hence of traffic, might be greater in the former, while the cost of construction and maintenance might be less. It was held that the reasonableness of rates on traffic wholly within the state must be deter mined without reference to the interstate business done by the carrier or to the profits derived from it.

The argument that a railroad line is an entirety; that its income goes into, and its expenses are provided for out of a common fund, and that its capitalization is on its entire line, within and without the state, can have no application where the State is without authority over rates on the entire line, and can only deal with local rates and make such regulations as are necessary to give just compensation on local business.

Whether the attempt thus made to sever the intrastate from the interstate business can be carried out successfully is a question involved in later litigation and not yet settled. It involves a determination of the proportion of value of plant and cost of traffic to be attributed to the lines within the state. In view of the interaction of the various elements of cost and of revenue within and without the state upon each other, the problem is most difficult, and may prove possible of solution only by an approximation.

The Court in the Nebraska case considered also the question on what amount the railroads were entitled to earn a revenue. The companies contended that they were entitled to such rates as would enable them at all times, not only to pay operating expenses, but also to meet the interest regularly accruing upon all outstanding obligations and to justify a dividend on all their stock; less than that, it was said, would deprive them of property without due process of law. The Court held, however, that this contention practically excluded from consideration the fair value of the property used, omitted the right of the public to be exempt from unreasonable exactions, would justify the railroad in trying to earn interest on bonds in excess of its fair value and dividends on fictitious capitalization. The court was still indefinite in laying down the basis of the valuation on which earnings might fairly be had. It said the rights of the public would be ignored if rates were exacted without reference to the fair value of the property used for the public or the fair value of the services rendered. But these two bases of calculation are far from leading to the same result. To base rates upon the value of the property, involves the value of the plant in its entirety and the net result of all the rates on thousands of items. To base them upon the value of the services rendered, involves a consideration only of particular items and may involve a consideration of the value of the services to the shipper. The two methods are incommensurate. What the court decided was that the basis of all calculations as to the reasonableness of rates must be the fair value of the property used; that in order to ascertain that value, the original cost of construction, the amount expended in permanent improvements, the amount and market value of the bonds and stock, the present as compared with the original cost of construction, the probable earning capacity of the property under the particular rates prescribed, and the sum required to meet operating expenses, are all matters for consideration, to be given such weight as may be just and right in each case. Justice Harlan was careful to add: " We do not say that there may not be other matters to be regarded in estimating the value of the property."

Many of these elements required and have received and are destined to receive further definition and analysis. What other elements are to be considered may never be finally settled, so infinitely various are the circumstances that distinguish each case as it arises.

The Court soon had occasion to apply the rule, and the opinion shows no greater certainty in the basis of valuation.[1] A water company insisted that the court should consider the cost of the plant, the annual cost of operation including interest on money borrowed and reasonably necessary to be used in constructing the same; the annual depreciation of the plant from natural causes resulting from its use; and a fair profit to the company either by way of interest on the money expended for the public use, or upon some other fair and equitable basis. All these matters the court conceded ought to be taken into consideration, but it held that the basis of calculation was defective in not requiring the real value of the property and the fair value in themselves of the services rendered to be taken into consideration.

[1] *San Diego Land Co.* v. *National City*, 174 U. S. 739 (1899).

The opinion, however, points to no more definite rule. " What the company is entitled to demand," says the Court, " in order that it may have just compensation, is a fair return upon the reasonable value of the property at the time it is being used for the public." This adopts present value as the standard, but leaves unsettled how the reasonable value of the property is to be ascertained, and what is a fair return.

The opinion in the next case [1] sought to make a distinction between public service companies and companies which without any intent of public service have placed their property in such a position that the public has an interest in its use. As to the first class, Justice Brewer said the owner intentionally devoted his property to the discharge of a public service, and undertook that which is a proper work for the state, and might be said to accept voluntarily all the conditions of public service which attach to like service performed by the state itself. As to the second class the owner placed his property in such a position willingly or unwillingly, that the public acquire an interest in its use, but he submits only to those necessary interferences and regulations which the public interests require. Of the former it was said that since the state was not guided solely by a question of profit but might conduct the business at a loss having in view a larger general interest, so perhaps an individual who had shown his willingess to undertake the work of the state might be held to perform that service without profit. The suggestion was put in the form of an interrogation, since it was confessedly unnecessary in the pending case to determine the question. It seems to conflict with *Smyth* v. *Ames*, and the Court has never yet decided that the legal right of regulation goes to this extent. The decided case involves a corporation of the other class, which was not doing the work of the state, was not performing a public service, and had acquired from the state none of its governmental powers. The business was that of a stock yard at Kansas City. The business was held to be so affected with a public interest, being at the gateway of a great commerce of which it was an important if not a necessary adjunct, that its charges like those

[1] *Cotting* v. *Kansas City Stock Yards Co.*, 183 U. S. 79 (1901).

of a grain elevator were subject to public regulation. But the Court said the

> business in all matters of purchase and sale is subject to the ordinary conditions of the market and the freedom of contract. He (the owner) can force no one to sell to him, he cannot prescribe the price which he shall pay. . . . If under such circumstances he is bound by all the conditions of ordinary mercantile transactions, he may justly claim some of the privileges which attach to those engaged in such transactions. And while he cannot claim immunity from all state regulation, he may rightfully say that such regulation shall not operate to deprive him of the ordinary privileges of others engaged in mercantile business.

The difference in practical result suggested in the opinion is that in the case of a business affected with a public interest although not devoted to the public service, the state's regulation of charges is not to be measured by the aggregate of profits determined by the volume of business, but by the question whether any particular charge to an individual dealing with him is, considering the service rendered, an unreasonable exaction.

> The question is not how much he makes out of his volume of business, but whether in each particular transaction the charge is an unreasonable exaction for the services rendered. He has a right to do business. He has a right to charge for each separate service that which is reasonable compensation therefor, and the legislature may not deny him such reasonable compensation, and may not interfere simply because out of the multitude of his transactions the amount of his profits is large. Such was the rule of the common law even in respect to those engaged in a quasi public service independent of legislative action. In any action to recover for an excessive charge, prior to all legislative action, who ever knew of an inquiry as to the amount of the total profits of the party making the charge?

The distinction suggested by Justice Brewer and his expressions with reference to the subject are interesting and suggestive ; but the opinion was not the opinion of the court. Six out of nine judges assented to the judgment upon the ground that the Kansas statute violated the Fourteenth Amendment because it applied only to one stock-yards company, and not to other corporations engaged in like business in Kansas, and therefore denied to that company the equal protection of the laws. They were careful to say that they expressed no opinion upon the question whether it deprived the company of its property without due process of law. This, and not Justice Brewer's elaborate opinion, expresses the view of the court. Under the facts of the case it amounted to saying that the answer was doubtful as to the question whether rates that enabled a company to earn 5.3 per cent on the value of the property used for stock-yards purposes, instead of about 10 per cent previously earned, amounted to depriving it of property without due process of law; the propriety of any rate of return was not decided.

The suggestion that a public service company, doing the work of the state, might properly do it for an unremunerative rate bore fruit in the Minnesota Coal Rate case.[1] That case is important because it sustained an unremunerative rate upon coal fixed by the state commission. The ruling is in conflict with the reasoning of *Smyth* v. *Ames* (the Nebraska cases) and the court recognizes the necessity of explaining the distinction. It says that while the reasonableness or unreasonableness of rates for intrastate traffic must be determined without reference to the interstate business, it does not follow that the companies are entitled to earn the same percentage of profits on all classes of freight carried. This hardly justifies the conclusion that the carrier may be compelled to carry some goods at a loss; for if so, the power to select those goods involves a power to discriminate quite at variance with fundamental principles; if the railroad can be compelled to carry coal at a loss, it may also be compelled to carry other goods at a loss; and since it is entitled to a fair return upon the whole business, this loss must be made up by the imposition of a heavier rate on other goods than would naturally fall thereon; the public authorities are then permitted to discriminate against some shippers and in favor of others, a discrimination which has always been condemned, and was held to be illegal by the New Jersey Supreme Court,[2] upon the ground that carriers were engaged in a public employment, three years before the United States Supreme Court decided the Granger cases.

[1] *Minneapolis & St. Louis R'd Co.* v. *Minnesota*, 186 U. S. 257 (1902).
[2] *Messenger* v. *Pennsylvania R.R.* 700, 407 (1873).

The court in the Minnesota Coal Rate case sought to justify the losing rate upon the ground that for purposes of ultimate profit and of building up a future trade, railways carry both freight and passengers at a positive loss. No doubt such is the fact, and if railways were to be left free to fix rates according to their own pleasure, and to discriminate at their pleasure between shippers, the practice of sowing seed to reap a future crop might be permissible. The difficulty is that considerations of that kind are not reducible to a legal rule, but involve considerations of business policy.

It is not only difficult to determine how much of the value of an entire railroad shall be attributed to the portion within a state, but since even that portion is used in part for intrastate and in part for interstate traffic, the value of the property used for local and for through traffic must also be determined; and since all the business is done by the same men, with the same equipment, the total cost of conducting the business must also be apportioned. As might be expected from the intricacy of the problem, the results thus far reached are not satisfactory. In the Gill case it was held that every mile need not pay; from which it would seem to result that the system must be treated as an entirety, and that losses on local traffic might be balanced by profit on through traffic or vice versa. *Smyth* v. *Ames* decided the contrary, and made necessary the determination of the proper basis for apportionment of value and cost. The South Dakota case [1] rejected gross receipts as a proper basis for the apportionment. The other basis suggested is that of the volume of traffic determined according to ton mileage. The tendency of the more recent cases in the lower Federal courts seems to be in the direction of apportioning cost and value according to gross receipts. The question is still unsettled in the Supreme Court. In the Florida Phosphate cases,[2] the court leaned to the ton-mile basis, at least as far as concerns the cost of doing the business.

[1] *Chicago, M. & St. P. Ry.* v. *Tompkins*, 176 U. S. 167.
[2] *Atlantic Coast Line* v. *Florida*, 203 U. S. 256 (1906). *Seaboard Air Line* v. *Florida*, 203 U. S. 261 (1906).

The question to be decided when the protection of the Fourteenth Amendment is invoked, is whether the rates as a whole afford a sufficient return, or are so low as to amount to confiscation. When, as in the South Dakota Coal case or the Florida Phosphate cases, the rate upon a single article only is involved, it is impossible to determine the effect of that single rate upon gross or net returns on the entire traffic, and hence impossible to prove that the rate fixed is so low as to amount to confiscation. Such was the result in the Florida Phosphate cases, and it is quite conceivable that the court might be forced to decide that one unremunerative rate after another was not in conflict with the property right of the carrier, until an entire schedule of unremunerative rates might have been sustained. In the Phosphate cases the question did not arise, since the rate permitted exceeded the average receipts per ton per mile under the previous tariff. But the possibility of the result I have indicated illustrates the danger of the decision in the Minnesota Coal case, that a carrier may be required to carry a particular commodity at an unremunerative rate.

IV

The reasonable value of the property used was by 1903 pretty well recognized as the proper standard upon which returns may be earned. In *San Diego Land & Town Co.* v. *Jasper* [1] the Court said: " It no longer is open to dispute that under the Constitution what the company is entitled to demand, in order that it may have just compensation, is a fair return upon the reasonable value of the property at the time it is being used for the public." That standard is adopted as against a standard based on actual cost, less depreciation. Actual cost, selling price, valuation for taxation, may all be evidence of the actual value. But actual value may sometimes be enhanced by the fact that the plant is larger than is needed. Is the company entitled to earn a revenue on an unnecessary expenditure ? To this question, the Court answers, no. Upon the value as fixed by the local board, rates

[1] 189 U. S. 439 (1903).

were fixed with the intention of securing a yield of 6 per cent. The court found no sufficient evidence that this rate was confiscatory. But the local board had fixed the rates as if the water company supplied the whole 6000 acres outside the city for which the works were intended. In fact it supplied less, and its receipts were therefore less than the supervisors estimated. The result might give the appellant less than 6 per cent on the value of the plant. But the court said that if the plant was built for a larger area than it could supply, the Constitution did not require that two-thirds of the contemplated area should pay a full return. The case is therefore important because it holds that a failure to pay six per cent on present value is not necessarily decisive of the question whether rates are confiscatory so as to violate the constitutional provision. The present value on which the company is entitled to a return is only the present value of what is reasonably necessary for the public service.

A water company in California[1] was incorporated under a statute which empowered the county board of supervisors to regulate rates, but not to reduce them so low as to yield to stockholders less than $1\frac{1}{2}$ per cent a month on the capital actually invested. After the company had invested about a million dollars in its plant, a new statute empowered the supervisors to so adjust the rates as to yield not less than 6 nor more than 18 per cent per annum upon the value of the property actually used and useful for the supply of water. The court held that there was no contract the obligation of which was impaired, and that even if there was a contract, the legislature might alter or amend the original statute under its reserved power. For our present purpose the important point decided is that it is not a confiscation nor a taking of property without due process, nor a denial of the equal protection of the laws, to fix water rates so as to give an income of six per cent upon the then value of the property actually used, even though the company had prior thereto been allowed to fix rates that would secure to it 18 per cent upon the capital actually invested. The right of property of a water company

[1] *Stanislaus County* v. *San Joaquin and King's River Canal and Irrigation Co.*, 192 U. S. 201 (1904).

under the California statute, so far as it is protected by the Fourteenth Amendment, is no more than a right to earn 6 per cent on present value, regardless of actual investment or previous statutory provisions permitting a larger return.

The method of determining present value still remains to be settled. To ascertain the value of tangible property, such as lands or buildings, for the purpose of determining the just compensation required to be made when it is taken for public use, has always been a sufficiently difficult question. To ascertain the value for the purpose of determining whether a schedule of rates is confiscatory is more difficult still.

In the Knoxville Water Company case,[1] the value had been based on cost of reproduction, to which there was added $10,000 for organization and promotion expenses, and $60,000 for value as a going concern. The court declined to decide upon the propriety of including these two items in the estimate, and expressly reserved them for consideration when the question necessarily arose. The Knoxville case turned upon the failure of the court below to make a proper deduction for depreciation arising from age and use. It was held that the water company was not entitled to value an old plant as if it were a new one. The more interesting question was as to the right of the company to add to the present value of its plant the cost of what had been lost through destruction or obsolescence, and what had been impaired in value although still in use. There was little discussion of the question in the opinion, no doubt because the circumstances of the particular case did not call for discussion. The court held that it was the duty of the company to use enough of its earnings to keep its plant good, before coming to the question of the amount of its profits, and that if it failed to keep its investment unimpaired, whether because it declared unwarranted dividends on over-issues of securities, or because it failed to exact proper prices for its output, it could not enhance the present value of its property by the addition of the costs of its mistakes. The question is likely to arise, as it has already in some cases, in a more difficult form, where fruitless but necessary

---

[1] *Knoxville* v. *Water Co.*, 212 U. S. 1 (1909).

experiments have been made, or plant has become obsolete in a rapidly advancing industry before it could possibly be made good out of current earnings. It arose before the Interstate Commerce Commission, in the converse case where the corporation, in order to reduce its apparent rate of earnings, sought to charge against current earnings the cost of betterments from which it was likely to profit for years to come. The Supreme Court approved the ruling of the Interstate Commerce Commission and held that the instrumentalities that are to be used for years should not be paid for by the revenues of a day or year.[1] A public service company cannot use more money in a year than is required for actual depreciation, and carry the excess as an addition to capital for the purpose of estimating the amount on which it is entitled to dividends, in determining whether a rate is confiscatory.[2] Novel questions of this character will arise with increasing frequency, and require the most careful consideration. Like most other questions in every department of the law, they are in their origin rather questions of fact than questions of law, although in course of time the rules become settled and thus become rules of law. In their origin, and as yet, many questions are questions of sound business management and engineering science. The law prescribes reasonable returns upon a reasonable valuation. What is a reasonable return and what is a reasonable valuation must vary with the circumstances of each particular case.

The basis of present value adopted in the Knoxville Water Company case was cost of reproduction less an allowance for depreciation in order to make up the difference between the value of new and old. Such a basis in the case of land, especially in a growing city, tends to make the cost of reproduction exceed the original cost, and in the case of railroads especially is almost sure to make present value greatly in excess of cost to the companies. It has therefore been contended with much ingenuity and force that the basis for rate regulation should not exceed the capital actually invested. In *Willcox* v. *Consolidated*

---

[1] *Illinois Cent. R.R.* v. *Inter. Com. Comm.*, 206 U. S. 441 (1907).
[2] *Louisiana R.R. Comm.* v. *Cumberland Tel. Co.*, 212 U. S. 414 (1909).

Gas Co.,[1] it was argued that one gas company should not be permitted to charge more than another for the sole reason that movements of population, uninfluenced by either company, had caused the site of its plant to be more valuable if vacated and sold; for it was said that although the fortunate company was entitled to obtain the full value of the land when sold, the unrealized profit meanwhile did not represent profit used in the manufacture and distribution of gas, but rather represented wealth which the manufacture and distribution of gas keeps out of use. This argument seems sound. The circumstances of the case did not call for an answer by the court. It did, however, distinctly reject the basis of actual cost even in the case of land. It held that the value of the property must be determined as of the time when the inquiry was made regarding rates; that the company was entitled to the benefit of any increase of value. That is in harmony with the general rule of law which permits the owner of real estate to profit by any increase in the value of his land. Obviously, however, if we are to uphold the rule that a public service corporation is entitled only to a reasonable return and that the public are entitled to be served at reasonable rates, we must apply the rule of reasonableness to the amount of the investment, as was done in the San Diego Water case. The Court recognized this, for it said there might be an exception to the rule where the property had increased so enormously in value as to render a rate permitting a reasonable return upon such increased value unjust to the public. This makes the reasonableness of the amount allowed for value of the property depend on the reasonableness of the rate to the public; but since the rate must afford a reasonable return to the company also, we are at once reasoning in a circle. The basis suggested by Mr. Whitney, in his argument as counsel, seems a better one, — that the value allowed should be the estimated cost of replacing the land in use with other land capable of accomplishing the same result. Probably no one would contend that if a gas company had been so fortunate as to locate its works at the corner of Broad and Wall Streets, and its land had attained the enormous value that there

[1] 212 U. S. 19 (1909).

prevails, it should be entitled to a return from its gas sales on the present value of the site. Prudent management would require removal to a less expensive site better adapted for the business.

The more difficult question that arose in the Gas Company case was the valuation of the franchise. As to the general question of the propriety of including the value of the franchise in the valuation of the property, the opinion gives little light. All that was decided was that it was proper to include in the valuation, the value attributed with the consent of the state to the franchises at the time of the consolidation of the companies, upon which investors had relied; and that it was wrong to hold, as the court of first instance did, that the value of the franchise had increased in the same ratio as the value of the tangible property. When it came to the general question, the Court said that to allow for increased value of the franchise was too much a matter of pure speculation and also opposed to the principle upon which such valuation should be made. Whether the Court meant merely that the evidence in the particular case was not sufficiently certain to justify the increased valuation, or whether it meant that upon principle the valuation of the franchise ought not under ordinary circumstances to be included, the opinion leaves in doubt.

The court calls attention to the fact that the franchise was subject to the legislative right to so regulate the price of gas as to permit no more than a fair return upon the reasonable value of the property. It would have been but a step to hold that to base the return to the company upon the value of such a franchise would be impossible, since the value of the franchise in turn depended on the rates. The two being dependent, one on the other, neither could furnish a substantial basis for fixing the other. As Judge Savage well said in a case in Maine,[1] "to say that the reasonableness of rates depends upon the fair value of the property used and that the fair value of the property used depends upon the rates which may be reasonably charged seems to be arguing in a circle." There is, however, as he points out, a sense in which the value of the franchise must be considered. It is the franchise, the right to operate and if possible to earn a dividend, that makes

[1] *Brunswick & T. Water District* v. *Maine Water Co.*, 59 Atl. Rep. 537 (1904).

the difference between a lot of junk, — old rails, pipes, and the like, — not worth recovering from their situation in and upon the ground, and a completed plant, railroad, water works, gas works, as the case may be. This is a part of the value of a going concern, the allowance for which the court refused to pass upon in the Knoxville Water Co. case. Even though the franchise is revocable, the fact that the plant has a legal right to exist gives added value to the physical structures. The value of a rightfully existing structure which may be lawfully used is very different from the value of the same structure without the legal right to use it for the purpose for which it was assembled. Quite recently, in the valuation of the Omaha Water Works,[1] the court has expressly approved an appraisal of the value as a going concern. " The difference between a dead plant and a live one," said Justice Lurton, " is a real value, and is independent of any franchise to go on, or any mere good will as between such a plant and its customers."

Although ordinarily the value of a franchise is not enhanced by the prospective profit from any particular schedule of rates, there is an exception where by reason of a contract protected by the contract clause of the Federal constitution, the corporation may continue to charge specified rates for a definite time.[2] The courts insist on finding the elements of a contract as they would between individuals. There must be an agreement upon sufficient consideration. Where the contract is made by a municipality, there must be legislative authority in the municipality to make the contract; and such legislation is construed strictly in favor of the public; authority to fix and determine rates does not authorize a municipality to make a bargain by which it ties itself

---

[1] *Omaha* v. *Omaha Water Co.*, 218 U. S. 180 (1910).

[2] *Los Angeles* v. *Los Angeles City Water Co.*, 177 U. S. 558 (1900) ; *Detroit* v. *Detroit Citizens Street Railway Co.*, 184 U. S. 368 ; *Cleveland* v. *Cleveland City Ry. Co.*, 194 U. S. 517 (1904) ; *Cleveland* v. *Cleveland Electric Railway Co.*, 201 U. S. 529 (1906) ; *Vicksburg* v. *Vicksburg Water Works Co.*, 206 U. S. 496 (1907). See also *New Orleans Water Works Co.* v. *Rivers*, 115 U. S. 674 (1885) ; (sustaining an exclusive right to supply water) ; *New Orleans Gas Co.* v. *Louisiana Light Co.*, 115 U. S. 650 (1885) ; (sustaining an exclusive right to supply gas) ; *Walla Walla* v. *Walla Walla Water Co.*, 172 U. S. 1 (1898).

up for the future.[1] Another exception may be suggested, — the investment by present owners in reliance upon the continuance or value of the franchise. To what extent, if at all, this element may enter into the calculation has not been expressly decided, nor does the Gas Company case settle the question. It settles indeed that under some circumstances such allowance must be made; but no attempt is made to define the circumstances with precision.

The Court held that the Gas Company case was not one for the valuation of good will because the complainant had a monopoly in fact and the consumer must take gas from it or go without; he must resort to the old stand whether he would or no. The Court held also that there was no particular rate of compensation which must in all cases and in all parts of the country be regarded as sufficient for capital invested in business enterprises; the amount of risk, the locality where the business is conducted, the rate expected and usually realized there upon investments similar in character, were all mentioned as factors, and it was held that under the circumstances of the gas business in the city of New York, six per cent was a proper return.

The element of wages of superintendence, which Mr. Whitney in his argument conceded must be covered by the returns to the company, was left out. In one sense this is not a return upon capital but wages of labor, and if it were possible for earnings due to the skill with which the business is managed to be secured to those alone whose skill produced the result, perhaps no more need be said. Practically, however, the earnings depend in part, sometimes in large part, not upon the skill in actual present-day management, but upon the satisfaction with which the public has been served in the past, perhaps by men long since dead. Given equal and reasonable rates, one company will be able to earn large dividends, and another perhaps unable to pay its way; and this result may be due not to any less efficient management,

---

[1] *Freeport Water Co.* v. *Freeport City*, 180 U. S. 587 (1901); *Danville Water Co.* v. *Danville City*, 180 U. S. 619 (1901); *Rogers Park Water Co.* v. *Fergus*, 180 U. S. 624 (1901); *Knoxville Water Co.* v. *Knoxville*, 189 U. S. 434; *Home Telephone Co.* v. *Los Angeles*, 211 U. S. 265 (1908).

but merely to the fact that one has been long in satisfactory
operation while the other is new and not yet in vogue. The
greater earnings of the one may even be due to the mere caprice
of fashion. But to whatever cause it is due, difficulty will arise
unless allowance be made, either by increasing the capital valuation on which the company is permitted to earn a return, by way
of a valuation of a going concern or the value of the probability
of an already assured income, or else by allowing an additional
return on the valuation minus this increment, by way of extra
compensation for the greater skill or the greater satisfaction with
which it serves the public. Even in the case of so close a monopoly as the Gas Company in New York City, it is not impossible
that some of its earnings may have been due to this cause; for
although it had a monopoly of the supply of gas through pipes
in the streets, it may have had competition, in the supply of
light, heat, and power, from the electric companies. Although
legally permissible, it would often be impracticable to cut down
rates to a level that would afford a fair return to one company
upon a valuation that failed to take into account the element of
value of a going concern or an assured income, without ruining
its weaker competitor. In some cases such lowering of rates
would prove inadvisable, especially in the case of railroads. One
road may through fortunate investments, the discovery of valuable minerals along its route, the opening of fertile territory, and
a rapid increase of population, prove a highly profitable investment; another at the same rates may barely pay its way; yet
to cut down rates on the prosperous road so as to reduce its
high dividends to a normal level, would emphasize and accen-
tuate the advantage already possessed by those along its line
over those along the line of the less prosperous road. Either
the prosperous road must be allowed to earn a higher return
upon the valuation or the valuation must allow for these
elements.

Up to the present time, the United States Supreme Court has
not been called upon to decide what elements are proper to be
considered in determining the present value of a plant of a
public-service company. That the value of the plant as a going

concern, not only ready for business but with business actually established, is greater than the bare cost of reproduction of the physical plant, is recognized by cases in other courts. It must be so, leaving out of view altogether the element of good will, which in the case of a strict monopoly ought to be disregarded. A going concern has necessarily expended money in various ways aside from the cost of physical plant in order to get going. The cost of promotion of the enterprise, of corporate organization, of obtaining the necessary franchises, permissions, and consents, of securing the necessary connections with other companies by rail or wire; the cost of experiments necessary in every new industry, and the often rapid substitution of improved appliances before the cost of the old can have been recouped out of earnings; the cost of developing the business including the oft-times necessary loss attending the incomplete stage of the plant, or the introduction of new appliances and methods; the cost of financing the enterprise, including interest on capital sunk before any returns begin to come in, — all go to make up the cost of a complete going plant, and are all expenses that a new enterprise must needs incur.

The United States Supreme Court has not as yet been called upon to analyze the costs of operation and to decide what items of cost of operation ought to be included in the annual charges before the profit can be ascertained. Professor Wyman has dealt with the subject in a satisfactory way [1] and the scope of this article does not call for its further discussion.

The question presented by a schedule of rates under the Fourteenth Amendment is whether the schedule permits a fair return upon a reasonable valuation or is so low as to amount to confiscation. This involves different considerations from those involved when the only question is the propriety of the rate on a single article. It cannot be foretold what effect a change of certain rates, for example on coal or gas, will produce on the net revenue of the business as a whole. This difficulty has been met by the adoption of a tentative course, leaving it for time

---

[1] Wyman on Public Service Corporations, § 1150 *et seq.*

and experience to determine whether constitutional rights have been infringed.[1]

A most serious difficulty is presented by our dual form of government. It is beyond the scope of the present discussion to treat the numerous cases dealing with the commerce clause, and the question what is interstate and what is intrastate commerce. The net return to a railroad company, — and it is to railway traffic that the questions most frequently relate, — depends on the relation between its income from whatever source derived and its outgoes whether for the conduct of interstate or intrastate business. The two are inextricably intermingled, and the problem of preserving the rights and powers of both the state and the federal governments is one of the problems of the future.

FRANCIS J. SWAYZE

[1] *Willcox* v. *Consolidated Gas Co.*, 212 U. S. 19 ; *Northern Pacific R'y* v. *North Dakota*, 216 U. S. 579.

XXVII

THE ENGLISH RAILWAY AND CANAL COMMISSION OF 1888 [1]

WHILE the law providing for the Commission of 1873 passed both Houses of Parliament with comparative ease and received but little opposition from the railway interest, the law of 1888 developed by small degrees, and met much opposition. The report of the Committee of 1881 had stated that a permanent railway tribunal was necessary.[2] Railway Commission legislation was introduced regularly between 1882 and 1886. In 1885 the nine principal railways submitted bills to Parliament embodying a general classification and a rearrangement of their maximum rates. But the protests of the traders led to the withdrawal of these measures. The defeat of the government in 1886 on the Irish Question prevented any further action at that time. In 1887 a regulative measure, which in some respects resembled the legislation of the following year, passed the House of Lords.

So far as the form of the Commission is concerned, the most important changes introduced by the legislation of 1888 were the court organization of the Commission and the limitation of the right of appeal. Under the old organization the Commission was considered to be in the same position as any inferior court, and might be prohibited from proceeding in matters over which it had no jurisdiction.[3] Now, by giving the Commission a definite

---

[1] From the *Quarterly Journal of Economics*, Vol. XX, 1905, pp. 1–55. The author was the expert employed by the Canadian Government in 1902 to draw up its Report upon Railway Rate Grievances and Regulative Legislation. British Railway Statutes and Regulations are reprinted in full in Hearings before the Senate (Elkins) Committee on Interstate Commerce, 1905, Vol. V, Appendix, pp. 133–264.   [2] Report of Select Committee on Railways, 1881, Part I, p. iii.

[3] *Toomer* v. *L. C. D. Ry. Co. and S. E. Ry. Co.*, 3 Ry. and Canal Traffic Cases, 98.

court organization and by making its decisions final on questions of fact, much strength was added.

The new legislation provided for a Commission of five members, composed of two lay and three *ex-officio* members. The *ex-officio* members are superior court judges, one for England, one for Scotland, one for Ireland. The active Commission at any one time has a membership of three, the two lay commissioners presided over by the designated superior court judge of the country in which the Commission is sitting.[1] While the judges who serve on the Commission are appointed for terms of five years, the lay commissioners hold office on a good-conduct tenure. The old provision whereby one of the lay commissioners was to be " of experience in railway business " was continued; and Mr. Price, the railway member of the former Commission, was reappointed. The qualification of the other lay commissioner was not specified. To this position Sir Frederick Peel, whose training was legal and who had been a member of the Railway Commission in 1873, was appointed. The lay commissioners were admonished of their judicial functions, for in their letters of appointment they were informed, " Doubtless you will feel that the judicial nature of your office is also incompatible with any active engagement in political controversies."

In every possible way the fact was emphasized that the Commission was a court, and therefore not concerned with rate making. The control of matters pertaining to rates was divided. Powers in regard to conciliation of rate difficulties were given to the Board of Trade. When the provision placing the revision of maxima and of classification in the hands of the Board of Trade was under consideration, an amendment to place such revision in the hands of the Commission was negatived.

The Act of 1888, while it repealed portions of the railway regulative acts already in existence, did not codify the portions remaining. Consequently there are still in effect sections of the

---

[1] The draft legislation of 1887 had provided a cumbrous arrangement whereby the judicial commissioner was to preside when a question of law was involved, while in other matters his attendance was to be invited by the lay commissioners, " if it was expedient for the better performance of the Commission's duties."

Railway Clauses Consolidation Act, 1845, the Railway and Canal Traffic Act, 1854, the Regulation of Railways Act, 1868, and the Regulation of Railways Act, 1873. Since 1888 jurisdiction in regard to actual rates has been given by an Act of 1894 ; while, under a law of 1904, the powers of the Commission in regard to private sidings have been made more definite by an interpretation of the " reasonable facilities " clause of the Act of 1854.[1]

While the jurisdiction given by the Act of 1888 embraces a variety of functions, the most important of which are undue preference, facilities for traffic, traffic on steamboats, through rates, rate books, terminals, legality of rates, provisions relating to private branch sidings, and references under the Board of Trade Arbitrations Act, 1874, the most important matters from the standpoint of the traders are (a) terminals, (b) reasonable facilities, (c) through rates, (d) undue preference, (e) control over actual rates.

TERMINALS, REASONABLE FACILITIES AND THROUGH RATES

The history of the terminal question is a long and involved one. When the earlier railways were chartered, the " canal toll " idea prevailed. For a time carriers, already in existence, quoted through rates over the railway lines, making such arrangements as they deemed proper in regard to payments for special services and for station terminals. It was not long, however, before the railways controlled the forwarding business, and complaint soon arose. The railways claimed the right, in addition to the powers given them under their maximum rates, to make charges for additional services and for terminals.[2] The traders contended that the maximum rates covered all that the railways were

---

[1] For detail concerning the unrepealed sections, see Woodfall, The New Law and Practice of Railway and Canal Traffic, etc., Appendix A.

[2] The question of terminals has come up in the United States. The charter of the Pittsburg & Connellsville Railway gave it the right to charge tolls. It was decided it had the right to charge terminals as well. *National Tube Works* v. *Baltimore & Ohio R.R.* (Penn.), 28 Am. and Eng. R'd Cases, 13.

legally empowered to collect. It was concerning the station terminals, however, that the keenest contention existed. The Select Committee of 1882 had recommended that terminal charges should be recognized, but that they should be subject to publication by the companies, and that in case of challenge they should be sanctioned by the Railway Commission.[1] A clause to this effect was contained in the regulative measure introduced by Mr. Chamberlain in 1884. In a decision of the Court of Queen's Bench in 1885 the right of the railways to collect terminals was definitely recognized.[2] But the traders did not recognize this decision as final ; for, because of a technical condition, it was impossible to carry the case before the higher courts. While the legislation of 1888 was in committee, various attempts were made to place the control of terminals under the Railway Commission, as well as to provide that in every case the maximum rates should include terminals. But the government took the position that terminals were legally established, and so they were given explicit recognition. *

The Act of 1888 had recognized terminals. The Provisional Orders Acts gave them definite form. The matter was finally passed on by the Commission in 1891 in a decision which upheld that of 1885.[3] Justice Wills, who gave the decision in the former terminal case, was at this time the judicial member of the Commission. On appeal the decision of the Commission was upheld. While the question of the legality of terminals has thus been settled, there still remains the question of the right of the trader to be exempt from the payment of terminals under special conditions. This question is of especial interest

[1] Select Committee on Railways, 1882, pp. v and xvii.

[2] *Hall* v. *London, Brighton, & South Coast Railway*, 15 Q. B. D. 505. This overruled a decision of the Railway Commission. A discussion of the question from the traders' standpoint will be found in Hunter, The Railway and Canal Traffic Act, 1888, pp. 38–50. See also British Railways and Canals, by " Hercules," chap. ii (a pro-trader brochure, published in London in 1885). A summary of the railway point of view will be found in the address of Mr. Pope, Q.C., representing the London & Northwestern Railway before the Board of Trade, October 29, 1889, reported in *Railway News*, November 2, 1889, pp. 778–780. See also Grierson, Railway Rates, English and Foreign, pp. 93–106.

[3] *Sowerby & Co.* v. *Great Northern Ry. Co.*, 7 Ry. and Canal Traffic Cases, 156.

in connection with the mining and manufacturing districts, where the establishments furnishing and receiving freight are usually situated on private sidings or on private railways. The importance of these sidings is shown in the fact that, while at the Sheffield freight station the tonnage in 1900 was 580,000, at a near-by siding it was 1,100,000. In 1894 the Commission was given jurisdiction in claims for exemption from payment of terminal charges at sidings when it was alleged that the services had not been performed. Under the provision of the Act of 1888, requiring the railway to distinguish conveyance from terminal charges, it had been held that the responsibility of the railway might be discharged by stating that the whole payment was for a conveyance rate.[1] But the Court of Appeal decided in 1897 that it was incumbent on the railway, in such a case to prove that it did not charge for terminals.[2] The Commission has power to allow a rebate from sidings charges without proof that any definite amount of terminal is included in the rate. A *prima facie* case for such a rebate is made out, if it is shown that, in respect of similar traffic between substantially the same termini, and passing over substantially the same routes, a sidings trader who does not require or use any terminal accommodation or services is charged the same amount as a trader who uses the station.[3] But the latter rate must not be simply a paper rate.[4] In calculating the amount of the rebate, it has, in general, been the practice of the Commission to follow the rule in Pidcock's case ; i.e., to assume that the service charges are in the same proportion to the rates actually charged as the maximum service charge would be to the sum of the maximum rates, — i.e., the maximum rate and the maximum terminals.[5]

[1] *New Union Mill Co.* v. *Great Western Ry. Co.*, 9 Ry. and Canal Traffic Cases, 160.

[2] *Salt Union, Ltd.* v. *North, Staffordshire Ry. and Others*, 10 Ry. and Canal Traffic Cases, 179.

[3] *Vickers, Sons & Maxim, Ltd.* v. *Midland Ry. and Others*, 11 Ry. and Canal Traffic Cases, 259.

[4] *Cowan & Sons* v. *North British Ry.*, 11 Ry. and Canal Traffic Cases, 271.

[5] *Pidcock* v. *Manchester, Sheffield & Lincolnshire Ry.*, 9 Ry. and Canal Traffic Cases, 45.

The through-rate clause of the Act of 1888 provides that through rates, stating the amount, route, and apportionment of the rate, may be proposed by a railway, a canal company, or a trader. In case of dispute regarding the rate or its apportionment the matter is brought before the Commission. In apportioning the through rate, the commissioners are to consider the special circumstances of the cases, and are not to compel any company to accept lower mileage rates than it may for the time legally be charging for like traffic, carried by a like mode of transit on any other line of communication, between the same points, being the points of departure and arrival of the through route.

Reasonable facilities in general must be such as can reasonably be required of the railway company, due allowance having been made for the way in which the service is already performed.[1] Similarly, in a reduced through rate there must always be considered whether there is a commensurate advantage to the railway company.[2] *Prima facie*, it is against public interest to interfere with vested legal rights, unless some compensation or equivalent is given. There must, therefore, be evidence both of public interest and reasonableness in favor of the rate and route sufficient to outweigh the former considerations.[3] The fact that two competing routes will tend to make either company treat the traders more reasonably is a consideration bearing on the question of public interest.[4] At the same time the Commission will not grant a through rate which creates unhealthy competition.[5] If there are grounds for the Commission granting something claimed as a proper facility for using railways, an objection grounded on its inconvenient consequences to railway companies

---

[1] *Newry Navigation Co.* v. *Great Northern Ry.* (Ireland), 7 Ry. and Canal Traffic Cases, 176.

[2] *Plymouth Incorporated Chamber of Commerce* v. *Great Western Ry. & L. & S. W. Ry.*, 9 Ry. and Canal Traffic Cases, 72 ; 10 *Ibid.* 17.

[3] *Didcot, Newbury & Southampton Ry.* v. *Great Western Ry. & L. & S.W. Ry.*, 9 Ry. and Canal Traffic Cases, 210.

[4] *Plymouth, Devonport & S. W. Ry.* v. *Great Western Ry. & L. & S. W. Ry.*, 10 Ry. and Canal Traffic Cases, 68.

[5] *Didcot, Newbury & Southampton Ry.* v. *L. & S.W. Ry. and Others*, 10 Ry. and Canal Traffic Cases, 17.

by reason of arrangements made by themselves will not be sufficient reason for not granting it.[1] The particular circumstances of the proposed route and rate must be considered. The reasonableness of a rate over a proposed route is not to be measured by an existing rate over an alternative route, even if the rate over the latter route may be reasonable.[2]

Incident to granting a through rate, a through booking (ticketing) arrangement may also be made.[3] While the Commission has not attempted to lay down any general principle on which through rates are to be apportioned, it will consider any special expenses in construction or special charges a company may have been empowered to make.[4] It is not clear that the Commission has power to rescind a through rate once established under the Act of 1888.[5] So far no such action has been taken.

In the claims made by canal and by dock companies to obtain through rates, considerable emphasis has been laid upon the technical interpretation of the word "railway." Thus it was decided in 1897 that the powers the Manchester Ship Canal possessed to construct railways on its quays, although these railways were simply for its own service, constituted it a railway company. In 1901 the action of the Commission in approving a through-rate arrangement for a dock company was overruled on the ground that the railways possessed by the dock company did not constitute a railway within the meaning of the act.[6] In

---

[1] *Corporation of Birmingham & Sheffield Coal Co., Ltd.* v. *Manchester, Sheffield & Lincolnshire Ry., Midland Ry., & L. & N. W. Ry.,* 10 Ry. and Canal Traffic Cases, 62.

[2] *Didcot, Newbury & Southampton Ry.,* etc. v. *Great Western Ry.,* etc., *ut supra.*

[3] *Didcot, Newbury & Southampton Ry.* v. *Great Western Ry. & L. & S. W. Ry.,* 10 Ry. and Canal Traffic Cases, 1.

[4] *Forth Bridge & North British Ry. Co.* v. *Great North of Scotland Ry. & Caledonian Ry.,* 11 Ry. and Canal Traffic Cases, 1. This would cover, for example, "bonus mileage," or an arbitrary, in the case of an expensive bridge.

[5] *Great Northern Central Ry.* (Ireland) v. *Donegal Ry.,* 11 Ry. and Canal Traffic Cases, 47.

[6] *London and East India Docks Co.* v. *Great Eastern Ry. & Midland Ry.,* 11 Ry. and Canal Traffic Cases, 57. This was a majority decision, Peel dissenting. The decision of the Court of Appeal was given by Mr. Justice Wright, who was a member of the Commission when the Manchester Canal case was decided. He distinguished the cases.

1903 a further application of the same company, subsequent to its acquisition of a short railway with which it had made connections, was refused on the ground that the difficulties of exchange of traffic did not justify the granting of such an application.

The Commission has looked at each through-rate case by itself. It has refrained from proposing a through rate. It has limited its action to the acceptance or rejection of the proposed through rate as brought before it. The power to propose through rates has been of little value to the traders. Normally, they have not been possessed of the exact knowledge necessary to the making of a through rate, with the result that they have been successful only in one out of five applications. The following summary gives details with reference to the through-rate applications formerly acted upon by the Commission :

YEAR	By Canal Company		By Dock Company*		By Railway Company*		By Traders		By Municipal Corporation and Traders	
	Granted	Refused	Granted	Refused	Granted	Refused	Granted	Refused	Granted	Refused
1895 ..	2	–	–	–	–	–	1	1	–	–
1896 ..	1	–	–	–	1	–	–	–	–	–
1897 ..	1	–	–	–	3	–	–	–	–	1
1898 ..	–	–	–	–	–	–	–	–	–	–
1899 ..	–	–	–	–	2	1	–	–	–	–
1900 ..	–	–	–	–	–	–	–	–	–	–
1901 ..	–	–	–	–	–	–	–	–	–	–
1902 ..	–	–	1	–	–	–	–	–	–	–
1903 ..	–	–	–	2	–	–	–	–	–	2

* No action prior to 1895.

UNDUE PREFERENCE

The question of " undue preference " has long engaged attention in England. Complaints were made during the investigations of 1882 that many anomalies existed in domestic rates. Thus London sugar refiners complained that, while Greenock was double the distance from given points, sugar was being carried to these points at the same rates as were given to London.[1] But it was against low import or *preferential* rates, which intensified the competition to which different industries were subjected, that special attention was directed.[2] The Act of 1873 had left much to the discretion of the Railway Commission in dealing with the question of undue preference. In the parliamentary discussions of 1887 and 1888 there were constant complaints of preferential rates. It was stated that no general measure dealing with railway traffic could be considered satisfactory which did not prevent preferential rates in favor of foreign products.[3] The government held, however, that no difference should be made between English merchandise and foreign merchandise because of origin.[4]

The undue preference section of the Act of 1888 provides that where, for the same or similar services, lower rates are charged to one shipper than are charged to another, or any difference in treatment is made, the burden of proof that such actions do not constitute an undue preference shall be on the railway. In considering whether the action complained of constitutes an undue preference, the commissioners are to consider " whether such lower charge or difference in treatment is necessary for the purpose of securing in the interests of the public the traffic in respect of which it is made. *Provided that no railway company shall make, nor shall the commissioners sanction, any difference in the tolls, rates, or charges made for or any difference in the treatment of home and foreign merchandise in respect of the same or similar services.*" [5] The final clause of the

[1] See evidence of J. H. Balfour Browne before the Select Committee of 1882, explanatory of the factors involved, answers to questions 1297 and 1298.

[2] In addition to the evidence bearing on this point contained in the Select Committee Report of 1882, see also detail in the Report of the Royal Commission on Depression of Trade and Industry, 1886.

[3] Motion of Earl of Jersey, Hansard, 1888, third series, Vol. 322, p. 1796. This was defeated by a vote of 72 to 45.

[4] Lord Salisbury, Hansard, 1888, third series, Vol. 323, p. 1052.

[5] I have italicized this so as to bring out the distinction of treatment between home and foreign traffic. In the bill, introduced in 1887, clause 25 provided that the commissioners were to consider whether the difference in charges or treatment was necessary " for the purpose of securing the traffic in respect of which it was made." The vague phrase, " in the interests of the public," contained in the legislation of 1888, was placed in the Bill of 1887 by amendment.

section prohibits a higher charge for similar services, for the carriage of a like description and quantity of merchandise, for a less than is charged for a greater distance on the same line of railway. The concluding clause of the section is not only wider than the "long and short haul" clauses of the American statute, it is also much wider than the prohibition hitherto existing in English legislation. An attempt was made by the railway interest to have a "long and short haul" clause placed in the legislation. It was argued that where a question of preferential rates came up, the comparison should in fairness to the railway be made with traffic carried over the same portion of the line.[1] It was held, however, that the consideration of this matter could safely be left to the discretion of the Commission.

Complaints concerning undue preferences have occupied a prominent place before the Commission. Broadly speaking, the subject-matter of these falls under the headings of : (a) *differential rates*, concerned with disparities in domestic rates and including as subheads export rates, group rates, and rebates in respect of quantity ; (b) *preferential rates,* concerned with disparities between home and import traffic. Before 1888 inequalities of charges for like services were only *prima facie* evidence, and the burden of proof was on the complainant: now it is on the railway. In the earlier decisions no rule is apparent. Each case was considered by itself. A decreased rate to develop a particular traffic in a particular district was an undue preference. The mere fact preference existed was not sufficient: it must be shown to be "undue" and "unreasonable." Differences in rate might be allowed where there were differences in the cost of conveyance.[2]

---

[1] The proposal was voted down, both in Grand Committee of the House of Commons and in the House itself. The motion will be found in Hansard, 1888, third series, Vol. 329, p. 452. The statement of Mr. Acworth, Hearings before the Committee on Interstate Commerce of the United States Senate, etc., 1905, Vol. III, p. 1851, that there is in the Act of 1888, a "long and short haul" clause — "the short distance included in the long distance" — is evidently attributable to the fact that he had not a copy of the act before him.

[2] For a summary of the law on this point, prior to 1888, see Woodfall, *op. cit.*, pp. 77–82. See also Darlington, Railway Rates, chap. iv.

Additional points have been made under the present Commission. A contract to give exclusive use of a given station to a particular colliery is an undue preference, as are also lower tolls given by a navigation company to prevent a large dealer moving his business.[1] Normally, similar charges should be made for similar services.[2] An unreasonable preference is a question of fact, and no general principle will be laid down.[3] Competition is a circumstance to be taken into consideration, and the extent to which it is to be considered is a question of fact, not law.[4] There can be no mathematical equality in regard to the charges or advantages between places which are outside of a group and the different members of a group. Competition and convenience to the neighborhood are to be considered as affecting the justifiability of a group rate.[5]

On the question of differential rates the Commission has reversed itself. As has been indicated, the Commission is empowered to consider whether the rate complained of " is necessary for the purpose of securing in the interests of the public the traffic in respect of which it is made." In 1890[6] complaint was made that lower rates on grain and on flour were given from Cardiff to Birmingham than from Liverpool to Birmingham. The distances were respectively 173 and $98\frac{1}{2}$ miles. The railway company contended that this was on account of competition and that the lower rate was necessary (1) in its own interest, (2) in the interests of the public. Direct inland communication

---

[1] *Rishton Local Board* v. *Lancashire & Yorkshire Ry.*, 8 Ry. and Canal Traffic Cases, 74 ; *Fairweather and Others* v. *Corporation of York*, 11 Ry. and Canal Traffic Cases, 201.

[2] *Timm & Son* v. *Great Eastern Ry.*, *Lancashire & Yorkshire Ry.*, *and Others*, 11 Ry. and Canal Traffic Cases, 214.

[3] *Per* Lord Herschell in *Pickering Phipps and Others* v. *London & N. W. Ry. and Others*, on appeal, 8 Ry. and Canal Traffic Cases, 100, 101 ; *Inverness Chamber of Commerce* v. *Highland Railway Co.*, 11 Ry. and Canal Traffic Cases, 218.

[4] *Pickering Phipps*, case cited, p. 87. Group rates are authorized by Section 29 of the Act of 1888. See in this connection the important decision given in *Denaby Main Colliery Co., Ltd.* v. *M. S. & L. S. Ry.*, 11 App. Cas. 97.

[5] *Pickering Phipps, etc.*, 87–88.

[6] *Liverpool Corn Traders' Association* v. *London & N. W. Ry.*, 7 Ry. and Canal Traffic Cases, 125.

exists between Bristol and Birmingham by way of the Severn river and canal navigation. There is also a combined sea and rail route.

Justice Wills pertinently said Parliament had dealt with the matter of undue preferences with a "faltering hand." It had left to the Commission the responsibility of deciding many things which would more naturally have been laid down in legislation.[1] The somewhat inchoate nature of the undue-preference clause is, however, more correctly attributed to its compromise origin. While it was intended, in a general way, that the phrase "in the interests of the public" should protect the interests of the consumers, Justice Wills was undoubtedly correct in saying that Parliament had no clear idea of what it meant. He considered that the "public interest" must be something wider than that of one of the two localities concerned, and stated that he could not see that any important "public interest" would be affected if the traffic in grain and flour should have to seek some other route from Cardiff to Birmingham.[2] The action of the railway in engaging in such competition created artificial conditions which interfered with the natural course of trade. Sir Frederick Peel put this point still more strongly: "A traffic which differs only from other traffic in being competitive can have no such a distinction made in its favor, however necessary a lower charge may be to meet the competition, or however much it may be to the benefit of the company to secure the traffic." The attempt of the railway to compete with the "natural advantages" of the traffic which went from the Severn ports [3] by sea and rail, or by inland water navigation, to Birmingham was unjustifiable. His general reasoning rested on the assumption that the low rail rate from Cardiff gave "little or no profit," and that therefore a penalty was being placed on Liverpool in the "highly remunerative rate" it paid.[4]

The unsatisfactory position taken by this decision in regard to the effect of competition, and the extent to which this was

[1] P. 137. [2] Pp. 136–138.
[3] These are Cardiff, Portishead, Avonmouth, Bristol, and Sharpness.
[4] Pp. 140, 141.

to be taken into consideration, was, however, apparently justified by the decisions on the matter. While the law was confused and contradictory, the leading decision — Budd's case — ruled water competition out of consideration.[1] The effect of water competition on the undue-preference clause was brought up again in 1892.[2] Complaint was made of an undue preference in flour and grain between the Severn ports and Birmingham, on the one hand, and Birkenhead and Birmingham, on the other. While the rate from Birkenhead to Birmingham, a distance of 98 miles, was 11s. 6d., the rate from Bristol to Birmingham, a distance of 141 miles, was 8s. 6d. The railway contended that the apparent anomaly was attributable to water competition. Both a majority and a minority decision were given. In the dissenting opinion, delivered by Sir Frederick Peel, it was held that, while the evidence justified low rates from the Severn ports, at the same time the Birkenhead rate should be reduced so as to give a lower mileage rate. The majority opinion upheld the railway position. The rates complained of were attributable to effective competition, maintained by a competing railway and by water competition. The existing inequality in rates was necessary to give the section of country around Birmingham the advantage of the supplies both from the Severn ports and from Birkenhead. Justice Wills stated that in the former decision he had construed " public interest " too narrowly. The public intended was the public of the locality or district. Any considerable portion of the population in general as opposed to an individual or an association was sufficient.[3]

While it is contended that one principle was applied in the first Corn Traders' case, because the amount of traffic affected

---

[1] *Budd* (*P. O.*) v. *L. & N. W. Ry.*, 4 Ry. and Canal Traffic Cases, 394. The cases bearing on this subject are dealt with by Justice Wills in his decision. See also Lord Herschell in *Pickering Phipps, infra*, 104, 105. See also Butterworth and Ellis, A Treatise on the Law relating to Rates and Traffic on Railways and Canals, etc., pp. 168–170.

[2] *Liverpool Corn Traders' Association* v. *Great Western Ry.*, 7 Ry. and Canal Traffic Cases, 114.

[3] *Liverpool Corn Traders' Association* v. *Great Western Ry.*, 7 Ry. and Canal Traffic Cases, 127.

was small, and that a different principle was applied in the second case because the amount of traffic affected was large,[1] it would appear that the change of position was, in reality, attributable to a decision in a case appealed from the Commission in 1891.[2] In this the construction of "public interest" had been involved. It was contended that a difference in rate complained of was not necessary for the purpose of securing the traffic in the public interest, and that the railway in making such a rate was seeking its own interest, not that of the public. This attempt to exclude the railway interest from "public interest" was denied by Lord Herschell. The point which should be considered, he stated, was not only the legitimate desire of the railway to obtain traffic, but also whether it was in the interest of the railway to secure this traffic rather than abandon it. The legislature, he continued, had recognized that there were cases where the traffic could not be obtained if the lower rate was raised, and where at the same time it would be unfair to demand as a condition of obtaining the traffic a reduction of the higher rate.[3] By judicial construction "public interest" has thus come to mean the controlling power of effective competition on particular rates. Undoubtedly there was a desire, when the legislation was under consideration in Parliament, to give the phrase a narrower construction. In 1887 it was stated that the railway, in carrying traffic on a rate competitive with sea-borne traffic, must show that there was a distinct public interest involved. The fact that some additional profit was obtained by engaging in such traffic was not sufficient.[4]

The "long and short haul" question comes before the Commission but seldom. When it does, it is not treated, as in the United States, as a form of preference demanding exceptional

---

[1] See Boyle and Waghorn, The Law relating to Railway and Canal Traffic, Vol. I, p. 4 ; also evidence of Mr. W. M. Acworth, Committee on Interstate Commerce, etc., 1905, Vol. III, p. 1849.

[2] *Pickering Phipps and Others* v. *L. & N. W. Ry. and Others*, 8 Ry. and Canal Traffic Cases, 83.

[3] *Pickering Phipps, etc.*, 102 and 103.

[4] See statement of Lord Salisbury, Hansard, 1887, third series, Vol. 314, p. 332.

treatment. The Commission has recognized effective competition as a justification of a lower rate for the longer distance. Where a higher rate is charged for the shorter than for the greater distance, the less being included in the greater, the Commission has held that, in the absence of effective competition at the longer distance point, such an arrangement is not justifiable, and that the shorter distance point should share on a mileage basis in the low rate given to the longer distance point.[1] The effect of competition has also been recognized in the case of export traffic. In 1903, in the Spillers & Bakers case, a low " shipment " rate was held necessary to obtain traffic. It was considered impossible to raise this rate, and the dissimilarity of circumstances did not warrant a comparison of the higher domestic rate with the lower export rate.[2] In 1904 a briquette manufacturing firm claimed that it was unduly prejudiced, since it paid the domestic rate on its raw material, while the manufactured product came into competition abroad with coal carried on a low export rate. The Commission upheld the principle of export rates, and further found that the railway was under no obligation to regulate its charges with reference to the ultimate competition complained of.[3]

From an early date English railway law has held that wholesale rates for large shipments do not constitute an undue preference. So early as 1858 in Nicholson's case, a leading case, it was decided that carrying at a lower rate in consideration of large quantities and full train loads at regular periods was justifiable, provided the real object was to obtain a greater profit by reduced cost of carriage. In taking this point of view, it was recognized that various shippers would necessarily be excluded from the advantage of the low rate granted on such conditions.[4] In the decisions of the Commission of 1873 it was recognized

---

[1] *Timm & Sons* v. *N. E. Ry.*, *Lanc. & York Ry.*, *and Others*, 11 Ry. and Canal Traffic Cases, 214.

[2] *Spillers & Bakers, Ltd.* v. *Taff Vale Ry.* ; 20 The Times L. R. 101.

[3] *Lancashire Patent Fuel Co.*, *Ltd.* v. *L. & N. W. Ry.*, *Great Central Ry.*, *and Others*. A summary will be found in the *Railway Times*, August 13, 1904.

[4] *Nicholson* v. *Great Western Ry.*, 5 C. B. (N. S.) 366. The test of the agreement complained of will be found in the footnotes to pp. 382–408. See also *Evershed* v. *L. & N. W. Ry.* (1877), 2 Q. B. Div. 267.

that lower rates might be given because of train-load shipments or of ability to load a greater weight into trucks.[1] The general justification of such arrangements has been recognized by the present Commission.

An example from a case decided in 1900 will indicate the nature of the arrangement.[2] A rebate of 3d. per ton from the established rate was to be made on condition that a minimum shipment of 25,000 tons of coal a year was guaranteed, and that the arrangement should last for five years. The Commission has, in various cases, held such rebates excessive.[3] The ground taken has been that the rebate is justified by a reduction in cost to the company, and that the rebate should not be in excess of the saving to the company. It is obvious that such a practice as this has dangers connected with it. A considerable number of complaints have been directed against the excessive advantages obtained by Messrs. Rickett, Smith & Co. under their rebate arrangement with the Midland Railway. In one case, though the evidence is contradictory, there are the earmarks of a secret rebate.[4] While the decisions of the old Commission recognized bulk of traffic as a justification for reduction of rates, the policy of the present Commission has not been clear cut. In some cases it has recognized quantity as a justification for a rebate.[5] But it has in other cases attempted to confine cost to mere economies of bookkeeping, attributable to more prompt settlements, etc.;[6] and it has expressed the dictum that rebates in respect of quantity would justify a differentiation of charges in so many cases that

---

[1] E.g. *Ransome* v. *Eastern Counties Ry.* (No. 2), 1 Ry. and Canal Traffic Cases, 109; *Girardot, Flinn & Co.* v. *Midland Ry.*, 4 Ry. and Canal Traffic Cases, 291; *Greenop* v. *S. E. Ry.*, 2 Ry. and Canal Traffic Cases, 319.

[2] *Daldy and Others* v. *Midland Ry. and Others*, 10 Ry. and Canal Traffic Cases, 305.

[3] E.g. *Charrington, Sells, Dale & Co.* v. *Midland Ry. Co.*, 11 Ry. and Canal Traffic Cases, 222; *Wallsall Wood Colliery Co.* v. *Midland Ry.*, *Railway Times*, July 25, 1903.

[4] *Charrington, Sells, Dale & Co.*, ut supra, p. 229.

[5] *Daldy and Others*, ut supra, p. 310. See also *Hickelton Main Colliery Co.* v. *Hull & Barnsley Ry.*, *Railway Times*, July 25, 1903. In this case the consideration of the lower rate was a minimum of 38,000 tons per annum.

[6] E.g. *Charrington, Sells, etc.*, ut supra, 230.

the rule against preference would be in danger of disappearing, " and the small trader would be in a more helpless position than the position in which he now is." [1]

While the traders recognize the value of export rates, and the effects of competition thereon, the conditions which affect the import rate are often neglected, and the low rail rates given on imported goods are often attributed to the stupidity, if not turpitude, of the railways in preferring home to foreign goods. When the Act of 1888 provided that the Commission should not " sanction any difference . . . in the treatment of home and foreign merchandise in respect of the same or similar services," it was claimed that this absolutely forbade preferential rates, and that the home traffic would therefore be carried at the same as that of foreigners.[2] Notwithstanding this enthusiastic prediction there is at present a reiterated demand for a select committee to investigate the question of preferential rates.

The discussion of preferential rates in England has proceeded along lines familiar to every student of the effects of water competition on railway rates. " Why," asks one, " if they (the railways) can carry at a profit from foreign countries, can they not carry home produce at the same rate ? " [3] If the London & Northwestern carried a train load of meat from Liverpool to London at 25s. because it was American, it should be able to do the same wherever the meat came from.[4] "Ex hypothesi they (the railways) already got a profit out of the produce they carried, . . . and what they would have to do was to put the English farmer and producer on the same footing as the foreigner." [5]

The question of preferential rates was brought before the Commission in 1895 in an exceedingly important case, which

[1] E.g. *Charrington, Sells, etc.*, *ut supra*, 231.

[2] Waghorn and Stevens, Report upon the Proceedings of the Inquiry held by the Board of Trade, 1889 and 1890, pp. 12 and 106. This report to the Lancashire and Cheshire, Devon and Cornwall, and Irish Conferences (traders' organizations), was published at Manchester in 1890. It contains a searching but extremely acrid and biased examination of the railway position.

[3] Lord Henniker, Hansard, 1885, third series, Vol. 315, p. 412.

[4] Mr. Mundella, Hansard, 1888, third series, Vol. 329, p. 413.

[5] Mr. Chamberlain, Hansard, 1888, third series, Vol. 339, p. 445.

lasted eight days.[1] Complaint was made that the railway charged
lower rates from Southampton docks to London on the following goods of foreign origin—wool, hay, butter, cheese, lard, hops,
fresh meat, bacon, hams—than it charged on similar articles
of home origin, which were normally carried a shorter distance,
and that the services rendered in respect of the foreign traffic
were not less than those rendered for the home traffic in the
proportion that the rates were lower. A few examples will serve
to show the nature of the disparity complained of:—

STATION	DISTANCE TRAVELED	RATES ON FRESH MEAT, HAY, AND HOPS TO LONDON		
		Rate for Meat	Rate for Hay	Rate for Hops
Southampton docks	76 miles	17s. 6d.	5s.	6s.
Southampton town	76 "	26s. 3d.	9s. 8d.	20s. 10d.
Alton	45 "	9s. 2d.	7s. 4d.	20s.
Botley	76 "	27s. 6d.	9s. 8d.	22s. 7d.

Back of the complaint lay a competition of ports for foreign
traffic. The London docks were in competition with the Southampton docks, which were owned by the London & Southwestern Railway.[2] Competition existed between the all water
route to London and the water and rail route *via* Southampton.

At first the railway endeavored to justify the apparent
anomalies on the grounds that the rates complained of were
made on the basis of water competition, and that, besides, they
were balances of through rates. But the Commission ruled that
such matters could not be considered in evidence under the
provisions of the Act. Under these conditions the railway had
to fall back on the unsatisfactory standard of cost of service.
It was shown that the rates for the home traffic covered a
variety of services—e.g., receiving, weighing, loading, covering,

---

[1] *Mansion House Association on Railway and Canal Traffic for the United Kingdom v. London & Southwestern Railway*, 9 Ry. and Canal Traffic Cases, 20.

[2] When these docks were acquired by the railway in 1892, it was anticipated
they would be a formidable competitor of the London docks. For information
descriptive of the highly developed facilities for handling traffic at the Southampton docks, see *Railway Age*, July 1, 1904; *Railway News*, January 7, 1905.

superintendence, provision of station accommodation, switching — which were not included in the rate on the foreign goods. The foreign merchandise was less valuable, less liable to damage, more easily and expeditiously handled, could be dealt with at times more convenient to the railway, always in larger quantities, and generally in a much more economical manner. On account of better baling, to cite one example, three tons of foreign hops could be loaded into a truck that would hold only two and a half tons of English hops.

The traders contended that such conditions of traffic as regularity and quantity, while admitted, were not capable of being included in the "similar services" spoken of in the undue preference section. Their contention was in substance that, while there might be differences in the case of home traffic because of dissimilarity of circumstances, in the case of the foreign traffic it was intended that there should not, on any account, be any difference in favor of foreign goods.

Had the contention of the traders been successful, it would have established a principle. But the decision of the Commission, which has been claimed as a victory by both parties, was of a compromise nature, and proceeded on the careful lines already laid down that undue preference is a matter of the facts of the particular case. The articles with which the decision concerned itself were hops, fresh meat, and hay. These were the only articles in which there was any considerable traffic from the stations intermediate between Southampton and London. The rates quoted on the other articles were simply "paper" rates. Sir Frederick Peel, who decided on the facts, held that the differences between the home and the import rates on meat, hops, and hay were not justified.[1] While his colleagues accepted this opinion, it was with hesitation. They both had doubts as to the alleged preference on meat,[2] and justly so. The average consignment of foreign meat from Southampton was 37 tons. In a period of seventeen months 10,638 tons of meat were shipped in 286 consignments. On the other hand, from Salisbury, the leading English meat center concerned, 231

[1] Mansion House case, pp. 38, 39. [2] *Ibid.*, pp. 32 and 43.

tons in 825 consignments were shipped in the same period. It is apparent that, where the whole series of costs would be so different, the Commission strained the idea of cost of service to the breaking point, and in doing so favored the home producer.

The decision was based on the idea, manifestly correct, that it was the intention of the statute to eliminate competition from the factors to be considered. At the same time the majority of the Commission are satisfied that the real factor controlling the rate situation in this case is water competition. As was said by Justice Collins, there was " no reason or principle in leaving out of account the fact of a rival route by rail or water from the point of departure to the point of arrival in the case of goods from abroad and taking it into account, as it clearly may be taken into account, where the comparison is between home goods only." [1]

This unsatisfactory decision, which cost the traders £2000 in law costs, obtained no general principle for the traders, and at the same time forced the railways to depend upon the artificial justification of cost of service. While the decision is of such a nature that in a case where there is real competition of home and foreign products a different verdict might be given, no further action in regard to preferential rates has been taken before the Commission. In 1899 the question of preferential rates was brought before the Board of Trade under the conciliation clause, but no satisfactory agreement could be obtained. [2]

It was Mr. Chamberlain who introduced into the legislation the clause under discussion. The agitation in regard to preferential rates has been given an added vigor by his preferential trade movement. Back of much of the outcry concerning preferential rates is a hazy protectionism. The support Mr. Chamberlain has obtained, for example, in the iron and steel industry is in considerable part due to preferential rates on iron and

[1] Mansion House case, p. 32. See also the statement of Lord Cobham in *Didcot, Newbury & Southampton Ry. Co.* v. *Great Western Ry. & L. & S. W. Ry.*, 9 Ry. and Canal Traffic Cases, 210.

[2] Case 16, Seventh Report of the Board of Trade, under Section 31 of the Act of 1888.

steel products, although the matter is complicated by the export rates given by the railways of competing countries.[1]

The control over docks by railway companies, which was objected to at an earlier date as a source of discrimination,[2] has been increasing of recent years. The railways have found it necessary to obtain control not only of docks, but also of steamer lines connecting with the Continent, in order to obtain the through rates which are necessary, if the import and export traffic are to balance, and thus permit a more economical use of rolling stock.[3] Complaint is made that the railways are spending large sums in erecting docks and warehouses at ports in order to encourage foreign trade, thereby still further increasing the number of preferential rates. The provisions of the Act of 1888 with reference to the right of the traders to have through rates from foreign points distinguished into their domestic and foreign portions are somewhat ambiguous. In the Southampton case the traders were unable to ascertain the foreign portion of the rate. As a result of this condition, an attempt was made in 1904 to obtain a provision in a special railway act, requiring that the railway should distinguish on its rate books, in the case of imports on a through rate, the portions attributable to (1) land carriage abroad, (2) dock, harbor, and shipping charges abroad, (3) conveyance by sea, (4) dock, harbor, and shipping charges at the British port, (5) railway charges in the United Kingdom. This was voted down by 103 to 79 on the ground that it was unfair to pick out a particular company in connection with what was a general matter.[4]

[1] See *Report of the Tariff Commission* (Chamberlain), 1904, Vol. I: The Iron and Steel Industry, under heading " Preferential Rates." *Contra*, see " British Railways and Goods Traffic: Is Preference given to Foreign Products? " (A. Dudley Evans, *Economic Journal*, March, 1905).

[2] Section 27 of the draft Report of the Select Committee of 1882, p. xxviii.

[3] The practice of consigning goods on through rates is increasing. At the same time Continental railways — e.g. those of Belgium — refuse to make through rates, except with railway companies. As to the alleged evil effects of such arrangements, see remarks of Mr. Hanbury, president of the Board of Agriculture, Hansard, 1902, fourth series, Vol. 108, p. 1640. See also Boyle and Waghorn, *op. cit.*, Vol. I, p. 304.

[4] Lancashire and Yorkshire Railway Bill. For text of the Instruction, see Hansard, 1904, fourth series, Vol. 131, p. 1473.

The farmers of the United Kingdom are subject to competition from many points.   To cite but a few examples : Algerian fruit and vegetables, French hops, Danish butter and eggs, compete with the home products.   The hop rates complained of when President Hadley wrote still exist.   Not only do the English farmers complain of preferential rates, there is also complaint from Ireland that the existing rate basis discriminates against Irish eggs, butter, and bacon.   It should be noted, although such a consideration is ruled out by the Railway Commission, that the low rates complained of are balances of through rates.   It costs about £10 for freight charges to place one ton of Algerian fruit or vegetables in London.   In fruit shipments the foreigners have had the advantage that a considerable number of the British growers are not giving sufficient attention to grading and packing and, in general, to the requirements of consumers.   The following may be taken as examples of the complaints in regard to Danish competition : —

	DISTANCE (mixed route)	RATE PER TON	
		Butter	Eggs
Esbjerg (Denmark) to Birmingham	553 miles	47s. 6d.	58s. 8d.
Armagh (Ireland) " "	358 "	42s. 6d.	50s.

The apparent disparity of rates on a distance basis disappears when it is remembered that on the Danish products there is a long water haul, and that there is also the difference between a car-lot and a less than car-lot basis.   The Danish rates are quoted on minimum consignments of ten tons, while the Irish rates are based on three hundredweight.

The more enlightened English farmers recognize the effects of water competition.   They know that it would not benefit them to have the through rate raised, as it would simply mean that the foreign produce would move more cheaply by an all water route.   When the London & Southeastern Railway in 1887 placed foreign hops on the same rate basis as domestic hops, the result was that the former moved by water to London.

The English producer was injuriously affected by the increased competition which lowered the price. At present approximately 90 per cent of the Continental produce imported by way of Boulogne and Calais goes by water to London. While the farmers recognize the superior facilities for handling foreign goods, they at the same time consider that the disparity between home and foreign rates is too great.[1]

Some part of the complaint in regard to preferential rates is attributable to misunderstandings in regard to rate conditions as well as to a lack of initiative on the part of the farmers. The Royal Commission on Agriculture stated in 1897 that, while coöperation among farmers was necessary in order to obtain lower rates, this matter could not be helped on by legislation.[2] But little has been done by the farmers to accomplish this.[3] While there is much unorganized complaint in regard to agricultural rates, the farmers are presenting very little evidence before the Departmental Committee, which is at present investigating the matter. The railways have been more willing than the farmers to coöperate. For forty years the London & Northwestern has been collecting small consignments of agricultural produce along its lines. These it forwards in bulk, delivers them to the London salesmen, pays market dues, collects the proceeds from the salesmen, and forwards the balance to the shippers. The London & Southwestern, which does a large business in package freight, undertook recently to supply the farmers along its lines with copies of Pratt's *The Organization of Agriculture*. All of the railways have been active in giving special rates to encourage agricultural shipments.[4] But, while

[1] E.g. evidence of W. W. Berry, a prominent hop grower of Kent, before the Royal Commission on Agricultural Depression, 1897, answers to questions 49,190, 49,226, 49,258. See also statement of Mr. Sinclair, Hansard, 1904, fourth series, Vol. 136, p. 295.

[2] Final Report, p. 529.

[3] See statement of the president of the Board of Agriculture, Hansard, 1902, fourth series, Vol. 108, p. 1639.

[4] For full detail concerning the special arrangements made by British railways in this regard, see Railway Rates and Facilities, copy of correspondence between the Board of Agriculture and Fisheries and the Railway Companies of Great Britain, etc., 1904. A large number of details bearing on the question of

the Danes are shipping produce into England on relatively low rates, which are the result of coöperation, 70 per cent of the domestic agricultural shipments on the Northeastern Railway are below three hundredweight, and 90 per cent fall below one ton.

CONTROL OVER ACTUAL RATES

In dealing with the rate policy of the Commission, a distinction must be made between the period prior to 1894 and that subsequent thereto. Though it had been stated in 1872 that legal maximum rates afforded but little real protection to the public,[1] the system was continued by the Act of 1888. While the work of the Board of Trade, as embodied in the Provisional Orders Acts, meant in all cases the systematization and in many cases the reduction of the maxima, the outcome was not satisfactory to the traders, some of whom wanted a general reduction of rates, regardless of the cost to the railways. The change of status in regard to *reasonable* rates introduced by the Act of 1888 was more apparent than real. The former Railway Commission had stated that, in addition to there being a necessity that rates charged should be within the maximum, there was also the added requirement that they must be reasonable.[2] No legal action had been taken, however, in regard to this matter. Two judicial decisions given in 1883 and in 1887 seemed to uphold the position that a maximum rate sanctioned by Parliament was conclusively reasonable.[3] But the statements in these decisions are simply dicta, since the question of reasonableness of rates was not directly involved. The Act of 1888, however, settled that the maximum rate was conclusive of reasonableness.[4]

preferential rates will be found in Pratt's Railways and Their Rates. This book has come to hand since the material contained in this section was set up.

[1] Report of the Joint Select Committee on Railway Companies Amalgamation, 1872, p. xxxiv.

[2] Fourth Report of the Railway Commissioners, p. 6, Section 14.

[3] See *Manchester, Sheffield & Lincolnshire Co.* v. *Brown*, 8 App. Cas. 715, and *Great Western Railway Co.* v. *McCarthy*, 12 App. Cas. 218. In the latter case Lord Watson took the position, "*Prima facie*, I am prepared to hold that a rate sanctioned by the legislature must be taken to be a reasonable rate."

[4] See Act of 1888, Section 24, Subsection 6 and Subsection 10. Report of Board of Trade, 1890, on Classification of Merchandise Traffic, etc., p. 17.

At the outset of its work the only way in which the Commission was brought in touch with rates was through the provisions concerned with undue preference and with through rates. The Commission will not state beforehand that a rate is preferential.[1] One of the commissioners, Sir Frederick Peel, has taken the position that certain powers over actual rates were given to the Commission. He has construed the statement in the " undue preference " clause which directs the commissioners to consider " whether the inequality cannot be remedied without unduly reducing the rate charged to the complainant " to give a power of reducing the higher rates.[2] Concerning this interpretation there is some doubt. Justice Wills holds that the words in question do not confer any rate-making power, but simply indicate the circumstances to be considered.[3] In an Irish case in 1897, in which the question of distributive rates was involved, it was held that the rate to a shorter distance point should be 3d. per ton less than the rate to the longer distance point; but no attempt was made to determine the longer distance rate.[4] In 1900 a temporary reduction of a canal toll was directed.[5] However, it cannot be said that these decisions have established the power of the Commission to reduce rates under the undue preference clause. Sir Frederick Peel also holds that the Commission may fix a through rate, no matter what the railways concerned may have agreed upon. While this matter has not been passed on, the weight of opinion is against such an interpretation.[6] It would appear, although this also has not been passed upon, that the Commission has no power to test the

---

[1] *In re* Taff Vale Ry. Co., 11 Ry. and Canal Traffic Cases, 89.

[2] Note his dissenting opinion in the Liverpool Corn Traders' Association case in 1892.

[3] Select Committee on Railway Rates and Charges, 1893, answer to question 8268.

[4] *Carrickfergus Harbor Commissioners and Others* v. *Belfast Northern Counties Ry.*, 10 Ry. and Canal Traffic Cases, 74.

[5] *Fairweather & Co. and Others* v. *Corporation of York*, 11 Ry. and Canal Traffic Cases, 201.

[6] Evidence before Select Committee of 1893, answers to questions 7963, 7964, 7966. See also the extremely guarded statement of Justice Wills before the same committee, answer to question 8264.

reasonableness of an established through rate. While the Commission has power to fix a through rate, if the parties do not agree, it would appear, although this is a moot point, that it has no power to apportion such a rate.[1] The Commission stated explicitly in 1895 that it had no power under the Act of 1888 to inquire into the reasonableness of a particular rate.[2] The various reductions of rate which have been ordered in connection with the workmen's trains applications are given under an entirely different jurisdiction.[3]

In the matter of group rates there has been some conflict between the English and the Irish decisions. The former regard competition and convenience as the most important factors. The latter lay more stress on distance. The appeals from the Commission have settled that competition is as important a factor in connection with rates as geographical position.

The question of the reasonableness of particular rates was suddenly brought before the Commission in 1894. The adjustments necessary in putting into force the rates under the revised maxima were great. The fact that fully one half of the traffic is carried on exceptional rates, which are below the class rates, still further complicated matters.[4] At the same time there was an apparent desire on the part of some of the railways to give the traders an object lesson in regard to the disadvantages of the legislative intervention which had brought some maxima below the actual rates formerly charged. And so the maximum class rates were published as the actual rates effective January 1, 1893. The outcry which followed quickened the work of adjustment, and led to an undertaking on the part of the railways that the rate increase should not be more than 5 per cent. But this

[1] This point was raised in the Forth Bridge case, 11 Ry. and Canal Traffic Cases, 5, but was not passed upon.

[2] *West Ham Corporation* v. *Great Eastern Ry.*, 9 Ry. and Canal Traffic Cases, 15.

[3] E.g. *In re London Reform Union* v. *Great Eastern Ry.*, 10 Ry. and Canal Traffic Cases, 280. See Ferguson, Railway Rights and Duties, pp. 206, 207.

[4] For detail concerning these rates, see "Report on the Question of Slow Freights (England)," by Henry Smart, *Bulletin of the International Railway Congress*, July, 1904.

did not prevent the enactment of a piece of panic legislation, passed hurriedly and without due consideration.[1] By this act it was provided that, where rates were directly or indirectly increased after December 31, 1892, they were *prima facie* unreasonable. The fact that the rate complained of was within the maximum was not to be a justification of the increase. The Commission was given power to deal with complaints arising under this act, subject to the provision that an application was first to be made to the Board of Trade. Over seventeen hundred complaints were brought before the Board of Trade between the date of the passage of the act and the end of February, 1895.

In the investigations leading up to the Provisional Orders legislation the traders had all along been desirous of having the actual rates serve as maxima.[2] The evident intention of the majority of the members of the Select Committee of 1893 was that the rates in force at the end of 1892 should be the maxima.

In taking up the new functions imposed by the revolutionary Act of 1894, the Commission had a full appreciation of the difficulties of the new jurisdiction. Justice Collins said, "I cannot suppose that Parliament intended to take the management of these great trading companies [the railways] out of the hands of the practical men who work them, and to place it in the hands of the Railway Commissioners." The Commission had no intention to exercise a rate-making power. It was its intention to construe the legislation strictly. In the interpretation of the statute there was, however, a difference of opinion between the commissioners. Lord Cobham held that the Commission was not competent, of its own knowledge, to say whether a rate was reasonable or not. "No tribunal, however expert, would undertake to say that a 6s. 6d. rate for the carriage of coal from Derbyshire to London is reasonable, but that 6s. 9½d.

[1] A mass of detail pro and con will be found in the evidence attached to the Report of the Select Committee of 1893. See also Mavor, "The English Railway Rate Question," *Quarterly Journal of Economics*, April, 1894; Acworth, The Elements of Railway Economics, pp. 147–154.

[2] E.g. speech of J. H. Balfour Browne, already cited, p. 171. Evidence of Marshall Stevens before the Select Committee of 1893, answers to questions 2448 and 2518.

is unreasonable." The legislature had, however, given a standard of reasonableness in the rate of 1892, and the rate could not be increased above this unless good reasons were shown.[1] In endeavoring to obtain some definite standard of measurement of reasonableness, the Commission ruled out all reference to competition, or to that more inclusive system, charging what the traffic will bear.[2] The opinion of the traders, that the rates in force at the end of 1892 should be maximum rates, received a partial support from Lord Cobham, who held that the fact that a rate had not been increased prior to 1892 created a strong presumption against the railway because it had not increased the rate when it had the unchallenged right to do so ;[3] but Justice Collins held that conditions prior to 1892 could be considered, and that the reasonableness of a rate was to be tested by conditions existing or apprehended before the legislation came into force.[4] Later decisions have taken into consideration conditions subsequent to 1894.[5] There still remained the question of the criterion of reasonableness. Justice Collins held that this should be cost of service. Reasonableness, he held, must be measured by reference to " the service rendered and the benefit received." This, in his opinion, pointed to cost of service as the base, because " the service rendered and the benefit received were unaffected by the prosperity or misfortune of the parties to the contract." [6] This squared with the views of the traders, who held that the true basis of a rate was cost of service.[7] The fact that the legislation provided, in the first

[1] *Derby Silkstone Coal Co., Ltd.* v. *Midland Ry.*, 9 Ry. and Canal Traffic Cases, 107.

[2] E.g. *Charlaw and Sacriston Collieries Co.* v. *Northeastern Ry.*, 9 Ry. and Canal Traffic Cases, 140. In *Black & Sons* v. *Caledonian Ry.*, etc., 11 Ry. and Canal Traffic Cases, 176, the Court of Sessions refused, on appeal, to grant the process which would enable the railway companies to investigate the books of the applicants to see what their profits had been during a given period.

[3] Derby Silkstone Coal Co. case, p. 130.   [4] *Ibid.*, p. 111.

[5] E.g. *Black & Sons, ut supra.*

[6] Derby Silkstone case, p. 113. The decision in this regard is based on *Canada Southern Ry. Co.* v. *International Bridge Co.*, 8 App. Cas. 731, 732.

[7] E.g., letter of Sir James Whitehead, president of the Mansion House Association, London *Times*, December 22, 1892 ; also speech of J. H. Balfour Browne, *ut supra*, p. 257.

instance, a rate of an antecedent period as a criterion of reasonableness would seem to show an intention of ruling out in the
present rate any consideration of what the traffic would bear;
for, if charging what the traffic would bear, in the present, were
admitted as a present criterion of reasonableness, it is difficult
to see how the past rate could serve as a standard of reasonableness, when, presumably, what the traffic would bear was
something essentially different.

The increases in rates complained of, which have for the most
part arisen in connection with coal traffic, have in a number of
cases been indirect, attributable to decreases in the allowance
made for wastage in the coal traffic, etc. The criterion the Commission has found it necessary to adhere to — cost of service —
has tied it down to an arbitrary arrangement. To meet this condition, the railways have had recourse to technicalities savoring,
in some instances, of subterfuge. It one case it was alleged that
the increase complained of was attributable to an increase in the
cost of cartage as distinguished from conveyance charges. The
former fell under terminal services, over which the jurisdiction
of the Commission was limited.[1]

No general principle has been established in the unreasonable-
rate cases. The railways had claimed the right in 1893 to increase the rates by 5 per cent as compared with the rates in force
in 1892. While the traders never recognized the validity of this
claim, the Board of Trade by 1898 had accepted this arrangement as justifiable. The important Smith & Forrest case, which
came up in 1899, was intended to test this arrangement.[2] Complaint was made by the oil refiners of Liverpool and Manchester
that an increase of 5 per cent was unreasonable. The increase
was in part direct, in part indirect, attributable to decreases in
cartage rebates. The matters involved were pertinent to the
whole freight traffic of the United Kingdom, and affected future

---

[1] *Mansion House Association, etc.* v. *L. & N. W. Ry.*, 9 Ry. and Canal Traffic
Cases, 174. See especially the remarks of Lord Esher in the appeal proceedings,
pp. 199, 200.

[2] *Smith & Forrest* v. *L. & N. W. Ry. and Others*, 11 Ry. and Canal Traffic
Cases, 156.

as well as past rates. The railways introduced statistical evidence showing that, because of various increases in cost, particularly in the case of labor, expenses were 5.1 per cent higher in 1892 than in 1888 and 6.3 per cent higher in 1898 than in 1892. The railways desired to carry the comparisons back to 1872, when many of the old rates had been fixed; but the Commission considered 1888 a sufficiently remote date, and comparisons were made with the conditions of 1891. It was found that an increase of 3 per cent would be justified. The Commission has thus shown its intention to look at each case by itself. If a 5 per cent increase should be found justifiable in a particular case, it would not necessarily have any bearing on a later decision.

The desire of the Commission not to engage in any rate-making experiments has kept it from making any statements as to general rates. It has concerned itself with the reasonableness of particular rates. The Commission has painstakingly endeavored to get at the cost involved. The decisions have been compromises. Where decisions have been against the railways, damages have been awarded on the basis of the difference between the increase and what was deemed a justifiable increase; and the railways have been ordered to desist charging the unreasonable rates. In a recent case an attempt was made to obtain an expansion of the unreasonable-rate jurisdiction.[1] It was contended that it was unreasonable to increase a rate, although the increased rate was still below the point to which it had been decreased in 1894. The Commission did not, however, pass upon this question. It is apparent that, if such a contention were accepted, still more rigidity would be introduced into the system. The traders' anticipations as to the effect of the Act of 1894 have been nullified by the willingness of the Commission to consider conditions antecedent to the legislation. The whole position, it must be recognized, is an exceedingly artificial one. While the position taken by the Commission is strained and unsatisfactory, it is difficult to see, when it was specifically referred back to the conditions of

[1] *Millom & Askam Hematite Iron Co.* v. *Furness Ry. and Others*, reported in *Railway Times*, January 21, 1903.

1892, what other method it could have adopted. By acting as it has, a degree of elasticity has been retained for the process under the legislation which it otherwise would not have possessed.[1]

It was objected at the outset, that the judicial member would dominate the Commission, owing to the difficulty of distinguishing between law and fact. It has happened, however, that in the performance of their duties the lay members determine on questions of fact. At the same time, while the opinion of the *ex-officio* commissioner is final on a point of law, the lay members also form and express their opinions.

The government has throughout considered the requirement that one member of the Commission shall " be experienced in railway business " to mean that he shall have been a railway director or a railway manager.[2] Exception has been taken to this by the traders. To the attempt to obtain a business representative on the Commission, in addition to a railway representative, the railways are not opposed. It is from the government that the objection has come. Mr. Mundella, when president of the Board of Trade, said he would be glad to appoint a " really " business man who should be an impartial authority, fairly representative of the trading class. Mr. Mundella had stated that the Commission as then constituted was generally unsatisfactory.[3] An attempt was made by the traders in 1894 to so amend the legislation that one of the commissioners should be " experienced in trade or commerce." This was not pressed beyond the first reading.[4] Mr. Bryce, who succeeded Mr. Mundella, held, however, that no such restriction as his predecessor had favored

---

[1] The criticism directed against the Commission by Grinling, in British Railways as Business Enterprises, pp. 161–163, contained in Ashley's British Industries, is not wholly justified.

[2] Mr. Price, before his appointment to the Commission of 1873, had been chairman of the Midland Railway. Viscount Cobham, who succeeded Mr. Price in 1891, had been deputy chairman of the Great Western. On Viscount Cobham's resignation, early in the present year, he was succeeded by Mr. Gathorne-Hardy, who had been deputy chairman of the Southeastern.

[3] Hansard, 1894, fourth series, Vol. 28, pp. 792, 793.

[4] The text of this bill will be found in the *Railway Times*, June 16, 1894, p. 782. See also Report of the Select Committee of 1893, p. xiii.

should be placed on the choice of the government. The desire to have a commercial representative is still active. Believing that the commissioners should be assessors, possessed of expert knowledge, rather than judges, the traders have urged that the terms of the commissioners should not exceed ten years, so that there might be an opportunity to keep constantly in touch with actual conditions.

Looking at conditions as they are, it is apparent that the presence of a railway representative on the Commission has meant that those appearing before it have been more careful to give essential details. There is no real cause for complaint, from the traders' standpoint, concerning the services which the lay members have performed. The railway representative, for example, in the enforcement of the legislation of 1894 has followed very closely the ideas favored by the traders. Sir Frederick Peel has been willing to give a broad construction to the legislative provisions concerned with control of rates.

The average English trader asks for a process which shall be " short, sharp, and decisive." And to him the process of the Commission has undoubtedly been unsatisfactory. As a minimum, six weeks elapse between the filing of the application and the decision of the case.[1] In a number of cases more than a year has elapsed between the initial hearing and the decision. In some cases the delays are attributable to adjournments in order to permit the obtaining of more evidence.[2] In other cases delays have been caused by an endeavor to get the parties to settle the questions in dispute. When cases are appealed, there are further delays. While one case has been decided on appeal within two months after the decision of the Commission, the usual period is from six months to one year.

Notwithstanding the assumption in 1887, that giving a *locus standi* to governing bodies and to traders' associations would cause much litigation, the number of complaints is not great.

[1] The Rules of Procedure of the Commission allow twenty-one days after the filing of the application for the filing of replies.

[2] E.g. the important case of Spillers & Bakers, etc., was heard first December 9 and 10, 1903. It was then adjourned for further evidence, and was decided in July, 1904.

In the period 1889–1903 there have been, on the average, fifty applications a year; but many of these have been of minor importance. In the same period there have been on the average twenty-three decisions a year. But here there are many cases where one decision covers a group of identical cases.[1] Complaint has been made of the small number of days on which the Commission sits. In the nine years, 1896–1904, the average period the Commission has sat annually as a court is thirty-two days. This, it is true, is exclusive of the days when the Commission has sat to consider applications for sanctioning working agreements between railways, the time taken up in connection with the administrative duties of the Commission, and the days on which the registrar of the Commission has inquired into damages and interlocutory proceedings which would otherwise come before the commissioners acting as a court. Of these no record is kept; but, after making all allowance, it is apparent that the Commission is not overworked. It is apparent, however, as has been recognized by the traders themselves, that the mere enumeration of the number of days on which the Commission has sat is no criterion of its usefulness.[2]

The Commission is criticised on account of its expense. This criticism is, however, directed only to a slight extent against its cost of maintenance.[3] It is the expense of obtaining a decision that the critics have in mind. In recommending a limitation of the right of appeal, the committee of 1882 intended to limit expense. By providing for the intervention of the Board of Trade in various matters, the legislation of 1888 hoped that the expense of proceedings might be kept down. The attempt of the legislation of 1894 to lessen expense, by providing that costs should not be granted by the Commission, except in cases where the claim or the defense is frivolous or vexatious, was intended to obviate the burden of the fees of the railway lawyers falling

[1] See Table I, on p. 793.

[2] In this connection see the statement of Sir B. Samuelson, who was very active, on the traders' side, in the steps leading up to the legislation of 1888. Hansard, 1883, third series, Vol. 278, p. 1887.

[3] In 1903 the cost of maintenance of the Commission amounted to £6497.

on the trader, when defeated in a case. The admittedly high
expenses are not attributable to the fees of the Commission,
which are moderate,[1] but to the development of a technically
equipped Railway Commission Bar. It was early seen that the
necessary prominence of the lawyers employed would make the
process relatively expensive. The same conditions existed in
connection with the Commission of 1873. In the body of lawyers found practicing before the Commission are many whose
names are prominent in the Parliamentary bar, — a practice
whose fees are high. The legal work before the Commission
has tended to fall into the hands of a relatively small number
of practitioners.[2] Prior to 1894 it was the practice to allow
costs for two lawyers, unless when some especially technical
matter was involved.[3] Since 1894 there have been, on the
average, two lawyers on each side in the traders' cases. Under
these conditions the expense, in a case contested before the Commission, runs from £150 to £200 a day. The individual trader
is able to lessen his expense where, as in the sidings' rent cases,
a group of traders bring action on a common set of facts. Only
in one case has a rate matter been presented before the Commission by the complainant himself; and he was unsuccessful.
The judicial members of the Commission are opposed to the
complainants appearing in person. While it is true that in one
case, which was settled before trial, the total court costs to the
complainant were £1; and these, with his other expenses, were
reimbursed to him by the railway, it is apparent that those who

[1] See Railway and Canal Commission Procedure, Schedule III, Woodfall,
op. cit. See also Senate Committee on Interstate Commerce, *ut supra*, Vol. V,
Appendix B, p. 220. The Commission fees in rate cases, as a maximum, do not
exceed £5.

[2] In the 58 traders' cases covered by the reported decisions down to 1902,
68 lawyers took part. Mr. J. H. Balfour Browne, K.C., who is the dean of the
traders' legal forces, appeared in 41 cases; Mr. C. A. Cripps, in 36; Mr. E. Moon,
in 31. In all there were 32 lawyers who appeared in more than three cases. Eight
of these appeared in more than ten cases each. The leaders have not practiced
exclusively on one side. For example, Mr. C. A. Cripps, who has appeared in
30 cases for the railways, has appeared in 6 cases on the traders' side.

[3] The registrar is the taxing officer of the Commission. See appeal from his
decision in this connection in *Glamorganshire County Council* v. *Great Western
Ry.*, 9 Ry. and Canal Traffic Cases, 1.

are aggrieved in small matters cannot afford to come before the Commission.[1] There have not been the migratory sessions of the Commission which the traders favor. The sessions are held in the capital cities of the countries concerned. It is cheaper to have the cases taken to the technically equipped lawyers in the capital cities than to have these come to the cases in local centers. If the case involves any matter of considerable moment, the contest has to be carried on against the Railway Association. This being so, the complaints have to be fought out by firms, groups of traders, trade associations, Chambers of Commerce, local governing bodies.[2] The cost of a suit before the Commission is, under these conditions, about the same as before any other high court.[3]

In view of the expense attaching to suits before the Commission, it has been urged that the power possessed by the Board of Trade under the Act of 1873 to institute proceedings before the Railway Commission should be utilized. While the railways would not object to the Board of Trade presenting before the Commission matters arising under the conciliation procedure of the Board, where its decisions have not been accepted by the railways, it has been held that this would interfere with the efficiency of the conciliation clause. The government has held that to make a government department public prosecutor in cases before the Railway Commission would savor rather of persecution than of prosecution.[4] One exception has been made to this general rule. In 1899 the Irish Department of Agriculture was empowered in its act of organization to present rate grievances before the Commission at the public expense. So far

---

[1] See evidence of T. Middleton before the Royal Commission on Agricultural Depression, 1897, answer to question 2361.

[2] One of the most interesting trade associations is the Mansion House Association, founded in 1889. It represented, before the Board of Trade in 1889–1890, 209 public and local authorities, 174 commercial and agricultural organizations, besides a large number of individuals.

[3] While the limitation of appeal reduces the expense, the powers of the Court of Appeal to grant costs in Commission cases is not affected by the legislation of 1894.

[4] Hansard, 1883, third series, Vol. 278, p. 1901, statement of Honorable Joseph Chamberlain.

there has been only one such case, in 1902. In this the Board of Agriculture was successful.

The Associated Chambers of Commerce urged in March, 1904, that, with a view to cheapness and expedition, the local county courts should be used in cases between the railways and the traders. This suggestion is especially intended to cover the case of the small trader. In one form or another it has been under discussion since the early nineties. Cases affecting railways already come before the county courts from time to time.[1] While the county court method of procedure might work fairly well in local matters, it is apparent that this procedure is unfitted for matters of more general interest. There would also be a defect in that the way is open for a lack of expedition. Appeals may be taken on points of law or equity from the decisions of the county court. In the consideration of these appeals the high courts are empowered to draw inferences of facts. Exceedingly small matters are appealed at present. In 1904 one appeal was concerned with an alleged overcharge of $11\frac{1}{2}d$. on a railway journey.[2] It has been suggested, however, that the cost of appeals under the proposed jurisdiction should, where the appeal is by a railway, be borne by the railway.[3]

When the Act of 1894 was under discussion, it was claimed that the legislation was defective, in that it had not restored the right possessed prior to 1888 to challenge the reasonableness of all rates. To the proposition to confer rate-making power on the Commission the government was strongly opposed. It considered that "to ask the Railway Commission, or any tribunal, to consider what is a reasonable rate would be to give them no firm ground on which they could stand." [4] Back of all the criticism directed by the trader against the Commission there is in

---

[1] E.g. cases arising under Section 5 of the Railway Rates and Charges Act of 1891. This section is concerned with special charges that may be made by railways for special services.

[2] *Ashton* v. *Lanc. & Yorkshire Ry.*, 2 K. B., 1904, 313.

[3] Waghorn and Stevens, *op. cit.*, p. 65.

[4] Statement of Honorable James Bryce, president of the Board of Trade, in an interview with the deputation on railway rates and charges, June 15, 1894, *Railway Times*, June 23, 1894.

reality a desire that the rate-making power should be exercised. But, while the desire exists, there is a lack of unanimity as to the means to use to accomplish this. In this uncertainty some are looking to the Board of Trade.

The Board of Trade was given jurisdiction, under the Act of 1888, to deal with rate grievances through a conciliation process modeled on that contained in the Act to Regulate Commerce. It is also empowered to attempt to settle complaints about unreasonable rates. The operation of the Board of Trade under its conciliation jurisdiction is recognized as having met with a considerable degree of success.[1] Agreements have been obtained in about one third of the cases brought before it. By the explanations it obtains from the railways the board is also able to settle incipient rate grievances. The process is simple and inexpensive. When a complaint is made, the railway is communicated with, so that a statement of its position may be obtained. If the matter cannot be settled by correspondence, an attempt is made to arrange a meeting at the Board of Trade between the complainant and a railway representative. Here the matter is taken up in an informal manner. Isolated cases have dragged on a year without a decision, but normally some settlement is obtained much more promptly. Complaints varying from an overcharge of $2d.$ on a lawn mower to questions concerned with preferential rates come before the board. In 1900 it was able to obtain a reduction in distributive rates affecting five hundred towns in England and in Ireland. Since 1888 over eleven hundred cases have been brought before the board.[2] Approximately one half of these were presented in the period 1899–1903. The table on the following page shows the result of the more important applications.

There were, then, under these headings satisfactory agreements in about one fifth of the applications made.

[1] This is admitted by so strong an advocate of the rate-making power as Mr. W. A. Hunter. See an article of his "Railway Rates and the Common Weal," *New Review*, Vol. VIII, p. 341.

[2] This is exclusive of over 1900 unreasonable-rate complaints dealt with by a special official prior to 1899.

PRINCIPAL APPLICATIONS, 1899–1903	SEVENTH REPORT		EIGHTH REPORT	
	Settled	Unsuccessful	Settled	Unsuccessful
Classification	4	9	2	12
Delays in conveyances, facilities, etc.	15	15	4	5
Facilities and tolls on canals . . .	2	4	—	—
Rates, differential	9	18	—	10
Rates, preferential	—	2	—	—
Rates, through rates obtained . .	2	7	2	4
Rates, through rates, reduction of .	2	2	—	1
Rates, unreasonable, reduction of .	37	82	18	29
Rebate, cartage	6	3	3	2
Rebate, station terminals	1	—	—	—

While the conciliation work of the Board of Trade has met with a fair degree of success in smaller matters, it has failed when larger matters have had to be dealt with. In Pidcock's case, which later came to the Railway Commission, there was involved the right of the complainant to receive rebates in respect of terminal services not performed at his sidings. The matter dragged on for seventeen months, and finally the railways stated they would take the matter to the Commission, although in the opinion of the Board of Trade the "matter was of no such intricacy or difficulty as to make the arbitrament of a more elaborate tribunal essential to a just decision." [1] The railways will not recognize the conciliation procedure in any matter which involves legal right. With a view to simplifying procedure the Act of 1888 provides that, when a trader desires to obtain a through rate, a preliminary hearing before the Board of Trade is necessary. However, since the determination of the board on such a matter has no legal effect, the preliminary hearing has become simply a perfunctory matter. The Board of Trade is unwilling to express an opinion; while the railways are unwilling to take any position that may be used against them before the Commission.

When the rate increases of 1893 were under discussion, the Mansion House Association proposed, on behalf of the traders,

[1] Fourth Report of the Board of Trade of Proceedings under Section 31 of the Railway and Canal Traffic Act, 1888, p. 6.

to accept the decision of the Board of Trade on these rates if the railways would also pledge themselves to accept the decision. But to this the railways would not agree. To the attempt to give the Board of Trade power over rates the railways are strongly opposed. This position is also supported by the Board of Trade itself. It has constantly claimed that the strength of the conciliation procedure of the board is wholly attributable to lack of compelling power. It is averse to any increased jurisdiction over rates being conferred upon it. It also believes that, if a new rate tribunal is organized, it should, while equipped with a commanding personnel, be of the "advisory" type.

Table I[1] indicates that, from the traders' standpoint, the most important matters brought before the Commission are sidings' rent charges, preference, unreasonable rates, charges for services at sidings, and reasonable facilities. Attention has already been directed to the importance of sidings' traffic in British railway working. For many years the small traders engaged in retailing coal had been using the trucks as storage warehouses. The railways objected to their sidings being crowded with loaded trucks. The colliery owners, to whom the rolling stock belonged, also objected. Formerly the railways had charged demurrage charges based on the average time a truck was detained on a siding. In 1895 the railways decided to charge demurrage based on the actual time a truck was detained on a siding over and above the time necessary to unload it. Since 1895 many applications dealing with this arrangement have been brought before the Commission. Some have come up under the heading of legality of rates, others under the heading of unreasonable rates. The complaints in regard to charges for services at sidings are attributable to the fact, already sufficiently explained, that in the English railway system there are various special charges over and above the conveyance rate. As is indicated in Table I, 779 applications have been made to the Commission.

The preventive effect of the Commission is in part measured by the details given in Table II.[2] A special example will make

---

[1] P. 793, *infra*.   [2] P. 793, *infra*.

the preventive effect clearer. In 1902 some forty-seven cases, which were brought before the Commission alleging that the Midland Railway was unduly preferring a prominent colliery, such favor being to the detriment of the complainants, were settled before trial. In all, 219 cases have been settled or withdrawn. Formal action has been taken in 346 applications,[1] leaving approximately one third of the applications concerning which there is no further record.

There has been only three cases in the history of the Commission in which anything savoring of a secret rebate has been brought before it. The work of the Commission, in so far as rates are concerned, has been almost entirely concerned with freight traffic. The Act of 1888 makes no direct provision for action in regard to passenger rates. It has, however, been settled in decisions arising out of the Commission's action that it has, as an incident of a through-rate arrangement, power to order through booking (ticketing) of passengers. It has also power to deal with passenger facilities under the question of "reasonable facilities." Of the rate cases formerly argued before the Commission the traders have won not far from three fifths. The tendency of the Commission has been to give compromise decisions. Not only have there been compromises as between the contending parties, there have been compromises as between the opinions of the commissioners themselves. In the Rickett, Smith case, in which the point involved was an increase in rates, Justice Collins thought all the increase was justifiable, Lord Cobham thought none of the increase was justifiable, Sir Frederick Peel occupied an intermediate position, and his opinion prevailed. Both in the traders' cases and in the cases between railways the Commission has been attempting to have the parties arrive at satisfactory settlements, without final action on its part. In some cases, when the parties have agreed, the Commission, in accepting the agreement, has incorporated it in its final order.

---

[1] This includes a large number of group decisions; i.e. where one decision covers identical facts in a set of cases, consent decisions, cases where a settlement arrived at by the parties is embodied in an order of the Commission, dismissal of applications, etc.

The presence of a judge on the Commission has meant a strict constructionist point of view in regard to the law. In general, powers have not been implied. Early in the history of the Commission Justice Wills said nothing could be more mischievous than to strain legislation to cover facts that had been left out of it. In 1892 the same judge, in speaking of a statute, said, " The legislature had reasons of its own, good, bad, or indifferent, which have nothing to do with me." In one case, however, where a railway had closed a branch railway, and pulled down the railway station, the Commission required, with much hesitation on the part of the judicial member, that the railway should give the reasonable facilities asked for; and this of necessity involved the rebuilding of the railway station. This implication from the law of 1854 was promptly overruled.[1]

Undoubtedly the presence of a judge on the Commission has made the relations with the higher courts more harmonious than was the case with the Commission of 1873. There has not been that tendency, so conspicuous in the relations of the Federal courts to the Interstate Commerce Commission, to regard the Commission as an amorphous interloper. In one case, it is true, the Scotch Court of Sessions claimed that, if a decision as to fact depended upon a conclusion in law, then there could be an appeal. This line of argument, which, if followed, would soon undermine the finality of the Commission's decisions on questions of fact, has not been adopted; and there has been a ready recognition by the courts of the finality of the Commission's decisions on questions of fact. The result of this is seen in the attitude of the courts to the decisions of the Commission. Down to 1904 there have been, as is indicated in Table III, thirty-eight appeals. The Commission has been overruled in four cases, while in two others it has been sustained in part and reversed in part. The decisions of the Commission in the traders' cases have more finality than in the cases between railways. While nine tenths of the applications before the Commission have been concerned with traders' rights, there have been only eighteen appeals in

---

[1] *Darlaston Local Board* v. *L. & N. W. Ry.*, 8 Ry. and Canal Traffic Cases, 216.

the traders' cases; while there have been fifteen appeals in cases where railways alone or railways and dock companies have been concerned.

From the standpoint of the trader a question of importance is the willingness of the railway to obey the orders of the Commission without fighting the matter to the last ditch. While, on the whole, the railways have been loyal to the decisions of the Commission, examples may be found on both sides. In 1902 the railway reconsidered its first intention to appeal the Charrington, Sells case. The result was that a large number of cases, in which the same set of facts was involved, were settled out of court. The London & Northwestern, as a result of the decision in the first Corn Traders' case, gave up the attempt to compete for the traffic with which the case was concerned, and readjusted its rates accordingly. On the other hand, it was necessary, in the case which the Mansion House Association won from the same railway in 1896, to have supplementary proceedings before the Commission in 1897 before the cessation of some of the rates complained of was obtained. The involved uncertainties of English railway law have also played their part. The railways have been able, acting within the law, but depending upon legal, not commercial, conditions, to modify the redress given by the Commission. In 1889 a decision, under the undue-preference clause, found that existing rates were interfering with the distributive business of the Irish town of Newry. Two years later complaint was made because one of the rates complained of had been raised. The railway successfully justified this, on the ground that the section of road, on which there was an increase of rate, was expensive to work on account of cost of gradients, etc. In 1900 the firm of Cowan & Sons, paper manufacturers, failed in an application to the Commission for a rebate on sidings' charges. In retaliation for this application the railway company, which for twenty-eight years had delivered coal at the private siding of the firm in question, refused any longer to deliver coal at the siding. While the railway was at the same time delivering coal at the sidings of adjacent competing firms, it delivered the coal for the Cowans at a near-by station, and they had to haul it *back* to their siding. The decision of the Commission in favor of the Cowans was overruled. It was held that the arrangement between the railway and the trader in this case was a purely voluntary arrangement, creating no prescriptive rights against the railway. It was not till 1904 that legislation, bringing such sidings within the facilities clause of the Act of 1854, and thus supporting the Commission's decision, was passed.

The Commission, whenever there is an identity of facts, — e.g., in many of the sidings' rent cases, — has dealt with cases in groups, giving a decision which covers a set of cases. The unwillingness of the courts to give the decisions of the Commission a more general effect has assisted in tying the decisions down to the facts of a particular case. In October, 1901, the Commission decided that certain coal rates charged by a number of Scotch railways were unreasonable. The rates were discontinued, as regards the complainants, in December of that year. Three other traders, who were subjected to the same rates, but who had not been parties to the suit, later brought action in the courts for damages because the railways had continued to charge them the rates complained of. The court held, however, that the decision of the Commission had no general effect. Although the rates had been found unreasonable, the court would take no cognizance of this unless they were also illegal.[1]

The functions committed to the Commission are extremely diverse. While it has, with evident innuendo, been called the Traders' Court, it has, in addition to dealing with rate matters, an extensive jurisdiction in regard to arbitration of matters referred to it by the Board of Trade; e.g., differences between railways involving such matters as running rights, number of trains under a running arrangement, arrangements in regard to connection in a through train service over a connecting line, division of expenses between the owning and the controlling company, differences between the Postmaster-General and railways in regard to postal payments, questions arising in connection

---

[1] *Lanarkshire Steel Co.*, Ltd. v. *Caledonian Ry.*, 11 Scots Law Times Reports, 407, 408. A preliminary decision of the court had held that the Commission's decision was of general effect. *Ibid.*, 225.

with the introduction of improved brakes, complaints in regard to the water supply of London. In addition it serves as a court of appeal from the Board of Trade in cases arising out of the rules made by the Board of Trade under the railway labor acts, and has alternative jurisdiction in the workmen's trains applications. In addition to jurisdiction under special acts the Commission exercises functions finding their legal sanction in some nineteen general acts.

Not only are there complaints at present in regard to preferences on imported products, there are also complaints concerning the rates and facilities given home products. Complaint is especially active in the case of Irish agricultural products. Comparisons, unfavorable to domestic rates, are constantly being made with foreign rates. The question of shipments on " owner's risk" rates gives rise to many complaints. The criticism of the Commission on Agriculture of 1897, that the rate regulative legislation has not given clear effect " to the intentions of Parliament," [1] is general among the traders. That the Commission has not accomplished much that was expected of it is a patent fact. Its procedure has not met the case of the small trader. At the same time the rate regulative procedure that accomplishes all that is expected of it is not absent from England alone. The Commission, it must be remembered, was organized, not to reduce rates or to intervene actively in matters of rate regulation, but as a court to settle differences. As a court, it has performed its functions. While there was, at the outset, some tendency on the part of the judicial members to look at matters from a legal standpoint rather than from the standpoint of facts, the tendency has been, in more recent years, to meet the conditions rather than to bend the conditions to meet preconceived theories. On questions of railway law the Commission has been, on the whole, more in touch with the facts than the ordinary law courts. While the expense attaching to litigation before the Commission is readily apparent, it may be queried in how far there is a justification for expecting either a cheap settlement or a settlement, at the public expense, of important business matters. So far as

[1] Final Report, paragraph 526.

England is concerned, the attempts to obtain cheap settlements, in the face of the existing involved body of railway law, would mean, if successful, results of little worth.

In the United States the Federal courts have recognized the debt of the Act to Regulate Commerce to the English regulative legislation. But, when comparison is made of the constitution and functions of the English Commission with those of the Interstate Commission, differences at once appear.

The English Commission is a court. The American Commission has the functions of a referee or special commissioner. The former has final decision in regard to fact and a limitation on the right of appeal, with the result that appealed cases are normally settled within a year. The latter has no finality of decision in regard to fact, and appeals from its decisions have taken from two to nine years to decide. While the English Commission has been overruled in the period ending 1904, wholly or partly, in six out of thirty-eight appeals, the American Commission has, in approximately the same period, been overruled in twenty-nine out of thirty-eight appeals.[1] While the Interstate Commerce Commission has, practically from the outset, claimed, as a necessary implication from the language of its enabling statute, an amendatory rate-making power, the English Commission, organized as a court, has, almost without exception, kept aloof from making implications extending its jurisdiction, and has denied any intention to exercise a rate-making power. While the members of the American Commission hold on a limited tenure and the Commission is a bipartisan organization, the tenure of the lay commissioners in the English Commission is for good conduct, there is a pension on retirement, no question of bipartisan organization enters in, and the provision is made that one of the commissioners shall have technical knowledge of railway affairs. The judicial members of the English Commission are assigned to it for five years; but during the period they are not engaged in the Commission work they perform their regular duties as judges of the high court.

[1] See Table III. See also Appendix D, Vol. V, p. 331, Hearings of Committee on Interstate Commerce, etc., 1905.

In the details of the regulative policy which has developed under the Commissions, resemblances and differences appear.[1] The English regulative policy is not in harmony with that of the United States in regard to the extent to which competition is to be considered as a justification of rate anomalies. While the English legislation eliminates competition in the case of import rates, the American position, as established in the Import Rate case, states that competition is to be considered as affecting both import rates and domestic rates. In the case of domestic rates the English Commission at first would not recognize competition as the justification of an anomalously low rate basis unless a well-defined "public interest" was thereby served. Later it accepted the same view as was set forth in the United States in the Alabama Midland case ; namely, that competition is one of the matters which may lawfully be considered in making rates. The grievance of secret rebates, one of the central evils in the United States, is practically nonexistent in England. There is no provision other than that of the undue preference clause to cover such a grievance. In both countries the principle that undue preference is a question of fact has been accepted. While the United States has singled out a particular form of preference for special treatment under the "long-and-short-haul" clause, England has allowed more elasticity by placing the matter under a general clause. On the question of the justifiability of granting wholesale rates in respect of quantities larger than car-load lots, the American decisions have been contradictory. The lower courts have shown a tendency to accept the decision in Nicholson's case, but in the Party Rate case the Supreme Court established as the law that a discrimination in respect of quantity, even if allowed to all doing the same amount of business, is to be considered from the standpoint of public policy and the effect of such an arrangement upon trade competition.[2] In so deciding

[1] There is no recognition, in the working of the English Commission, of results arrived at in the regulative policy of the United States.

[2] *I. C. C.* v. *Baltimore & Ohio Rd. Co.*, 145 U. S. 263. This upholds the general position taken at an earlier time by the Interstate Commerce Commission in *Providence Coal Co.* v. *Providence & Worcester R. Co.*, 1 I. C. C. Decisions, 363. See also Judson, The Law of Interstate Commerce and its Federal Regulation, p. 194.

there has been accepted as a principle what is, so far, only a tendency in the English regulative policy.

The dissimilarities of the matters dealt with by the two Commissions will be seen by referring to Table I. The items common to the two Commissions are legality of rates, unreasonable rates, reasonable facilities, and undue preference.[1] In all, about one half of the applications made to the English Commission are concerned with matters of a kind coming before the American Commission.

The English Commission has used two sets of rate principles: competition as an important factor in differential rates, export rates, and in general in the home side of undue preference; cost of service in regard to preferential rates, and unreasonable rates. This has been in great degree attributable to the legislation. The traders have desired free trade in exports, not in imports. Admitting that there has been a certain *judicial* bias in favor of the cost-of-service principle, it is at the same time apparent that legislation, like that of 1894, which makes a past rate the *prima facie* criterion of reasonableness rules out the possibility of considering present competition. The defects of the legislation of 1894 are its own. The Commission has made the legislation less unworkable than could have been expected.

A considerable part of the desire to control and lower actual rates in England pertains to that hysterical belief in England's industrial decadence which has found some favor in recent years. A considerable part of the criticism arises from the endeavor to prove, on the basis of foreign statistics not properly comparable with English statistics, that English rates are unduly high. Some rearrangements in the Commission's machinery would, however, effect improvements. An arrangement whereby, when a question of principle is established in a decision of the Commission as distinct from a mere finding on facts, the enforcement should be placed in the hands of the Board of Trade

[1] I omit sidings' rent (demurrage) charges, because the conditions under which these arise in England differ entirely from those existing in the United States.

instead of leaving it as a question of possible dispute to be fought out in individual cases, would effect an improvement. A closer articulation of the conciliation procedure of the Board of Trade with the process of the Commission, whereby the findings of the former would have a status before the latter, would also be expedient. The Commission is becoming more and more a technical court, whose decisions are modified by an attempt to obtain settlements rather than legal decisions. Notwithstanding the criticism directed against it, it is difficult to see how, considering the peculiar geographical, industrial, and railway conditions it has faced, the Commission could have accomplished more than it has done.

S. J. McLean

Leland Stanford Jr. University

TABLE I

SUBJECT-MATTER OF APPLICATIONS DEALT WITH BY THE COMMISSION, 1889–1903 [1]

	1889	1890	1891	1892	1893	1894	1895	1896	1897	1898	1899	1900	1901	1902	1903
Board of Trade (Prevention of Accidents Act, 1900)	–	–	–	–	–	–	–	–	–	–	–	–	–	6	26
Classification	–	–	–	–	–	–	–	–	–	1	–	–	–	–	1
Facilities, reasonable	3	8	3	3	1	6	–	1	4	2	2	5	4	4	3
Postmaster-General, applications concerning	–	–	–	–	–	–	–	–	–	2	2	2	–	1	–
Preference, undue	3	4	5	4	5	5	4	6	–	1	6	3	97	10	8
Rates, distinction of	2	3	–	–	–	–	–	1	–	–	–	–	–	–	–
Rates, legality of	–	2	–	1	–	–	–	2	–	–	–	2	–	–	–
Rates, through	–	–	–	–	–	2	13	4	3	3	6	2	1	–	–
Rates unreasonable	–	–	–	–	–	1	63	10	2	24	–	–	3	–	1
Sidings, rent (demurrage)	–	–	–	–	–	–	–	6	–	–	25	3	–	108	91
Sidings, rebate from sidings' charge	–	–	–	–	–	1	6	3	–	4	9	8	6	–	3
Sidings, services on, charges for	–	–	–	–	–	–	1	4	5	1	–	2	–	23	24
Terminal charges	–	1	–	–	–	1	–	1	–	–	–	–	–	–	–
Trucks, rebates because not supplied	–	–	–	–	2	–	–	–	1	–	–	–	–	–	–
Railways, differences under special acts, etc.	3	10	1	2	4	5	3	7	6	3	3	4	2	1	2
Railways, working agreements approved	3	2	5	5	2	–	2	2	2	2	–	1	2	3	1
Workmen's trains applications	–	–	–	1	–	–	–	–	–	23	1	3	–	1	–
Water Act, Metropolitan (1897), applications	–	–	–	–	–	–	–	–	–	2	–	2	–	–	–
Miscellaneous	–	–	1	2	1	2	3	3	1	2	–	1	1	1	1

TABLE II

CASES WITHDRAWN OR SETTLED EITHER IN COURT OR OUTSIDE, 1889–1903 [1]

	1889	1890	1891	1892	1893	1894	1895	1896	1897	1898	1899	1900	1901	1902	1903
Facilities, reasonable	1	–	–	2	–	1	1	–	2	2	–	4	1	3	2
Postmaster-General, applications concerning	–	–	–	–	–	–	–	–	–	1	–	–	–	–	–
Preference, undue	–	–	1	–	2	2	2	–	2	2	2	–	–	2	15
Rates, legality of	–	1	–	–	–	–	–	2	3	–	–	–	–	–	–
Rates, through	–	–	–	–	–	–	–	1	2	–	1	1	–	1	–
Rates, unreasonable	–	–	–	–	–	–	2	16	20	19	8	1	4	30	–
Sidings, rent (demurrage)	–	–	–	–	–	–	–	2	2	–	–	–	–	1	1
Sidings, rebate from sidings' charge	–	–	–	–	–	–	1	2	1	3	2	3	1	–	–
Sidings, services on, charges for	–	–	–	–	–	–	–	1	2	–	–	1	–	–	–
Railways, differences under special acts, etc.	–	–	1	–	1	1	–	2	–	2	–	1	–	–	–
Workmen's trains applications	–	–	–	–	–	–	–	–	–	12	1	3	1	–	–
Water Act, Metropolitan (1897), applications	–	–	–	–	–	–	–	–	–	–	1	–	–	–	–
Miscellaneous	–	–	–	–	–	2	–	2	1	–	–	1	1	–	–

[1] In various cases a number of points are dealt with. In constructing the table, I have selected the most important point in each case.

TABLE III

CASES APPEALED FROM THE RAILWAY AND CANAL COMMISSION, 1889–1904[1]

YEAR	NAME OF CASE	APPEALED BY	POINT INVOLVED IN APPEAL	RESULT
1890	Traff Vale Ry. Co. v. Barry Docks & Ry. Co.	Defendant	Differences under special act	Com. sustained.
1891	Sowerby & Co. v. Great Western Ry. Co.	Plaintiff	Terminal charges	"
1891	Rhymney Ry. Co. v. Bute Docks Co.	"	Facilities between parties	"
1892	Pickering, Phipps, et al. v. L. & N. W. Ry. et al.	"	Undue preference	"
1892	Liverpool Corn Traders' Ass'n v. Gt. W'n Ry.	"	Undue preference	"
1894	Northeastern Ry. v. Scarborough & Whitby Ry.	"	Construction of working agreement	"
1894	Darlaston Local Board v. L. & N. W. Ry.	Defendant	Reasonable facilities	overruled.
1895	Mansion House Ass'n v. Gt. W'n Ry.	"	Unreasonable rates	sustained.
1896	Greenwood & Sons v. Lanc. & Yorkshire Ry.	Plaintiff	Rebate on sidings' charges	"
1896	Watson, Todd & Co. v. Midland Ry. & L. & N. W. Ry.	Defendant	Terminal rebates	"
1896	Mansion House Ass'n v. L. & N. W. Ry. & L. & S. W. Ry.	"	Unreasonable rates	"
1896	Didcot, N. & S. Ry. v. Gt. W'n Ry. & L. & S. W. Ry.	Both parties	Through booking of passengers	"
1887	Northeastern Ry. v. North British Ry.	Defendant	Running rights	"
1888	Salt Union v. North Staffordshire Ry.	"	Rebate on sidings' charges	"
1888	Gt. Northern Ry. v. N. E. Ry. & N. B. Ry.	"	Differences under special act	"
1889	Huntingdonshire County Council v. Simpson	"	Reasonable facilities	"
1900	Postmaster-General v. Corp'n of London	"	Telegraph connections	"
1900	Postmaster-General v. Corp'n of Glasgow	"	Telegraph connections	"
1900	Forth Bridge v. N. B. Ry., Gt. N. Ry., et al.	Plaintiff	Through rates	overruled.
1900	L. T. & S. Ry. v. Gt. Eastern Ry.	"	Differences between railways	sustained.
1901	Cowan & Sons v. North British Ry. (No. 2)	"	Rebates on sidings' charges	"
1901	Black & Sons v. Cal. Ry., N. B. Ry., & G. & S. W. Ry.	Defendants	Application for details of plaintiffs' profits to use in suit	"
1901	Cowan & Sons v. North British Ry. (No. 3)	Defendant	Reasonable facilities	{ sustained.[2] / overruled.[2]
1901	Huntington et al. v. Lanc. & Yorkshire Ry.	Plaintiff	Ownership of a siding	sustained.
1901	Rhymney Ry. v. Great Western Ry.	Defendant	Differences between parties	"
1901	Gt. Western Ry. v. Metropolitan Ry.	"	Differences between parties	"
1902	Crompton & Co. v. Lanc. & Yorkshire Ry.	Defendant	Rebate on sidings' charge	{ sustained.[2] / overruled.[2]
1902	Vickers, Sons & Maxim v. Midland Ry. et al.	Defendants	Power to propose through rate	sustained.
1902	London & India Dock Co. v. Gt. Eastern Ry. & Midland Ry.	"	Connection of siding with railway	overruled.
1902	Lanc. Brick & Terra Cotta Co. v. Lanc. & Yorkshire Ry.	Defendant	Difference between parties	overruled.
1902	Gt. Western Ry. v. Metropolitan Ry.	Plaintiff	Difference between parties	sustained.[2]
1902	Mold & Denbigh J'n Ry. v. L. & N. W. Ry.	Defendant	Undue preference	"
1903	Abram Coal Co. v. Gt. Central Ry.	Plaintiff	Refusal of proposed through rate	"
1903	London & India Docks v. Midland Ry. & Gt. Eastern Ry.	Plaintiff	Compensation for mail	"
1903	Great Western Ry. v. Postmaster-General	Defendant	Undue preference	"
1903	Ackers, Whitley & Co. v. Gt. Central Ry.	"	Undue preference	"
1904	North British Ry. v. Caledonian Ry.	"	Running rights	"
1904	Lancashire & Yorkshire Ry. v. Wright	Plaintiff	Point of law	overruled.

[1] The official report of cases for 1904 is not yet available.

[2] In part.

XXVIII

RAILWAY REGULATION IN FRANCE[1]

THE railway policy of France is based on the view that railways should be exploited, not by the State, but by strong independent companies under strict government control. National purchase has again and again been considered, but has always been rejected. When last it was proposed in the French Parliament that the State should buy out four of the large railway companies, one hundred Chambers of Commerce voted against, and one only for, the proposal. While the companies are encouraged to earn large profits,[2] they are never allowed to compete with one another, or to invade one another's territory, and their arrangements for sharing traffic or earnings constantly receive official sanction. The State has refrained from dictating their tariffs, and confined itself to exercising a veto over those which they propose. Under the Railway Conventions of 1883, as under those of 1859, the government has no power either to fix or to alter rates. The proposal of a rate must emanate from one of the companies, but before taking effect it has to be approved by the Minister of Public Works.

The official machinery by which this control over rates is exercised consists of three parts: a salaried corps of expert officials for gathering information; a large nonsalaried committee made up of high officials, members of the legislature, and representatives of the business community, to give advice

[1] From the *Quarterly Journal of Economics*, Vol. XX, 1906, pp. 279-286. Further details are given in translations from Colson's "Abrégé de la Législation des Chemins de Fer, etc.," in Hearings before the Senate (Elkins) Committee on Interstate Commerce, 1905, Vol. V, Appendix, pp. 265-297.

[2] M. Pelletan, in his report of May 12, 1889, pointed out that French railway shares paid from 10 to 24 per cent of their original cost; since then there have been some increases in dividends.

based on that information; and, lastly, the Minister who acts on that advice.

The permanent officials who investigate and report on all questions concerning rates number 68, and cost the State 400,-000 francs a year; that is, 10 francs for each kilometer of railway at present in operation.[1] Of this amount 258,500 francs represent the salaries of the chief experts, 32 in number.[2] At their head, receiving 20,200 francs a year, is the Director of Commercial Supervision (*Directeur du Contrôle Commercial*), who studies the tariffs and commercial workings of all the French companies. Under his orders are the General Supervisors of Commercial Exploitation (*Contrôleurs Généraux de l'Exploitation Commerciale*), each of whom has similar duties in respect to a single railway, receives 11,400 francs a year, and is assisted in his work by one Principal Inspector and several Special Inspectors. To each railway is assigned one Principal Inspector (*Inspecteur Principal*) of Commercial Exploitation, receiving 8000 francs a year, and from three to five Special Inspectors (*Inspecteurs Particuliers*), each of whom receives from 6500 to 5500 francs a year. These inspectors are all under the orders of the General Supervisor in charge of that particular railway.

There is at the Ministry of Public Works a bureau of Railway Direction, one of the divisions of which investigates tariffs and charges, and the head of which is known as the Director of Railways (*Directeur des Chemins de Fer*). This high official acts as counselor to the Minister on all points connected with railway administration.

But the Minister's chief adviser is the Consultative Committee of Railways (*Comité Consultatif des Chemins de Fer*) over which he presides, and which examines questions of rates as well as all others affecting the relations between the railway companies and the State. The organization of this Committee has been several times changed. In its present form, which

---

[1] The 40,000 kilometers "of general interest" are alone to be counted, since tariffs of local lines are, as a rule, passed upon by the prefects of the several departments.

[2] M. Sibille's Report on Budget of 1905 (*Ch. des Députés*, No. 1962), pp. 148, 183.

dates from 1898, it has 100 unpaid members, 10 *ex officio* and 90 appointed for two years by the President of the Republic. The present membership consists of 36 government officials (6 *ex officio*), 34 members of the legislature (4 *ex officio*), and 30 men holding no political office. A combination is thus secured of administrative, legislative, and general opinion.

Among the officials are the Director General of Customs, a brigadier general on the general staff, the Directors of Forests, of Agriculture, of Commerce, and of Labor, the Director of Roads, Navigation and Mines, the Director of Commercial Supervision, the Director of Railways, and five other members of the Council of State. Among these last is M. Picard, well known as the author of the two principal works on French railways, who, as vice chairman, presides over the Committee in the absence of the Minister; while M. Colson, another member, is almost equally well known for his book, Transports et Tarifs, and for the articles on Transportation which he contributes to the *Revue Politique et Parlementaire*. Both these officials have heretofore filled the post of Director of Railways.

Among the Deputies MM. Baudin, Barthou, Bourrat, and Sibille, and among the Senators M. Waddington, are specially conversant with railway problems, the first two being ex-Ministers of Public Works, and the three others having written elaborate reports on various railway questions.

In the general group we find twelve presidents or members of Chambers of Commerce (Paris, Lille, Hâvre, Lyons, Bordeaux, and Marseilles being among the cities represented), six presidents or members of national Agricultural Societies, two workingmen, the Governor of the Bank of France, seven business men or civil engineers, two of whom represent internal navigation, one judge, and one representative of the International Railway Congress. This last member, M. Griolet, is also vice chairman of the Railway du Nord, and is the only railway official belonging to the Consultative Committee.[1]

---

[1] For further particulars, see J. de la Ruelle, Contrôle des Chemins de Fer (Paris, 1903), p. 218, and for the names of present members, see Annuaire du Min. des Travaux Publics, 1905, p. 34.

General meetings of the Committee are seldom held, most of its business being transacted by its "permanent section," a sub-committee of 40 members (4 *ex officio*, 36 annually chosen by the Minister), which meets at least once a week. This "section" comprises twelve Senators and Deputies, six representatives of commerce, industry, and agriculture, three civil engineers, two workingmen, and the member of the Railway Congress, besides sixteen of the government officials. Matters of importance may be referred to the whole Consultative Committee by the Minister, or by the Vice President either on his own initiative or upon the request of five members of the "section."

When a company wishes to introduce a new rate or to change an old one, the regular procedure is the following. The text of the proposed rate must be posted up or otherwise advertised in the company's stations, and sent to the Minister of Public Works, to the Director of Commercial Supervision, to the Prefects of departments, and to the Chambers of Commerce of districts affected by the rate. The Chambers of Commerce and the Prefects are expected to forward to the Minister in writing any protests or comments which they may wish to make.

The proposal is then carefully examined by the General Supervisor of Commercial Exploitation in charge of the railway proposing the rate, whose duty it is to report thereon. In this task he is assisted by the Principal Inspector and the several Special Inspectors of the railway in question. These officials are instructed personally to inform themselves as to the needs of trade and the views and wishes of business men. Having done so, they prepare a written report, which must embody "a thorough discussion of the prices proposed, and a comparison between them and other tariffs in force on the French railways at the various shipping points with which this traffic competes." [1] The report is submitted to the Director of Commercial Supervision, who transmits it with or without revision to the Minister of Public Works. As soon as these documents reach the Minister he lays them before the Consultative Committee. If this Committee makes a favorable report, the Minister approves the

[1] Ministerial Circular of July 16, 1880.

rate, and it usually goes into effect within fifteen days from that date. Thus on March 25, 1904, a proposed addition to one of the special tariffs of the Railway de l'Ouest was duly advertised. It was officially approved on the 11th, and took effect on the 26th of April, 1904.[1] No rate can become operative until one month after having been advertised. In order to keep the public fully informed, the text of the proposal and that of the ministerial approval are published in the *Journal Officiel*.

The ministerial sanction given to any rate may be withdrawn at any time, and, in accepting a rate proposed, the Minister may attach to his approval certain conditions to which the company must assent before the rate can take effect. A passenger rate cannot be increased till it has been in force three months, nor a freight rate till it has been in force one year.

The interval between the proposal and the approval of a rate, which is normally one month, is sometimes a great deal longer. Should it, however, be necessary to put a rate into immediate effect, the Minister often grants a provisional "homologation," whereby the rate becomes at once available pending its formal consideration and approval.

The French tariffs that have been thus approved are published in the two large folio volumes of the *Recueil Chaix*, a revised edition of which is issued quarterly. The edition bearing date July, 1905, but not actually issued till last September, has 1712 pages in the volume containing the tariffs for slow freight, and 980 pages in that containing the rates for fast freight and passengers. These manuals would be less bulky if they embodied only the tariffs of the large companies, but they also include the rates of all the light railways, narrow-gauge lines, and tramways throughout France. In the intervals between the editions of this work newly approved rates are published in a special weekly bulletin, as well as in the *Journal Officiel*. Thus the authorized railway tariffs are at all times readily accessible to the French public.

Since the French regard railway tarification from a commercial standpoint, their tariffs, like those of England and the

---

[1] *Journal Officiel*, April 3 and 25, 1904.

United States, are based on the so-called "value" system,
which consists in charging such rates as the traffic will bear.
Their system of classification would take too long to explain.
Suffice it to say that, in compliance with the demands made by
the government in 1879, the classification and description of
freight was made uniform on all the French railways by their
reformed tariffs approved between August, 1884, and December, 1890. At the same time the number of reduced tariffs and
special rates was much cut down, and the *Recueil Chaix* considerably simplified. Since those reforms, however, the large
family of special rates has continued to multiply, under the
pressure of commercial needs, though the Consultative Committee is on principle opposed to them, and seeks, whenever
possible, to procure in their stead reduced kilometric scales of
rates drawn up on the Belgian differential plan, and applicable
in any direction and on any line of the given railway.

In sanctioning a special rate, the Committee almost always
insists, as a condition of approval, that intermediate stations
shall also be entitled to it, and that a special rate, say from
Toulouse to Orleans, shall be enjoyed as far as Orleans by
goods shipped from Toulouse to points beyond Orleans.

The Minister of Public Works having no power to fix rates,
the principal function of the Consultative Committee is to check
unjust, discriminating, or capricious tarification, and thus by
degrees to produce throughout France an equitable system of
rates. It often suggests to the companies what changes it deems
desirable, and, though it can only suggest, yet the possession of
its veto often enables it, when granting one of the companies'
requests, to gain its own point as a *quid pro quo*. This influence
is all the stronger because the authority vested in the Minister,
and through him in the Consultative Committee, covers not
only the commercial (i.e., rate-making), but also the technical
and financial [1] sides of railway administration.[2]

---

[1] E.g. no railway company can issue bonds without the assent of the Consultative Committee and of the Minister.

[2] It is clearly to the companies' interest not to offend an authority on which
they are in so many ways dependent. A different system of administration,
interfering only in commercial matters, would be far from having the same
influence (Colson, Transports et Tarifs, 1898, p. 350).

The Committee always declines to indorse any special rate savoring of undue preference or discrimination; for instance, a rate in favor of goods produced by a particular factory or of materials ordered by a particular contractor. It also rejects any rate calculated to draw away traffic from any other French railway or to ruin the business of coasting steamers or canal boats. Thus in April, 1899, a special rate of 15 francs on mineral waters shipped to Paris was requested by the P.-L.-M. Company. This rate was approved in April, 1900, but, the canal men of Roanne having pointed out that it was ruining them, the approval was withdrawn on August 24, 1901.

The Committee endeavors to adjust the tariffs enjoyed by competing industrial centers in such a way as to secure to each the natural advantages of its location. If, however, a particular place or industry has long had the benefit of certain special rates, and has thus acquired a quasi-vested right to them, the Committee will not allow them to be abolished without stipulating that they shall be reëstablished, "if within a year their disappearance gives rise to well-founded complaints."

A good illustration of the manner in which the Committee may obtain concessions from the companies is furnished by the negotiations leading up to the approval on October 27, 1900, of the new tariff of Accessory Charges (*Frais Accessories*). The companies had for twenty-five years been urging that the registration fee for luggage should be raised to 15 centimes, while the Committee still insisted on maintaining it at 10 centimes. The Committee also wished that the companies should guarantee to the consignor of freight using the lines of several companies the route offering the cheapest combination of rates, even when not demanded by him, as they had been doing since 1883 for the consignor of freight using the lines of a single company. The companies, on the other hand, had been anxious to suppress certain special rates affecting about 1350 kinds of freight. The matter was settled by a compromise, in which the companies waived their claim for the 15-centime registration fee, and consented to guarantee the cheapest route in the manner mentioned, while the Committee advised the Minister to sanction the suppression of the special rates on the ground that they were practically obsolete.[1]

In Algeria and in the Regency of Tunis the service of commercial supervision has been organized in a manner practically identical with that above described, and proposals of rates are referred either to the Minister of Public Works in Paris or to the Resident-General in Tunis. This latter personage is assisted by a consultative committee of eight or ten members most of whom are officials connected with the administration of the Regency.

W. H. BUCKLER

JOHNS HOPKINS UNIVERSITY

[1] Arrêté du 27 October, 1900, Impr. Nat., 1902.

XXIX

RAILROAD OWNERSHIP IN GERMANY[1]

*   *   *   *   *   *   *   *

THE Prussian railway administration was reorganized on April 1, 1895.[2] Previous to that time there had existed two distinct official bodies, or "resorts," immediately below the minister of public works. The latter was then, and is now, the executive head of the railway administration, and the two bodies subordinated to him were known as Eisenbahndirektionen and Eisenbahnbetriebsämter, respectively, the one having direct charge of the operation of the railways and the other performing purely administrative functions. Of the Direktionen there were 11, and of the Betriebsämter 75. The functions of both of these have now been consolidated in the royal State railway directories, of which 20 have been created,[3] with their seats at Altona, Berlin, Breslau, Bromberg, Cassel, Cologne, Danzig, Elberfeld, Erfurt, Essen, Frankfurt a. M., Halle a. S., Hannover, Kattowitz, Königsberg, Magdeburg, Münster, Posen, St. Johann-Saarbrücken, and Stettin. Each directory is composed of a president, appointed by the King, and the requisite number of associates, two of whom, an Ober-Regierungsrath and an Ober-Baurath, may act as substitutes of the president under the direction of the minister. Each directory has complete administrative control over all the railways within its limits, although the subordinate civil administrative organs of the State, such as the Oberpräsident, Regierungspräsident, and Landrath, have certain powers in the granting of concessions, police regulations,

---

[1] From *Annals of the American Academy of Political Science*, 1897, Vol. X, pp. 399–421. *Ibid*. Vol. XIX, March, 1907, is another good description.

[2] Only a few minor changes have been introduced since.

[3] Since this was written (1897) the Hessian railways have been associated with the Prussian and the number of directories increased to 21.

etc. The directory decides all cases arising out of the action of special and of subordinate branches of the administration ; and, representing the central administration, it may acquire rights and assume responsibilities in its behalf. The directories may be characterized as general administrative organs, one of whose great functions is the proper coördination of all the parts of the railway system.

Below and subordinated to them are special administrative organs, upon whom falls the duty of local adaptation and supervision. There are 6 classes of these local offices, and their names indicate in a general way their functions : operating, machine, traffic, shop, telegraph, and building offices or Inspektionen, as they are called. Shortly before the new system went into operation the minister of public works issued special business directions for each class of offices. The contents of each of these ministerial orders may be grouped under 3 heads : (1) the position of the office in the railway service ; (2) its jurisdiction in matters of business ; (3) general provisions. To give a detailed analysis of the functions of the local offices is out of the question here. It should be added, however, that all phases of the service, whether from the point of view of the railways or of the public, are carefully provided for. Thus one of the foremost duties — " die vornehmste Aufgabe " — of the local traffic office is to maintain a " living union" between the railway administration and the public. For this purpose the chief of the office is in duty bound, by means of numerous personal interviews and observations, to inform himself concerning the needs of the service in his district, to investigate and to remedy complaints and evils without delay, and to take such measures as will secure the most efficient service. It is also one of his duties to inform the public concerning the organization and administration of the railways, so as to avoid idle complaints. This single provision in the rules governing one of the local offices illustrates the spirit of them all.

Private railways, which before April 1, 1895, had been supervised by a special railway commission, are now subject to the jurisdiction of the president of a directory and his alternates.

This was another step toward greater unity in the system. The directories upon whom the supervision of the private roads devolves are those at Altona, Berlin, Breslau, Cassel, Cologne, Elberfeld, Erfurt, Essen, Frankfurt a. M., Halle, Hannover, Königsberg, Magdeburg, Münster, St. Johann-Saarbrücken, and Stettin. As there are 20 directories, and only 16 supervise private railroads, it is evident that jurisdictions for private roads are not identical with those of directories. Nor does each directory have an equal number of miles of private or State roads within its jurisdiction. This depends largely upon the geographical distribution of the railways and upon the intensity of the traffic. Thus, the Berlin directory supervises 587 kilometers of State roads, while Halle has 11,884 kilometers. The other directories lie between these two extremes. It may be added that on April 1, 1895, the private roads represented together only 2200 kilometers (not including Anschlussbahnen, and 71 kilometers rented to private parties) against 27,060 kilometers[1] of State roads, of which 10,479 kilometers contained two or more tracks.

All Prussian railways, then, whether State or private, are subject to the jurisdiction of a carefully graded administrative system — local, intermediate, and central — each part of which is connected with every other part in such a manner that, without interfering with the ability to act promptly in cases of emergency, every act not only finds its responsible agent, but the central organ can also make its influence felt in the remotest branch of the system and at the same time not transcend its responsibility to the public.

Advisory councils and other bodies. Whether we regard the interests of the railways and of the public as identical or not, there are certainly times when harmony between the two does not exist. This may be due to the failure of each to understand the other, or to some wrongful act which one of them may have committed. Whatever the cause, if such circumstances do arise any organ which can promptly and prudently remove the friction performs an admirable service in the interests of public traffic. Such an agent is found in Prussia in the advisory councils and

---

[1] Increased to 37,161 kilometers by the close of 1900.

other bodies which coöperate with the legally responsible parts of the railway administration. These councils are created by law, and are required to meet regularly for the purpose of coöperating with the State administration upon all the more important matters pertaining to the railway traffic, especially time-tables and rate schedules.

The first German advisory council was organized in the federal domain of Alsace-Lorraine. Through an impulse given by the chamber of commerce of the city of Mülhausen a conference between the representatives of the chambers of commerce of Alsace-Lorraine and the general imperial railway directory at Strassburg was held at Mülhausen on October 21, 1874. Organization, composition, and functions of the council were agreed upon during the first session. Originally its membership was confined to the chambers of commerce of Alsace-Lorraine, but later representatives of the various agricultural and industrial bodies were also admitted. All matters falling within the domain of at least 2 chambers of commerce could be brought before the council.

The proceedings of this conference made such a favorable impression upon the federal railway commissioner that he attempted, although without immediate success, to induce the other German railways, both State and private, to assist in this movement toward a closer union and a better understanding between the commercial and railway interests by instituting similar councils. The circular letter of the commissioner, addressed to the railways on January 11, 1875, is one of the most significant steps in the development of the councils.

"This arrangement," says the letter, "primarily strives to establish an intimate connection between the places intrusted with the administration of the railways and the trading classes. It will keep the representatives of the railways better informed as to the changing needs of trade and industry and maintain a continued understanding between them ; and, on the other hand, it will impart to commerce, etc., a greater insight into the peculiarities of the railway business and the legitimate demands of the administration, and consequently, by means of earnest and moderate action, it will react beneficially upon both sides through an exchange of views."

This statement sounds the keynote of the whole movement. For a time the railways were not very ready to respond, and the movement made little progress until the policy of the State to purchase private railways was about to be inaugurated. The Prussian Landtag made its approval of the first bill for the nationalization of railways dependent upon certain wirthschaftliche Garantien (economic guarantees) which it demanded of the Government. A resolution to this effect was adopted by the Landtag in 1879. The ministry of trade and industry had already taken active steps during the previous year. In 1880 a bill embodying the motives of the resolution of the Landtag was introduced, and after having undergone various changes and modifications was approved and published as the law of June 1, 1882.

Prussia was thus the first, and, up to the present time is the only,[1] country in which advisory bodies of this nature were placed upon a legal basis. The law is entitled Gesetz, betreffend die Einsetzung von Bezirkseisenbahnräthe und eines Landeseisenbahnraths für die Staatsbahnverwaltung. As the name indicates, it creates a class of advisory boards or councils known as Bezirkseisenbahnräthe (circuit councils), and one national council, called Landeseisenbahnrath. The national council is the advisory board of the central administration, and the circuit councils of the railway directories. Since the reorganization of the railway administration, April 1, 1895, 8 circuit councils have been in existence, with their seats in Bromberg, Berlin, Magdeburg, Hannover, Frankfurt a. M., Cologne, Erfurt, and Breslau. It will be remembered that there are 20 directories, so that a circuit council serves as an advisory board for more than one directory. The national council is composed of 40 members, holding office for 3 years. Of these, 10 are appointed and 30 are elected by the circuit councils from residents of the province or city, representing agriculture, forestry, manufacture, and

---

[1] Japan and Switzerland have since then established similar councils on a legal basis.

trade, according to a scheme of representation published in a royal decree. Of the appointed members, 3 are named by the minister of agriculture, domains, and forests ; 3 by the minister of trade and industry ; 2 by the minister of finance ; and 2 by the minister of public works. An equal number of alternates is appointed at the same time. Direct bureaucratic influence is guarded against by the exclusion from appointment of all immediate State officials. The elective members are distributed among provinces, departments, and cities, by the royal order to which reference has just been made, and both members and alternates are elected by the circuit councils. The presiding officer and his alternate or substitute are appointed by the King. In addition, the minister of public works is empowered to call in expert testimony, whenever he may think it necessary. Such specialists, as well as regular members, receive for their services 15 marks (about $3.60) per day and mileage.

The national council meets at least twice annually, and deliberates on such matters as the proposed budget, normal freight and passenger rates, classification of freight, special and differential rates, proposed changes in regulations governing the operation of railways, and allied questions. It is required by law to submit its opinion on any question brought before it by the minister of public works ; or, on the other hand, it may recommend to the minister anything which it considers conducive to the utility and effectiveness of the railway service. Its proceedings are submitted regularly to the Landtag, where they are considered in connection with the budget, thus establishing " an organic connection " between the national council and the parliament. In this way the proceedings are made accessible to every one, and an opportunity is given to approve or disapprove what the council does, through parliamentary representatives. The system is one of reciprocal questioning and answering on part of the minister of public works, the national council, and the parliament.

The circuit councils are equally important and interesting. Since January 1, 1895, 9 of these have been in existence. Their membership, which varies considerably with the different councils, was fixed by the minister of public works in December, 1894. Any subsequent modifications which may have been made have no bearing on what we are considering here. At that time the council at Magdeburg had only 24, while that at Cologne had 75 members. The nature of their composition can best be illustrated by presenting an analysis of the membership of one such council. The council of Hannover, comprising the railway directories of Hannover and Münster-Westphalen, seems to be a fair type. In that council we find 1 representative from each of the chambers of commerce of Bielefeld, Geestemünde, Hannover, Harburg, Hildesheim, Lüneburg, Minden, Münster, Osnabrück, Ostfriesland and Papenburg, Verden and Wesel ; 1 representative from each of the following corporations or societies : Society of German Foundries in Bielefeld, German Iron and Steel Industrials in Ruhrort, Craftsmen's Union of the Province of Hannover, Branch Union of German Millers in Hannover, Union of German Linen Industrialists in Bielefeld, Society for Beet Sugar Industry in Berlin, Society for the Promotion of Common Industrial Interests in the Rhine Country and Westphalen, in Düsseldorf, and the Society of German Distillers in Berlin; 4 representatives from the Royal Agricultural Society in Celle ; 3 from the Provincial Agricultural Society for Westphalen, in Münster ; 1 from the German Dairy Society in Schladen and Hamburg, the Society of Foresters of the Hartz, the North German Foresters in Hannover, the Union of Forest Owners of Middle Germany in Birnstein, and from the Society for the promotion of Moor Culture in the German Empire ; and, lastly, 1 from the Society of German Sea Fishers in Berlin. This one illustration is probably sufficient to show the thoroughly representative character of the circuit councils. If a circuit comprises railways covering territory of other German States, the chambers of commerce, industrial, and agricultural societies of such territory may also be represented in the council. The minister of public works has power to admit other members, and frequently does so when the nature of the questions upon which the council deliberates makes it desirable. Thus, at a meeting in which the rates on coal and coke — to be noted hereafter — from the Rhenish mining districts to the seashore were to be considered, there were present an Oberpräsident, accompanied by an assessor, a deputy of a Regierungspräsident, a Landrath (these three are civil administrative officers presiding over a province, circuit, and department, respectively), a representative of the Upper Mine Office at Bonn and at Dortmund, of the Royal Mine Directory at Saarbrücken, of the Royal Railroad Directory at Hannover, of the Dortmund and Gronau and Enscheder Railroad Company (private), in addition to the regular representatives and voting members.

The circuit council, as has been indicated above, stands in a relation to the railway directory similar to that of the national council to the minister. The law makes it mandatory upon the directory to consult the circuit council on all important matters concerning the railways in that circuit. This applies especially to time-tables and rate schedules. On the other hand, the council has the right, which it freely exercises, of making recommendations to the directory. In case of emergency the directory may act according to its own judgment independently of the council, but it is required to report all such cases to the standing committee of the council and to the council itself. This provision supplies the elastic element, which enables the railways to meet momentary wants. The standing committee of the council is an important body. It meets regularly some time before the full council holds its sessions, and its proceedings form the basis of the deliberations in the council. The committee receives petitions, memorials, and other communications. The bearers of these are invited to appear before the committee and to advocate their cause. Questions are asked and answered on both sides, and after all the questions have been presented the committee votes upon the petition or request, usually in the form of a resolution adopted by majority vote, recommending the council to accept or reject the demands made in the petitions. The action of the committee is reported on each question by a member designated for that purpose to the full council at its next session. While the decision of the committee is usually accepted by the council, it in no way binds